‘A must-read for students and managers who want to understand and act upon the challenges that ‘borderless’ firms and their leaders face in a world revolutionized by disruptive change of all types, with a renewed emphasis on corporate governance and environmental and social sustainability.’ – Africa Ariño, **IESE Business School, Spain**

‘This book provides a fantastic base to develop critical thinking skills around the topics of global strategic management and globalization. It offers clear explanations of important frameworks coupled with real world examples and data which students can use to understand and analyze firms, industries and countries.’ – Heather Berry, **George Washington University, USA**

‘The uncertainty in today’s business world is greater than ever with climate change, geopolitical fragmentation and the aftershocks of the pandemic making decision-making harder than ever. This textbook provides a route map through this uncertainty with lots of fresh case studies and bang up-to-date explanations of what is happening today. It provides both practical advice and theoretical insights for students of business at every level.’ – Julian Birkinshaw, **London Business School, UK**

‘I highly recommend this book on global business strategy. Including numerous real life case studies, a summary of the relevant literature and useful pedagogical tools, it is the perfect companion for both students and instructors. It analyses the environmental, social and governance issues international businesses face and covers contemporary important developments, such as cryptocurrencies. Congratulations to the authors on a very well-researched and comprehensive text!’ – Lourdes S. Casanova, **Cornell University, USA**

‘This book is perfect for undergraduate and graduate students interested in global strategy. It offers complete coverage of the foundation knowledge needed to understand how companies navigate and thrive in the current global landscape. The latest theoretical insights are explained in a rigorous and practically relevant way and are supported by a wide range of up-to-date activities and examples that bring these topics to life.’ – Ilya Cuypers, **Singapore Management University, Singapore**

‘Lasserre and Monteiro’s textbook on global strategic management is essential reading for all students of corporate management. I recommend it to both business executives and students alike for learning both the conceptual foundations of global strategy and examining the practical applications of these concepts.’ – Soumitra Dutta, **University of Oxford, UK**

‘*Global Strategic Management* is an invaluable textbook for students studying globalization, seamlessly blending theory and practice. The international case studies and examples are particularly useful, encouraging students to engage in the complex issues facing globalizations.’ – Ehsan Khajeh, **Coventry University, UK**

'Lasserre and Monteiro's book provides a comprehensive analysis of how companies operate in the global arena, beginning with a rich analysis of the global environment, followed by a discussion of corporate and competitive global strategies, and concluding with a pragmatic application of those concepts to functional areas of the organization. The text is didactic and accompanied by a set of interesting and informative cases. It is an invaluable resources for students of global strategy.' – Sergio Lazzarini, **Insper Learning Institution, Brazil**

'Lasserre and Monteiro provide a solid overview of the strategies of globally operating multinationals and the evolving global business environment. The book excels at providing tools for managers and is rich in contemporary data and case examples originating from a wide variety of industries and national contexts.' – Klaus Meyer, **Ivey Business School, Canada**

'This latest edition of *Global Strategic Management* continues to be the best choice for business students looking to develop a deeper understanding of global business. It contains numerous practical cases and explains concepts from literature in a way that allows for their immediate application. I strongly recommend it to readers and instructors alike.' – Michael Mol, **Copenhagen Business School, Denmark**

'This book offers comprehensive treatment of contemporary global strategy, including coverage of born globals, emerging markets and open innovation, topics on which Monteiro is a leading authority. By highlighting the Sustainable Development Goals and the need for a post-Covid-19 'green recovery', the text equips business leaders of the future for the Decade of Action and beyond.' – Shameen Prashantham, **China Europe International Business School, China**

'Lasserre and Monteiro's new version of *Global Strategic Management* is the best global strategy book on the market. It covers both western and emerging market contexts with a wide range of theories, models and cases, and highlights emerging issues including sustainability, digitalisation and national competitiveness. Organised in three key sections – context, strategy and management – it's easy-to-follow, pedagogical approach ensures *Global Strategic Management* is ideal for undergraduates and postgraduate students alike.' – Mohammad B. Rana, **Aalborg University, Denmark**

'This textbook combines academic rigor with practical relevance, addressing fundamental concepts as well as current and future trends in globalization. It provides a truly multi-faceted global perspective with 33 case studies from more than 20 countries, as well as an even larger number of practical examples.' – Karlheinz Schwuchow, **Hochschule Bremen University of Applied Sciences, Germany**

FIFTH EDITION

Global Strategic Management

Philippe Lasserre and
Felipe Monteiro

BLOOMSBURY
NEW DELHI • LONDON • OXFORD • NEW YORK • SYDNEY

BLOOMSBURY INDIA
Bloomsbury Publishing India Pvt. Ltd
Second Floor, LSC Building No. 4, DDA Complex, Pocket C–6&7,
Vasant Kunj, New Delhi 110070

BLOOMSBURY, BLOOMSBURY ACADEMIC INDIA and the Diana logo are trademarks of Bloomsbury Publishing Plc

First published in India 2023
First published in Great Britain 2002
This edition published 2023

This edition published with permission from Bloomsbury Publishing Plc, 50 Bedford Square, London, WC1B3DP, UK.

ISBN: 978-93-56403-48-2
10 9 8 7 6 5 4 3 2 1
For sale in the Indian subcontinent only

Typeset by Integra Software Services Pvt. Ltd.
Printed and bound in India by Thomson Press India Ltd

To find out more about our authors and books visit www.bloomsbury.com and sign up for our newsletters

Philippe Lasserre:

Pour mes enfants Virginie, Benoit, Marion, mes petits-enfants Abigail, Noé, Hélio, mon arrière-petite-fille Brianna, ma compagne Aline et à la mémoire de Michelle

Oh! combien de marins, combien de capitaines
Qui sont partis joyeux pour des courses lointaines …

Victor Hugo, *Oceano Nox* (1840)

Felipe Monteiro:

Para minha esposa Mariana, meus filhos Bernardo e Clara, minha mãe Carmen e em memória do meu pai Luiz Felipe

Navegar é preciso; viver não é preciso

Fernando Pessoa

About the Authors

Philippe Lasserre is Emeritus Professor of Strategy and Asian Business at INSEAD. He obtained his Master's degree from ESSEC (Paris) and his PhD from the University of Texas at Austin. Since 1975 he has been involved in teaching, researching and consulting in strategic management and international business. He is the author of various articles on strategy, international business, business in Asia and joint ventures and he has co-authored *Strategies for Asia Pacific* (Palgrave Macmillan: 1995, 1999, 2006) and *Strategy and Management in Asia Pacific* (McGraw-Hill: 1999), as well as *Global Strategic Management* (Palgrave Macmillan: 2002, 2007, 2012, 2018). He participated in the development of the Euro-Asia Centre of INSEAD and the INSEAD Asian campus in Singapore in the early 2000s. He has been a visiting professor in various universities in Singapore, at the China European Business School in Beijing and Shanghai, at the University of Texas in Dallas, at Curtin University in Perth, at Thunderbird University in Glendale, Arizona and at the Université de Geneve. He currently lives in France.

Felipe Monteiro is Senior Affiliate Professor of Strategy and the Academic Director of the Global Talent Competitiveness Index (GTCI) at INSEAD. He is also a Senior Fellow of the Mack Institute for Innovation Management at The Wharton School, University of Pennsylvania. He obtained his Ph.D. in Strategic and International Management from the London Business School. He has taught at the London School of Economics (LSE) and worked as a Senior Researcher at the Harvard Business School's Latin American Research Center. His research focuses on global open innovation and the role of boundary spanners in multinational corporations, and he has received important awards from the Academy of Management, the Academy of International Business and the Strategic Management Society. He has also received the INSEAD Deans' Commendation for Excellence in MBA Teaching on multiple occasions, along with Wharton's 'Goes Above and Beyond the Call of Duty' Teaching Award. He is a prolific and award-winning case writer, and consults and gives talks for companies and governments worldwide. He currently lives in France.

Brief contents

Part I Global contexts 1

1 Globalization of markets and competition 3
2 The emerging global environment 38
3 Globalization, societies and cultures 71
4 Globalization, sustainable development and social responsibility 112

Part II Global strategies 173

5 Designing a global strategy 175
6 Assessing countries' attractiveness 226
7 Entry strategies 257
8 Global mergers, acquisitions and strategic alliances 284

Part III Managing globally 351

9 Global marketing 353
10 Global operations and digital networks 381
11 Global innovation 424
12 Global financial management 453
13 Global human resource management 482
14 Designing a global organization 522

Part IV Conclusions 559

15 Current and future trends in globalization 561
16 Global strategic management in action: Haier – the building of a global champion, 1984–2020 594

Glossary 607
Index of subjects 624
Index of names 628
Index of organizations and companies 637

Long contents

About the authors vii
Figures xxi
Tables xxvii
Mini-cases and examples xxxi
Tour of the book xxxv
Companion website xxxvii
Acknowledgements xxxviii

Introduction to the fifth edition xxxix

Part I Global contexts 1

1 Globalization of markets and competition 3
Introduction 3
The phenomenon of globalization 4
Globalization from a macro perspective 8
What are the factors that push for globalization? 8
What are the factors that work against globalization? The localization push 13
Globalization at the level of the firm 17
The global/multi-local mapping 25
Summary and key points 32
Learning assignments 33
Key words 33
Web resources 34
Notes 34
References and further reading 34

2	**The emerging global environment**	38
	Introduction	38
	Emerging countries and their development	40
	Emerging countries and their institutional and business environments	47
	Importance of business conglomerates	51
	Significant presence of 'bottom-of-the-pyramid' market segments	52
	Emerging countries and global firms	53
	Summary and key points	65
	Learning assignments	67
	Key words	67
	Web resources	67
	Notes	67
	References and further reading	68
3	**Globalization, societies and cultures**	71
	Introduction	71
	The different facets of culture	72
	National cultural differences	73
	Economic cultures and business systems	83
	The impact of cultures on global management	87
	Summary and key points	104
	Learning assignments	107
	Key words	108
	Web resources	108
	Notes	108
	References and further reading	109
4	**Globalization, sustainable development and social responsibility**	112
	Introduction	112
	Sustainable development	113
	Globalization and environmental issues	118
	Globalization and societal issues	126
	Global corporations' ethics and corporate social responsibility	141
	Global companies and business ethics	143

Social responsibility and global firms: an ongoing challenge 148
Summary and key points 158
Learning assignments 162
Key words 163
Web resources 163
Notes 163
References and further reading 166

Part II Global strategies 173

5 Designing a global strategy 175
Introduction 175
A company business strategy 176
Framework for a global strategy 180
Global strategies and the multi-business firm 203
Global strategies and the small and medium-sized enterprise (SME) 203
Born global 208
Born global and born digital 209
Summary and key points 217
Learning assignments 220
Key words 221
Web resources 222
Notes 222
References and further reading 223

6 Assessing countries' attractiveness 226
Introduction 226
Why is a country attractive? 227
Market, resources and industry opportunities 228
Assessing market opportunities 229
Plotting trends 231
Assessing resource opportunities 234
Competitive context 238
Socioeconomic, political and cultural distance 242

Country risk analysis 244
Putting it all together 246
Summary and key points 251
Learning assignments 253
Key words 253
Web resources 253
Notes 254
References and further reading 254

7 Entry strategies 257
Introduction 257
Why enter? Defining strategic objectives for a country presence 259
When to enter? First mover, follower, or acquirer? 261
The pace of entry 262
Entry modes: How to enter? 263
Comparing entry modes 270
Choosing an entry mode 270
Entry strategies in the digital space 271
Summary and key points 276
Learning assignments 280
Key words 280
Web resources 281
Notes 281
References and further reading 281

8 Global mergers, acquisitions and strategic alliances 284
Introduction 284
Global mergers and acquisitions 285
Cross-border acquisitions performance 289
The process of mergers and acquisitions 290
Pre-acquisition 291
Strategic fit 293
Capabilities fit 294
Cultural fit 294
Organizational fit 295
Integration framework 300

Integrating the companies: the transition phase 302
Integrating the companies: the consolidation phase 305
Global alliances and joint ventures 307
Partner analysis 313
Negotiation and design 317
Implementation 323
Global multilateral alliances 326
Global industrial ecosystems 331
Joint ventures for local market entry 333
Joint venture decay and failure 336
Summary and key points 343
Learning assignments 345
Key words 346
Web resources 346
Notes 347
References and further reading 347

Part III Managing globally 351

9 Global marketing 353
Introduction 353
Customer behavior, convergence and global segmentation 354
Product standardization 355
Global branding 356
Advantages of global branding 358
Disadvantages of global branding 359
Building a global brand 361
Advertising 362
Online global advertising 363
Global pricing 364
Global account management 365
Global solution selling 367
Global sales and distribution 369
Global marketing positioning 370
Fair trade marketing 370

Global marketing and its limits 371
Summary and key points 374
Learning assignments 378
Key words 378
Web resources 378
Notes 379
References and further reading 379

10 Global operations and digital networks 381
Introduction 381
The globalization of value chains: offshore production and outsourcing 382
Selecting operational sites 383
Global manufacturing networks 385
Global sourcing 388
Global logistics 392
The global management of infrastructure projects 395
The internet and global operations 397
Summary and key points 413
Learning assignments 420
Key words 421
Web resources 421
Notes 421
References and further reading 422

11 Global innovation 424
Introduction 424
The international product life cycle model 424
Global R&D networks 426
Globalization of R&D: benefits and constraints 428
Management of global R&D networks 430
The Global Innovation Index 431
Systems 432
International transfer of technology 434
Global knowledge management 435
Global Open Innovation 438

Summary and key points 446
Learning assignments 449
Key words 449
Web resources 449
Notes 450
References and further reading 450

12 Global financial management 453

Introduction 453
Currency risk 454
Strategic exposure 455
Transaction exposure 456
Hedging techniques 456
Non-hedging techniques 458
Translation exposure 458
Project finance 458
Project valuation 459
Project financing 461
Global capital structure 462
Crosslisting 464
International bond market 465
Benefits of raising debt globally 466
Concerns with raising debt globally 466
International bond market credit ratings 466
Development finance 467
Sovereign funds 468
Targeted financing 468
Cryptocurrencies 469
Trade finance 471
Documentary credit 471
Export credit agencies 472
Countertrade 473
Global financial management and taxation 473
Summary and key points 474
Learning assignments 477

Key words 478
Web resources 478
Notes 478
References and further reading 479

13 Global human resource management 482
Introduction 482
Assignment of personnel: the global human resource wheel 484
Expatriate management 485
Virtual assignments vs relocation 496
Destination challenges 497
International remote work appeals to many 499
Localization 499
The Global Talent Competitiveness Index 500
Skills development 506
Individual skills 507
Developing skills through job rotation and training 509
Working from anywhere (WFA) 509
Summary and key points 513
Learning assignments 517
Key words 517
Web resources 518
Notes 518
References and further reading 519

14 Designing a global organization 522
Introduction 522
The merry-go-round organizational challenge 523
The international division model 525
The global functional model 526
The geographical models 529
The multi-business global product division models 532
The matrix models 534
Alternative structural models 540
Regional headquarters in global management 545
Summary and key points 553

Learning assignments 554
Key Words 554
Web resources 555
Notes 555
References and further reading 555

Part IV Conclusions 559

15 Current and future trends in globalization 561

Introduction 561
Global challenges 562
Geopolitics and globalization 564
Demography and migration 564
Asymmetric development 566
Regional blocs 568
Sustainable development 570
Technological developments 572
Global risks 574
Ethnic, religious and cultural friction 575
The future of global corporations 581
Summary and key points 584
Learning assignments 587
Key words 587
Web resources 587
Notes 588
References and further reading 589

16 Global strategic management in action: Haier – the building of a global champion, 1984–2020 594

Introduction 594
Phases 1 and 2: building the brand and diversification (1984–1998) 595
The competitive battlefield of China in the 1990s 596
Phases 3 and 4: internationalization and global brand strategy (1998–2012) 598
Phase 5: global integrated network (2012–2019) – consolidating global leadership 601

Phase 6: ecosystem strategy (2019–) 603
Learning assignments 605
Notes 605
References and further reading 606

Glossary 607
Index of subjects 624
Index of names 628
Index of organizations and companies 637

Figures

0.1	Structure of the book	xlii
1.1	DHL Global Connectedness Index	5
1.2	Tariff reductions and international trade	9
1.3	Globalization push factors	12
1.4	Localization push factors	15
1.5	A multinational competitive configuration – Otis Elevators in the 1960s	18
1.6	A global competitive configuration – Otis today	19
1.7	The three steps in globalization	20
1.8	World trade evolution since 1870	22
1.9	Migration Chart	22
1.10	DHL Global Trade Barometer from 2013 to 2019	23
1.11	Global-local mapping: different industries have different competitive requirements	26
1.12	Global-local mapping: different segments have different competitive requirements – example of banking	26
1.13	Total cost of drug development (average US$ m)	27
1.14	Pattern of pharmaceutical R&D	28
1.15	An example of global M&A in the pharmaceutical industry: a German, American and French group	28
1.16	US pharmaceutical distribution channel	30
2.1	Globalization indicators, 2000–2020 (base 100 = 2000)	39
2.2	Globalization growth indicators, 2000–2019	40
2.3	GDP growth rates: emerging countries versus the world (1990–2019)	42
2.4	Shares of middle class, 2015–2020	43
2.5	Capital formation, 2001–2019	44
2.6	Foreign trade and investment, 2001–2019	45
2.7	Rule of law and control of corruption indicators (2019)	48
2.8	Government effectiveness and regulatory quality indicators, 2020	48

2.9 Selected ease of doing business scores, 2020 (From 0=Not Easy, 100=Easy) 51
2.10 The three segments in emerging markets 53
2.11 Advantages and disadvantages of offshoring and offsourcing in emerging countries 55
2.12 The strategic development of emerging market champions 56
2.13 Number of emerging market multinationals on Fortune Global 500 58
3.1 The architecture of business systems 83
3.2 Framework for negotiation with reference to international contracts 89
3.3 Negotiation Process Source: authors' own construction adapted from Fisher, Ury and Patton 90
3.4 Negotiation attributes and cultural differences 93
4.1 Sustainable development and the global firm 113
4.2 Temperatures worldwide: earth surface (land and oceans) 119
4.3 Total world GHG emissions 121
4.4 Variation in spot prices for CO_2 122
4.5 Ecological investment components 125
4.6 Corruption and development 129
4.7 Example of tax evasion 140
4.8 The global ethical web 142
5.1 The purpose of strategy 178
5.2 Global development of Samsung Electronics 180
5.3 Global strategy framework 181
5.4 A mapping of several global companies using the TNI index 184
5.5 Mapping of global ambition 185
5.6 Comparative mapping of global ambition: comparison of Walmart (retailing), Michelin (tyres), Airbus (aircraft), Nestlé (food) 186
5.7 The evolution of Whirlpool's globalization (measured by GRI) 187
5.8 The three dimensions of the value proposition 189
5.9 Example of customers' value curve 189
5.10 Generic value chain 191
5.11 Typical globalization of the value chain 192
5.12 A generic global distribution of activities in the value chain 193
5.13 Sources of competitive advantage 196
5.14 The Transfer, Adapt, Create model applied to the globalization of mass retailing 199
5.15 Global/multi-local mapping and global structures 202

5.16 Essilor's business process 214
5.17 Perspective on Essilor's market development (figures as of 2014) 214
6.1 The foreign market entry decision 226
6.2 General investment framework 227
6.3 Framework for assessment of a country's market, resources and industry attractiveness 229
6.4 Relationship between GDP per capita and mobile subscriptions per 100 people, 2019 (R = 0.85) 230
6.5 Relationship between GDP per capita and the production of cement, 2019 (R = 0.36) 230
6.6 The 'middle-class effect' 232
6.7 Illustration of the middle-class effect in Indonesia between 2002 and 2019 232
6.8 Market segmentations 233
6.9 Natural resource per capita 235
6.10 Pay and productivity and skills of current workforce 236
6.11 Summary of the CAGE Distance Framework model 243
6.12 Framework for country risk analysis 244
6.13 Variability of economic growth, Hungary versus Czech Republic, 2000–2019 245
6.14 Political and economic risks in selected countries 246
6.15 Foreign direct investment and country risks, 2000–2019 247
7.1 Entry modes 263
7.2 Factors influencing entry modes 264
7.3 Mapping of entry mode choices 272
8.1 Number and value of global mergers and acquisitions from 1985 to 2020 287
8.2 The process of mergers and acquisitions 290
8.3 Fit analysis in mergers and acquisitions 293
8.4 Framework for capabilities analysis in mergers and acquisitions 294
8.5 Cash-flow-based valuation for M&As 298
8.6 A model of a step-by-step integration framework 300
8.7 Contingent integration modes 301
8.8 Various types of alliance in a global context 308
8.9 Framework for the analysis of strategic alliances 310
8.10 Economic value potential for each partner in an alliance 312
8.11 Partner's fit analysis in strategic alliances 314
8.12 Assessing the strategic fit based on the criticality of the alliance for partners 315

8.13 Strategic fit against partners' strategic agendas 316
8.14 Organizational designs in alliances 317
8.15 Typical items in a joint venture agreement 319
8.16 Management skills needed in alliances 321
8.17 The death valley spiral 323
8.18 Types of alliance constellations 326
8.19 Nestlé Alliances Portfolio 327
8.20 Arqus European Universities alliances 328
8.21 Alliance partners in GAVI 330
8.22 Lead firm ecosystem: a simplified view of Apple iPhone ecosytem 331
8.23 Simplified example of a value proposition ecosystem: long-distance travel ecosystem 332
8.24 Example of a technology-centred ecosytem: electrical vehicle ecosystem 332
8.25 Organization of the cross-company teams and global alliance committee in the Renault–Nissan Alliance 338
8.26 The Nissan Revival Plan and the cross-functional teams 339
8.27 New organization of the Renault–Nissan Alliance 340
8.28 Renault's alliances and global acquisition network 340
9.1 Western versus Asian hierarchy of needs 355
9.2 Customer segmentation 355
9.3 Global product standardization types 356
9.4 Global brand positioning 359
9.5 Principle of global account management 365
9.6 A financial global account management network servicing a leading European manufacturer 367
9.7 Global solution selling: an international bid for a power plant in China 368
9.8 Sales and distribution 369
10.1 The global operations network 381
10.2 Forms of offshoring 383
10.3 Different models of internationalization of services 387
10.4 Different global sourcing designs 389
10.5 Reverse auction process 391
10.6 Bidding profile for reverse auction 391
10.7 Apple supply chain 393

10.8 Amazon's global logistics 394

10.9 Airbus logistics 394

10.10 Players in an international infrastructure project 396

10.11 Global use of the internet, April 2020 398

10.12 Players in the internet space 400

10.13 Reach vs richness trade-off 403

10.14 Traditional supply chain model 408

10.15 Integrated supply chain ecosystem 408

10.16 Ericsson global sites and centres 412

11.1 The international product life cycle 425

11.2 Nestlé's global R&D architecture 427

11.3 Evolution over time of global R&D activities 429

11.4 Global Innovation Index (GII) Framework 431

11.5 Knowledge creation, sharing and 'melding' in global firms 439

12.1 Key issues in global financial management 454

12.2 Variation of major currencies against the euro, 2000 to 2021, yearly average 454

12.3 Bitcoin price (January–May 2021) 470

12.4 Documentary credit in international trade 472

13.1 Global human resource issues 483

13.2 The global human resource wheel 485

13.3 Human resource wheels 486

13.4 The expatriate challenges 487

13.5 Expatriates' acculturation: the 'four Fs' 488

13.6 The primary ingredients of individual managerial behaviour required for success in expatriate assignments in Asia 490

13.7 Selected indices of cost of living excluding rent 492

13.8 Expatriate tenure 494

13.9 Human resources practices supporting expatriation 495

13.10 Percentage of respondents who would work remotely for an employer with no physical presence in their country 499

13.11 The Global Talent Competitiveness Index (GTCI) model 501

13.12 Hiring and firing practices 506

13.13 Global leadership capabilities 508

13.14	Global management development in a global oil company	509
14.1	The evolution of global organizational models	526
14.2	The global functional organizational design	527
14.3	Geographical organizational models	529
14.4	The multi-business global product division organizational model	533
14.5	Matrix organizational simplified models	535
14.6	The Olam three-dimensional organization matrix	537
14.7	Convergence of global organizational designs	542
14.8	New business models for a new global landscape	544
14.9	Profiles of regional headquarters in global firms	546
14.10	Organizational structure of regional headquarters	547
14.11	Siemens' new company structure on 1 January 2008	549
14.12	Siemens' company structure in 2020	550
14.13	ACER's organizational model	551
15.1	Global challenges and the global corporation	562
15.2	The global income gap, ratio of GDP per capita in OECD countries to low-income countries, 1990–2019	567
15.3	Projected changes in temperature according to different projected levels of greenhouse gas emissions	571
15.4	Energy demand and gas emission projections according to two scenarios	571
15.5	A new organizational model	581
16.1	Evolution of market share in China in major appliances (2014–2019)	597
16.2	The competitive battlefield in China, 1990s to 2010	598
16.3	Schematic representation of *Rendanheyi 2.0* as applied to water purifiers	602
16.4	Haier's inverted pyramid organizational structure	603

Tables

1.1	Globalization data	4
1.2	The societal benefits of globalization	16
1.3	Major global acquisitions and mergers from 1999 to 2020	29
1.4	Manufacturing and R&D facilities outside country of origin	29
1.5	Major producers of generics	30
1.6	Pharmaceutical market historical data and forecasts, US$ bn (global 2019–2025)	31
2.1	Estimated evolution of middle-class populations in China, India and Indonesia (millions)	43
2.2	Evolution from agriculture to industry and services	46
2.3	Possible institutional voids in emerging countries	49
2.4	Ease of doing business indices	50
2.5	Differences between traditional middle-class strategies and bottom-of-the-pyramid strategies	53
2.6	Differences in internationalization patterns between traditional multinational companies and emerging markets multinationals	57
2.7	Comparison of revenues growth rate between 2011 and 2016 between BCG Global Challengers in various industries and traditional multinational companies	58
2.8	Selected examples of global challengers from emerging countries	59
2.9	Charoen Pockphand: diversification and globalization	62
3.1	Hofstede values orientation (selected countries)	76
3.2	Trompenaars' six value orientations	77
3.3	The eight dimensions of Meyer's culture map	78
3.4	Country clusters for regions covered in the GLOBE project and the salient cultural and leadership characteristics they present	81
3.5	Assessing a business system	84
3.6	Differences in business systems	86
3.7	Monocultural vs multicultural teams	88
3.8	Impact of culture on negotiating behaviour: a comparison of American and Japanese responses	93

3.9	Chinese business negotiation style	96
3.10	Business practice differences	97
3.11	Brazilian indicators	102
4.1	Sustainable development issues	114
4.2	Total world GHG emissions including land-use change and forestry (billion tons equivalent CO_2)	119
4.3	Depletion of natural resources	122
4.4	Corruption indices including rankings	127
4.5	Five corruption cases from 'clean' countries	132
4.6	A checklist of anti-corruption measures	133
4.7	The ten principles of the UN Global Compact	146
5.1	Business, corporate and global strategy	177
5.2	Distribution of the world market by regions in selected industries, 2019 (as a percentage of US$ value)	183
5.3	Distribution of markets and revenues in tyres, 2019 (%)	184
5.4	Global positioning alternatives	190
5.5	Capabilities leading to competitive advantage	194
5.6	Sources of competitive advantage of global companies	196
5.7	Building global sustainable advantage	197
5.8	Organizational designs for global strategies	200
5.9	SMEs' economic weight measured by contribution to employment and value added in selected countries in Europe, North and South America, Asia Pacific	204
5.10	Typology of international SMEs	205
5.11	Obstacles to internationalization as perceived by SMEs	207
5.12	Differences between born global and traditional global firms	209
5.13	Examples of three major born global firms	210
5.14	HSBC distribution of revenues, employment and customers	212
6.1	Macro indicators used in international market assessments	231
6.2	Characteristics of demand according to country life cycle clusters	234
6.3	Quality of infrastructures	237
6.4	Porter's industry analysis as applied to international business entry	238
6.5	Major types of incentive for foreign investments	241
6.6	Cluster characteristics, Asia Pacific	249
6.7	Country profiles	250

7.1 Entry strategy objectives 260
7.2 Advantages and disadvantages of being a first mover 262
7.3 Advantages and disadvantages of country-based joint venture partnerships 267
7.4 Comparing various entry modes 271
7.5 Three models of entry 272
8.1 Value creation in M&As 292
8.2 Failures in the integration process 299
8.3 Main strategic objectives pursued in various types of alliance 311
8.4 Value creation and distribution 313
8.5 Receptivity in learning 326
8.6 Types of local partner for market entry joint ventures 333
9.1 Customer needs and value curves 354
9.2 Top five leading global brands comparison between 2020 and 2000 357
9.3 Examples of corporations using global and local brands 357
9.4 Top ten relevant brands 362
9.5 Major global advertising agencies, 2019 362
9.6 Capabilities required for global solution selling 369
9.7 Various global marketing positions 370
10.1 Criteria for facilities location 384
10.2 Ferdow's classification of globally set-up factories 386
10.3 Phases in international infrastructure projects 396
10.4 Digital platforms 400
10.5 Effects of the internet on globalization 404
10.6 The evolution of Industry 4.0 407
10.7 Comparison of supply chains 409
10.8 Organizational requirements for e-business 410
11.1 R&D capabilities, 2000 and 2018 425
11.2 Top ten R&D spenders as % of GDP 426
11.3 Total R&D spend US$PPP (purchasing power parity) 426
11.4 Performance evaluation criteria 430
11.5 Global Innovation Index top 20 countries 432
11.6 Classification of technology 434
11.7 Opportunities and constraints for knowledge management in global companies 436
11.8 Tools and approaches used for knowledge management in the metanational corporation 437

11.9 Intellectual property rights and their infringement 442
11.10 Protection of intellectual property rights 443
11.11 Scout locations 444
12.1 Classification of risk linked to infrastructure assets 459
12.2 Financial risk mitigants and incentives for infrastructure finance 460
12.3 Correlation coefficients of monthly returns for selected stock markets, 1 January 2016 to 1 March 2021 463
12.4 Regional distribution of domestic and foreign listed companies for various stock exchanges, 2021 464
12.5 Types of international bond 466
12.6 List of the main multinational DFIs 467
12.7 The main bilateral DFIs 467
12.8 Top ten largest sovereign wealth fund rankings by total assets 468
13.1 The changing nature of international staffing 486
13.2 Eight global trends for global mobility 2021 498
13.3 Top twenty countries 501
14.1 Characteristics of global functional organizational design 527
14.2 Characteristics of geographical organizational models 530
14.3 Characteristics of the multi-business global product division organizational model 533
14.4 Characteristics of matrix organizational models 535
15.1 World population, 2015 to 2100 565
15.2 Pros and cons of migration 566
15.3 Global and regional inequalities 567
15.4 Regional trade agreements 568
15.5 Selected global risks 2021 575
15.6 Simplified list of the 15 Global Challenges identified by The Millennium Project 578
15.7 The Millennium Project Global Challenges 579
15.8 Management of new roles for the individualized corporaton 582
15.9 Data relating to Pulau Vicente 584
16.1 Haier's six strategic stages 594
16.2 Head-to-head comparison of Haier Smart Home and Midea groups 597
16.3 Haier vs. global competitors, 2018–2021 599
16.4 Haier's key international industrial investments 600

Mini-cases and examples

Mini-cases				
Chapter	**MC #**	**MC title**	**Area covered**	**Page number**
1 Globalization of Markets and Competition	1.1	Pharmaceutical Industry: a global and local Industry	Global	27
2 The Emerging Global Environment	2.1	Stefanini and the Global Digital Revolution	Brazil, Global	60
2 The Emerging Global Environment	2.2	Charoen Pokphand (CP)	Thailand/ SE and East Asia	62
2 The Emerging Global Environment	2.3	BYD (Build Your Dreams)	China	64
3 Globalization, Societies and Culture	3.1	Working across cultures: the engineering consultants' clashes	Indonesia/ various	98
3 Globalization, Societies and Culture	3.2	Brazil	Brazil	100
4 Globalization, Sustainable Development and Global Responsibility	4.1	Shell and Cosan	Brazil	123
4 Globalization, Sustainable Development and Global Responsibility	4.2	Jack Cumberland	SE Asia	131
4 Globalization, Sustainable Development and Global Responsibility	4.3	Operation Car Wash	Brazil, Latin America	151
4 Globalization, Sustainable Development and Global Responsibility	4.4	Enel	Italy, Global	154
4 Globalization, Sustainable Development and Global Responsibility	4.5	Etisalat's philanthropic activities	UAE	156
4 Globalization, Sustainable Development and Global Responsibility	4.6	Light Up The World (LUTW)	Canada/ Peru	157
5 Designing a Global Strategy	5.1	HSBC: the world's local bank	China, Hong Kong, UK	211
5 Designing a Global Strategy	5.2	Essilor: a global player	France, Global	213
5 Designing a Global Strategy	5.3	Quinta do Vallado	Portugal, Global	215
6 Assessing Countries' Attractiveness	6.1	TAG Heuer	Switzerland, US	240

Mini-cases				
Chapter	MC #	MC title	Area covered	Page number
6 Assessing Countries' Attractiveness	6.2	Izmir Industrial Electric: Exercise	Turkey (Fictional)	249
7 Entry Strategies	7.1	Schneider Electric and the power backup market in India	India	273
7 Entry Strategies	7.2	Entry and development of Transsion in Africa	SE China/ Africa	274
8 Global Mergers, Acquisitions and Strategic Alliances	8.1	The long road of global mergers in the telecoms equipment industry	Global	306
8 Global Mergers, Acquisitions and Strategic Alliances	8.2	General Motors' global alliances: a Sisyphean task	US/Global	341
9 Global Marketing	9.1	waterdrop®	Austria, Global	372
9 Global Marketing	9.2	Halo Top – using digital marketing to disrupt the global ice cream giants	US/Various	373
10 Global Operations and Digital Networks	10.1	The globalization of the sharing economy: Airbnb, Uber and BlaBlaCar	US/France/ Global	410
10 Global Operations and Digital Networks	10.2	Ericsson global value chain	Sweden, Global	412
11 Global Innovation	11.1	FC Barcelona, Barça Innovation Hub (BIH)	Spain, Global	441
11 Global Innovation	11.2	Global giants' R&D networks – Siemens and BASF	Germany, Global	445
12 Global Financial Management	12.1	Cleanwater in Vietnam	Australia/ Vietnam	474
13 Global Human Resource Management	13.1	Global managers – Pedro Aguilar	Argentina/ US	511
13 Global Human Resource Management	13.2	Global managers – Joseph Laval	France-Thailand	512
14 Designing a Global Organisation	14.1	Siemens Vision 2020+	Various	549
14 Designing a Global Organisation	14.2	ACER's global organizational evolution	Taiwan/ Global	551
15 Current and future trends in globalization	15.1	Threat of a pandemic	Asia (Fictional)	583

Examples				
Chapter	Example #	Example title	Region	Page number
1 Globalization of Markets and Competition	1.1	Otis Elevators	EU/UK/US	18
2 The Emerging Global Environment	2.1	The multi-segment approach in emerging countries	Germany/ China/Brazil/ India	54
4 Globalization, Sustainable Development and Global Responsibility	4.1	An introduction to issues of corporate social responsibility – Shell in Nigeria	Nigeria	114
4 Globalization, Sustainable Development and Global Responsibility	4.2	Child labour and the global firm: Sialkot and Reebok	Pakistan/UK	136
5 Designing a Global Strategy	5.1	Samsung Electronics	South Korea	179
5 Designing a Global Strategy	5.2	Whirlpool	US	186
5 Designing a Global Strategy	5.3	Yellow Tail: a blue ocean strategy in action in the global market space	Australia	195
5 Designing a Global Strategy	5.4	Gemplus: from Marseille to the world	France	210
5 Designing a Global Strategy	5.5	Sunna Design: a born global start-up	France	210
5 Designing a Global Strategy	5.6	Cochlear: an Australian born global high-tech company	Australia	211
7 Entry Strategies	7.1	IKEA's market-seeking entry strategy in India	Sweden/ Various	258
7 Entry Strategies	7.2	Cargill's market- and resource-seeking entry strategies	US	259
8 Global Mergers, Acquisitions and Strategic Alliances	8.1	Getinge's growth via international acquisitions	Sweden	285
8 Global Mergers, Acquisitions and Strategic Alliances	8.2	An ongoing global alliance: the Renault–Nissan Alliance	France/ Japan	338
9 Global Marketing	9.1	Global/local branding – L'Oréal in China	France/ China	360
10 Global Operations and Digital Networks	10.1	Li & Fung's 'virtual factory' concept	China	389
10 Global Operations and Digital Networks	10.2	E-procurement and reverse auctions	Global	390
10 Global Operations and Digital Networks	10.3	Apple's vs Amazon's global supply chains	US/Global	392
10 Global Operations and Digital Networks	10.4	Enron in India: the Dabhol Power Plant[8]	US/India	397

Examples				
Chapter	Example #	Example title	Region	Page number
10 Global Operations and Digital Networks	10.5	Yahoo! and anti-racist legislation in France	France, US	404
11 Global Innovation	11.1	Nestlé – a global network	Switzerland	427
11 Global Innovation	11.2	Global virtual lab at Merck Sharp and Dohme (MSD)	US	443
13 Global Human Resource Management	13.1	Appointing a divisional manager in France	Switzerland/ France	483
13 Global Human Resource Management	13.2	ABB's localization programme in China in the late 1990s	Sweden/ Switzerland/ China	504
14 Designing a Global Organisation	14.1	Evolution of two global organizations: Unilever and Procter & Gamble	UK/ Netherlands/ US	523
14 Designing a Global Organisation	14.2	Global functional organizational design at Apple	US	528
14 Designing a Global Organisation	14.3	Geographical organizations – Zee Entertainment and ISS	India	531
14 Designing a Global Organisation	14.4	Philips	The Netherlands/ Global	534
14 Designing a Global Organisation	14.5	Matrix organizations – Olam and BASF	Nigeria/ Germany	536
14 Designing a Global Organisation	14.6	Strategy and organizational structure: IBM from the 1990s to the 2020s	US	542
14 Designing a Global Organisation	14.7	Example of a digitally enabled structure: GitLab	Ukraine/ Global	544
15 Current and Future Trends in GSM	15.1	The Millennium Project	US/Global	578
15 Current and Future Trends in GSM	15.2	The 'Future Possibilities Report'	UAE/United Nations	580

Tour of the book

Chapter 1

Globalization of markets and competition

By the end of the chapter you should be able to:

- Define globalization from a macro environment perspective
- Identify the forces pushing towards globalization and the forces pushing for localization
- Define what globalization means for firms
- Identify the various steps of globalization for firms
- Make a distinction between multinational and global firms
- Spell out the benefits and pitfalls of globalization
- Analyse the recent trend of deglobalization
- Discuss the consequences of the Covid-19 pandemic on globalization
- Position an industry or a business on the global/multi-local mapping

1 Chapter introductions and learning objectives | provide a guide to the material in each chapter and allow progress to be checked.

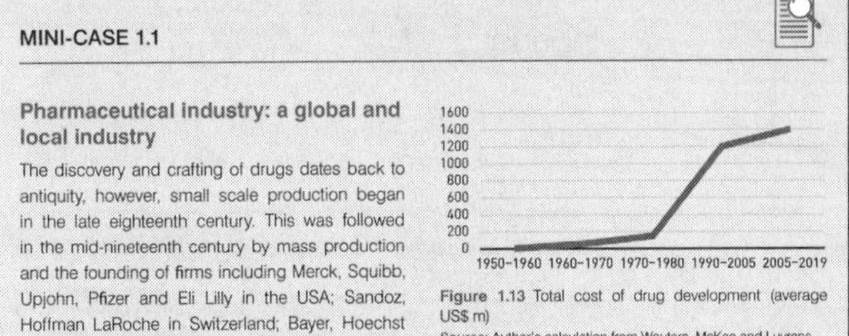

MINI-CASE 1.1

Pharmaceutical industry: a global and local industry

The discovery and crafting of drugs dates back to antiquity, however, small scale production began in the late eighteenth century. This was followed in the mid-nineteenth century by mass production and the founding of firms including Merck, Squibb, Upjohn, Pfizer and Eli Lilly in the USA; Sandoz, Hoffman LaRoche in Switzerland; Bayer, Hoechst in Germany; Beecham, Wellcome in the UK; and Clin-Byla in France. At the beginning of the twentieth

Figure 1.13 Total cost of drug development (average US$ m)

Source: Author's calculation from Wouters, McKee and Luyrens (2020).

2 Mini-cases | help students to apply key concepts in global strategy to the real world of business. They are largely based on a diverse range of 'transnational' companies which operate across the world.

3 Inserts | provide additional information that expands upon and contextualizes key information.

Insert 1.1 Theories of globalization

Macro theories: free trade and globalization

The *theory of comparative advantage*, proposed in the early nineteenth century, stated that under free trade, nations will maximize wealth if they export the goods for which they have a relative advantage (Ricardo 1967). The idea is that countries should concentrate on the production of those goods and services at which they are most efficient and export them, whilst buying in other products from abroad. The total global production of goods and services will then be higher than when separate countries try to produce everything themselves. As a theoretical example, imagine two similar industrial parks, one in Malaysia and the other based in the Philippines, both with 10,000 workers, and both producing electrical products. Both sites employ 5,000 workers (half their total effort) to produce computer

Table 1.1 Globalization data

	US Sbn Current Price					Average Growth rate
	1990	2000	2010	2019	2020	1990–2019
World GDP (US $bn)	22800	33700	66200	87600	84700	5.10%
Gross Capital formation	5880	8150	16200	23000	*na*	5.20%
Trade (Export of goods and Services)	4300	7940	22900	24800	22600	6.90%
Foreign Direct Invesments (Inward Stock)	2196	7377	19899	36377	41354	11%
Foreign Direct Investments (Inflows)	205	1356	1393	1530	999	10%
Cross Border Mergers and Acquisitions (Value)	98	960	347	423	379	18%
Sales of Foreign Affiliates	7615	17000	32960	33200*	*na*	8.43%
Royalties and Licences fees	31	75	191	427*	*na*	9.80%
Employment of Foreign Affiliates (Thousand)	30860	54000	62900	85500	*na*	5.40%
Daily Foreign Exchange Transactions (US $bn)	539	1240	3972	6592	*na*	9%

Source: Authors' own, based on data from World Bank, World Development Indicators: https://databank.worldbank.org/source/world-development-indicators; UNCTAD: https://unctad.org/statistics; BIS (Bank of International Settlements): https:///www.bis.org/statistics/rpfx19.htm?m=6%7C381%7C677.

4 Figures and tables | are used extensively to illustrate the theory.

EXAMPLE 1.1 Otis Elevators

Otis Elevator Company started in 1853 in New York and was soon selling elevators in Canada and Europe as well. In the 1960s it had many plants, service operations and sales offices all over Europe, where the company grew organically as well as by acquisition. Each subsidiary fought for a share of local markets. Competitors were either local national companies or subsidiaries of rival multinational companies. The Otis subsidiaries managed all the activities of the value chain (marketing, design, production, installation and service). For instance, the French subsidiary designed elevators for the French market, manufactured them in French factories, sold them with French sales forces and maintained them with a French after-sales organization – the

5 In-chapter examples | are scattered throughout the text to reinforce how the theory is put into practice. Longer examples are highlighted and exemplify global strategy at work.

Summary and key points

1 Globalization is the process by which people, products, information and money can move freely across borders
   a Four factors are pushing globalization:
      - Political: liberalization of trade and investment reduces trade barriers
      - Technological: technology reduces the cost of coordination and increases economies of scale
      - Social: convergence of customer choices encourages standardization and global branding
      - Competitive: emergence of new competitors induces integration companies to compete on all fronts with strong coordination

6 Summary and key points | provide an abbreviated version of the main concepts and theories. They are useful for revision and checking understanding of the key points.

Learning assignments

1 Among the enterprises that you know, can you identify one that qualifies as a global company? Why?
2 In Figure 1.9, why are saving accounts positioned low on global approach and high on local approach while investment banking is high on global approach and low on local approach?
3 In Figure 1.8, food retail is positioned as a local business, with a very low globalization score. However, in the press, companies like Tesco, Walmart or Carrefour are described as 'global retailers'. Explain this discrepancy.
4 What are the social factors that have pushed for globalization, and which have been pushing against it?

7 Learning assignments | test understanding of the chapter and encourage further thought.

8 Key words | appear at the end of each chapter and can be used as checklists for revision.

Key words

- Arbitrage benefits
- Comparative advantage
- Global companies
- Global industries
- Global/multi-local mapping
- Globalization
- International product life cycle
- Multinational companies

9 Web resources | are included for students who want to delve a little further.

Web Resources

INSEAD:
http://knowledge.insead.edu/
Businessweek magazine:
https://www.bloomberg.com/businessweek
McKinsey Quarterly:
http://www.mckinseyquarterly.com/
UNCTAD:
http://unctad.org/en/Pages/Home.aspx
Boston Consulting Group:
https://www.bcgperspectives.com/
Provides information about the WTO:
http://www.wto.org/
Provides statistics and papers from the IMF:
http://www.imf.org/
https://www.globaltradealert.org/

References and further reading

Books and articles

Altman, S. and Bastian, P. (2020) *DHL Global Connectedness Index*. https://www.dhl.com/content/dam/dhl/global/dhl-spotlight/documents/pdf/spotlight-g04-global-connectedness-index-2020.pdf (accessed 1 February 2022).
Baker, M. and Hart, S. (1999) *Product Strategy and Management* (London: Prentice-Hall).
Bank for International Settlements (2014) 84th Annual
Dunning, J. (1993) *Multinational Enterprises and the Global Economy* (Wokingham: Addison-Wesley).
Dunning, J. H. (2001) 'The Eclectic (OLI) Paradigm of International Production: Past, Present and Future', *International Journal of the Economics of Business*, 8 ((2): 17–190.
Evenett, Simon J. (2019) 'Protectionism, State Discrimination and International Business Since the Onset of the Global Financial Crisis',

10 References and further reading | identify key texts for further research and include books and journal articles.

Companion website

Visit the companion website at **bloomsbury.pub/global-strategic-management-5e** for a range of teaching and learning resources including:

Global Strategic Management
5th Edition
by Philippe Lasserre and Felipe Monteiro

Home
Instructor Resources
Student Resources

Seamlessly blending academic rigour and practicality, this textbook provides an introduction to global business strategy. Assuming a born global perspective, *Global Strategic Management* is supported by ample pedagogical features, including numerous case studies and examples featuring both established multinationals and unknown SMEs from across the globe.

The book takes an applied approach to global business strategy, emphasising functional parts of international business (managing marketing, operations, HR and finance). New to this fifth edition is increased material on sustainability and corporate social responsibility, including discussion of climate change, NGOs and sustainable development goals. Subjects such as the impact of technology, cryptocurrency and global strategy in the digital space are discussed in more detail.

For instructors:

- Microsoft® PowerPoint presentations for each chapter
- Answers to mini-case questions
- Answers to learning assignments
- A testbank of multiple choice and essay questions
- Videos illustrating issues covered in the chapters of the book

For students:

- Multiple choice questions for revision
- Appendices

Acknowledgements

The authors would like to give particular recognition to Anne Marie Carrick for her collaboration in the preparation, documentation and editing of the book.

We would also like to thank our colleagues at INSEAD who gave us useful advice, as well as their blessing, to use some of their work in this new edition: David Dubois, Horacio Falcão, Wesley Koo, Michael Lee, Joerg Niessing, Yadav Prashant, Phanish Puranam and Anna Szerb.

We would also like to thank our colleagues at INSEAD who gave their support for the previous editions: Henri Claude de Bettignies, Amitava Chattopadhyay, Gabriel Hawawini, Philip Parker, Jose Santos, Hellmut Schütte, Jasjit Singh, Claude Viallet (†) and Michael Witt.

Many thanks also to all our colleagues in the INSEAD Strategy area for their continuous support while we were writing this book. In particular, our gratitude goes to Michael Bikard, Laurence Capron, Yves Doz, Javier Gimeno, Ilze Kivleniece, Chengyi Lin, Subi Rangan, Andrew Shipilov, Ithai Stern and Peter Zemsky. Having them around–even during Covid times– has been a major source of inspiration for us. Our thanks also goes to our faculty assistants namely Elodie Poulain and Typhanie Vasseur.

Thanks also to Mary Boldrini from the INSEAD Library who helped us to retrieve useful data and Andrew Lee who helped with additional research. We are also grateful to the research department of INSEAD who provided some financial support and to the INSEAD Case Publishing team, Isabel Assureira, Carine Dao Panam, Claire Derouin, Hazel Hamelin, Emilie Lescalier Traquet and Larisa Shikhova. We would also like to thank the global leaders who generously gave us their time and opened the doors of their organizations for us to write about their challenges and accomplishments. In particular, we would like to thank Joao Alvares Ribeiro, Jean-Claude Biver, Ernesto Ciorra, Celso Ferrer, Yannick Fierling, Jean-Marc Frangos, Mariano Gomide, Paulo Kakinoff, Joao Roquette Ribeiro, Vincent Rotger, Zhang Ruimin, Javier Sobrino, Francesco Starace, Shubao Sun, Marco Stefanini, Fabio Tentori and Geraldo Thomaz.

Our gratitude also goes to our collaborators in other projects, which inspired a number of the ideas and examples presented in this book. Our special thanks go to Tulio Alburquerque, Tina Ambos, Niklas Arvidsson, Sergio Averbach, Jose Miguel Benavente, Julian Birkinshaw, Daniel Blake, Claudio Conti, John Davies, Benoit Decreton, Denise Dunlap, Lisa Friedman, Sumantra Ghoshal (†), Gustavo Herrero, Susan Hill, Katia Kachan, Suzana Kertesz, Thomas Klueter, Bruno Lanvin, Sergio Lazzarini, Luiz Mesquita, Michael Mol, Caterina Moschieri, Aldo Musacchio, Nikita Pillai, Marta Pimentel, Gabriel Rozman, Jose Santos, Don Sull, Betania Tanure, Katherine Tatarinov and Ivanka Visjnic.

Christian Ritter, Elizabeth Holmes, Sophie Harrington and Isabelle Cheng from Bloomsbury and Deborah Maloney from Integra gave us their competence and patience in editing the text. Our final wholehearted thanks goes to our families and friends for all their support and love.

Introduction to the fifth edition

The fifth edition of this book was prepared from 2020 to mid 2022, a time in which the Covid-19 pandemic severely impacted economic, social and health conditions. More than 500 million people were infected with the Coronavirus and more than 6.3 million people have died as of June 2022. In early 2022 Russia invaded Ukraine affecting global trade and investments and disrupting global supplies.

Those events have triggered large-scale government support for businesses and industries and the recovery presents a unique occasion to rethink and reset priorities when rebuilding, focusing efforts on the sustainability, resilience and inclusiveness aspects of governments' policies and businesses' strategies and actions.

During this unprecedented time, businesses adapted rapidly to both changes in consumers' behaviours and a shift to remote working, rapidly deploying digital systems to accommodate these changes. The general consensus is that the move to digital, hybrid ways of working and work from everywhere trends are likely to persist even after the pandemic subsides.

Covid-19 has brought globalization front and centre of the debate, highlighting interconnectedness (the virus went global in a few weeks) and deglobalization (the difficulties in international cooperation and the re-emergence of nationalisms in the provision of vaccines, medical supplies, protective masks, etc.). The pandemic and the Ukrainian war have also highlighted the interdependence of global production and supply chains, as well as the risks and fragilities that they are exposed to, forcing multinationals to revise their localization and procurement strategies to gain resilience in the current uncertain environment.

Furthermore, a resurgence of several forms of nationalism in Russia, Turkey, China, Central Europe and the USA have given a new momentum to protectionism. The European Union itself, one of the most ambitious international integrative organizations, showed some signs of both disillusion and dissolution, with Brexit being the most notorious example. Even the emerging world is experiencing some economic slowdown. As a response to the Russian invasion of Ukraine in early 2022, Western democracies, lead by the US, UK and EU, imposed a series of economic and financial sanctions against Russia that affected global trade and finances in energy, food and disrupted global supply chains. In spite of uncertain signs, many corporations from all over the world have shown a willingness to pursue their quest for global markets. OECD (Organisation for Economic Co-operation and Development) firms are still looking at emerging economies in order to capture the consumption appetite of their expanding middle classes. New champions from emerging countries are progressively planting investments outside their boundaries and developing an appetite for acquiring companies in the industrial world.

On the technological front, the recent period has seen confirmation that the world has fully entered into a digital era that permeates nearly all segments of human activities: health, industrial production, entertainment, communication research and development and more.

This new edition considers that globalization is still an ongoing, fundamental economic phenomenon, but tries to take into consideration the above-mentioned geopolitical, technological and climatic trends. The objectives of this edition are to help students and managers to understand the forces that drive globalization and to put together all aspects of global strategic management to provide firms with the relevant skills to support their global ambitions. It is still about global firms and global management. Its objective remains to help graduate and undergraduate students to understand the main issues that companies and their managers confront when they 'go global' or 'manage globally', and how to cope with them. Data and narratives have been updated in light of the aforementioned new developments, and several case examples added. At the end of each chapter there are now one or two Mini-cases that students may discuss in class.

The book has been designed as a support for specialized courses on strategic management for global firms or courses on international business, and is equivalent to a series of course notes to be read in preparation for a class or afterwards. Students will normally be assigned a case study for each of the topics covered in the book. It can also be used as a reference guide for managers and executives.

There are a number of excellent textbooks on international business already available.[1] How does this book compare?

First, the focus of the book is on business firms and their employees. It has eliminated from the text the macroeconomic and political factors that traditional international business textbooks cover, such as international trade and investment flows, the problems of economic development in emerging countries, analysis of international and regional institutions (such as the World Trade Organization (WTO), the United Nations (UN), the World Bank and other development banks, the European Union (EU), the North American Free Trade Agreement (NAFTA), the Association of Southeast Asian Nations (ASEAN)), as well as geopolitical analysis of diplomacy and defence. It is assumed that students who are interested in those topics will read specialized books or attend courses taught by economists or political scientists.

Second, the book takes the view that the traditional international business paradigm, based on the study of investments in 'foreign' countries by 'home'-country firms, is no longer sufficient for studying global firms. International and multinational firms controlling a vast array of 'foreign subsidiaries' have been in existence for a long time but, since the 1970s, the concept of 'global' firms has progressively imposed itself at the nexus of borderless strategic thinking. Global firms have increasingly shed their original nationality to manage a network of firms in an integrated and coordinated way out of 'centres' that are no longer necessarily located in their country of origin. Those firms 'without borders' make up the vanguard of the modern industrial architecture. More and more 'born global' companies and small and middle-sized firms have improved their global presence.

Some chapters have been strengthened to deal with the new reality of multinational corporations as they put environmental, social and corporate governance (ESG) at the front and centre of their strategies and operations.

New sections have been added to emphasize the role of digital technologies, which have revolutionized consumer behaviours, impacted core business models and blurred borders between industries and sectors. In the case of multinational corporations, these disruptive digital tools have also enabled productive and innovative networks, supply chain management and marketing of products and services at a distance. The chapter on global alliances has been augmented with references to global ecosystems.

This edition, like the previous ones, is inspired largely by theoretical and empirical work. Obviously, classical issues such as entry strategies or expatriate management will not be forgotten, but the overall tone of the book looks at how, ultimately, international or multinational firms become global and are managed globally.

Third, the book aims to describe and analyse the key strategic and managerial challenges for firms, but does not pretend to be exhaustive or encyclopaedic. Many theoretical developments have been deliberately omitted: transaction costs theory, locational theory and agency theory, for instance. We have also avoided the temptation to provide long lists of publications. Instead, we have concentrated solely on the most relevant literature in each discussion. A more extensive list of references and further reading is available at the end of each chapter.

Several Examples and Mini-cases have been inserted in the chapters in order to illustrate the points made in the text. In addition, a number of online appendices can be found on the companion website, which provide further information on cryptocurrency, global/local mapping, country profiles, government support programs, globalization indices, country comparisons, cash flow adjustment, different types of risk, organizational design and scenario construction. These can be accessed and downloaded via the companion website, at **bloomsbury.pub/global-strategic-management-5e**.

Finally, the book owes a considerable debt to the work done by professors or ex-professors at INSEAD Business School, and has favoured their works rather than those of others. This has been a deliberate choice, given the long-standing involvement of the authors in the intellectual life of this institution.

The structure of the book

As Figure 0.1 shows, the bulk of the book is organized into three parts of unequal length according to the classical strategic framework of Environment, Strategy, Implementation: which in this case translates to Global Contexts, Global Strategies and Managing Globally. The Current and Future Trends in Globalization and the long case study on Global Strategic Management in Action (Chapter 16) tie up the arguments presented in that structure.

How can this book be used?

This book can be used in three ways:

1. As a stand-alone textbook for a course based on lectures and exercises. At the end of each chapter there are questions that can serve as learning assignments to prepare for such lectures, or to follow them.
2. As background reading for a course based on case studies. To that end Appendix I.1 (see companion website) lists potential cases that can be used to support each chapter of the book. Those cases

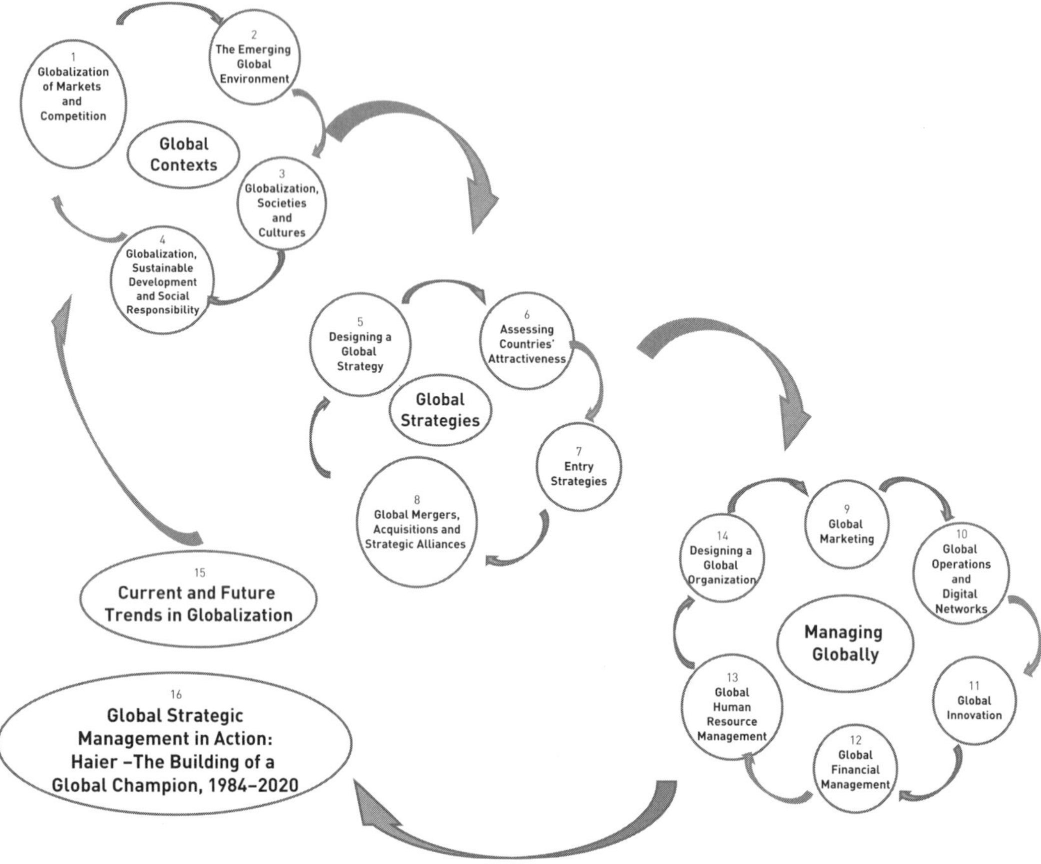

Figure 0.1 Structure of the book

are available from the most important case platforms, such as INSEAD Publishing, Harvard Business School Publishing and The Case Center. There are also some excellent casebooks available.[2]

3 As a reference book, particularly in executive programmes or for individual readers who wish to get acquainted with global strategic management without being burdened by too much theory and background reading.

Notes

1 Inkpen and Ramaswamy (2006); Tallman (2009); Peng (2021).

2 De la Torre, Doz and Devinney (2001); Bartlett and Ghoshal (2002).

References and further reading

Recent (since 2015)

Hill, C. W. L. and Hult, G. T. M. (2021) *International Business: Competing in the Global Marketplace*, 13th edn (New York: McGraw-Hill).

Peng, M. (2021) *Global Strategy*, 5th edn (Boston, MA: Cengage Learning).

Schlege, B. and Winer, R. (2020) *The Routledge Companion to Strategic Marketing* (Milton, Oxford: Routledge).

Berck, J. and Demarzo, P. (2020) *Corporate Finance* (London: Pearson Education).

Weihrich, H., Cannice, M. and Koontz, H. (2020) *Management: A Global, Innovative, and Entrepreneurial Perspective*, 15th edn (New York, NY: McGraw-Hill).

Geringer, M., McNett, J., Minor, S. and Ball, D. (2020) *International Business* (New York, NY: McGraw-Hill).

Hawawini, G. and Viallet, C. (2019) *Finance for Executives: Managing for Value Creation*, 6th edn (Mason, OH: South-Western Cengage Learning).

Wild, J. and Wild, K. (2019) *International Business: The Challenges of Globalization*, 9th edn (London: Pearson).

van Tulder, R., Verbeke, A. and Piscitello, L. (2019) *International Business in the Information and Digital Age* (Bingley, UK: Emerald Publishing).

Eun, C. and Resnick, B. (2017) *International Financial Management*, 7th edn (New York, NY: McGraw-Hill).

Jensen, K. R. (2017) *Leading Global Innovation: Facilitating Multicultural Collaboration and International Market Success* (London: Palgrave).

Pucik, V., Evans, P. A. L., Björkman, I. and Morris, S. S. (2017) *The Global Challenge: International Human Resource Management*, 3rd edn (Chicago, IL: Chicago Business Press).

Tell, F., Berggren, C., Brusoni, S. and van de Ven, A. (2017) *Managing Knowledge Integration Across Boundaries* (Oxford: Oxford University Press).

Lehmacher, W. (2017) *The Global Supply Chain: Technology, Transformation and Circular Economy* (Wiesbaden: Springer International).

Westland, C. (2016) *Global Innovation Management*, 2nd edn (London: Palgrave).

Before 2015

Johansen, J., Farooq, S. and Cheng, Y. (2014) *International Operations Networks* (London: Springer-Verlag).

Kotler, P. and Kotler, M. (2014) *Winning Global Markets: How Businesses Invest and Prosper in the World's High-Growth Cities* (Hoboken, NJ: Wiley).

Hayton, J. (ed.) (2012) *Global Human Resource Management Casebook* (New York, NY: Routledge).

Yip, G. and Hult, G. T. M. (2012) *Total Global Strategy*, 3rd edn (Harlow: Pearson Education).

Bartlett, C. and Beamish, P. W. (2011) *Transnational Management: Text, Cases and Readings in Cross-Border Management*, 6th edn (New York, NY: McGraw-Hill).

Hitt, M. A., Ireland, R. D. and Hoskisson, R. E. (2011) *Strategic Management: Competitiveness and Globalization: Concepts and Cases*, 9th edn (Mason, OH: Thomson South-Western).

Tallman, S. (2009) *Global Strategy: Global Dimensions of Strategy* (Chichester: Wiley).

Dunning, J. H. and Lundan, S. M. (2008) *Multinational Enterprises and the Global Economy*, 2nd edn (Cheltenham: Edward Elgar).

Inkpen, A. and Ramaswamy, K. (2006) *Global Strategy: Creating and Sustaining Advantage Across Borders* (Oxford: Oxford University Press).

Ariño, A., Ghemawat, P. and Ricart, J. E. (2004) *Creating Value Through International Strategy* (Basingstoke: Palgrave Macmillan).

Bartlett, C. A. and Ghoshal, S. (2002) *Managing Across Borders: The Transnational Solution*, 2nd edn (Boston, MA: Harvard Business School).

De la Torre, J., Doz, Y. L. and Devinney, T. (2001) *Managing the Global Corporation: Case Studies in Strategy and Management*, 2nd edn (New York, NY: McGraw-Hill).

Doz, Y. L., Santos, J. and Williamson, P. J. (2001) From *Global to Metanational: How Companies Win in the Knowledge Economy* (Boston, MA: Harvard Business School).

Bartlett, C. A., Doz, Y. L. and Hedlund, G. (1990) *Managing the Global Firm* (London: Routledge).

Prahalad, C. K. and Doz, Y. L. (1987) *The Multinational Mission: Balancing Local Demands and Global Vision* (New York, NY: Simon & Schuster).

Journals

Academy of Management Journal: https://aom.org/research/journals/journal

California Management Review: https://cmr.berkeley.edu/

Global Strategy Journal: https://onlinelibrary.wiley.com/journal/20425805

Harvard Business Review: https://hbr.org/

Journal of International Business Policy: https://link.springer.com/journal/42214/volumes-and-issues

Journal of International Business Studies: http://www.springer.com/business+%26+management/journal/41267

Journal of Management Studies: https://onlinelibrary.wiley.com/journal/14676486

Journal of World Business: https://www.journals.elsevier.com/journal-of-world-business

Long Range Planning: https://www.journals.elsevier.com/long-range-planning

MIT Sloan Management Review: http://sloanreview.mit.edu

The International Journal of Human Resource Management: http://www.tandfonline.com/toc/rijh20/current

The International Journal of Logistics Management: http://www.emeraldinsight.com/journal/ijlm

Thunderbird International Business Review: http://onlinelibrary.wiley.com/journal/10.1002/(ISSN)1520-6874

Part I

Global contexts

Chapter 1 Globalization of markets and competition | Chapter 1 defines what 'globalization' means, first from a geopolitical and economical point of view and second for business enterprises. It looks at the many political, technological, social and economic factors that have driven globalization as well as the ones restraining it. It describes how companies have over time moved from being national to international, then to multinational and finally becoming global firms. It ends by proposing a mapping of industries and firms according to the extent to which they are exposed to globalization or localization drivers.

Chapter 2 The emerging global environment | Chapter 2 underlines the growing importance of emerging countries, their companies and their markets in the world since the 1980s. It describes the main characteristics of emerging countries, their development paths and their attractiveness as markets and as offshore operational bases, as well as their competitiveness and the role of their global champions. Strategies for doing business in emerging countries will also be discussed.

Chapter 3 Globalization, societies and cultures | Chapter 3 discusses how in different parts of the world societies still differ in terms of the ways economic activities are structured, coordinated and managed, and how cultures influence the behaviour of people and organizations. It begins with a presentation of different streams of research showing international differences in business cultures and economic organizations. Various cross-cultural studies will be presented, followed by a discussion of the impact of cultural differences on management, cross-cultural teams, negotiations and business practices. The last part of the chapter deals specifically with international negotiations.

Chapter 4 Globalization, sustainable development and social responsibility | This chapter addresses some of the issues that global companies face concerning environmental and ethical challenges. Particular emphasis is put on the kind of ethical dilemma global firms and managers have to confront in their worldwide operations – issues such as corruption, tax evasion, environmental protection, human rights, labour laws and gender equality.

Chapter 1

Globalization of markets and competition

By the end of the chapter you should be able to:

- Define globalization from a macro environment perspective
- Identify the forces pushing towards globalization and the forces pushing for localization
- Define what globalization means for firms
- Identify the various steps of globalization for firms
- Make a distinction between multinational and global firms
- Spell out the benefits and pitfalls of globalization
- Analyse the recent trend of deglobalization
- Discuss the consequences of the Covid-19 pandemic on globalization
- Position an industry or a business on the global/multi-local mapping

Introduction

Chapter 1 defines what 'globalization' means: firstly from a geopolitical and economic point of view, and secondly for business enterprises. It looks at the many political, technological, social and economic factors that have driven globalization, as well as those restraining it. It describes how many companies have evolved, over time, from 'national' to 'international', then 'multinational' and finally 'global'. Using an example, the chapter looks at how a *multinational* company having foreign subsidiaries can become *global* by extending its operations worldwide and adopting a competitive configuration through strong coordination and integration of its international activities across borders. Both the benefits and constraints of globalization are described. Some factors still push towards a local approach to management, on a country-by-country basis, and the elements inducing this localization are analysed.

Finally, the global/multi-local mapping matrix is presented as a tool to position industries, companies and businesses according to the relative importance they place on global versus local approaches. The chapter ends by introducing some of the societal issues associated with globalization.

The phenomenon of globalization

Since the 1960s, international trade, investment and migration have all grown much faster than the world economy. Firms have multiplied their presence outside their country of origin, employing more and more people and selling and buying technology internationally (see Table 1.1 and Figure 1.1). More products are sold in similar stores, with similar features carrying a common brand across the globe. Factories that were prosperous in the Western world have been closed and transferred to lower-cost countries. English is now considered the *lingua franca* for major business transactions. Events happening in one location are visible in real time everywhere thanks to the internet and social networks. This is what is commonly referred to as the process of 'globalization'.

Table 1.1 Globalization data

	US$ bn Current Price					Average Growth Rate
	1990	2000	2010	2019	2020	1990–2019
World GDP (US $bn)	22800	33700	66200	87600	84700	5.10%
Gross Capital Formation	5880	8150	16200	23000	*na*	5.20%
Trade (Export of Goods and Services)	4300	7940	22900	24800	22600	6.90%
Foreign Direct Invesments (Inward Stock)	2196	7377	19899	36377	41354	11%
Foreign Direct Investments (Inflows)	205	1356	1393	1530	999	10%
Cross Border Mergers and Acquisitions (Value)	98	960	347	423	379	18%
Sales of Foreign Affiliates	7615	17000	32960	33200*	*na*	8.43%
Royalties and Licence fees	31	75	191	427*	*na*	9.80%
Employment of Foreign Affiliates (Thousand)	30860	54000	62900	85500	*na*	5.40%
Daily Foreign Exchange Transactions (US $bn)	539	1240	3972	6592	*na*	9%

Source: Authors' own, based on data from World Bank, World Development Indicators: https://databank.worldbank.org/source/world-development-indicators; UNCTAD: https://unctad.org/statistics; BIS (Bank of International Settlements): https:///www.bis.org/statistics/rpfx19.htm?m=6%7C381%7C677.

In today's business world, managers, politicians, journalists and academics commonly refer to concepts such as 'globalization', 'global industries', 'global competition', 'global strategies' and so on. While those terms are widely used, their exact meaning is often not well understood. For some people, globalization is considered to be the intrusion of foreigners into local communities. Its effect is viewed as a destruction of the social fabric within nations. For others, it means freedom of movement, entrepreneurship, an exchange of cultures and harmonization. As far as the corporate world is concerned, some are certain it means 'to expand the company's presence abroad'; for others, it means 'standardizing a product and selling it to the world'; for others still, it denotes an approach to management in which decision making is centralized at corporate headquarters. There are many reasons for this confusion. One relates to the fact that the phenomenon of globalization

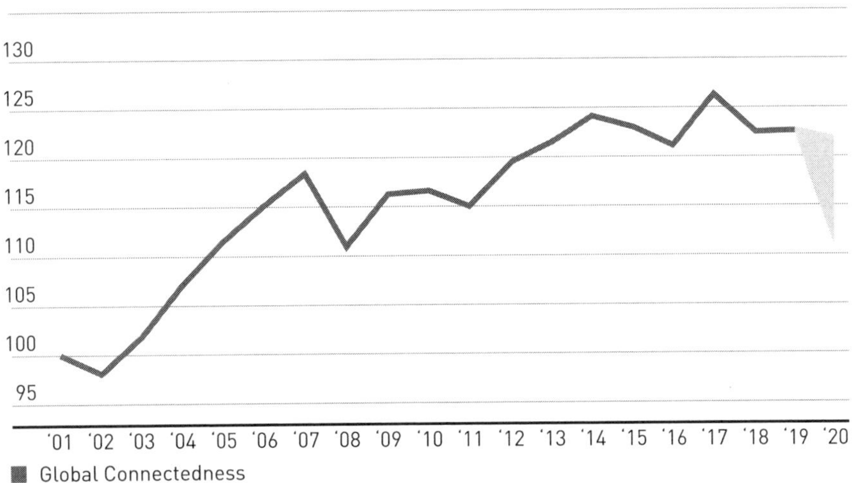

Figure 1.1 DHL Global Connectedness Index

Source: The Global Connectedness Index is a combination of measures concerning the global movement of trade, capital, Information and people, https://www.dhl.com/content/dam/dhl/global/dhl-spotlight/documents/pdf/spotlight-g04-global-connectedness-index-2020.pdf.

describes macroeconomic and political change, while for the business world it denotes a strategic and managerial issue. While the concept of globalization is relatively new, the phenomenon is not. There have been periods in history when the world was without borders, and citizens, products and money could move freely. Theories have been developed to explain and advocate free trade and globalization from the macro point of view, and to explain the process of globalization from the business point of view (see Insert 1.1). As far as the business world is concerned, before the 1970s the most frequently used terminology, when referring to integrated operating across the world, was 'international', 'multinational' or occasionally 'transnational'. Even if we ignore the East India Company, which started in the early seventeenth century, modern corporations such as Unilever, Nestlé and Procter & Gamble were operating all over the world by the end of the nineteenth century. They are known as multinational companies, but nobody would have called them global fifty years ago. The global concept appeared in the early 1970s and progressively invaded boardrooms, classrooms and business literature. What is the exact meaning of globalization? What forces generated it? And what are the consequences for firms?

There is no single, well-established definition of globalization. Here we will posit as a working definition: 'The process by which people, products, information and money can move freely across borders'. As a consequence, markets may tend to converge, providing opportunities for the standardization of products, for production centres to be (re)located to more economical places, and for R&D labs to be distributed across countries. As we will see, this implies a more centralized management of firms. Before examining the many aspects of corporate life impacted by the phenomenon of globalization, we will first look at the macroeconomic, technological and political factors that have generated such a global environment, and then look at how firms have changed their operations to take advantage of the new opportunities this environment offers.

Insert 1.1 Theories of globalization

Macro theories: free trade and globalization

The *theory of comparative advantage*, proposed in the early nineteenth century, stated that under free trade, nations will maximize wealth if they export the goods for which they have a relative advantage (Ricardo 1967). The idea is that countries should concentrate on the production of those goods and services at which they are most efficient and export them, whilst buying in other products from abroad. The total global production of goods and services will then be higher than when separate countries try to produce everything themselves. As a theoretical example, imagine two similar industrial parks, one in Malaysia and the other based in the Philippines, both with 10,000 workers, and both producing electrical products. Both sites employ 5,000 workers (half their total effort) to produce computer motherboards and 5,000 workers to make videogame consoles. The Malaysian operation is able to produce 10 million motherboards per year and the Philippines 8 million, while the Malaysians produce 200,000 consoles to the Philippines' 250,000. Malaysia has, therefore, demonstrated a comparative advantage over the Philippines for motherboards and Philippines has a comparative advantage over Malaysia for consoles. The total global output in the current situation will be 18 million motherboards and 450,000 consoles per year. For better results, Malaysia should concentrate on producing motherboards and trading them, while the Philippines should focus its efforts on consoles. In this situation the global output rises to 20 million motherboards and 500,000 consoles, marking an 11 per cent increase in both motherboards and consoles.

World-system theories suggest that globalization is the product of nationalistic, capitalistic, colonial and international expansion (Wallerstein 1974, 2000; Robinson 2004). For instance, from the sixteenth century the colonial expansion of Spain, Portugal, the Netherlands, Britain and France created a global market for a certain number of commodities. Later, the USA and Japan became colonial imperialistic global powers. In other words, since the appearance of modern shipping vessels and navigation systems, truly global trade has become possible.

Marxism views globalization as the result of the tendency of the return on capital to decrease, forcing capitalists to find new territories to exploit. Lenin argued that the ultimate stage of capitalism was imperialism (Marx and Engels 1848; Lenin 1917). The argument is that the profits of firms tend to decrease because of intense competition. Firms react by merging and looking for markets outside their national boundaries, creating global oligopolies, for example Holcim Group, Apple and Samsung.

Network society theories see globalization as the result of the vested interests of a transnational capitalistic class (managers, politicians, bureaucrats, bankers), as well as of supranational organizations such as the WTO, UN and EU (Castells 1996; Sklair 2000). Advances in telecommunications and the rise of the internet have made it possible for business to be conducted globally, both in terms of financial transactions and internationally connected production systems.

Technological cultural theories propose that information technologies have led to a convergence of culture (Robertson 1992; Ritzer 1993). Very similar in essence to McLuhan's 'Global Village' concept,[1] these theories state that thanks to technology, people in different countries increasingly tend to share a common culture and consumer choices, making global product design and production possible and desirable.

The *World 3.0* theory, developed by Professor Pankaj Ghemawat,[2] holds that humanity has followed four stages of social, political and economic organization and trade. The first stage (World 0.0) refers to the prehistoric period in which societies were organized into thousands of tribes surviving by hunting and gathering, and where human interactions were limited to those between the members of tribes, with practically no external trade. The second stage (World 1.0) refers to the formation of political entities in the forms of cities or empires (China, Sumer, Aztec), governing several thousands to millions of peoples (mainly farmers) under a political power structure (an empire or kingdom). Mostly economically self-sufficient, these states introduced some international transactions, but limited exchange mechanisms (such as trade via the Silk Road). World 2.0 started in the seventeenth century with the colonial expansion of European powers and the creation of nation states. The first multinationals, such as the British East India Company, extended their reach as far as Asia. During the nineteenth century, thanks to transportation and communication innovations, multinational firms from Europe, America and Japan developed. After a decline between the two world wars, global development exploded and saw the formation of the modern business juggernauts such as Nestlé, General Electric and Siemens that we see today. The driving force of World 2.0 in the postwar years was a progressive deregulation and integration of markets. World 3.0 is predicted to evolve, following the global financial crisis of 2008, as a world that is characterized by a high level of market integration but also a high level of government regulation, in what has been called *semiglobalization*.

Micro theories: corporate globalization

Transaction cost theories posit that multinational firms result from the economic benefits of internalizing costs of transaction rather than relying on contracts to regulate contact with international economic agents (Buckley and Casson 1976).

Resource-based theories suggest that firms take advantage of their proprietary assets (technology, capital) to expand their presence in international markets (Barney 1991).

Resource seeking theories explain the global expansion of firms by their desire to obtain resources they don't have (Dunning 1993).

The Eclectic (OLI) theory of International production asserts that internationalization of firms is determined by three sets of forces: the ownership of a competitive advantage (O), the location of an attractive external country where to invest (L) and the benefits of internalizing the operations (I) (Dunning 2001).

The Uppsala model of Internationalization (Johnson and Vahine 1977) proposes that the process of internationalization is a process of gradual resources commitments based on the knowledge about foreign markets possessed by a firm and the perceived risks and opportunities.

Globalization from a macro perspective

Historically the world has experienced various periods of intense trade across continents and free movement of people and capital (see Insert 1.2), in particular during the nineteenth century after the Napoleonic wars. After a decrease due to the two world wars of the twentieth century, several factors generated the emergence of the new economic environment that we call 'global'.[3] During the 1950s and the 1960s the convergence of several political, technological, social and competitive factors began to shape this new environment.[4]

Insert 1.2 History of globalization

In a book published in 2020, Jeffrey Sachs, from Columbia University, states that 'Humanity has always been globalized, since the dispersal of modern humans from Africa some seventy thousand years ago'.[5] He identifies seven distinct periods (ages) of globalization determined by the interplay of three major sets of factors: Geography, Institutions and Technology, and Know-how. The seven ages are:

1. Paleolithic (70,000–10,000 BCE): When the migration from the African nest of Homo sapiens reached sites along the Middle East coastal areas.
2. Neolithic (10,000–3000 BCE): Further global expansion in this period is linked with the development of agriculture progressively replacing hunting and allowed the settlement of population in the temperate zones of Europe and the Middle and Far East.
3. Equestrian (3000–1000 BCE): Fostered by the progressive domestication of animals (goat, camel, sheep, cattle, horses). The horse allowed the transport of goods on long distances and permitted the migrations and trade to northern Europe, India and China.
4. Classical (1000 BCE–1500 CE): Fostered by the creation of empires motivated by political and/or religious motives. Mongols, Roman, Assyrian, Persian, Greek, Arab, Ottoman empires are examples of such cultural, economic global developments.
5. Ocean (1500–1800 CE): The development of trans-oceanic sailing vessels initiated the Spanish and Portuguese implantation in America and Asia followed by British, Dutch and French explorers, creating the first global capitalism and colonialism illustrated by the advent of global trading houses.
6. Industrial (1800–2000 CE): The steam engine was the initiator of industrialization in Britain in the nineteenth century, which cumulated with the technological development of communication, transport and the expansion of the multinational firms.
7. Digital (twenty-first century): The global connectivity of the internet and artificial intelligence offers multiple possibilities for designing new global transactions reinforcing the world.

What are the factors that push for globalization?

Political factors: liberalization of trade and investments

The main political factor has been the stabilization of postwar peace in Organisation for Economic Cooperation and Development (OECD) countries, which allowed the development of free trade among nations. Two main organizations have been the source of trade liberalization – the General

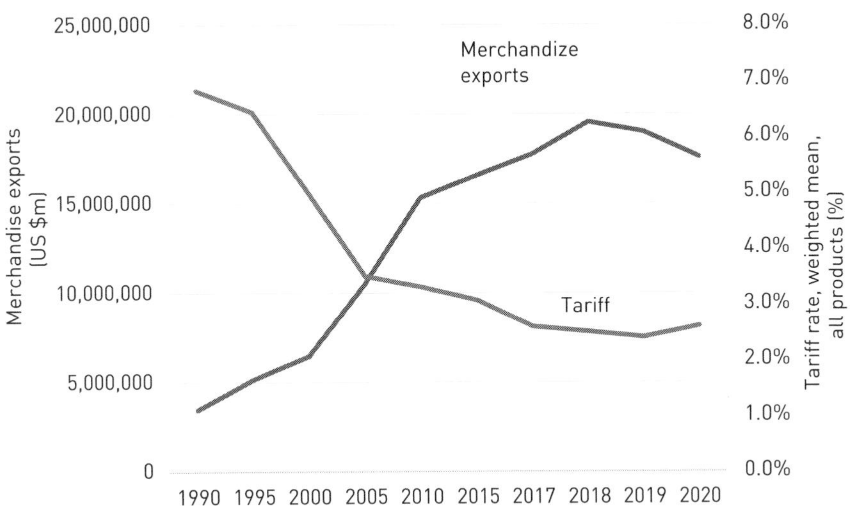

Figure 1.2 Tariff reductions and international trade
Source: Authors' creation using data from various World Bank Indicators.

Agreement on Tariffs and Trade (GATT) (replaced by the World Trade Organization (WTO) in 1995) and the European Union – to which one may add the progressive opening of emerging nations to foreign investments.

The GATT, founded in 1946 by twenty-three nations, initiated a series of negotiations, called 'rounds', aimed at reducing tariff concessions to encourage the liberalization of trade. The Kennedy Round in the mid-1960s, the Tokyo Round in the early 1970s, the Uruguay Round in late 1980s and the Doha Round in 2001 created an environment that fostered international trade, as shown in Figure 1.2.

The European Economic Community (EEC), later subsumed by the European Union (EU), was established on 25 March 1957 by the Treaty of Rome, which was signed by Belgium, France, Italy, Germany, Luxembourg and the Netherlands. The aim was to create a common market, and economic and political integration among the six member states. As a result, goods, people and financial flows could move freely across countries. During the 1970s, the EEC was enlarged with the entry of the UK, Ireland and Denmark, followed by Spain, Portugal and Greece in the 1980s, Sweden, Austria and Finland in the 1990s, and Poland, Lithuania, Latvia, Czech Republic, Slovakia, Slovenia, Malta, Hungary, Estonia, Cyprus, Romania, Bulgaria and Croatia in the early 2000s. In 1993, a single market which eliminated most legal and bureaucratic barriers was established among the member states. In 1999, a single currency, the euro, was adopted by nineteen countries, and passport-free travelling without any border controls was allowed between twenty-six countries as part of the Schengen Agreement signed in 1985. Companies could integrate their operations across Europe to take advantage of a market of 500 million customers and gain economies of scale by specializing and concentrating their operations. In 2020 the UK Left the European Union.

In addition, from 1948 to 2020 the number of preferential trade agreements (PTA) and regional trade agreements (RTA) notified to the GATT/WTO increased from practically none to around 600 in 2020 with

Insert 1.3 Some global definitions

Globalization is the process by which people, products, information and money can move freely across borders.

Global industries are industries in which, in order to survive, competitors need to operate in the key world markets in an integrated and coordinated way. Industries such as aerospace, computers, telecommunications, appliances, power generation, insurance and corporate data transmission are examples of global industries. In these sectors it is difficult to sustain competition if one does not cover (nearly) the whole world as a market, and if one does not integrate operations to make them cost and time effective.

Multinational companies are the companies that operate in various countries outside their countries of origin.

Global companies are multinational companies that operate in the main markets of the world in an integrated and coordinated way. Companies such as HSBC, Apple, Nestlé, Unilever and Samsung are global companies.

'Born global' companies have become multinational immediately upon or soon after being founded. Examples of born global companies include Airbnb, Netflix, Spotify and Uber.

Globalizing is the phenomenon whereby the competitive structure of industries changes progressively from multinational to global. Industries such as telecommunications, processed food, personal care and retail are in the process of globalization.

Global integration and coordination are the organizational structure and management processes by which various activities scattered across the world are made interdependent. As examples, global manufacturing integration implies the specialization of factories and the cross-shipment of parts between different production sites; global product development requires the coordination of various research centres and marketing teams; global account management demands that different country subsidiaries provide a service according to a plan negotiated centrally, and so on.

an acceleration in the twenty-first century. In particular from 2008, more than 300 PTA and RTAs were notified to the WTO, including the United Kingdom's post-Brexit generalized systems of preferences in January 2021.

Finally, in parallel with what was happening in the industrialized countries, the developing nations progressively adopted more positive attitudes towards foreign direct investment (FDI). At first, investment laws were designed to attract foreign investors in order to induce them to produce locally, but over the years the legislation has evolved toward a more open stance, favouring cross-border investments. According to the WTO, between 1958 and May, 2021 3,760 Bilateral Investment Treaties (BIT) that promote and protect investment in two respective countries or block of countries were signed and 2,298 are still in force.

Technological factors: transport, communication, education, science and production technology

Another set of 'push factors' for globalization are related to technological progress, which has lowered the cost of transport and communication, as well as the unit cost of production, through economies of scale or the localization of productive capacities and sourcing in low-cost economies.

Air, rail and road transport and the use of containers in maritime logistics have reduced the cost of shipping goods from country to country, as well as, in the case of air transport, enabling the travel of business managers. The development of telecommunications has reduced the cost of information exchange between business units scattered around the globe. On the scientific front, from 2005 to 2018 the percentage of foreign university-level students studying in OECD countries increased from 5 per cent to 9 per cent.[6]

Progress in manufacturing technology has given tremendous impetus to the need to concentrate production in world-class factories benefitting from huge economies of scale, thus encouraging the rationalization and integration of production systems. Besides manufacturing concentration, companies have also been able to source components or services from low-cost countries, either by setting up their own operations or by purchasing locally. Global value chains involving production of goods in two or more countries grew from 10 per cent of world GDP in 2000 to 14 per cent in 2017.[7]

Another motivating factor behind globalization is the need to quickly amortize increasing R&D costs. Companies are confronted with dual pressures: R&D budgets are increasing and the time elapsing between invention and commercialization is becoming shorter. For instance, it took fifty-two years for television to move from invention to large-scale commercial adoption and production, but the same step took nine years for the first personal computer (IBM 610) and just three years for the iPhone. For major appliances, it took seven years in the 1950s and 1960s to introduce a new model versus two years in the 1970s. The life cycle of Intel's 286 microprocessor was seven years while the 486 model lasted five years.[8] As a consequence, companies need to launch products and services at the same time in all major markets to be able to recoup their investments.

Finally, the advent of the internet has fostered the immediate transfer of media, social networking and the long-distance communication and online transactions that constitute the backbone of global communities today. During the Covid-19 pandemic, the global aspect of technology has been further demonstrated by the unprecedented global scientific cooperation necessary to develop new vaccines.

Social factors: convergence of consumer needs

International air transport and the diffusion of lifestyles by movies and TV series have increased the brand awareness of consumers worldwide. Brands like Sony, Nike, Levi's or Coca-Cola are known nearly everywhere. Kenichi Ohmae,[9] in his book *Triad Power*, has discussed the 'Californization of society' – teenagers in São Paulo, Mumbai, Milan or Los Angeles listening to the same music, using the same iPhone, wearing the same pair of blue jeans and using TikTok, Instagram and YouTube. The convergence of customer behaviour and needs is also facilitated by the urbanization and industrialization of societies. The less cultural and the more technical the product, the more likely that it can be standardized and appeal to consumers in all countries: smartphones, PCs, elevators, cranes, robots and internet platforms are products for which national differences do not matter much.

Competitive factors

The 1960s saw the emergence of Japanese competitors in markets that traditionally had been dominated by American or European companies. Japanese, and later Korean, firms adopted a global approach at the very beginning of their international expansion. One of the reasons behind this global outlook was that they did not have many national subsidiaries, while their international expansion coincided with the opening of trade barriers. From the start they designed products for the world market, creating global brands such as Sony, Panasonic and Hyundai, and their efficient production systems gave them a cost advantage in electronics and automotive parts. Competitors had to adopt a similar strategy to survive. During the 1990s emerging competitors from China, India and Brazil also entered the global game. China became 'the factory of the world' by offering offshore low-cost production sites. In other parts of the emerging world, local manufacturers in Thailand, Indonesia, Vietnam, Turkey and Mexico provided OECD industries and retailers with low-cost garments, toys, tools and furniture.

Another competitive force that pushed companies to globalize was the globalization of customers. During the 1970s, Citibank created a Global Account Management Unit to service corporate customers with international subsidiaries. Similar phenomena developed in the IT, telecom and consulting sectors, and also in the luxury segment of fashion and perfumes. Figure 1.3 summarizes these political, technological, social and competitive 'push factors' that have fostered globalization.

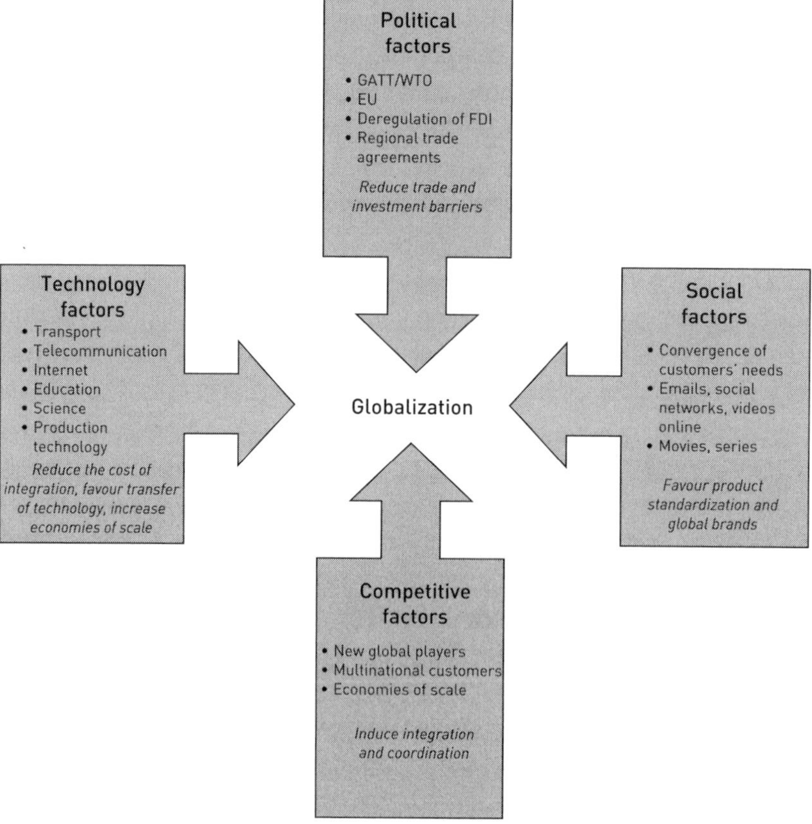

Figure 1.3 Globalization push factors

What are the factors that work against globalization? The localization push

As mentioned earlier, globalization is associated with some degree of standardization of products and practices plus a high level of coordination and integration of activities in a company's value chain. Factors that oppose standardization, coordination and integration therefore work against globalization. One can group those factors into four main categories: cultural, commercial, technical and legal.

1. Cultural factors: attitudes, tastes, behaviour and social codes

When the consumption of a product or a service is linked to traditions and national or religious values, global standardization is not effective. Some products – for instance, Kretek (tobacco and clove) cigarettes in Indonesia or the Pachinko (pinball) game in Japan – are unique to one society and their globalization is nearly impossible, although one can argue that with innovative marketing it may not be. For example, Beaujolais nouveau wine, the consumption of which was typically a Burgundian and Parisian bistro event before the 1970s, is now available in Tokyo, Paris or New York; while Halloween (trick or treat) masquerades, a traditional US festivity, are now common in Europe. This shows that even highly culture-specific items can be appreciated by customers all over the world. However, it remains true that food and drink tastes, social interactions in business negotiations, attitudes towards hygiene, cosmetics or gifts vary from culture to culture, thus hampering a global product design or approach. In the Asia Pacific and Latin American regions, for instance, personal relationship building rather than legal contracts is the normal way to conduct business. One has to spend time and effort in building these personal ties, which in a US context would be largely considered a waste of time.

Religion may play an important role in limiting the effects of globalization, particularly in the domains of national cuisine or cultural products (such as films).

Nationalism can also be considered as an obstacle to globalization to the extent that it promotes a return to trade protectionism and a retreat from international agreements in certain societies (as shown by Brexit).

2. Commercial factors: distribution, customization and responsiveness

In some sectors, distribution networks and practices differ from country to country and as a consequence the ways of managing the network, motivating dealers and distributors, pricing and negotiation are hardly amenable to global coordination. For instance, the marketing and distribution of pharmaceutical products differs according to the country's health system. In some countries, such as Japan, doctors sell medicine, while in other countries pharmacists sell to patients who get a refund (or not) from their insurance company, while in yet other cases pharmaceutical products are delivered freely to the patient.

Responsiveness to customers' demands, as well as customization, are other factors which almost by definition defeat standardization. Private savings or current accounts to individuals, loans to small and medium-sized enterprises (SMEs), mortgages, consulting activities and individual architectural designs are activities in which a local presence and a fast reaction to customers' requirements are needed for competitive success. Although some practices, processes or methodologies can be standardized on a worldwide basis (consulting, engineering, architecture or auditing, for example), specific customer requests have to be taken into consideration, thus limiting globalization.

3. Technical factors: standards, spatial presence, transportation and languages

Technical standards in electrical, civil, chemical or mechanical engineering can create a burden for global companies. The economies of scale and cost benefits of global integration and standardization cannot be exploited fully when technical standards vary greatly. In certain cases, standards can be changed without major modification – for instance, mobile telephony does not represent a major hurdle for global manufacturing. In other instances, standards are not that easy to accommodate and require a specific local production line. This is mainly the case for beer or foods, for instance.

Spatial presence is a requirement for those industries which need to occupy a physical space in order to create and distribute their products and services. Retail banking, retailing, hotels, local telephone services, hospitals, entertainment and car dealerships are examples of industries where the services have to be produced locally. There are still some advantages in globalizing certain tasks (such as the back office functions of accounting, data processing, global sourcing and transfer of best practices), but the location constraint still limits globalization benefits. In the future, e-commerce is likely to reduce the spatial constraint considerably, particularly when it comes to non-physical services such as banking or movies on demand. E-commerce in physical products can also eliminate the spatial constraint as far as the customer interface is concerned, but it is still hampered by logistical constraints. The example of Amazon demonstrates that it is possible for a customer in Paris or Rio de Janeiro to order a book but the customer will have to bear shipping costs that may eliminate the basic cost advantage of the e-bookstore. This is the reason why Amazon has established 175 fulfilment centres outside the USA, thus moving toward a more multinational business design.

The impediments of transportation are important if the cost of transport cancels out the benefits of concentrating production. Bulk commodities such as cement or basic chemicals are more economically produced in local plants than in global centralized units, despite the scale economies that could be gained: the cost and the risks of transport cancel out the benefits of centralized production. Similarly, when production systems are not scale-intensive and small productive units can achieve similar costs to large plants – in plastic moulding, for instance – there are no major benefits in building a global production system.

Finally, language can be an additional constraint to global approaches. This can be significant when it comes to customer services, of which training services, personal banking, personal telecommunication and retailing are examples. English has become more and more the 'global language', and industries such as graduate business training or high-level consulting can use English without bothering with translation.

4. Legal factors: regulation and national security issues

Governments impose regulatory constraints that often work against globalization, either because they limit the free flow of personnel (regulation on working permits), cash (exchange controls, tax), goods (customs duties, quotas), or data (censorship, the internet and controls on electronic data interchange), or because they impose localization constraints (local content, local ownership and joint venture policies).

Over the years, thanks to the GATT/WTO, multilateral agreements (EU, ASEAN, NAFTA and so on), and International Monetary Fund (IMF) requests, government legislation is leaning towards more open contexts that favour globalization. However, some constraints still exist. Some sectors such as telecommunications, media, banking and insurance are still tightly controlled and some countries (such as China and India) or regional blocs (EU) still impose local content requirements.

Finally, governments are deeply concerned with national security and will prevent foreigners gaining too much control of their defence or strategic sector industries. In the defence sector, for instance, where R&D costs are huge and economies of scale significant, globalization would appear to be fully justified, but is in fact limited because of national security constraints. Since the 2001 World Trade Center attack in New York and similar incidents in London, Madrid, Moscow, Beirut, Nairobi and Paris, governments have adopted measures that constrain the movement of people and products. Security has become the chief priority.

Recent geopolitical issues, translated into commercial wars, have affected the globalization process. One can give as an example the constraints put on Huawei's development of its 5G network, the ban on export to Iran imposed by the USA and the economic and financial sanctions imposed on Russia in 2022.

Finally the Covid-19 pandemic and the Russian invasion of Ukraine have illustrated the fragility of global value chains in pharmaceutical energy, food, or semiconductor products. For instance, the production of medical masks is concentrated in China and this generated a shortage in the USA and Europe, leading these countries to relocalize production domestically.

Figure 1.4 summarizes these localization push factors.

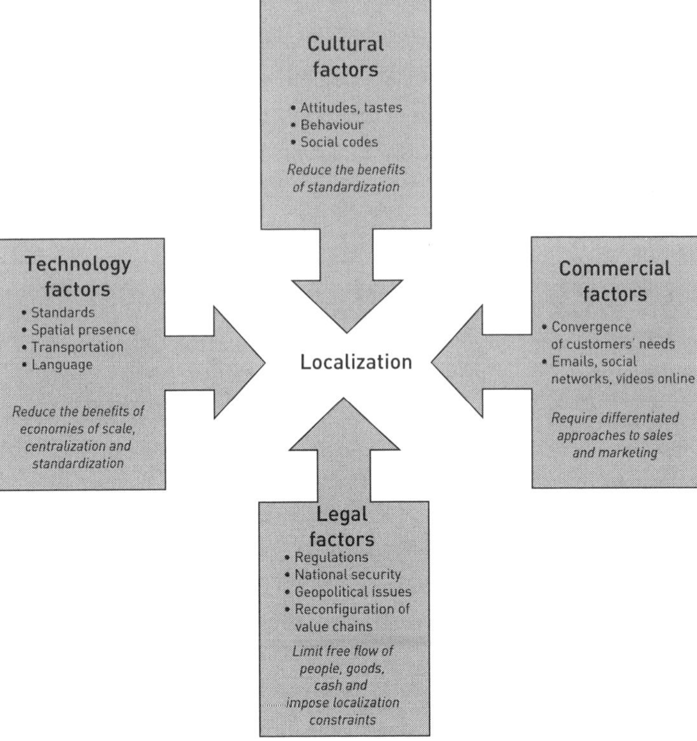

Figure 1.4 Localization push factors

The benefits of localization

The benefits of localization, instead of a global integrated and coordinated approach, are essentially customer-oriented benefits that give firms increased market power and ultimately an increased market share. Those benefits are proximity, flexibility and quick response time.

- **Proximity** is the capability to be close to the market, to understand the customer's value curve.
- **Flexibility** is the capability to adapt to customer demands in the various dimensions of the marketing mix: product/service design, distribution, branding, pricing and services. Ultimately, flexibility leads to customization.
- **Quick response time** is the ability to respond at once to specific customers' demands and increased resilience in case of global shocks (e.g. pandemics).

These three benefits are closely interrelated: proximity provides the basis for flexibility and flexibility provides the basis for a quick response time. All three give a competitive advantage when local cultural, technical, commercial and legal contexts vary so much from country to country.

The benefits and pitfalls of globalization: the macro picture

In 1817, David Ricardo in his theory of comparative advantage[10] showed that it was beneficial to nations to specialize and trade goods in which they had a comparative advantage. This laid the foundation of trade theory, which itself is the underlying foundation of globalization: in a perfect global setting where goods, people, data and money flow freely, companies can adopt an integrated and coordinated approach to their operations and the competitive battlefield would be the world. Since Ricardo's time, partisans and adversaries of free trade have exchanged heated debates about the advantages and disadvantages of globalization for society. Table 1.2 summarizes those arguments.

Table 1.2 The societal benefits of globalization

Arguments in favour of globalization	Arguments against globalization
Creates overall wealth for all nations because specialization increases trade	Imposes a massive strain on labour forces both in developed countries (job destruction) and developing countries (sweatshops, child labour)
Reduces inflation because of cost efficiencies	Standardizes customer tastes. Reduces diversity
Benefits customers because of price reductions arising from cost efficiencies	Induces concentration of power in a few global corporations Introduces a 'law of the jungle' leading to domination by the strongest multinational
Better allocation of natural, financial and human resources	Harms the environment because of unrestrained exploitation of natural resources such as forests
Reduces corruption because of free-market trade	Reduces the capacity for nations to protect their national interests, cultures and values

The globalization debate gained political visibility during the 1990s. In Europe, the Treaty of Maastricht (signed in 1992) adopted the euro as a single currency, generating a heated debate on the loss of sovereignty and the advantages of further political and economic integration. In 1995, the North America Free Trade Agreement (NAFTA) created similar discussion. In Asia, after the 1997 financial crisis, globalization was questioned and, at the end of that decade, the WTO at the Seattle ministerial conference could not set up an agenda for launching another trade round because of public criticism of the whole concept of globalization. Since 2000 and particularly after the world 'subprime' crisis of 2008, there has been growing debate about the future of globalization. Some have announced the 'end of globalization' or 'deglobalization': a concept that will be discussed later in the chapter.

Despite all this political turmoil, some analysts think that the world is becoming progressively more integrated. According to the consulting firm McKinsey,[11] by 1997 the value of truly global markets represented approximately $6 trillion out of a total world output of $28 trillion (21 per cent). In 1999, the firm anticipated that by 2030 the proportion of global markets would amount to $73 trillion out of $91 trillion (80 per cent). However, there is an ongoing debate about the future of globalization (see Chapter 15), fuelled by the pandemic that struck the world in 2020 and the Russian invasion of Ukraine in early 2022.

Globalization at the level of the firm

As mentioned previously, many firms from Western Europe extended their operations outside their country of origin into the Americas, Asia or Africa, most of them in the form of colonial implantations, from the seventeenth century onwards. Arab merchants penetrated the Southeast Asian region in order to organize trade. Following the industrial revolution, large corporations started the capitalistic movement of international investments in infrastructure projects and in the setting up of subsidiaries. The first wave of modern multinational expansion began in 1880 and declined after the First World War. This wave was made of 'free-standing' firms, legally incorporated in their native country but extending rapidly internationally via the creation of local subsidiaries. Except for the resource-based multinational, each local subsidiary was self-standing. By the end of the nineteenth century, firms such as Nestlé, Lever Brothers (Unilever), General Electric and Bayer were representative of this generation of multinational corporations. A second wave of corporate international expansion through local subsidiaries took place after the Second World War, launched by US and European companies and augmented later by Japanese companies. In the 1960s local subsidiaries were extended to more and more countries but started to progressively lose their autonomy and become part of an integrated global network.[12] Classically, over time firms have followed a sequential evolution, from being exporters, to the setting up of foreign subsidiaries, to the integration of operations across the world.[13] From local, they became international, then multinational and now global. More recently, 'born global' companies have assumed a global setting from the beginning,[14] a development that will be discussed in Chapter 5.

To illustrate the traditional phenomenon of globalization let us take the simplified example of Otis Elevator Company.

EXAMPLE 1.1 Otis Elevators

Otis Elevator Company started in 1853 in New York and was soon selling elevators in Canada and Europe as well. In the 1960s it had many plants, service operations and sales offices all over Europe, where the company grew organically as well as by acquisition. Each subsidiary fought for a share of local markets. Competitors were either local national companies or subsidiaries of rival multinational companies. The Otis subsidiaries managed all the activities of the value chain (marketing, design, production, installation and service). For instance, the French subsidiary designed elevators for the French market, manufactured them in French factories, sold them with French sales forces and maintained them with a French after-sales organization – the management was essentially French. In Germany, Otis designed, manufactured, sold, installed and serviced elevators for the German market; and the same applied in nearly every major country – see Figure 1.5. In smaller countries, products or components were exported from major countries' subsidiaries. The operations were self-contained in each country and the results were evaluated on a country-by-country basis. Such a situation had prevailed for over five decades, since the early 1900s. It corresponds to what was referred to as a multinational or multi-domestic world, in which multinational companies like Otis were competing in each main market of the planet.

By the end of the 1960s several key elements played a role in changing this competitive structure. One country manager at Otis perceived that the European business context was changing. First, the Treaty of Rome in 1957 had created the European Economic Community (EEC), at that time called the Common Market. This meant that tariff barriers across Europe were coming down; it became viable to produce components in one country and export them to other countries. This allowed the company to concentrate on the production of components in a network of specialized factories across Europe, each of them making one product category or one component. Components could be cross-shipped for ultimate installation in the various client countries. In 2015 Otis operated all over the world as six regional organizations, with 200 factories and twelve engineering facilities.

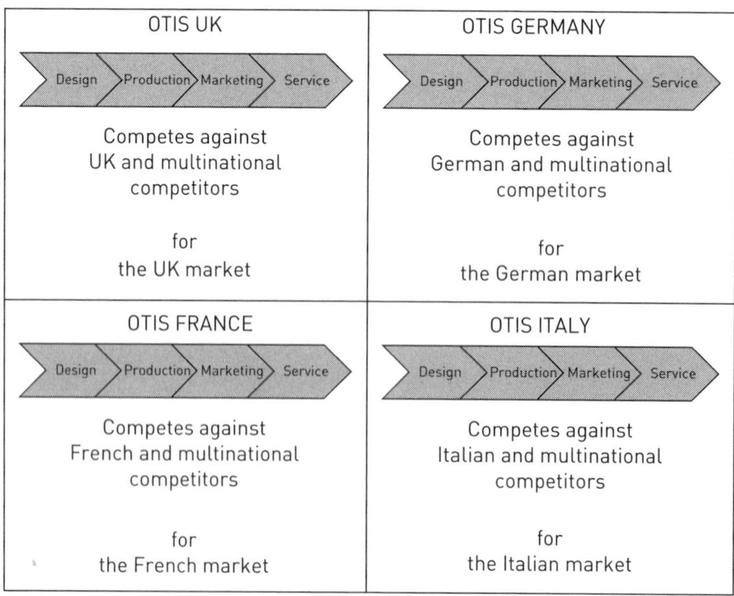

Figure 1.5 A multinational competitive configuration – Otis Elevators in the 1960s

The benefits of such a system were obvious – by concentrating production the company could benefit from economies of scale, and some of the reduction in costs could be passed to the customers in the form of lower prices, leading to higher market share. Products could be designed for an entire market (standardized). Instead of having country segmentation one would have pan-European segmentation based on utilization, that is, high-rise buildings, low-rise buildings and so on.

Standardization would be possible only if customers in Europe – architects, engineers, real estate developers, housing departments and so on – shared a common view about what an elevator should be. Despite the differences in housing organization across countries, elevators were essentially technical products with very little cultural content and therefore able to be standardized. Only selling methods would vary from country to country. The Otis management perceived this as an opportunity to gain market share in Europe and engaged in the pan-European strategy depicted in Figure 1.6 in which design centres and factories were specialized and interdependent.

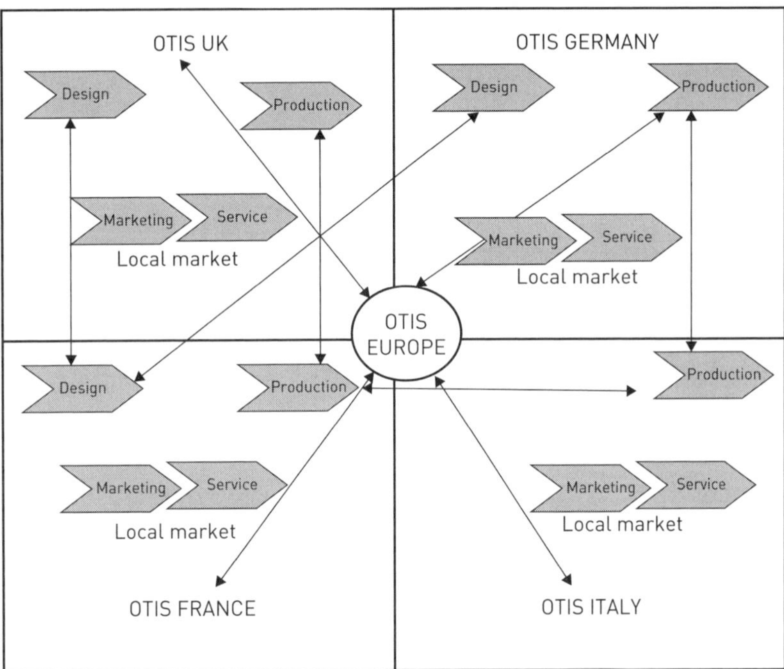

Figure 1.6 A global competitive configuration – Otis today

From a management point of view this was a radical change: country managers were no longer responsible for the whole value chain, but only for part of it. They were obliged to coordinate with other countries through the European headquarters. This led to a very successful story. By 1975, Otis had captured 40 per cent of the European market, while limiting penetration from Japanese corporations which were rapidly expanding and succeeding internationally. If Otis had not adopted the regional strategy it would have been uncompetitive and competitors were obliged to adopt a similar strategy if they wanted to survive. This concept was further expanded and today Otis is organized by product line on a worldwide basis. There are still country subsidiaries, which take care of installation, maintenance, public relations and personnel, but product development and manufacturing are coordinated globally by product line. From being a 'multinational', Otis has become the 'global' company shown in Figure 1.6.

The phenomenon of an active coordinated and integrated presence in the main regions of the world is what 'global company' means. It is important to observe that this change gave Otis a competitive advantage and that competitors were obliged to adopt a similar approach if they wanted to survive. Globalization is neither a consultant's fad nor a management buzzword, it is a competitive imperative in an increasing number of industries. The development of information technologies, the fluidity of capital markets, the advent of megamergers in the telecoms, computer, oil, pharmaceutical, power and car industries – all of these demonstrate that business firms are increasingly behaving as if they were already living in a global world (see Insert 1.3, Some global definitions).

Historically, the globalization process, according to the stage theory of internationalization,[15] can be best described as shown in Figure 1.7. It has evolved in three steps: 1) international trade: export and sourcing; 2) multinational investments: setting up value-adding activities in different countries; and 3) integration and coordination of activities across regions and countries.

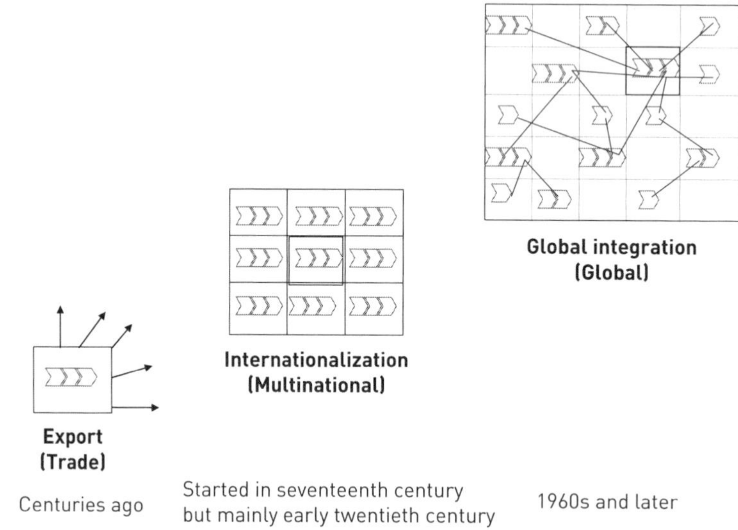

Figure 1.7 The three steps in globalization

Globalization called into question: deglobalization

From a historical perspective, the globalization phenomena experienced at the end of the twentieth century were not new. Some economic historians have observed that at the end of the nineteenth century the world was more 'global' than it is today. Obviously, the state of affairs was different: global powers such as Britain, France and the United States were globalized because of their colonial influence. Trade barriers were limited, and people, money and goods moved easily across borders. Nationalism, epitomized by the First and Second World Wars, provoked protectionism and restriction of exchange. Then postwar technological, political and economic factors, as described previously, reintroduced globalization and generated new management paradigms. But at the dawn of the twenty-first century, while globalism seemed triumphant, some dissonant voices are increasingly calling into question the concept of a borderless, free-market, monocultural world after the financial 'subprime' crisis, Covid-19 pandemic and more recently Russia's invasion of Ukraine; there has been an increasing number of arguments stating that the world is entering a period of de-globalization.[16] Table 1.2 summarizes those arguments.

The globalization debate gained political visibility during the 1990s. The *dissenting* voices are still increasing in the countries that have benefited the most from globalization – the OECD countries – and their point of view can be best summarized by Rodrik:[17]

- 'First, reduced trade barriers and investment accentuate the asymmetry between the groups that can cross international borders (either directly or indirectly, say via outsourcing) and those that cannot.' These semi-skilled and unskilled workers can be replaced by other cheaper workers abroad. This undermines the social fabric in the developed world.
- 'Second, globalization engenders conflicts within and between nations over domestic norms and the social institutions that embody them' (such as pension funds, social security, values and culture).
- 'Third, globalization has made it increasingly difficult for governments to provide social insurance.' The welfare state is under attack.
- 'The question therefore is how the tension between globalization and the pressures for socialization of risks can be eased. If the tension is not managed intelligently and creatively, the danger is that the domestic consensus in favour of open markets will ultimately erode to the point where a generalized resurgence of protectionism becomes a serious possibility.'

From a macroeconomic point of view, deglobalization is characterized by the decrease or slowing down of growth in international flow of trade, investment, capital and people migration (Figures 1.8, 1.9 and 1.10). Figure 1.10 presents the Global Trade barometer, an indicator established by DHL, the logistics company. It shows that from 2011–2019 international trade growth declined following the 'subprime' crisis, then regained momentum up to 2017 but declined again since to become negative.

From a political viewpoint deglobalization is materialized by the upsurge of economic nationalism, leading to trade disputes and discriminatory measures. Economic and political factors are interrelated: international trade declines negatively affect the desire for MNCs to invest in foreign lands and consequently impact on capital flows and migrant workers.[18]

Altogether these deglobalization trends can be due to the combination of several factors:

a A slowdown in global demand

b Protectionist policies

c Calamities such as wars, pandemics and industrial hazards in key countries

d Societal scepticism about the benefits of globalization (caused by the unequal distribution of benefits of growth and rising inequalities, the loss of cultural identity and the inability to influence decisions).

The Covid-19 pandemic crisis and the invasion of Ukraine in 2022 fuelled a resurgence of nationalism all over the world. Economic nationalism was epitomized by the policy of President Trump under his slogan 'Make America great again' and engagement in a series of tariffs increases against China and Western Europe. Similarly the decision by Britain to leave the European Union can be attributed to this social discontent. The Global Trade Alert Index created by the University of St Gallen noted that

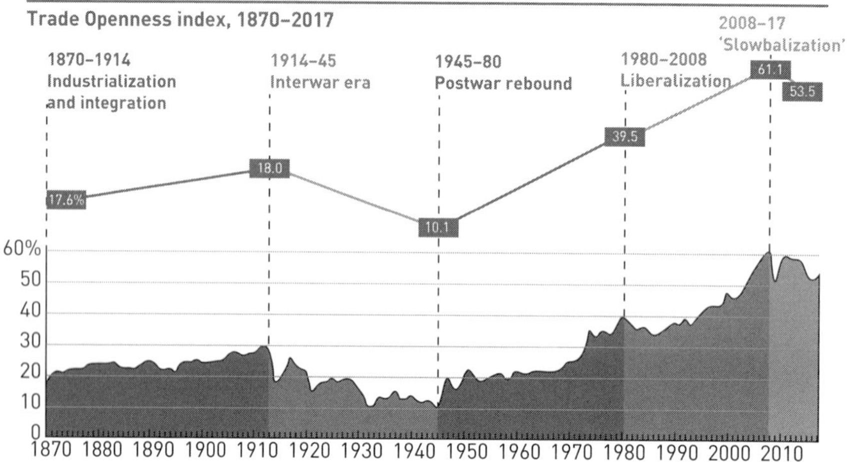

Figure 1.8 World trade evolution since 1870

Source: PIIE, https://www.piie.com/research/piie-charts/globalization-retreat-first-time-second-world-war.

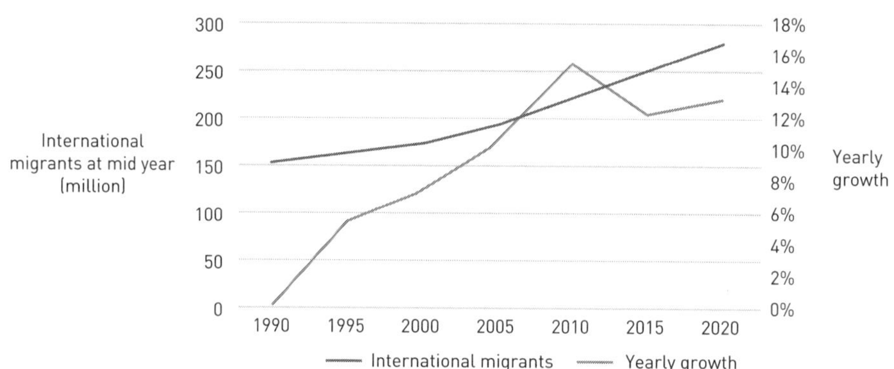

Figure 1.9 Migration Chart

Source: Authors' own using data from https://www.un.org/development/desa/pd/content/international-migrant-stock.

since 2011, the number of state interventions discriminating against international trade outpaced the number of interventions favouring international trade. The most frequent measures are import tariffs, subsidies to local companies and limitations for foreign bodies to participate in public procurement. Out of the 21,092 discriminatory measures implemented since 2019, 88 per cent were related to trade discrimination (Global Trade Alert 2021).

Globalization in turmoil: Covid 19 and the Ukrainian war

Whether the future will consist of further globalization or an increase in deglobalization due to the Covid-19 pandemic and to the Russian invasion of Ukraine in early 2022 is still being debated. In the short and medium terms, the global economy will be subject to important '*disruptions in commodity markets especially food and energy, logistic networks, supply chains and foreign direct investment*'. (World Bank report 2022.)

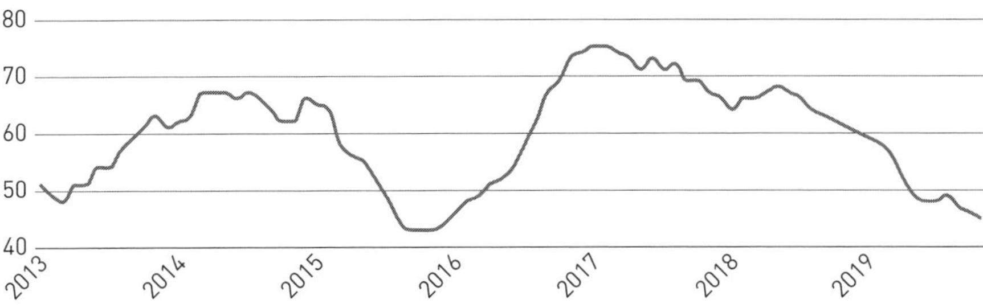

> 50 Expansion, 50 = Stable, < Contraction

Figure 1.10 DHL Global Trade Barometer from 2013 to 2019
Note: *The DHL Global Trade Barometer forecasts short-term trade growth over a three-month period.*
Source: https://lot.dhl.com/global-trade-barometer-gtb/reports/global/.

What is for certain is that one can expect direct economic results to be at least as devastating as in the years following the financial crisis, with the drop in global demand 'compounded by the effect of governments protecting their own and implementing policies to boost local employment at the expense of imports' (Toulan 2020). Others stress the uncertainties surrounding future growth in various industrial sectors and their impact on global trade and investments (McKinsey Global Institute March 2021). For Yip (2021), the final economic global outcome of the pandemic depends on three factors:

a The attitude of national policies with respect to limitation of tree trade and repatriation of production to domestic territories
b The fiscal and investment policies to stimulate demand
c The attitude of multinational companies with respect to their global value chains and safety of supply.

The stimulus package of $1.9 trillion in the USA, the €1.8 trillion from the European Union recovery plan and the $500 billion from China are indicative of the fact that public policies are determined to encourage both growth in demand and in productive capacities.

The benefits and pitfalls of globalization for business

The benefits of globalization can be assessed from two points of view: the business or competitive perspective and the macro, socioeconomic perspective.

The benefits viewed from the macro/socioeconomic perspective have been discussed earlier, so this section will focus on the benefits to a corporation of adopting a global strategy.

Business and competitive benefits can be grouped into four categories: cost, timing, learning and arbitrage.

- **Cost benefits.** These come, on the one hand, from economies of scale owing to the standardization of products and processes as well as increased bargaining power over suppliers of raw materials, components, equipment and services; and, on the other hand, from the ability to organize a logistic and sourcing network based on location factors. Examples of economies of scale through standardization are numerous. Otis Elevators was able to lower the cost, and hence the price, to consumers of elevators in Europe by 30 per cent by introducing a pan-European manufacturing system.

- **Timing benefits.** These come from a coordinated approach to product launching in the early stage of the product life cycle. In a multinational setting, each subsidiary is more or less free to adopt products for its own market. This is sometimes called 'the shopping caddy' approach to product adoption. Such an approach generates inefficiencies in the management of the product life cycle since the optimal volume is obtained only after a lengthy process of product adoption by all subsidiaries. A classic example of the deficiency of the 'shopping caddy' approach is Philips America's refusal to adopt the V2000 video system, developed by Philips' mother company in the Netherlands. As a result, this innovation was not able to gain the volume of sales it needed in the most important world market and lost competitiveness compared to Japanese manufacturers such as Sony and Matsushita. In the late 1960s, the 'international product life cycle' theory of multinational product introduction postulated the progressive adoption of products over time according to the level of economic and scientific development of countries (see Figure 1.2). Such a theory is no longer valid. When industries globalize, waiting too long to launch a product can be fatal, particularly if the product has a short life cycle, which is more and more frequently the case. For example, Microsoft launched Windows 2000 at the same time everywhere in the world.
- **Learning benefits.** These accrue from the coordinated transfer of information, best practices and people across subsidiaries. Such transfer eliminates the costly 'reinvention of the wheel' and facilitates the accumulation of experience and knowledge. In Thailand, Unilever formulated and implemented an innovative strategy to produce and market ice cream. The Thai experience served as a template for other countries in the Asia Pacific region, giving the company a first-mover advantage. This example illustrates the benefits that can be gained from a coordinated transfer of best practice.
- **Arbitrage benefits.** These come from the advantages that a company can gain by using the resources in one country for the benefit of its subsidiary in another country. These can be direct competitive advantages or indirect cost advantages. A competitive advantage can be gained by playing a 'global chess game': for instance, engaging in a price war in one country in order to tie up the resources of competitors in that country, thus depriving them of cash flow which could be used elsewhere. This strategy was used by the Korean car manufacturer Hyundai, who avoided targeting European car companies in their home countries. Instead, they entered the UK market with the Pony car model. In the UK continental European competitors enjoyed a strong position and were very profitable. To counter the Korean assault European firms were obliged to lower their prices, diminishing their cash flow that could have been used to reinforce their competitiveness in other markets. Another type of arbitrage comes from differential cost elements such as taxes, interest and possibly risk reduction through the pooling of currencies.

These four benefits are real but achieving them is subject to certain conditions, and their adoption has to be measured against the real competitive advantage they provide to the firms adopting them.

The benefits in cost reduction obtained by economies of scale are contingent upon the market responsiveness to standardization and whether customers are price sensitive. If customers are not responsive and prefer tailored products and services to standardization, a global approach is less appropriate. A similar reasoning applies to the benefits of timing. As for purchasing power, it may be limited for culturally sensitive services such as advertising.

The benefits of learning are positive if the experience gained in one country is applicable to another. If this is not the case, there is a timing deficit: the time spent in realizing that one has made a mistake plus the time to learn the new environment. When Disneyland Paris opened near Paris, Disney transferred its know-how and operational methods to France but encountered a lot of cultural and legal problems in implementing these. It is estimated that around two years were lost to adjust the format to local conditions.

The benefits of arbitrage can be offset by the cost of managing the arbitrage and any legal barriers to it that may exist. In the case of tax arbitrage, governments are careful to ensure that global companies do not abuse their arbitrage power.

Despite those limitations, more and more companies recognize the competitive benefits of globalization. However, one should be aware there are still some factors that work against globalization and in favour of localization.

The global/multi-local mapping

Two sets of forces – globalization and localization – shape the competitive structure of industries and induce companies to configure their worldwide business systems with the right mix of coordination, integration and decentralization. Global/multi-local mapping is a tool that has been developed to position industries and industry segments according to the relative importance of each set of forces. Figure 1.8 represents a mapping for various industries, while Figure 1.9 does the same for various segments of the banking industry.

The mapping in Figures 1.8 and 1.9 reveals that industries and segments can be broadly positioned into three types of competitive situations:

- **Type I:** Global forces dominate and firms in those industries can sustain competitive advantage by operating across the world in a coordinated way. There are few advantages to push for local adaptation of products, services and approaches. Efficiency, speed, arbitrage and learning are the competitive drivers. These industries are global, as in the case of microchips, bulk chemicals or civil aircraft.
- **Type II:** Local forces dominate and flexibility, proximity and quick response are determining capabilities for competitive advantage. Firms can operate independently in different countries; their approaches are different from country to country. Food retailing, consumer banking or voice telephony fall in this category.
- **Type III:** In these industries there is a mix of global and local forces at play and competitiveness cannot be achieved without achieving the benefits of global coordination and, at the same time, the benefits of flexibility, proximity and quick response time. This positioning is increasingly becoming the dominant competitive battleground for a vast majority of sectors.

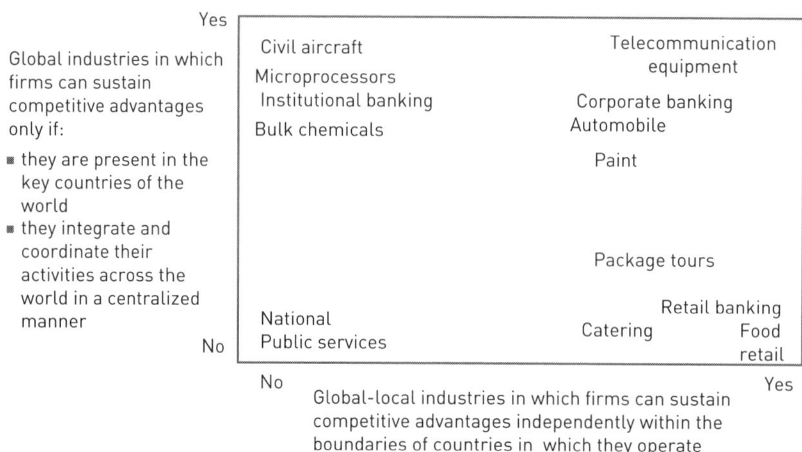

Figure 1.11 Global-local mapping: different industries have different competitive requirements

Global/multi-local mapping can be used to assess a situation at a point in time or to anticipate evolution over time. It can also serve as mapping for the various activities of the value chain. As we will see in Chapters 7, 8 and 14, a good understanding of industry positioning will help the formulation of business and country strategies, as well as the implementation of an effective organizational design.

In online Appendix 1.1 there is a questionnaire that will help analysts and managers to position their business on the global/multi-local mapping matrix.

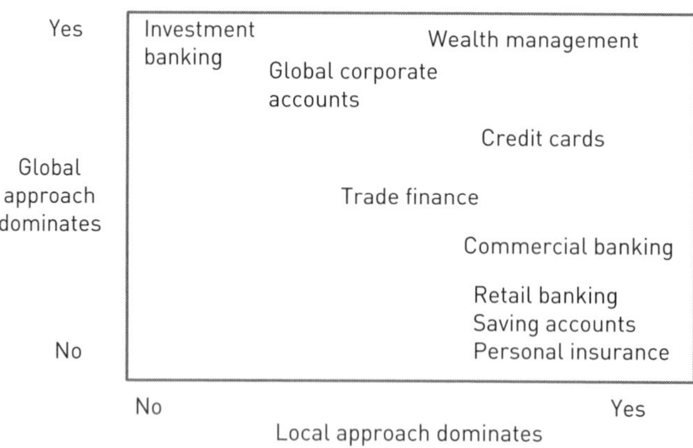

Figure 1.12 Global-local mapping: different segments have different competitive requirements – example of banking

MINI-CASE 1.1

Pharmaceutical industry: a global and local industry

The discovery and crafting of drugs dates back to antiquity, however, small-scale production began in the late eighteenth century. This was followed in the mid-nineteenth century by mass production and the founding of firms including Merck, Squibb, Upjohn, Pfizer and Eli Lilly in the USA; Sandoz, Hoffman LaRoche in Switzerland; Bayer, Hoechst in Germany; Beecham, Wellcome in the UK; and Clin-Byla in France. At the beginning of the twentieth century, some of the early players opened foreign subsidiaries that were mainly transatlantic. The First World War, which began on 28 July 1914 and ended on 11 November 1918, put a stop to the trend. In the 1920s, foreign expansion restarted. Despite this, by the end of the Second World War in 1945, the industry was a collection of national domestic players exporting products and producing in a small number of foreign subsidiaries.

The discovery of penicillin and insulin changed the industry's economics. It marked the need for capital to fund research and development (R&D) as well as the industrial assets of production. After the 1950s, there were three major developments: 1) the increasing cost of R&D, coupled with the birth of biotechnologies; 2) the concentration of the industry through mergers and acquisitions; and 3) the globalization of production. The 1970s to the 1990s marked the end of patent protection that led to the development of generics and the birth of biotechnologies.

1 R&D

Figure 1.13 shows the evolution of R&D costs. It illustrates the increasing capital required for the

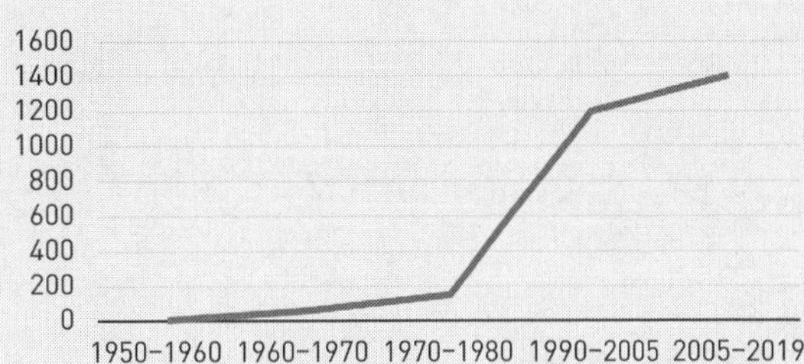

Figure 1.13 Total cost of drug development (average US$ m)

Source: Authors' calculation from Wouters, McKee and Luyrens (2020).

discovery, testing, approval and commercialization of drugs. The figures are averages and the ranges can be high. For instance, for the period between 2005–2019 the average cost is $1,400 million, but the range varies from $670 million for anti-infective drugs, to $6,000 million for cancer immunotherapies.

In addition to the large sums required, drug development is also a lengthy process. The pattern of drug development is shown in Exhibit 1.14. The time to recoup initial investment is relatively short during the period of patent protection (fifteen years) compared with the development time (twelve years). This encouraged firms to enlarge their markets and open subsidiaries or acquire companies. In addition to the increase in R&D, new technologies based on biotechnologies emerged forcing traditional pharmaceuticals to invest in their development either internally or through acquisition or alliances with biotech firms.

2 Mergers and acquisitions

The concentration of pharmaceutical firms followed two trends: First, domestic mergers such as the

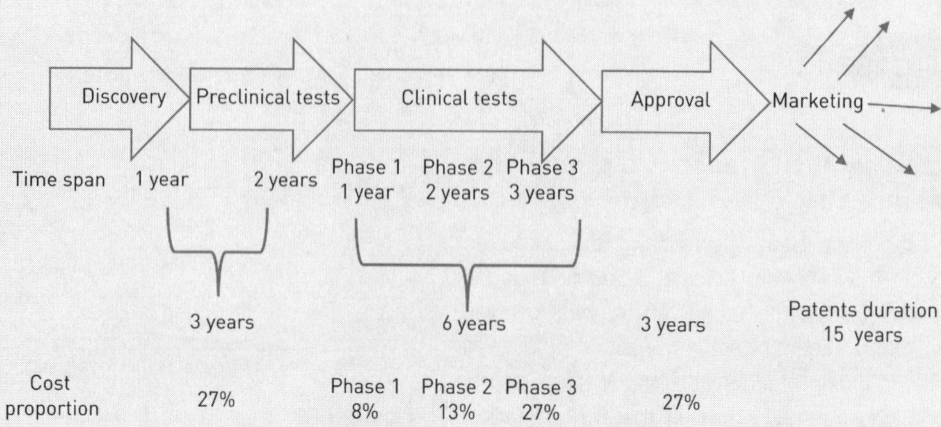

Figure 1.14 Pattern of pharmaceutical R&D
Source: Authors' illustration based on various sources.

creation of Novartis that resulted from the merger of four Swiss companies: Sandoz, Ciba-Geigy, Hexal and Chiron. Similar examples include SmithKline and Beecham with Glaxo in the UK. Second, global mergers illustrated in Figure 1.15 with the creation of Sanofi (France, Germany, USA).

1987	1995			
Hoechst (G)+	=Hoechst-Celanese (G)+			
Celanese (USA)				
	Marion Merrill Dow (USA)	1999		
	=Hoechst Marion (G)	Hoechst Marion (G)+		
		+		
1990	1990			
Rhone Poulenc (Fr)+	=Rhone Poulenc Rorer (FR)	Rhone Poulenc Rorer (FR)+		2004
Rorer (USA)		=Avantis (Fr)		Avantis (Fr)+
				Sanofi (fr)
				=Sanofi Avantis (Fr)

Figure 1.15 An example of global M&A in the pharmaceutical industry: a German, American and French group

From 1999 to 2020, there was a large increase in global mergers and acquisitions, in particular with the acquisition of biotechnologies and genetic engineering firms (Table 1.3).

3 Globalization of production

Before the post-1999 acquisition fever, global pharmaceutical firms had established a network of productive capacities across the globe to

Table 1.3 Major global acquisitions and mergers from 1999 to 2020

Year	Acquirer	Acquiree	Value (US$ bn)
1999	Astra (Sweden) merged with	Zeneca (UK)	64
2006	Merck (USA)	Serono (Switzerland)*	13
2009	Roche (Switzerland)	Genetch (USA)*	44
2010	Novartis (Switzerland)	Alcon (USA)	39
2011	Sanofi (France)	Genzyme (USA)*	20
2015	Actavis (Ireland)	Allergan (USA)	70
2016	Teva (Israel)	Allergan Generic (USA) *	40
2017	Johnson & Johnson (USA)	Actelion (Switzerland)*	30
2018	Sanofi (France)	Bioverativ (USA)*	12
2019	Takeda (Japan)	Shire (UK)*	62

Source: Various sources. * indicates biotechnology and genetic engineering firms.

capitalize on the growth of markets. This enabled them to be close to the market; overcome constraints of localization in certain countries; and to organize a global value chain to benefit from low cost of production for some elements. Table 1.4 shows the number of manufacturing and R&D facilities of major pharmaceutical groups in 2019.

Table 1.4 Manufacturing and R&D facilities outside country of origin

	Revenues 2019 US$ m	Manufacturing sites outside country of origin	R&D sites outside country of origin
NovoNordik	18.3	15	4
Bayer (Pharma Division)	20.8	11	12
Gilead	22.1	3	*NA*
Amgen	22.2	*NA*	*NA*
Eli Liklly	22.3	8	*NA*
Astra Zeneca	24.4	2	2
Bristol-Myers Squibb	26.5	10	4
GlaxoSmithKline (GSK)	33.6	36	15
AbbVie	33.7	11	1
Sanofi	36.15	31	15
Merck	46.84	14	8
Novartis	48.7	5	3
Pfizer	51.8	25	1

Source: Companies' websites.

4 The production of generics

After a patent expires, generic drugs can be produced at a lower cost. Traditional large pharma firms have created subsidiaries that specialize in this type of production; however, a significant proportion of production comes from emerging countries, in particular India (Table 1.5).

Table 1.5 Major producers of generics

Generic producer	Revenues 2020 US$ m	Country	Part of
TEVA Pharmaceutical	16,700	Israel	
Industries	9,600	Switzerland	Novartis
Sandoz Division	8,300 (9 months only)	USA	Viatris (result of merge between Mylan and Upjohn)
Mylan	8,100	Germany	Fresenius Group
Fresenius Kabi Hospira	4,500	USA	Pfizer
Sun Pharma generic Segment	4,500	India	Sun Pharmeceutical Industries

Source: Companies' websites.

5 Pharmaceutical distribution and retailing

Pharmaceutical distribution varies according to geography and regulations. In OECD countries, private wholesalers and distributors largely supply drugs and medicinal products to hospitals, clinics and retail pharmacies. Some hospitals and retail pharmacy chains buy directly from manufacturers and receive products through a manufacturer-appointed logistics company. However, in the US and the EU, the majority of drugs are delivered by wholesalers and distributors (Figure 1.16).

Pharmaceutical full-line wholesalers are still central in the supply chain, however, new distribution models have emerged in recent years. In some territories direct sales from manufacturers has increased while in countries such as in the UK, new distribution models like Direct to Pharmacy

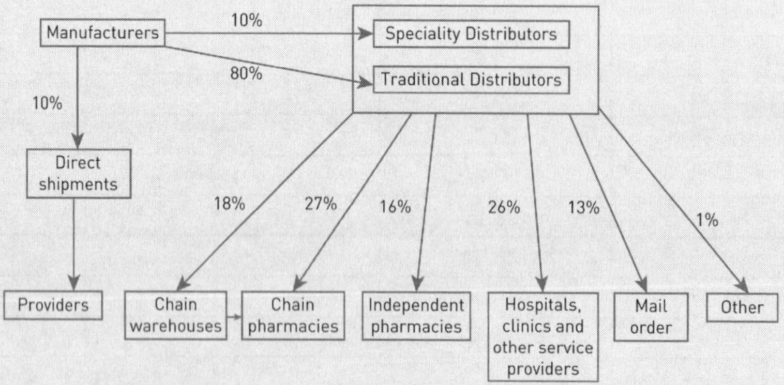

Figure 1.16 US pharmaceutical distribution channel

Source: Yadav and Anupindi, Case study in FIP Report on Pharmacists in the Supply Chain, 2018.

(DTP) or Reduced Wholesale Arrangements (RWA) have arisen.[18]

Pharmaceutical distribution is a consolidated industry in OECD countries, for example in the US, three large wholesalers/distributors – McKesson, Cardinal and Amerisource-Bergen – control 90 per cent of pharmaceutical distribution. Branded drug manufacturers (such as Johnson & Johnson) generally used third-party distributors due to the cost of meeting the highly regulated conditions for correct storage and transportation of drugs. Generic drug producers, however, compete on price, therefore a good distribution deal can leverage negotiation power for pricing.

For pharmaceutical retailers, some have their own internal distribution service while others opt for third-party companies. In the US, three companies account for 50 per cent of the market (CVS Pharmacy, Walgreens Company and Express Scripts Holding Company). New retailers have emerged in recent years such as Amazon and other online players.

In emerging markets, affordability is a concern for access to pharmaceuticals but also availability and reliability of supply chains. Many private sector pharmaceutical supply chains in emerging markets experience considerable inefficiencies that are caused by complex networks of importers, wholesalers, distributors, sub-distributors and a mass of retail outlets. There is often little tracking of purchases resulting in stock-outs and substandard medicines entering the supply chain. Technological innovation offers an impactful way of increasing supply chain efficiency, especially for markets with transport infrastructure deficiencies. Digital innovations range in sophistication from text messaging systems that update stock levels, to 'smart' vaccine fridges that automatically send stocking and temperature control reports.

6 Pharmaceutical industry and the production of a vaccine against Covid-19

The Covid-19 pandemic exposed the global nature of the pharmaceutical industry, mainly with regard to the production of vaccines. The alliance between BioNtech, a German Biotech company, and the pharmaceutical giant, Pfizer, resulted in the development in record time of a vaccine based on a new technology – the RNA messenger. Astra Zeneca has also developed a vaccine in Oxford, UK, which is now manufactured in factories throughout Europe.

7 The global industry by 2020 and estimated future

In its 2020 Global Pharmaceutical and Healthcare report, Fitch Solutions, an industry data analysis foundation, predicted a 33 per cent increase in the industry's total revenues.

Table 1.6 Pharmaceutical market historical data and forecasts, US$ bn (global 2019–2025)

Geography	Indicator	2019	2020	2021f	2022f	2023f	2024f	2025f
Sub Saharan (Region)	Pharmaceutical sales, US$ bn	16.907	16.312	17.157	18.025	18.904	20.186	21.930
Asia (Region)	Pharmaceutical sales, US$ bn	350.932	365.605	401.129	417.88	436.567	459.791	482.566
Europe (Region)	Pharmaceutical sales, US$ bn	352.583	361.384	406.079	428.828	445.681	462.727	483.715
Latin America (Region)	Pharmaceutical sales, US$ bn	56.738	50.801	53.363	56.512	59.359	62.647	66.280
MENA (Region)	Pharmaceutical sales, US$ bn	35.444	36.062	37.518	39.369	40.959	42.840	45.091
North America (Region)	Pharmaceutical sales. US$ bn	391.97	409.276	431.476	445.882	460.557	475.203	490.334

f =forecast

Source: Fitch Solutions (2021: 23).

Questions

1 Have R&D costs fostered the globalization of the industry? Why/why not?

2 What is the benefit for a pharmaceutical company in dispersing its R&D facilities?

3 Why have emerging countries invested in the production of generics?

4 Why did it take less than one year to discover and produce a vaccine for Covid-19, when normally the average time to produce a new drug is estimated at twelve years, as shown in Figure 1.14?

Summary and key points

1 Globalization is the process by which people, products, information and money can move freely across borders

   a Four factors are pushing globalization:

   - Political: liberalization of trade and investment reduces trade barriers
   - Technological: technology reduces the cost of coordination and increases economies of scale
   - Social: convergence of customer choices encourages standardization and global branding
   - Competitive: emergence of new competitors induces integration companies to compete on all fronts with strong coordination

   b Four driving forces are acting against globalization:

   - Cultural: differences in taste, behaviour and social codes reduce the benefits of standardization of products or services
   - Commercial: differences in distribution channels and customer interfaces require differentiated approaches to sales and marketing
   - Technical: differences in standards, transportation and language constraints reduce the benefits of economies of scale, centralization and standardization
   - Legal: differences in regulations and security measures limit free flow of resources and impose localization constraints.

2 A global company can be defined as a company that operates in the main markets of the world in an integrated and coordinated way. A global company carries out one activity (e.g. manufacturing) or a component of the activity (e.g. manufacturing one sub-part only) of the value chain in one country which serves the company's worldwide market. A multinational company is a company that operates in the many markets of the world with little or no integration and coordination among operations.

3 Localization has three benefits:

   a Proximity

   b Flexibility

   c Quick response time to customers

4 Globalization has four benefits:
   a Cost
   b Timing
   c Learning
   d Arbitrage
5 The globalization of companies traditionally followed a three-step sequential development: export, multi-countries, global.
6 Deglobalization. There are recent trends indicating a decline in the speed of globalization. The Covid-19 pandemic reinforces this trend.
7 Global/multi-local mapping is used for identifying the competitive requirements of an industry or a business segment and can assist companies in formulating business and country strategies.

Learning assignments

1 Among the enterprises that you know, can you identify one that qualifies as a global company? Why?
2 In Figure 1.9, why are saving accounts positioned low on global approach and high on local approach while investment banking is high on global approach and low on local approach?
3 In Figure 1.8, food retail is positioned as a local business, with a very low globalization score. However, in the press, companies like Tesco, Walmart or Carrefour are described as 'global retailers'. Explain this discrepancy.
4 What are the social factors that have pushed for globalization, and which have been pushing against it?
5 What are the benefits of having a local approach?
6 When the Otis Elevator Company introduced the change described in Example 1.1 (p. 18), there was a lot of resistance from the various heads of the European subsidiaries. Why? What arguments do you think the people hostile to globalization used?
7 Can Apple be classified as a global firm? Why did you make that assessment?
8 Can we qualify the champions of the digital economy such as Facebook, Amazon and Netflix as global?
9 What are the effects of the Covid-19 pandemic on globalization of industries and firms?

Key words

- Arbitrage benefits
- Comparative advantage
- Global companies
- Global industries
- Global/multi-local mapping
- Globalization
- International product life cycle
- Multinational companies

Web Resources

INSEAD:
http://knowledge.insead.edu/
Businessweek magazine:
https://www.bloomberg.com/businessweek
McKinsey Quarterly:
http://www.mckinseyquarterly.com/
UNCTAD:
http://unctad.org/en/Pages/Home.aspx
Boston Consulting Group:
https://www.bcgperspectives.com/
Provides information about the WTO:
http://www.wto.org/
Provides statistics and papers from the IMF:
http://www.imf.org/
https://www.globaltradealert.org/

Companion website

Visit the companion website at bloomsbury.pub/global-strategic-management-5e for a multitude of weblinks and resources, self-test questions for revision and appendices.

Notes

1 McLuhan (1962).
2 Ghemawat (2011).
3 James (2001).
4 Yip (1992).
5 Sachs (2020).
6 OECD (2021).
7 Xin L. (2019).
8 Ohmae (1985).
9 Ricardo (1967).
10 Lowell and Fraser (1999).
11 Jones (2005).
12 Johanson and Vahlne (1977).
13 Chetty and Campbell-Hunt (2003); Li, Qian and Qian (2015); Tanev (2012).
14 Johanson and Vahlne (op, cit).
15 Rodrik (1997).
16 Piketty (2013, 2019).
17 Cuervos-Cazurra et al. (2020).
18 Walter, Dragosits and Said (2012).

References and further reading

Books and articles

Altman, S. and Bastian, P. (2020) *DHL Global Connectedness Index*. https://www.dhl.com/content/dam/dhl/global/dhl-spotlight/documents/pdf/spotlight-g04-global-connectedness-index-2020.pdf (accessed 1 February 2022).

Baker, M. and Hart, S. (1999) *Product Strategy and Management* (London: Prentice-Hall).

Bank for International Settlements (2014) 84th Annual Report, Bank for International Settlements. http://www.bis.org/publ/arpdf/ar2014e.pdf (accessed 4 May 2017).

Barney, J. B. (1991) 'Firm resources and sustainable competitive advantage', *Journal of Management*, 17 (1): 99–120.

Bartlett, C. A. and Ghoshal, S. (1989) *Managing Across Borders: The Transnational Solution* (Boston, MA: Harvard Business School Press).

Buckley, P. and Casson, M. (1976) *The Future of the Multinational Enterprise* (London: Macmillan).

Buckley, Peter J. and Hashai, N. (2020) 'Skepticism toward globalization, technological knowledge flows and the emergence of a new global system', *Global Strategy Journal*, 10: 94–122.

Castells, M. (1996) *The Rise of the Network Society*, vol. I of *The Information Age: Economy, Society, Culture* (Oxford: Blackwell).

Chetty, S. and Campbell-Hunt, C. (2003) 'A strategic approach to internationalization: a traditional versus a "born-global" approach', *Journal of International Marketing*, 12 (1): 57–81.

Cuervo-Cazurra A., Doz, Y. and Gaur, A. (2020) 'Skepticism of globalization and global strategy: Increasing regulations and countervailing strategies', *Global Strategy Journal*, 10: 3–31.

Dunning, J. (1993) *Multinational Enterprises and the Global Economy* (Wokingham: Addison-Wesley).

Dunning, J. H. (2001) 'The Eclectic (OLI) Paradigm of International Production: Past, Present and Future', *International Journal of the Economics* of *Business*, 8 ((2): 17–190.

Evenett, Simon J. (2019) 'Protectionism, State Discrimination and International Business Since the Onset of the Global Financial Crisis', *Journal of International Business Policy*, 2 (1): 9–36.

Fitch Solutions (2021) *Global Pharmaceutical & Healthcare Report Q2*, 2021.

Frankopan, P. (2015) *The Silk Road, A New History of the World* (London: Bloomsbury).

Fraser, J. N. and Oppenheim, J. (1997) 'What's new about globalization?', *McKinsey Quarterly*, 2: 168–79.

Ghemawat, P. (2011) *World 3.00, Global Prosperity and How to Achieve it* (Boston, MA: Harvard Business Review Press).

Goodwin, J. (2001) *Otis: Giving Rise to the Modern City* (Chicago, IL: Ivan R. Dee).

Harvard Business School (1994) *Global Strategies: Insights from the World's Leading Thinkers* (Boston, MA: Harvard Business School Press). (This book contains a collection of *Harvard Business Review* (*HBR*) articles.)

Humes, S. (1993) *Managing the Multinational: Confronting the Global–Local Dilemma* (London: Prentice-Hall).

International Bank for Reconstruction and Development (2007) *Global Economic Prospects, Managing the New Wave of Globalization* (Washington: World Bank).

International Telecommunication Union (2014), *Measuring the Information Society Report*. http://www.itu.int/dms_pub/itu-d/opb/ind/D-IND-ICTOI-2014-SUM-PDF-E.pdf (accessed 1 February 2022).

James, H. (2001) *The End of Globalization: Lessons from the Great Depression* (Cambridge, MA: Harvard University Press).

Johanson, J. and Vahlne, J. E. (1977) 'The internationalization process of the firm', *Journal of International Business Studies*, 8 (1): 23–32.

Jones, G. (2005) *Multinationals and Global Capitalism: From the Nineteenth to the Twenty-first Century* (Oxford: Oxford University Press).

Lang, Austin (2020) *Why Disney would like you to forget Disnyeland Paris' opening day*. https://allears.net/2020/06/18/why-disney-would-like-you-to-forget-disneyland-paris-opening-day/ (accessed 1 February 2022).

Langlet, F. (2013) *La Fin de la Mondialisation* (Paris: Fayard).

Lenin, V. (1917) *Imperialism, the Highest Stage of Capitalism* (available in Penguin Classics, 2010).

Li, L., Gongming, Q. and Zhengming, Q. (2015) 'Speed of internationalization: mutual effects of individual- and company-level antecedents', *Global Strategy Journal*, 5 (4): 303–20.

Lowell, L. B. and Fraser, J. N. (1999) 'Getting to global', *McKinsey Quarterly*, 4: 68–81.

McLuhan, M. (1962) *The Gutenberg Galaxy: The Making of Typographic Man* (Toronto: Toronto University Press).

Marx, K. and Engels, F. (1848) 'Manifesto of the Communist Party', reproduced in *Marx and Engels Selected Works* (New York, NY: International Publishers, 1968).

Michel, D., Salle, R. and Valla, J. (1996) *Marketing Industriel* (Paris: Economica).

Micklethwait, J. and Wooldridge, A. (2000) *A Future Perfect: The Challenge and Hidden Promise of Globalization* (London: Heinemann).

Mirza, H. (ed.) (1998) *Global Competitive Strategies in World Economy: Multilateralism Regionalization and the Transnational Firm* (Cheltenham: Edward Elgar).

Mischke, J. (2021) *Will productivity and growth return after the COVID-19 crisis*? McKinsey Global Institute, March 2021, https://www.mckinsey.com/~/media/McKinsey/Industries/Public%20and%20Social%20Sector/Our%20Insights/Will%20productivity%20and%20growth%20return%20after%20the%20COVID%2019%20crisis/Will-productivity-and-growth-return-after-the-COVID-19-crisis-Report-final.pdf?shouldIndex=false (accessed 1 February 2022).

Novela, S. (2017) *Case Study Disney in France for Cross Culture Management*. https://bbs.binus.ac.id/ibm/2017/06/case-study-disney-in-france-for-cross-culture-management/ (accessed 1 February 2022).

OECD (2010) *Measuring Globalization: OECD Economic Globalisation Indicators* (Paris: OECD).

OECD (2021) *International Students Mobility*. https://data.oecd.org/students/international-student-mobility.htm#indicator-chart (accessed 1 February 2022).

Ohmae, K. (1985) *Becoming a Triad Power* (New York, NY: McKinsey).

Peng, M. (2001) 'The resource-based view and international business', *Journal of Management*, 27: 803–29.

Piketty, T. (2014) *Le Capital au XXI Siecle* (Paris: Seuil); English translation: *Capital in the Twenty First Century* (Cambridge, MA: Belknap Press, 2014).

Piketty, T. (2019) *Capital et Ideologie* (Paris: Seuil); English translation: *Capital and Ideology* (Cambridge, MA: Harvard University Press, 2020).

Porter, M. E. (ed.) (1986) *Competition in Global Industries* (Boston, MA: Harvard Business School Press).

Porter, M. E. (1998) *The Competitive Advantage of Nations* (New York, NY: Free Press).

Prado-Wagner, C. (2014) 'Trends on telecommunication/ICT services regulation and costs and tariff policies', Report to the ITU/BDT Regional Economic and Financial Forum of Telecommunications/ICT for Asia Pacific, Yangon, Myanmar, 1–2 September. https://www.itu.int/en/ITU-D/Regulatory-Market/Documents/Myanmar/Session5_Prado_costing%20trends.pdf (accessed 6 June 2017).

Prahalad, C. K. and Doz, Y. L. (1987) *The Multinational Mission: Balancing Local Demands and Global Vision* (New York, NY: Free Press).

Qualls, W., Olshavsky, R. W. and Michaels, R. E. (1981) 'Shortening of the PLC: an empirical test', *Journal of Marketing*, 45 (4): 76–80.

Rangan, S. and Lawrence, R. Z. (1999) *A Prism on Globalization* (Washington, DC: Brookings Institution).

Ricardo, D. (1967) *On the Principles of Political Economy and Taxation* (Homewood, IL: Irwin).

Ritzer, G. (1993) *The McDonaldization of Society* (London: Sage).

Robertson, R. (1992) *Globalization: Social Theory and Global Culture* (Thousand Oaks, CA: Sage).

Robinson, W. I. (2004) *A Theory of Global Capitalism: Production, Class and State in a Transnational World* (Baltimore, MD: The Johns Hopkins University Press).

Rodrik, D. (1997) *Has Globalization Gone Too Far?* (Washington, DC: Peterson Institute for International Economics).

Rugman, A. (2000) *The End of Globalization: A New and Radical Analysis of Globalization and What it Means for Business* (London: Random House).

Ruta, Michele (Ed) World Bank. 2022. *The Impact of the War in Ukraine on Global Trade and Investment*. Washington, DC. © World Bank. https://openknowledge.worldbank.org/handle/10986/37359 License: CC BY 3.0 IGO.

Sachs, J. D. (2020), *The Ages of Globalization: Geography, Technology, and Institutions* (Chichester, NY: Columbia University Press).

Sklair, L. (2000) *The Transnational Capitalist Class* (London: Blackwell).

Tanev, S. (2012) 'Global from the start: the characteristics of born-global firms in the technology sector', *Technology Innovation Management Review*, 2 (3): 5–8.

Toulan, O. (2020) *Globalization After Covid-19: What's in Store?* IMD, May. https://www.imd.org/research-knowledge/articles/globalization-after-covid-19-whats-in-store (accessed 1 February 2022).

UNCTAD (2008) 'Countries continue to compete for FDI but not unconditionally', Investment Brief no. 3.

UNCTAD (2015) *World Investment Report 2015: Reforming International Investment Governance* (United Nations).

Vahlne, J-E. and Johanson, J. (2020) 'The Uppsala model: Networks and micro-foundations', *Journal of International Business Studies*, 51 (1): 4–10.

Wallerstein, I. (1974) *The Modern World System*, vol. I (New York, NY: Academic Press).

Wallerstein, I. (2000) 'Globalization or the Age of Transition?', *International Sociology*, 15 (2): 249–65.

Walter, E., Dragosits, A. and Said, M. (2012), 'Access to pharmaceutical products in six European countries – analysis of different pharmaceutical distribution systems Farmeconomia', *Health Economics and Therapeutic Pathways,* 13 (1): 33–41.

Witt, Michael A. (2019) 'De-globalization: Theories, predictions and opportunities for international business research', *Journal of International Business Studies*, 50 (7): 1053–77.

Wouters, O., McKee, M. and Luyrens, J. (2020) 'Estimated research and development investment needed to bring a new medicine to market, 2009–2018', *American Medical Association*, 323 (9): 844–53. https://jamanetwork.com/journals/jama/fullarticle/2762311 (accessed 1 February 2022).

WTO (World Trade Organization) (2008) *World Trade Report 2008: Trade in a Globalizing World* (Geneva: WTO).

Xin, L., Meng, B. and Wang, Z. (2019) 'Recent patterns of global production and GVC participation', in World Trade Organization, Global Value Chain Development Report 2019. https://www.wto.org/english/res_e/booksp_e/gvc_dev_report_2019_e_ch1.pdf (accessed 1 February 2022).

Yip, G. (1992) *Total Global Strategy: Managing for World Wide Competitive Advantage* (Englewood Cliffs, NJ: Prentice-Hall).

Yip, G. (2021) *Does COVID-19 Mean The End For Globalization?*, Imperial Business Insights, Forbes, January. https://www.forbes.com/sites/imperialinsights/2021/01/08/does-covid-19-mean-the-end-for-globalization/?sh=2425648671e4 (accessed 1 February 2022).

Journals

Business

Business Week: https://www.bloomberg.com/businessweek

Economist: https://www.economist.com/

Financial Times: https://www.ft.com/

Fortune: https://fortune.com/

Semi-academic

California Management Review: https://journals.sagepub.com/home/cmr

Columbia Journal of World Business: https://www.journals.elsevier.com/journal-of-world-business

European Management Journal: https://www.journals.elsevier.com/european-management-journal

Harvard Business Review: https://hbr.org/

Multinational Business Review: https://www.emeraldgrouppublishing.com/journal/mbr

Sloan Management Review: https://sloanreview.mit.edu/

Academic

Global Strategy Journal: https://strategicmanagement.net/

International Human Resources Management: https://www.tandfonline.com/

Journal of International Business Studies: http://www.palgrave.com/gp/journal/41267

Strategic Management Journal: https://strategicmanagement.net/

Chapter 2

The emerging global environment

By the end of the chapter you should be able to:

- Understand the characteristics of emerging countries
- Identify the market and outsourcing opportunities they offer to global firms
- Understand the strategic development of competitors coming from emerging countries

Introduction

During the first two decades of the twenty-first century, the seemingly unstoppable ascent of globalization that had characterized the 1970s, 1980s and 1990s continued its momentum but experienced significant volatility due to geopolitical, economic and public health events. First, the terrorist attacks in New York in 2001 induced the 'War on Terror' and subsequent terrorist attacks followed in London, Madrid, Nairobi and later in Paris. By 2016, the Middle East had become the theatre of extreme tensions with the birth of the Islamic State, the Syrian and Yemeni civil wars and underlying tension between Iran and Saudi Arabia. That series of events led to a reconsideration of the free movement of people and the adoption of drastic security measures. Second, in 2008 a financial crisis (known as the 'subprime crisis') in the USA spread across the world and generated a deep slowdown in global growth, trade and investments. Finally, by 2020 the Covid-19 pandemic created a severe reduction in growth on many dimensions of global economy (Figure 2.1). A similar trend was observed in early 2022 with the invasion of Ukraine by Russia.

Starting with the end of the Korean war and the decolonization of the British and French empires, a group of countries traditionally named 'developing countries' embarked on economic development to become what was known as 'emerging countries'. By 2000, until the 2020s, most countries in Asia and Latin America and some in Africa and Central Europe exhibited rates of growth of foreign direct investment (FDI) and international trade that were higher than in the industrialized countries (Figure 2.2).

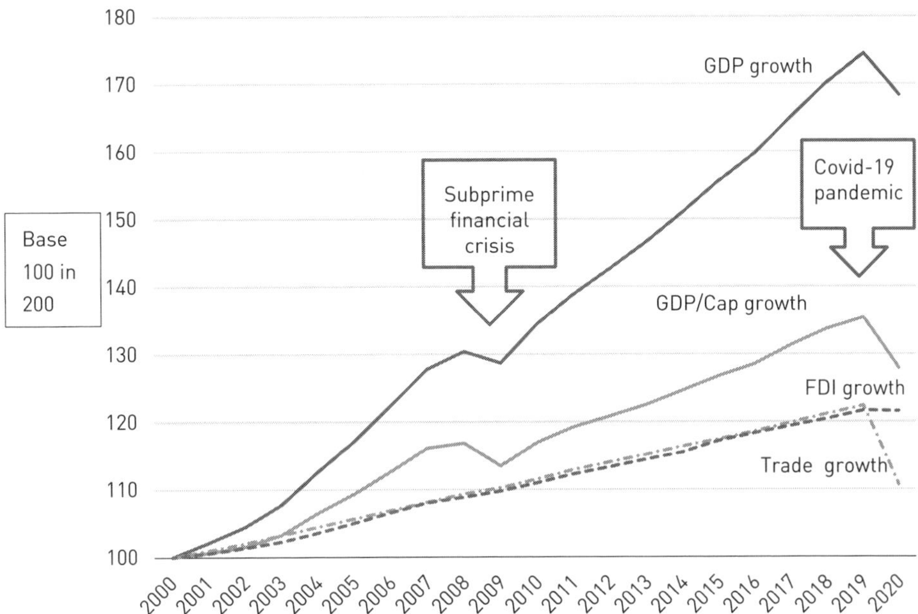

Figure 2.1 Globalization indicators, 2000–2020 (base 100 = 2000)
Source: Authors' own based on data from World Bank World Development Indicators and UNCTAD, Statistical database 2020.

By 2015, a significant slowdown in emerging countries had been observed, particularly in China, Brazil and Russia, but this slowdown did not hide the fact that emerging countries had become more and more important in the global arena, both in terms of markets and competition. A 2010 report on global development by the Organisation for Economic Co-operation and Development (OECD) stated: 'Over the past decade, a group of emerging and developing economies has been leading the way in terms of growth and development, shifting the world's economic center of gravity.'[1] At the micro level, companies such as Lenovo or Haier from China, Ranbaxy and Infosys from India, Embraer from Brazil, Gazprom from Russia, SAB from South Africa and Petronas from Malaysia joined the league of global players that traditionally was occupied by Western or Japanese multinationals.

In 2006 the *Financial Times* FT 500 Global list included just fifteen firms from emerging countries; by 2020 that number had risen to 122. The largest proportion (46 out of 122) of those firms were from China. The growing international importance of companies and markets from emerging countries is one of the key characteristics of today's global business environment. In this chapter we will describe the main characteristics and development paths of emerging countries, as well as strategies for dealing with them. Their attractiveness as markets and as offshore operational bases will also be addressed, as well as their competitiveness and the role of their global champions.

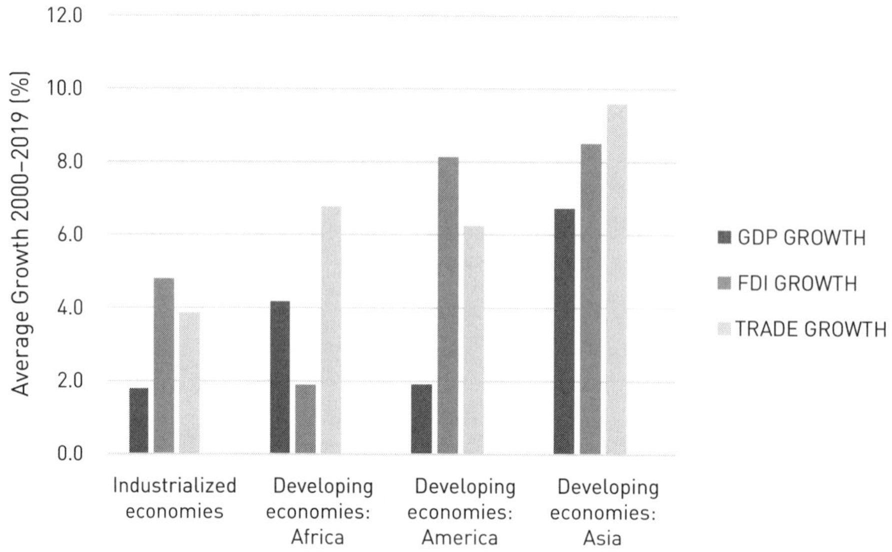

Figure 2.2 Globalization growth indicators, 2000–2019

Source: Authors' own construction, using data from UNCTAD, Statistical Database 2016.

Emerging countries and their development

There is no clear definition of an 'emerging country'. The phrase is used often to describe countries that exhibit:

a High economic growth;

b The increasing development of a middle class;

c A high degree of infrastructure and educational investment;

d A progressive shift from agriculture to industry and services;

e An economy in which market mechanisms play an increasing role;

f The opening of their markets to international trade and investment.

There have been several groupings of countries that qualified as 'emerging'. By the 1980s the term 'Asian Tigers' was introduced to qualify the tremendous economic success of four Asian countries or territories: South Korea, Singapore, Taiwan and Hong Kong, which by 2020 had joined the group of industrialized countries or territories. In 2003, a Goldman Sachs paper identified four countries (Brazil, Russia, India, China), to which South Africa was later added, to form the BRICS. This group of five emerging giants was considered representative of the growing importance of the emerging world in the global economy, and were seen as likely to overtake most OECD countries. Later, in 2005, Goldman

Sachs introduced a new group named 'The Next Eleven'. Consisting of Bangladesh, Egypt, Indonesia, Iran, South Korea, Mexico, Nigeria, Pakistan, Philippines, Turkey and Vietnam, it was thought that these countries could potentially have a BRICS-like impact rivalling the G7.[2]

Following the fall of the Berlin wall and the dissolution of the Soviet Union in the late 1980s and early 1990s, a new category of emerging countries appeared in the international literature: the 'transition economies'. These consisted of the countries that were satellite states of the USSR, such as Poland, Hungary and Czechoslovakia, or states that were part of the union such as Ukraine. Some of these have subsequently joined the European Union, thus leaving their emerging classification.

In this chapter, we will pinpoint some of the key characteristics of emerging countries through the course of their historical development. For the sake of simplicity, for most of the figures in this chapter we will adopt the World Bank categories clustered by income level (Growth National Income (GNI in US$) per capita):[3]

- Low income countries: GNI/cap less than $1,026
- Lower middle-income countries: GNI/cap between $1,027 and $3,995
- Upper middle-income countries: GNI/cap between $3,996 and $12,375
- High income countries: above $12,376

Emerging countries are represented in the upper and lower middle-income categories. A list of countries included in each category is given in online Appendix 2.1.

In this chapter we will identify three categories of emerging country:

1. The **BRICS:** these five emerging giants are considered representative of the growing importance of the emerging world in the global economy, and are likely to overtake most OECD countries in the not-so-distant future. Their profile is detailed in Appendix 2.1.
2. The **newly industrial economies** (NIEs) that have reached a degree of wealth, in terms of GDP per capita and industrial activities, similar to the traditional economies of Europe, North America and Australia–New Zealand. These NIEs can be found:

   a. in the Middle East and Turkey or among oil-rich countries such as Saudi Arabia and the United Arab Emirates;
   b. in Asia with the so called 'tigers' such as Hong Kong, Taiwan, South Korea and Malaysia;
   c. in Latin America. Argentina, Mexico, Chile do not belong to the BRICS but have nevertheless achieved a high level of industrialization and market economy. In this category we find companies that have achieved the status of global champion despite the fact that their domestic economies are still considered to be 'developing'.

3. The **industrializing economies:** countries such as Egypt, Nigeria, Indonesia, Morocco, Tunisia, Ivory Coast, Philippines, Thailand, Vietnam and Colombia that have left the status of least developed countries and have achieved a significant level of industrialization and market economy.

Growth

As Figure 2.3 shows, one of the key characteristics of the emerging world economies is that their pace of development has surpassed the rest of the world. Among those, the upper-middle income countries are by far the fastest growing, with China taking the lead. China's GDP in dollar terms overtook Japan as the second world economy in 2010. The incremental growth of the five BRICs countries by themselves overtook the G7 countries by $2,000 billion between 2010 and 2019.

This incremental demand is due to three factors: a rapidly growing urban middle class, investment in infrastructure and a drive to conquer international markets.

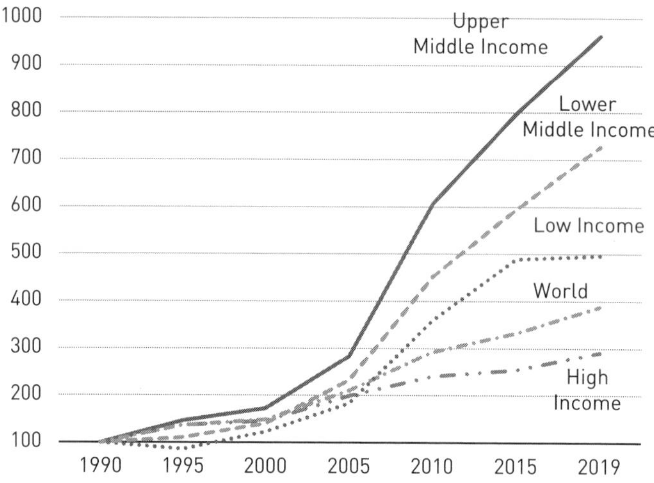

Figure 2.3 GDP growth rates: emerging countries versus the world (1990–2019)

Source: Authors' own construction using data from World Bank development indicators database, http://databank.worldbank.org/data/reports.aspx?source=world-development-indicators.

Emerging middle class

The concept of 'middle class', although widely used by economists and sociologists, is vague. The definition of the Swedish middle class, for instance, would differ considerably from the definition in Indonesia. The definition of middle class can be purely statistical (the population that occupies the centre point on the distribution of income) or it can refer to purchasing power (the population that can afford to purchase goods and services beyond the traditional subsistence level but does not belong to the country's wealthy elite). When looking at doing business in emerging countries, the second definition is the most relevant because the ability of the consumer to afford to purchase products and services is what drives demand. Interestingly, the demand for most mass consumer goods and their related inputs is often triggered by the presence of an affluent middle class.

Emerging markets, particularly, experience what is known as the 'middle-class effect', which derives from the skewed original nature of income distribution in emerging countries. At an early stage of economic development, a large proportion of the population is poor and the proportion of middle-class people is relatively low. With economic development the proportion of middle-class people increases faster than that of the poor (Table 2.1). This effect is more visible in urban centres such as Shanghai, Beijing or Guangzhou, due to the huge inflow of foreign investment into those cities.[4]

In 2009, an OECD report estimated that the global middle-class population was 1.8 billion people consuming $21 trillion – of which around 850 million people were from emerging countries, consuming $7.5 trillion. The forecast was that 2.02 billion middle-class people from emerging countries would be consuming $19 trillion by 2020, and 3.8 billion consuming $38 trillion by 2030.[5] For its part, the McKinsey Institute estimated that around 2 billion people in 24 emerging countries were middle class and consumed $6.9 trillion per year in 2010, a figure that it expected to rise to $20 trillion by 2020.[6] Globally, the Asia Pacific region is forecast to become the area with the largest middle-class group (see Figure 2.4 and Table 2.1).

Table 2.1 Estimated evolution of middle-class populations in China, India and Indonesia (millions)

	China		India		Indonesia	
Population	**2012**	**2022**	**2015**	**2025**	**2012**	**2020**
Total	1,350	1,418	1,263	1,400	250	280
Middle class	435	705	255	585	177	358
Proportion	32%	50%	20%	42%	43%	60%
	People living in households earning $16,000–34,000 (around $6,400–13,000 per capita)		People living in households earning $7,700–16,500 (around $27,00–5,500 per capita)		People whose expenditures are $2,400–6,000 per capita	

Source: Authors' own construction based on data from: China – Barton et al. (2013); India – Narayanswamy and Zainulbhai (2007); Indonesia – Rastogi et al. (2013). These are estimates: there are no official records of middle-class demographic definitions.

The middle-class population, because of its ability to consume beyond subsistence level, drives the demand in consumer goods (both durable and fast moving) and services, as well as demand for the raw materials, components and intermediate products that support these goods and services.

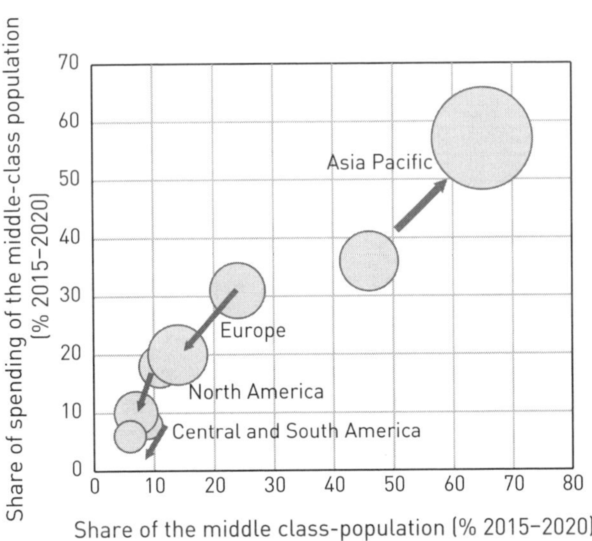

Figure 2.4 Shares of middle class, 2015–2020

Note: Bubble size indicates actual spending in PPP dollars. Local currency units can be converted to purchasing power parity (PPP) dollars. A PPP exchange rate reflects the number of units of a country's currency required to buy the same amount of goods and services in that domestic market that one US dollar would buy in the USA. The figures for 2020 are estimated.

Source: Authors' own construction based on Homi Kharas, *The Unprecedented Expansion of The Global Middle Class An Update*, Global Economy & Development Working Paper 100, February 2017, Brooking Institute.

Investment

The second driver of incremental demand is investment in infrastructure. The proportion of growth in capital formation, representing investments in roads, telecommunications, energy and similar infrastructure, over GDP in emerging countries is above the average of industrialized high income countries (Figure 2.5). In its 2008 *World Investment Report*, the United Nations Conference on Trade and Development (UNCTAD) stressed the vital need for infrastructure in the developing world and also the opportunities on offer to international, as well as local, firms for investing in those much-needed infrastructure projects.[7] An OECD report in 2017 estimated that global infrastructure investment needs $6.3 trillion per year over the period 2016–2030 to support growth and development, without considering further climate action (relative to mid-2016).[8]

Infrastructure projects, because of their contribution to demand for equipment, raw materials, services and labour, have a multiplier effect on income and ultimately on demand.[9]

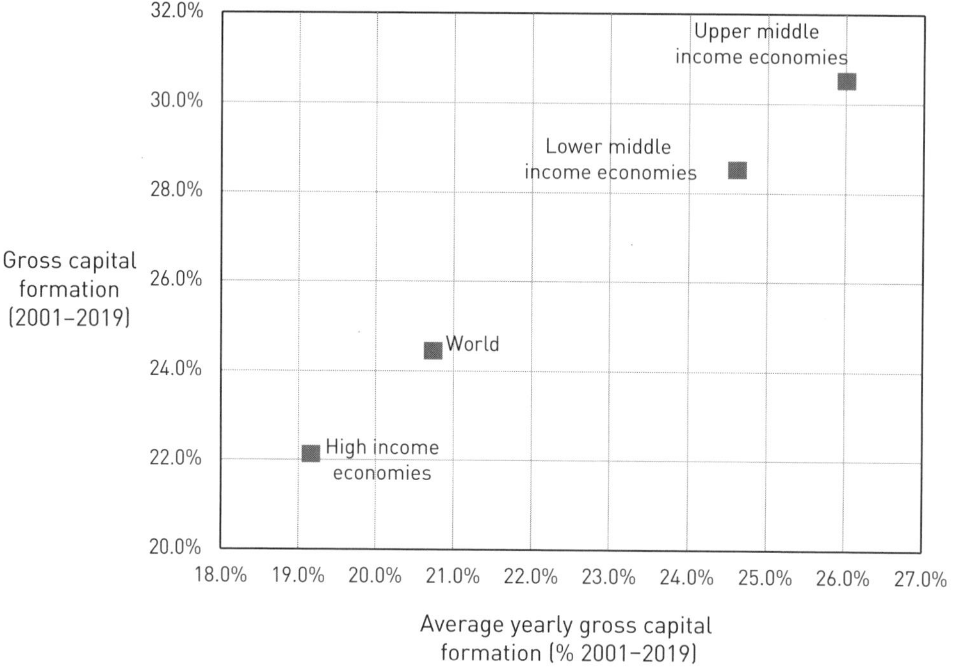

Figure 2.5 Capital formation, 2001–2019

Source: Authors' own construction calculated from World Bank development indicators, http://databank.worldbank.org/data/reports.aspx?source=world-development-indicators.

Opening of markets to international trade and investment

The third driver of economic development in emerging countries is the opening of their economies to international trade and investment. Since the 1990s, emerging countries have seen a significant increase in their inflow of FDI as well as their participation in international trade (Figure 2.6). Overall, industrialized countries dominate the total value of exports ($1.7 trillion versus $0.7 trillion for upper middle and lower middle economies in 2019), but the weight of emerging countries is growing very quickly. In 1999, the upper and lower middle income economies' share of world trade was 18 per cent; by 2019 it rose to 27 per cent while their flow of FDI rose from 13 per cent to 25 per cent during the same period. This, together with the two other drivers of growth, makes the emerging economies attractive to global, as well as local, firms.

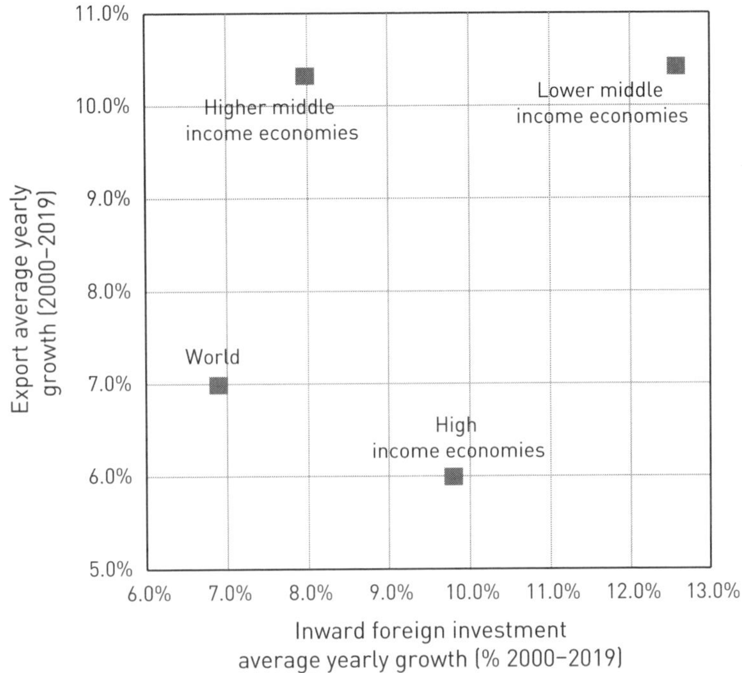

Figure 2.6 Foreign trade and investment, 2001–2019

Source: Authors' own construction based on several World Bank development indicators, http://databank.worldbank.org/data/reports.aspx?source=world-development-indicators.

Progressive shift from agriculture to industry and services

Development economists have observed the structural changes happening when an economy 'takes off' from a stage of poverty and low economic growth to a progressive increase in national wealth fostered by investments and trade. One key element of this structural change is the relative decline of the agricultural share of GDP to the benefit of industry and service sectors (Table 2.2).[10]

Market mechanisms play an increasing role

After the progressive opening of China, which began under Premier Deng Xiao Ping in 1979, and the fall of the Berlin Wall in 1989, the centrally managed economies of China, Russia and Eastern Europe have increasingly relied on market mechanisms for resource allocation. In other parts of the world, especially in

Table 2.2 Evolution from agriculture to industry and services

Agriculture, forestry and fishing, value added (% of GDP)	1990	2019
BRICS		
Brazil	6.8	4.4
India	26.9	16.01
China	26.5	7.0
Russian Federation	15.4	3.4
South Africa	4.2	1.9
Least developed countries (UN classification)	35.6	16.8
East Asia and Pacific	10.3	4.7
Latin America and Caribbean	8.1	4.7
Euro area	2.4	1.6
North America	3.0	0.9
WORLD	7.6	3.4

Source: Authors' own construction based on World Bank development indicators, http://databank.worldbank.org/data/reports.aspx?source=world-development-indicators.

South America, what is known as the 'Washington Consensus'[11] has induced emerging and developing countries to liberalize their economies, privatize government-owned companies and deregulate government control[12] (see Insert 2.1). The extent to which China has adopted market mechanisms is subject to debate since in practice government intervention is still present in key strategic sectors.

Insert 2.1 What is the Washington Consensus?

The Washington Consensus is a series of prescriptions established in 1989 at the Institute of International Economics Conference in Washington, DC that reflect liberal policy recommendations for emerging countries. They are:

- Fiscal discipline: limit budget deficit
- Public expenditure priorities should be directed toward fields offering both high economic returns and the potential to improve income distribution, such as primary healthcare, primary education, and infrastructure
- Tax reform: broaden the tax base and adopt lower marginal rates; tax foreign holdings
- Interest rate should be market determined

- Maintain a competitive exchange rate
- Trade liberalization: eliminate quantitative restrictions and replace with low tariffs
- Liberalize inflow of foreign direct investment
- Privatization of state enterprises
- Deregulate to abolish entry barriers or restrictions on competition
- Secure property rights

Source: Author's summary of some of the arguments in Williamson (1990, 1993).

Market mechanisms do not mean that the emerging economies are entirely free of control and intervention but that there has been for the past thirty years the development of a buoyant market-led sector.

Emerging countries and their institutional and business environments

In addition to the characteristics described in the previous section, emerging countries share (to a certain extent, although to different magnitudes) certain traits related to their institutional and business environments:

- Governance
- Market imperfection
- Ease of doing business
- Importance of business conglomerates
- A significant presence of 'bottom-of-the-pyramid' market segments.

Governance

Before the 1980s most emerging countries were governed by Marxist-inspired or authoritarian regimes. Political turbulence such as the cultural revolution in China or *coups d'état* in Latin America, Africa and Indonesia marked the political life of many countries. As a result, the quality of government and the formulation of policies were hampered by frequent disruptions. Despotism, favouritism, corruption and the absence of clear and impartial rules of law contributed to uncertainties in the conduct of business affairs. The past four decades have seen changes in the governance of emerging countries, which now favour more stable regulations and judicial systems. However, there is still a distance between emerging and OECD countries with regard to the quality of governance. Figures 2.7 and 2.8 illustrate some world governance indicators for 2019 for a selected number of emerging and OECD countries.

If we compare Figures 2.7 and 2.8 with Figures 2.1 and 2.2, we can see a discrepancy that may be detrimental to the stability and continuity of development.

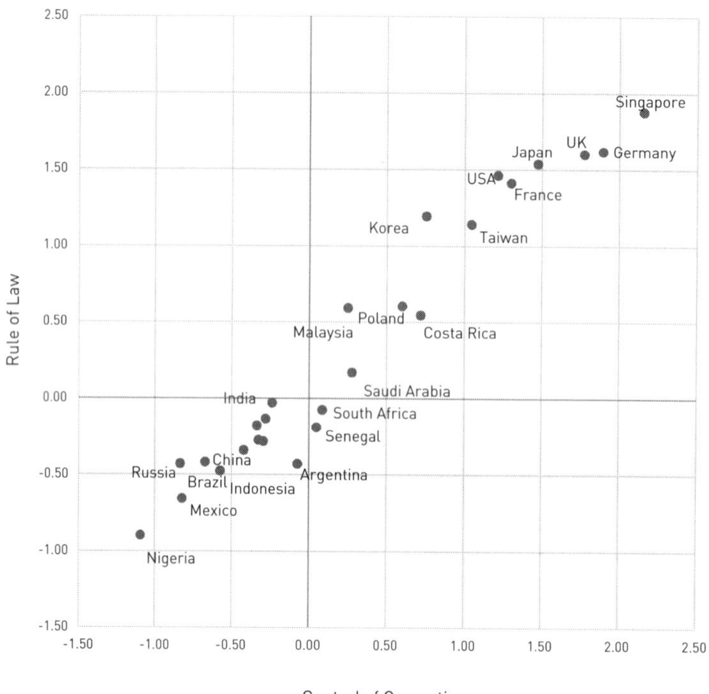

Figure 2.7 Rule of law and control of corruption indicators (2019)

Source: Authors' own construction based on several World Bank development indicators, http://databank.worldbank.org/data/reports.aspx?source=world-development-indicators.

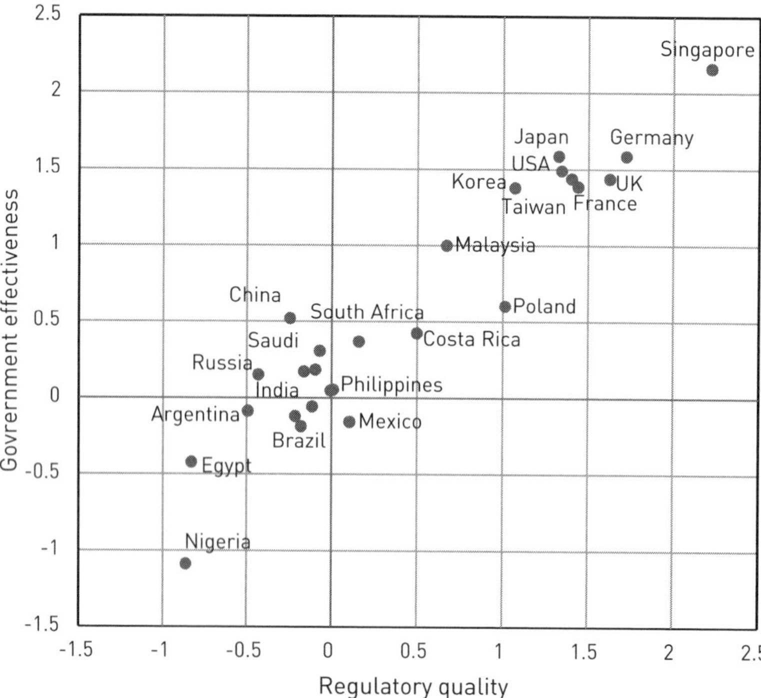

Figure 2.8 Government effectiveness and regulatory quality indicators, 2020

Source: Authors' own construction based on several World Bank development indicators, 2020 http://databank.worldbank.org/data/reports.aspx?source=world-development-indicators.

Market imperfection

In 1997 Professors Khanna and Palepu from the Harvard Business School proposed that what differentiates emerging countries from OECD countries is a number of market failures due to institutional contexts. They pinpointed three such market failures: information problems, misguided regulations and inefficient judicial systems. They later redefined those market failures as 'institutional voids' that directly affect business (Table 2.3).

Khanna and colleagues developed a set of questions that companies must address in order to identify their institutional context in relation to the political and social system, openness of government and administration, product markets, and labour and capital markets. Their overall conclusion is that investing companies need to understand these differences and adapt their strategies accordingly, but they also need to be aware of the rapid evolution in those contexts that may at any time demand further adaptation.

Table 2.3 Possible institutional voids in emerging countries

Political and social systems	• Uncertain stability of political cohesiveness • Lack of clarity in the distribution of power • Strong interference in regulating business • Uncertain protection of property rights • Lack of independence of judiciary system • Ethnic, religious, family, linguistic tensions • Control of media • Control or prohibition of non-governmental organizations • Corruption
Openness	• Investments and preferential treatment for national companies • Bureaucratic constraints on foreign business concerning the opening of businesses, acquisition of property, transfer of dividends, local borrowing, imports and exports, labour and currency
Product markets	• Lack of socioeconomic and market data • Lack of information on quality of products and services • Difficulties in accessing suppliers • Weak logistical infrastructure • Intricate distribution and retailing systems • Poor product-related environmental and safety regulations • Unsophisticated consumer credit and payment mechanisms • Poor consumer protection
Labour markets	• Weak educational system • Poor mobility of personnel • Ethnically/politically biased performance and remuneration of employees • Feeble protection of employees and restriction or prohibition of trade unions • Difficulties in fluidity of hiring and firing employees

Capital markets	• Low liquidity of equity market • Limited effectiveness of banking and financial institutions in collecting savings and channelling investments • Lack of transparency on financial performances of corporations • Predominance of government banking sector • Poor protection for minority shareholders • High predominance of diversified conglomerates • Politically motivated allocation of licences • Unclear bankruptcy process

Note: Not all characteristics apply to all emerging countries, and some of those can be found in some OECD countries.
Source: Author's own construction based on findings of Khanna and Palepu (1997).

Ease of doing business

Another way to look at a country's environment is to observe their friendliness to the conduct of business. Since 2002, the World Bank has compiled an annual 'ease of doing business ranking'. This gives a composite ranking of eleven sub-indices, which measure how easily and quickly business issues are dealt with (see Table 2.4).

Table 2.4 Ease of doing business indices

• **Starting a business procedures:** Time, cost and paid-in minimum capital to start a limited liability company
• **Dealing with construction permits**: Procedures, time and cost to complete all formalities to build operational facilities, and the quality control and safety mechanisms in the construction permitting system
• **Getting electricity**: Procedures, time and cost to get connected to the electricity grid, the reliability of the electricity supply and the cost of electricity consumption
• **Registering property:** Procedures, time and cost to transfer a property and the quality of the land administration system
• **Getting credit**: Movable collateral laws and credit information systems
• **Protecting minority investors:** Minority shareholders' rights in related-party transactions and in corporate governance
• **Paying taxes:** Payments, time and total tax rate for a firm to comply with all tax regulations
• **Trading across borders:** Time and cost to export the product of comparative advantage and import spare parts
• **Enforcing contracts:** Time and cost to resolve a commercial dispute and the quality of judicial processes
• **Resolving insolvency:** Time, cost, outcome and recovery rate for a commercial insolvency and the strength of the legal framework on insolvency
• **Labour market regulation**: Flexibility in employment regulation and aspects of job quality

Source: World Bank (2020).

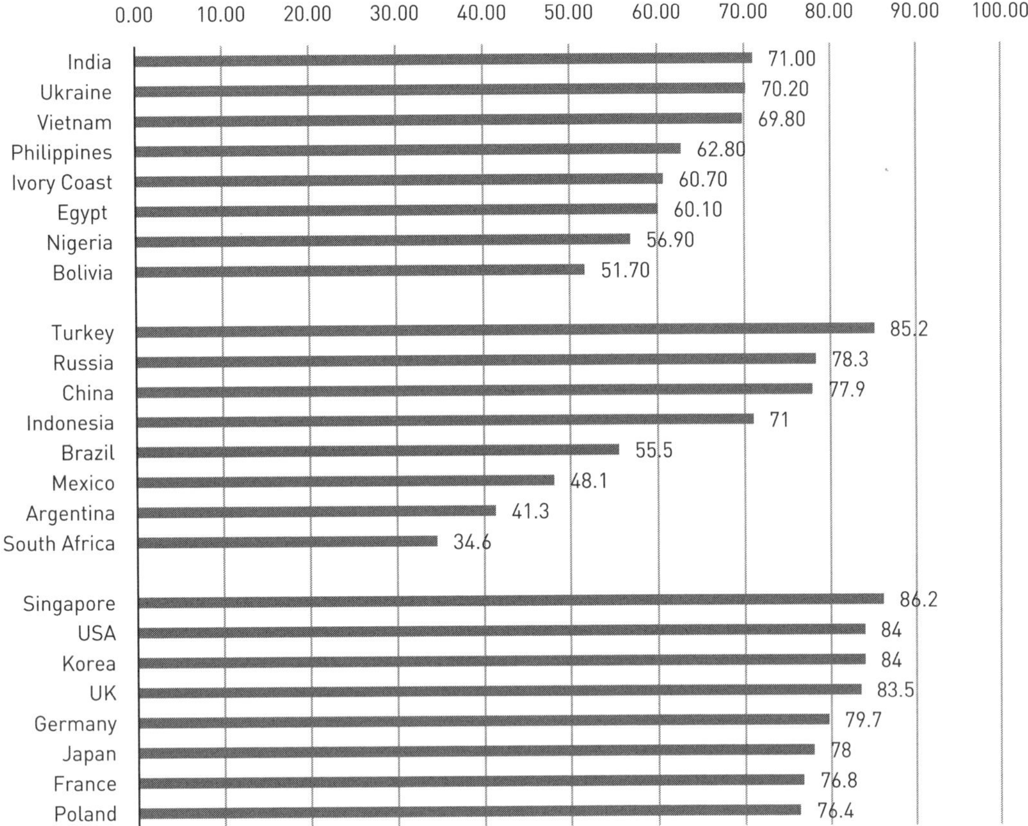

Figure 2.9 Selected ease of doing business scores, 2020 (From 0 = Not Easy, 100 = Easy)
Source: Authors' own construction using data from World Bank, http://www.doingbusiness.org/rankings.

In Figure 2.9, a sample of countries' (out of 189 countries examined) ease of doing business scores shows that emerging countries tend to have lower scores than traditional or newly industrialized economies. The overall scores do not mean much, and for a deeper analysis one should look at the individual subcomponents described in Table 2.4.

Importance of business conglomerates

Conglomerates, in the forms of publicly or privately owned highly diversified groups, are common in most emerging countries. As Khanna and Pepalu have observed, 'diversified business groups remain the dominant form of enterprise throughout most emerging markets'.[13] There are several reasons for that situation. Khanna and Palepu attribute it to institutional voids such as illiquidity of capital markets and politically motivated resource allocation. In some cases, countries have abandoned Marxist-inspired state management and given opportunities to individual entrepreneurs, who are often close to the authorities, to take advantage of the new opportunities opening in many sectors. This was the case after the demise of the Soviet Union when many oligarchs took over newly privatized state-owned enterprises. Similarly in China, ex-bureaucrats and 'red princes' seized similar opportunities. In other cases in less developed countries, postcolonial governments gave privileged access to licences to affiliated business partners, who then entered many industries. This was the case for overseas Chinese family conglomerates in Southeast Asia and family *groupos* in Latin America. In nearly all cases, the scarcity of financial and qualified human resources made it easy for economic power to become concentrated in the hands of a few large diversified groups. In the 1960s, South Korea, at the time an emerging country, diversified *chaebol* (large family-controlled firms) such as Daewoo, Samsung and Lucky Goldstar dominated the economy. Over the years, with globalization, conglomerates have tended to reduce their diversity in order to focus on their core strengths, but still play an important role.

Significant presence of 'bottom-of-the-pyramid' market segments

As mentioned earlier, an emerging middle class generates strong demand for fast-moving consumer goods as well as consumer durables. This, in turn, creates demand for the supply of intermediate products and natural resources along the value chain. However, emerging countries also feature a large non-middle-class population, what C. K. Prahalad called the 'bottom of the pyramid'.[14] According to Prahalad, in emerging countries, the largest proportion of the population located at the lowest level of income are willing to consume goods that are of good quality but obviously at a price level they can afford, and with formulation and packaging adapted accordingly. This population, contrary to conventional wisdom, is brand conscious and, given that their aim is to become middle class, multinational firms need to capture those market opportunities and brand loyalty. This implies that in emerging countries global firms are advised to adopt a dual strategy: one for the middle class that looks more or less like their traditional approach, and one for the bottom-of-the-pyramid customer that is very different. Table 2.5 shows the difference between these two approaches.

At the opposite end of the spectrum, firms making luxury goods find emerging markets very attractive due to the appearance of a class of 'nouveaux riches' who built their fortune by taking advantage of the benefits of deregulation, economic growth and, to a certain extent, 'wild capitalism'. For example, the French company LVMH saw its revenue from emerging countries rise from 2 billion euros in 2004 to over 21 billion in 2021.[15] Emerging markets then accounted for 39 per cent of the firm's total revenues. Similar trends are observed in companies such as Mercedes, BMW, Gucci and Swiss watchmakers.

Altogether, emerging markets see dynamism in the three major segments of the market: upper high-end nouveaux riches, middle class and bottom of the pyramid (Figure 2.10). Each has its own characteristics and offers opportunities to local and international firms that approach it with the appropriate strategy.

Table 2.5 Differences between traditional middle-class strategies and bottom-of-the-pyramid strategies

Traditional middle-class strategy	Bottom-of-the-pyramid strategy
• Value pricing based on differentiation and segmentation • Product life cycles of designed obsolescence and renewal • Products, services functionalities and packaging are adaptation of industrialized markets • Advertising on mass TV and media • Products designed for 'regular' environments • Urban focus • Transfer of technology • Use of skilled resources • Build supply chains similar to industrialized world	• Find new price–performance relationships leading to quality at low prices • Products built to last • Products, services functionalities and packaging are 'reinvented' to fit local conditions • Communication and advertising rely less on mass advertising and more on educational campaigns using government programmes and non-governmental organizations • Products designed for 'hostile' environments • Rural focus • Hybrid technology: combination of advanced and adaptation • Unskilled work process • Adapt supply chains to local conditions

Sources: Based on concepts discussed in Prahalad (2005) and Dawar and Chattopadhyay (2002).

Figure 2.10 The three segments in emerging markets

Emerging countries and global firms

For global firms the growth and opening up of emerging countries has far-reaching consequences for market development, as well as for sourcing and localization of production capacities. Also, emerging countries have created strong firms that raise a competitive challenge to the traditional global firms in their local as well as global markets.

Global firms' strategies for emerging markets

Beyond the classic steps in strategic analysis and formulation that require companies to perform a proper assessment of environments, markets, and competition, emerging countries require three specific considerations: 1) the kind of product/service redesign and adaptation needed according to the selected segments; 2) the localization of strategic capabilities; 3) whether to engage in strategic partnerships with local firms.

Decide on the kind of service redesign and adaptation needed according to the selected segment

As seen earlier, there are three distinct market segments, each of them offering high levels of growth opportunities. Global firms will have to decide whether they want to concentrate on one segment or several. This applies particularly to entering the bottom-of-the-pyramid segment and designing products and services for it. This approach implies a simplification of products' characteristics. The three examples that follow show companies adopting a dual strategy; one approach for the middle-class segment and one for the bottom-of-the-pyramid segment.

EXAMPLE 2.1 The multi-segment approach in emerging countries

Saurer

In 2003, Volkman (the German subsidiary of Saurer from Switzerland) was a global leader in textile twisting machines. In China, the company had achieved dominance in the high-end market but was not present in the low-end market that represented 70 per cent of demand. The low-end market was dominated by Chinese competitors that sold machines at half the price of Volkman's. The company had to decide whether to develop a simple low-cost machine. The decision was difficult because this type of machine was not part of the engineering culture of the company. Eventually, after the mobilization of a team of young Chinese and German engineers, they put a machine on the market that sold at a competitive price for much simpler performance (although still of superior quality to its competitors). This move proved very successful, not only in China but in other emerging countries.

Unilever Brazil

In 1996, while Unilever was the dominant player in the detergent market in Brazil, it developed and marketed 'Ala', which was targeted at low-income customers in the northeast of the country. This detergent was positioned as a perfumed hand-washing detergent giving the sensation of cleanliness at an affordable cost.

General Electric

In 2010, General Electric in India launched the Mac 400, a portable electro-cardiograph equipped with a small printer and rechargeable batteries that doctors could transport easily and operate in remote villages. This machine was priced at one-third of the price of conventional machines.

Sources: Saurer – Ryans (2006); Unilever Brazil – Charndon (2004). Copyright © 2007 INSEAD; GE Healthcare – Singh (2011). Copyright © 2011 INSEAD.

Decide on the localization of strategic capabilities

The practices of purchasing products in emerging countries (offsourcing) and relocating manufacturing operations (offshoring) are not new, but they increased considerably during the 1990s and 2000s. China has been the main recipient of offshore plants, followed by Mexico and Eastern Europe. On the service side, India has been a leading destination for offsourcing IT and business processes. Previously, offshoring and offsourcing were based solely on low costs and were essentially limited to manufacturing and the procurement of parts, components and original equipment manufacturing (OEM) products. For instance, Walmart bought around $13 billion of Chinese products in 2004 and Carrefour purchased $1.6 billion. Nowadays, offshoring and offsourcing encompass all elements of the value chain: R&D, manufacturing and services. Although the cost advantage of buying and producing in emerging countries can be significant (on average, 50 per cent of the costs of production in the USA or Europe), global firms have found other advantages too: higher flexibility and speed, better responsiveness to change in environments, higher service orientation. Figure 2.11 gives a pictorial representation of the advantages and disadvantages of offshoring and offsourcing in the various elements of the value chain.

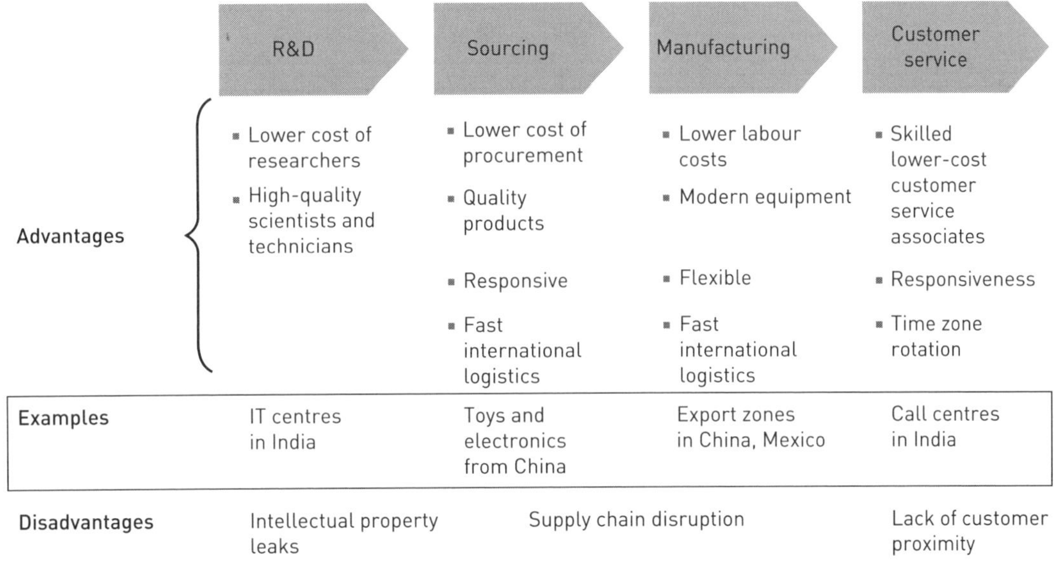

Figure 2.11 Advantages and disadvantages of offshoring and offsourcing in emerging countries

Decide whether to engage in strategic partnerships with local firms

While the authorities of emerging countries tend to welcome foreign investors, they must also balance this with encouraging the growth and development of national enterprises. They see foreign investors as a source of knowledge that can be acquired. Foreign firms may benefit from the support of local partners in order to speed their company's development and navigate the maze of cultural, social and political intricacies. In some cases, governments force foreigners to ally with a local partner when they consider that the industry is too strategic to be left in the hands of foreigners, such as natural resources or defence. When this is not the case, the decision is left to the investor who has to weigh the benefits and costs of engaging in a joint venture, as will be discussed in Chapter 8.

Emerging competitors

Until the 1970s, corporations from the emerging world were viewed as exploiters of cheap labour or imitators of outdated technologies. This perception started to change in the 1990s when some corporations followed the development path adopted by Japanese firms such as Toyota, Sony and Mitsubishi in the 1950s, and by Korean *chaebols* or Taiwanese groups such as Acer in the 1970s. Big corporations from China, Brazil, India and more recently Russia have climbed the global competitive ladder described in Figure 2.12. Starting in domestically protected markets or by exploiting natural resources, they progressively moved up to become fully fledged global players.

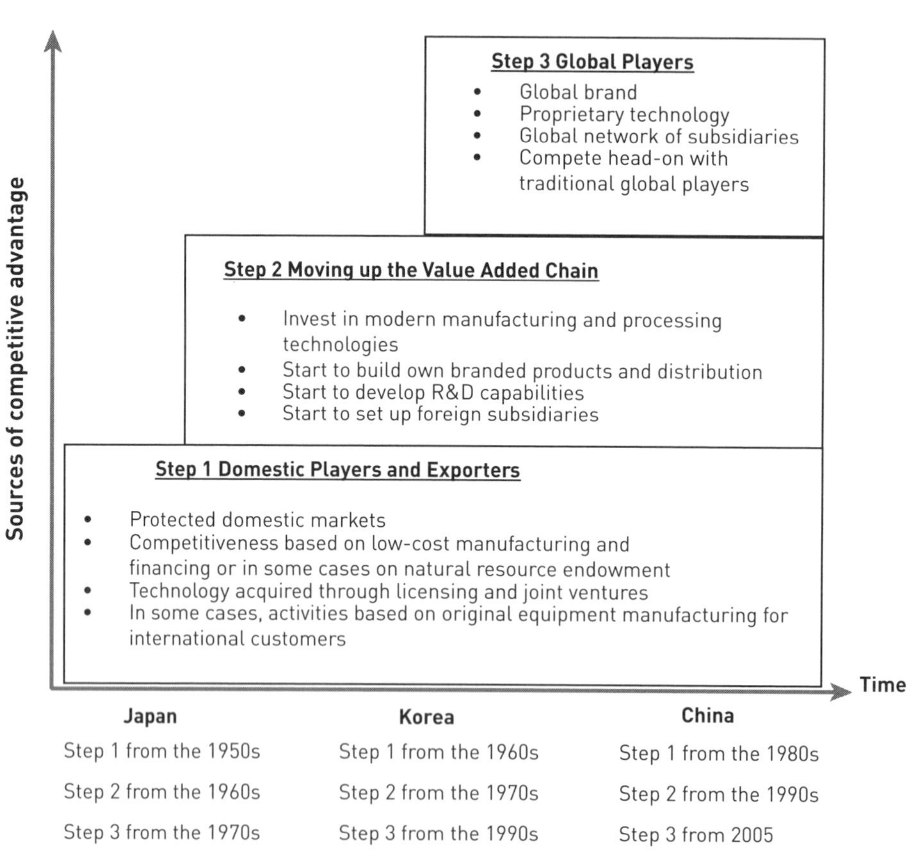

Figure 2.12 The strategic development of emerging market champions

From a competitive point of view, while multinational firms traditionally concentrated their efforts on the differentiated segments of markets, deploying their competitive advantages of technology and marketing competencies, emerging market champions adopted a two-step approach:

1. In their protected home markets they concentrated on the lower-end segments, benefitting from a low-cost base, from imported technology and from their knowledge of the local environment. They succeeded in building volume in a market that was largely ignored by multinational firms.
2. In the international markets they started by exporting low-priced products through OEM and distributors' brands, and progressively built their own distribution network and later their foreign presence via acquisitions.

Typical differences in patterns of internationalization in terms of speed, pace, and deployment of competitive advantages found between the traditional multinational companies from the developed world and the multinational firm from the emerging countries are described in Table 2.6.

Table 2.6 Differences in internationalization patterns between traditional multinational companies and emerging markets multinationals

Globalization characteristics	Traditional multinationals	New multinationals from emerging countries
Starting sources of competitive advantages	Technology developed in home country	Low cost of input: Natural resources Labour
Pace of development	Sequential Recently born global	Dominance in local markets followed by rapid expansion in key markets
Modes of development	Foreign Direct Investments search for wholly owned subsidiaries	Mainly acquisitions and alliances
Management systems	Complex structures: matrix types	Simple structures: mainly geographical
Human resources	Large number of global staff	Few global staff Reliance on local staff

Source: Author's own construction based on various sources.

Emerging multinationals momentum

The 2020 edition of the annual report published by Cornell University (Casanova and Miroux 2020) mentioned that 'the leading firms of the new millennium now come from new corners on the map. Eight out of the 20 largest economies qualify as emerging markets whose companies are among the world's most prized.' The report quotes the evolution of Emerging Multinationals in the Fortune 500 report for the period ranging from 2010 to 2020 (see Figure 2.13).

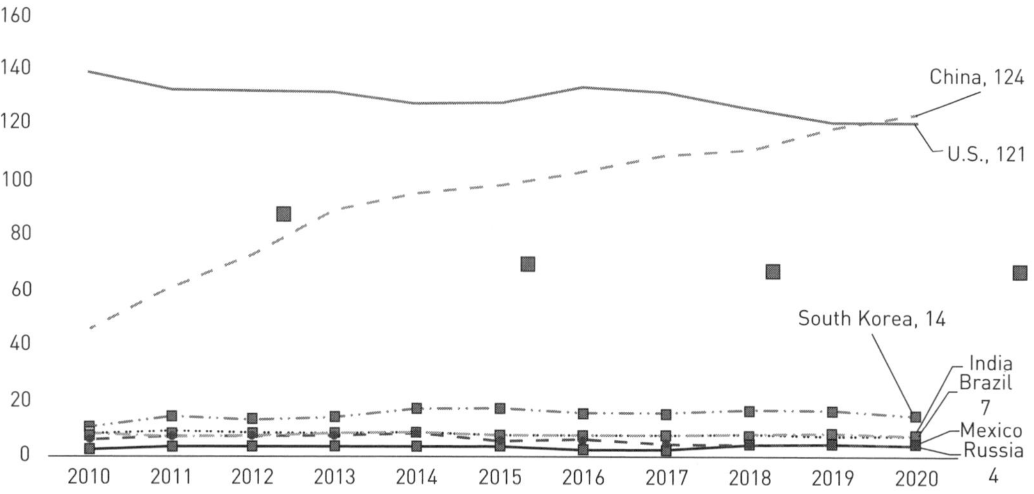

Figure 2.13 Number of emerging market multinationals on Fortune Global 500

Every year UNCTAD publishes a World Investment Report, giving a view of the relative importance of multinational companies from emerging countries.

Between 2008 and 2018, the foreign assets of the 100 largest multinational companies from emerging countries grew from $808 billion to $2,581 billion (an increase of 210 per cent), and the number of their foreign employees grew from 2.6 million to 4.6 million (a 77 per cent increase). During the same period, the 100 largest non-financial multinational enterprises worldwide saw their foreign assets increase by 51 per cent and their foreign employees by 8 per cent.

Every year, the Boston Consulting Group (BCG) identifies 100 corporations from emerging countries with at least $1 billion of sales, a minimum of 10 per cent of revenues generated, and 10 per cent of foreign assets from overseas operations. BCG calls those companies the 'global challengers'. According to the latest report[16] the global challengers between 2011 and 2016 enjoyed an annual growth rate of revenues significantly higher than the ones enjoyed by traditional multinational companies operating in the same sectors (Table 2.7) of 18 per cent between 2000 and 2013, compared with 7 per cent for other multinational firms. Table 2.8 presents a sample of global challengers coming from different continents.

Table 2.7 Comparison of revenues growth rate between 2011 and 2016 between BCG Global Challengers in various industries and traditional multinational companies

Industry	BCG Global Challengers	Multinational Global Peers*
Health Care	25%	3%
Technology, Media and Telecommunication	11%	1%
Consumer Goods	12%	4%
Industrial Goods	10%	–3%

*** = Global peers are multinational companies operating in the same sector**

Source: BCG Global Challengers: Digital Leapfrogs, May 2018, Boston Consulting Group.

Table 2.8 Selected examples of global challengers from emerging countries

Country of origin	Name	Activities	Date of creation	Revenues 2019 (US$ m)	Percentage of foreign revenues (%)	Presence in foreign countries
Brazil	BRF	Foods	1934	8.4	45	130
Russia	Lukoil	Oil and gas	1995	125	84	30
India	Wipro	Foods	1934	8.4	45	130
China	BYD	Batteries, Automotive	1995	17	16	5
South Africa	SASOL	Chemical and Energy	1950	14.9	52	37
Mexico	FEMSA	Foods and Distribution	1890	26.8	45	27
United Arab Emirates	Etisalat	Telecom services	1976	14.2	38.5	16
Indonesia	Golden Agri-Resources	Palm oil products	1972	6.4	83	70
Turkey	Sabanci Holding	Energy, Cement, Banking, Retail	1925	13.9	34	12
Philippines	Universal Robina	Food and Beverages	1950	2.75	31	35
Argentina	Mercado Libre	E-Commerce	1997	2.3	80	18
Kenya	Suparicom	Telecommunication	1999	2.27	*NA*	3
Nigeria	Dangote Cement	Cement	1981	2.33	40	9
Peru	Alicorp	Food and Personal care	1997	2.71	44	30
Morocco	OCP group	Fertilizers (Phosphate)	1920	6.07	*NA*	16

Sources: Authors' own construction based on data from the various companies' Annual Reports, 2019.

In a more recent report the BCG identified what it calls 'Tech challengers' which according to the authors are 'companies with the ambition and potential to reinvent and reshape the industries in which they operate. Their innovative advances, rapid growth, and expanding global positions merit close attention.'[17] Half of those Tech challengers are coming from China.

Insert 2.2 China: The New Incoming Global Giant

When China joined the World Trade Organization in 2001, its share of global trade of goods and service was 3 per cent, however by 2019 it climbed to 10 per cent and to 18 per cent in terms of its share of world manufacturing exports. During the same period the USA's share declined from 15 per cent to 11 per cent. Regarding foreign investments inflow China's share increased from 5 per cent to 10 per cent.

China became the 'factory of the world' with regards to low-cost labour-intensive industrial goods. After 2015, China's competitive advantage in labour-intensive industry declined, but this was replaced progressively by an increase in technology-intensive sectors such as IT, health products, machinery and appliances, and transportation equipment. According to a report from the NSB National Science Board:

> In high-technology manufacturing industries (which totalled US$1.6 trillion in value-added terms in 2016), the United States and China were the largest global providers (31% and 24% of the global share, respectively); China's output rose sharply over time and now exceeds that of the EU.[18]

MINI-CASE 2.1

Stefanini and the Global Digital Revolution

Stefanini – A Brazilian Global IT Player[19]

Founded in 1987 by Marco Stefanini in Brazil, Stefanini became one of the largest ICT service providers in Latin America. However, unlike most Latin American companies, Stefanini focused on international markets, making it a truly global company. By 2020, it was a $1 billion global provider of technology services, present in 41 countries, with 25,000 employees operating in 35 languages and providing 80 solutions working in 20 industries.[20] The company offered a wide range of IT services, following the 'one-stop-shop' model. Through its Digital Services, Stefanini provided strategy and technology consulting, helping customers innovate and transform their business models, and adapt them to the market context of the digital economy. These included:

- Business Process Outsourcing (BPO) outsourcing operational processes such as purchasing and payroll.
- IT Outsourcing (ITO) providing IT support services onsite.
- Application Development Centres that centralized the development and integration of software according to client needs.
- Selling licences and providing maintenance to large global software and hardware partners such as IBM, SAP, Oracle and Dell.

Over the thirty-year period, with no external investment, Marco had taken on global competitors such as IBM, Tata Consultancy Services (TCS) and Accenture and had to contend with the vicissitudes of Brazil, a complex home base.

History

Stefanini IT Solutions' first partner was IBM, a company that at the time was undergoing issues with its mainframe training. Marco expanded operations, offering training services to other companies. In 1989, as the company started to take off, Brazil was undergoing turbulent times economically. In the 1990s, the 'Collor Plan' blocked all liquidity and the savings of the population in an attempt to control inflation. Marco reduced operations and looked for new opportunities – outsourcing applications and technical support professionals.

By 1993, Stefanini had reached its first million billing and developed its first independent software factory in Brazil. In 1994, as demand for application development and maintenance accelerated, ERPs (Enterprise Resource Planning) emerged that threatened IT outsourcing services because they were standardized, low maintenance and did not require new development. Marco saw it as an opportunity – the person who carried out the services needed to be better qualified, therefore the price of the service could be up to three times higher. In addition, ERPs required new technical services such as infrastructure.

As the internet was widely adopted by business and society in Brazil and competition increased, Marco expanded internationally, beginning in 1995 with its first acquisition in Argentina, followed by further expansion in Latin America in 2000. Stefanini continued to expand, moving into the US the following year and setting up operations in Italy and Portugal in 2003. In 2005 a London hub was created, and the first unit was created in India the following year.

By 2009, Stefanini had a portfolio of global customers, including J&J, GE and Caterpillar. CIOs were pleased with its service delivery, helping its entry into new markets. Stefanini continued to expand, acquiring its largest company in 2011: Tech Team. This was followed by the first non-IT company the following year, Orbitall. The same year, Stefanini launched its global brand 'our DNA Powering Your Business'. The company continued to acquire companies throughout the world with acquisitions and joint ventures in cyber security and Internet of Things (IoT), among others.

Despite the company's success and growth, Marco realized that the industry was transforming radically; what had been successful in the past would not work in the future. The effects of the digital revolution applied to many of Stefanini's activities. He knew the company had to evolve the supply of products and services. Stefanini's sales and delivery models would also need to be strengthened. Stefanini was creating a global ecosystem that enhanced its ability to create unique solutions. It was also building digital business solutions in workplace infrastructure and applications services, among others.

There were several options for further geographic expansion. Stefanini could acquire more companies worldwide as it had in the past or form strategic alliances with local or multinational technology companies. However, some geographies could prove more challenging. Did it want to target the US where there were many customers but fierce competition? Should Stefanini pursue a similar strategy to Johnson & Johnson where they had taken its successful Brazilian operations and worked backwards helping the company in other ways? Another option was to bolster its presences in other countries, for example key European markets such as the UK where it had a small market share. Stefanini could expand through joint ventures and/or create strategic alliances with local or multinational technology firms. Its hubs and offices throughout the world could facilitate this. Ultimately, Stefanini needed to decide which 'geographical battles' it should fight.

Source: Based on Monteiro, Rozman and Carrick, 'Stefanini and the Digital Revolution: Transforming and Being Transformed', INSEAD case no. 09/2018-6328 (2017); Figures: https://stefanini.com/en.

Questions:

1 What are the factors that have made Stefanini so successful over the company's thirty-year history?

2 How and why did they expand globally?

3 How has technology impacted the business over the years?

MINI-CASE 2.2

Charoen Pokphand (CP)

When in 1920 the Chia brothers opened their first shop in Bangkok selling seeds for farmers, they did not know that they were on the way to launching the development of one of the most successful global conglomerates in the Asia Pacific region. After the Second World War, in 1953, they started the first vertical integration move by opening an animal feed mill in their garage, which was soon modernized. A series of developments followed drawing on their knowledge of agricultural industries.

Table 2.9 Charoen Pokphand: diversification and globalization

Date	Industry	Date	Country
1959	Vegetable seed farm		
1970	Chicken farming		
		1979	Shenzen, China: JV with US Continental Grain for animal feed
1980	Swine farming support to farmers		
1983	Enter property development		
1986	Tiger prawn farming in JV with Mitsubishi	1986	Turkey: Animal feed and chicken farming
1988	Enter retailing with Makro and Seven Eleven		
1990	Enter telecom industry. Pasteurized dairy products	1990	China: Motorcycle production in Henan Province
		1993	Vietnam: Livestock feed mill
		1996	Chennai, India: Aquaculture Pudong, China: Lotus Supercenter mall
2000	Frozen foods Pharmaceutical	2000	China: Opening of Sino Bio Pharma

		2001	Vietnam: Aquaculture
		2006	Russia: Livestock feed, swine and chicken farming Laos: Integrated livestock
		2007	Philippines: Animal feed and farming
		2012	Beijing, China: Egg production 'Three million layers' Belgium: investment in frozen foods
2014	E-Commerce	2014	Indonesia, Philippines, Cambodia and Myanmar: Expansion of e-commerce
		2015	Alliance with Itochu (Japan) and Citic (China) for sourcing
2016	Beverage and food distribution	2016	Expansion of beverage and food distribution to China, Thailand, India, Cambodia, Laos and Myanmar
		2017	Cambodia: Rice mill USA and Canada: Food distribution
		2017	Cambodia: Rice mill
			CP is also present under one form or another in Australia, New Zealand, Kenya, Tanzania, South Africa, Germany, France and Italy

With a total turnover of $19 billion in 2019, CP is a significant representation of the business drive of overseas Chinese entrepreneurs that characterize the Southeast and East Asia region.

The company website (https://www.cpgroupglobal.com/) states that

> the CP Group has many business entities which comprise individual companies and/or groups of companies operating in multiple industries ranging from traditional backbone industries such as agriculture to technology–driven forefront industries such as e-commerce/digital. Moreover, these companies consist of both listed and private companies.
>
> Through business diversification we recognize new opportunities and adapt our businesses to remain competitive in evolving markets. And most important, the synergy resulting from our related businesses enable us to deliver higher quality and better products and services with greater value to consumers.

Questions:

1 Why can a company be so diversified and still be successful?

2 When looking at the internationalization of CP what kind of competitive advantages does it possess and in which part of the world?

MINI-CASE 2.3

BYD (Build Your Dreams)

Founded in 1995 by Mr Wang Chuanfu in Shenzhen, Southern China, BYD (Build Your Dreams) is today the largest supplier of rechargeable batteries in the world and has diversified into electronic components, car manufacturing and solar energy. It has operations primarily in China, India, Hungary and Brazil and employs more than 180,000 people. Its turnover in 2010 was 46 billion Yuan RMB ($6.8 billion).

Mr Wang was a chemist and researcher at Beijing Non-Ferrous Metal Research Institute who was assigned to be the general manager of a government-owned battery factory. After reading that Japan was going to stop the production of the NiCd1 battery because of environment concerns, Wang quit his job and founded Shenzhen BYD Battery Company Limited with 2.5 million Yuan RMB borrowed from his cousin. The company started with 20 employees.

When BYD started out, making rechargeable batteries for tools like electric drills, Wang and his engineers built their own production line on which the cheap cost of labour replaced expensive machinery, giving BYD a competitive advantage on price. In 2000, it qualified as a Li-ion battery supplier for Motorola and, in 2002, for Nokia. BYD had to compete not only with traditional Japanese battery makers but more and more with local newcomers who tried to copy BYD's production system.

With increased competition, Wang diversified into making components such as LCD screens, keypads and modules for mobile phone manufacturers. Those electronic manufacturing activities became the second pillar of the BYD corporate portfolio. In 2008, this division bought Sino MOS, which specialized in semiconductor technology and became a significant part of BYD activities.

However, the major strategic move came on 22 January 2003 when BYD purchased Xi'an Tsinchuan Auto Co. and entered the auto industry. Immediately Wang replicated in the car industry his method of production based on cheap labour-intensive methods rather than expensive automation. But BYD also had to build an R&D capability, so Wang went to top universities and hired thousands of new mechanics and engineering graduates. By the end of 2009, BYD had more than 12,000 engineers working in basic R&D functions. Wang remarked that he was blessed with engineers who worked hard for only 3,600 Yuan RMB a month. He also engaged in reverse engineering practices, dismantling competitors' products in order to understand and possibly replicate some components. Another practice derived from the battery business was the vertical integration and manufacture of most of the parts internally. Wang bought a mould-making factory in Beijing and another in Japan.

The first car produced by the company, the BYD F3, was very much like the Toyota Aygo. In order to fight a possible law suit, BYD hired 200 legal staff.

In 2007, Warren Buffett's Berkshire Hathaway bought 10 per cent of BYD shares for $230 million.

In 2008, Wang announced the launch of a hybrid model and a fully electric car for 2009.

By 2009 the F3 was a success with 290,000 cars sold, and Wang announced his intention to become the number 1 car maker in China by 2015 and the world's best car maker in 2025.

In the electric car business, Wang claimed a competitive advantage in electric car battery with BYD's lithium-ion ferrous phosphate (LFP) technology.

The launch of the first purely electric vehicle was announced in January 2010.

However, 2010 was marked by a decline in profits due to distribution problems.

In 2011, BYD and Daimler signed a memorandum of understanding and announced they would jointly launch electric cars under a new brand in China in 2013 through Shenzhen BYD Daimler New Technology Co. Ltd. This joint venture had a capital of 600 million Yuan RMB, combining Daimler's proprietary technologies in vehicle structure and safety with BYD's auto battery.

On the battery side of the business, in 2008, BYD signed an agreement with the local government of Shangluo, Shannxi, to build a solar-powered battery plant and announced that it would build 5,000 MW per year of solar photovoltaic cell manufacturing capacity at a cost of 22.5 billion Yuan RMB by 2015. This was considerably more than Suntech Power Holdings Co. Ltd, a major Chinese player in this market, whose capacity was about 100 MW per year.

In October 2011, BYD opened its North American headquarters in Los Angeles.

In 2014, it opened the first iron phosphate battery production plant in Manaus (Brazil) and expanded to the production of lithium phosphate in 2020.

In 2015, it began producing a new electric bus model, in Brasilia, in cooperation with the local bus body maker Marcopolo.

The BYD revenues grew from from $12 billion in 2015 to $18 billion in 2019.

Its revenues come from the following sources: China (84 per cent), Asia Pacific (8 per cent), USA and rest of the world (8 per cent).

Questions:

1 How do you account for the success of BYD?

2 Given what you know of the global car industry, do you think that BYD is on course to realize Wang's dream of becoming the number 1 global player? What elements are in its favour? What elements may prevent this goal from being achieved?

Source: Anna Wang and Hellmut Schütte, term paper 'BYD Build Your Dream', 2010. Adapted with kind permission of Hellmut Schütte.

Summary and key points

1 Since the start of the twenty-first century, emerging countries from Asia, Latin America, Africa and Central Europe have exhibited rates of growth in GDP, foreign direct investment and international trade higher than industrialized countries

2 'Emerging countries' describes countries that exhibit:

a High economic growth

b The increasing development of a middle class

c A high degree of infrastructure and educational investment

- d A progressive shift from agriculture to industry and services
- e An economy in which market mechanisms play an increasing role
- f The opening of their markets to international trade and investment

3 The World Bank groups emerging countries that fulfil those requirements into three categories:

- a Low income countries: GNI/cap less than $1,026
- b Lower middle-income countries: GNI/cap between $1,027 and $3,995
- c Upper middle-income countries: GNI/cap between $3,996 and $12,375

4 Economic growth is due to three factors:

- a A rapidly growing urban middle class
- b An investment in infrastructure
- c A drive to conquer international markets

5 The major differences between emerging countries and OECD countries are a number of market failures due to institutional contexts:

- a Governance marked by weak rule of law, poor control of corruption and regulatory quality
- b Institutional voids and market imperfections
- c Ease of doing business needs to be improved
- d Importance of business conglomerates
- e A significant presence of 'bottom-of-the-pyramid' market segments

6 Global firms benefit from emerging countries for:

- a Market development
- b Sourcing and localization of production capacities

7 Strategies for emerging countries consist of:

- a Deciding on the kind of product/service redesign and adaptation needed according to the selected segments
- b Deciding on the localization of strategic capabilities
- c Deciding whether one engages in strategic partnership with local firms

8 Emerging market champions:

- a Concentrate on the lower-end segments in their protected home markets
- b Succeed in building volume in a market that is largely ignored by multinational firms
- c In international markets they start first importing low-priced products through OEM and distributors' brands, and progressively build their own distribution network and, later on, their foreign presence via acquisitions

Learning assignments

1 What are the differences between an emerging country and a developing country?

2 Why does a growing middle class contribute to growth?

3 What benefits do emerging markets champions get from OEM contracts?

4 What are the threats coming from emerging markets champions to Western global firms?

5 How do you explain the paradoxical position of China being the second largest economy in the world and still classified as an emerging economy?

Key words

- BRICS
- Emerging countries champions
- Emerging country
- Institutional voids
- Middle class
- Bottom of the pyramid
- OEM
- Offshoring
- Offsourcing

Web resources

https://www.unido.org/
http://info.worldbank.org/governance/wgi/index.aspx#home
http://unctad.org/en/Pages/Home.aspx

Companion website

Visit the companion website at bloomsbury.pub/global-strategic-management-5e for a multitude of weblinks and resources, self-test questions for revision and appendices.

Notes

1 OECD (2010).

2 https://www.goldmansachs.com/insights/archive/BRICs-and-Beyond.html. For a complete review of the BRICS and the next eleven.

3 Gross national income (GNI is equal to product (GDP) plus net income (positive or negative) received from abroad.

4 Youval and Magni (2012).

5 Kharas (2009).

6 Court and Narasimhan (2010).

7 UNCTAD (2008).

8 https://www.oecd.org/env/cc/g20-climate/Technical-note-estimates-of-infrastructure-investment-needs.pdf
9 Ifzal and Pernia (2003).
10 Soubbotina (2010).
11 Williamson (1990, 1993, 2004).
12 Huang (2010).
13 Khanna et al. (2005).
14 Prahalad (2005).
15 https://www.lvmh.com/investors/profile/financial-indicators/#groupe.
16 BCG Global Challengers: Digital Leapfrogs, Boston Consulting Group, May 2018.
17 5 BCG Tech Challengers: The next generation of innovation in Emerging Markets, Boston Consulting Group, 2020.
18 National Science Board, Science & Engineering Indicators 2018, https://www.nsf.gov/statistics/2018/nsb20181/
19 Based on the INSEAD case study: Reference 6328, L. F. Monteiro, G. Rozman, A-M Carrick, 'Stefanini and the Digital Revolution: Transforming and Being Transformed', 2017.
20 Stefanini company brochure 2020.

References and further reading

Aguiar, M., Bradtke, T., Carlisle, E. et al. (2014) *Redefining Global Competitive Dynamics: 2014 BCG Global Challengers*, BCG Perspectives.

Barton, D., Chen, Y. and Jin, A. (2013) 'Mapping China's middle class', *McKinsey Quarterly*, June.

Besouri, C. P. (2006) 'A grassroots approach to emerging market consumers', *McKinsey Quarterly*, 4: 61–71.

Boston Consulting Group (2009) *The 2009 Multilatinas*. https://www.bcg.com/publications/2009/2009-bcg-multilatinas (accessed 24 May 2017).

Boston Consulting Group (2010, May) *The African Challengers*. https://www.bcg.com/publications/2010/african-challengers (accessed 8 February 2022).

Boston Consulting Group (2010, September) *Winning in Emerging-market Cities*. https://reclaimistanbul.files.wordpress.com/2011/04/bcg-raporu.pdf (accessed 8 February 2022).

Boston Consulting Group (2014) *The 2014 BCG New Global Challengers*. https://www.bcg.com/publications/2014/growth-meet-global-challengers (accessed 8 February 2022).

Casanova, L. and Miroux, A. (2020), Emerging Market Multinationals Report 2020: 10 Years that Changed Emerging Markets, Cornell University. https://doi.org/10.7298/cvhn-dc87 (accessed 11 February 2022).

Court, D. and Narasimhan, L. (2010) 'Capturing the world emerging middle class', *McKinsey Quarterly*, July, 1–6.

Dawar, N. and Chattopadhyay, A. (2002) 'Rethinking marketing programs for emerging markets', *Long Range Planning*, 35: 457–74.

Deloitte (2014) *Deloitte's 2014 Global Outsourcing and Insourcing Survey, 2014 and Beyond*.

Deloitte Research (2006) *Unlocking the Value of Globalisation: A Deloitte Research Global Manufacturing Study*.

Euromonitor International (2010) 'Consumer Lifestyles in China', December.

Farrell, D., Gersh, U. and Stephenson, E. (2006) 'The value of China's emerging middle class', *McKinsey Quarterly*, Special Edition, 60–9.

Guillén, M. F. and García-Canal, E. (2009) 'The American model of the multinational firm and the "new" multinationals from emerging economies', *Academy of Management Perspectives*, 23 (2): 23–35.

Gupta, A. K. and Wang, H. (2009) *Getting China and India Right* (San Francisco, CA: Jossey-Bass).

Gwartney, J., Lawson, R. and Hall, J. (2016) *Economic Freedom of the World: 2016 Annual Report*, Fraser Institute. https://www.fraserinstitute.org/sites/default/files/economic-freedom-of-the-world-2016.pdf (accessed 24 May 2017).

Huang, Y. (2010) 'Debating China's economic growth: The Beijing consensus or the Washington consensus', *Academy of Management Perspectives*, 24 (2): 31–7.

Ifzal, A. and Pernia, E. M. (2003) 'Infrastructure and poverty reduction: what is the connection?', ERDB Policy Brief Series, No. 13, Asian Development Bank.

Kearney, A. T. (2008) *The Rise of Emerging Markets in Mergers and Acquisitions*. https://silo.tips/download/the-rise-of-emerging-markets-in-mergers-and-acquisitions-developing-countries-ar (accessed 29 January 2022).

Khanna, T. and Palepu, K. (1997) 'Why focused strategies may be wrong for emerging markets', *Harvard Business Review*, 75 (4): 41–51.

Khanna, T., Palepu, K. and Sinha, J. (2005) 'Strategies that fit emerging markets', *Harvard Business Review*, 84 (10): 63–76.

Kharas, H. (2009) 'The emerging middle class in developing countries', OECD Development Centre, Working Paper no. 285, OECD.

Kharas, H. (2011) 'The emerging middle class in developing countries', Global Economy and Development at Brookings (Washington, DC: Brookings).

Kharas, H. (2017) 'The unprecedented expansion of the global middle class: an update', Global Economy and Development at Brookings (Washington, DC: Brookings).

Kim, D., Kandemir, D. and Cavusgil, S. T. (2004) 'The role of family conglomerates in emerging markets: what Western companies should know', *Thunderbird International Business Review*, 46 (1): 13–38.

Lasserre, P. (1993) 'The coming of age of Indonesian-Chinese conglomerates', INSEAD Euro Asia Centre, Working paper no. 13.

Lazzarini, S. G., Mesquita, L. F., Monteiro, F. and Musacchio, A. (2021) 'Leviathan as an inventor: leader or laggard? Patenting intensity, originality, and impact in state-owned multinational firms', *Journal of International Business Studies*, 52: 560–94.

Narayanswamy, S. and Zainulbhai, A. (2007) 'India's consumption evolution', *Business Standard* (India), May.

OECD (2010) *Perspectives on Global Development 2010, Shifting Wealth*, OECD.

Prahalad, C. K. (2005) *The Fortune at the Bottom of the Pyramid* (Upper Saddle River, NJ: Wharton School Publishing).

Rastogi, V., Tamboto, E., Tong, D. and Sinburimsit, T. (2013) 'Asia's next big opportunity: Indonesia's rising middle-class and affluent consumers', BCG Perspectives, March., https://www.bcg.com/publications/2013/center-consumer-customer-insight-consumer-products-indonesias-rising-middle-class-affluent-consumers (accessed 4 July 2017).

Satish, S., Ormiston, C., Bloch, N. et al. (2008) 'How to win in emerging markets', *Sloan Management Review*, Spring: 19–23.

Soubbotina, T. P. (2010) *Beyond Economic Growth: Meeting the Challenges of Global Development*, International Bank for Reconstruction and Development.

Tahilyani, N., Tamhane, T. and Tan, J. (2011) 'Asia's $1 trillion infrastructure opportunity', *McKinsey Quarterly*, March.

UNCTAD (2008) 'Transnational corporations and the infrastructure challenge', *World Investment Report 2008*, UNCTAD.

UNCTAD, Statistical Database (n.d.). http://unctadstat.unctad.org/wds/ReportFolders/reportFolders.aspx-?sCS_ChosenLang=en (accessed 6 June 2017).

UNCTAD, World Investment Reports (2016). http://unctad.org/en/pages/DIAE/World%20Investment%20Report/WIR-Series.aspx (accessed 24 May 2021).

Vestring, T., Rouse, T., Reinert, U. and Varma, S. (2005) *Making the Move to Low-cost Countries* (Boston, MA: Bain and Company).

Williamson, J. (ed.) (1990) 'Latin American adjustment: how much has happened?', Institute for International Economics, Conference volume.

Williamson, J. (1993) 'Democracy and the "Washington Consensus"', *World Development*, 21 (8): 1329–36.

Williamson, J. (2004) 'A short history of the Washington Consensus', Paper commissioned by Fundación CIDOB for the conference 'From the Washington Consensus towards a new global governance', Barcelona, 24–5 September 2004.

Wilson, D. and Purushothaman, R. (2003) 'Dreaming with BRICs: the path to 2050', Goldman Sachs, Global Economic paper no. 99, 1 October.

World Bank (n.d.), Global Indicators Database. http://databank.worldbank.org/data/reports.aspx?-source=world-development-indicators (accessed 6 June 2017).

World Bank (2016) *Doing Business 2016*. http://www.doingbusiness.org/~/media/WBG/DoingBusiness/Documents/Annual-Reports/English/DB16-Full-Report.pdf (accessed 24 May 2017).

World Bank (2020) *Doing Business 2020*. https://documents1.worldbank.org/curated/en/688761571934946384/pdf/Doing-Business-2020-Comparing-Business-Regulation-in-190-Economies.pdf (accessed 8 February 2022).

Youval, A. and Magni, M. (2012) 'Meet the Chinese consumer of 2020', *McKinsey Quarterly*, March.

Zoubir, Y. and Lhabitant, F. S. (2003) *Doing Business in Emerging Europe* (Basingstoke: Palgrave Macmillan).

Chapter 3

Globalization, societies and cultures

By the end of the chapter you should be able to:

- Understand the meaning of culture and the various layers of culture
- Understand the variety of different forms of economic organization and business system
- Identify the key characteristics of international cultural differences
- Understand the different management issues associated with cultural differences
- Understand the managerial issues associated with cross-cultural teams
- Understand how cultural differences affect international negotiations
- Identify the key characteristics of an economic culture
- Be aware of differences in the ways of conducting business across cultures

Introduction

When Samuel Huntington wrote *The Clash of Civilizations* in 1993 he made the prediction that 'the great divisions among humankind and the dominating source of conflict will be cultural'.[1] While his argument was essentially addressing geopolitical conflicts, it stressed the fact that economic globalization reaches its limits when confronted with the diversity of values, beliefs, behaviours and codes of conduct. In different parts of the world societies still differ in terms of the ways social, political and economic activities are structured, coordinated and managed, and the behaviours of people and organizations are influenced by what is commonly called 'culture'. Global corporations are by nature organizations that *interact* with customers, employees, partners, suppliers and government bodies from different national cultures, giving rise to the anecdotal gaffes well documented by David Ricks.[2] Beneath the surface of these 'travellers' tales' lies one of the main challenges that global firms have to confront. Do the various players in the global ecosystem give the same meaning to the same concepts, behaviours and attitudes? Do employees around the world get the same message when policies are enacted, memos exchanged or rewards distributed? Do customers of the same age, urbanization and wealth value similar product or service attributes? Do employees in multinational teams share similar assumptions and causal relationships about decision parameters? When a contract, a business venture or a loan is being negotiated, do the parties understand each other's 'silent language'? These are the questions that all global companies have to address in their cross-cultural management competencies.

This chapter presents the results of academic and empirical research on societal and cultural diversity. It begins with a presentation of the variety of business cultures and economic organizations. Various cross-cultural studies will be presented, followed by a discussion of the impact of cultural differences on management, team members, negotiations, categories of player and business practices.

The different facets of culture

There is no universal definition of culture. Schneider and Barsoux (1997) identified 164 different definitions made by anthropologists. More relevant broad definitions of culture include 'a shared pattern of behaviour' (Mead 1953), a 'system of shared meaning or understanding' (Levi-Strauss 1971; Geertz 1973), or 'a set of basic assumptions, shared solutions to universal problems … handed down from one generation to another' (Schein 1985). All these definitions have in common the concept that culture is *shared*, and contain an implicit decoding of an underlying pattern of *cause and effect relationships*, whether cognitive (meaning, assumptions), attitudinal/emotional (behaviour) or decisional (solutions). Schein adds the dimension of *generational transmission*, which implies a certain degree of consistency of culture over time.

Instead of a definition, some scholars have attempted to describe the content of culture. According to André Laurent[3] there are three major layers of culture. In ascending order, they are:

1 **Basic assumptions and meaning:** the elements of belief that are the least visible and probably the most entrenched, since they deal with ingrained models of understanding, meaning and causal relationships that have been largely shaped by historical factors and transmitted through the educational process to the next generation. Religious faith and assumptions about human nature belong to this category (e.g. 'all men are equal', 'time is limited').

2 **Values, beliefs and preferences:** the explicit expression of what people consider as good or appropriate in one's personal or social life. Values can be challenged and possibly changed to some extent by new information and confrontation with new situations. A manager whose assumption about human nature is that people are fundamentally greedy, for example, will probably believe that only materialistic rewards will motivate employees. They may change this belief if exposed to situations in which people sacrifice their own financial reward for the benefit of others.

3 **Behaviour:** the most visible part of the iceberg. It is manifested in action and can be modified through education as well as through some forms of 'conditioning'. Behavioural change does not necessarily indicate a genuine modification of the beliefs or assumptions underneath it. An autocratic leader may be told to change their style of leading a meeting although they still believe that employees 'have to be told' (belief) based on the assumption that human beings are fundamentally divided into 'born leaders' and 'passive followers'. In such a case, behavioural change is superficial.

In the management field which, by its very nature, is concerned with the economic achievement of social groups (companies), culture manifests in four key dimensions:

- **National or ethnic culture:** derived from the national, religious or ethnic origin of citizens or social groups.
- **Corporate culture:** the accumulated assumptions, values, beliefs and behavioural norms resulting from the history of the company (good and bad experiences), its existing and past leadership (the legacy of charismatic CEOs), its ownership structure (family-owned, publicly listed, private, government-owned) and its size.
- **Industry culture:** any accepted values and codes of conduct derived from the professional norms of a particular industry such as heavy manufacturing, services, oil and gas and so on.
- **Professional culture:** derived from the training and professional norms and constraints of different corporate functions such as accountants, researchers, production personnel, sales and marketing people and so on. As Lawrence and Lorsh (1969) have described, professional orientation introduces a large amount of differentiation within organizations.

All companies are confronted by corporate, industrial and professional cultural diversity in their home country even if they do not operate in foreign countries. What is specific to multinational and global firms is that this diversity is compounded by national and ethnic differences encountered from their worldwide implantation. In this chapter we will limit our presentation to national and ethnic cultural differences.

National cultural differences

Nations are political constructs resulting from historical evolution. Nation states may not be the best unit of analysis of cultural differences since within nations one may find different sub-cultures according to the variety of ethnic, linguistic and religious groups (for instance, Balinese in Indonesia and Roma in Romania). Religion may be another valid way of categorization, although it is not perfect: an Indonesian Muslim will think and act differently from a Saudi Arabian Muslim.

From a practical perspective, most cultural research in management has used nations as their unit of grouping for cultural categories. Analysis of national cultural differences in a business management context suggests four main streams of differences:

1. **Ethnological research:** 'silent language' differences (Hall and Reed Hall 1990).
2. **Managerial values and assumptions:** work-related value differences (Hofstede 1980); value orientation differences (Trompenaars 1993; Hampden-Turner and Trompenaars 2000); management assumption differences (Laurent 1986; Meyer 2014a, 2014b, 2015a, 2015b).
3. **Country clusters:** the grouping of nations according to similarities in cultural traits (Ronen and Shenkar 1985; Huntington 1997).
4. **Economic cultures:** how business systems are organized and interactions governed (Albert 1991; Berger and Dore 1996; Whitley 1999; Redding 2001).

Ethnological research: 'silent language' differences

According to Hall, cultures differ in the way they communicate through non-verbal signs or **'silent language'**.[4] He identifies six silent languages: *time*, *space*, *material goods*, *friendships*, *agreements* and *context*.

- Cultures differ according to their perception of **time.** Time can be seen as *sequential and scarce,* as in the case of the Germanic culture, leading to the quest for preciseness, punctuality and deadline-keeping. Some cultures see time as *fluid*, *circular and abundant*, as in Arab countries, where people will be less punctual and not really disturbed by delays and postponements.
- Differences in the perception of **space** relate to the concept of *social distance* that measures not only the physical proximity in social interactions but also the emotional intimacy. In high-social distance cultures, people will tend to avoid physical and emotional proximity – a typically British trait. However, in low-social distance cultures – such as the Latin countries – people have no objection to physical contact and the sharing of emotions.
- The language of **material goods** is linked to the importance attached to financial wealth as a sign of status – a materialistic trait of Americans – as opposed to other status signifiers such as family, education or seniority.
- **Friendship** is built and maintained quite differently. In some societies, one can make friends rapidly but the relationship may be superficial and may not last long. The silent language of this sort of friendship may shock people coming from societies where friendships are not so quickly built but last longer.
- The silent language of **agreement** quite often differentiates Western cultures from Eastern. In Western societies, most agreements or disagreements are explicitly stated and documented in writing. In Eastern cultures, verbal and sometimes ambiguous agreements are accepted. In Indonesia, for instance, it is often difficult for a business partner to say a straight 'no', but a 'maybe' might in fact have the same negative connotation.
- The silent language of **context** attaches importance to the person rather than the content in a communication. In high-context societies – mostly Asian, South American or Latin – the important part of an interaction is the person (with *whom*) and the emphasis given to the setting, the ambiance and ceremonials. In low-context societies – Anglo-Saxon, Nordic or Germanic – the *what* dominates the communication, hence the importance attached to written documents and technical specifications.

Differences in managerial values and assumptions

Several scholars have posited theories of managerial cultural difference at the level of nationalities, notably:

- Hofstede's work-related values
- Trompenaars' value orientation

- Laurent's management assumption
- Meyer's culture map

Hofstede's work-related values

Hofstede's research is probably one of the most frequently quoted in the international management literature because of the vast amount of data he collected. Hofstede's original (1980) survey was made with 116,000 employees at IBM worldwide. He asked questions related to their preferences in management styles and work values, and related the answers to national origin; he found that national cultures differed according to four main dimensions: *power distance*, *individualism*, *uncertainty avoidance* and *masculinity*.[5]

- **Power distance** is the extent to which people in certain societies accept *inequality in power distribution* or, on the contrary, have a more *egalitarian view* of power distribution. High-power distance societies will accept hierarchical control and respect authority – as, for instance, in Malaysia – while egalitarian societies will have a more democratic view of social control, with no particular reverence for high-ranking functions – as, for instance, in Denmark.
- **Individualism** characterizes a culture in which individuals look after their own or immediate relatives' interests. This is the case in most Western cultures and translates into individual *assertiveness and initiative* in business contexts. Collectivist cultures, on the other hand, will put group interests above individuals: *consensus and harmony* will be preferred to assertiveness. East Asian cultures commonly put society ahead of the individual.
- **Uncertainty avoidance** is typical of societies in which ambiguity and unpredictability are not accepted, and there is a continual search to codify, plan and regulate the environment (Japan, Spain). At the opposite end of the scale are social groups in which tolerance and risk taking are accepted and rewarded (USA, Sweden).
- **Masculinity** refers to the high value given to assertive, competitive behaviour. Femininity, on the other hand, refers to societies where quality of life, non-aggressive behaviour, interpersonal relations and concern for the weak are dominant values.

The forty countries in Hofstede's original study were clustered around the four dimensions. It appears that Asian, Latin American and Arab countries are high on power distance and low on individualism, while Anglo-Saxon and Nordic countries show the reverse. South European countries such as Italy, Spain or France are high on power distance and on individualism. The dimensions related to masculinity and uncertainty avoidance are less based on regions. For instance, in Asia, Japan scores very high on masculinity and uncertainty avoidance while India, Indonesia or Singapore are relatively low on those two dimensions.

In 2010 Hofstede added two more dimensions and increased his sample of countries to seventy.

- **Long-term orientation** refers to societies that encourage thrift and efforts in modern education as a way to prepare for the future, as opposed to societies showing a short-term orientation: preferring to maintain traditions and norms and viewing social change with suspicion.
- **Indulgence** stands for societies that allow relatively free gratification of basic and natural human drives related to enjoying life, while restrained societies suppress gratification of needs and regulate it by means of strict social norms. Table 3.1 presents the positioning along those six dimensions of a selection of sixteen nationalities.

Table 3.1 Hofstede values orientation (selected countries)

Values	High	Low
Power distance (*)	Brazil, China, Egypt, France, India, Indonesia, Japan, Mexico, Russia, Thailand	Australia, Denmark, Germany, Sweden, UK, USA
Individualism (*)	Australia, Denmark, France, Germany, Sweden, UK, USA	Brazil, China, Egypt, France, India, Indonesia, Japan, Mexico, Russia, Thailand
Uncertainty avoidance (*)	Australia, Brazil, Egypt, France, Germany, Mexico, Russia, UK	China, Denmark, India, Indonesia, Japan, Sweden, Thailand, USA
Masculinity (*)	Australia, Brazil, Egypt, France, Germany, Japan, Mexico, UK, USA	Brazil, Denmark, Egypt, Indonesia, Sweden, Russia, Thailand
Long-term orientation (**)	China, Germany, Denmark, France, Indonesia, Japan, Russia, Thailand	Australia, Brazil, Canada, Denmark, Egypt, India, Mexico, Sweden, UK, USA
Indulgence (***)	Australia, Brazil, Mexico, France, Thailand, Russia, UK, USA	China, Egypt, Germany, Indonesia, India, Japan

Sources: Table constructed with data from: * Hofstede (1980); ** Hofstede and Minkov (2010); *** https://www.hofstede-insights.com/country-comparison

Trompenaars' value orientation

The cultural differentiation proposed by Trompenaars (1993), also based on survey data, identifies six value orientations that differentiate cultures and impact the way countries conceive organizations (see Table 3.2). Trompenaars found significant differences in national groups; most Asian cultures, for instance, differ from Western cultures in all dimensions.[6]

Laurent's management assumption

André Laurent (1986) asked precise questions related to organizational and managerial issues of international managers of various nationalities attending executive seminars over twenty-five years. He found a systematic pattern of national differences[7] in their replies:

- 'Most managers seem to be more motivated by *obtaining power than by achieving objectives*' (Latin European countries – Italian, French, Spaniards – agree with this statement, while Danes, Swedes and Norwegians disagree).

Table 3.2 Trompenaars' six value orientations

Value orientation	Description	Examples
Universalism vs Particularism	Rule-based behaviour; general application	Nordic countries
	Circumstance, relation-based behaviour; specific application	Southeast Asia, China, African countries
Individualism vs Communitarism	Individual rights are supreme; individual performances are valued	Western countries
	Group's rights are supreme; harmony and cohesion are valued	Asian countries
Specificity vs Diffusion	Objective, analytical, reductionist reasoning	Germany, France
	Holistic, synthetic reasoning	Middle East, Asia
Achieved status vs Ascribed status	Status and respect achieved by 'doing'	United States
	Status and respect achieved by 'being'	Malaysia, China
Inner direction vs Outer direction	Knowledge of 'right' and 'wrong' lies inside the individual ('guilt culture')	Protestant countries
	Knowledge of 'right' and 'wrong' comes from society ('shame' culture)	Confucian societies
Sequential time vs Synchronous time	Time is a straight line that is consumed in one direction	Western
	Time is a circle	Arabic, African, Asian countries

Sources: Authors' own, based on texts by Trompenaars (1993) and Hampden-Turner and Trompenaars (2000).

- 'It is important for managers to have at hand *precise answers to most of the questions that a subordinate may raise about their work*' (Asian and Latin individuals strongly support this statement, while Anglo-Saxon and Nordic cultures do not).
- 'In order to have efficient working relationships, it is often necessary to *bypass the hierarchical lines*' (Nordic and Anglo-Saxon cultures agree, while Chinese, Italian, Spanish or Indonesian nationals strongly disagree).
- 'An organization structure in which subordinates have *two direct bosses should be avoided at all costs*' (Chinese, Italians, French and Indonesians reject this organizational model, while Americans and Swedes accept the idea of working for two bosses).
- 'The main reason for having a hierarchical structure is that everybody knows *who has authority over whom*' (Chinese, French, Japanese and Indonesian nationals agree, while Americans, Swedes and British disagree).

Laurent's results consistently show that basic managerial and organizational assumptions concerning power, structure, clarity of roles and hierarchy are still deeply embedded in national cultures. These differences in assumptions pose a challenge to global firms that need to organize, lead and motivate people of diverse cultural heritage. Laurent even found that 'cultural differences in managerial assumptions were not reduced as a result of working for the same multinational companies', thus rejecting the idea that national cultures converge thanks to corporate cultures.

Meyer's culture map

Based on her extensive research and consulting practice, Erin Meyer (2014a) proposed eight scales that correspond to the eight key cultural issues that managers working in an international context should understand and take into consideration.[8] They are:

- Communication
- Evaluation of people
- Persuasion
- Leadership
- Decision making
- Trust
- Disagreements
- Scheduling.

For each of these issues she mapped countries' 'cultural traits' on a polarized continuum. Table 3.3 summarizes these eight dimensions.

Table 3.3 The eight dimensions of Meyer's culture map

Low context Messages are expressed clearly and directly without any implied subtextual meaning. *(Examples: USA, Germany, UK, Denmark)*	**Communicating across cultures**	High context Messages are often implied and not expressed directly (reading between the lines). (*Examples: China, Indonesia, Russia, France*)
Direct negative feedback Negative feedback is frank and honest. (*Examples: Russia, Germany, France*)	**Evaluating performances and providing negative feedback**	Indirect negative feedback Negative feedback is provided diplomatically. Positive messages soften the negative. (*Examples: Japan, Thailand, Indonesia, and to an extent USA, UK*)
Applications-first Arguments are presented with facts, figures and logic. (*Examples: USA, Canada, Australia, UK*)	**Persuasion**	Principles-first Arguments are presented conceptually, theoretically. (*Examples: Italy, France, Germany, Russia*)
Egalitarian Low distance between subordinate and boss. Hierarchy can be bypassed. (*Examples: Sweden, Israel, Australia*)	**Leadership**	Hierarchical High distance between subordinate and boss. Communications follow hierarchy. (*Examples: India, Korea, Nigeria*)

Top-down Decisions are made by the boss. *(Examples: India, China, Russia)*	**Decision making**	Consensual Decision are made in groups. *(Examples: Japan, Sweden, Netherlands)*
Task-based Trust is based on the quality of work and performance. *(Examples: USA, Denmark, Netherlands)*	**Trust**	Relationship-based Trust is based on social relationships and network. *(Examples: China, Saudi Arabia, India, Brazil)*
Confrontational Open confrontation can be seen as positive. *(Examples: Israel, France, Germany)*	**Disagreements**	Confrontation avoidance Disagreement is seen as negative. *(Examples: China, Indonesia, Thailand)*
Time is linear Tasks are scheduled according to a time sequence, one step at a time. *(Examples: Germany, Sweden, Japan)*	**Scheduling**	Time is flexible Tasks are scheduled to run simultaneously. *(Examples: India, Mexico, Turkey)*

Source: Authors' own, based on text of Meyer (2014a).

Country clusters

The clustering approach consists of grouping countries according to their degree of geographical, linguistic, religious, historical and social proximity. Several approaches have been proposed:

a Ronen and Shenkar (1985) divided the world into nine clusters: Anglo, Germanic, Nordic, Near Eastern, Arab, Far Eastern, Latin American and Independent (Brazil, Japan, India, Israel).

b Huntington (1997) grouped countries by what he calls 'civilizations' based on language, religion, values, beliefs and institutional and social structures. He identified eight modern 'civilizations': Sinic (China and Chinese communities as well as Vietnam and Korea), Japanese, Hindu, Islamic, Orthodox, Latin American, African and Western (Western Europe, North America and Australia). Huntington's grouping has more to do with *geopolitics* than with management. He asserted that more and more conflicts in the world will be due to clashes of 'civilizations'.

c The GLOBE (Global Leadership and Organizational Behavior Effectiveness) study is a collaborative ongoing research project based on multi-phase, multi-method, multi-sample research data collection. It assesses two measures:

i *Societal Culture*, defined as the 'shared motives, values, beliefs, identities, and interpretations or meanings of significant events that result from common experiences of members of collectives that are transmitted across generations'. The dimensions of societal cultures are:

- **Performance orientation:** how far societies encourage performance improvement and excellence.
- **Assertiveness:** the extent to which individuals in the society tend towards being assertive, confrontational and aggressive in their relationships with others.
- **Future orientation:** how much individuals engage (or should engage) in future-oriented behaviours such as planning, investing in the future and delaying gratification.
- **Humane orientation:** how far a society encourages and rewards (or should encourage and reward) individuals for being fair, altruistic, generous, caring and kind to others.
- **Collectivism:** how far a society promotes the collective distribution of resources and collective action and how far individuals express pride, loyalty and cohesiveness in their organizations or families.
- **Gender egalitarianism:** how much societies minimize gender inequality.
- **Power distance:** to what extent societies accept and endorse authority, power differences and status privileges.
- **Uncertainty avoidance:** how much societies rely on norms, rules and procedures to alleviate the consequences of unpredictable future events.

ii *Cultural Leadership*, defined as 'the ability of an individual to influence, motivate, and enable others to contribute toward the effectiveness and success of the organizations of which they are members'. GLOBE identifies six global leadership dimensions:

- **Charismatic/value-based leadership:** reflects the ability to inspire, motivate and expect high performance from others based on firmly-held core values.
- **Team-oriented leadership:** emphasizes effective team building and implementation of a common purpose or goal among team members.
- **Participative leadership:** reflects the degree to which managers involve others in making and implementing decisions.
- **Humane-oriented leadership:** reflects supportive and considerate leadership and includes compassion and generosity.
- **Autonomous leadership:** refers to independent and individualistic leadership attributes.
- **Self-protective leadership:** focuses on ensuring the safety and security of the individual and group through status enhancement and face-saving.

The result is a clustering of societies, as presented in Table 3.4, that indicates the dominant features appearing in both dimensions.

Table 3.4 Country clusters for regions covered in the GLOBE project and the salient cultural and leadership characteristics they present

CLUSTERS									
Anglo	Confucian Asia	Eastern Europe	Germanic Europe	Latin America	Latin Europe	Middle East	Nordic Europe	Southern Asia	Sub-Saharan Africa
UK South Africa Ireland Australia Canada (English-speaking) New Zealand USA	Taiwan Singapore Hong Kong South Korea China Japan	Hungary Russia Kazakhstan Albania Poland Greece Slovenia Georgia Czech Republic	Austria Switzerland Netherlands Germany	Costa Rica Venezuela Ecuador Mexico Colombia Guatemala Bolivia Brazil Argentina	Italy Israel Portugal Spain France French Switzerland	Iran Qatar Morocco Turkey Egypt Kuwait	Finland Sweden Denmark	India Indonesia Philippines Malaysia Thailand	Namibia Zambia Zimbabwe Nigeria
SOCIETAL CULTURES									
High power distance Low collectivism High gender equality Low uncertainty avoidance	High power distance High collectivism High assertiveness Low gender equality High performance orientation	Low future orientation High uncertainty avoidance Low collectivism High power distance Low performance orientation Low future orientation Low power distance Low uncertainty avoidance Low collectivism Low power distance Low assertiveness High gender equality	High uncertainty avoidance High future orientation High collectivism Low power distance Low assertiveness High gender equality High performance orientation	Low power distance High gender equality	Low future orientation High uncertainty avoidance High collectivism High power distance Low gender equality	Low future orientation Low uncertainty avoidance Low collectivism Low power distance Low assertiveness High gender equality	High future orientation High uncertainty avoidance High collectivism High assertiveness Low gender equality	High future orientation High uncertainty avoidance High assertiveness Low gender equality High performance orientation	High future orientation High uncertainty avoidance High assertiveness Low gender equality High performance orientation

LEADERSHIP STYLES									
Anglo	Confucian Asia	Eastern Europe	Germanic Europe	Latin America	Latin Europe	Middle East	Nordic Europe	Southern Asia	Sub-Saharan Africa
HIGH									
Charismatic leadership Participative leadership	Autonomous leadership Self-protective leadership	Autonomous leadership Self-protective leadership	Charismatic leadership Participative leadership Autonomous leadership	Charismatic leadership Team-oriented		Self–protective leadership	Charismatic leadership Participative leadership	Charismatic leadership Humane orientation Self-protective leadership	Humane orientation
MEDIUM									
Team-oriented Autonomous leadership	Humane orientation	Humane orientation Team-oriented	Team-oriented Humane orientation	Participative leadership Humane orientation Self-protective leadership	Charismatic leadership Team-oriented Participative leadership Autonomous leadership Self-protective leadership	Autonomous leadership Humane orientation	Team-oriented Autonomous leadership	Team-oriented	Charismatic leadership Self-protective leadership Team-oriented
LOW									
Self-protective leadership	Participative leadership	Participative leadership	Self-protective leadership		Humane orientation	Participative leadership Charismatic leadership	Self-protective leadership Humane orientation	Participative leadership	

Sources: Authors' own construction based on various GLOBE project literature and data.

The Lewis model

According to Richard Lewis (1996), cultures can be classified into three groups: linear active, multi-active and reactive.

- In **linear active cultures** people are task-oriented, highly organized planners. They prefer direct discussion and use facts and figures. They are prone to accepting compromise to achieve results. In this category we find German, Swiss, North American and Scandinavian cultures.
- **Multi-active cultures** group people who are loquacious, emotional and relationship-oriented. They tend to do several things and talk at the same time. In this category we find Latin American, Southern European, Western and Northern African and Middle Eastern cultures.
- In **reactive cultures** people are introverted, show respect to an interlocutor and listen without interrupting. In this category one will find most of the Asian cultures.

Economic cultures and business systems

In the early nineteenth century, Max Weber, a German sociologist, explained the differences in competitive and business behaviour between Latin European countries and Nordic/'Anglo-Saxon' countries as being caused by the influence of religions. In Northern Europe, Protestantism encouraged *individual achievement* leading to free enterprise and favouring the emergence of modern 'capitalism', while Catholicism in Spain, and to a certain extent in France, induced *state control*.[9] Several scholars have identified various *economic cultures* or *forms of capitalism*[10] (Weber, Berger, Dore, Trompenaars, Albert) that explain international variation in institutional governance and competitive behaviours. Based on these earlier works, Whitley, Redding and Witt developed a methodology explaining the differences using what they call a *business system analysis*.[11]

A *business system* is the way economic activities are structured, coordinated and managed. It is the result of the interaction between three sub-systems: governance, culture and institutional fabric (Figure 3.1).

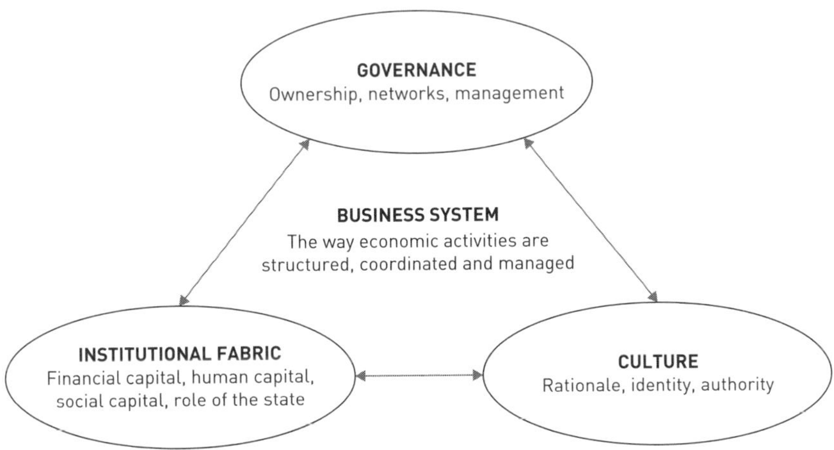

Figure 3.1 The architecture of business systems
Source: Authors' own, based on text in Witt and Redding (2014).

- **Governance** reflects the dominant mode of control, interdependencies and exercise of authority in business firms. This is made up of three components:
  - The **ownership system**: How the ownership of enterprises is distributed between the public and private sectors (corporate, family, associative).
  - The **networking system**: How firms collaborate and do deals among themselves (contractual, ethnic, religious relationships).
  - The **management system**: Do employees participate in decision making in business enterprises? Do the employees have access to top managers or are those functions concentrated within a social elite?
- The **social culture** is constituted by the norms, values and social codes which form the basis of social interactions and shared beliefs. This is made up of three components:
  - **Rationality**, which describes the way societies set objectives and the importance they attach to formal systems and processes in setting objectives.
  - **Authority**, which describes how societies set rules for vertical order (and determines the legitimate source of power).
  - **Identity**, which describes the rules of horizontal order (what makes the citizens stick together).
- The **institutional fabric** represents the organization, development and allocation of resources, and comprises four components:
  - **Financial capital**, its formation and allocation.
  - **Human capital**, how human skills are developed.
  - **Social capital**, the way trust is created among members of economic agents.
  - **Role of the state** in the regulation and control of business activities.

Table 3.5 gives a list of questions to address when evaluating the business system of a society while Table 3.6 summarizes some differences in business systems in America, Europe and Asia.

Table 3.5 Assessing a business system

Governance	
Ownership system	• How is the ownership of companies distributed among the public sector, the corporate private sector, the family controlled sector, the associative sector (cooperatives, associations)? • What is the relative weight of big business vs small business? • How is power practically distributed in business between shareholders, managers, trade unions, authorities, pressure groups? • What is the weight of diversified conglomerates?
Networking system	• What is the relative weight of vertical integration, conglomeration vs contractual relationships in the coordination of firms? • What is the relative importance of alliances, partnerships, joint venture business associations in the business landscape? • What is the importance of ethnic, religious, regional or alumni networks?

Management system	• Is the decision making primarily autocratic, participative or bureaucratic? • On which criteria does career advancement depend: performance, loyalty, nepotism, membership of a particular group?
Social culture	
Rationality	• How far does society agree that the main mission of business is to create value for shareholders, stakeholders and society? • Are goals set for the long or short term, and are they growth or profit oriented? • Does society consider that the appropriate process for reaching business objectives should be democratic or autocratic, through negotiation or dialogue?
Authority	• Is hierarchy or egalitarian democracy the main basis for authority? • What are the sources of power in the society: religion, castes, wealth, ethnic belonging, university degree and so on?
Identity	• Is individualism or group-oriented collectivism prevalent in the society? • If group orientation, what is the relevant grouping (family, clan, company, religion, region, ethnicity)?
Institutional fabric	
Financial capital	• How is capital allocated: planned economy, banks, financial markets or informally? • Are financial markets open and transparent? • Is foreign capital welcomed?
Human capital	• What is the quality of primary, secondary and tertiary education? • Is education primarily practical or theoretical? • Are on-the-job training and apprenticeships encouraged? • What is the role (if any) of trade unions? • Are trade unions organized at the level of companies, industries or nationally? • How strong are the craft-based unions? • Does the employment system encourage long-term tenure? Flexibility? Turnover? • Is there a healthcare social security system? Unemployment compensation?
Social capital	• Is the society based on interpersonal trust, institutionalized trust (in the law) or hierarchical trust (in leadership)? • In the case of interpersonal trust, what is the reference group (family, school, religious, clans and so on)?
Role of the state	• Is the government interventionist in business or labour conflicts? • Is the market highly regulated? • Is there a central planning authority?

Table 3.6 Differences in business systems

	Anglo/ American	German and Nordic European	French and Latin European	Japanese	Korean
Social culture					
Rationality How objectives are set Importance of systems and procedures	Democratic process Rules led	Democratic Consensus led	Democratic Negotiation led conflict resolution	Democratic Consensus led	Autocratic
Authority The ground rules for vertical order Origin of power	Constitution Laws Decentralization	Laws Decentralization	The state Laws Centralization	The state Corporations Decentralization	The state Corporations Centralization
Identity The ground rules for horizontal order (What makes society stick)	Individual rights Contracts Heterogeneity (Micro cultures)	Social welfare Homogeneity	Social welfare Cultural identity Heterogeneity (Micro cultures)	National belonging Cultural identity Homogeneity	Nationalism Cultural identity Homogeneity
Institutional fabric					
Capital How financial capital is found and channelled	Financial markets Low gearing	Banks Medium gearing	State and market Medium gearing	Banks High gearing	State High gearing
Human capital How human skills are developed	Academic Performance	Academic Apprenticeships	Academic Elitist	Academic plus On the job Elitist	Academic Elitist
Social capital How trust is created	High trust in contracts and legal institutions	High trust in contracts and negotiation	Low trust Confrontational Negotiation	High trust within groups Low outside	High trust within groups Low outside
Role of state Regulation and control of business	Limited	Collaborative with trade unions	State interventionist	Incentives	High
Governance					
Ownership Who owns enterprises	Shareholders	Banks Employees Shareholders	State Shareholders	Banks Cross-shareholding	Business groups Cross-shareholding

Networking How economic agents relate to each other (the rules of business transactions)	Contracts	Contracts Some elitist relationships	Elitist relationships State interventionism	Elitist relationships	Personal relationships State intervention
Managing How employees are induced to cooperate in the firm	System-led motivation Performance measures	Hierarchical Technical competence	Hierarchical bureaucracy Negotiation	Corporate identity Corporate loyalty	Hierarchical Corporate loyalty

Sources: Authors' own construction based on Albert (1991); Berger and Dore (1996); Whitley (1999); Trompenaars (2000); Hampton-Turner and Trompenaars (2000).

The impact of cultures on global management

The effects of cultural difference on the management of global companies are pervasive: there is no aspect of corporate life that is not impacted by culture. Six aspects of corporate life are particularly influenced by cultural differences:

- Marketing and customer communications (see Chapter 10)
- Human resources (see Chapter 14)
- Partnerships, mergers and acquisitions (see Chapter 9)
- Multi-cultural teams
- Negotiations
- Business practices.

Marketing, partnership/acquisition and human resources are covered in later chapters. This chapter focuses on teamwork, negotiations and business contexts.

Multi-cultural teams

In most activities, global firms rely on teamwork – committees, task forces, cross-functional teams and so on. Many departments at corporate, regional or subsidiary levels are staffed by managers of different nationalities and cultures. Multicultural teams in multinational firms are used in the form of task forces, business planning activities, research and development, joint ventures activities as well as top management teams in global and regional headquarters (Schneider and Barsoux 1997). The productivity of multinational teams has been widely discussed in academic circles (Stahl et al. 2010, 2020). The summary of the hypothesis and findings are summarized in Table 3.7.

Table 3.7 Monocultural vs multicultural teams

Monocultural Teams		Multicultural Teams	
Advantages	**Disadvantages**	**Advantages**	**Disadvantages**
• Proximity of values, beliefs and attitudes • Similar educational background	• Group think • Narrower span of alternatives	• Diversity of contributions • Broader range of perspectives	• Divergence of point of views • Misunderstanding of meanings • Longer time of clarification
Possible results	**Possible results**	**Possible results**	**Possible results**
• Better cohesion • Quicker consensus	• Lower creativity	• Higher creativity	• Divergence • Possible conflictual stereotyping

Source: Authors' own based on Stahl et al. (2010, 2021).

Given the variety of cultural heritage, communication and decision-making processes can be blunted by *cultural noise*: multi-cultural teams can perform either significantly worse or better than mono-cultural firms. The performance of multicultural groups is a function of three factors:[12]

1 Multiplicity of perspectives, experiences and viewpoints increases the *richness of information.*
2 Possible *loss of cohesion* owing to miscommunication, misunderstanding and stereotyping.
3 The ability of team leaders to combine the variety of perspectives and achieve group *synergy.*

The relative impact of these three factors can lead to polarized performance. In an interesting study made with German- and American-staffed work teams, two researchers found that the Germans' rational, analytical approaches to problem-solving combined with the action-oriented, free-wheeling, innovative approaches of American members contributed to high performance. However, performances were poor when the team leader was not able to introduce team-building procedures that facilitated information-sharing and group awareness of cultural assumptions.[13]

Cross-cultural negotiations[14]

International operations require managers to be involved in a large variety of negotiations: it may involve suppliers, agents, distributors, licensees, joint venture partners, government authorities, trade unions and employees, but also offices within the same company in other countries. The difference between international and domestic negotiations is not limited to the cultural backgrounds of the parties involved. While culture as seen so far has a significant influence on how people negotiate, some other variables can become quite relevant once one moves into international negotiations. For example, when dealing across borders, one needs to worry about exchange rates. Wild exchange rate fluctuations can quickly either create a profit windfall or wipe out profits. That is not usually a concern when one is negotiating within one's own country. Other elements to take into account are international and national political instabilities, the potentially different degree of governmental interventionism in the economy and the different political, economic and judicial systems. While on a day-to-day basis some of these may not seem particularly important, a lack of consideration of these international negotiation variables can doom investments, destroy relationships or end with contracts that mean nothing more than an empty piece of paper.

In the next section we will look at three frameworks of analysis and negotiations: the bargaining framework, the process framework and the ritual framework. These will be followed by the international and cultural dimensions of negotiations.

The bargaining framework

A very simple model of negotiation is provided in Figure 3.2. In this model negotiations are reduced to a buyer and a seller seeking to settle a transaction: an export contract or a project, the acquisition of a company or part of it, a licensing contract or a joint venture agreement, to more subjective or non-monetary negotiations such as the settlement of a court dispute or the agreement on a partnership strategy, where one party sells their preferred idea to their counterparty (buyer). In more monetary-focused or price negotiations, the seller implicitly (and sometimes explicitly) has a reservation price which is the price below which the seller is ready to walk away because there is a better alternative at this price.[15] For the buyer the situation is symmetrically similar. Notice that some negotiations are not just about price or not about price at all, in which case the negotiation may take a different direction.

Generally, in price negotiations, the reservation price will be modified by an uncertainty factor because forecasts of the potential benefits or costs are always affected by risks. In such cases, it is common for the parties to resort to a bargaining process, where the seller's opening offer (usually reflective of their aspiration prices and perceived uncertainties) in the negotiation will generally be higher than their reservation price and the buyer's will be lower than their reservation price. Culturally speaking,

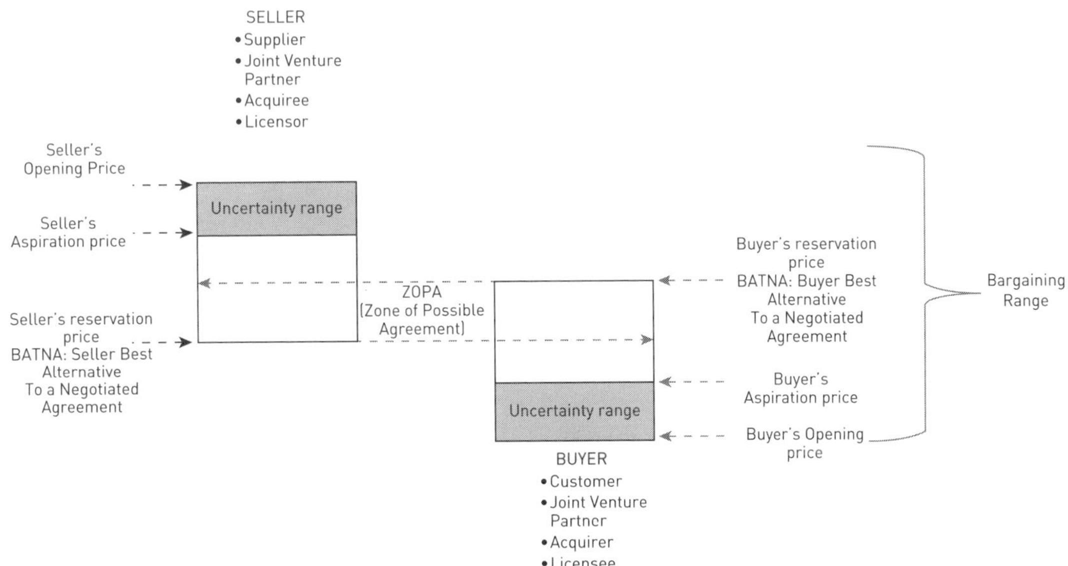

Figure 3.2 Framework for negotiation with reference to international contracts

the distance between initial offers and the final deal may differ dramatically. In some cultures, it is expected that the parties will open with offers close to a reasonable final price, where in other cultures it is accepted and even expected that the parties may start with offers significantly far away from a final price, reasonable or not. The negotiation then takes the form of a *ritual*, which again can differ significantly from country to country, through which the negotiators will seek to bargain in the hopes of finding an agreement in the bargaining range (a.k.a. ZOPA or Zone of Possible Agreement), as seen in Figure 3.2. If the seller is a better bargainer the price may end up close to the buyer's reservation price and vice versa. But at the end, provided the agreement is within the bargaining range, one obtains a *compromise* in which both parties get a deal that is better than their walk-away alternatives.

The negotiation process framework

Fisher, Ury and Patton (2011) define seven elements of a negotiation, which work together like the different parts of anatomy. Each move of a negotiation can be classified as one or more of these elements (Figure 3.3).

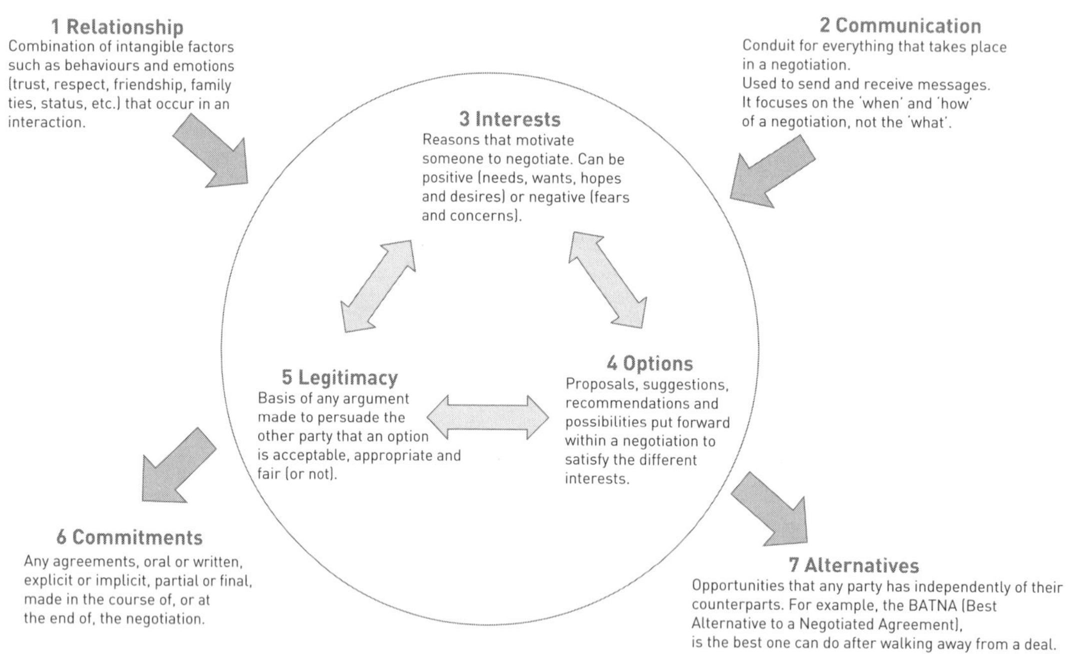

Figure 3.3 Negotiation Process Source: authors' own construction adapted from Fisher, Ury and Patton (2011).

According to the authors a successful process of a negotiation can be evaluated according to these seven attributes:

1 **Relationship between the parties:** A good working relationship is the ability of negotiators to work together productively and respectfully, despite their differences and without suspicion and abrasiveness.

2 **Effective two-way communication:** In good two-way communication negotiators are listening as well as speaking with clarity and patience. A well-crafted message can minimize the need for repetition and the risk of misunderstanding.
3 **Satisfy interests, not positions:** Positions are the parties' inflexible demands. Fights over positions are at the heart of win–lose negotiations while focusing on interests that are the real motivations for the negotiation is conducive to a win–win conclusion.
4 **Many possible options:** Bringing as many options as possible can enhance the likelihood of finding at least one solution that works for all parties.
5 **Arguments based on legitimacy so that all parties believe them to be fair:** A legitimate argument is an argument that is considered as fair, based on real facts and not a game played on deceptive or manipulative arguments. In practice, each negotiator can come up with several legitimate arguments per option. It is the exercise of working together to find an option that makes sense to all parties and encourages them to continue negotiating in a win–win way.
6 **Well-planned commitment:** Agreements made in the course of, or at the end of, a negotiation should be:
   - **Clear:** The parties should have the same understanding of what is agreed without reading between the lines.
   - **Sufficient:** It should cover the negotiators' important issues, thus reducing the need for additional negotiations or renegotiations.
   - **Operational:** The parties should be sure of their abilities and resources to implement the deal.
7 **Deal better than the best alternative to a negotiated agreement (BATNA) for each party:** Before agreeing, it is helpful for each party to compare the deal at hand to the BATNA. This helps to recognize if a deal is realistically good or bad and allows the parties to accept or reject it.

The negotiation ritual framework

From a normative point of view negotiation should generally follow a 'ritual' sequential six-stage pattern:

a **Pre-negotiation:** each party prepares its negotiation strategy
b **Climate setting:** introduction of negotiators, greetings, physical context
c **Presentation:** agenda-setting, opening statements
d **Mid-point bargaining:** substantive debate, request for clarification, search for common ground, trial 'concessions'
e **Closure:** binding concessions offered, search for agreements, final drafting/signing
f **Post-negotiation:** ratification of agreements by corporate headquarters, or government bodies.

Cultural aspect of negotiating

As mentioned in the beginning of the chapter there are many dimensions of cultural differences such as corporate cultures, industry cultures, professional cultures and national or ethnic cultures. As such one can say that any negotiation is a cross-cultural exercise to which the international dimension is only one element. However, international managers are confronted with this additional dimension when negotiating with foreign counterparts. This dimension can be made more complex when dealing with negotiating teams made of members of different nationalities, as is often the case when dealing with multinational companies.

There can be a large amount of cultural diversity in approaches and behaviours during these stages. According to Jeswald W. Salacuse,[16] international negotiations are affected by culture in ten ways:

1 *Goal*: is the negotiation conceived as a way to conclude a contract (generally US approach) or to build a relationship (generally Asian or Latin approach)?
2 *Strategy*: is the choice of using or not using power an approach to lead to a mutual benefit (*win–win*) or to have one side winning over the other (*win–lose*)?
3 *Style*: is it formal (stick to strict rules) or informal (personal, friendly, off-the-record talks)?
4 *Communication*: is the negotiation direct (to the point, business-like, clear messages) or indirect (implicit messages, ambiguous gestures)?
5 *Time*: does it involve punctuality and firm deadlines or flexibility and elasticity of deadlines?
6 *Emotions*: showing personal emotion or not during negotiations?
7 *Form of agreement*: is it very specific and detailed or a general framework?
8 *Flow process*: is the negotiation to start from general principles and proceed to specific items (*deductive process*) or is it considered a collection of specific items (*inductive*)?
9 *Team organization*: is there one team leader or is there consensus among negotiators?
10 *Risk taking*: do negotiators accept ambiguity and show willingness to find new approaches and share information or try to avoid revealing too much and departing from a well-known negotiation platform?

Another factor not mentioned in this list is the difference of approach used for *influencing the behaviour* of the other party: whether one will use a *direct* approach (either threatening, persuading or demonstrating) or an indirect one (calling for sympathy, referring to personal stakes).[17]

Figure 3.4 gives a pictorial representation of those cultural negotiating traits, with some indication of which type of culture tends to one side or the other, while Table 3.8, using different criteria, summarizes the key differences between American and Japanese approaches. However, we should observe that, with the increased globalization of firms, multi-cultural teams are more and more engaged in negotiation, making the cultural stereotypes less and less relevant. It may well be that a British firm will send a negotiating team led by a French division head, with an Irish lawyer, a Singaporean controller and a Brazilian engineer. Which negotiation culture would prevail remains to be seen!

Examples of cultures following this style			Negotiation attributes			Examples of cultures following this style
US, UK, French	*Contract*	⟸	GOAL	⟹	*Relationship*	Asian, Arabic
US, German	*Win-Lose*	⟸	ATTITUDE	⟹	*Win-Win*	Japanese
Asian	*Formal*	⟸	STYLE	⟹	*Informal*	US
Western European, North American	*Direct*	⟸	COMMUNICATION	⟹	*Indirect*	Asian, Arabic
US, Germany	*Strict*	⟸	TIME	⟹	*Flexible*	Arabic, Chinese, Latin
Japanese	*Hidden*	⟸	EMOTIONS	⟹	*Expressed*	Latin
US	*Specific*	⟸	FORM OF AGREEMENT	⟹	*General*	Japanese
French	*Deductive*	⟸	FLOW PROCESS	⟹	*Inductive*	Asian
Chinese	*One leader*	⟸	TEAM ORGANIZATION	⟹	*Consensus*	Japanese
US, French	*Risk taking*	⟸	RISK TAKING	⟹	*Risk averse*	Japanese
US, German	*Direct*	⟸	INFLUENCING	⟹	*Indirect*	Asian, Arabic

Figure 3.4 Negotiation attributes and cultural differences

Source: Authors' own figure, based on text of Salacuse (2003) and Brett (2001).

Table 3.8 Impact of culture on negotiating behaviour: a comparison of American and Japanese responses

Negotiation parameters	Typical American response	Typical Japanese response
Basic approach to business in general	Transactional; profit-oriented; detail-conscious; legalistic	Structured; strategic; starting from trust
Central purpose of negotiation	Reaching agreement on a contract	Launching a long-term relationship
Selection criteria for negotiator(s)	Verbally articulate generalists; technical competence; 'rational abilities'	Rank; position; 'social competence'
Appropriate **number of negotiators**	Few	Many: in order to demonstrate seriousness and for functional coverage, including learning
Appropriate **role(s) of lawyers(s)**	Key participant: leader, contract advisor, and/or draftsperson	None: seen as adversarial trouble-makers
Attitude toward **decision-making process**, and appropriate degree of delegation of authority to negotiators	Top-down decision making; very high degree of delegation of authority	Consensual, middle-up decision making (*ringi seido*); little or no authority delegated to negotiators
Appropriate **tone** for negotiation and communication	Direct; informal; familiar; egalitarian; candid	Highly indirect; highly formal; hierarchical; reserved
Negotiators' interest in **personal feelings** and values of counterparts	Little or none; irrelevant or improper; logic more important than emotions; issues more important than personalities	Acute; personal rapport essential to establish trust (*ningen kankei*)

Table 3.8 *(Continued)*

Negotiation parameters	Typical American response	Typical Japanese response
Appropriateness of **socializing** with counterparts	Inappropriate; unacceptable; risks conflicts of interest and loss of personal control	Highly appropriate; traditional behaviour; also ritualized gift-giving
Attitude toward **time** during negotiations	Acutely time-conscious; 'time is money'; impatient	Patience is the key
Attitude toward **silence** during negotiations	Strongly averse; uncomfortable; 'fill the void'	Essential: for decorum and for non-verbal communication and empathy (*haragei*)
Reaction to **cross-cultural** signals	Unaware; or consider them unimportant	Aware of differences
Attitude toward **sequential bargaining** and negotiating progress	Strongly attracted to both	Unimportant
Attitude toward **sharing information**	Open; willing	Collect it avidly, but do not give it out
Attitude toward **closure**	Essential for a successful negotiation; results-oriented, not process-oriented	Not necessary or even important; take the long view
Form of the contract	Long; detailed; covering all foreseeable contingencies	Prefer very short; and limited to general principles and affirmations
Commitment to the contract	Totally binding	Weak; the relationship is what counts, not the document; changing conditions will necessitate later amendments

Source: Sunshine (1990). Reproduced with permission from International Development Law Institute.

Recommendations in international negotiations

Different negotiating styles have different impacts on outcomes, and managers engaged in international negotiations should be aware that a certain number of precautions should be taken, and recommendations followed to minimize failure owing to cultural hang-ups. The following checklist provides a useful list of prescriptions.[18]

Sunshine's checklist:

1 Anticipate objective differences across borders such as exchange rate history among the currencies of the different negotiation parties, international and national political instabilities, the potentially different degree of governmental interventionism in the economy in different countries and the different political, economic and judicial systems.

2 Understand one's own cultural 'lens' using a list of negotiation parameters such as those in Figure 3.3 and Table 3.7.

3 Understand the other party's cultural 'lens' using a similar checklist. Table 3.8 shows the typical attitudes of Chinese negotiators.
4 List negotiation items that are likely to be affected by cultural differences and anticipate counterparts' responses. Normally, how to build trust and express emotions, as well as the different process preferences, or the amount or manner of information sharing are some of the negotiation aspects most affected across cultures. To a lesser extent, look at how cultures differ in their preference for different interests and what values and arguments are considered most persuasive when allocating resources (e.g. some cultures are more convinced by seniority arguments, while others value more meritocracy). Finally, cultures differ in how they make decisions, how binding commitments are, how to reach them and how to interpret them if there are problems, as well as their willingness to walk away from bad deals.
5 Assess potential responses and list those that are likely to fit and those that are likely to conflict.
6 Try to disentangle 'cultural' divergences from 'business' divergences in order to be ready to adjust behaviour and avoid being trapped in 'cultural' clashes.
7 While negotiating, translate not only language, but also behaviours and the intention behind them.
8 Ask, ask, ask to learn, challenge assumptions and stereotypes, and adjust your negotiation strategy as you progress.
9 Be ready to invest more time because international negotiations have more variables, obstacles and differences than national negotiations, and thus they will on average take longer.

In a Harvard Business School article, Erin Meyer gives some practical recommendations for communication in a cross-cultural negotiation.

Meyer's checklist:

1 *Adapt the way to express disagreement*: In some cultures open disagreement may be seen as positive if it's expressed calmly and factually (for example in Russia) while in other cultures the same behaviour would provoke anger (for example in Thailand).
2 *Know how to calibrate self-expression*: In some cultures it's common – and entirely appropriate – during negotiations to voice when excited, laugh passionately, touch counterparts on the arm or even put a friendly arm around them (for example in Brazil). In other cultures such self-expression not only feels intrusive or surprising but may even demonstrate a lack of professionalism (for example in Germany).
3 *Learn how the other culture builds trust*: Trust can be divided into two categories: cognitive and affective. Cognitive trust is based on the confidence you feel in someone's accomplishments, skills and reliability. It comes from the head (Cartesian Northern European for instance). Affective trust arises from feelings of emotional closeness, empathy, or friendship. It comes from the heart (most Asian or African cultures).
4 *Avoid yes-or-no questions*: In some societies the word 'yes' may be used when the real meaning is no. This is particularly so in Indonesia where a blunt no is considered as a loss of face for the other party.

5 *Look for cultural bridges*: A third party who is knowledgeable about the two cultures of the negotiators can be very helpful in minimizing misunderstandings or communication failures.

6 *Be careful of the binding strength of written agreements*: One has to consider that in some societies where the legal system is based on traditions a written document does not carry the same binding strength as in Napoleonic or common law legal systems.

Table 3.9 Chinese business negotiation style

	Chinese negotiation characteristics	Relevance for foreign negotiators
Team composition	• Often large team of varying competence • Team leader is not necessarily the most competent or the most influential, but has the highest status • Some team participants may rotate	• Appoint a team leader of equal or higher status to that of the Chinese leader • Identify who is knowledgeable and who are the 'real' negotiators • Appoint a competent business negotiator • Maintain the same team over time
Courtesy, etiquette, social relationships and trust	• Dignity has to be maintained • Social status • Ritual and protocol must be observed • Importance of saving/not losing face • Importance of personal relationships in forming business link • Banquets, gifts are signs of trust and good relationships	• Keep conversations polite • Save face (yours and colleagues') by not openly criticizing other team members or Chinese delegates • Cultivate personal relationships • Participate in banquets, give gifts and respect etiquette • Resist any temptation to question the honesty or motives of the other party (implies mistrust) • Eye contact should be avoided
Negotiation approaches	• A successful negotiation should lead to a win–win situation • 'Yes' is not often 'yes' • Take time over negotiations • 'Sweet and sour' (carrot and stick) approaches	• Make sure that the other party is never left in the position of a 'loser' • Avoid showing undue haste to conclude deals • Don't jump to conclusions • Don't speak too much, take time to listen as well

Source: Authors' compilation based on discussions in Fang (1997, 2006); Woo and Prud'homme (1999); Herbig and Martin (1999).

Business practices

'Business practices' refers to the day-to-day interactions that managers have with customers, suppliers, partners and government officials. As well as the negotiation styles described earlier, three categories of practice are impacted by cultural differences: etiquette, relations and competition:

- **Business etiquette** represents the set of rituals that take place when people communicate in business dealings. It includes the way people address each other, speak, dress, eat, stand, sit, gesticulate, pose and deal with time.
- **Relations** involves the way business transactions are established, whether personal relationships or legal/technical matters are the prime ingredient of transactions.

- **Competition** indicates how competitive advantages are obtained. In some countries, competition is perceived and practised as a fair game in which products, services and performances are compared and the winner ultimately decided on. In other countries, different criteria such as ethnic belonging, family connections or political considerations can determine the winner.

  Table 3.10 shows examples of such practices.

Table 3.10 Business practice differences

Practice	Definition	Examples
Etiquette		
Addressing	How to name the other person	• In Malaysia, nobility titles are the proper form of address (*Encik, Tan*) • In France, people are addressed by their title (*Monsieur le Directeur*) • In the USA, the first name is normal • In Japan, the exchange of business cards is critical
Gesturing	How to position oneself and how to use body language	• Showing the soles of the feet offends Arabs • Left-hand shaking is not proper in Muslim countries • Finger-pointing is considered to be highly threatening and impolite in Asia
Dressing	Dress code	• Malaysian businessmen use jacket and tie while in Singapore a long-sleeved shirt is normal business attire
Eating	Importance of meals in business dealing Behaviour at the table	• French business transactions usually take place at a lunch or dinner table • Chinese banquets and sometimes drinking punctuate deals
Timing	How to manage time	• Signs of impatience are considered improper in many cultures • Lengthy preliminaries are usual in the Middle East
Talking	Importance of verbal communication	• Silent pauses are the norm in China or Japan
Relations		
Engaging	Importance given to establishing personal relationships in business	• Most Asian countries prioritize the personalization of contacts before engaging in business transactions
Contracting	Importance given to overall agreement on principles versus details	• Legal contracting is the norm in the USA while broad-brush agreements are considered satisfactory in Japan
Competing		
Advantages	Product technology versus personal connections as a source of competitive advantage	• In China, connections (*guanxi*) are still a very important factor in competitive advantage
Supplying	Preference given to friends and families in supply contracts	• In Asia the notion of 'extended families' implies that preferential treatment will be given to families/friends for supply contracts

MINI-CASE 3.1

Working across cultures: the engineering consultants' clashes

In mid-2005 Gunawan Wiboto (Gunawan), an ethnic Chinese Indonesian entrepreneur and founder of the Ramayana Group, decided to build a steel mill incorporated as a new company: PT Hanuman Steel. His team began the search for an experienced engineering consultant for the project. The company approached several consulting firms reputed for their engineering services. The difficulty, as they quickly discovered, was finding a consultant who believed they could do it their way and be successful.

The required services fell into four stages: basic design, detailed engineering, procurement and construction. Representatives from four selected reputable international consultants submitted their proposals. On 3 January 2006, the John Smith Engineering Consultant Corp., headquartered in Melbourne, was awarded the contract for the basic design development phase.

John Smith and the basic design – development phase

The John Smith team began work quickly and efficiently. According to Hanuman Steel's Chief Engineer, 'The rapport was excellent. They treated us as personal guests, and we did the same when they came to Surabaya.'

The first ripples of disturbance appeared when a team of specialists from John Smith travelled to Indonesia for an on-the-spot investigation. On matters related to engineering work, the relationship between the two firms remained good. It was the financial side, and specifically the construction budget and the overall cost of the project, that caused the first rifts to appear. When Hanuman Steel looked at Smith's costing, they found they were 'way out – they were engineers, not commercial people'. If the design side went well, the commercial side proved far more contentious; the relationship finally foundered over budget disagreements concerning the three remaining phases. Smith's estimated cost for the procurement and the construction of the mill was $100 million. Hanuman Steel estimated it at $50 million. Smith's schedule for completion of the project was thirty-six months, Hanuman Steel's was eighteen months.

At this stage, Gunawan concluded that his interests were no longer being served, and, as the basic design phase of the project was coming to an end, he decided to opt for a different consultant for the following phases.

A failed attempt: Lars Corp

Gunawan and his Chief Engineer visited Stockholm to sound out Lars Corp, a Swedish firm that had already worked on the preliminary blueprint of the project. Lars was selected for the phases of detailed engineering, procurement and construction. At the end of November 2006, draft contract in hand, Hanuman Steel negotiators went to Stockholm to finalize the agreement. Negotiations were difficult because Lars adopted a very legalistic approach. But finally an agreement was reached and Gunawan flew to Stockholm to sign the contract. A celebration dinner was held. The next morning, Gunawan discovered that Lars' president had left for the USA. However, before leaving he had drawn up a letter of understanding, signed it and sent it to the hotel. Inserted in this document, Gunawan found a clause concerning performance guarantees that was 'totally against the spirit of everything we had discussed'. The clause, which had not been previously seen or discussed by the Hanuman Steel people, had 'turned a fixed price contract into an open contract'. Other clauses, already agreed, had also been changed. To Gunawan, the message was clear – it indicated a lack of trust in him and his company. Utterly frustrated by this development, Gunawan refused to sign the document and flew directly to Pittsburgh to meet Tom Brown, a short-listed US consultant.

Another try: Tom Brown

Shortly after Gunawan's visit to Brown, a meeting was held between the staff of the two companies. On Hanuman Steel's side, concern centred on the juxtaposition of low costs and high quality, and achieving the right balance. The director of engineering at Brown's was 'a polished, very polite and persuasive gentleman'. He and the Hanuman Steel team discussed the project in Pittsburgh for two weeks, aided by visits from Gunawan and the Brown director's boss. Between them, they covered all the ground in deciding who should do what; what should be Hanuman Steel's responsibility and what Brown's, and what they should do jointly. Shortly after, Brown's president, Tom Brown, accompanied by the man who would be in charge of the project, flew to Surabaya to sign a letter of understanding. In February 2007, a cross-cultural seminar organized by Hanuman Steel's two European consultants took place in Pittsburgh, attended by people from Hanuman Steel and Brown's. The practical outcome, it was hoped, would be to resolve problems before they arose and forge a team spirit.

Despite these efforts, a feeling of uneasiness began to surface on the Hanuman Steel side during the early meetings to prepare for the supplier negotiations. Hanuman Steel found that Brown's was 'building in safety feature after safety feature, which gave us serious doubts about the eventual cost of the project'. The breaking point came over a much more important issue. Brown's had agreed to give Hanuman Steel two almost unconditional bank bonds which it could cash if the project failed. However, Brown's appeared to have second thoughts about the bank bonds, and its failure to issue them turned into a serious problem. Hanuman Steel then withdrew its team and sent Brown's a letter noting that 'under the circumstances, we feel we cannot work together. Thank you very much.'

Gunawan had learnt his most important lesson: 'Even when you have everything in a written contract, it doesn't mean you will get it.' These problems had been exacerbated by the cultural gulf between the two sides. Gunawan's entrepreneurial approach and determination to keep his budget adjusted for local conditions, coupled with the Indonesian preference for keeping their financial plans flexible and in shades of grey, was diametrically opposed to the European and North American desire to play it safe – to have everything set in concrete down to the finest detail, with every guarantee possible and every contingency allowed for. As Hanuman Steel eventually discovered, what they were asking for was outside the experience of the conservative Western consultants. It created a clash of two very different cultures.

Questions:

1 How do you assess the situation?

2 Do you think Gunawan was being unreasonable?

3 Do you think the Western consultants did not understand the Indonesian context and culture?

4 How much were the clashes caused by cultural differences as opposed to commercial ones?

Source: Based on authors' own work.

MINI-CASE 3.2

Brazil

The Republic of Brazil is the largest country in South and Central America. Numerous indigenous tribes predated the arrival of the explorer Pedro Álvares Cabral who claimed the territory for Portugal in 1500. Brazil remained a Portuguese colony until independence in 1822, and the creation of the Empire of Brazil. The country became a presidential republic in 1889. A military junta governed from 1964 to 1985. Brazil's Constitution (established in 1988) formed the Federal Republic which is made up of the Federal District, 26 States and 5,564 Municipalities.

Civil society

Brazilians make up a diverse multi-racial society composed of descendants of indigenous peoples, Portuguese settlers, enslaved people and European and Japanese immigrants. Interracial marriages have created a tolerant and mixed society. The Roman Catholic religion predominates, with two-thirds of the population identifying as Catholic. There is a high income inequality (Gini index = 55). Most of the poor are concentrated in enclaves known as '*favelas*'.

Government

Brazil is a Federal Republic headed by the President and the Vice President, elected every four years with the right to re-election for one more consecutive term. The president appoints cabinet ministers who are directly responsible to them and whom they can dismiss at any time. The legislative body is the National Congress, consisting of a Senate and a Chamber of Deputies.

The Heads of the Senate and Chamber of Deputies play a critical role in consensus building prior to key votes. They also control large budgets and can authorize congressional inquiries. In addition, the president of the Chamber of Deputies is third in the line of succession in the event of the president's impeachment or early death, and the president of the Senate is fourth. Such an event took place in 2016 when President Dilma Rousseff was deposed.

Government in each state reflects the structure at the federal level. States possess those powers that are not specifically reserved for the federal government or granted to municipal councils. States are led by a governor, elected by direct vote. They are only allowed to serve for two consecutive terms. Each state has an elected State Assembly.

Economy

The Brazilian economy is characterized by a huge internal market in terms of population and natural resources. After the dictatorship of the 1960s and 1970s, Brazil enjoyed a period of growth but with high inflation. An austerity measure, 'the Plano Real' of 1994 reduced inflation but the country still experienced a high account deficit. During President Lula's presidency from 2003 to 2010 the economic situation improved, and inflation was reduced. Despite external debts, Brazil's middle class is growing, and poverty is declining. Although in 2015 there were still 40 million people living in poverty, this statistic compares favourably with the early 2000s, when the figure was 60 million. However, the economy remains vulnerable to fluctuations caused by global crises or domestic politics. After 2010, with a reduction in China's imports and a decline in commodity prices, Brazil entered a period of recession: investors' confidence declined, and corporate debts and bankruptcy increased. Brazil still relies on a significant degree of government intervention to protect its local industry, such as quotas, tariffs and local-content rules, to implement tax breaks and subsidies to encourage demand for locally produced goods. However, it has been estimated that 85 per cent of small businesses do not pay taxes.

Labour markets

The acceleration of economic growth during the first decade of the twenty-first century produced increased demand for labour. The jobless total fell to below 6 per cent, but by 2016 it had increased to 11 per cent.

The 'informal' sector is estimated to account for 40 per cent of GDP (90 per cent of workers in agriculture and fishing are believed not to have formal work contracts). This informal sector has long provided a social safety net for low earners amongst the urban poor, and this group continues to account for the largest proportion of workers employed in the informal sector.

Trade union density (i.e. the proportion of salaried workers that belong to a trade union) is around 18 per cent, a relatively high percentage compared to other emerging countries.

Financial system

The Brazilian banking sector, both private and state-owned, is growing rapidly. With more than 140 listed banking institutions, the sector is still of a moderate size relative to the economy, with a credit-to-GDP ratio of less than 50 per cent. The mix of state-owned, private and foreign banks is highly concentrated, with the five largest banks accounting for about 70 per cent of sector assets. Banco do Brasil, the National Bank for Economic and Social Development (BNDES), and Caixa Econômica Federal (CAIXA) are the first-, third- and fourth-largest banks, respectively, with nearly 40 per cent of sector assets in total – all of them at least partly state-owned.

Brazil also has a buoyant fintech ecosystem, being the headquarters of Nubank, the largest digital bank in the world, with more than 48 million customers.

Business entities

Instead of pure privatization, the Lula administration promoted public–private partnerships (PPP). PPP companies are enterprises with the majority of their stock owned by the government, but also having shares owned by the private sector and usually traded on stock exchanges. The take-up of this scheme has been disappointing and state-owned companies are still playing a dominant role in the financing and construction of large infrastructure projects. In 2017, the government considered rule changes for the PPPs that could make them more attractive. Banco do Brasil, Petrobras, Sabesp and Eletrobras are examples of mixed-economy companies. Other major companies such as Vale (mining) or Embraer (aircraft manufacture) are former state-owned enterprises. The Brazilian corporate landscape also includes family-owned conglomerates such as the Votorantim group.

Society

As already noted, interracial marriages have long been a key characteristic of Brazilian society. The cultural mixing comes from centuries of historical development. In addition to the original indigenous population, the colonization brought Portuguese settlers who brought four million enslaved Africans. Since independence around 5 million people have migrated from different countries of origin (mainly Germany, Italy, Spain and Japan). This high rate of mixing explains two socio-cultural practices of contemporary Brazilian society: *cordiality* and *jeitinho*.

Cordiality denotes cheerful, friendly, welcoming and hospitable people. Brazilians know they are all implicitly mixed and no one is more or less ethnically 'pure' than another; in other words, nobody is going to feel or start acting superior to anyone else.

Jeitinho is a process by which someone reaches a goal in spite of constraints such as laws, orders, rules and so on. It is the antithesis of bureaucracy. While bureaucracy is theoretically rational, impersonal and anonymous, *jeitinho* is emotional and affective. So when someone is confronted by an obstructive regulation, they will immediately fall back on their interpersonal relationships in an attempt to get around the regulation by appealing to the human beings behind it.

Brazilian organizational cultures have, in general, been traditionally seen as closed systems in which leaders with strong personalities, rigid values, paternalistic patterns and highly centralized hierarchical structures prevail. The *jeitinho* culture translates in business as lack of planning and improvization: 'Well, there is no clear way to reach the goal, but somehow, with the help of God, we will achieve it anyway.' The weakness of most employees' commitment to and engagement with corporate life encourages an unchallenged bureaucratic structure, which, in turn, stifles initiative and promotes the prevalence of regimented rules.

Since the early 2000s, profound changes in the Brazilian economy have been gradually transforming the business climate from paternalistic and protectionist to one of free enterprise, especially in the economically well developed and heavily industrialized southeastern part of the country. The co-existence of old and modern business structures underlines differences in working conditions, such as retirement prerequisites and rights, guarantees of job stability, personal and professional advantages and so on.

Question:

Based on this mini-case and your own research, sketch a business system analysis of Brazil.

Sources: This mini-case was compiled by the author from data collected from IHS Markit (www.ihs.com), Wikipedia (https://en.wikipedia.org), World Bank data (http://www.doingbusiness.org/data/exploreeconomies/brazil/) and Ferreira et al. (2004) 'Organizational culture in Brazilian public and private companies', Gama Filho University.

Table 3.11 Brazilian indicators

Economy and demography (2020)		
GDP (US$ billion)		1445
GDP, PPP (US$ billion)		3152
GDP per capita (US$)		6797
GDP per capita, PPP (US$)		14830
Population, total (million)		213
Urban population (%)		87%
Gini Index		53
Governance indicators (2020) from –2.5 to +2.5		
Government effectiveness		–0,447
Voice and accountability		0,261
Political stability and absence of violence		–0,422
Regulatory quality		–0,162
Rule of law		–0,176
Control of corruption		–0,342

Ease of doing business (2020)		
Starting a business	Rank	138
	Procedures (number)	10.6
	Time (days)	16.6
	Cost (% of income per capita)	3.6
Getting electricity	Rank	98
	Procedures (number)	5
	Time (days)	132
	Cost (% of income per capita)	333
Registering property	Rank	133
	Procedures (number)	14
	Time (days)	24.5
	Cost (% of property value)	3.6
Getting credit	Rank	104
Protecting minority investors	Rank	35
Paying taxes	Rank	175
	Total tax rate (% profit)	64.7
Trading across borders	Rank	108
	Cost to export (border compliancer hours)	12
	Cost to export (documentary compliance §)	226
Enforcing contracts	Rank	58
	Time (days)	731.0
	Cost (% of claim value)	20.7
	LU	
Resolving insolvency	Rank	77

Note: *Overall ranking is out of 190.*

Source: Data from World Bank, Ease of Doing Business Index, http://www.doingbusiness.org/data/exploreeconomies/brazil/ (accessed 22 January 2022).

Summary and key points

1 Cross-cultural management:

a Potential issues are concepts, behaviours or attitudes being interpreted differently by different nationalities

b Culture can potentially encompass:

- Layers of culture
  - Assumptions and meaning
  - Values, beliefs and preferences
  - Behaviour

2 National culture:

a Differences in national cultures:

- Ethnological research ('silent language')
- Differences in work-related values
  - Power distance
  - Individualism
  - Uncertainty avoidance (tolerance towards ambiguity)
  - Masculinity
- Differences in value orientation
  - Rule-based versus relation-based behaviour
  - Individualism versus collectivism
  - Objective analytical reasoning versus holistic/synthetic reasoning
  - Status and respect achieved by doing versus being
  - Knowledge of 'right' or 'wrong' arises from within versus from society
  - Sequential time versus synchronous time
- Cultural map

  Eight dimensions of cultural differences
  - Communication
  - Evaluation of people
  - Persuasion
  - Leadership
  - Decision making
  - Trust
  - Disagreements
  - Scheduling

3 Country clusters

- **a** National grouping according to cultural traits proximity
- **b** Globe's societal culture
- **c** Performance orientation
- **d** Assertiveness
- **e** Future orientation
- **f** Humane orientation
- **g** Collectivism
- **h** Gender egalitarianism
- **i** Power distance
- **j** Uncertainty avoidance
- **k** Economic culture and business system
  - The '*business system*' is the way economic activities are structured, coordinated and managed. It is the result of the interaction between three sub-systems:
    - *Governance* reflects the dominant mode of control, interdependencies and exercise of authority in business firms. It is made of:
      - Ownership system
      - Networking system
      - Management system
    - *Culture* is constituted by the norms, values and social codes of society. It is made of:
      - Rationality
      - Authority
      - Identity
    - *Institutional fabric* represents the organization, development and allocation of resources. It is made of:
      - Financial capital
      - Human capital
      - Social capital
      - Role of the state

4 Impact of culture on management:

- **a** Multi-cultural teams:
  - Types:
    - Business development
    - Regional headquarters

  - Corporate headquarters
  - Joint ventures and alliances
  - Task forces
- Performance depends on:
  - 'Rich information' resulting from a multiplicity of perspectives, experiences and viewpoints
  - Possible loss of cohesion
  - Ability for team leaders to achieve group synergy

b Negotiations:

- Seven elements work together in a negotiation:
  - Relationships
  - Communication
  - Interests
  - Options
  - Legitimacy
  - Commitment
  - Alternatives
- There are commonly six stages:
  - Pre-negotiation: each party prepares for negotiation
  - Climate-setting: introduction, physical context
  - Presenting: agenda-setting and opening statements
  - Mid-point bargaining
  - Closure: search for agreements, final drafting/signing
  - Post-negotiation: ramifications of agreements
- Impact of culture on negotiations: diversity of culture affects negotiations in nine ways:
  - Goal
  - Attitude
  - Style
  - Communication
  - Time
  - Emotions
  - Forms of agreement
  - Flow process

  - Risk taking
- Checklist for negotiators:
  - Understand the 'cultural' lens of your own and your counterparty's positions
  - List negotiation items which risk being affected by cultural factors
  - Assess potential responses
  - Disentangle cultural divergence from business divergence
  - Anticipate counterparts' responses
- Negotiation style:
  - Business etiquette: includes the way people talk, dress, eat, stand, pose and deal with time
  - Relation practices: the way transactions are established either personal or legal/technical
  - Competition: how competitive advantages are obtained
  - Cultural aspects of business practices:
    - Etiquette
    - Relations
    - Competition

Learning assignments

1 What types of cultural differences can business managers experience? Give examples.

2 What is the 'silent language' of negotiation?

3 A lower-level manager discovers that his boss has made a wrong decision that could affect the company negatively. Looking at the various cultural norms described in the chapter, how would you expect this manager to behave if they were:

a Indonesian?

b Danish?

4 What consequences can you draw from Laurent's assumptions of management differences for the organization of a subsidiary in China?

5 Looking at Erin Meyer's cultural mapping, what kind of problems would you anticipate for a German manager in Indonesia?

6 What cultural issues would you anticipate in a planned partnership between a UK listed e-company and a Korean family conglomerate?

7 Why have East Asian counties been more efficient in containing the Covid-19 pandemic?

8 How would you recommend an American manager plan a negotiation with a Japanese counterpart?

9 What real-life examples of 'cultural misbehaviour' or misunderstandings have you experienced personally, or heard of? How could these have been avoided?

10 In your opinion, what is the usefulness of doing a business system analysis when considering whether to invest in a country?

11 Are the theories, models and principles taught in business schools all over the world progressively eliminating cultural differences in the management of business enterprises?

Key words

- Business etiquette
- Corporate culture
- Cultural heritage
- Economic cultures
- Individualism
- Industry culture
- National/ethnic culture
- Power distance
- Professional culture
- 'Silent language'
- Uncertainty avoidance

Web resources

McKinsey Quarterly – Teams:
http://www.mckinsey.com/featured-insights

A brief overview of the GLOBE project:
http://globe.bus.sfu.ca/study_2004_2007

Companion website

Visit the companion website at bloomsbury.pub/global-strategic-management-5e for a multitude of weblinks and resources, self-test questions for revision and appendices.

Notes

1 Huntington (1993: 22).
2 Ricks (1993).
3 Laurent (1986).
4 Hall (1960).
5 Hofstede (1980).
6 Trompenaars 1993).
7 Laurent (1986).
8 Meyer (2014b).
9 Weber ([1905] 1930).
10 Albert (1991); Berger and Dore (1996); Trompenaars (1993); Whitley (2007).
11 Redding (2005); Redding and Witt (2007); Whitley (1999); Witt (2010); Witt and Redding (2014).
12 Adler (1997); Neeley (2015).
13 Stumpf and Zeutchel (2001).
14 *This part benefited from the contribution of Horacio Falcao Affliate Professor of Decision Sciences, INSEAD*
15 Negotiation theorists call this point the BATNA: best alternative to a negotiated agreement. See Raiffa (1982) as well as Fisher and Ury (1991).
16 Salacuse (2003).
17 Salacuse (2003); Brett (2001)
18 This list is from Sunshine (1990: 77–81).

References and further reading

Adler, N. (1997) *International Dimension of Organizational Behavior* (Cincinnati, OH: South Western College Publishing).

Albert, M. (1991) *Capitalisme contre Capitalisme* (Paris: Seuil).

Berger, P. (1986) *The Capitalist Revolution* (New York, NY: Basic Books).

Berger, S. and Dore, R. (eds) (1996) *National Diversity and Global Capitalism* (Ithaca, NY: Cornell University Press).

Brake, T., Medina, D. and Walker, T. (1994) *Doing Business Internationally: Guide to Cross Cultural Success* (New York, NY: McGraw-Hill).

Brett, J. M. (2001) *Negotiating Globally* (San Francisco, CA: Jossey-Bass).

Chhokar, J. S., Brodbeck, F. C. and House, R. J. (2007) *Culture and Leadership Across The World: The GLOBE Book of In-Depth Studies of 25 Societies* (New York, NY: Lawrence Erlbaum Associates).

Chu, C. (1991) *The Asian Mind Game: Unlocking the Hidden Agenda of the Asian Business Culture: A Westerner's Survival Manual* (New York, NY: Rawson Associates).

Coyle, D. (2018) *The Culture Code: The Secrets of Highly Successful Groups* (New York, NY: Bantam Books).

Daher, N. (2019) 'Elaboration on the relationship between cultural intelligence and the expatriates cross-cultural adaptation', *International Journal of Business and Public Administration*, 16 (1), Spring: 56–73.

Dorfman, P., Javidan, M., Hanges, P., Dastmalchian, A. and House, R. (2012) 'GLOBE: a twenty year journey into the intriguing world of culture and leadership', *Journal of World Business*, 47: 504–18.

Falcao, H. (2010)) *Value Negotiation: How to Finally Get the Win–Win Right* (London: Pearson Education).

Fang, T. (1997) *Chinese Business Negotiation Style: A Socio-Cultural Approach* (Linköping: Linköping University Press).

Fang, T. (2006) 'Negotiation: the Chinese style', *Journal of Business and Industrial Marketing*, 21 (1): 50–60.

Fisher, R. and Ury, W. (1991) *Getting to Yes* (New York, NY: Penguin Books).

Fisher, R., Ury, W. and Patton, B. (2011) *Getting to Yes: Negotiating Agreement Without Giving In* (London: Random House Business).

Gahuri, P. and Usunier, J. C. (1996) *International Business Negotiations* (Oxford: Pergamon Press).

Geertz, C. (1973) *The Interpretation of Culture* (New York, NY: Basic Books).

Hall, E. (1960) 'The silent language in overseas business', *Harvard Business Review*, May–June: 87–96.

Hall, E. and Reed Hall, M. (1990) *Understanding Cultural Differences* (Yarmouth, ME: Intercultural Press).

Hampden-Turner, C. and Trompenaars, F. (2000) *Building Cross-Cultural Competence* (Chichester: John Wiley).

Helmold, M., Dathe, T., Hummel, F., Terry, B. and Pieper, J. (eds) (2020) *Successful International Negotiations: A Practical Guide for Managing Transactions and Deals* (London: Springer).

Herbig, P. and Martin, D. (1999) 'Negotiating with Chinese: a cultural perspective', *Cross Cultural Management: an International Journal*, 5 (3): 40–54.

Ho-Won Jeong (2016) *International Negotiations: Process and Strategies* (Cambridge: Cambridge University Press).

Hofstede, G. (1980) *Culture's Consequences: International Differences in Work-related Values* (Beverly Hills, CA: Sage).

Hofstede, G. and Minkov, M. (2010) 'Long- versus short-term orientation: new perspectives Asia', *Pacific Business Review*, 16 (4), October: 493–504.

House, R. J., Hanges, P. J., Javidan, M., Dorfman, P. W. and Gupta, V. (2004) *Culture, Leadership and Organizations: The GLOBE Study of 62 Societies* (Thousand Oaks, CA: Sage).

Huntington, S. P. (1993) 'The clash of civilizations?', *Foreign Affairs*, 72 (3): 22–49.

Huntington, S. P. (1997) *The Clash of Civilizations and the Remaking of World Order* (London: Simon & Schuster).

Inglehart, R. and Baker, W. (2000) 'Modernization, cultural change and the persistence of traditional values', *American Sociological Review*, 65 (1): 19–51.

Jackson, T. (1995) *Cross Cultural Management* (London: Butterworth-Heinemann).

Kremenyuk, V. (1996) *International Negotiation: Analysis, Approaches, Issues* (San Francisco: Jossey-Bass).

Laurent, A. (1986) 'The cross-cultural puzzle of global human resource management', *Human Resources Management*, 25 (1): 91–102.

Lawrence, P. R. and Lorsch, W. J. (1969) *Organization and Environment* (New York, NY: Irwin).

Levi-Strauss, C. (1971) *L'Homme Nu* (Paris: Plon).

Lewis, R. D. (1996) *When Cultures Collide: Managing Successfully Across Cultures* (London: Nicholas Brealey). See also http://www.crossculture.com/about-us/the-model/ (accessed 1 February 2022).

Mead, M. (1953) *Coming of Age in Samoa* (New York, NY: Modern Library).

Meyer, E. (2014a) *The Culture Map: Breaking Through the Invisible Boundaries of Global Business* (New York, NY: Public Affairs).

Meyer, E. (2014b) 'Navigating the cultural minefield: learn how to work more effectively with people from other countries', *Harvard Business Review*, 92 (5): 119–23.

Meyer, E. (2015a) 'When culture doesn't translate: how to expand abroad without losing your company mojo', *Harvard Business Review*, 93 (10): 66–72.

Meyer, E. (2015b) 'Getting to sí, ja, oui, hai, and da: how to negotiate across culture', *Harvard Business Review*, 93 (12): 74–80.

Meyer, E. (2017) 'Being the boss in Brussels, Boston, and Beijing', *Harvard Business Review*, 95 (4): 70–7.

Neeley, T. (2015) 'Global teams that work', *Harvard Business Review*, 93 (10): 74–81.

Raiffa, H. (1982) *The Art and Science of Negotiation* (Cambridge, MA: Belknap Press).

Redding, G. (1990) *The Spirit of Chinese Capitalism* (Berlin: De Gruyter).

Redding, G. (ed.) (1995) *International Cultural Differences* (Brookfield, VT: Dartmouth College, International Library of Management).

Redding, G. (2001) 'Convergence or divergence at the Millennium', INSEAD Euro Asia Centre, Working Paper No. 70.

Redding, G. (2005) 'The thick description and comparison of societal systems of capitalism', *Journal of International Business Studies*, 35: 122–55.

Redding, G. and Witt, M. A. (2007) *The Future of Chinese Capitalism: Choices and Chances* (Oxford: Oxford University Press).

Ricks, D. A. (1993) *Blunders in International Business* (Malden, MA: Blackwell Business).

Ronen, S. and Shenkar, O. (1985) 'Clustering countries on attitudinal dimensions: a review and synthesis', *Academy of Management Review*, 10 (3): 435–54.

Salacuse, J. (2003) *The Global Negotiator: Making, Managing, and Mending Deals around the World in the Twenty-First Century* (Basingstoke: Palgrave Macmillan).

Schein, E. (1985) *Organizational Culture and Leadership* (San Francisco, CA: Jossey-Bass).

Schneider, S. C. and Barsoux, J.-L. (1997) *Managing Across Cultures* (London: Prentice-Hall).

Stahl, G., Maznevski, M., Voigt, A. and Jonsen, K. (2010) 'Unraveling the effects of cultural diversity in teams: a meta-analysis of research on multicultural work groups', *Journal of International Business Studies*, 41: 690–709.

Stahl, G., Maznevski, M. and Jonsen, K. (2021) 'Unraveling the effects of cultural diversity in teams: a retrospective of researchon multicultural work groups and agenda for future research', *Journal of International Business Studies*, 52: 4–22.

Stumpf, S. and Zeutchel, U. (2001) 'Synergy effects in multinational work groups: what we know and what we don't know', in M. Mendenhall, T. Kühlman and G. Stahl (eds), *Developing Global Business Leaders* (Westport, CT: Quorum Books), 175–94.

Sunshine, R. B. (1990) *Negotiating for International Development*, International Development Law Institute (Dordrecht: Martinus Nijhoff).

Trompenaars, F. (1993) *Riding the Waves of Cultural Differences: Understanding Cultural Differences in Business* (London: Nicholas Brealey).

Trompenaars, F. and Hampden-Turner, C. (2000) *Riding the Waves of Cultural Differences: Understanding Cultural Differences in Business*, 3rd edn (London: Nicholas Brealey).

Weber, M. ([1905] 1930) *The Protestant Ethic and the Spirit of Capitalism*. Trans. T. Parsons and A. Giddens (London: Unwin Hyman). Originally published in 1905 as *Die protestantische Ethik und der Geist des Kapitalismus*.

Whitley, R. D. (1992) *Business Systems in East Asia: Firms, Markets and Societies* (London: Sage).

Whitley, R. D. (1999) *Divergent Capitalisms* (Oxford: Oxford University Press).

Whitley, R. D. (2007) *Business Systems and Organizational Capabilities: The Institutional Structuring of Competitive Competences* (Oxford: Oxford University Press).

Witt, M. A. (2010) *Guide to Business Systems*, Technical Note, INSEAD.

Witt, M. A. and Redding, G. (eds) (2014) *The Oxford Handbook of Asian Business Systems* (Oxford: Oxford University Press).

Woo, H. S. and Prud'homme, C. (1999) 'Cultural characteristics prevalent in the Chinese negotiation process', *European Business Review*, 99: 313–22.

World Bank (2020) Ease of Doing Business Index. http://www.doingbusiness.org/data/exploreeconomies/brazil/ (accessed 1 February 2022).

Chapter 4

Globalization, sustainable development and social responsibility

At the end of the chapter you should be able to:

- Understand the domains of sustainable development and social responsibility
- Participate in the formulation of environmentally friendly policies
- Understand the social responsibility of global firms in maintaining appropriate practices with regard to child labour, human rights and labour conditions
- Understand the causes and effects of corruption in business and the role that a global company can play in fighting corruption
- Understand the many aspects of global citizenship
- Understand the role of codes of conduct and of global non-governmental organizations (NGOs)

Introduction

Globalization has had, and still has, deep social, political and environmental consequences. The effects of globalization on society and general welfare are often challenged on the grounds that globalization tends to affect the environment, widens the gap between rich and poor and encourages practices that are detrimental to the well-being of the world population, particularly people in developing countries. On the environmental front, global firms are accountable for the acceleration of mining, agricultural and transportation activities, generated by foreign investments and global trade, that have added additional stresses on climate, resource depletion and species diversity. On ethical issues, multinational firms, as the agents of globalization, are front-line targets of critics who blame them for misconduct in a vast array of domains, such as corruption, encroachment on human rights, child labour, tax evasion and poor citizenship. This chapter tries to address some of the issues that global companies face in dealing with the natural environment and the societies in which they operate, with a particular emphasis on the kind of ethical dilemmas that firms and global managers have to confront in their worldwide operations.

Most of these ecological, ethical and societal issues are not limited to global enterprises (for instance, a purely domestic firm can be accused of corruption or pollution), and this chapter does not pretend to give exhaustive coverage of business ethics in general. It concentrates only on how these affect global operations. Figure 4.1 shows the two main categories considered in this chapter: environmental issues and societal issues complemented by the role of global firms as global citizens.

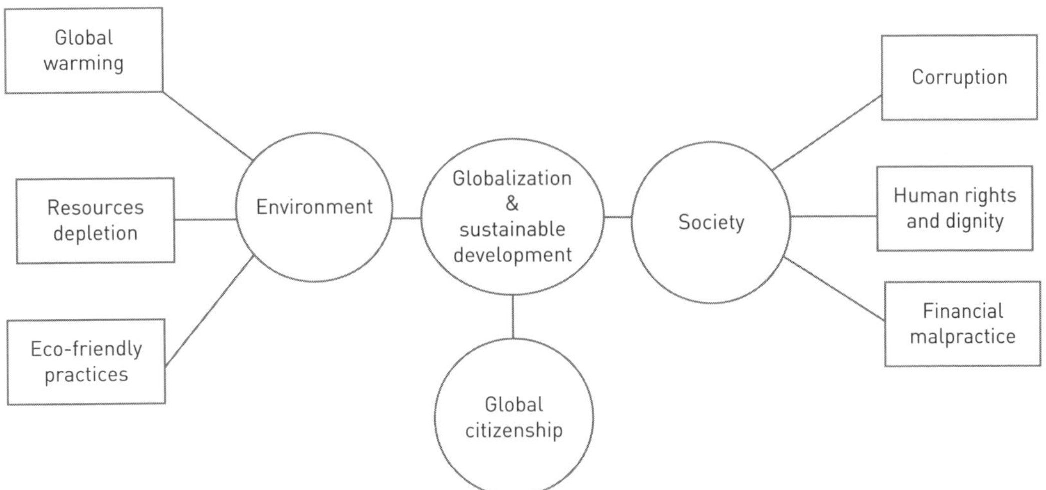

Figure 4.1 Sustainable development and the global firm

Sustainable development

The concept of sustainable development was first introduced in 1987 by the World Commission on Environment and Development, in what is known as the 'Brundtland Report'.[1] It was defined as 'development that meets the needs of the present without compromising the ability of future generations to meet their own needs'. According to the World Business Council for Sustainable Development, 'development means the building of societies in which people are able to enjoy security, good health, decent housing, clean water and modern power supplies'.[2] In order to be sustainable, development demands a respectful, careful and, ideally, renewable utilization of natural resources, as well as the protection of the ecological system. Sustainable development is the subject of global meetings of political leaders discussing what measures can be taken to preserve the planet. The first such meeting was held in Rio de Janeiro in 1992 and contained a declaration of principles within twenty-seven recommendations.[3] In September 2015, the United Nations (UN) set an agenda for sustainable development with goals to be achieved by 2030.[4] A report based on scientific research was produced to support the recommendations.[5] In this report seventeen sustainability issues were identified; Table 4.1 lists these with their possible impacts.

Table 4.1 Sustainable development issues

Description of issue	Sustainable development impact
Environmental issues	
Agriculture, hunger and food security • Industrial agriculture vs subsistence farming • Use of pesticides and fertilizers • Use of water • Intensive vs extensive agriculture • Deforestation	• Ecosystem conversion to agriculture or forest • Fragmenting habitats • Introduction of non-native species • Pollution of ecosystems through farm chemical run-off • Genetic homogenization through monoculture • Erosion, siltation, etc.
Climate change • Global warming	• Emission of greenhouse gas
Energy • Renewable electricity • Fossil fuel energy systems • Energy conservation practices • Nuclear energy	• Pollution of ecosystems through spills • Pollution of ecosystems through extraction (e.g. effluent, noise, etc.) • Nuclear waste management
Industrialization and infrastructure • Socially efficient investments	• Destruction of ecosystems through infrastructure construction • Facilitating access to fragile ecosystems, fragmenting habitats, pollution • Use of land for transport infrastructure
Natural resources • Renewable resources	• Pollution of ecosystems linked to use of inputs in extraction (e.g. effluent, noise, etc.) • Over-mining, over-fishing
Oceans • Marine ecosystem • Micro plastics • Ocean acidification • Ocean temperature	• Destruction of habitats through damaging fishing practices • Potential over-fishing of target and by-catch species • Introduction of non-native species • Pollution of marine and freshwater ecosystems through effluent discharge, excessive nutrient and chemical loading (aquaculture, noise)
Sustainable consumption and production • Mode of consumption • Food waste	• Waste disposal (e.g. electronic components, batteries, etc.) • Packaging
Terrestrial biodiversity • Wetlands • Conservation of species • Genetically modified organisms	• Facilitating access to fragile ecosystems, fragmenting habitats, pollution • Pollution of forest ecosystems through effluent and noise • Erosion and associated effects

Water and sanitation • Sustainable water infrastructure • Water pollution	• Water pollution and over-use destroying habitats and ecosystems • Pollution associated with transport use, including greenhouse gas and air pollution emissions
Societal issues	
Cities and human settlement • Urbanization and sub-urbanization	• Emission of greenhouse gases (GHGs) due to transportation and energy production
Economic growth and employment • Large-scale production and transportation systems • Territorial expansion to production	• Use of non-renewable resources • Impact on emission of GHGs and attrition of resources due to economic activities • Decoupling of growth and GHG emission • Promotion of community-based systems of production • Generalization of recycling
Education • Schooling programmes	• Unequal access to education • Inclusion of sustainable development issues in programmes
Gender equality • Mode of consumption	• Role of women in the management of water and energy resources, food security
Governance • Rule of law	• Role of lobbies in distribution of forestry, mining and construction permits • Fight against corruption • Protective legislation and enforcement favourable to environmental protection
Health • Access to healthcare	• Effects of environmental hazards on health
Peaceful and inclusive societies • Community participation in decision making • Institutions • Human rights	• Accepted role of environmental local and international NGOs
Poverty eradication • Unbalanced development	• Child poverty and child labour

Source: Data from CAIT Climate Data Explorer, 2015, Washington, DC: World Resources Institute, http://cait.wri.org.

EXAMPLE 4.1 An introduction to issues of corporate social responsibility – Shell in Nigeria

Shell's oil exploration in Nigeria began in 1937 when Nigeria was still a British colony. After Nigerian independence, Shell formed a joint venture with the Nigerian government. Oil resource exploration and exploitation took place, among other locations, in an area of southeast Nigeria around the Niger Delta in which lived the Ogoni, a small ethnic group of about half a million people. In 1990, the leaders of the Ogoni created the Movement for the Survival of the Ogoni People (MOSOP) which demanded more benefits from the Nigerian government and also compensation for the environmental damage created by Shell's operations. In 1993, several clashes between Nigerian security forces led to MOSOP protests being brutally repressed, including the killing of several protesters. Subsequently, nine leaders of MOSOP were hanged after a trial by a military court. Shell was accused of complicity despite repeated denials from the company. Shell pulled out of Ogoniland and in 1997 revised its 'Statement of General Business Principles', reaffirming its support for human rights. In 1998, Shell produced its first social and environmental publication, *Profits and Principles*.

The Ogoni case has been a trigger for wider recognition of the responsibility of a global firm with regards to environmental protection and safeguarding human rights. Shell's experience in Nigeria illustrates the need for global corporations to consider the issues related to sustainable development.

Source: Wheeler et al. (2001a, 2001b, 2001c).

The 17 Sustainable Development Goals (SDGs)[6] were adopted by all United Nations (UN) Member states in 2015. They are a universal call for action to end poverty, protect the planet and improve the lives and prospects of everyone, everywhere.[7] The 17 Goals are part of the UN 2030 Agenda for Sustainable Development – a fifteen-year plan to achieve the goals. By 2021, progress had been made, but action to meet the goals was not advancing at the speed or scale necessary. Despite this, more people worldwide were living better lives compared to the previous decade with better access to healthcare, decent work and education than before.

Businesses and the SDGs

In the Paris Agreement on Climate Change in 2015, members committed to work to limit global temperature rise to below the 2 degrees Celsius that is essential for the achievement of the SDGs.[8] According to the UN and other international organizations, achievement of these goals relies on joint effort from both the public and private sectors. To this end, while the Trump administration took significant steps to withdraw the US from the Paris Agreement, immediately after his inauguration in January 2021, President Biden signed an executive order to reverse the previous administration's withdrawal and the

Sustainable Development Goals

1 No poverty
2 Zero hunger
3 Good health and well-being
4 Quality education
5 Gender equality
6 Clean water and sanitation
7 Affordable and clean energy
8 Decent work and economic growth
9 Industry, innovation and infrastructure
10 Reduced inequality
11 Sustainable cities and communities
12 Responsible consumption and production
13 Climate action
14 Life below water
15 Life on land
16 Peace and justice-strong institutions
17 Partnerships to achieve the goals

Paris Agreement came into force in the US on 19 February 2021.[9] Businesses in Europe have also taken steps to influence climate change policy when more than 150 business leaders, including those of Microsoft, Google, IKEA, Deutsche Bank and EDF, signed an open letter to urge the EU to set higher than planned climate goals for 2030,[10] including a 55 per cent reduction in greenhouse gas emissions by the end of the decade, which was agreed on at the end of 2020.[11]

Companies have taken different approaches to playing their role in sustainable development in terms of pursuing largely symbolic or substantive sustainability efforts, even in the same industries and with comparable size and resources. The apparel company H&M has been accused of inflating its positive environmental impact, through advertisement campaigns such as that for its 'Conscious Collection', while masking considerable harm caused by its production processes.[12] This corporate behaviour is often referred to as 'greenwashing'.[13] There is increasing evidence on the negative effects of 'greenwashing' in terms of companies' perceived reputation and integrity, which dampen consumer purchase intentions.[14] On the other hand, other companies in the same industry, like Patagonia, openly advertise the environmental costs of their productions and actively discourage their customers from supporting 'fast fashion'.[15] While the evidence is still inconclusive in terms of corporate social responsibility efforts and financial performance, including consumer behaviour, most studies report a non-negative or positive effect[16] and socially responsible firms may expect greater effort and lower wage requirements from their employees.[17]

Some organizations go even further in driving change towards achieving the SDGs by entering (competitive) collaborations with their competitors or using novel organizational forms to tackle grand societal challenges. The Electronics Industry Citizenship Coalition (EICC) is an initiative to create industry-wide standards on social, environmental and ethical issues in the electronics industry supply chain; founding members include IBM, Dell and HP. Such 'co-opetitive' efforts in the context of corporate sustainability are considered a viable strategy to considerably improve industry-wide corporate social performance.[18] In terms of new organizational forms to support sustainability, social enterprises, such as Fair Trade organizations and microfinance institutions, combine logics from both for-profit and non-profit businesses to create positive social impact in a financially sustainable way.[19] The creation of new legal entities[20] to accommodate these new organizational forms also supports the notion that companies play a crucial role in driving worldwide efforts towards the achievement of the 2030 Agenda for Sustainable Development.

All companies are concerned with sustainability but some industries bear the largest responsibility in dealing with sustainable development. Those are the extractive and energy industries (oil, mining, forestry), biotechnology and agribusinesses (genetically modified organisms (GMOs)), chemicals, pulp and paper. Multinational and global firms in those sectors, and others, are constantly being challenged on the grounds that they are contributing to the degradation of the environment. The most common issues confronting multinational corporations are:

- Global warming and carbon dioxide (CO_2) emissions;
- Depletion of natural resources, effects of monocultures, deforestation and intensive agriculture;
- Waste disposal.

In order to contribute to sustainability, global firms must pay attention to:

- Control of suppliers;
- Eco-friendly capital investments;
- Green management of resources.

Globalization and environmental issues

Global warming and CO_2 emissions

One of the most prominent environmental issues is the increasing warming of the planet due to the emission of greenhouse gases (GHGs) constituted mainly of CO_2, methane, nitrous oxides and fluorinated gases. Their 'greenhouse effect' is to trap heat within the atmosphere, creating global warming which raises the average temperature of the globe (Figure 4.2), increases sea levels and creates climatic catastrophes and agricultural disruptions. In turn, population migration may result,

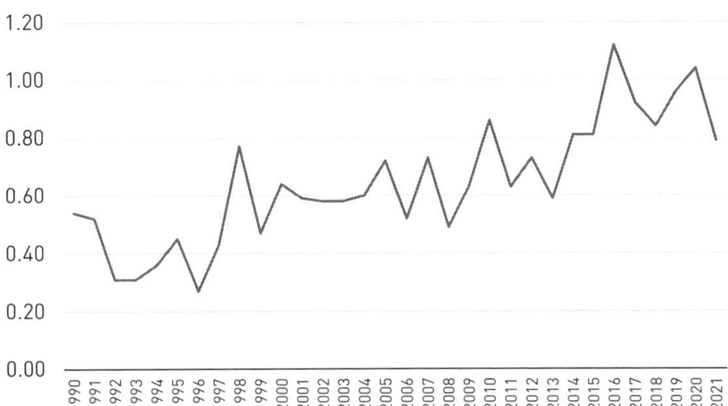

Figure 4.2 Temperatures worldwide: earth surface (land and oceans)

Source: NOAA National Centers for Environmental information, *Climate at a Glance: Global Time Series*, published August 2021, retrieved on 17 August 2021 from https://www.ncdc.noaa.gov/cag/.

generating further potential impacts and conflict. Global emissions of GHGs were 52 billion tons in 2019,[21] 70 per cent more than in 1990 (33 million tons) and seven times the level of 1950 (7 million tons). China and industrialized countries are the major producers of CO_2. The energy sector plays the largest part (Table 4.2), although it should be noted that CO_2 emissions do have natural as well as artificial/industrial sources. Without proper controls, the whole ecology of the planet may be disrupted. The long-term effects of global warming are potentially dramatic in terms of human health, natural disasters, farming and human settlement.

Table 4.2 Total world GHG emissions including land-use change and forestry (billion tons equivalent CO_2)

Country	2019	%
World	52.4	100
China	14.01	26.7
United States	6.59	12.6
European Union	4.34	8.3
India	3.72	7.1
Other OECD G20	3.71	7.1
Russian Federation	2.54	4.8
Japan	1.36	2.6
South Korea	1.24	2.4

Turkey	1.08	2.1
Indonesia	0.82	1.6
Canada	0.79	1.5
Brazil	0.77	1.5
South Africa	0.72	1.4
Mexico	0.71	1.4
Australia	0.63	1.2
Argentina	0.60	1.1
Saudi Arabia	0.38	0.7
Others	8.40	16.0
SECTORS		
Energy	35.87	68
Agriculture	6.47	12
International transport	1.36	3
Waste	2.90	6
Others	5.80	11

Source: Authors' own from PBL Netherlands Environmental Assessment Agency, 'Trends in mondiale uitstoot van CO_2 en alle broeikasgassen: 2020 rapport', https://www.pbl.nl/publicaties/trends-in-mondiale-uitstoot-van-co2-en-alle-broeikasgassen-2020-rapport (accessed 15 May 2021).

There is political controversy on the exact role that industries play in this phenomenon but the magnitude of the potential consequences is such that in 1992, following a UN assessment of climatic change published in 1990, 154 nations signed the UN Framework Convention on Climate Change in Rio de Janeiro, inciting members to adopt policies to reverse the trend. This led to the Tokyo Protocol of 1997, which provided binding commitments from industrialized countries to reduce their yearly emission of GHGs by 5 per cent between 2008 and 2020.[22] Since 1995, annual Conference of the Parties (COP) meetings have taken place. In 2009, there were high hopes for the Copenhagen meeting (COP15), where ambitious goals were proposed, but unfortunately no agreement could be found. At the meeting in Paris in 2015 (COP21), 195 governments agreed in principle to limit gas emissions so that the global temperature rise would be limited to 1.5 degrees Celsius above pre-industrial levels. As a consequence of the ratification of the treaty by many industrialized countries, companies in those countries are committed to implement reduction of CO_2 emissions.

One initiative conducive to the reduction of CO_2 is carbon trading through regulated market mechanisms. The most utilized market mechanisms are the *cap-and-trade* schemes, under which a regulatory body sets a limit (the cap) on the amount of CO_2 that companies are allowed to emit. Companies that emit more than their cap have to purchase credits from a company that has kept below the cap. Carbon credits can be traded in exchanges such as the European Union Emission Trading System (EU ETS) launched in 2005[23] (see Insert 4.1).

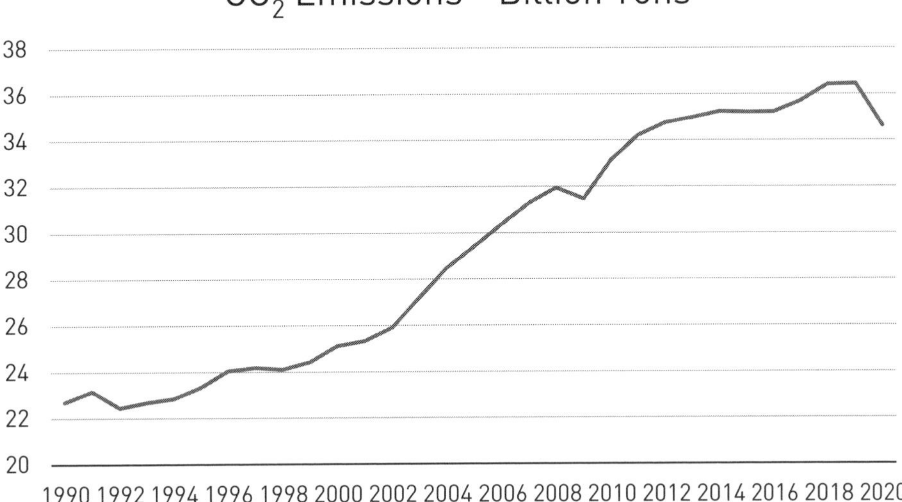

Figure 4.3 Total world GHG emissions

Source: GitHub, https://github.com/owid/co2-data (downloaded 15 May 2021).

Insert 4.1 The EU Emissions Trading Scheme (EU ETS)

The EU Emissions Trading Scheme (EU ETS)[24] is a cap-and-trade system in which participation is mandatory for businesses in the following sectors: energy production (power and heat generation), energy-intensive industries including oil refineries, steel works and production of iron, aluminium, metals, cement, lime, glass, ceramics, pulp, paper, cardboard, acids and bulk organic chemicals and aviation. Under the scheme individual industrial sites are granted an allowance (the EUA allowance) that gives the right to emit a certain level of CO_2. Companies that emit below the level of their allowance can sell their excess allowance at a market price (as shown in Figure 4.4). Companies that emit more than their allowance can buy an extra allowance on the market. Allowances are granted for each individual plant via a National Allocation Plan in each EU member state and approved by the Commission. It is mandatory for companies producing CO_2, NO_2 and perfluorocarbon (PFC) emissions to participate in the scheme. In 2020, the EU ETS market for CHG global emission of the twenty-eight European countries was valued at 201 billion euros for a volume of 8 billion tons with an average price of 25 €/T (Source: Refinitiv, https://www.refinitiv.com/content/dam/marketing/en_us/documents/reports/global-carbon-market-emission-trading-system-review-2019.pdf).

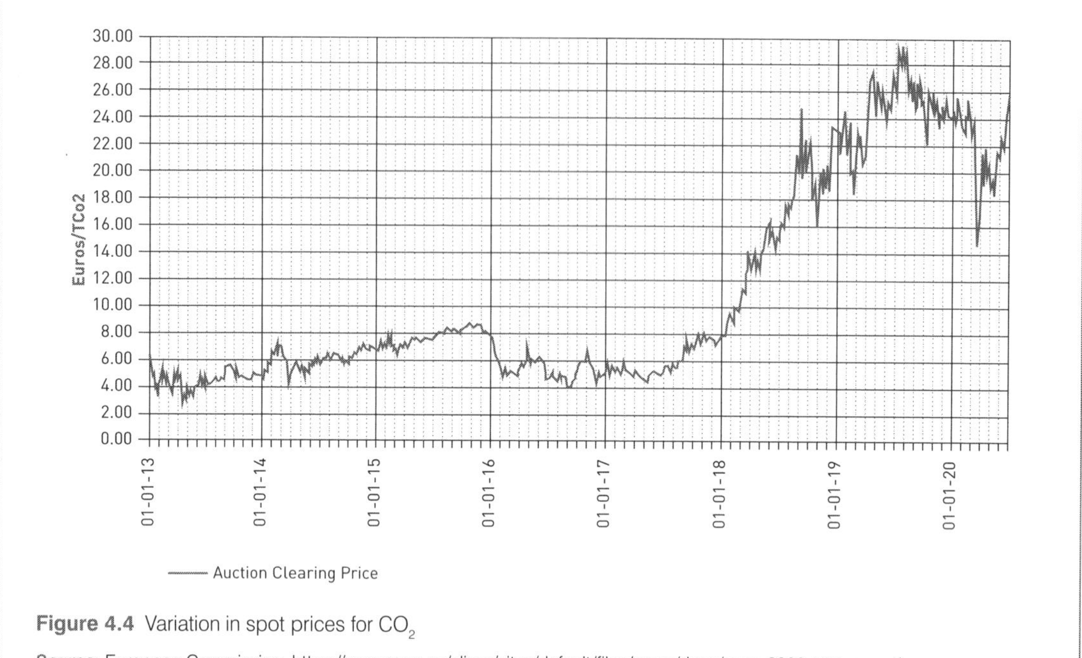

Figure 4.4 Variation in spot prices for CO_2

Source: European Commission, https://ec.europa.eu/clima/sites/default/files/news/docs/com_2020_740_en.pdf

Depletion of natural resources

Humanity currently needs the regenerative capacity of 1.5 earths to provide the ecological goods and services we use each year. This is because we 'cut trees faster than they mature, harvest more fish than the oceans can replenish, and emit more carbon […] than the forests and oceans can absorb'.[25] Table 4.3 shows some examples of the depletion of natural resources.

Table 4.3 Depletion of natural resources

Resource	Signs of depletion
Living species	The 2020 global LPI (Living Planet Index) shows an average 68 per cent decline in living species populations between 1970 and 2016.*
Fish	'Around 33% of all freshwater fish are threatened with extinction. Since 1970, the number of fishes that weigh over 66lbs—have declined by 94% and migratory freshwater fish by 76% .'**
Water	Over 2 billion people already live in areas subject to water stress. Some 3.4 billion people, 45 per cent of the global population, lack access to safely managed sanitation facilities. At the current rate, there will be a 40 per cent gap between global water supply and demand by 2030.***
Deforestation	Between 2015 and 2020, 10 million hectares of forest were converted to other uses every year (approximately the size of Iceland per year).****

Sources: * WWF 2021[26]; ** WWF 2021[27]; *** UNESCO (2021)[28]; **** UNEP 2021[29]

Waste production and disposal

According to UNEP (UN Environment Programme), 4 billion tons of municipal and industrial waste are produced every year. The global issues related to waste production and disposals are twofold:

1. It is the rich industrialized countries that are the major producers of waste that contains or exposes a lot of hazardous materials (municipal, construction material, dismantled electronics and computers, vessels, machinery, nuclear power residue), due to their high rate of consumption and lifestyles.
2. The disposal of this waste is very often delegated to the developing world. Because of their lack of financial resources and their hunger for international currencies, many developing countries are willing to accept waste that is not tolerated in the developed world.

Global firms and environmental issues

Multinational firms are often accused of being unresponsive or not sufficiently active on sustainable development issues regarding the environment[30] (see Mini-case 4.1 below).

MINI-CASE 4.1

Shell and Cosan

In June 2011, Royal Dutch Shell (usually known as Shell) and Cosan announced the start of operations at Raízen, a 50/50 joint venture to produce ethanol, sugar and electricity from sugar cane, as well as to distribute and market fuel. The Raízen operation started with 40,000 employees, and is among the five largest companies by revenue in Brazil, with a market value estimated at $12 billion, and producing and selling over 2 billion litres of ethanol a year. Shell indicates that turning sugar cane into ethanol offers a number of environmental benefits over other biofuel production processes. As it grows, sugar cane generally absorbs CO_2 at a greater rate than other biofuel crops such as soy.

In a press release, Shell stated: 'Ethanol made from Brazilian sugar cane produces around 70% less CO_2 than petrol and by-products from turning sugar cane into ethanol are recycled as organic fertiliser. Plant waste, called bagasse, is burned to produce power for the processing mills and surplus energy is supplied to the national grid.'

But critics of ethanol are also pinpointing its harmful effects on the environment and society. According to the Transnational Institute:

> sugarcane is grown as a monocrop, predominantly in southern and central Brazil as well as in parts of Asia and Africa. It relies on heavy quantities of inputs, particularly fertilizer. Harvesting is often done by hand, and working conditions are notoriously harsh. A number of studies in Brazil have shown that demand for land for sugarcane is leading to the conversion of grasslands and wooded savannah for crops, releasing stored carbon dioxide, and displacing previous users like cattle farmers

who move into tropical forests. Sugarcane also has devastating effects on biodiversity – with the Cerrado savannah of Central Brazil, where sugarcane is grown, being one of the world's most biodiverse and also most threatened habitats. Sugarcane expansion is also affecting Brazil's Atlantic Forest, and indirectly the Amazon, as cattle farmers move into the forest in the search for new pasture.

Sugarcane expansion may lead to land conflicts, as rural communities are forced off land to make way for the plantations. Small-scale farming has become unviable in the plantation areas and many small farmers feel they have no financial choice but to sell up. Sugar plantations are displacing small farms, food crops and subsistence food systems – leading to food shortages and price rises.[31]

Questions:

1 Imagine you are a socially responsible Shell shareholder. What is your view on the issue?
2 Shell has been criticized over environmental concerns and human rights in Africa, Europe and the USA. What can an energy company do to answer such criticisms?

Control of suppliers

Sustainable development does not stop at a firm's own national boundaries. Outsourcing across the world is a key feature of global firms and it is the responsibility of such firms to ensure that their foreign suppliers are engaged in sustainable development. This is particularly true in countries that are less demanding in terms of environmental and social protection. Often known as *green purchasing*, environmental preferable purchasing (EPP) consists of the selection and acquisition of products and services that minimize negative environmental impacts over their life cycle (through energy and water conservation, reduction of waste and pollutants, use of recycled materials, use of energy from renewable resources, use of alternatives to hazardous chemicals or components). It also demands that suppliers pursue human resource practices that prohibit the use of forced labour, child labour and workplace discrimination.

Green purchasing is adding sustainable issues to the classical price/performance criteria used in the evaluation of suppliers. It requires that the buyer audits and controls the fulfilment of these criteria, and it also requires suppliers to have appropriate training in the adoption of good practice in sustainable development.[32]

Eco-friendly capital investments

The IMF defines socially responsible investment as 'the incorporation of environmental, social, and governance (ESG) principles into business decisions, economic development, and investment strategies'[33] and it is estimated that by 2020, these investments reached $49.1 trillion in total assets.[34]

Figure 4.5 represents all the ecological factors that need to be taken into consideration when planning an industrial investment.

In the developing countries of Asia, Africa and Latin America, careful attention has to be given to:

a potential disruption in the ecosystem: deforestation, water requirements;

b potential disruption in the social and cultural environment;

c the appropriateness of the technology transfer with regard to the existing environment and capabilities.

Green management of resources

Agribusiness industries, forestry and pulp and paper, in particular, need to engage with deforestation and land depletion issues. The main sustainability problems associated with these industries are:

- soil erosion due to intensive agriculture;
- loss of rainforest due to deforestation;
- reduction of biodiversity;
- depletion of water resources;
- disruption of traditional farming.

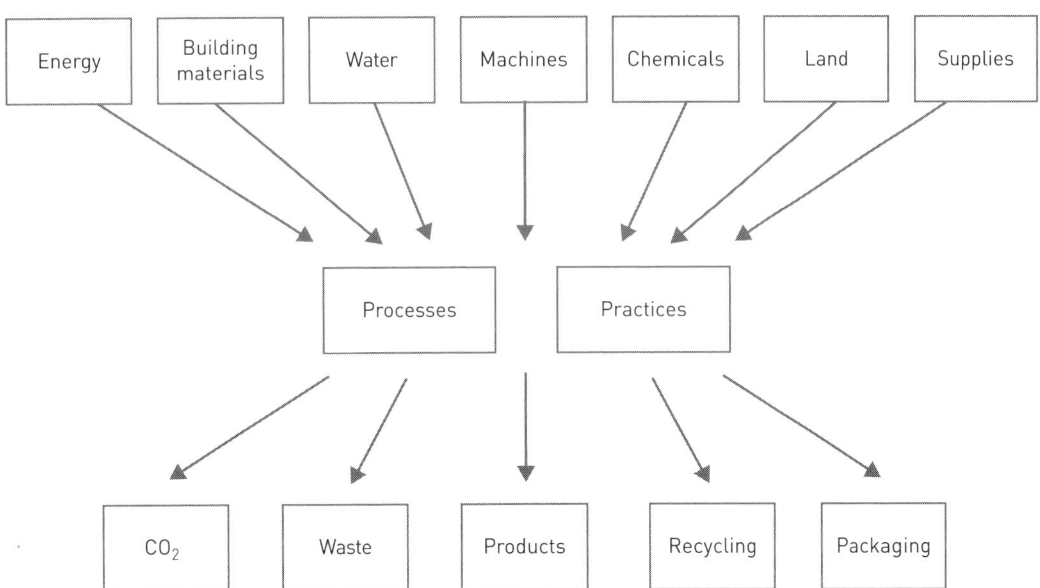

Figure 4.5 Ecological investment components

However, it was estimated by the Food and Agriculture Organization in 2009 that, due to population growth, global agriculture production would need to increase by at least 70 per cent by 2050.[35] Global firms engaged in agribusiness need to adopt practices that preserve bio-capacity.

Examples of such practices are:

- reforestation;
- adoption of agricultural techniques that reduce soil erosion and preserve water quality such as strip cropping, planting trees on croplands and adoption of agro-forestry systems.[36]

In addition to the measures mentioned earlier, firms engaged in environmentally problematic industries can implement a series of industry-specific eco-efficient actions. According to Holliday et al. and Lehni,[37] eco-efficiency can be improved in seven ways:

- reduction in material intensity
- reduction in energy intensity
- reduction in waste dispersion
- enhancement of recyclability
- maximum use of renewables
- extension of product durability
- increase of service intensity.

Globalization and societal issues

Societal issues encompass all activities that are relevant to the harmonious development of human societies. In the process of their globalization, firms may be involved directly or indirectly in practices that are disrupting societal well-being. Those practices can be classified in three categories:

- corruption and bribery
- human dignity
- financial malpractice.

The remainder of this section will be devoted to one of the most predominant and worrying ethical issues in global business: the practice and effects of corruption and bribery.

Corruption and bribery

According to the OECD, 'estimates show that the cost of corruption equals more than 5% of global GDP (US$ 2.6 trillion) with over US$ 1 trillion paid in bribes each year'.[38] Overall, corruption distorts market mechanisms, allocates resources to non-optimal projects and increases the cost of doing business by 10 per cent. Corruption is therefore considered to be one of the main global business issues.

Corruption can be simply defined as 'the abuse of entrusted power for private gain'.[39] This definition applies to public officials as well as employees of private companies who receive personal gain (a *bribe*) in the form of cash or other benefit (such as a car, family travel or the employment of a relative) and, in return, give a preferential advantage to the donor. Transparency International (TI) regularly publishes one index: the Corruption Perceptions Index (CPI) – see p. 132 for more about TI. The CPI is a score that relates the perceptions of corruption in the public sector in different countries as seen by businesses, academics and risk analysts. It represents a compilation of different surveys. Transparency International used to publish the Bribe Paying Index (BPI) that ranked the leading exporting countries in terms of the degree to which their companies are perceived to be paying bribes abroad. This BPI has not been published since 2011 but is reported in Table 4.4.

Table 4.4 gives the 2020 CPI and the BPI for 2011.

The chairperson of Transparency International, in the brochure presenting the 2020 index, declared that 'COVID-19 is not just a health and economic crisis. It's a corruption crisis. And one that we're currently failing to manage.'[40]

In 2015, their statement was: 'The 2015 Corruption Perceptions Index clearly shows that corruption remains a blight around the world. But 2015 was also a year when people again took to the streets to protest corruption.'[41]

The industries in which corruption is most acute are: public works contracts and construction, arms and defence, power (including petroleum and energy), mining, telecoms, aerospace and banking. Although the practice of corruption is not limited to global enterprises, their visibility and power give them particular responsibility to, as well as a greater impact on, the societies in which they operate. Corruption tends to be more prevalent in developing countries. As Figure 4.6 shows, there is a positive correlation between GDP per capita and the CPI. Countries that formerly had a planned economy score lower on the scale.

There is vigorous debate about the exact limits of corruption, its origin, its real effects and its practice.

Table 4.4 Corruption indices including rankings

Corruption Perceptions Index 2020 *0 = High level of corruption* *100 = Low level of corruption*			Bribe Payers Index 2011 *0 = High level of paying bribes* *10 = Low level of paying bribes*		
Low corruption			Low propensity to bribe		
1	Denmark	88	1	Netherlands	8.8
1	New Zealand	88	1	Switzerland	8.8
3	Finland	85	3	Belgium	8.7
4	Singapore	85	4	Germany	8.6
4	Sweden	85	4	Japan	8.6

4	Switzerland	85	6	Australia	8.5
7	Norway	84	6	Canada	8.5
8	Netherlands	82	8	Singapore	8.3
9	Germany	80	8	UK	8.3
9	Luxembourg	80	10	USA	8.3
10	Australia	77			
	High corruption			**High propensity to bribe**	
170	Democratic Republic Congo	16	19	Taiwan	7.5
170	Haiti	15	19	India	7.5
170	North Korea	13	22	Turkey	7.5
173	Libya	12	23	Saudi Arabia	7.4
174	Equatorial Guinea	9	23	Argentina	7.3
174	Sudan	1.5	25	UAE	7.3
176	Venezuela	1.5	26	Indonesia	7.1
176	Yemen	1.2	27	Mexico	7
178	Syria	1.1	28	China	6.5
179	Somalia	0.8	29	Russia	6.1
179	South Sudan	0.8			

Source: Transparency International Corruption Perceptions Index 2020.

When gifts become bribes, where does corruption start?

It is standard practice in some countries to offer gifts as recognition of friendship and relationships.[42] The dividing line between a bribe and a gift is frequently ambiguous, but the general rule would be to consider as a gift any present offered openly whose content can be disclosed in the person's professional and social environment. Gifts can also be offered to communities (school sponsorship, donation to communities, etc.), the rule still being that it be openly offered. Beyond the frontiers of transparency, the land of bribery begins.

In the USA the Foreign Corrupt Practices Act of 1977 that exposes American executives to criminal sanctions strictly forbids bribery. Such legislation does not exist in other countries, although the Convention on Combating Bribery of Foreign Public Officials in International Business Transactions, adopted by the OECD on 21 November 1997, has been ratified by thirty-four OECD countries and seven non-OECD members. This convention prohibits the use of bribes, states that criminal sanctions should be applied to the persons engaged in bribery and recommends that tax deductibility of bribes not be permitted.[43] The OECD Convention, however, has a lower dissuasive power than the American Foreign Corrupt Practices Act.

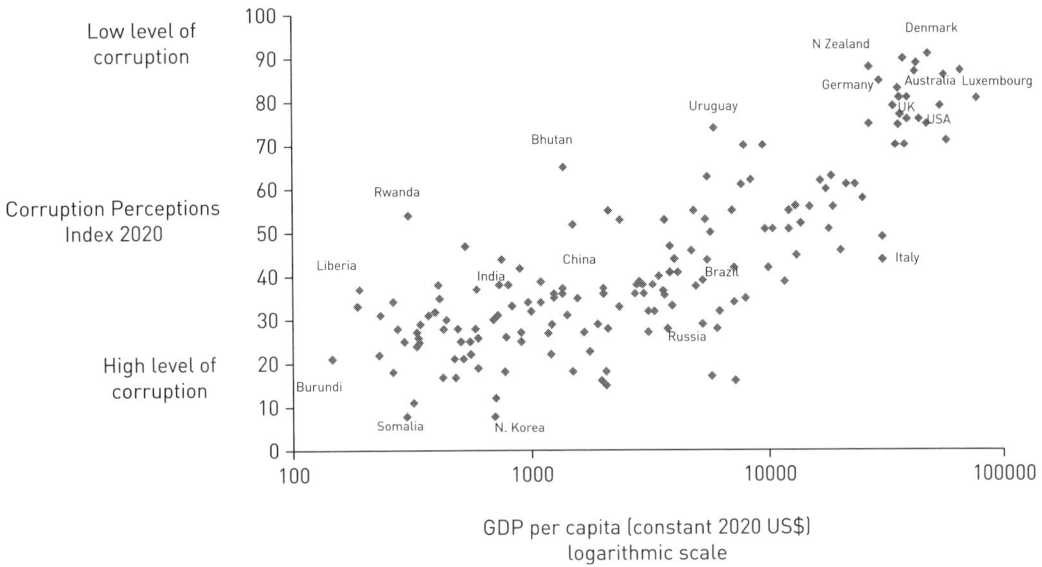

Figure 4.6 Corruption and development

Sources: Authors' own construction. Data from Transparency International Corruption Perceptions Index 2020 and World Bank Development Indicators, https://datatopics.worldbank.org/world-development-indicators/.

Causes and effects of corruption

The causes of corruption are diverse,[44] and belong to five main categories:

1. **Administrative resource allocation:** the substitution of transparent market mechanisms by administrative authorization and distribution. Price controls, multiple exchange rates, subsidies and administrative authorizations granted without competitive bidding are mechanisms that induce corruption.
2. **Lack of institutional checks and balances and information:** absent or powerless public audit, single source of power without right of appeal, cowed legal system and media.
3. **Insufficient funding of public services:** leading to low remuneration of public officials relative to private sector, lack of proper financing of political parties or under-supply of public goods for hospitals, transport and schools.
4. **Social and cultural factors:** such as a societal division along ethnic and linguistic lines leading to nepotism.
5. **Natural resources:** abundant natural resources are also an incentive for bribery.[45]

Several studies converge to demonstrate the adverse effects of corruption on the economy.[46] The effects are both direct and indirect.

Direct effects

We can list three in particular:

a It *discourages domestic and foreign indirect investment (FDI)* because of the additional cost burden on projects: it amounts to another *hidden tax*. In 1998, it was estimated that if India could reduce its corruption level to that of Singapore, the effect on foreign investment would be the same as reducing the corporate tax rate by 22 per cent.[47] Corruption thus hampers economic growth. In 2018, the Secretary-General of the United Nations indicated that the global cost of corruption was at least 5 per cent of world GDP.[48]

b It *skews public capital expenditure* in favour of new equipment as opposed to maintenance and operational expenditure. It also discriminates against educational and health expenditure that is less amenable to bribery.

c It *reduces the productivity of public investments* and reduces the *collection of taxes*.

Indirect effects

The most common are:

a *Reduction in work productivity* as a result of demotivation.

b *Dislocation of social fabric.*

c *Loss of integrity* inside the bribe-giving companies: employees may feel authorized to benefit from corrupt practices for themselves.

d Corruption money is often *linked to criminal and terrorist activities*.

Although some economists have argued that corruption facilitates transactions in inefficient markets and therefore is a form of 'grease, speeding the wheels of commerce',[49] the negative effects are overwhelmingly dominant.

The practice of corruption and the role of global companies

Many companies, despite the damaging economic and social effects, engage in bribery to obtain contracts. Companies coming from countries that are themselves 'immune' from corrupt practices bribe officials or executives from other countries. This paradoxical behaviour[50] is attributed to competitive necessities ('If I don't my competitor will, and my shareholders and employees will lose out') as well as cultural justifications (see Mini-case 4.2). Performance and rewards systems that focus entirely on economic achievements also tempt local managers to engage in corrupt practices in order to 'make the figures', even in corporations that officially assert a global code of ethics.

MINI-CASE 4.2

Jack Cumberland

Jack Cumberland was the Managing Director of IndoMedia, a leading advertising agency in [the fictional Southeast-Asian country] Indoland. IndoMedia was formed as a joint venture between EuroMedia from the UK and a local entrepreneur. Jack, born in Scotland in 1975, joined Procter & Gamble as a junior brand manager after graduating from London University Business School in 1998. Six years later he was recruited by EuroMedia. He was attached to a client group in London for five years, then moved to Spain for four years and finally was named Managing Director of IndoMedia.

IndoMedia had a good reputation in Indoland as a very creative agency that was well connected to the media. It also had the reputation of being reliable in a country where media charges could be discounted by up to 60 per cent from the 'official' rate. Most agencies charged the 'official' rate to their clients and pocketed the discount for themselves. IndoMedia charged only a 20 per cent commission on top of the discounted rate, giving them a competitive advantage over other agencies despite the fact that its artwork charge was higher. For printing jobs, quotations were requested from at least three competitors in order to obtain the best price.

A few months after his appointment, Jack was approached by Eddy, a representative of a big printing company in Indoland. Eddy was very upset because he saw the volume of his business with IndoMedia declining although his work was of the highest price/quality ratio. He mentioned that IndoMedia's manager in charge of buying print jobs, Omar, was asking that the quotation include 'not only the usual 10 per cent, but then it was 15 per cent and recently 25 per cent' to be paid as soon as the printer received the money from the agency.

Jack asked Eddy if he was ready to repeat his allegations in front of Omar. The answer was immediate: 'No way, It would kill my business', Eddy replied, and walked away.

Later Jack talked to Andreas, the Finance Director, a man of experience and wisdom. Jack became angrier as he was talking. But Andreas was smiling and finally, when Jack stopped talking, Andreas asked him: 'Haven't you realized that you work in Indoland?'

Questions:

1 What options does Jack have in this situation?

2 What do you think that he should do?

Source: Adapted from Schütte (1986).

As a result, many global firms implicitly put their managers in a conflictual position.[51] The distribution of bribes is often delegated to a third party such as an agent or a joint venture partner.

In the late 1990s, some firms, as well as private and public international institutions, created platforms to fight against corruption and introduce practical codes of conduct within global firms. In addition to the OECD Convention on Combating Bribery of Foreign Public Officials in International Business Transactions, and the US Foreign Corrupt Practices Act mentioned earlier, the most prominent private, non-governmental organization is Transparency International, whose corruption and bribery indices we covered on p. 127.[52]

Transparency International (TI) is an international NGO based in London with national chapters in seventy-seven countries. Its stated mission is 'to curb corruption by mobilising a global coalition to promote and strengthen international and national integrity systems'. TI's activities consist of distributing information about corrupt practices and ways to fight against them and it has also launched an annual awards programme to honour individuals and organizations around the globe that are making a difference in ending corruption. The goal is to give greater recognition to the efforts of journalists, civil society workers, activists, government and corporate whistleblowers who work to investigate and unmask corruption, often at great personal risk. The Integrity Awards also seek to encourage those whose example provides leadership in the global anti-corruption effort. TI publishes a Global Corruption Report as well as the CPI and BPI. It gives free access to a Corruption On-Line Research and Information System and its national chapters implement a large variety of activities to inform about and fight against corruption. TI has published thirty-two lessons that constitute a source of inspiration and guide for action.[53] Table 4.5 gives five examples of corruption involving companies from countries that have a high score on the CPI index and Table 4.6 gives a checklist of the most common measures that governments and companies can take to fight corruption.

Table 4.5 Five corruption cases from 'clean' countries

Corporations involved (country of origin)	Case	Countries involved
Airbus (France)	In February 2020, the European manufacturer of civilian and military aircraft agreed to pay nearly $4 billion in combined penalties to the US, France and UK to resolve foreign bribery charges.	Taiwan Malaysia Indonesia Sri Lanka Ghana
Semlex (Belgium)	Semlex, a Belgian company that manufactures passports, licences and other biometric documents, is currently embroiled in a long-running corruption and money-laundering investigation involving several countries in Africa, including DRC and Madagascar. The company is also linked to investigations in Kyrgyzstan and stands accused of arming the Côte d'Ivoire civil war in 2010.	Democratic Republic of Congo Madagascar Kyrgyzstan Ivory Coast
Gunvor (Switzerland)	In 2019, a commodities trading company was condemned by Swiss authorities to pay approximately $96.7 million for failing to put adequate measures in place to prevent the bribery of foreign government officials in Cote d'Ivoire and the Republic of Congo in exchange for lucrative oil deals.	Cyprus Ivory Coast

Bombardier (Canada)	One of the world's leading plane and train manufacturers based in Canada was under investigation in 2020 for foreign bribery in Indonesia, only a few years after similar charges of foreign bribery were brought against the Swedish branch of the company in Azerbaijan.	Azerbaijan Indonesia
San Faustin (Luxembourg)	San Faustin, a financial holding company in Brazil, for foreign bribery and money laundering.	Argentina Italy Brazil

Source: Transparency International(2020), https://images.transparencycdn.org/images/CPI2020_Report_EN_0802-WEB-1_2021-02-08-103053.pdf (accessed 15 May 2021).

Table 4.6 A checklist of anti-corruption measures

Public sector
Transparency • Provide an adequate degree of transparency in the entire procurement cycle in order to promote fair and equitable treatment for potential suppliers. • Maximize transparency in competitive tendering and take precautionary measures to enhance integrity, in particular for exceptions to competitive tendering.
Good management • Ensure that public funds are used in public procurement according to the purposes intended. • Ensure that procurement officials meet high professional standards of knowledge, skills and integrity.
Prevention of misconduct, compliance and monitoring • Put mechanisms in place to prevent risks to integrity in public procurement. • Encourage close cooperation between government and the private sector in order to maintain high standards of integrity, particularly in contract management. • Provide specific mechanisms to monitor public procurement as well as to detect misconduct, and apply sanctions accordingly.
Accountability and control • Establish a clear chain of responsibility together with effective control mechanisms. • Handle complaints from potential suppliers in a fair and timely manner. • Empower civil society organizations, media and the wider public to scrutinize public procurement.
Private sector
• Strong, explicit and visible support and commitment from senior management to the company's internal controls, ethics and compliance programmes or measures for preventing and detecting foreign bribery. • A clearly articulated and visible corporate policy prohibiting foreign bribery. • Compliance with this prohibition and the related internal controls, ethics and compliance programmes is the duty of individuals at all levels of the company. • Oversight of ethics and compliance programmes or measures regarding foreign bribery. • Ethics and compliance programmes designed to prevent and detect foreign bribery, applicable to all directors, officers and employees, including subsidiaries, and to third parties such as agents and other intermediaries, consultants, representatives, distributors, contractors and suppliers, consortia, and joint venture partners.

Public sector

- A system of financial and accounting procedures, including a system of internal controls, reasonably designed to ensure that accounts cannot be used for the purpose of foreign bribery or hiding such bribery.
- Ensure periodic communication and documented training for all levels of the company on measures regarding foreign bribery.
- Appropriate measures to encourage and provide positive support for the observance of ethics.
- Appropriate disciplinary procedures to address, among other things, violations, at all levels of the company, of laws against foreign bribery, and the company's ethics and compliance programme or measures regarding foreign bribery.
- Effective measures for: a) providing guidance and advice to directors, officers, employees and, where appropriate, business partners on complying with the company's ethics and compliance programmes; b) the protection of employees willing to report breaches of the law or professional standards or ethics occurring within the company, and undertaking appropriate action in response to such reports.
- Periodic reviews of the ethics and compliance programmes and improvements to their effectiveness in preventing and detecting foreign bribery.

Sources: Public sector – OECD (2008); Private sector – OECD (2009).

Other anti-corruption initiatives

Other organizations have issued guidelines and regulations to prevent corrupt practices:

- The **UN General Assembly** in 1996 adopted a *Declaration against Corruption and Bribery.*
- The **International Chambers of Commerce** in 1977 issued the *Rules of Conduct on Bribery.*
- The **World Bank** in 1995 issued *procurement guidelines* in order to prevent corruption in projects financed by the Bank.
- The **Council of Europe** in 1994 created a Multidisciplinary Group on Corruption. In 1997 it issued the *Guiding Principles for the Fight against Corruption* and in 1999 a *Criminal Law Convention on Corruption.*
- The **Caux Round Table**, founded in 1986, is a network of senior business leaders from both the industrialized and the developing nations that recognize that business must take a leadership role in developing a more fair, free and transparent society, leading to greater world prosperity and sustainability of resources.

Despite all these efforts, there is still a long way to go before bribery disappears, but global firms and global executives are under increasing public scrutiny and the most progressive firms have made considerable progress in the implementation of ethical behaviour.

Human dignity

Global executives are often confronted with the issue of procuring components, materials or services in countries that do not respect labour practices that are illegal in the developed world, though are sometimes considered normal. The most significant are the utilization of school-aged children as workers, unacceptable working hours and working conditions, forced labour, the exploitation of legal and illegal immigrants and the obstruction or elimination of trade unions. Other issues are linked to the activities of global companies in countries where human rights are not protected and abuses occur, such as forced labour, arbitrary detention of trade unionists and political opponents and repression against ethnic or religious minorities. In such cases multinational companies stand accused of complicity with the government or at least of indirectly benefitting from those practices.

Child labour

Child labour has become a globalized issue and the one that provokes a typical ethical dilemma. In a thought-provoking article, Martha Nichols (1993) explained the dilemma of choosing between respecting a code of ethics and cancelling an order to a supplier employing young children, and therefore accepting the consequences of depriving their families of much-needed income and putting the children back on the street, or accepting the order knowing that children are working to fulfil it.[54] According to UNICEF, 'about 168 million children aged 5 to 17 are engaged in child labor accounting for almost 11 per cent of all children'.[55] According to the International Labour Organization (ILO) in 2017 'out of the 168 million children worldwide that are engaged in child labour, 85 million at least, are in hazardous work',[56] although a steady decline of those numbers has been observed since 2000. Around 70 per cent of children work in agriculture and many work in dangerous conditions (mines, working with chemicals and pesticides or dangerous machinery). Girls are found to be exploited as household help. They are everywhere but invisible, toiling as domestic servants in homes, labouring behind the walls of workshops, hidden from view in plantations. Quoting UNICEF again: 'Some of them are trafficked (1.2 million), forced into debt bondage or other forms of slavery (5.7 million), into prostitution and pornography (1.8 million), into participating in armed conflict (0.3 million) or other illicit activities (0.6 million).'[57] The main domain in which multinational companies can be indirectly involved in child labour is in procurement from companies that use children as a labour force. Mass retailing companies with their billion dollar purchases of goods from the developing world are often confronted with this issue. In a 2018 report the US Department of Labors (ILAB) provided a list of countries and the respective commodities that are using child labour, as well as the list of the involved commodities.[58] Global firms are not generally involved directly in child labour in their production centres but indirectly through subcontractors or suppliers. Neither UNICEF nor the Department of Labor publish a list of such firms but a certain number of claims by NGOs such as Amnesty International or Human Rights Watch have mentioned some global firms whose suppliers use child labour, mainly in the three sectors mentioned earlier. Most of the shamed firms have taken measures to modify their sourcing process but the tracking of the long chain of supply makes the exercise difficult.

EXAMPLE 4.2 Child labour and the global firm

Soccer balls (Sialkot and Reebok)

By the mid-1990s, Sialkot, located in the Punjab province of Pakistan, was the centre for the production of customized, high-quality sporting goods and surgical equipment: 25,000 workers were involved in these activities. The production and export of 35 million soccer balls accounted for $45 million in 1995. Since the stitching of soccer balls is labour-intensive, children were used to perform this task. In Pakistan, it was estimated that 3.6 million children were employed as labourers; one-third earning wages, the remaining children being engaged as family helpers for agricultural tasks.

In the mid-1990s, child labour cases were brought to public notice via television reports and news magazines, and this drew attention to soccer ball production. Reebok, a leading sporting goods global firm, implemented its own policy in order to abolish child labour. Reebok's policy was 1) to buy finished goods from a child labour-free factory so stitching was taken out of the home; 2) to set up a monitoring programme; and 3) to start an educational programme. David Husselbee, Programme Director of Save the Children Fund's UK office, came to Sialkot and facilitated dialogue between the industry and the ILO. This resulted in the Sialkot Partnership to End Child Labour, which led to an agreement with the Sporting Goods Manufacturers' Association in Atlanta in 1997. The Atlanta Agreement stated that:

- Stitching centres were to be established which would bring the work out of households
- Workers would be systematically registered in order to check their age
- Alternative educational programmes would be created for children
- Rewards, warnings and penalties were set up to encourage vendors not to use child labour
- Members of the World Federation of Sporting Goods would favour vendors that did not use child labour.

The programme was a success from the point of view of child labour in the soccer ball industry, but it had some indirect negative effects. For example, by taking the work out of the household, it also prevented Punjabi women for doing these jobs because they could not work in the factory for religious reasons. Furthermore, other industries were still employing children and so some of the children who left stitching moved to more hazardous or arduous work, such as carpet-making or in brickworks.

Source: Crawford et al. (1999).

Human rights

With regard to **human rights**, global corporations are often confronted with their direct or indirect complicity in all sorts of abuses. This happens when global firms operate in countries whose political regimes use methods of enforcement that do not respect the principles of the Universal Declaration of Human Rights (UDHR) as adopted by the United Nations. These prohibitions include arbitrary detention, execution of political dissidents, non-respect of legal procedures for trials of opponents, deportation of population, use of military force to quell civilian unrest, rape or torture by security forces or by factions in civil wars and so on. Global firms can be involved directly, when human rights abuses are committed to protect their operations, or indirectly, when their activities contribute to maintaining political regimes involved in human rights abuse. Insert 4.2 gives an example of global firms being criticized for association with human rights abuses.

Insert 4.2 Global firms and human rights

Oil companies in Myanmar

Unocal and its partner, Total of France, are building a natural gas pipeline (the Yadana project) from the Andaman Sea through the rainforests of southern Myanmar into Thailand. This represents the country's largest foreign investment. The pipeline has become the target of intense lobbying by international human rights groups. Groups who oppose Unocal's investment in Myanmar filed lawsuits against Unocal in the USA and Total in France in order to link this investment to forced labour and human right abuses committed by the Myanmar military. Both Unocal and Total settled the case by compensating people who were subjected to forced labour by the military without admitting any culpability.

Source: Hennebel (2006).

In 2000, Pierre Sane, the then General Secretary of Amnesty International, pinpointed five reasons why business should care about human rights.

1 The moral argument:

We do not need to convince managers and boardrooms that the amputation of children's limbs in Sierra Leone in order to terrorize a population and win a war is wrong, or that the gang rape of women by Serb soldiers in Kosovo is evil, or that the killing of civilians in East Timor or Chechnya is to be condemned. These acts are wrong, invidious. They have been prohibited internationally.

2 The legitimacy argument:

Human rights have been codified in treaties ratified by governments. People around the world are struggling to hold their governments accountable for the implementation of international law.

3 The self-interest argument:

I believe it is in the interest of business to see human rights protected. The rule of law protects investments by guaranteeing political stability. An educated and healthy population increases economic productivity. A company tarnished by controversies around human rights violations can see its reputation destroyed and its profitability threatened.

4 The responsibility argument:

Companies, and more specifically, multinational corporations, have secured for themselves freedoms to operate which have given them enormous power to affect the lives of people, but with power comes responsibility.

5 The universal argument:

The Universal Declaration of Human Rights (UDHR) calls upon all organs of society to protect and promote human rights. The ILO conventions protect the rights of the workers. Other conventions place direct responsibility on companies to act in accordance with international human rights law.[59]

Amnesty International proposes a checklist of conduct principles for global firms to adopt (see Insert 4.3).

Insert 4.3 Human rights principles for companies: a checklist

Non-discrimination

Businesses are required not to discriminate on grounds unrelated to the job (for example, race, colour, sex, language, religion or political opinion) but to promote equal opportunities.

Protection of civilians and laws of war

Businesses will have to ensure that they do not aid or abet human rights violations, nor benefit from war crimes such as plunder and pillage, crimes against humanity, genocide, torture, forced labour, hostage-taking or other violations of international human rights or humanitarian law.

Use of security forces

Businesses using security forces should establish policies to: ensure that security-related *employees or contractors* are not known human rights violators; provide adequate training in human rights procedures to security forces; and incorporate human rights obligations in security contracts.

Workers' rights

The UN Norms and Commentary reiterate, on the one hand, the prohibitions against the use of forced or compulsory labour, and against exploitation of children. On the other hand, businesses should follow mandates for safe and healthy working conditions, remuneration that ensures an adequate standard of living, freedom of association and the right to collective bargaining.

Corruption, consumer protection and human rights

Businesses should not engage in corruption of governmental officials and should use fair and honest business practices according to consumer protection laws and standards; this includes a duty to refrain from producing or marketing harmful or even potentially harmful products.

Economic, social and cultural rights

Businesses should respect all human rights, and contribute to their realization. They should do what they can 'within their respective spheres of activity and influence' to uphold the rights to adequate food, drinking water, the highest attainable standard of physical and mental health, housing and education. They also forthrightly support the right to development and the rights of indigenous peoples.

Human rights and the environment

Businesses are obliged to comply with international and national laws, policies and regulations on preserving the environment. This includes complying with the precautionary principle and conducting their activities so as to contribute to the wider goal of sustainable development.

Indigenous peoples' rights

Companies should respect the principle of free, prior and informed consent of communities to be affected by development projects.

As a consequence it is recommend that companies and business associations should:

- Adopt, disseminate and implement a code of conduct which complies with the UN Human Rights Norms for Business.
- Prepare and implement operational guidelines to apply the UN Human Rights Norms for Business.
- Apply the UN Human Rights Norms for Business in contracts and other dealings with contractors, sub-contractors and any other associates.
- Organize training seminars and workshops for staff and facilitate similar events with associates and within industry associations to raise awareness of the UN Human Rights Norms for Business.

Source: Amnesty International (2004) (reproduced with permission).

Financial malpractice

Financial malpractice in a global context refers to the ability of global corporations to use their multinational presence to deprive states of their normal share of taxes through tax evasion. It also concerns their ability to interfere in local politics through the sponsoring of 'friendly' political parties or movements, and in some cases even helping provoke the overthrow of 'unhelpful' governments.

Tax evasion

Tax evasion is the practice of artificially shifting profits from high-taxation countries to low-taxation countries (whereby taxable income is generated in the former but transferred for reporting and taxation purposes to a local subsidiary in the latter). In the USA, it is estimated that hundreds of billions of dollars are lost in tax revenues.[60] This can be achieved by inflated interest on loans provided to a local subsidiary or via inflated transfer pricing. Another method is to harbour profits in tax havens in order to avoid paying taxes in the home country. In that respect, tax havens play a major role in facilitating tax evasion.[61] Contractor has identified seven methods of tax avoidance by multinational companies:[62]

- Exemption/deferral: not remitting profit from subsidiaries;
- Transfer pricing: high price in high-tax country;

- Royalties payments: overcharging in high-tax country;
- Intracorporate loans manipulating interests between affiliated companies;
- Charging overheads;
- Round tripping: using tax havens;
- Shifting corporate office to a low-tax country using an acquired company in that country.

Figure 4.7 demonstrates these methods of tax avoidance using a fictitious example.

The OECD's 132 member states have implemented the recommendations of the Global Forum on Transparency and Exchange of Information for Tax Purposes.[63] The European Union established in 2016 an Anti-Tax Avoidance Package to coordinate member countries' efforts to prevent tax evasion; a difficult undertaking given the disparity of corporate taxes among members.[64]

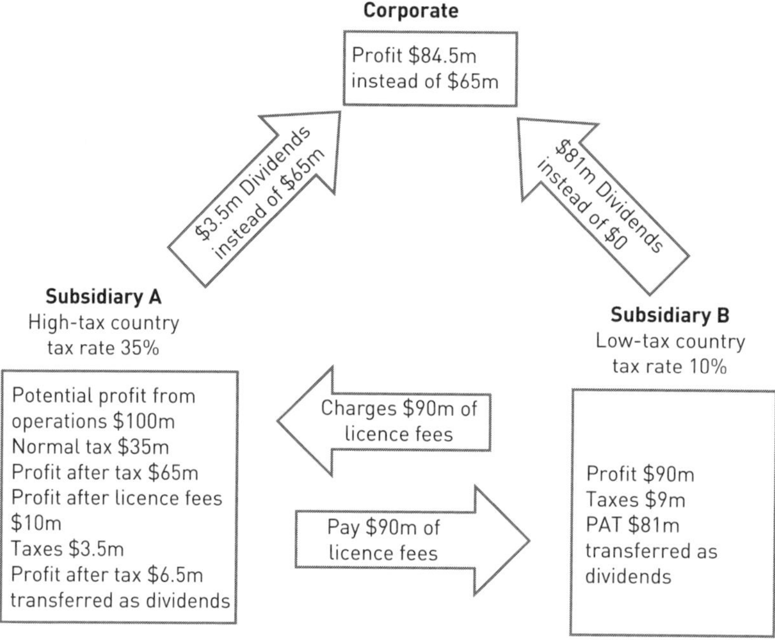

Figure 4.7 Example of tax evasion

Political financing

Another concern that has often been expressed about some multinational companies is their interference in internal politics and the promotion of legislation designed to protect their interests. This can be a case of directly financing a political opposition party in order to remove a government. It can also take the form of intensive lobbying in order to change unfavourable legislation or promote the sponsoring of biased research programmes. The oil and gas, mining, agro-chemicals, pharmaceuticals and tobacco industries have been particularly involved in the past in such practices.

Lobbying activities are not in themselves illegal, as long as there is a certain level of transparency in the activities of the lobbyists.[65] It is estimated that there are 30,000 registered lobbyists at the European Commission in Brussels.

Global corporations' ethics and corporate social responsibility

Business ethics has been defined as 'how a company integrates core values such as honesty, trust, respect and fairness into its policies, practices and decision-making'.[66] It encompasses issues of conflicts of interests, financial and accounting integrity, corruption and bribery, ethical advertising, bio-ethics and employee privacy. These issues are not specific to international business but the differences in legislation, cultures and practices make the implementation of ethical behaviour more subject to what is known as an 'ethical dilemma'.[67] 'Ethical dilemma' describes the moral conflicts that occur when making a morally right choice that may generate a bad outcome or when making a morally wrong choice that may result in a good outcome. For instance, terminating the contract to a supplier who employs children is an example of making a morally right choice that may result in a bad outcome: the loss of income to poor families. Paying a bribe to buy back the freedom of prostitutes is a morally wrong choice that may result in a good outcome. It has been argued that, despite a strong temptation to postpone or shelve those difficult decisions, the resolution of ethical dilemma is the responsibility of business managers who need to be guided by the key principle of transparency. According to Sir Adrian Cadbury, 'actions are unethical if they don't stand scrutiny'.[68]

Business ethics as a moral obligation has led to the development of the corporate social responsibility (CSR) movement, defined as 'the obligations of firms to society or more specifically to those affected by corporate policies and practices'.[69] CSR is not new, although for a long time dealing with social issues was left to the conscience of individuals, to religious sermons[70] or to legislators. However, since the 1960s, a series of events (see Insert 4.5) have generated a vast global public opinion movement that has questioned the role of multinational corporations (MNCs) with respect to the environment and social matters, and pushed corporations to enforce policies and communicate their practices with regard to their responsibilities in those domains. The need for communication has led to the development of social reporting. Today, environmental, ethical and social issues are considered to be near the top of the list of corporate concerns and they engage a multiplicity of organizations that interact to form an 'ethical web', as described in Figure 4.8.

An ongoing debate

In 1970, Milton Friedman wrote an article in the *New York Times* entitled 'The social responsibility of business is to increase its profits',[71] in which he claimed first that only individuals can have responsibilities and second that it is not the responsibility of business executives to spend shareholders' money on tasks that are elected legislators' duties. This extreme line of thinking has been strongly challenged on philosophical grounds as well as practical ones. Today it is well established that 'the debate is no longer whether to make substantial commitments to corporate social responsibility, but how'.[72] For some, being

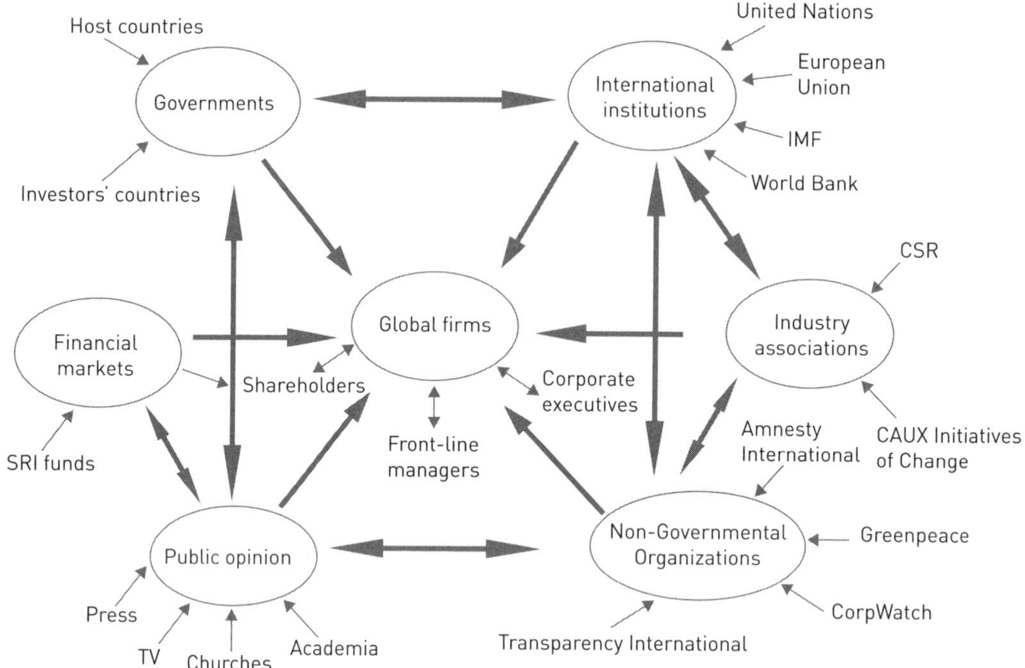

Figure 4.8 The global ethical web

Note: The list of organizations shown here is not exhaustive.

Insert 4.4 Doing well by doing good

Some academic studies suggest that ethically and socially responsible behaviour and investment by corporations is not an economic losing proposition, and is often associated with profitability. The causality is not direct and not necessarily visible in the short term. It requires the corporation to consider that, beside shareholders, external stakeholders play an important role in the well-being of the enterprise. It also means that the incentive systems motivate employees to behave with a socially responsible view.

The opponents to that view point out that such an approach is a defensive one that does not contribute to profit but instead avoids loss. Given the negative image attached to misconduct and the loss of sales or investment that may ensue, companies can be better off by being seen to address some significant sustainable development issues such as protection of human rights, environmental protection or anti-corruption measures.

responsible is a good value proposition (see Insert 4.4, 'Doing well by doing good') and, for others, it is a hypocritical application of self-interest. Although CSR seems now to be well accepted, there are still some companies that deny the responsibility of corporations on certain ecological or social issues such as global warming or free licensing of medical treatment for AIDS in the developing world. Hypocritical behaviour is also experienced by managers who 'feel strong organisational pressure to do things that they believe are sleazy, unethical and sometimes illegal',[73] despite the fact that officially their company adopts a socially responsible position. With the increasing globalization of the world and the variety of ethical dilemmas faced, as well as increasingly global ecological and social issues, multinational firms have been forced, willingly or not, to confront their responsibility in some areas (see Table 4.1). Since the 1970s, CSR has increasingly been on the agenda of business leaders, governments and international institutions.[74]

Global companies and business ethics

Global corporations as global citizens

Corporate social responsibility is not limited to restrictive practices of corruption, environmental protection or human dignity: those are the don'ts of global management behaviour. There are more positive aspects of doing business internationally: the dos that encompass the contributions to economic, social, technological and human development in the country in which the global firm operates. This is what is called 'global citizenship'. There is no accepted definition of global citizenship but, according to Hewlett-Packard (which has appointed a Senior Vice President for Corporate Affairs and Global Citizenship since 2005), it represents a commitment to 'Conducting business with uncompromising integrity, to engage with a variety of external stakeholders – from local communities to the United Nations, to provide resources to improve access to technology and educational opportunities, to develop products and

Insert 4.5 What sparked the corporate responsibility movement

- In the 1970s, the campaign against apartheid imposed a boycott of British and US banks which lent money to South Africa.
- In February 1976, a Lockheed executive revealed that the company had paid bribes to Japanese government officials to buy its aircraft. The ensuing scandal accelerated the enactment of the Foreign Corrupt Practices Act.
- In 1984, a gas leak at Union Carbide's pesticide plant in Bhopal, India killed more than 2,000 people.
- In 1988, the Asian-American Free Labour Association (AAFLA, a branch of the AFL-CIO trade union) found that Nike, the sporting goods company, used contractors in Indonesia who were breaking Indonesian labour laws and paying workers below-subsistence wages.
- In 1990, a Burma Campaign against Chevron called for a halt to oil extraction in Burma, where human rights were not protected. Similar calls were made subsequently against Total.
- In 1995, environmentalists from Greenpeace occupied the Brent Spar oil rig in the North Sea to prevent Shell going through with their original plan to dump the decommissioned rig into the water. This triggered a complete re-evaluation of company policies and practices that led Shell to produce an annual report on sustainable development.

services that are environmentally sustainable, to protect the privacy of our customers, partners and employees.'[75] As can be seen, three out of the five commitments are on the proactive, positive side of conducting business. The kinds of actions that can be exhibited in these three categories are:

a Dialogue and engagement with local stakeholders and communities:

- Contribute actively to community development in the form of grants, social, cultural and sporting events.
- Engage with schools and universities by offering research funds, individual grants and opportunities for internships.
- Offer educational opportunities.
- Participate in the local chamber of commerce and contribute to dialogue with authorities in any debate concerning ecological, technical or economic issues.
- Sponsor medical campaigns.
- Facilitate the ad hoc detachment of in-house experts to local councils, schools and community institutions.

b Provide resources to improve access to technology and educational opportunities:

- Donate computers to schools and institutions.
- Donate machinery that can foster rural development.
- Engage in training campaigns and development programmes such as internet usage, irrigation and preventive medicine.

c Develop products and services that are environmentally sustainable:

- Use biodegradable packaging.
- Favour renewable energy when possible.

The Triple Bottom Line

The Triple Bottom Line (TBL) was developed by a British management consultant, John Elkington, in 1994 while he was working for the think tank SustainAbility. It is the belief that companies should commit to social and environmental concerns as much as to profits. Thus, instead of one bottom line (that traditionally means profits) there should be three: profit, people and the planet. A TBL gauges a company's commitment to corporate social responsibility (CSR). Elkington used the phrase as a way of measuring performance in American companies – measuring their impact on the environment over time.

TBL measures the financial, social and environmental performance of a company. The TBL theorizes that if a firm concentrates on profit uniquely, thus ignoring people and the planet, it does not account for the full cost of doing business. Companies should work simultaneously on all three bottom lines:

1. Profit: traditional measure of corporate profit (P&L);
2. People: how socially responsible the company has been historically;
3. Planet: how environmentally responsible a business has been over time.

Insert 4.6 Examples of global citizen programmes

Carrefour Start-up Challenge in Brazil

In 2017, with the support of Carrefour, the French NGO Hello Tomorrow promoted the Start-up Challenge in Brazil to encourage start-ups and businesspeople to propose solutions for the development of foods that are healthier (production, distribution, handling, storage and nutritional information), more sustainable (development, production, distribution) and with less waste (production, handling, storage, marketing, usage and recycling). Winners are granted financial rewards to implement their projects.

HSBC Water Programme in Mexico

As part of its global Water Programme the bank is working with the NGO Urbana to provide sustainable sources of water to families in Mexico who suffer from chronic shortage. The investment in the project is part of HSBC's $100 million Water Programme which aims to provide hundreds of thousands of people with access to safe water and sanitation and to protect the biodiversity of important river systems. Over the course of the project, 641 rainwater harvesting systems will be installed in low-income communities in the Huichol mountains in Jalisco and on the southern edge of Mexico City, where many houses are not connected to the water system.

Unilever Perfect Village initiative

Launched first in India in 2000 and extended to Vietnam in 2013 and Pakistan in 2015, the Perfect Village initiative consists of helping local communities and small-scale retailers to grow their businesses while becoming more aware of Unilever's products and their uses. This means educating and employing 'Women Ambassadors' in the selected village.

Danone's Naandi Community Water Services funding

Naandi Community Water Services (NCWS) is a company that builds micro-factories in villages. The factories filter water using simple, effective and inexpensive technology (reverse osmosis or ultra-violet filtration), and communities come to buy their water at a very reasonable price of around four cents (three pence) per 20-litre jug. This initiative is funded by the Danone Communities Fund and the Danone Ecosystem Fund.

Google Global Fishing Watch (GFW) platform

Google, in association with SkyTruth, an NGO focused on satellite-based environmental monitoring, and Oceana, an NGO devoted to ocean protection, developed the Global Fishing Watch (GFW) platform that identifies vessels suspected of fishing illegally, and tracks them.

Sources: Companies' sustainability reports.

Integrating social responsibility policies into business strategies

Confronted with criticism, some firms have developed policies and practices designed to integrate social responsibility issues into their business strategies. Forest Reinhart at the Harvard Business School found that those strategies were based on three inter-related developments:[76]

a Design and implementation of **information systems**, both internal and external, in order to understand the environmental impact of products over their entire life cycle, as well as the concerns and expectations of customers, employees, environmentalists, international institutions and governments. Such information is complemented by proactive communication such as the yearly *Shell Report: People, Planet and Profit,* in which the company documents the actions that it has taken to meet its economic, environmental and social responsibilities.[77] The UN Global Compact has developed a Communication on Progress model for companies to follow for social reporting implementation. In parallel with this, 250 companies are participating in Business for Social Responsibility (BSR), a non-profit corporate membership organization that has developed a Global Reporting Initiative proposing a series of indicators to measure and disclose their performance regarding social responsibility.[78] These indicators are compatible with the Global Compact guidelines.

b Design and implementation of **incentive systems** devoted to fostering sustainable development performances, such as tying bonuses to good environmental practice.

c Contribution to **institutions,** such as the Global Compact (see Table 4.7), the World CSR (which groups different organizations such as the Business Impact), The Center for Corporate Citizenship at Babson College, The Prince of Wales Business Leader Forum (PWBLF), CSR Europe and Business Impact, Global Sullivan Principles. Online Appendix 4.1 lists organizations that are active in promoting corporate social responsibility.

Table 4.7 The ten principles of the UN Global Compact

Human rights
Principle 1: Businesses should support and respect the protection of internationally proclaimed human rights; and Principle 2: make sure that they are not complicit in human rights abuses.
Labour standards
Principle 3: Businesses should uphold the freedom of association and the effective recognition of the right to collective bargaining; Principle 4: the elimination of all forms of forced and compulsory labour; Principle 5: the effective abolition of child labour; and Principle 6: the elimination of discrimination in respect of employment and occupation.
Environment
Principle 7: Businesses should support a precautionary approach to environmental challenges; Principle 8: undertake initiatives to promote greater environmental responsibility; and Principle 9: encourage the development and diffusion of environmentally friendly technologies.

Anti-corruption
Principle 10: Businesses should work against all forms of corruption, including extortion and bribery.
The Global Compact's ten principles enjoy universal consensus and are derived from: The Universal Declaration of Human Rights The International Labour Organization's Declaration on Fundamental Principles and Rights at Work The Rio Declaration on Environment and Development The United Nations Convention Against Corruption

Source: UN, *The Ten Principles of the UN Global Compact,* https://www.unglobalcompact.org/what-is-gc/mission/principles (accessed 1 February 2022).

At the World Economic Forum, Davos, on 31 January 1999, UN Secretary-General Kofi Annan challenged world business leaders to 'embrace and enact' the Global Compact's ten principles, both in their individual corporate practices and by supporting appropriate public policies. These principles cover topics in human rights, labour and the environment.

The Global Compact is now a network of organizations and corporations that adhere to the ten principles. It asks companies to embrace, support and enact, within their sphere of influence, a set of core values in the areas of human rights, labour standards, the environment and anti-corruption (see Table 4.7).

Codes of conduct

As mentioned earlier, many public and private organizations have tried to provide guidelines to companies in the form of codes of conduct.

There are five types of code of conduct.[79]

1 Company codes

Codes that are adopted unilaterally by companies such as Levi Strauss, Marks & Spencer, Starbucks, HP, Adidas, 3M, Apple, Nestlé, Novartis, Google, HSBC and Reuters.

2 Trade association codes

These are adopted by a group of firms in a particular industry. Like company codes, they tend to be a unilateral measure adopted by the firms. They may be adopted by associations of firms based in developed countries, as in the case of the British Toy and Hobby Association code, or by firms in developing countries, such as the Bangladesh Garment Manufacturers and Exporters Association (BGMEA) code and the Kenya Flower Council code.

3 Multi-stakeholder codes

These are adopted as a result of negotiations between several stakeholders, including firms or their industry representatives, NGOs and/or trade unions. Governments may also be involved in the development of such codes. The UK's Ethical Trade Initiative Base Code is an example of such a multi-stakeholder approach.

4 Model codes

These are designed to provide a benchmark of what a particular organization regards as good practice. They are not generally applied in practice, but intended as a model which companies or trade associations could follow. These have been proposed by trade unions, for example, the ICFTU's Basic Code of Conduct covering Labour Practices, and by NGOs such as Amnesty International.

5 Inter-governmental codes

These are negotiated at an international level and are agreed by national governments. They date back to the 1970s when both the OECD's Guidelines for Multinational Enterprises and the ILO's Tripartite Declaration of Principles Concerning Multinational Enterprises were adopted.

Appendix 4.2 gives a list of codes alongside the organization that provides them. The first and most prominent is the *OECD Guidelines for Multinational Enterprises* (see Appendix 4.3).[80] The guidelines are recommendations addressed by governments to multinational enterprises operating in or from adhering countries (the thirty OECD member countries plus nine non-member countries: Argentina, Brazil, Chile, Estonia, Israel, Latvia, Lithuania, Romania and Slovenia). They provide voluntary principles and standards for responsible business conduct in a variety of areas including employment and industrial relations, human rights, environment, information disclosure, competition, taxation, and science and technology. The Guidelines were first published in 1976 and have been regularly reviewed since then. Those guidelines serve as a template for other initiatives.

Codes of conduct are important instruments of communication, education and reporting for the firms that are genuinely willing to accept their social responsibilities. These codes have been criticized on the ground that 'codes are little more than general statements of business ethics with no indication of the way in which they are to be implemented'.[81]

Social responsibility and global firms: an ongoing challenge

We have described the most salient issues concerning the social responsibilities of global firms. The list is not exhaustive and every day new cases appear; firms are caught off guard and have to react and adjust their policies. Some adopt a very defensive attitude, but soon realize that it does not work. A multiple dialogue between governments, NGOs, international institutions, the media and public opinion and industry associations has been going on since the 1990s, and will progressively align corporate strategies relating to human dignity. The 'ethical dimension' has now reached the financial markets with the development of socially responsible investing (SRI) in which investors select companies that are considered to be socially responsible.[82] However, as the case of corruption demonstrates, improvement is slow and regressive behaviour can still be exhibited. On climate change, the US government refused, on behalf of American industrialists, to sign the 1997 Kyoto Treaty on the reduction of carbon dioxide emissions. During the Obama administration the US adopted a more positive stand by signing the Paris COP21 in 2016, a decision that was reversed by the Trump administration. New ethical debates arise daily, as in the cases of bio-ethics, genetically modified (GM) organisms and the right of pharmaceutical companies to limit the development of alternative HIV drugs in developing countries. More and more, global firms are being held accountable for impacts that were traditionally the domain of government, and this looks likely to be one of the most challenging tasks for the future.

The role of business schools

In response to the many challenges the world is facing in all aspects of society from economic, political, social to environmental and technological ones, the member states of the United Nations drew up the UN Sustainable Development Goals (SDGs). These are a cohesive and centralized framework for discussing a new development model, good for people and the planet. Business schools play a key role in training future leaders to address these challenges (see Figure 4.1). The Responsible Research for Business and Management (RRBM) is a virtual organization designed to encourage and support research in business and management disciplines. It was developed by a group of twenty-four leading scholars in five disciplines at twenty-three university-based business schools in ten countries but has grown into a larger community. Among its partners are AACSB, EFMD, PRME, Aspen Institute's Business and Society Program and GRLI as well as many business schools worldwide.

Students of business are increasingly demanding management skills in sustainable and responsible business practices. One example of how business can work as a force for good is INSEAD's Hoffmann Global Institute for Business and Society (HGIBS) that aims to align business education with the SDGs, as business leaders discuss the SDGs and use them to account for their contributions to society. Founded in August 2018, its goal is to integrate sustainability across all activities and mobilize all stakeholders for impact. The institute does this through researching and developing sustainable business models; exploring means of operating sustainably and inspiring a diverse group of future leaders whilst engaging with its global alumni community to expand the impact.

Covid-19 and the green recovery

'We need to turn the recovery into a real opportunity to do things right for the future'. – *UN Secretary-General António Guterres*[83]

What is a 'green recovery'?

The Covid-19 pandemic, which was declared by the World Health Organization (WHO) on 11 March 2020,[84] resulted in an unprecedented global economic downturn due to entire sectors of the economy, such as tourism and hospitality, being partially or completely shut down during national lockdowns. The World Bank estimated the global economic contraction to be 4.3 per cent in 2020[85] with a slower than expected recovery due to the emergence of variants and resurgence of Covid-19 cases worldwide.

According to S&P, the most impacted sectors of the pandemic are airlines, leisure facilities and restaurants.[86]

Governments across the globe have mobilized significant resources and deployed extraordinary policy measures to support recovery from the crisis and these efforts were further boosted by the approval of the first Covid-19 vaccine by the Food and Drug Administration[87] and the European Medicines Agency[88] in December 2020. As governments plan the road out of the crisis and into recovery, it is increasingly recognized that the Covid-19 pandemic and the reduction in economic activity have important implications for how the 2030 Agenda for Sustainable Development, with the 17 Sustainable Development Goals adopted by United Nations Member States in September 2015,[89] is implemented across countries. International organizations like the International Monetary Fund (IMF) and the Organisation for Economic Co-operation and Development (OECD) have called on governments to implement a 'green recovery' through stimulus packages that integrate economic, social and climate change objectives with recovery policy needs.[90]

Opportunities associated with a 'green recovery'

The reduction in economic activity caused by the Covid-19 pandemic, especially transportation and industrial activity, resulted in unprecedented reductions in greenhouse gas emissions; it is estimated that global energy-related CO_2 emissions fell by 5.8 per cent in 2020, which is the largest annual percentage decline since the Second World War.[91] A 'green recovery' would involve policy measures that support further reduction in greenhouse gas emissions even as the economy recovers, through raising the cost of emissions and providing fiscal stimulus to 'green' activities such as climate-smart infrastructure and technologies, that both boost aggregate demand and employment.[92]

One of the key enablers of a 'green recovery' is argued to be transitioning to a circular economy, which has the potential to drive multiple policy objectives including the reinvigoration of the economy in a climate-friendly way. It is estimated that global transition to a circular economy could reduce greenhouse gas emissions by 25 per cent, generate savings of $200 billion per year and create 700,000 jobs by 2040.[93] The European Union (EU) has been at the forefront of this transition through developing a Circular Economy Action Plan, a key building block of the European Green Deal, which lays out the roadmap to achieve the EU's 2050 climate neutrality target.[94]

Finally, the Covid-19 pandemic has also induced considerable changes in individual behaviour and preferences, which are expected to have long-term consequences in terms of the way people work and travel. It is expected that increased demand for work-from-home from employees will remain high and that airline travel will see a slow return to pre-pandemic levels driven by uncertainty surrounding the future of business travel.[95] Sustaining these changes is considered an important driver of a 'green recovery' through reduced greenhouse gas emissions and energy usage, which will therefore likely shape future preferences and demand that companies across the globe need to prepare for.

Challenges to a 'green recovery'

While there are considerable opportunities and optimism associated with a 'green recovery', there are severe challenges in terms of its implementation and a risk that quick economic recovery is prioritized over climate change considerations. The OECD estimates that only 17 per cent of the total sums allocated to global Covid-19 recovery so far have been allocated to environmentally positive measures, with the rest of the funding either not considering environmental dimensions or reversing progress made so far.[96] The OECD calls for governments to increase the component of total Covid-19 spending on a green recovery, to align policy measures across sectors such as agriculture, waste management and forestry, and finally, to invest in skills and innovation required for a sustainable recovery.

MINI-CASE 4.3

Operation Car Wash

Brazil, one of the world's largest emerging markets with the ninth largest economy, has a population of 208 million and GDP of $1.8 trillion.[97] In 2014, a federal police superintendent in Brazil began an operation codenamed *'Lava Jato'* (Car Wash),[98] one of largest anti-corruption investigations in the world. It unveiled the shady relationships between government contractors, political campaign agencies and high-profile politicians in what were known as 'pay-for-play' schemes – bribes and campaign contributions paid by major corporations to government officials and political parties in exchange for lucrative government contracts which were over-invoiced to 'cover the costs'. A number of state-owned companies including Petrobras, the national oil company (over $88.8 billion in revenues in 2017),[99] were part of a system of institutionalized corruption whereby corporate executives overpaid an average of 3 per cent for contracts that were awarded on the basis of their political ties. Operation Car Wash uncovered 'backstage' agreements struck by public officials involving billions of dollars (Petrobras alone was estimated to have paid out over $2 billion).

Federal Judge Sérgio Moro was a key protagonist in Operation Car Wash and subsequently named among the 'World's Greatest Leaders' by *Fortune*, the '100 Most Influential People' by *Time* and the 'Fifty Most Influential' list by *Bloomberg Magazine*. Moro's convictions included former president Luis Inácio Lula da Silva (one of the most popular politicians in Latin America), a former speaker of the House of Representatives, two former ministers of state and a former governor of Rio de Janeiro (the state with the second-highest GDP). Operation Car Wash also resulted in the imprisonment of some of Brazil's most powerful businessmen.

By 2019, $3.4 billion in public funds had been recovered and 445 people indicted, many officials from the leftist Workers Party who had been in power since 2003. By June 2020, the investigations had led to prison sentences totalling over 2,200 years for 165 prominent Brazilians.[100] The combined efforts of Operation Car Wash in Curitiba, Rio de Janeiro and São Paulo resulted in more than 200 penal actions, with 217 defendants convicted, 256 individual plea bargains, 21 corporate agreements and 121 investigations.[101]

Operation Car Wash prompted a number of reforms in Brazil that forced companies to take measures against corruption. Among 250 Brazilian companies interviewed by KPMG in 2015, 57 per cent had ethics and compliance programmes in place; a year later the figure had risen to 76 per cent and by 2019 only 3 per cent did not have compliance procedures. However, 18 per cent of respondents in 2019 said they had no dedicated area for compliance, 32 per cent thought their resources were inadequate and 16 per cent believed there was a lack of independence/ autonomy.[102]

Operation Car Wash had repercussions in other Latin American countries, including the resignation in March 2018 of Peru's president, Pedro Pablo Kuczynski, who was accused of taking bribes from engineering company Odebrecht when he was a cabinet minister.[103] Others involved in scandals were Colombian president Juan Manuel Santos and Venezuelan president Nicolas Maduro.[104]

New president: After a turbulent campaign, Jair Messias Bolsonaro was sworn in as President of Brazil on 1 January 2019. He appointed Sergio Moro as Minister of Justice and Public Security. Moro accepted the post believing it was an opportunity to consolidate the achievements of Operation Car Wash and permanently strengthen the rule of law from Brasilia. Moro was replaced in the Car Wash cases, resulting in a slowdown in the speed cases were judged. Some said it was because the judge had to get acquainted with the cases, others blamed his profile. On average, it took Moro eleven and a half months to issue a verdict. In September 2019, cases awaiting a decision from Judge Luis Antonio Bonat had taken twenty-six months.[105]

From the start, Minister Moro and the Operation Car Wash team experienced difficulties. As Moro had been responsible for the conviction of former president Lula, Moro's new role in the government led to accusations of a conflict of interest. Lula would have been the Workers' Party (PT) presidential candidate in 2018 and was ahead in the polls even from jail. Some said that Lula being blocked from running paved the way for Bolsonaro's victory.[106]

In June 2019, a whistleblower delivered files containing thousands of confidential messages exchanged among the leaders of Operation Car Wash to *Intercept*, an investigative left-leaning website.[107] The recordings and text messages appeared to show prosecutors colluding with Moro during the investigations, prompting claims that the trials were unfair.[108] Moro and the prosecutors claimed that the alleged recordings had been obtained illegally by hacking their accounts and insisted there was nothing illegal in the leaked dialogues.

Congress passed legislation in 2019 aimed at preventing the abuse of power by prosecutors[109] and later by rejecting an anti-corruption package proposed by Moro to strengthen the fight against corruption, notably the institutionalization of prison after the first appellate court conviction.[110]

In April 2020, Sergio Moro resigned as Justice Minister, alleging that Bolsonaro had interfered in the federal police by replacing its main leaders in an attempt to protect his family and friends from ongoing investigations. His resignation triggered a political crisis for Bolsonaro, adding to the health crisis sparked by the Covid-19 pandemic. On resigning, Moro said, 'I didn't enter the government to serve a master. I entered it to serve the country, the law.'[111]

When Moro returned to Curitiba, he could not resume his previous role since when agreeing to become Justice Minister he had had to resign and renounce all benefits associated with the twenty-two years he had served as federal judge.[112]

Covid-19: In March 2020 Brazil was in crisis following the outbreak of Covid-19. Lockdowns and social distancing measures were responsible for economic debacle. Brazil was one of the most affected countries globally.[113] Bolsonaro's opponents blamed the president as he downplayed the pandemic, railed against lockdown and promoted unproven cures.[114] Covid-19 showed that systemic corruption was still alive and kicking in Brazil. During the pandemic, local and state governments had to make urgent purchases of ventilators and other medical equipment using more flexible procurement processes because of the emergency situation. It soon became clear Brazil was facing not only a new disease but an old one: widespread corruption was back. The press started to disclose corruption cases linked to Covid-19 purchases. As of June 2020, purchases under investigation amounted to more than R$1 billion (US$200 million). A new probe opened every three days in response to allegations of financial irregularities involving public budgets intended for coronavirus relief.[115]

Impact on the private sector: The impact of Operation Car Wash on corruption in the public sector was significant, but was even more profound in some business sectors. As a consequence of the investigations, construction companies such as OAS, UTC, Engevix, Camargo Correia and Queiroz Galvão had serious financial problems and had to substantially restructure and create compliance functions.[116]

According to Sergio Moro, Operation Car Wash worked as a wake-up call to the private sector in Brazil.[117] 'Doing the right thing, having effective compliance, doing your homework, all this is good for business and for profits.'[118] Petrobras was one example of how Car Wash had changed corporate Brazil. With a complete change in the leadership team in 2014, it created the role of Chief Governance and Compliance Executive Officer with the goal of strengthening internal practices and mitigating risks related to fraud and corruption. The objective was to make the new director as independent as possible: they could only be dismissed with the permission of board members who represented minority non-government shareholders.[119] The company had to work fast to mitigate risks, first by creating a robust compliance system with new controls and procedures. This generated a perception by some of increased bureaucracy and loss of agility. In a second phase it moved to an 'Integrity system' whereby compliance was instilled in every employee. Almost 200 employees across every area were trained as 'Integrity Agents' in compliance and integrity issues. Employees were obliged to take so-called 'integrity pills' – short videos broadcast internally to create awareness.[120] To reinforce compliance and integrity principles, the company created a series of mandatory trainings (online and in-person); non-attendance would prevent an employee from being promoted or advancing to a higher level. Specific trainings were made available for external stakeholders such as vendors and contractors.

Its efforts were recognized externally. In September 2020, the World Economic Forum agreed to allow Petrobras to re-join the PACI (Partnering Against Corruption Initiative), one of the main international organizations in the fight against corruption, formed by compliance officers from large multinational companies, international institutions and government bodies. Petrobras was a member of this initiative until 2014, when the scandal broke. The company also joined other external groups that discuss and share best practices in compliance-related issues, such as the Compliance Commission of IBP (Brazilian Petrol Institute) and the Entrepreneurial Act for Integrity, Prevention and Fight Against Corruption of Instituto Ethos.

At the end of 2020, Sergio Moro declared: 'I really believe that Operation Car Wash changed things in Brazil. It's not difficult to go back to the anti-corruption agenda. It will depend on political will.'[121]

Questions:

1 What do you believe were the most important achievements of Operation Car Wash in the fight against corruption?

2 Do you believe Brazil will be a better place to do business going forward or will the achievement brought by Operation Car Wash be ephemeral?

This Mini-case is based on two INSEAD Case Studies: Monteiro and Albuquerque (2018) and Monteiro and Kertesz (2021).

MINI-CASE 4.4

Enel

Enel was one of the largest power utilities companies in the world, with €80 billion in revenues for 2019. Its gross operating margin of €17.7 billion was generated from renewables (43 per cent), thermal (45 per cent) and nuclear (12 per cent). Enel worked in thirty-two countries across five continents, with 67,000 employees. It generated energy with a managed capacity of more than 89.8 GW, selling gas and distributing electricity across a network spanning 2.2 million km for 74 million end users, making it the largest private electric distribution network globally.[122]

The Enel Group was the first private renewable player worldwide, with a renewable footprint of over forty-six GW managed capacity in 2019. Half the energy generated was with zero CO_2 emissions. The company was the first to replace traditional electromechanical meters with smart electronic meters, enabling real-time readings and remote-control management for greater energy efficiency. This was critical for the development of intelligent grids, smart cities and electric transportation.[123]

Francesco Starace had been responsible for the success of Enel Green Power, before he was appointed Enel's CEO in 2014. He introduced a new strategy to capture value in the energy transition. Sustainability was the key to growth in this new environment. He made sustainability a pillar of growth and aligned the strategic plans of Enel with the UN SDGs aiming to be carbon-free by 2050.

Enel's goal was to create long-term sustainable value for all its stakeholders by adhering to UN Sustainable Development Goals (SDGs) in its investment decisions. Its plan was to reduce specific CO_2 emissions by 2030 (SDG13: 0.23 g/kWheq) and to promote the economic and social growth of the local communities where it operated. Other goals by 2030 were: SDG4 quality education for 2.5 m beneficiaries, SDG7 affordable and clean energy for 10 million people, SDG8 decent work conditions for 8 million beneficiaries. They moved from a CSR approach to one that aimed to change the way a utility could stay in the market in the long run, running a sustainable business through innovation. Enel translated the academic Creating Shared Value approach into a methodology applied to its value chain, so that sustainability was integrated into daily activities not by a central function, but by the people managing the business, from Business Development to Engineering, Construction, and Procurement up to Operation.

To capture value from the four macro trends, innovation had a key role in a world that was changing faster than its ability to adapt. Starace then hired Ernesto Ciorra, an entrepreneur and former consultant, to lead Enel's innovation and sustainabilitiy efforts.

The result was '*innovability*' – *innovation* and *sustainability* combined.

Enel built an Open Power platform that allowed electricity access to more people and opened the world of energy to new technologies, uses, ways of managing and partnerships. An international network of 'Innovation Hubs' were set up in Israel, USA, Spain, Italy, Russia, Brazil and Chile, and 'Open Innovability' (the first energy crowdsourcing platform) launched – connecting outside innovations with the company's internal needs. Corporate culture was transformed with a matrix structure implemented based on lines of business and geographical regions. The business lines (Thermal Generation, Trading, Infrastructure & Networks, and Enel Green Power) were responsible for managing and developing assets, with the goal of optimizing performance and increasing return on capital for all the regions where Enel was present.

The geographic units were responsible for the sale of electricity and natural gas, and managing relationships with external stakeholders (P&L was reflected in the matrix structure: revenues were the responsibility of the country manager, costs (CAPEX and OPEX) were the responsibility of the business lines, while EBITDA was a shared objective). Prior to this restructuring the organizational structure had been vertical with decisions made from the top down with each division operating separately. When Starace become CEO in 2014, Enel was a portfolio of companies operating almost independently. Each country manager was in charge of P&L along the entire value chain (generation, distribution, marketing and sales) but there was little communication among countries or divisions, and no sharing of ideas.

Under the new matrix structure innovability teams were set up in every business line, managed by innovation managers. The innovability teams looked for *challenges* at every level of their respective business lines, scouted and tested solutions, and supported their colleagues in implementing these solutions into the real business. Having the innovability teams working within the business lines and in a matrix structure allowed the company to test projects more efficiently and avoid duplication across countries and business lines, reducing the cost of innovation. Innovation and sustainability were embedded in the lines, hence they became more direct, faster and efficient.

Another major change was the creation of the Digital Solutions staff function in 2018, formed from the merger of the ICT department with business people. The aim was to work towards the digitalization of the Group's assets, its client relationships and the way employees worked. Over 2,000 people in the Group adopted 'agile' methodology to support the quest for innovation and digitalization. Digital Solutions had its own dedicated Innovation Manager.

A complete change of mindset was also required. Several programmes were launched including 'My Best Failure', launched in 2015. The idea was to encourage employees to share their 'failure stories' online within the Group, reward entrepreneurial spirit and replace fear of mistakes with an 'open, no blame culture' that thrived on lessons learned. A corporate entrepreneurship programme was launched called 'Make it Happen!', where employees were encouraged to form teams and develop ideas for new start-ups or ways to improve Enel's business. To ensure the success of the open innovation approach, Enel needed fast access to new ideas, technologies and business models from start-ups, SMEs, universities and researchers around the world.

Innovation hubs: The company set up ten innovation hubs worldwide connecting the Group to the best innovation ecosystems in the world. These hubs continuously scouted new opportunities for Enel's traditional businesses and created new valuable businesses that were sustainable long term for Enel and its customers. Enel deployed local innovation hubs in countries where it had a strong industrial presence – Chile (Santiago), Brazil (Rio de Janeiro together with Sao Paulo) and Russia (Moscow) – to be close to the people who implemented the technology. By 2019, four years after the opening of the first innovation hub in Tel Aviv, Enel had scouted more than 6,000 start-ups around the world and had done a preliminary assessment on over 1,000 of them.

In 2020, six years after Starace took control, Enel's stock had increased from €4.06 to €7.84 for a total market capitalization of €99 billion.[124] In November the same year Enel announced it would invest €160 billion over ten years to become a green 'super major' and carbon free by 2050. It planned to expand its green hydrogen capacity to more than 2 GW by 2030 and phase out coal by 2027. In 2018, Enel ranked number 28 on Fortune's list of companies that can 'change the world'.[125]

Questions:

1 Does it make sense to put innovation and sustainability together? Why or why not?

2 What are the main benefits of having innovation hubs in different parts of the world, including emerging markets?

This Mini-case is based on an INSEAD case study: Monteiro and Benavente (2019).

MINI-CASE 4.5

Etisalat's philanthropic activities

Etisalat Group is a telecoms corporation from the United Arab Emirates, headquartered in Abu Dhabi. With revenues amounting to AED 51.7 billion (US$14 billion), it operates in seventeen countries across the Middle East, Asia and Africa.

As part of its sustainability and social responsibility strategy, Etisalat has developed a company policy of developing relationships with multiple local stakeholders in the various countries where it operates, referred to as 'stakeholder engagement'. As part of its engagement, the group considers itself to be the 'national champion for the UAE and ... a quasi-government'. As such, it pursues a series of philanthropic activities worldwide, in conjunction with the UAE's Ministry of International Co-operation. It intervenes in the domain of education, health, charities and civic infrastructure works. The table gives a sample of these activities, performed directly or in partnership with Dubai Cares, a philanthropic organization created by the Emirati government to improve children's access to quality primary education in developing countries.

EDUCATION	
• Sri Lanka	Donation of laptop computers to schools Financing of fully equipped libraries
• Nigeria	Financing of schools infrastructure Financing of teacher training programme (in association with the British Council)
• Ivory Coast	Scholarships School renovation
• Afghanistan	Financing of computer labs in schools Educational assistance for adults
• Niger	School improvement programmes

HEALTH • Egypt	Water purification and distribution programmes
• Pakistan	Free wifi zones in public and private hospitals
• Niger	Providing air-conditioned maternity units for patients Providing mosquito nets to combat malaria
• Ivory Coast	Building hospitals
• Sri Lanka	HIV and AIDS awareness programme
CHARITY • Sri Lanka	Flood relief programme Career counselling programme
• Pakistan	Water supply for suburban areas
• Niger	Food aid
CIVIC WORKS • Sri Lanka	Recycling of packaging material Tree planting
• Afghanistan	Reconstruction of mosques Women's empowerment programmes Sponsoring National Volleyball Federation
• Pakistan	Tree planting programme School enrolment programmes for girls in remote areas Emergency flood response programmes

Questions:

1 What benefits does a global corporation such as Etisalat draw from its philanthropic activities?

2 In financing these philanthropic activities, and in choosing which ones to support, does a global corporation run the risk of being seen as a substitute for the local government? If so, what are potential drawbacks to this?

Source: Etisalat CSR & Sustainability Report 2012, http://www.etisalat.com/en/system/docs/reports/Etisalat-CSR-Sustainability-Report-2012_lowres.pdf (accessed 2012).

MINI-CASE 4.6

Light Up The World (LUTW)

Light Up The World (LUTW) is an international development organization whose goal is to provide renewable energy technologies and high-efficiency lighting to communities around the world that do not have access to appropriate and affordable energy solutions.

This Canadian non-profit organization implements projects in communities that do not have access to electricity. These projects provide sustainable energy solutions and lighting to off-grid areas (communities without a connection to the main electrical power grid). This helps communities transition away from using fuel-based lighting and spending a significant amount of their income on batteries and charging cell phones.

LUTW has two offices: the head office based in Calgary, Canada, and a field office serving projects in South America, based in Lima, Peru.

Supported by donations from individuals, corporations, host country NGOs, international foundations and industrial partners (totalling some $750,000 annually), LUTW has brought light to homes in fifty-four countries around the world, from Afghanistan to Zambia.

The example of Peru

LUTW established its first field office in Peru to serve the estimated 4 million people in the country without access to electricity. Most of them live in the foothills of the Andes at high altitude. Traditionally they used candles and kerosene as a substitute for electricity. As of 2022 LUTW has powered over a million projects helping more than a million families in fifty-five countries around the world since its creation.

LUTW designs and provides simple solar photovoltaic (PV) systems that consist of a solar PV module (to generate electricity) connected to a cable (to transport the electricity), a controller (to regulate the voltage and current), battery (to store the electricity) and devices such as light bulbs (which convert the electricity into a useful service, light!). These low-voltage systems provide a basic electrification service that includes lighting and communications (by charging cell phones and powering radios) to homes in small, rural, off-grid communities.

The installation of a system is carried out by thirty-five community solar technicians that are trained by LUTW.

The cost of a system is around $360, out of which a household has to pay $220, spread over the first year. This has to be compared with an annual average of $240–360 spent on kerosene and candles. The money saved can be used for children's education, improving nutrition or to finance small businesses.

Question:

How can this organization globalize further?

Sources: LUTW's website, http://lutw.org/; some data reproduced with permission of INSEAD from R. Nair and P. Parker, 'Light up the World (A): Lighting up the Developing World', INSEAD case no. 6231, https://publishing.insead.edu/case/light-world-peru-a-lighting-developing-world (accessed 1 February 2022).

Summary and key points

1 Sustainable development is defined as 'development that meets the needs of the present without compromising the ability of future generations to meet their own needs'

2 Sustainable development encompasses three main issues facing global companies:

a Environmental:

- Global warming
- Resource depletion
- Eco-friendly practices

b Societal issues:

- Corruption
- Human rights and dignity
- Financial malpractice

c Global citizenship

3 Main environmental issues:
  a Destruction of ozone layer
  b Climate change and global warming
  c Natural resource depletion:
    - Deforestation
    - Over-fishing
    - Over-mining
  d Waste production and disposal
  e Persistent organic pollution
  f Radioactive waste
4 Global warming is linked to CO_2 emissions:
  a At the Paris Conference in 2015 (COP21), 159 governments agreed to limit temperature rise from gas emissions to 1.5 degrees Celsius above the pre-industrial level
  b The EU Emissions Trading Scheme organizes a market for CO_2 emissions
5 Global firms can participate in environmental protection by:
  a Controlling suppliers
  b Making eco-friendly capital investments
  c The green management of resources:
    - reduction in material intensity
    - reduction in energy intensity
    - reduction in waste dispersion
    - enhancement of recyclability
    - maximum use of renewables
    - extension of product durability
    - increase of service intensity
6 Business ethics encompasses issues of conflicts of interest, financial and accounting integrity, corruption and bribery, ethical advertising, bio-ethics and employee privacy
7 Corruption can be defined as the abuse of public office for private gain; a gift can be offered openly but a bribe cannot

  Two indices related to corruption were published up to 2011:
  - *Corruption Perceptions Index (CPI)* is a score which relates to the perception of the degree of corruption, assessed by businesses, academics and risk analysts
  - *Bribe Payers Index (BPI)* ranks exporting countries in terms of the degree to which their companies are perceived to be paying bribes abroad (not published since 2011)

a There are five *causes* of corruption:

- *Administrative resource allocation*: when administrative authorization and distribution replaces transparent market mechanisms
- *Lack of institutional checks,* balances and information
- *Inadequate funding* of public services leading to relatively low remuneration of public servants and under-supply of public goods
- *Social and cultural factors* leading to nepotism
- *Abundance of natural resources* leading to discrimination in the allocation of funds

b *Effects* of corruption:

- Direct:
  - Discourages domestic and foreign investments owing to additional cost burden on projects
    - Skews public capital expenditure in favour of new equipment instead of operating existing equipment
    - Reduces the productivity of public investments and reduces tax collection
- Indirect:
  - Decreased work productivity through demotivation
    - Dislocation of social fabric
    - Loss of integrity within firms
    - Link with terrorism and criminal activities

c Global companies *engage in bribery* because of:

- Need to keep up with competitors' practices
- Cultural justifications
- Result of an incentive system which emphasizes economic achievements

d Anti-corruption measures:

- Disclose publicly and make widely known the company's endorsement of anti-corruption measures
- Establish a clearly articulated written policy prohibiting employees from paying/receiving bribes
- Implement policies with due care and take disciplinary action for any violations
- Provide training and support to employees to carry out the policy
- Maintain full and proper accounting records, subject to periodic internal audit review
- Report annually on the firm's bribery and corruption policy and describe the company's experience in its enforcement; the annual report should be independently audited

- Require all agents/suppliers to affirm that they have neither made nor will make any improper payments
- Establish a monitoring and auditing system to detect any improper payments made by the firm's employees/agents
- Report publicly any solicitation for payments
- Establish a system for employees/agents to report any improper payment without fear of retribution

8 Child labour

a Main ethical dilemma

b Global firms can be involved in child labour through their suppliers

9 Human rights are concerned with:

a Forced labour

b Racial or gender discrimination

c Health and safety

d Freedom of association

e Fair working conditions

10 Involvement in human rights abuses:

a Direct involvement: human rights infringed or ignored by global companies to protect their operations or profitability

b Indirect involvement: contributions to political regimes that are involved in human rights abuse

11 Financial malpractices

a Financial malpractice refers to the ability of global corporations to use their multinational presence to deprive states of their normal share of taxes through tax evasion

b It also concerns their ability to interfere in local politics through the sponsoring of 'friendly' political parties or movements

12 Principles for global firms:

a Formulate a company policy on human rights

b Security arrangements should protect human rights and be consistent with international standards of law enforcement

c Get involved in community initiatives or bodies that promote human rights

d Company policy should not approve discrimination, slavery or child labour practices

e Provide safe and healthy working conditions and products

f All employees should have the freedom to associate with and the right to join collective bargaining mechanisms

- **g** Mechanisms should be established to monitor a company's compliance with international human rights standards

13 Corporate social responsibility describes the obligations of firms to society or, more specifically, to those affected by corporate policies and practices

14 Global citizenship covers the following areas:

- **a** Dialogue and engagement with local stakeholders and communities
- **b** Provision of resources to improve access to technology and educational opportunities
- **c** Development of products and services that are environmentally sustainable
- **d** Use of biodegradable packaging
- **e** Favouring renewable energy when possible

15 Global companies can handle their increasing responsibility for social issues that were traditionally the domain of governments by:

- **a** Design and implementation of information systems and social reporting
- **b** Design and implementation of incentive systems devoted to fostering sustainable development
- **c** Contribution to public and private institutions

Learning assignments

1 What are the main causes of corruption?

2 Which corrupt practices involving global firms have you heard of?

3 What dilemma may a country manager face when confronted by a request to solicit a bribe to obtain a major contract?

4 Which policies should a global firm implement to prevent corrupt practices?

5 How can corporate policies be designed to contribute to the protection of the global environment?

6 What should the country managers do if a local supplier in a developing country is employing twelve-year-old labourers?

7 Should a global company pull out of, or avoid investing in, a country well known for human rights abuses by its military rulers?

8 Draw a global ethical web for a pharmaceutical company engaged in anti-HIV drug production.

9 What are SRI funds? Select an SRI fund and track its performance as compared to the general evolution of the stock market.

10 What are the SDGs?

11 How can business schools play a further role in achieving the SDGs? Give an example of one way they can help.

12 What are the challenges facing companies in measuring their triple bottom line? How can they get buy in from all stakeholders to adopt the TBL rather than the traditional bottom line?

13 What are the main challenges to a green recovery post Covid-19?

Key words

- Bribe
- Child labour
- Corporate social responsibility (CSR)
- Corruption
- Covid-19 green recovery
- Environmental crisis
- Ethics
- Human rights
- Socially responsible investment (SRI)
- Sustainable Development Goals (SDGs)
- Transparency International (TI)
- Triple Bottom Line

Web resources

In addition to the resources mentioned in Appendices 4.1 and 4.2, the following may be useful:

Corpwatch:
http://www.corpwatch.org
European Commission, Energy, Climate, Energy:
https://ec.europa.eu/clima/index_en
European Commission on Sustainable Development:
https://ec.europa.eu/info/strategy/international-strategies/sustainable-development-goals_en
McKinsey:
https://www.mckinsey.com/featured-insights/climate-change
World Business Council for Sustainable Development:
www.wbcsd.org
World Bank Development Indicators:
https://databank.worldbank.org/source/world-development-indicators
World Resources Institute:
https://www.wri.org
United Nations Environment Program:
https://www.unep.org
UNICEF (United Nations International Children Emergency Fund):
https://www.unicef.org

Companion website

Visit the companion website at bloomsbury.pub/global-strategic-management-5e for a multitude of weblinks and resources, self-test questions for revision and appendices.

Notes

1 Brundtland Report: https://sustainabledevelopment.un.org/content/documents/5987our-common-future.pdf
2 World Business Council for Sustainable development: https://www.wbcsd.org/Overview/About-us/Vision_2050
3 Rio de Janeiro Conference(1992) https://www.un.org/en/development/desa/population/migration/generalassembly/docs/globalcompact/A_CONF.151_26_Vol.I_Declaration.pdf
4 United Nation: https://www.undp.org/sustainable-development-goals

5 https://sustainabledevelopment.un.org/topics/science
6 Sustainable Development goals: https://sdgs.un.org/goals
7 Ibid
8 United nations: https://www.un.org/sustainabledevelopment/ climate-action/ (accessed 23 May 2021).
9 https://www.npr.org/2021/02/19/969387323/u-s-officially-rejoins-paris-agreement-on-climate-change?t=1651657261721 (accessed 4 May 2022).
10 https://www.corporateleadersgroup.com/reports-evidence-and-insights/news-items/eu-business-leaders-urge-higher-2030-emissions-reduction-targets (accessed 23 May 2021).
11 https://euobserver.com/green-deal/150364 (accessed 23 May 2021).
12 https://www.independent.co.uk/climate-change/news/hm-greenwashing-sustainable-circulose-venetia-falconer-manna-a9312566.html (accessed 23 May 2021).
13 Delmas and Burbano (2011).
14 De Jong, Harkink and Barth (2018).
15 https://www.patagonia.com/stories/dont-buy-his-jacket-black-friday-and-the-new-york-times/story-18615.html (accessed 23 May 2021).
16 Awaysheh et al. (2020); Friede, Busch and Bassen (2015).
17 Burbano (2016); Bode and Singh (2018).
18 Kumar, Connell and Bhattacharyya (2020).
19 Battilana and Lee (2014).
20 Eldar (2017).
21 Global Emission of CO2: https://www.pbl.nl/sites/default/files/downloads/pbl-2020-trends-in-global-co2-and-total-greenhouse-gas-emissions-2019-report_4068.pdf
22 Tokyo protocol: https://unfccc.int/kyoto_protocol
23 European Trading Scheme: https://ec.europa.eu/clima/eu-action/eu-emissions-trading-system-eu-ets_en
24 Ibid
25 WWF International (2014) p.10
26 Living Planet report: https://c402277.ssl.cf1.rackcdn.com/publi- cations/1371/files/original/ENGLISH-FULL. pdf?1599693362 (accessed 15 May 2021). The Living Planet Index (LPI) is a measure of the state of the world's biological diversity based on population trends of vertebrate species from terrestrial, freshwater and marine habitats.
27 https://www.unep.org/explore-topics/forests (accessed 15 May 2021).
28 https://www.worldwildlife.org/stories/one-third-of-freshwater-fish-face-extinction-and-other-freshwater-fish-facts (accessed 15 May 2021).
29 https://unesdoc.unesco.org/ark:/48223/pf0000375724 (accessed 15 May 2021).
30 Husted (2013)
31 FAO: https://www.fao.org/3/i6583e/i6583e.pdf
32 Plas and Erdmenger (2000)
33 IMF Global Financial Stability Report, chapter 6, P81 'Sustainable Finance', https://www.imf.org/en/Topics/climate-change/green-finance (accessed 1 February 2022).
34 https://www.pionline.com/esg/global-esg-data-driven-assets-hit-405-trillion(accessed 1 February 2022).
35 Food and Agriculture Organization: https://www.fao.org/fileadmin/user_upload/lon/HLEF2050_Global_Agriculture.pdf
36 World Business Council for Sustainable Development (2010)
37 Holiday et al (202), Lehni (2000)
38 OECD (2014).
39 Transparency International, 2001 index.
40 Transparency International, 2020 index.
41 Transparency International, 2015 index.
42 Fadiman (1986).
43 OECD (2007).
44 Mauro (1997); Tanzi (1998).
45 Leite and Weiman (1999).
46 Besides the IMF papers cited earlier, a series of World Bank reports showing the negative effects of corruption are available at http://econ.world- bank.org/ (accessed 30 May 2017).
47 Wei (1998).
48 United Nations : https://www.un.org/press/en/2018/sc13493.doc.htm
49 Kaufmann and Wei (1999).
50 Hess and Dunfee (2001).

51 Badaracco and Webb (1995).
52 http://www.transparency.org.
53 Pope (2000).
54 Nichols (1993).
55 UNICEF (2014).
56 ILO (2017).
57 See UNICEF (2014). See also the Child Labor Coalition at http://www.stopchildlabor.org.
58 ILAB 2018, https://www.dol.gov/sites/dolgov/ files/ ILAB/ListofGoods.pdf(accessed 1 February 2022).
59 Sane (2001).
60 Gravelle (2015).
61 Gravelle (2015) gives a list of tax havens on p. 3.
62 Contractor (2016).
63 106 OECD (2015)
64 European Commission (2016).
65 Hadjikhani and Ghauri (2006)
66 BSR (2003).
67 Donalson and Dundee (1999).
68 Cadbury (1987).
69 This definition is from Smith (2003). There are many definitions of CSR but this one is the most comprehensive in its simplicity
70 In 1891 Pope Leo XIII published the encyclical 'Rerum Novarum' in which he set up recommendations to firms about their rights and duties to society and particularly to their labour force.
71 *New York Times Magazine*, 13 September 1970.
72 Smith (2003: 2).
73 Badaracco and Webb (1995).
74 Katsoulakos et al. (2004).
75 Hewlett-Packard (2005).
76 Reinhart (1999).
77 Shell Corporation (2015).
78 BSR (2003).
79 This classification is from Jenkins (2001).
80 Those guidelines are available on the OECD website: http://www.oecd.org.
81 Jenkins (2001: 28).
82 Awaysheh et al. (2020)
83 United nation: https://news.un.org/en/story/2020/08/1070652
84 WHO (2020): https://www.who.int/director-general/speeches/detail/who-director-general-s-opening-remarks-at-the-media-briefing-on-covid-19-11-march-2020 (Accessed 22nd May 2021)
85 World Bank (2021): https://www.worldbank.org/en/publication/global-economic-prospects. (Accessed 22nd May 2021)
86 S&P: www.spglobal.com/marketintelligence/en/news-insights/blog/industries-most-and-least-impacted-by-covid19-from-a-probability-of-default-perspective (Accessed 22nd May 2021)
87 FDA (2020): https://www.fda.gov/news-events/press-announcements/fda-takes-key-action-fight-against-covid-19-issuing-emergency-use-authorization-first-covid-19#:~:text=Today%2C%20the%20U.S.%20Food%20and,years%20of%20age%20and%20older. (Accessed 22nd May 2021)
88 EMA (2020): www.ema.europa.eu/en/news/ema-recommends-first-covid-19-vaccine-authorisation-eu. (Accessed 22nd May 2021)
89 UN (2015): https://www.un.org/ga/search/view_doc.asp?symbol=A/RES/70/1&Lang=E. (Accessed 22nd May 2021)
90 OECD (2020) : https://www.oecd.org/coronavirus/policy-responses/covid-19-and-the-low-carbon-transition-impacts-and-possible-policy-responses-749738fc/. (Accessed 22nd May 2021)
91 IAE: https://www.iea.org/articles/global-energy-review-co2-emissions-in-2020. (Accessed 22nd May 2021)
92 IMF: (2020): https://www.imf.org/en/Topics/climate-change/green-recovery#Topic%201. (Accessed 22nd May 2021)
93 https://www.ellenmacarthurfoundation.org/assets/downloads/The_circular_economy_solution_to_plastic_pollution_July_2020.pdf. (Accessed 22nd May 2021)
94 EU (2020): https://ec.europa.eu/environment/strategy/circular-economy-action-plan_en (Accessed 22nd May 2021)
95 Forbes (2021) : https://www.forbes.com/sites/oliverwilliams1/2021/04/29/welcome-to-the-post-covid-business-trip/?sh=299e81f51ae8 (Accessed 22nd May 2021)

96 OECD:https://www.oecd.org/coronavirus/en/themes/green-recovery (Accessed 22nd May 2021)
97 *The Economist Pocket World in Figures* (2018).
98 According to Rodrigo Chemim in his book, *Mãos Limpas e Lava Jato: A Corrupção Se Olha no Espelho* (p. 94), the investigation led police to several companies that used it to launder money. When officers realized the size of the crimes and the profile of those involved, the petrol station Torre in Brasilia was under investigation. Most petrol stations offer car wash services, but the amount of money being laundered was much larger, hence the name chosen was Operação Lava Jato (or Operation Jet Wash). It later became Operation Car Wash.
99 Statista, https://www.statista.com/statistics/279719/revenue-of-petrobras/ (accessed 16 June 2018).
100 Harris and Schipani (2020).
101 Minitério Público Federal – 'Caso Lava Jato – Resultados', http://www.mpf.mp.br/grandes-casos/lavajato/resultados (accessed 15 October 2020).
102 KPMG, 'Pesquisa Maturidade do Compliance no Brasil', 4th edition, 2019.
103 Rocharun and Casey (2018).
104 Felter and Cara Labrador (2018).
105 Konchinski (2019).
106 Schipani (2019).
107 Schipani, Stott and Webber (2019).
108 Greenwald and Linhares (2019).
109 Harris (2020).
110 Onofre (2019).
111 Nugent (2020).
112 Fonseca (2018).
113 G1, 'Brasil tem 5,3 milhões de casos confirmados de Covid, com médias de casos e mortes em estabilidade', 21 October 2020, https://g1.globo. com/bemestar/coronavirus/noticia/2020/10/21/ casos-e-mortes-por-coronavirus-no-brasil-em-21- de-outubro-segundo-consorcio-de-veiculos-de- imprensa.ghtml (accessed 22 October 2020).
114 The Americas, 'An increasingly prickly partnership', The Economist, 3 September 2020.
115 Harris, Schipani and Long (2020).
116 Philips (2017).
117 Webinar to INSEAD, 30 November 2020.
118 Ibid.
119 Interview with Marcelo Zenkner, 24 August 2020.
120 Ibid.
121 Webinar for INSEAD, 30 November 2020.
122 https://www.enel.com.co/en/about-enel/enel-group.html(accessed 1 February 2022).
123 Ibid.
124 https://ycharts.com/companies/ESOCF/market_cap (accessed 21 December 2020).
125 https://fortune.com/change-the-world/2018/enel/ (accessed 1 February 2022).

References and further reading

Books and articles

Amnesty International (2004) *The UN Human Rights Norms for Business: Towards Legal Accountability* (London: Amnesty International Publications). http://www.amnesty.org (accessed 21 June 2017).

Anderson, T. L. and Leal, D. R. (1997) *Enviro-Capitalists: Doing Good While Doing Well* (Lanham, MD: Rowman & Littlefield).

Awaysheh, A., Heron, R. A., Perry, T. and Wilson, J. I. (2020) 'On the relation between corporate social responsibility and financial performance', *Strategic Management Journal*, 41 (6): 965–87.

Badaracco Jr., J. and Webb, A. P. (1995) 'Business ethics: a view from the trenches', *California Management Review*, 37 (2): 8–29.

Banerjee, N. (2001) 'US lawsuit snares Exxon', *International Herald Tribune*, 22 June.

Battilana, J. and Lee, M. (2014) 'Advancing research on hybrid organizing – insights from the study of social enterprises', *The Academy of Management Annals*, 8 (1): 397–441.

Bode, C. and Singh, J. (2018) 'Taking a hit to save the world? Employee participation in a corporate social initiative', *Strategic Management Journal*, 39 (4): 1003–30.

Bode, C., Rogan, M. and Singh, J. (2019) 'Sustainable cross-sector collaboration: building a global platform for social impact', *AMD*, 5: 396–414. https://doi.org/10.5465/amd.2018.0112 (accessed 1 February 2022).

Brammer, S., Branicki, L. and Linnenluecke, M. K. (2020) 'COVID-19, societalization, and the future of business in society', *Academy of Management Perspectives*, 34 ((4): 493–507.

BSR (*Business for Social Responsibility*) (2003) *Overview of Business Ethics*, BSR Brief, October.

Burbano, V. C. (2016) 'Social responsibility messages and worker wage requirements: field experimental evidence from online labor marketplaces', *Organization Science*, 27 (4): 1010–28.

Burns, J. L. and Spar, D. L. (2000) 'Hitting the wall: Nike and international labor practices', Harvard Business School Case 9-700-047.

Cadbury, A. (1987) 'Ethical managers make their own rules', *Harvard Business Review*, Sept–Oct: 69–73.

CAIT Climate Data Explorer (2015) Washington, DC: World Resources Institute. http://cait.wri.org (accessed 1 February 2022).

CEO (Corporate Europe Observatory) (2017) 'Sugarcane ethanol: a sweet solution for Europe's fuel addiction?'. http://archive.corporateeurope.org/ethanolfueladdiction.html (accessed 15 June 2017).

Contractor, F. (2016) 'Tax avoidance by multinational companies: methods, policies, and ethics', *Rutgers Business Review*, 1 (1): 27–43.

Cramer, J. (2017), *Corporate Social Responsibility and Globalisation: An Action Plan for Business* (London: Routledge).

Crane, A. and Matten, D. (2020) 'COVID-19 and the future of CSR research', *Journal of Management Studies*, 58 (1): 280–4.

Crawford, R., Cadot, O. and Trap, D. (1999) 'Soccer balls: made by children for children? Child labor in Pakistan', INSEAD Case Study 12/1999-4865.

Cushman Jr., J. H. (1998) 'Nike pledges to end child labor and apply U.S. rules abroad', *New York Times*, 13 May.

De Jong, M. D. T., Harkink, K. M. and Barth, S. (2018) 'Making green stuff? Effects of corporate greenwashing on consumers', *Journal of Business and Technical Communication*, 32 (1): 77–112.

Delmas, M. A. and Burbano, V. C. (2011) 'The drivers of greenwashing', *California Management Review*, 54 (1): 64–87.

Donalson, T. and Dundee, T. W. (1999) 'When ethics travel: the promise and perils of global business ethics', *California Management Review*, 40 (4): 45–63.

Dunchin, F. and Lange, G.-M. (1994) *Our Common Future* (Oxford: Oxford University Press).

The Economist Pocket World in Figures (2018) (London: Profile Books).

EFMD (European Foundation for Management Development) (2005) *Globally Responsible Leadership: A Call for Engagement* (Brussels: EFMD).

Eldar, O. (2017) 'The role of social enterprise and hybrid organizations', *Columbia Business Law Review*.https://scholarship.law.duke.edu/faculty_scholarship/3637 (accessed 24 May 2021).

European Commission (2008) *EU Action Against Climate Change* (Brussels: European Commission).

European Commission (2016) *Anti Tax Avoidance Package* (Brussels: European Commission). http://ec.europa.eu/taxation_customs/business/company-tax/anti-tax-avoidance-package_en (accessed 15 June 2017).

European Union (2016) *EU Emissions Trading System (EU ETS)* (Brussels: European Union Publication Office). https://ec.europa.eu/clima/sites/clima/files/factsheet_ets_en.pdf (accessed 15 June 2017).

Fadiman, J. A. (1986) 'A traveller's guide to gifts and bribes', *Harvard Business Review*, July–August: 4–12.

Falck, O. and Heblich, S. (2007) 'Corporate social responsibility: doing well by doing good', *Business Horizons*, 50 (3): 247–54.

Felter, C. and Cara Labrador, R. (2018) 'Brazil's Corruption Fallout', Council on Foreign Relations, 11 January. www.cfr.org/backgrounder/brazils-corruption-fallout (accessed 1 February 2022).

Fonseca, A. (2018) 'Moro pede exoneração do cargo de juiz federal para ser ministro no novo governo' G1, 16 November. https://g1.globo.com/pr/parana/noticia/2018/11/16/presidente-do-trf-4-assina-ex-oneracao-de-sergio-moro.ghtml (accessed 15 October 2020).

Food and Agriculture Organization (2009) *How to Feed the World in 2050*. http://www.fao.org/wsfs/forum2050/wsfs-forum/en/ (accessed 30 May 2017).

Friede, G., Busch, T. and Bassen, A. (2015) 'ESG and financial performance: aggregated evidence from more than 2000 empirical studies', *Journal of Sustainable Finance and Investment*, 5 (4): 210–33.

Ganson, B., He, T. L. and Henisz, W. J. (2021) 'Business and peace: the impact of firm-stakeholder relational strategies on conflict risk', *Academy Of Management Review*.

García-Feijoo, M., Eizaguirre, A. and Rica-Aspiunza, A. (2020) 'Systematic review of sustainable-development-goal deployment in business schools', *Sustainability* 12 (1): 440.

Gatignon, A. and Capron, L. (2020) 'The firm as an architect of polycentric governance: building open institutional infrastructure in emerging markets', *Strategic Management Journal*: 1– 38. https://doi.org/10.1002/Smj.3124 (accessed 1 February 2022).

Gravelle, J. (2015) *Tax Havens: International Tax Avoidance and Evasion*, Congressional Research Service Report, R40623, January.

Greenwald, G. and Linhares, J. F. (2019) 'Russo deferiu uma busca que não foi pedida por ninguém', *The Intercept*, 19 October.

Hadjikhani, A. and Ghauri, P. (2006) 'Multinational enterprises and their lobbying activities in the European Union', in L. Oxelheim (ed.), *Institutional Transparency for Economic Growth in Europe* (Oxford: Elsevier), 371–98.

Harris, B. (2020) 'Investigators fear the end in near for Brazil's Lava Jato probe', *Financial Times*, 16 August.

Harris, B. and Schipani, A. (2020) 'Sergio Moro, the Brazilian "Judge Dread" who brings down presidents', *Financial Times*, 8 May.

Harris, B., Schipani, A. and Long, G. (2020) 'Coronavirus corruption cases spread across Latin America', *Financial Times*, 7 July.

He, H. and Harris, L. (2020) 'The impact of Covid-19 pandemic on corporate social responsibility and marketing philosophy', *Journal of Business Research*, 116: 176–82.

Hennebel, L. (2006) 'L'affaire Total-Unocal en Birmanie jugée en Europe et aux Etats Unis', CRIDHO Working Paper 2006/09. http://cridho.uclouvain.be/documents/Working.Papers/CRIDHO.WP.2006.09.pdf (accessed 6 July 2017).

Hess, D. and Dunfee, T. (2001) 'Fighting corruption: a principled approach', Wharton School Working Paper.

Hewlett-Packard (2005) *2005 HP Global Citizenship Report*. http://www8.hp.com/us/en/pdf/hp2005gcreport_tcm_245_1368286.pdf (accessed 15 June 2017).

Holliday, C., Schmidheiny, S. and Watts, P. (2002) *Walking the Talk: The Business Case for Sustainable Development* (Sheffield: Greenleaf Publishing).

Husted, B. (2013) 'Global environmental and social strategy', *Global Strategy Journal*, 3: 195–7.

ILO (International Labour Organization) (2017) *Facts on Child Labour 2010* (Geneva: ILO).

Jenkins, R. (2001) *Corporate Codes of Conduct Self-Regulation in a Global Economy*, United Nations Research Institute for Social Development, Technology and Society Programme Paper no. 2.

Johnsson-Latham, G. (2007) 'A study on gender equality as a prerequisite for sustainable development', Report to the Environment Advisory Council, Sweden.

Katsoulakos, P. et al. (2004) *A Historic Perspective of the CSR Movement*, White Paper SFAID, Athens University, December.

Kaufmann, D. and Wei, S. (1999) 'Does "grease money" speed up the wheels of commerce?', National Bureau of Economic Research, Working Paper No. w7093, April.

Kolk, A. (2016) 'The social responsibility of international business: from ethics and the environment to CSR and sustainable development', *Journal of World Business,* 51 (1): 23–34.

Kolk, A., van Tulder, R. and Welters, C. (1999) 'International codes of conduct and corporate social responsibility: can transnational corporations regulate themselves?', *Transnational Corporations*, 8 (1): 143–80.

Konchinski, V. (2109) 'Substituto de Moro, reduz velocidade de julgamentos da Lava Jato no Paraná' UOL, 14 September. https://noticias.uol.com.br/politica/ultimas-noticias/2019/09/14/saida-de-moro-reduz-velocidade-de-julgamentos-da-lava-jato-no-pr.htm (accessed 11 June 2020).

Kumar, A., Connell, J. and Bhattacharyya, A. (2020) 'Co-opetition for corporate social responsibility and sustainability: drivers and success factors', *Sustainability Accounting, Management and Policy Journal*. https://www.researchgate.net/publication/347728567_Co-opetition_for_corporate_social_responsibility_and_sustainability_drivers_and_success_factors (accessed 24 May 2021).

Lehni, M. (2000) *Eco-efficiency: Creating More Value with Less Impact* (Geneva: World Business Council for Sustainable Development).

Leite, C. and Weiman, J. (1999) 'Does Mother Nature corrupt natural resources? Corruption and economic growth', IMF Working Paper, WP/99/85, July.

Li, C. and Reuer, J. J. (2020) 'The impact of corruption on market reactions to international strategic alliances', *Journal of International Business Studies*: 1–16.

Mauro, P. (1997) *Why Worry About Corruption*?, Economic Issues Series, 6 (Washington, DC: IMF).

Monaghan, P. (2013) 'Corporate social responsibility: how the movement has evolved since the 90s', *Guardian*, 11 May.

Monteiro, L. F. and Albuquerque, T. (2018) *Doing Business in Brazil after Operation Car Wash (A)*, INSEAD Case study. https://publishing.insead.edu/case/car-wash (accessed 1 February 2022).

Monteiro, L. F. and Kertesz, S. (2021) *Doing Business in Brazil after Operation Car* Wash *(B)*, INSEAD Case study. https://publishing.insead.edu/case/doing-business-brazil-after-operation-car-wash-b (accessed 1 February 2022).

Monteiro, L. F. and Benavente J.M.G. (2019), *Enel's Innovability: Global Open Innovation and Sustainability*, INSEAD Case Study. https://publishing.insead.edu/case/enel.

Netherlands Environmental Assessment Agency (PBL) (2020), 'Trends in mondiale uitstoot van CO_2 en alle broeikasgassen: 2020 rapport'. https://www.pbl.nl/publicaties/trends-in-mondiale-uitstoot-van-co2-en-alle-broeikasgassen-2020-rapport (accessed 1 February 2022).

Nichols, M. (1993) 'Third-world families at work: child labor or child care?', *Harvard Business Review*, 71 (1): 12–23.

Nugent, C. (2020) 'I didn't enter the government to serve a Master. Brazil's Star Justice Minister on His Resignation and Clash With President Bolsonaro', *Time Magazine*, 21 May.

Odziemkowska, K. and Henisz, W. (2020) 'Webs of influence: secondary stakeholder actions and cross-national corporate social performance', *Organization Science*, 32 (1): 233–55.

OECD (Organisation for Economic Co-operation and Development) (2000) *No Longer Business as Usual* (Paris: OECD).

OECD (Organisation for Economic Co-operation and Development) (2001) *Sustainable Development* (Paris: OECD).

OECD (Organisation for Economic Co-operation and Development) (2007) *Integrity in Public Procurement* (Paris: OECD).

OECD (Organisation for Economic Co-operation and Development) (2008) *Enhancing Integrity in Public*

Procurement: A Checklist (Paris: OECD). http://www.oecd.org/gov/41760991.pdf (accessed 30 May 2017).

OECD (Organisation for Economic Co-operation and Development) (2009) *Recommendation of the Council for Further Combating Bribery of Foreign Public Officials in International Business Transactions*, Working Group on Bribery in International Business Transactions (Paris: OECD). http://www.oecd.org/daf/anti-bribery/44176910.pdf (accessed 30 May 2017).

OECD (Organisation for Economic Co-operation and Development) (2014) *The Rationale for Fighting Corruption*, CleanGovBiz, Background briefing (Paris: OECD). https://www.oecd.org/cleangovbiz/49693613.pdf (accessed 30 May 2017).

OECD (Organisation for Economic Co-operation and Development) (2015) *Tax Transparency 2015: Report on Progress*, The Global Forum on Transparency and Exchange of Information for Tax Purposes 2015. https://www.oecd.org/tax/transparency/global-forum-annual-report-2015.pdf (accessed 31 May 2017).

Onofre, R. (2019) 'Deputados retiram prisão em 2ª instância de pacote de Moro', *O Estados de S.Paulo*, 9 July. https://politica.estadao.com.br/noticias/geral,grupo-de-trabalho-da-camara-rejeita-proposta-de-prisao-apos-condenacao-em-2-instancia,70002914370 (accessed 19 October 2020).

Philips, D. (2017) 'Car Wash Launches Revolution in Transparency and Compliance', *Financial Times*, 15 May 2017. https://www.ft.com/content/885536a6-30ae-11e7-9555-23ef563ecf9a (accessed 1 February 2022).

Plas, G. and Erdmenger, C. (2000) *Green Purchasing Good Practice Guide*, An ICLEI 'Policy and Practice' Publication (Freiburg: ICLEI).

Pope, J. (2000) *Confronting Corruption: The Elements of a National Integrity System* (London: Transparency International).

Rangan, S. (ed.) (2015) *Performance and Progress: Essays on Capitalism, Business, and Society* (Oxford: Oxford University Press).

Reinhart, F. L. (1999) *Down to Earth: Applying Business Principles to Environmental Management* (Boston, MA: Harvard Business School Press).

Rocharun, M. and Casey, N. (2018) 'Peru's president offers resignation over vote-buying scandal', *The New York Times*, 21 March. www.nytimes.com/2018/03/21/world/americas/peru-kuczynski-resigns.html (accessed 1 February 2022).

Sane, P. (2001) *Why Human Rights Should Matter, Earth Times News*, 8 January. https://www.globalpolicy.org/component/content/article/225/32149.html (accessed 21 June 2017).

Schipani, A. (2019) 'Sergio Moro takes his crusade inside Brazil's halls of power', *Financial Times*, 14 January.

Schipani, A., Stott, M. and Webber, J. (2019) 'Latin America: Brazil's anti-corruption drive faces a backlash', *Financial Times*, 11 August.

Schütte, H. (1986) *Peter Clausen*, INSEAD Case Study.

Shell Corporation (2015) *Sustainable Reporting and Performance.* http://www.shell.com/sustainability/sustainability-reporting-and-performance-data.html (accessed 31 May 2017).

Smith, C. (2003) 'Corporate social responsibility: whether or how?', *California Management Review*, 45 (4): 1–25.

Soubbotina, T. P. (2004) *Beyond Economic Growth: An Introduction to Sustainable Development*, WBI Learning Resources Series (Washington, DC: World Bank).

Stevens, C. E. and Newenham-Kahindi, A. (2021) 'Avoid, acquiesce … or engage? New insights from sub-Saharan Africa on MNE strategies for managing corruption', *Strategic Management Journal*, 42 (2): 273–301.

Tanzi, V. (1998) 'Corruption around the world: causes, consequences, scope and cure', International Monetary Fund Staff Paper, 559.

Tashman, P., Marano, V. and Kostova, T. (2019) 'Walking the walk or talking the talk? Corporate social responsibility decoupling in emerging market multinationals', *Journal of International Business Studies*, 50 (2): 153–71.

Transparency International (various years) *Corruption Perceptions Index*. http://www.transparency.org/research/cpi/overview (accessed 26 April 2021).

UNEP (United Nations Environment Programme) (2011) *Towards a Green Economy: Pathways to Sustainable Development and Poverty Eradication* (Nairobi: UNEP). https://sustainabledevelopment.un.org/index.php?page=view&type=400&nr=126&menu=35 (accessed 8 February 2022).

UNFCC (United Nations Framework Convention on Climate Change) (2004) *The First Ten Years* (Bonn: UNFCCC). http://unfccc.int/resource/docs/publications/first_ten_years_en.pdf (accessed 1 February 2022).

UNICEF (2014) *Child Labour and UNICEF in Action: Children at the Centre* (New York: UNICEF).

United Nation Global Compact (2011) Business Against Corruption – A Framework for Action. https://www.unglobalcompact.org/library/162 (accessed 1 February 2022).

United Nations Conference on Environment and Development (1992) *Rio Declaration on Environment and Development*. http://www.unesco.org/education/pdf/RIO_E.PDF (accessed 15 June 2017).

United Nations (2011) *Cities and Climate Change: Global Report on Human Settlements 2011 – Policy Directions* (Nairobi: United Nations Human Settlements Programme). http://unhabitat.org/books/cities-and-climate-change-global-report-on-human-settlements-2011-abridged/ (accessed 30 May 2017).

United Nations (2015) *Transforming our World: The 2030 Agenda for Sustainable Development*. https://sustainabledevelopment.un.org/post2015/transformingourworld/publication (accessed 1 February 2022).

United Nations (2020) *The Sustainable Development Goals Report 2020*. https://unstats.un.org/sdgs/report/2020/ (accessed 1 February 2022).

United Nations World Commission on Environment and Development (1987) *Our Common Future, World Commission on Environment and Development* ['the Brundtland Report'] (London: Oxford University Press).

United States Environmental Agency (2021) *EPA's Climate Change Indicators in the United States*. https://www.epa.gov/climate-indicators (accessed 26 April 2021).

US Department of Labor (2018) Bureau of International Labor Affairs '2018 List Of Goods Produced By Child Labor Or Forced Labor'. https://www.dol.gov/sites/dolgov/files/ILAB/ListofGoods.pdf (accessed 1 February 2022).

Van Tulder, R. and Kolk, A. (2001) 'Multinationality and corporate ethics: codes of conduct in the sporting goods industry', *Journal of International Business Studies*, 32 (2): 267–83.

Wei, S. (1998) 'Corruption in economic development: beneficial grease, minor annoyance or major obstacle?', Harvard University and National Bureau of Economic Research Working Paper.

Wheeler, D., Retchman, R., Heike, F. and Boele, R. (2001a) 'Shell Nigeria and the Ogoni. A study in unsustainable development: the story of Shell Nigeria and the Ogoni people: conflict and prospects for resolution', *Sustainable Development*, 9: 74–86.

Wheeler, D., Retchman, R., Heike, F. and Boele, R. (2001b) 'Shell Nigeria and the Ogoni. A study in unsustainable development: corporate social responsibility and stakeholder management versus a rights-based approach to sustainable development', *Sustainable Development*, 9: 121–35.

Wheeler. D., Retchman, R., Heike, F. and Boele, R. (2001c) 'Shell Nigeria and the Ogoni. A study in unsustainable development: the story of Shell Nigeria and the Ogoni people: analysis and implications of Royal Dutch Shell Group's strategy', *Sustainable Development*, 9: 177–98.

World Bank (2012) *Inclusive Green Growth: The Pathway to Sustainable Development* (Washington, DC: World Bank).

World Business Council for Sustainable Development (2010) Vision 2050. https://www.wbcsd.org/Overview/About-us/Vision-2050-Time-to-Transform (accessed 30 May 2017).

World Resources Institute (2015) CAIT Climate Data Explorer (Washington, DC: World Resources Institute). http://cait.wri.org (accessed 30 May 2017).

WWF International and Zoological Society of London (2014) *Living Planet Report 2014: Species and Spaces, People and Places*. https://www.wwf.or.jp/activities/lib/lpr/WWF_LPR_2014.pdf (accessed 30 May 2017).

Xavier, C. V., Pitta, F. T. and Mendonça, M. L. (2011) 'Social and environmental impacts of sugarcane production in Brazil', Transnational Institute. https://www.tni.org/en/sugarcane-brazil (accessed 31 May 2017).

Yandle, B. (1999) 'Enviro-capitalists: doing good while doing well', in T. A. Anderson and D. R. Leal (eds), *Capitalism and Environmentalism Go Hand* (Irvington-on-Hudson, NY: The Freeman Foundation for Economic Education).

Journals

Journal of World Business: https://www.journals.elsevier.com/journal-of-world-business

Sustainability: https://www.mdpi.com/journal/sustainability

Sustainable Development: https://onlinelibrary.wiley.com/journal/10991719

Journal of International Business Studies: https://www.palgrave.com/gp/journal/41267

Journal of Sustainable Development (*JSD*): http://www.ccsenet.org/journal/index.php/jsd

Part II

Global strategies

Chapter 5 Designing a global strategy | Chapter 5 defines the various approaches to business strategy and its components and how these apply to global businesses. It covers the formulation of objectives, the choice of countries and regions, the competitive positioning of products and services, the design of and investment in a global business system to create and sustain global competitive advantages and the choice of a global organization design. It will also explore the processes by which firms globalize, making a distinction between large multinational firms, small and medium-sized enterprises and 'born global' start-ups. The chapter will also discuss the measurement of corporate globalization.

Chapter 6 Assessing countries' attractiveness | Chapter 6 looks at the first step in the decision to develop globally – the selection of countries in which to invest. It presents the various steps in the analysis of opportunities and risks. This covers such aspects as country risk analysis, business system analysis, industry and competitive analysis, market opportunities and host government incentives.

Chapter 7 Entry strategies | Chapter 7 discusses the various decision choices in entering a country market. It considers issues of timing and the various forms of entry, ranging from wholly owned subsidiaries to joint ventures, licensing or other types of franchising, distributors' agreements or a representative office, each form being analysed in terms of its advantages and disadvantages.

Chapter 8 Global mergers, acquisitions and strategic alliances | Chapter 8 focuses on the many ways of combining capabilities between two or more firms in order to increase and obtain the competitive advantages needed in the global marketplace. The chapter will look first at mergers and acquisitions (M&As) as a means of achieving economies of scale and scope. It offers an analysis of the various phases of global M&As, from pre-acquisition, to valuation and post-acquisition. Then it turns the reader's attention to the various forms of strategic partnerships linking two or several independent firms. Those partnerships can be global strategic alliances, local joint ventures or simply any form of long-term contract. A framework for the analysis of strategic alliances and practical recommendations for their implementation are then given.

Chapter 5

Designing a global strategy

At the end of this chapter you will be able to:

- Identify a global strategy by breaking down all its elements
- Contribute meaningfully to the formulation of a global strategy
- Describe a global business system
- Identify the sources of competitive advantages in a given company

Introduction

The globalization of industries discussed in Chapter 1 was led by a few pioneering companies that identified early on the opportunities offered by designing and implementing global strategies. The majority of those companies have developed their global presence progressively while some other 'born global' firms have globalized very soon after their creation. In this chapter, a framework for the formulation of global strategies is proposed, based on the experience of leading global companies. The chapter starts by defining what *business strategy* is about and how it applies to *global companies*. It uses the example of how Samsung Electronics has developed its global strategy. The framework for the strategy consists of:

- *Global ambition*: stating the long-term objectives of the corporation as well as the relative importance of the regions in its global footprint.
- *Global positioning*: choice of countries, customer segments and value proposition.
- *Global business system*: investment in resources, assets and competence to create a global value chain and global capabilities, either directly or through alliances and acquisitions.
- *Global organization*: global structure, processes, coordination and human resources (HR) management.

This chapter details all of these elements and provides some tools:

- The *Transnational Index*, the *Global Revenue Index* and the *Global Capabilities Index*, which measure the extent to which a company can be considered a global or a regional player
- The classification of countries according to their *strategic importance* (key countries, emerging countries, platform countries, marketing countries)
- The definition of *global positioning* according to the scope of markets, value proposition and competitive approach based on cost leadership or differentiation
- *Business system* design
- *Competitive advantages* analysis
- *Sustainability* of competitive advantages.

The chapter then describes three stages in the process of globalization: export, multinational and global. It ends by sketching the various forms of organizational structures found among multinational and global firms.

A company business strategy

A company business strategy is a set of *fundamental choices* which defines its long-term objectives, its value proposition to the market, how it intends to build and sustain a competitive business system and how it organizes itself. (See Insert 5.1 for a more detailed definition of strategy.)

Insert 5.1 Origin, content, purpose and drivers of strategy

Strategy (from the Greek, *stratos* (an army) and *agein* (to lead)) has traditionally been a military art. The ancient Chinese military theorist, Sun Tzu (*c*. 500 BCE) stated that 'the supreme art of war is to subdue the enemy without fighting'.

Strategy as an art of war was transferred into a business context in the early 1960s (Ansoff 1965). This does not mean that there was no 'strategy' behind business decisions before this; there were just no formal theories of business strategy.

There are several schools of thought about what business strategy is, but all schools recognize that business strategy has to do with *choice* and *investments*. A business strategy will generally cover the following:

- **Ambition:** Choice of *long-term objectives* for the business.
- **Positioning:** Choice of products and customer *segments* and of a *value proposition* to customers.
- **Capability building:** Choice of investments in order to create a business system that is able to *deliver value competitively*.

- **Organization:** Choice of *people*, *structures*, *processes and systems*.

The concept of strategy may apply at various levels in a corporation (see Table 5.1). The most frequent distinctions are:

- **Business strategy** (also called *competitive strategy*) is applied at the level of a business operating in a particular industry segment. It defines the way the business wants, and is able, to compete in its segment.
- If the market in which the firm operates is global, its business strategy will be a **global business strategy** that defines its long-term objectives and selects its value proposition for the world market. A global business strategy will also build, integrate and coordinate its business system to gain and sustain a global competitive advantage, and put in place an organizational system to manage its operations worldwide.
- **Corporate strategy** is applied at the level of a company engaged in different business segments: the multi-business corporation. It essentially defines the portfolio of businesses in which the corporation wants to operate and the resource allocation pattern among those businesses.
- If the corporation operates globally, the corporate strategy will be a **global corporate strategy** which will integrate the various global strategies of the different businesses in the corporate portfolio.

Purpose and drivers of strategy

The purpose of business strategy is to build and sustain a competitive business system in selected markets leading to economic value creation. Economic value is created when the revenues generated by the business is equal to or larger than the total cost of doing business (see Figure 5.1).

Economic value is driven by two major forces:

- the macro structural characteristics of the industry in which the company operates (Porter 1980);
- the ability to build and sustain competitive advantages (Porter 1985).

Hence, the key choices of strategy are firstly to decide where the company will compete and secondly to invest in capabilities leading to competitive advantages.

Table 5.1 Business, corporate and global strategy

	Business strategy: competing in one industry	Corporate strategy: competing in several industries and/or industry segments	Global strategy: competing in several countries
Ambition	• Business definition • Mission/vision • Long-term objectives	• Business definition • Mission/vision • Long-term objectives • Relative importance of businesses	• Business definition • Mission/vision • Long-term objectives • Relative importance of regions and countries

Positioning	• Which customer segments • Which countries • Our value proposition	• Which businesses • Degree of integration • Our competitive principles (differentiation/costs)	• Which regions/ countries • Degree of integration • Our competitive principles (global/local)
Capabilities building	• Business system design • Key investments • Acquisition, mergers, joint ventures, alliances?	• Resource allocation among businesses • Mergers, acquisitions, alliances • New entries/exit	• Resource allocation among regions/ countries • Designing global value chain • Mergers, acquisitions, alliances • New entries/exit
Organization	• HRM development • Structure • Processes • Policies • Values and culture	• Corporate internal governance • Corporate HRM • Structure • Policies • Values and culture	• Corporate internal governance HRM policies • Global structure • Degree of autonomy of subsidiaries • Integration and coordination among subsidiaries • Values and culture

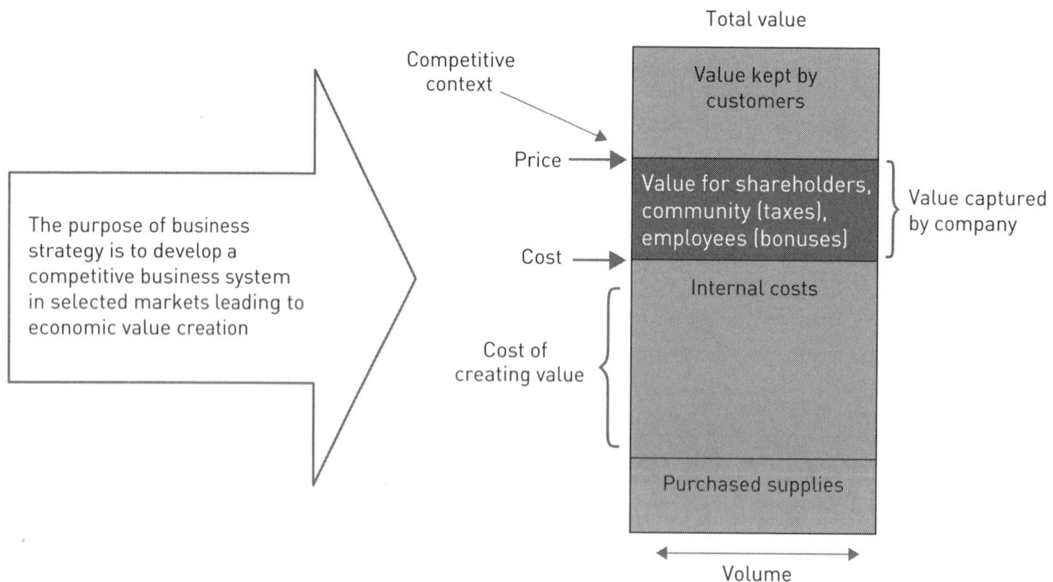

Figure 5.1 The purpose of strategy

Source: Authors' own, see Besanko et al. (2007) for further discussion.

A business strategy is global when a company competes in key markets across the world and when its business system consists of integrated and coordinated activities across borders.

The case of Samsung Electronics illustrates how their global strategy has been developed over time.

EXAMPLE 5.1 Samsung Electronics

The Samsung Group is one of the leading Korean conglomerates (known as *chaebol*). It was created in 1938 by its founder and first chairman Byung-Chull Lee as a trading firm which then diversified into many other activities after the Korean War ended in 1953. Samsung Electronics is the leading subsidiary of the Samsung Group. In 2014, with consolidated sales of $216 billion and 286,000 employees in eighty counties, it accounted for 70 per cent of the turnover of the group.

Created in 1969, Samsung Electronics initially focused production on electronic components, transistors, integrated circuits and microchips. Then it developed products that incorporated those components, such as TV sets and microwave ovens, for its domestic market. Because of the already-established trading links and capabilities of the wider Samsung Corporation, Samsung Electronics was able to engage in international business very early in its life. The earliest international development for Samsung Electronics was in exporting electronic components: TV sets followed by microwave ovens on an original equipment manufacturer (OEM) basis in the late 1970s. Early in the 1990s the company started to market its products internationally under its own brand name. By the late 1980s/early 1990s, assembly plants had been set up in Thailand, Indonesia and Malaysia, followed by China, Brazil and Vietnam. Three factories opened in 1994 in Texas, USA, and in 1995 the company opened regional headquarters in the USA, Germany, Singapore and China. Subsequently, R&D centres were set up in the USA, Russia, India, Japan, China, Israel, Poland and Brazil. The global strategy was formalized in the mid-1990s and was based on 'a dedication to making world-class products, providing customer satisfaction and being a good corporate citizen, all under the vision of quality first'. After the Asian financial crisis of 1997, the Samsung Group reduced the number of its businesses and divested from some activities such as car manufacturing in order to focus on more promising sectors such as electronics. In the late 1990s, the company launched a line of mobile telephones that eventually led to entry into the smartphone and tablet markets and to direct (and successful) competition with Apple's iPhones and iPads. By 2015, Samsung Electronics had become the world leader in a large number of products, including LCD TV panels, smartphones and DRAM, relying on a network of eleven regional headquarters, thirty-seven production centres, thirty-four research centres and fifty-six local sales organizations.

Analysis of Samsung Electronics' global strategy

Created before the Second World War, when Korea was under Japanese rule, Samsung was a trading company similar to the Japanese *Sogo Shosha*.[1] It was only after the Korean War that it became a *chaebol*, a diversified group that started to produce and export products: insurance in 1958, electronics in 1969, heavy industry in 1976, aerospace and chemicals in 1979, IT in 1985, plus many others over time. Samsung Electronics was only one of several companies within the Samsung Group. The *ambition* of Samsung Electronics shifted from being an exporter to becoming a multinational firm with assembly factories scattered across Asia, Europe and America. After the 1997 Asian crisis, the focus was to become a global player, primarily – but not exclusively – in mobile telephony.

The *positioning* of Samsung Electronics is to offer world-class quality, standardized products, based on innovation and relying on thirty-four research and development centres. Since its founding, Samsung has become a global brand (see Figure 5.2).

A global integrated network of factories, R&D centres and sales organizations was set up over time while the company concentrated on limited leading product lines.

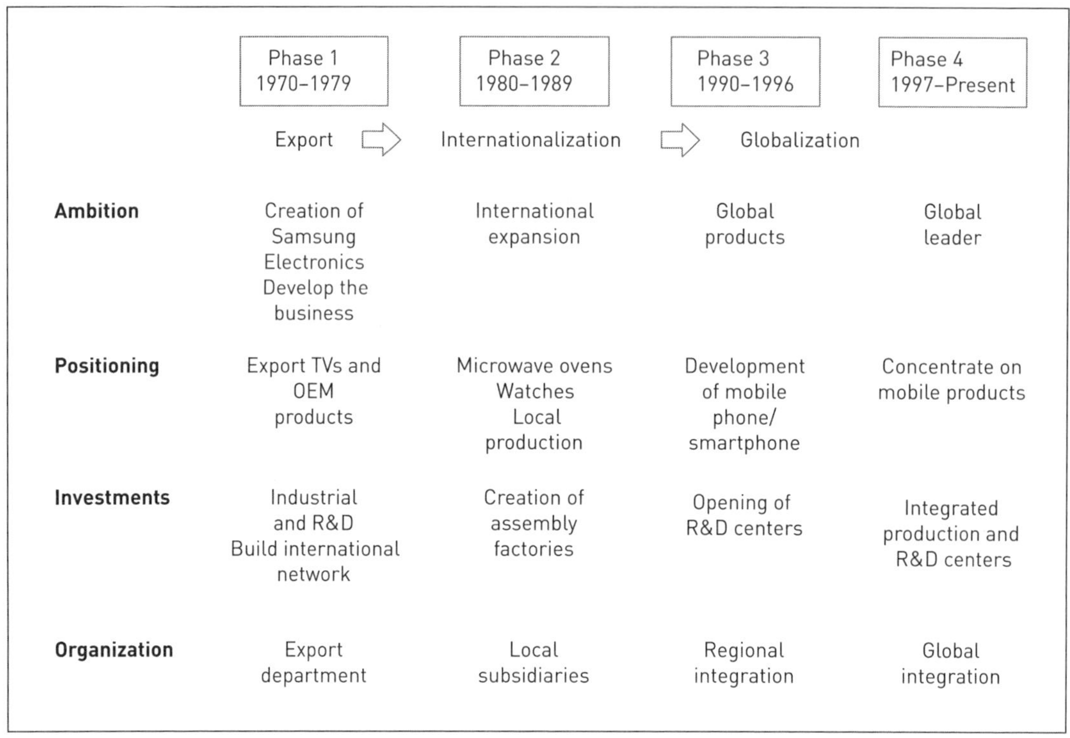

Figure 5.2 Global development of Samsung Electronics

Based on the Samsung example, it is now possible to describe more formally the components of a global strategy.

Framework for a global strategy

A global strategy is made up of four major components (see Figure 5.3):

- Global strategic *ambition*
- Strategic global *positioning*
- Global *business system*
- Global *organization*.

Global ambition

The global strategic ambition expresses the role a company wants to play in the world marketplace. It defines two types of perspective: the rationale for globalization and the scope of the global presence.

Rationale for globalization: market/resource/capability-seeking objectives

According to John Dunning,[2] global expansion can be driven by three kinds of motive: market-seeking, resource-seeking and capability-seeking.

- *Market-seeking* objectives relate to the pursuit of sales expansion in international territories. This can be achieved by exports or local operational subsidiaries.
- *Resource-seeking* objectives relate to accessing natural and human resources in international territories in order to use those resources for global competitiveness. This is achieved by contractual sourcing, direct exploitation of mining or agriculture, or by setting up offshore production centres.
- *Capability-seeking* objectives are aimed at capturing innovative or logistical capabilities that international territories may offer. This can be achieved by setting up local R&D centres, logistic or hub centres, research alliances or intelligence offices.

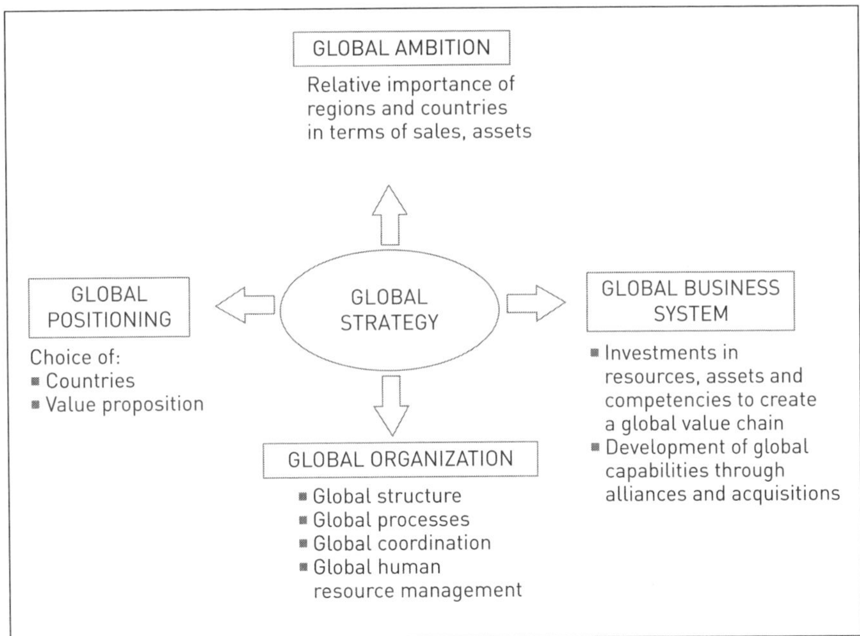

Figure 5.3 Global strategy framework

Scope of the global presence

The scope of the global presence expresses how the company views the future distribution of its sales and assets in key regional clusters worldwide, and can be formulated into four types of role:

- Global player
- Regional player
- Global exporter
- Global sourcer.

A company whose ambition is to be a **global player** aspires to establish a *sustainable competitive position in the key markets of the world* and to build an integrated business system of designs spread over those key markets. Sony and Samsung Electronics fit such a description, as would Nestlé, Unilever, Ericsson, Nokia, Siemens, Shell, Canon, Procter & Gamble, Toyota and HSBC.

A **regional player** aims to capture a *strong competitive advantage in one of the key regions of the world* – North America, Europe or Asia – and to remain a marginal or relatively weak competitor in the other parts. Companies such as Peugeot, Shiseido or Barclays would be examples of such an ambition. The distinction between a global player and a regional player is more about the relative importance of each major region of the world in the company's portfolio, rather than the stated ambition of the company in its external communications. Many companies assert that they are 'global', when their accounts reflect a strong concentration of their sales to one region.[3] However, this situation may change if the company has a real ambition to become a global player that is supported by the appropriate investment. Renault, for instance, a traditional European player, has acquired controlling positions in Nissan, Samsung automobiles, Mitsubishi and Avtovaz, transforming the company into a European, Asian and North American player thanks to Nissan's operations in the USA.

A **global exporter** is a company whose role is to *sell in the key markets of the world* products manufactured or services operated in its home country, and that builds foreign operations only to support the export drive. The major aerospace or defence companies such as Boeing, Airbus and Raytheon can be classified in this category despite the fact that they have some supporting assets (maintenance, sales offices, etc.) outside their home region.

A **global sourcer** is a company that procures a large fraction of its product components from factories located outside its base market and concentrates its sales in its *domestic market*. In such a case the ambition would hardly qualify as global. However, many managerial issues of integration and coordination of activities, such as in-house factories or long-term subcontracting, would be quite similar to those that a global company would have to face.

In order to assess the degree of global ambition exhibited by companies, we will look at the distribution of their sales, assets and personnel.

In 2019, the world economy produced $87,700 billion worth of goods and services: 33 per cent in America (North and South), 35 per cent in Asia and Oceania, 26 per cent in Europe and 6 per cent in Africa. The global GDP was expected to exceed $100 trillion in 2022.

In certain industries the distribution of markets can differ from the distribution of GDP, and growth differentials will make the future distribution of world markets different from what it is today. Table 5.2 gives a distribution of world markets by regions.

Table 5.2 Distribution of the world market by regions in selected industries, 2019 (as a percentage of US$ value)

Industry	Asia Pacific	Europe	Americas	Middle East and Africa
Advertising	35	20	38	7
Apparel and Footwear	39	26	29	7
Appliances	48	19	28	5
Automotive components	35	25	36	4
Chemicals	60	18	14	8
Construction	53	21	24	2
Consumer Electronics	47	19	26	7
Defense	31	22	39	8
IT services	24	31	44	1
Life insurance	42	31	25	2
Medical Equipment	37	30	26	7
Personal care	36	25	33	6
Retailing	38	25	30	7
Telecom services	40	22	26	12
Tyres	42	26	28	4
GDP (2019)	35	26	33	6

Source: Authors' own, based on data from various sources.

A *pure*, global company should ideally exhibit three major characteristics:

1. The distribution of its sales would be proportional to the distribution of markets in its industry. For instance, Sony's distribution of sales is 28 per cent in North America, 23 per cent in Europe and 39 per cent in Asia, which closely replicates the percentage distribution of consumer electronic industry markets (23 per cent in North America, 36 per cent in Europe and 38 per cent in Asia).
2. The distribution of its assets and workforce would be proportional to the distribution of markets in its industry.
3. It would manage its activities in an integrated and coordinated way across the globe.

Obviously, this may not apply to all industries, given that no two industries have the same degree of global pressure towards globalization, as has been discussed in Chapter 1. In a global industry such as the tyre industry, where the distribution of the market is 31 per cent in North America, 30 per cent in Europe, 35 per cent in Asia and 4 per cent in the rest of the world, the distribution of revenues of the five major players differs substantially from the industry distribution, as shown in Table 5.3.

Table 5.3 Distribution of markets and revenues in tyres, 2019 (%)

Company	Americas	Europe	Asia and rest of the world
Bridgestone	42	15	43
Continental	26	49	25
Goodyear	54	32	14
Michelin	37	37	26
Pirelli	34	48	18
Global Tire Industry	33	26	46

Source: Companies' annual reports.

The globalization indices

There are two useful globalization indices for evaluating the extent to which a company has followed a global ambition. Online Appendix 5.1 gives a technical explanation of the measurement of those indices.

- The Transnational Index (TNI), used by the United Nations Conference on Trade and Development (UNCTAD), is a composite ratio of the proportion of activities outside the home country of a multinational firm.

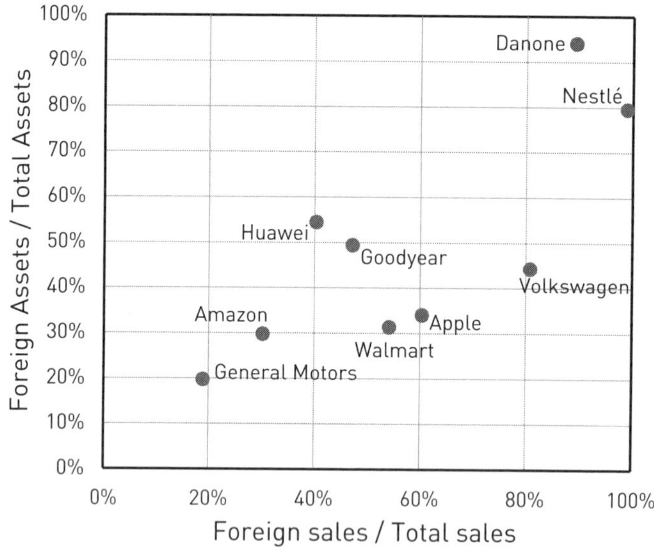

Figure 5.4 A mapping of several global companies using the TNI index

- The Global Revenue Index (GRI) represents a company's distribution of sales in the major world regions as a percentage of the industry distribution of demand in the same regions.[4] If the world market in an industry is divided in the proportion of 30 per cent in North America, 30 per cent in Europe, 30 per cent in Asia and 10 per cent in the rest of the world, the GRI will compare the actual distribution of sales of a company in those four major regions with sales distribution for the industry as a whole. A company with a low GRI is more concentrated in one region, while a company with a high GRI will have a distribution of sales similar to the distribution of the global demand in that industry.

- The Global Capability Index (GCI) represents the distribution of *assets* or *personnel* in a similar way to the GRI. Companies which rely heavily on external sourcing will have a low GCI score. This is because the company cannot deploy resources and capabilities at will, but relies on external parties to supply the capability. This reliance on external parties also means that the company can face potential problems such as product/service unavailability, time delays in delivery or price pressure from its overseas suppliers.

By combining the GCI and the GRI in one chart, we obtain a mapping of the *global ambition of players* (Figure 5.5).

A company low in both GRI and GCI would be a regional player, a company low in GRI and high in GCI would be a global operator, a company low in GCI and high in GRI would be a global exporter, while a company high in both dimensions would be a global player and a company with an average score in both dimensions would be a regional player.

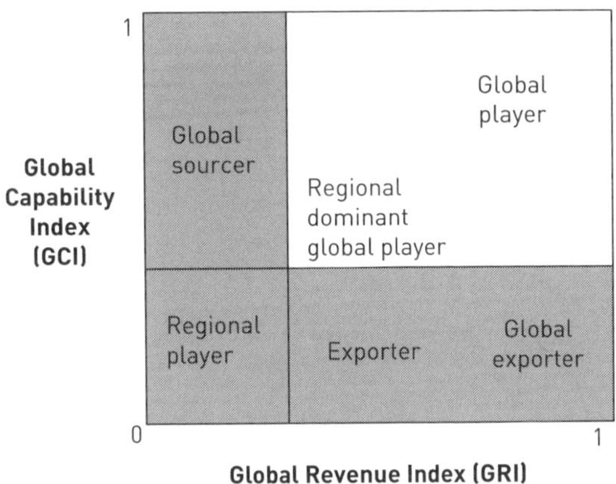

Figure 5.5 Mapping of global ambition

Figure 5.6 shows the mapping of four leading companies: Michelin in the tyre industry, Airbus in the aircraft industry, Walmart in retailing and Nestlé in foods. Michelin and Nestlé can be considered as global players while Walmart is positioned as a regional player and Airbus as a global exporter.

None of these indices is perfect. The UNCTAD index favours companies from smaller exporting countries (Switzerland, for instance) to the detriment of corporations from large countries (the USA, for instance). For their part, the GRI and GCI still assign a global score to companies that concentrate their operations in one region or country. For instance, a US company having 100 per cent of its sales in the USA would still obtain a global score, which would be equivalent to the relative size of the US presence in the world.

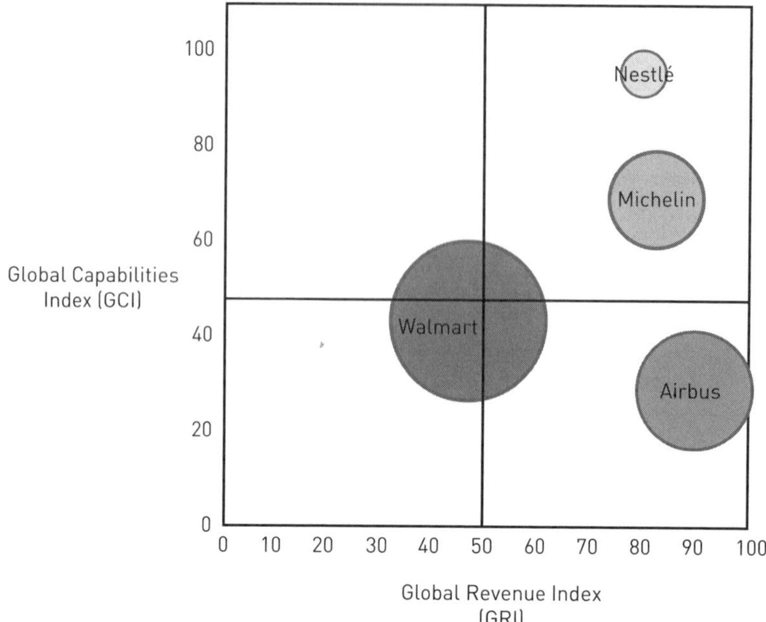

Figure 5.6 Comparative mapping of global ambition: comparison of Walmart (retailing), Michelin (tyres), Airbus (aircraft), Nestlé (foods)

Note: *The size of the bubbles is proportional to total sales in 2014.*

Source: Authors' own construction using data from the companies' websites.

Dynamic utilization of the global indices

As part of the strategy formulation process, companies can use the global indices to analyse their position and set their global ambition.

To illustrate, we will take the example of Whirlpool and the global appliance industry.

EXAMPLE 5.2 Whirlpool

In 1980 Whirlpool was essentially a regional operator. Its sales and assets were concentrated in the United States. Its GRI was 0.35 and its GCI 0.40. The white goods industry (refrigerators, washers, cookers) was at that time primarily a regional industry. For instance, American refrigerators tended to be too big to fit easily in European or Japanese homes. However, the industry gradually moved towards globalization because of the huge economies of scale to be gained in manufacturing components, branding and R&D. The Swedish company, Electrolux, moved aggressively within Europe to become a pan-European company and invested in the United States and Asia to become a global player. The Whirlpool management realized that the company's future would be at stake if it did not follow a globalization path. The first step of this process was an alliance with the Philips appliance business, which became an acquisition. From a single regional player, Whirlpool moved into the position of a dual regional player with a strong delocalization of its factories, particularly in Latin

America. Then, in the early 1990s, Whirlpool realized that the Asia Pacific region was going to represent 40 per cent of world sales for refrigerators, washers and cookers. It set a target of gaining a significant position in Asia. By the year 2010, Whirlpool had become a global player but retreated from China then lowering its Global GRI by 2019 (see Figure 5.7).

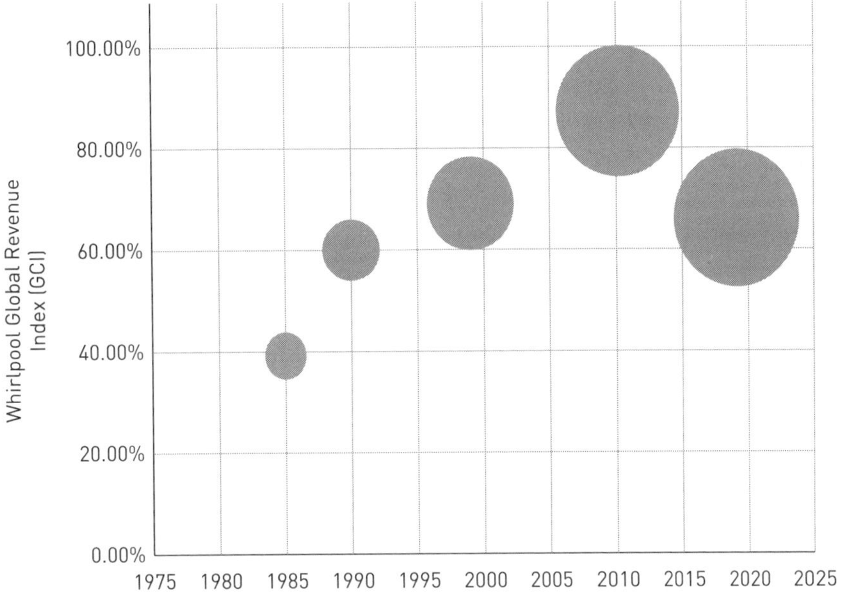

Figure 5.7 The evolution of Whirlpool's globalization (measured by GRI)
Note: *Bubbles are proportional to sales.*
Source: Authors' own using data from www.whirlpool.com.

Global positioning

Global positioning consists of two types of choice:

- First, the *choice of countries* in which the company wants to compete and the role that those countries play in the global portfolio.
- Second, the definition of the various *value propositions* for the products or services of the company, corresponding to the type of segments and countries in which the company wants to compete.

Choice of countries

Depending on the industry, countries differ in the opportunities they offer to companies for their strategic development. Some countries, given their size, growth or the quality of their human, natural or locational resources, are critical for companies' long-term competitiveness. Those countries are classed as **key**

countries. Not to be present in these countries is a serious handicap for companies who want to be global players. As mentioned earlier, Europe, North America and Asia are the three regional clusters that a global player would consider, but within those clusters some countries are more important than others, and should be given priority. In Asia, for instance, in the automotive sector, Japan, Korea and China can be considered as key. In Europe, Germany and, to a certain extent, the UK and France are key countries. In the pulp and paper industry, in which natural resources are a key component of competitive advantage, countries like Indonesia can be considered as key, while California (Silicon Valley) would be key for internet players.

The second category of countries is countries that exhibit a high growth rate, making them strategically attractive in the near future. These are the **emerging countries** (as defined in Chapter 2). Today China, India, Brazil and Poland would generally qualify for that definition but, again, it is difficult to generalize since opportunities are industry-specific.

The **platform countries** constitute a third category. These are the countries that, because of locational advantage, good logistical, financial, regulatory and legal infrastructure or qualified personnel, can serve as a 'hub' for setting up regional centres, that is, global factories that are 'platforms' for further development. Singapore, Hong Kong, Ireland and Taiwan are examples of such countries. For example, Carrefour, the French hypermarket giant, has used Taiwan as a platform for strategic development in Asia.

A fourth category would be **marketing countries**, where the market is attractive without being as strategically critical as the key countries. Countries such as Vietnam in Asia, Tunisia in North Africa or Colombia in Latin America may not be considered as key or emerging for an automobile company on industrial or investment grounds, but may be interesting from the marketing point of view.

The type of presence suitable for such countries should be assessed on its own merits, depending on the political, economic and business contexts. Countries with a strong resource base but limited market prospects would be classified as **sourcing countries**; for instance, Malaysia for rubber or Saudi Arabia for petroleum.

Typically, a global company will control a portfolio of operations in these different categories of country. The benefit of such categorization is to establish *priorities* in investments and to guide *entry strategies* (a topic that will be discussed in Chapter 7).

Value proposition

The value proposition is defined by the value attributes and the market to which the company seeks to appeal. It comprises:

- Choice of value attributes prioritized.
- Choice of customer segments targeted.
- Degree of worldwide standardization adopted for the product/service offering.

These three factors interrelate, as shown in Figure 5.8.

Value attributes are the elements of the products or services that customers value when making their purchasing decision. These include the product design, functionality, performance, quality,

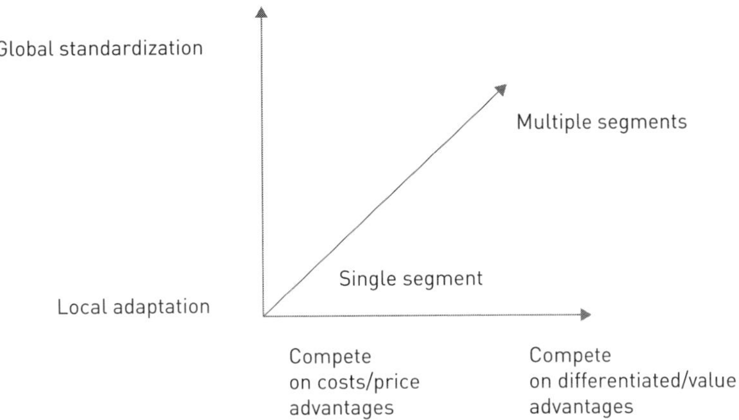

Figure 5.8 The three dimensions of the value proposition

customization and price, as well as the related service, brand, availability, and other features. The set of those attributes for a particular group of customers and a particular product or service gives the customers' value curve as illustrated in Figure 5.9.

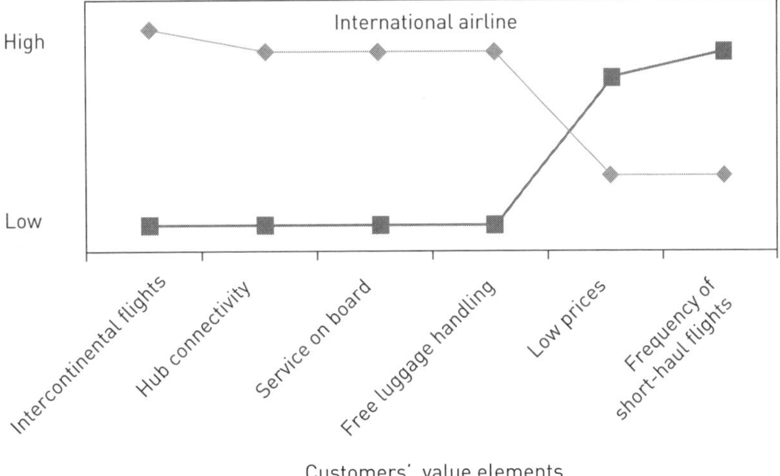

Figure 5.9 Example of customers' value curve

Professor Michael Porter of Harvard Business School has identified two 'generic' strategies corresponding to two types of value attributes:[5]

- A proposition based on value-enhancing attributes such as performance, quality, service and customization. Porter calls this a *differentiated* attribute.
- A proposition based on price for standardized products or services. Porter calls this *cost leadership*.

The same typology can apply to global positioning: the company can either position itself as a global differentiator or a global cost leader.

Customer segments are groups of customers that have similar *value curves*. Those customer groups can be identified by income level, geographical location, age and lifestyle attributes for consumer goods and service industries; or by industry, size and purchasing behaviour for business-to-business (B2B) industries. The strategic choice at this level is to decide whether the company should prioritize one or two segments – a positioning that Michael Porter qualifies as *focused* – or whether it attempts to embrace many or all customer segments – a positioning qualified as *broad*.

The third component of the value proposition is the choice between a standardized versus an adaptive value proposition across countries. If you aim to appeal to similar value attributes or the same type of customer segments across the globe, your approach is qualified as *standardized*; if you try to appeal to different value attributes or segments according to the country or regions, the approach is qualified as *adaptive*.

Thus the company's value proposition consists of trying to identify the customer groups it wants to serve (focused or broad), the type of value attribute it wants to offer to those customers (cost versus differentiation) and whether it is homogeneous or not across countries (standardized versus adaptive). Coca-Cola, Swatch and Sony, for instance, have a standard value proposition across the globe and serve similar segments. Unilever and Procter & Gamble adjust their value proposition and their segmentation in different countries.

The combination of those three choices can lead to eight different positionings, which are illustrated in Table 5.4 with some examples.

Table 5.4 Global positioning alternatives

Global niche players				Broad global players			
Standard differentiated	**Cost leader**	**Adaptive differentiated**	**Cost leader**	**Standard differentiated**	**Cost leader**	**Adaptive differentiated**	**Cost leader**
Standardized niche differentiator	Low-cost standardized niche	Differentiated niche adapter	Low-cost niche adapter	Broad standardized differentiator	Broad standardized cost	Broad adaptive differentiator	Broad adaptive cost leader
Example: Swatch, Intel	**Example:** Acer	**Example:** McDonald's	**Example:** Carrefour	**Example:** Sony	**Example:** Matsushita	**Example:** Unilever, P&G, Philips	**Example:** Electrolux

The strategic choice of a value proposition dictates the type of capabilities that are needed to compete globally, and therefore the type of business system in which the company needs to invest.

Global business system

The third of our four elements to global strategy consists of the business system deployed across countries in order to transfer and reinforce the company's existing competitive advantages and build new ones. We will first define what a business system is and describe the components of a global business system, and second consider how global firms (re)create, reinforce and transfer their competitive advantages.

Global business system and its components

A *business system* is the configuration of the various activities that a firm carries out (either internally or externally through alliances) in order to design, produce and deliver value to customers, and ultimately to capture value for itself. Professor Porter describes a company business system as a 'value chain'.[6] Global business system design consists of breaking down this company value chain into elements that are spread and integrated across the world. Each company has a different value chain according to the type of industry in which it operates and the degree of vertical integration it has adopted.

However, three major generic components of a value chain can be distinguished:

- *Innovative activities*: R&D, knowledge creation, design.
- *Productive activities*: procurement, manufacturing, back office, operations, logistics.
- *Customer relationship activities*: marketing, sales, distribution, customer services.

In each of these activities, the company deploys resources, assets and competencies. Figure 5.10 represents a generic value chain, showing the key resources, assets and competencies that are typically found in each activity.

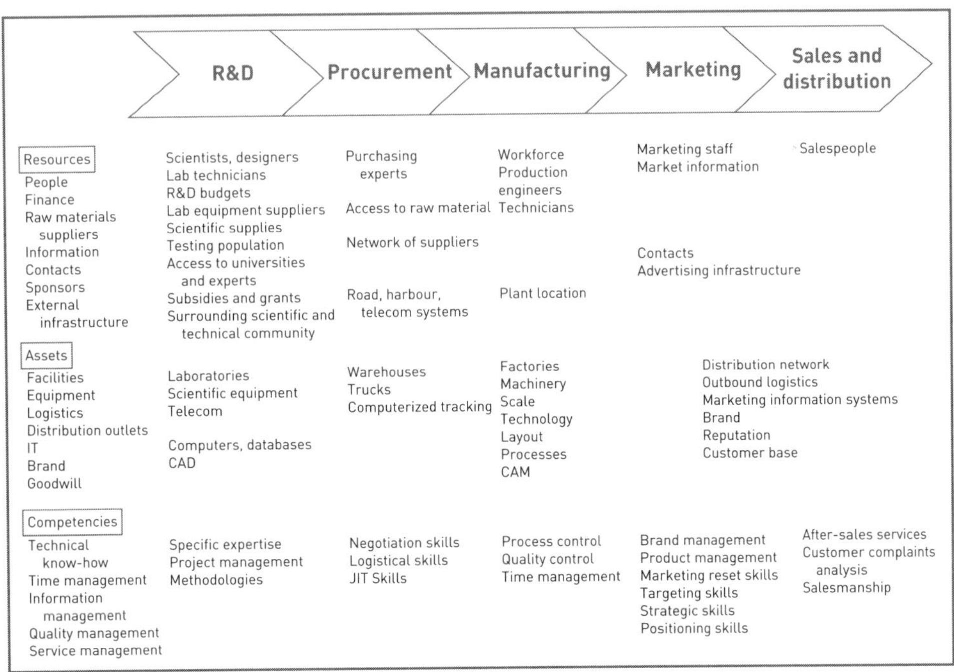

Figure 5.10 Generic value chain

During the process of globalization, companies split their value chain by spreading their activities across the world. The typical path of globalization of the value chain is described in Figure 5.11.

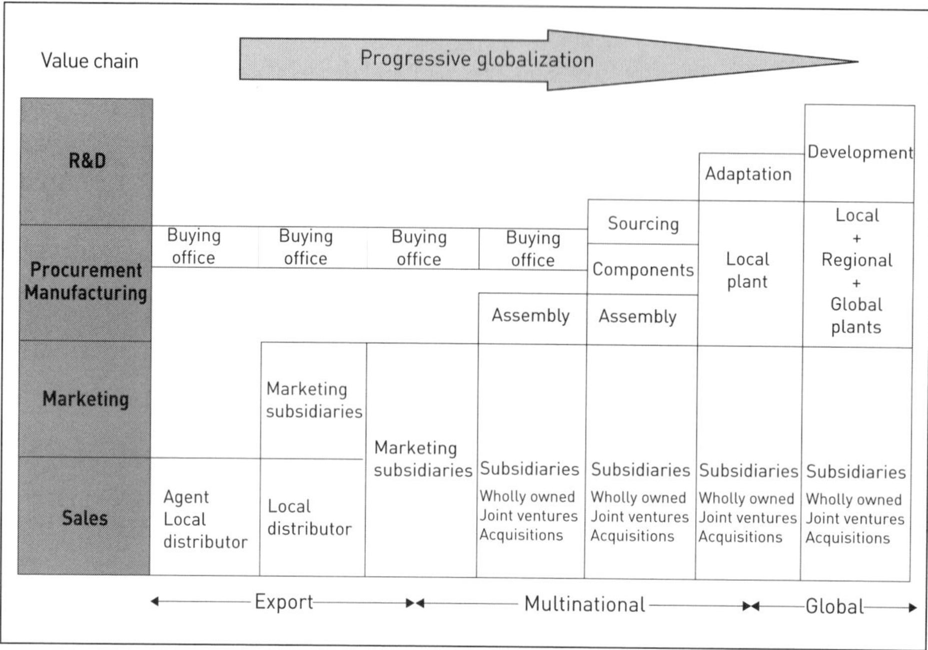

Figure 5.11 Typical globalization of the value chain

The first stage is the *export stage* in which the only element of the value chain to be set up in foreign countries is sales, and even then this is not through direct investment but through local distributors, agents or licensing. The only direct investment at this stage is, if the size of the market justifies it, the creation of a representative office for one country or region. Those representative offices are set up to seize opportunities, identify agents, distributors and partners, organize trade flow and prepare the way for future substantial investments.

The second stage is to actively invest in *marketing subsidiaries* to manage the marketing mix. Those subsidiaries are staffed with expatriates plus local recruits and their role is to coordinate the activities of the distributors, organize promotions, set up logistics and service centres and, in some cases, some operational facilities, such as testing laboratories or assembling operations to support the sales effort. Those marketing subsidiaries may eventually take over the local distribution. When the market justifies the expense, or when local governments require the localization of value-adding activities, companies invest in manufacturing or operational facilities for the service sectors. Some R&D facilities may be localized as well, in order to better adapt products or services to local conditions. These foreign investments are made either as wholly owned subsidiaries, as joint ventures or via acquisitions of local firms. At this stage, as the number of those investments increases, the company is a multinational, managing a portfolio of relatively independent worldwide subsidiaries.

During the final stage of globalization, multinational companies integrate and coordinate their worldwide operations to take advantage of economies of scale, transfer of know-how and resource optimization. This leads to an interlocking set of value chain activities which falls broadly into three categories: the activities which have a global role to serve the whole world (*global activities*, such as global research centres, or global plants), those which have a regional role (*regional activities*) and those which are purely local (*local activities*). Figure 5.12 shows how these three categories interact.

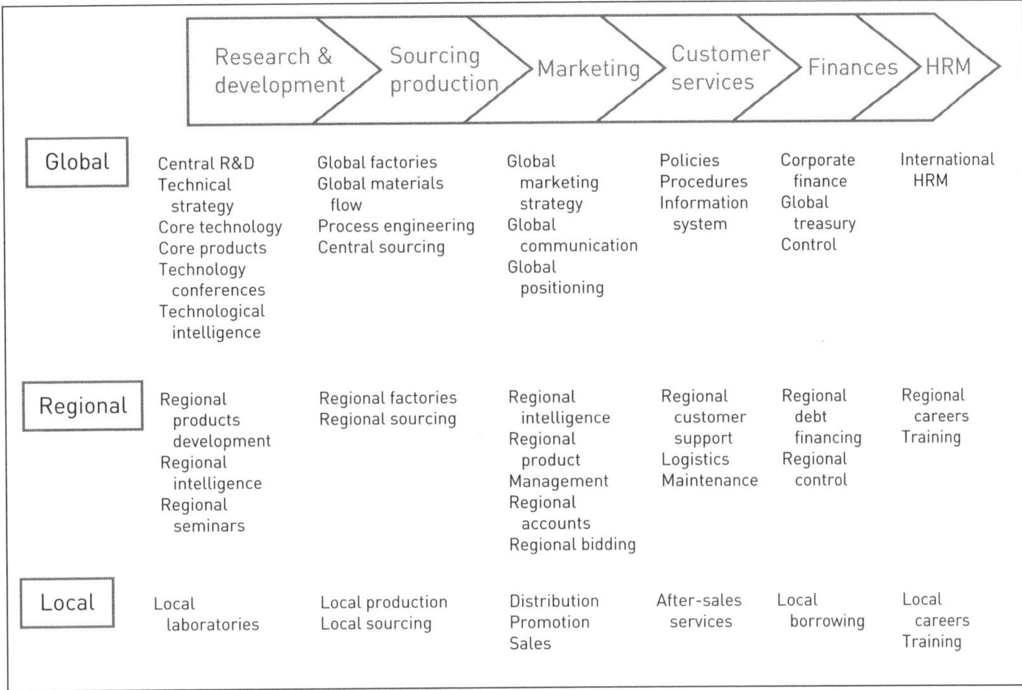

Figure 5.12 A generic global distribution of activities in the value chain

Competitive advantages

Competitive advantages are capabilities that are difficult to replicate or imitate and are non-tradable. Traditionally, there were seen to be two types of capability that lead to competitive advantage (Porter 1985):

- Capabilities leading to an increase in customer value through performance, quality and brand services: a *differentiated* value proposition.
- Capabilities leading to a lower cost base, such as low-cost labour, low-cost sourcing, economies of scale in production, efficiency: a *cost leadership* value proposition.

More recently, three other types of competitive advantage have been identified:

- Capabilities that allow companies to be ahead of the competition in developing new products or services, leading to an *innovative advantage*.[7]
- Capabilities that allow companies to be faster in adapting to change and delivering value to customers, leading to a *time-based advantage*.[8]
- Adopting a 'blue ocean strategy' – that is, by-passing the existing competition and creating a new market space. This approach, as initiated by Chan Kim and Renée Mauborgne,[9] is based on four principles:
  - eliminating those elements of the value curve that are not necessary;
  - reducing some elements that are less important;
  - augmenting those elements that need more emphasis; and
  - creating new elements as needed.

An example of such an approach is the Australian wine maker Yellow Tail (see below).

These capabilities are shown in Table 5.5.

Table 5.5 Capabilities leading to competitive advantage

Differentiation Capabilities leading to enhanced customer value	**Cost leadership** Capabilities enabling a low-cost position	**Innovative advantage** Capabilities enabling companies to take the lead in developing new products or services	**Time-based advantage** Capabilities making companies faster in adapting to change and delivering value to customer	**Blue ocean strategy** Ability to create a new market space offering a different value curve to customers
• Superior technology • Superior quality • Innovative design • Better functionality • Customization • Better related services • One-stop shopping • Solution selling • Brand image • Responsive distribution • Customer relationships • Customer services • Financing	• Low-cost raw material • Low-cost labour • Economies of scale • Economies of scope • Cumulative volume • Customer base • Network externalities • Efficient process technology • Time management • Productivity management	• Create new market spaces • Find new solutions • Develop radical change in value chain management • Create new business designs	• Faster R&D • Faster logistics • Quick response time	• Eliminate some elements of products offering that are not adding value • Decrease some elements • Increase some elements • Add new elements

EXAMPLE 5.3 Yellow Tail: a blue ocean strategy in action in the global market space

Yellow Tail, a mid-sized Australian wine maker, successfully entered the highly competitive US market (and later on, the European and Asian markets) by creating a new market space based on the following features:

- Targeting consumers that usually do not buy wine, intimidated by its complex lexicology and the wide ranges of variety and price on offer.
- Limiting the offer to two simple understandable types of wine; Cabernet Sauvignon for red wine, Chardonnay for white.
- Establishing a simple, strong and recognizable 'Yellow Tail' brand.
- Affordable price range and distribution via supermarkets.

Source: Kim and Mauborgne (2007).

Sources of competitive advantages

These competitive advantages find their sources in the proprietary ownership of, or access to, valuable resources, assets or competencies, as shown in Figure 5.13.

Sustainability of competitive advantage

Competitive advantage, in order to be valuable, needs to be long-lasting.[10] From an economic point of view, a competitive advantage is similar to a monopoly that the company creates for itself and which gives the company a *profit advantage* over its competitors. This happens only if this monopoly is not immediately neutralized by imitation.

There are four ways of achieving sustainability:

- Customer loyalty due to a strong brand or a unique customer value.
- Positive feedback due to accumulated experience or network effects.[11]
- Pre-emption of key resources such as location, key personnel, distribution networks, patents and so on.
- Imitation barriers such as inimitable competencies or costly capabilities to copy or replicate.

Global firms' competitive advantages

For global firms, the central issue is to be able to utilize their existing advantages in multiple-country leverages in order to compete successfully with local players and other global competitors. This can be done in two ways:

- By being among the first competitors to enter a given market: *first-mover advantages*. This will be discussed in more detail in Chapter 7.
- By exploiting capabilities already built up in other countries in order to displace and dominate existing competitors: *leveraging advantages*.

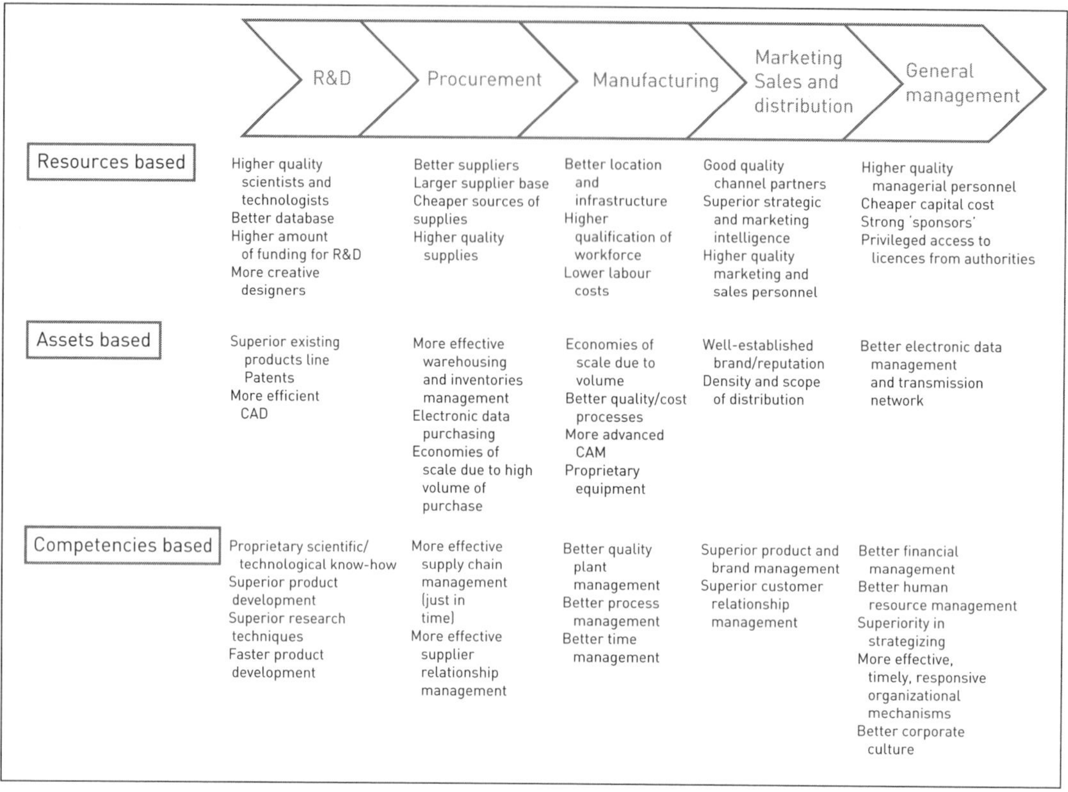

Figure 5.13 Sources of competitive advantage

The determining factors in gaining leveraging advantages are linked to the ability to transfer existing competitive capabilities from one country to another, to adapt some capabilities to local conditions and also to create new ones fitted to local markets. These abilities to transfer, adapt and create will be discussed later in this chapter. Table 5.6 describes the typical sources of competitive advantages of global firms and Table 5.7 shows how such global firms typically achieve sustainability.

Table 5.6 Sources of competitive advantage of global companies

Manufacturing	Services
Access to a globally scarce resource Access to natural resources: agribusiness, mining, etc. Access to low-cost labour if in a labour-intensive industry Access to a supply network	**Access to a globally scarce resource** Access to financial resources: banking, insurance Access to qualified human resources: designers, entertainment, etc. Access to information: consulting activities

Manufacturing	Services
Critical mass built at home Efficient manufacturing system size	**Critical mass built at home** Credit cards, courier services, airlines, transport
'Network' effect Specialized network of production sites Established product performance, quality	**'Network' effect** Consulting, engineering, financial services, brokerage, buying services, shipping agency, news agencies, hotel chains
Competencies built over time Technology management	**Competencies built over time** Consulting, engineering, hospital management, legal, education, etc.
Image, brands and reputation Long-lasting relationships with customers, well-established brands (e.g. Coca-Cola, Apple, Mercedes)	**Image, brands and reputation** Hotel, fast foods, distribution, training, etc. (e.g. McDonald's, Walmart, Harvard Business School)
'Piggybacking' Associated with the international development of another firm or industry	**'Piggybacking'** Associated with the international development of another firm or industry Some consulting activities, banking, engineering, hotels

Table 5.7 Building global sustainable advantage

Mode of building advantages	Type of sustainability			
	Customer loyalty	Network externalities	Accumulated volume	Pre-emption
First mover	Introduce new concept or product Create new brand	Create standard in key countries right at the beginning of the product life cycle	Build volume rapidly	Capture locations, distribution, available talent, partners, etc.
Leverage	Use global brand leverage R&D to innovate and differentiate	Use existing global customer base to expand globally	Use experience effect from global operations to be a cost leader	

Global, regional, multinational deployment of competitive advantages

One particular aspect of leveraging competitive advantage in a global setting is related to the way in which a company will distribute and organize its capabilities. From that point of view, three types of configuration can be identified:

- *Global configuration*: the world is considered as a single market, therefore products will be standardized across the globe and organization will be centralized.

- *Regional configuration*: the competitive approach will be differentiated according to regional characteristics and the organizational structure will be designed around regions. Many authors have advocated the benefits of a regional approach rather than a global or multinational one.[12]
- *Multinational configuration*: the world is a collection of different countries, and competitive strategies will be adapted to the different environment.

Global competitive advantages and liability of foreignness

It has been argued that when developing in foreign countries, global firms face the difficulty of being unfamiliar with the new environment as well as not having a local network and having to manage operations from a distance. Companies operating abroad not only have less knowledge of the host markets, they are likely to encounter discrimination by clients, suppliers and governments, additional transportation and coordination costs, and the risk of foreign exchange rate fluctuations and asset expropriation. Their difficulties are amplified when the host country is more distant from the home country in terms of culture, economic development, political systems and business practices. Doing business in distant countries often means increased organizational complexity, higher transportation, adaptation and monitoring costs. Other challenges include understanding and transferring knowledge and competences to the host market, and dealing with local customers, suppliers, governments and employees.

This constitutes a handicap known as the liability of foreignness.[13] Therefore it is necessary for the global firm to compensate for this weakness with a set of competitive advantages that are superior to those of the local or international firms that are already established in the host markets.[14]

Global chess

In addition to leveraging their intrinsic competitive advantages, global companies possess the ability to play a global 'chess game', meaning that they can *cross-subsidize* one country with another in order to compete more effectively. A company uses its cash flow in one country in order to subsidize the development of the business in another country, or loses money in one country in order to gain a higher profit to compensate those losses in another country. Finally, tax arbitrage through transfer pricing mechanisms allows global companies to optimize their overall return given the constraints imposed by the various regulatory authorities.

An example of the global 'chess game' was provided in the 1970s, when the French company Michelin entered North America with radial tyre technology that American tyre producers could not reproduce on a large scale. In order to delay Michelin's entry and to make it more painful, Goodyear engaged in a price war in Europe where it had a relatively small market share. This forced Michelin, the market leader in Europe, to also lower its prices and therefore be deprived of a source of cash flow that could have been used to finance its expansion in the United States. Another example of cross-subsidization is provided by Citibank's Global Account Management Program by which a global marketing plan is negotiated by the Citibank parent account manager with a corporate client for its financial needs worldwide. For instance, Citibank may give 'sweetener' financing for a project in Argentina, but as a *quid pro quo* it will get a large share of a securitization in Hong Kong. In this case, Argentina subsidizes Hong Kong for the overall benefit of the company.

The transferability of capabilities in multinational and global firms: the transfer, adapt, create model

Obviously one of the central issues when firms globalize is to know which capabilities can be easily transferred internationally to new territories without any change (*Transfer*), which capabilities can be transferred with some adaptation to local conditions (*Adapt*) and which ones have to be created from scratch when entering new countries (*Create*).

Figure 5.14 gives an example of the application of the *Transfer*, *Adapt*, *Create* model in the case of mass retailers such as Walmart, Tesco or Carrefour. For instance, in supply chain management, electronic data processing can be transferred without change. Nearly all competencies that form the basis of the companies' competitive strengths need to be adapted to take into consideration the behaviour of local consumers, suppliers and employees. Physical assets cannot be transferred and need to be created on the spot, and even intangible assets such as well-known brands need to be 're-created' in the localities if they are not known by local consumers.

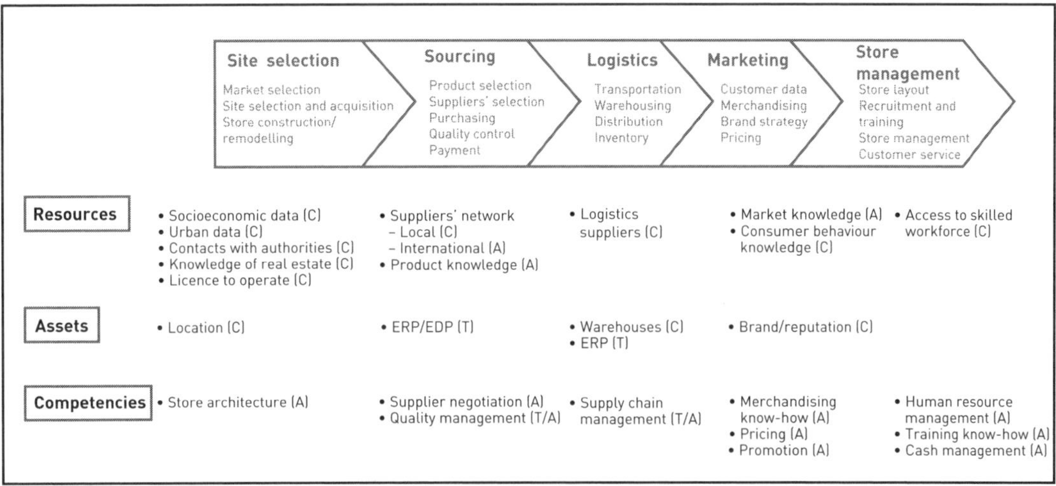

Figure 5.14 The Transfer, Adapt, Create model applied to the globalization of mass retailing
Note: *For each component of the value chain the capabilities that can be transferred (T), adapted (A) or created (C) are identified.*

The role of partnership and strategic alliances in building global capabilities

In the process of globalization, companies may well need to acquire and complement their capabilities by setting up *partnerships*. Although we will discuss global strategic partnership in Chapter 8, it is useful, at this stage, to note that partnerships are very often critical for achieving a global presence and building global competitive advantages. This applies to even for the most alliance-allergic firms, such as Michelin, which tried to build a global presence by itself, but eventually was forced to make an acquisition in the United States (Uniroyal) and undertake several joint ventures in Asia (Japan, Korea, Thailand). Strategic alliances for globalization can take several forms:

- *Global alliances*: the role of which is to pool complementing capabilities to reach world markets, or to achieve a critical mass in R&D. Good examples of world market partnerships are the airline alliances such as Star or One-World, or Concert in the telecoms sector between BT and AT&T. R&D global alliances are frequent in aerospace, life sciences, electronic defence industries and oil exploration.
- *Partnerships for market entry*: such as *joint ventures*, *franchises* or *licensing:* the role of which is to comply with local government requirements (as has been the case in China) or to facilitate entry or minimize risks in a particular country.
- *Acquisitions*: from an ownership point of view, these are not partnerships, since one party takes over the other, but from a management point of view they are not dissimilar to an alliance, since different national and corporate cultures have to be combined. Acquisitions may be either global or local in scope.

Global organization

The final element of a global strategy is the design of an *organizational architecture* which is able to support and implement the global ambition, global positioning and global business system already described. In Chapter 15, we will discuss in more depth the various types of global organizations and the issues associated with their implementation. Here, we will limit our comments to the key elements of choices that may be considered during the strategy formulation process.

Alongside the global development path described in Figure 5.11, several authors have identified different types of structures, systems and cultures in the management of global firms;[15] see Table 5.8.

Table 5.8 Organizational designs for global strategies

Phases of global development	Structure	Process	Culture
Early export	Export department Within marketing and sales All activities at home Distributors, agents in foreign countries Export managers travel Possible foreign representative offices	Domestic process plus: International database (market research) International financing Instruments (trade financing)	Domestic corporate culture dominates Pioneering phase Export managers as missionaries
Large export and early multinational subsidiaries	International division as distinct from domestic activities Subsidiaries report to international division on a country-by-country basis	Specific planning and control processes for international operations International careers distinct from domestic ones	Ethnocentric culture Expatriate domination High degree of operational autonomy in subsidiaries

Full multinational	Geographical structure The world is organized by region National subsidiaries report to regional headquarters which report to corporate headquarters The company is a confederation of national units	Localization Multiple processes fitted to national requirements Only a few central policies Careers essentially national except for a few international managers	Pluricentric Except for a few international managers, each national entity reflects its national culture International diversity prevails
Global	Integrated approaches Three types: a Global-functional structure: each key function is managed centrally b Single matrix structure: dual line of reporting, geographical and functional c Transnational network: not really a structure but more a way of managing global companies so that efficiency, responsiveness and innovation are optimized	Global standardization Common processes and standard procedures across borders Activities coordinated centrally Synergies systematized Careers international	Global mind Strong corporate values Common themes Corporate culture prevails above any national culture including culture of the mother company
		Dual information process: Global and local but working in integrated manner Transfer of people and knowledge A large number of policies to define responsibilities and avoid conflicts Multidimensional information system: transfer of people and knowledge	Negotiating culture Ability to solve conflicts Requires strong corporate values Team mind Culture of sharing, transfer and cooperation
Multi-business	The business diversity adds another dimension of complexity in the organization of global operations		
Global product When the company is at the same time multi-country and diversified	Three types of structure, processes and culture may apply depending on prevailing competitive context of the industry: a Multi-business geographical structure The company is organized by regions/countries which are in charge of managing multiple-product businesses in each country Each country is in charge of formulating the appropriate strategy for each business line and is responsible for profits. Business managers support national policies but do not have profit responsibilities		

	b Global business structure Each business is integrated centrally The country subsidiaries are implementers of centrally formulated strategies and policies Profit responsibilities are assigned to global business managers who manage their global business according to competitive conditions c Multi-business matrix structure Dual-line business/geography Profit responsibilities are in the hands of both business managers and national managers

Source: Authors' own figure. Adapted from text in Stopford and Wells (1972); Prahalad and Doz (1987); Bartlett and Ghoshal (2000); Heenan and Perlmutter (1979).

These different organizational choices have been mapped by Bartlett and Ghoshal in a grid that positions the various types of global structure according to the competitive requirements of global integration and local responsiveness, as in Figure 5.15.

The choice of an adequate organizational model is contingent upon the following factors:

- The nature of the *competitive context in the industry*. As discussed in Chapter 1, the more 'global' the industry, the more integrated and coordinated the activities and the more the organizational structure should reflect this integration. The world functional structure, the global business structure or the matrix structure fulfil this requirement.
- The *strategic positioning* adopted by the firm. A standardized positioning using cost leadership as a competitive advantage will require a tightly integrated organization such as the centralized hub or the global business structure.

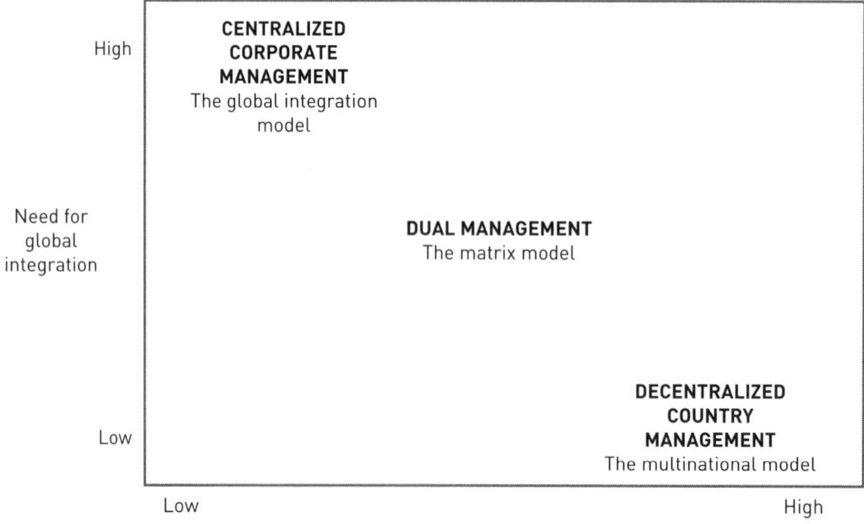

Figure 5.15 Global/multi-local mapping and global structures
Source: Authors' own figure, based on Bartlett and Ghoshal (1989).

Global strategies and the multi-business firm

In the previous sections of this chapter we developed a framework for the formulation of global strategies made up of four elements: ambition, positioning, investment and organization. This framework applies when a company operates in a homogeneous industry environment. If the company is multi-business, and controls a portfolio of different business sectors, the framework applies at the level of each business but not directly at the level of the total corporation. As is often the case, in a given corporation, some businesses are more global than others and the rules of competition differ from business to business. For instance, in the telecommunications industry, voice telephony and mobile telephony are essentially local or national businesses, while corporate data is a global business. France Telecom's stated strategic ambition is to be a national player in France for voice telephony, a European player in mobile and a global player in corporate data.

However, the global corporate strategy of a multi-business corporation is more than the mathematical sum of the global strategies of each business it controls.[16] It may be defined in terms of the four elements described earlier, but with modified content:

- *Corporate global ambition*: overall strategic direction assigned to the group for its globalization. Does the corporation want to be a global player in all businesses it controls or does it assign different global profiles to different businesses? What is the overall mission for the group?
- *Corporate global positioning*: which businesses does the corporation want to be in? Does the corporation view its business portfolio as homogeneous in terms of competitive positioning? Does it want to be a cost leader across the board? Does it want the businesses to share a common global brand?
- *Global business system*: to what extent do business units share resources, assets and competencies in order to optimize synergies? What are the corporate priorities in resource allocation among businesses?
- *Global organization*: is the global structure organized according to a geographical design, a global business design or a matrix design? What is the role of the corporate headquarters in the strategic and operational control of the business units? Does the corporation set up regional headquarters to coordinate activities at regional level? What kind of human resource management (HRM) has the corporation put in place? Are the key managerial functions managed globally for all businesses, at business level or at regional level?

All these questions boil down to one key consideration: What is the *value added of corporate activities* in fostering the global competitiveness of the business units?

In Chapter 14 we go into this issue in more detail and some examples will be presented.

Global strategies and the small and medium-sized enterprise (SME)

Small and medium-sized enterprises (SMEs) represent a significant proportion of employment activities in the world (Table 5.9). Their participation in international trade and investment remains relatively limited;

their main global activities are sourcing and exporting. According to the OECD, SMEs account for about 60 per cent of employment and between 50 per cent and 60 per cent of value added and are the main drivers of productivity in many regions and cities.[17] 'The SME contribution to overall exports is for most countries similar to their contribution to value added between 20% to 40% for most OECD economies.'[18] The European Commission in 2010 indicated that 25 per cent of European SMEs are engaged in exports, 29 per cent in imports, 2 per cent in foreign direct investments and 7 per cent in technological partnerships.[19] However, 'when the role of SMEs as suppliers of inputs to larger direct exporters is taken into account, the importance of SMEs as exporters increases considerably'.[20]

Table 5.9 SMEs' economic weight measured by contribution to employment and value added in selected countries in Europe, North and South America, Asia Pacific

	% of enterprises		% of employment		% of value added	
	Micro 1–9 employees	SMEs 10–249 employees	Micro 1–9 employees	SMEs 10–249 employees	Micro 1–9 employees	SMEs 10–249 employees
Turkey	96	4	41	33	20.2	33.7
Poland	96	4	37	31	16.7	34.5
Mexico	95	5	31	37	12.0	25.2
France	95	5	30	33	23.0	32.5
Italy	95	5	45	34	27.8	39.5
Spain	95	5	39	34	24.0	36.8
Korea	93	7	19	35	19.3	28.5
UK	90	10	29	51	13.6	47.9
Brazil	85	15	23	39	17.1	33.1
China	67	33	16	50	10.3	47.8
Russia	86	14	1	32	NA	NA
Canada	81	19	23	35	NA	NA
USA	79	21	10	32	NA	NA

Source: The MSME Economic Indicators Database 2019 consulted on 15 September 2020, https://www.smefinanceforum.org/data-sites/msme-country-indicators (accessed 1 February 2022).

Does the framework presented here apply to SMEs as well as large multinational and global enterprises? The answer to that question is 'yes and no'. 'No', because of SMEs' limited resource base; they are not generally able to create global capabilities by deploying assets, resources and competencies in the twenty to thirty countries that represent 90 per cent of world demand. 'Yes', because these companies also need to 'think global' if they are competing in sectors that are confronted with global competition and if new market opportunities are located outside their national boundaries.

Obviously, their global strategic design will probably not be as comprehensive and complex as the one that has been developed here, but the ambition, position, investment and organization framework may be a useful tool for marshalling their thinking.

Different types of SMEs and their globalization potential

Not all SMEs are candidates for global expansion. A large proportion, estimated at around 40 per cent of SMEs, are involved in activities that are not subjected to international sourcing, exporting or producing. Those are the traditional local services, small shops or artisans. A small proportion, estimated at around 5–10 per cent, are strategically affected by globalization, either because their products or services are challenged by global competitors, because they contribute to the global value chains of bigger multinational companies, or because their innovative products need to be deployed globally for economic or competitive reasons. These would include high-tech entrepreneurial firms, subcontractors or niche players in advanced services or luxury products. The remaining 50 per cent could be involved or are marginally involved in international activities but a number of barriers deter them.

Based on a survey in the east of England with 1,200 SMEs,[21] a typology of international SMEs was developed at different stages of internationalization (Table 5.10).

Table 5.10 Typology of international SMEs

The Curious	Only marginal consideration of export activities
The Frustrated	Have experienced international activities but do not push very hard to expand them
The Tentative	Some experience but are still limited by a lack of market intelligence
The Enthusiastic	Considerable experience of international activity but still limited by access to skills and resources
The Successful	High levels of experience and skills

Source: Lloyd-Reason and Mughan, quoted in OECD (2008: 20–1).

Globalization of large multinational companies has created opportunities for SMEs to participate in global value chains as suppliers or subcontractors.[22] One such opportunity is known as 'piggybacking' whereby large firms help their smaller subcontractors or suppliers to set operations close to their own foreign investments. Another form of involvement in the global value chain is the generalization of outsourcing by large firms who want to concentrate on their core competencies and open opportunities for external suppliers to provide the goods and services that were previously produced internally.

Insert 5.2 Piggybacking

Piggybacking is a form of indirect internationalization of a firm which uses the capabilities of another firm to export or invest into international markets. The exporting firm is called the 'rider' and the supporting firm is called 'the carrier'. This practice can take several forms:

1. The carrier uses its sales network to market the rider's products. This is the most ancient form of indirect export carried by traditional trading firms such as Japan's *sogo shoshas* or the hongs in Hong Kong.
2. The carriers invite the riders to participate in a construction project as subcontractor, a frequent practice in infrastructures such as airports, refineries, factories, power plants.
3. The carrier as an established foreign investor in a country invites and facilitate a supplier to invest close to their foreign facilities facilities

Piggybacking can be very helpful to small and medium-sized companies in developing a global presence without carrying the entry costs.

Sources: Terpstra and Chwo-Ming (1990); Djärf and Engström (2003).

Most SMEs will perceive themselves as 'global exporters', relying on local distributors and agents for the sales and marketing of their products. Some more daring companies will set up representative offices in key countries in order to support their marketing efforts, and control and coordinate their distributors. The most resourceful will establish operational subsidiaries either directly or through partnerships of resources to 'globalize'.

In all cases, they will have to address the question of their competitive positioning and the deployment of capabilities to capture the market opportunities. In any case SMEs will have to overcome the barriers to internationalization and find ways to enhance their global capabilities.

Barriers to internationalization for SMEs

Table 5.11 provides a list of the barriers to internationalization for SMEs.

As Table 5.10 shows, those barriers belong to two categories: one related to financial issues and the other to the ability to deal with a foreign environment. In fact SMEs have to deal with two sorts of liabilities when they engage in international/global business: the liability of size and the liability of foreignness. Both liabilities end up being a problem of resources, whether financial, human or bargaining power.

Overcoming the barriers

Two major sources of intervention may help SMEs to overcome the barriers to internationalization: government-led initiatives and company-led initiatives.

Table 5.11 Obstacles to internationalization as perceived by SMEs

Rank – weighted factor	Description of barrier
1	Shortage of working capital to finance exports
2	Difficulty identifying foreign business opportunities
3	Limited information to locate/analyse markets
4	Inability to contact potential overseas customers
5	Difficulty obtaining reliable foreign representation
6	Lack of managerial time to deal with internationalization
7	Inadequate quantity of personnel and/or untrained personnel for internationalization
8	Difficulty in matching competitors' prices
9	Lack of home government assistance/incentives
10	Excessive transportation costs

Note: *Barriers ranked by SMEs using the top ten ranking method.*

Source: OECD (2009), Table 1. Reused with permission from the Organisation for Economic Co-operation and Development.

Many governments or international organizations, being conscious of the difficulties that many SMEs face, have tried to implement specific programmes. In 2009 the OECD grouped government support initiatives into four categories: financial help programmes, business environment facilitators, capability-enhancement programmes and assistance in information gathering.[23] The OECD published a report detailing the various programmes implemented in seventeen OECD countries to facilitate SMEs' internationalization.[24] The following approaches are the kind of actions that governments can implement in order to foster the global capabilities of SMEs.

- *Information gathering and distribution*. Most governments, thanks to their diplomatic networks, have access to a myriad of information about business opportunities and risks in many countries. Factual and legal information can be made available online, and special reports on countries and industries can be provided to the public. Tailor-made, customized studies can be proposed at affordable costs.
- *Advice and consulting*. When an entrepreneur is considering exporting or investing in a particular region, a specialized government agency can provide consultancy and advisory services about various alternatives, potential partners, market access and legal issues that can help the company to evaluate the costs and benefits as well as the specific risks.
- *Trade fairs*. One useful way to raise a company's profile in international markets is to participate in trade fairs. Costs are generally quite high and government agencies can provide an umbrella for presenting the products and services of SMEs. In some cases, specific conferences on industrial sectors can be organized and sponsored, and entrepreneurs can present papers about their company and products.

- *Training*. Organizing specialized training programmes on international marketing, market entry, joint venturing, cross-cultural issues, languages and so on.
- *Financing*. Providing insurance for risks taken by firms. Sponsored loans for SMEs.
- *Logistical and market access support*. Helping companies in their dealings with authorities, finding agents, distributors and partners. Providing offices from which entrepreneurs can initiate their business. Helping in negotiations.

Appendix 5.2 gives some information about selected government agencies and their various programmes.

Government support is not the only requisite for small and medium-sized businesses to start exporting and investing internationally. In 2004 the European Community carried out a study[25] to analyse the characteristics of successful exporters. The study pinpointed the following factors that enhanced exporting capabilities:

- Owner/CEO personal involvement
- International experience of founder
- Consistency and persistence.

In addition, the study pinpointed the significant benefits of the internet for SMEs in their internationalization process, both in terms of information gathering and e-market opportunities.

Born global

So far this chapter has presented the traditional views of global strategic development, mainly a step-by-step progressive international deployment known as the Uppsala model.[26] However, some companies have moved rapidly to globalize and adopt an international presence from the beginning of their existence. Those firms are described as 'born global' or sometimes 'international new ventures'. There are many definitions of 'born global'.[27] The earlier proponents of the concept defined born global firms as 'firms that intended to export immediately upon inception',[28] or firms that 'succeed in world markets without an established domestic base',[29] thus concentrating on the early exporting drive of those companies. The concept has since evolved to include 'business organizations that, from inception, seek to derive significant competitive advantage from the use of resources and the sale of outputs in multiple countries',[30] thus encompassing firms that perform operational activities in foreign countries: a positioning which is similar to the definition of a 'global firm' that is adopted in this textbook.

Many researchers[31] have found the following characteristics of born global firms:

- A small domestic market inciting entrepreneurs to find a larger market for starting a new venture.
- The presence of multinational customers (a piggybacking perspective).
- The emergence of global niches markets particularly in the technology intensive sectors.[32]
- The firm's products or services have significant first-mover advantages or network effects.

- Born global firms offer high value-added products or services – technology start-ups in particular tend to quickly find partners, distributors and sometimes production or service in foreign markets.
- Internationally experienced and highly motivated company leaders.
- Strong capabilities in building partnerships.

The differences between born global firms and traditional globalizing ones is presented in Table 5.12 below.

Table 5.12 Differences between born global and traditional global firms

Born global SMEs	Traditional stepwise internationalizing SMEs
• The world is seen as one market	• The world is seen as multiple markets
• The market of origin is simply one market among others	• The market of origin is a stepping stone for internationalization
• Learning by doing	• Learning in the original market is prerequisite for engaging in internationalization
• Standardization of products and services	• Most often tailor-made products and services to fit local markets
• Speed is important (first-mover advantage)	• Step-by-step progress
• Rely early on networks (intermediaries, banks, consultants, etc.)	• Build networks progressively

We shall examine the examples of three born global firms: Gemplus (a French smartcard manufacturer), Sunna (a French company involved in lighting solutions) and Cochlear (an Australian high-tech firm).

Born global and born digital

There is some evidence that digital platforms and applications have been globalizing their presence more rapidly after their inception than traditional non-digital firms (see Table 5.13). Firms that base from the start their business model on internet-based transactions can be qualified as 'born digital firms'. The propensity for a large fraction of born digital firms to become global players rapidly after their inception can be due to several factors. First, the ease that technology provides to connect with potential customers, partners and suppliers across the world. Second, the automated interactions in computer-to-computer and computer-to-user relationships allow these newcomers to benefit from network effects, both direct and indirect. Third, their physical presence is more often limited to low capital-intensive local offices in global markets giving them flexibility to operate and change their local profile. Often in many cases born digital firms deal with non-physical products or services such as social networks and booking platforms that are easily scalable providing the opportunity to build rapidly economies of scale (economies of 'clicks').

Table 5.13 Examples of three major born global firms

Born global firms	Business	Date of creation	Date of first international move	Global presence by 2020
Meta Platforms, Inc. (formerly known as Facebook)	Social network	2004	2007	70 offices; 17 data centres
Airbnb	Peer-to-peer rental	2008	2009/2011	750 million guests; 220 countries
Netflix	Online TV streaming	2007	2010	14 offices; customers in 190 countries

EXAMPLE 5.4 Gemplus: from Marseille to the world

In the late 1980s, the French company Gemplus was one of the first companies to enter the market for smartcards. Immediately after its formation in Marseille in the south of France, it created a subsidiary in Germany, a joint venture company in Singapore and a marketing company in the United States. This strategy reflected the nature of the industry: the technology of the smartcard is pervasive; it has numerous applications in banking, telecommunications, transport and internet transactions; and it has the potential to become global. National boundaries do not provide strong entry barriers, but national legislations and established infrastructures make national presence a competitive requirement. Network externalities, customer base and first-to-enter are significant competitive advantages in this industry. Gemplus, which is a medium-sized technology firm, realized this competitive imperative and, right from the start, devoted a large proportion of its limited resources to global expansion.

In 2006 Gemplus merged with Axalto to create Gemalto, headquartered in Amsterdam.

In 2016 it operated in forty-eight countries with 15,000 employees and €3.1 billion turnover.

EXAMPLE 5.5 Sunna Design: a born global start-up

Sunna Design was created in 2010 near Bordeaux (France) by a young engineer. His project was to develop a public lighting solution based on solar energy and separate from the public electricity grid. The applications of such a system could be widespread, particularly in rural areas of emerging countries. Initially, the young start-up received financial support from the French government as well as corporate partners to develop prototypes and support early sales. The company was able to raise €6.6 million to fund its development. Applications were rapidly sold to twenty countries including Senegal, Nigeria, Cameroon, South Africa and Saudi Arabia. R&D and production are located in France but system installation is handled by a network of twenty local installers. In 2015 the company achieved a turnover of €1.4 million, 95 per cent of which was generated outside France.

See http://www.sunna-design.fr/en.

EXAMPLE 5.6 Cochlear: an Australian born global high-tech company

Cochlear Pty Ltd was founded in Melbourne in 1981 in order to commercialize the multi-channel ear implant technology developed by Professor Graeme Clark (with the support of the University of Melbourne). Following the opening of a second office in Sydney in 1982, the company rapidly expanded its presence outside Australia with its first US office opening in 1984, followed by Europe and Japan. In 2005 the company acquired Philips Hearing Instruments in Belgium, thus establishing its first global research centre. In the same year, it acquired Entific Medical System, a Swedish hearing-aid company, and in 2012 acquired Otologist, a middle-ear-implant firm in Boulder, Colorado. It has now established research agreements and arrangements with more than 100 external research partners around the world. Cochlear has a global supply chain and sells into more than 100 countries. Components are sourced across Europe, Asia and the Americas. Manufacturing operations are primarily located in Australia and Sweden, with smaller sites in Belgium and the USA. Cochlear has direct local operations in twenty countries and 2,800 employees. It operates with three regional headquarters:

- USA for the Americas (accounting for 45 per cent of their global sales across four national offices);
- Europe (37 per cent of global sales to more than nine countries);
- Asia Pacific/Australasia (18 per cent of global sales to ten countries).

In its annual company report for 2015–2016, Cochlear stated that manufacturing operations are primarily located in Australia and Sweden, with smaller sites in Belgium and the US. Suppliers and the manufacturing sites are aligned to enable the company to deliver products of the highest quality and reliability.

See http://www.cochlear.com/.

MINI-CASE 5.1

HSBC: the world's local bank

The Hong Kong and Shanghai Banking Corporation was created in Shanghai in 1865. Its primary business was to finance trade with China. Up until the Second World War, it expanded rapidly in the Asia Pacific region (Japan, Malaysia, the Philippines and Thailand), with only a limited presence in the USA and Europe. After 1950, the bank embarked on a series of acquisitions in Europe (UK, France), the Middle East, Latin America (Mexico, Argentina, Brazil) and the USA. It listed on the New York, London, Paris and Hong Kong stock exchanges, and also moved its corporate headquarters from Hong Kong to London in 1993. In 1999 it adopted the name HSBC and positioned itself as 'the world's local bank', defining itself as a global bank with strong local presence and knowledge. The principal holding company, HSBC Holdings plc, is a public limited company incorporated in England. HSBC has a matrixed management structure organized according to its global businesses and global support functions. These are underpinned by the legal entity structure, which is made up of a global network of locally incorporated subsidiary companies that provide oversight at a country and regional level. Each of these subsidiaries has a board and management structure that reflects its activities and complexity. To strengthen accountability and flows of information, there are seven principal subsidiaries that are responsible for the oversight of Group companies in their region and accountable to the board of HSBC Holdings plc.

HSBC's structure is also influenced by the regulatory framework that applies to it. Many of the Group's entities are locally regulated. While HSBC Holdings plc is not itself a regulated entity, it owns – directly or indirectly – a number of operating subsidiaries that are regulated and supervised as banks, insurance companies or securities firms in the countries and territories where they operate. In addition, the HSBC Group is subject to the consolidated supervision of the UK Prudential Regulation Authority.

It is the largest bank in Europe, with total assets of $2.715 trillion (as of August 2020). Its network comprises 3,900 offices in sixty-five countries and territories across Africa, Asia, Oceania, Europe, North America, and South America, and around 38 million customers.

HSBC is organized within four business groups: Commercial Banking, Global Banking and Markets (investment banking), Retail Banking and Wealth Management, and Global Private Banking. In 2020, the bank announced that it would consolidate its Retail Banking and Wealth Management arm with Global Private Banking, to form Wealth & Personal Banking. As of 30 October 2020, it had a market capitalisation of £66.1 billion ($90.1 billion [as of January 2022]).

The bank has developed a strategy of building networks within the world's largest and fastest growing trade corridors (streams of products, services and information moving between geographic entities) and economic zones. The company states that: 'Our network of businesses covers the world's largest and fastest growing trade corridors and economic zones. More than 43 per cent of our client revenue derives from businesses and individuals with an international presence' (http://www.hsbc.com/about-hsbc/our-strategy/the-value-of-our-network).

The distribution of the bank's net income and profit before tax are given in Table 5.14.

Table 5.14 HSBC distribution of revenues, employment and customers

By geography	Total	Asia Pacific	Europe	North America	Latin America	Middle East and North Africa
Employees	239,712	54.2%	27.1%	6.4%	8.3%	4%
Revenues (US$ m)*	50,429	26,922 (47%)	18,419 (32.1%)	6,375 (11%)	3,020 (5.3%)	2, 628 (4.6%)
Customer accounts by country (US$ m)	1,642,780	38.3%	46.4%	11.1%	1.7%	2.5%
By business	**Total**	**Retail Banking and Wealth Management**	**Commercial Banking**	**Markets**	**Corporate**	
Revenues (US$ m)	50,429	43.6%	26.4%	30.3%	0.3%	

* Reported revenue per region is not additive and will not sum with total revenue due to intra-HSBC transfer of $6,935 million. Percentages in revenues are calculated by: Reported revenue per region/Sum of reported revenue per region (which exceeds HSBC's reported revenue for 2020).

Source: HSBC Annual report 2020.

Questions:

1 The bank defines its businesses as 'global'. What is your opinion of this definition? Are all the businesses really global? What are the implications for decision making?

2 What is your assessment of HSBC's strategy of focusing on trade corridors?

MINI-CASE 5.2

Essilor: a global player

Essilor is the result of the merger in 1972 of two French ophthalmological companies: Essel, a specialist in corrective glass lenses, and Silor, a specialist in plastic lenses. Its products used to be exported through an international network of local distributors but, in 1979, the company embarked on a global strategy with the opening of its first international factory in the Philippines and the progressive acquisition of local distributors. Global development has occurred through a mixture of greenfield investments, acquisitions and alliances. Between 2008 and 2010 it acquired or allied with 83 companies worldwide, and since 2011 an additional 45 partnerships have been completed.

By 2019 Essilor was the number one player for corrective optical lenses with a global market share of around 25 per cent, a turnover of €7.5 billion with a profit of €757 million and 64,000 employees worldwide. In January 2017, Essilor announced a merger with the Italian Luxottica Group, a global player in the design, manufacture and distribution of eyewear, creating a new entity with combined sales in excess of €17 billion, more than 140,000 employees and sales in more than 150 countries.

The Essilor corrective lenses business process is built around five elements:

- *Retail optical shops* (opticians) providing customer contact, with ophthalmologists determining the type of lens required. Essilor relies on 300,000 independent optical shops around the world.
- *Prescription laboratories* which deliver lenses to professional customers (opticians, independent optometrists, wholesalers and optical chain stores) as quickly as possible. Essilor's network includes 449 prescription laboratories and numerous independent laboratories which distribute its lenses.
- *Factories* that manufacture the lenses either in a semi-finished or finished form. Finished lenses are mass produced, with both sides prepared in the plant. For semi-finished lenses, only the front of the lenses is prepared in the plant. The back and coatings are applied later by prescription laboratories, before the lenses are delivered to stores. Essilor has 33 factories worldwide.
- *Distribution centres* (14 in total) cover every stage in the distribution process: from the delivery of raw materials to plants to the delivery of finished products to optician customers. Essilor ships lenses from 14 production sites to 332 finishing laboratories, before they are distributed to 300,000 opticians around the world.
- *Technology and innovation centres* undertake R&D for the development of new lenses as well as the anticipation of future needs. Essilor employs more than 600 researchers, in ten R&D centres and laboratories, some of which are its own and others in the form of joint ventures or joint partnerships.

The interaction of these components is represented in Figure 5.16.

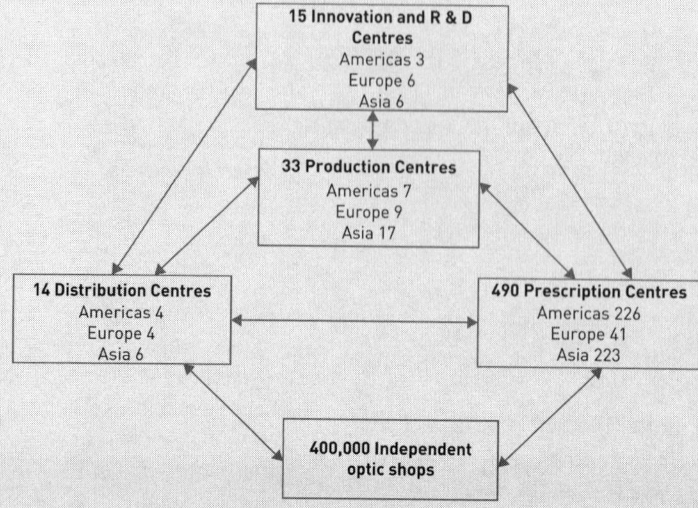

Figure 5.16 Essilor's business process

Source: Authors' own, constructed using information available from https://www.essilor.com.

Essilor's strategy is based on four pillars:

- Innovation in products, services and marketing as well as the quality of its relationships with opticians all over the world.
- The growth and development of middle markets in emerging countries. Figure 5.17 represents the company's views about the perspective of market development.
- The pursuit of acquisitions and partnerships.
- Offering check-ups and supplying lenses in regions where access to optical care is difficult, in order to develop new markets.

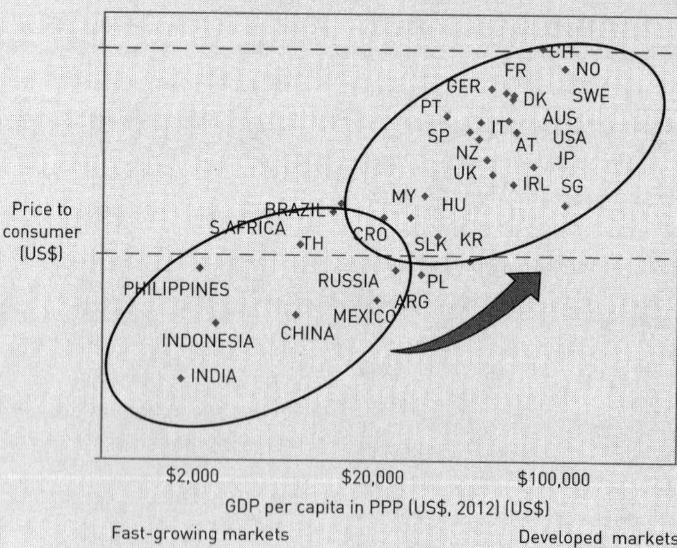

Figure 5.17 Perspective on Essilor's market development (figures as of 2014)

Source: Redrawn by the author from Estin & Co's analysis on behalf of Essilor. Reproduced with permission of Estin from *Growing in a Bigger Playing Field: Essilor Investor Day 2014*, https://www.essilor.com/essilor-content/uploads/2016/08/Essilor_2014-Investor-Day_Booklet_25062014.pdf (accessed 1 February 2022).

EssilorLuxottica

By December 2018, EssilorLuxottica, resulting from the merger of Essilor and Luxottica, claimed that it had formed a global leader in the design, manufacture and distribution of ophthalmic lenses, frames and sunglasses, combining complementary expertise in advanced lens technologies and in eyewear, creating a vertically integrated business positioned to serve the global market of eyecare and eyewear industry. EssilorLuxottica directly operates 7,700 stores (50 per cent in North America, 14 per cent in Europe, 20 per cent in Asia, Oceania, Africa and 16 per cent in Latin America) plus 3,200 franchises. The sales of the group amounted to €17.4 billion with a net profit of 11.8 per cent.

Questions:

1. Based on the description of the business system and Figure 5.16, what are the strategic and organizational challenges for Essilor's global management?
2. From Figure 5.17 it appears that the most potentially attractive markets are in emerging countries. Do you think that Essilor's strategic pillars are compatible with these market prospects?
3. What issues would be involved in developing the business in China, India, Indonesia and Russia?
4. Can EssilorLuxottica as an integrated group become a dominant global player in eyewear and lens products? What are the benefits of vertical integration?

MINI-CASE 5.3

Quinta do Vallado

Quinta do Vallado (Vallado), a Portuguese vineyard founded in 1716 and situated in the Douro Valley, had been run by the Ferreira family and their descendants for 200 years. It produced Port wine and in the late 1990s high quality table wines. Other recent activities included wine tourism, an onsite shop and own-label olive oil. It was recognized globally as a high-quality wine producer – winning many awards and continued ratings above 90 points (96 times) by *Wine Spectator* and Robert Parker in 2020. Over the past twenty years, globalization had become of utmost importance with exports accounting for 40 per cent of its total revenues by 2020. Its geographic reach had expanded tenfold from 5 international markets in 2000 to 48 in 2020, with a sixfold increase in growth rate in the last twelve years.

The challenge was how to continue growing revenues. Vallado could continue to push into international markets but which should it prioritize given it would be competing with the largest wineries in the world? There was also Covid-19 to consider and the long-term impact on the industry. Vallado could concentrate on its premium and super premium wines with high prices and margins but low volumes, or develop entry-level wines with low prices and margins but high volumes, sold through off-trade channels with discount/promotion strategies. Alternatively, it could remain a niche vineyard.

The Portuguese wine industry

Wine production in Portugal had always been an important part of agriculture, related to domestic economic conditions but also with a strong export tradition. In the eighteenth century, Port wine exports were big business for the Portuguese, with Great Britain the most important market. Regulation in the 1930s led to improved wine quality and conditions for wine producers. A slogan at the time was 'To drink wine is to feed one million people in Portugal.' When Portugal joined the European Union in 1986 the production of dry wines took off – with the abolishment of the Port lodges' monopoly wine producers including those in the Douro valley could produce and bottle their own wine: Port or dry Douro wines.

Quinta do Vallado

Vallado's wines were uniquely positioned between the tradition of the 'Old World' and the innovation of the 'New World'. While Port was a traditional Portuguese wine, the Douro region's dry wines had adopted some of the practices, marketing and mind-set of the New World. The Douro winemaking region was declared a World Heritage Site in 2001. In 2003, Quinta do Vallado joined forces with four other vineyards in the region forming the *Douro Boys* group with the goal of promoting the region's wine. They pooled their efforts, organizing joint presentations, seminars and tastings. The Boys' reputation grew globally, recognized by respected critics including *The New York Times*.

In 2009 a new winery was completed, combining state-of-the art technology with high-quality architectural design; it was one of the most visited places in the Douro Valley.

The Vallado wines

Vallado invested in the design of the bottles and the labels, a far cry from the Portugal of the past. In 2009, Vallado moved from a single national distributor in Portugal to several regional ones. The goal was to be present in each region – this meant getting a bottle of wine into a restaurant would be faster. The same year, they decided to sell directly to large supermarket chains in Portugal – another major change to its operations.

Premium brands

Vallado produced unique wines in small volumes targeted at the 'luxury' sector – a crucial contribution to the prestige of the Vallado brand and its profitability. The Vallado Adelaide was the top dry red wine from an old single vineyard. The name was a tribute to the vineyard's ancestor Dona Antonia Adelaide Ferreira. It was only produced in very special years (2005, 2007, 2008, 2009, 2011, 2012, 2014) and in small volumes (3,500 bottles). Other premium brands included Vallado Tributa Port 1866 (99 Parker Points and mainly sold in China at a time when the market was strong in luxury) and Vallado ABF Port 1888 (98 Parker Points – launched in 2016 to celebrate the 300th anniversary of Quinta do Vallado. It was a limited edition of 933 numbered bottles – sold at more than €3,000 per bottle).

International markets

Two-thirds of Vallado's production was destined for the domestic market, giving a strong local base. Portugal's domestic market was growing progressively (mainly through tourism, hospitality, restaurants, etc.) leading to steady wine sales. Vallado had initially focused on the domestic market although its market share was fairly small. It was also established in foreign Portuguese-speaking markets (Angola, Brazil, Macau), where it had a strong position and from there expanded into new potential markets (USA, Canada, UK, China). Brazil and Angola had become priority markets for Vallado wines.

New opportunities included the US, one of Vallado's largest markets, where a 25 per cent tariff was imposed on imported wines from France, Germany, Spain and the UK in 2019. President Trump had then threatened to raise this tariff to 100 per cent tax on all European wines.

The UK was another potential market for Vallado, but with the country's withdrawal from the European Union, the long-term effect on taxes and trade regulations was unclear. China was also on the company's radar – potentially a game-changer for sales of Vallado's wines as they opened an exclusive Vallado store in November in Wenzhou, although a few months later it was closed due to Covid-19. Poland was the vineyard's largest export market in value and volume. It was an example of the benefits of the good relationship with the Portuguese supermarket chains – Jeronimo Martins – that also owned the largest Polish retail chain, with over 3,500 shops.

Questions:

1 What are the opportunities and risks for global strategists in the wine industry?

2 How can Quinta do Vallado continue to grow its revenues? Should it maintain its push into international markets? If so, which markets should be prioritized?

3 How can it compete with the largest wineries in the world to serve the global market?

4 Should it concentrate on: a) premium and super premium wines with high prices/low volumes or b) entry-level wines with low prices and margins but high volumes sold through off-trade channels with discount/promotion strategies?

5 Should it remain a niche vineyard?

6 Will Covid-19 have a long-term impact on the industry?

This mini-case is based on Monteiro, Pimentel and Carrick, Quinta do Vallado: From Douro to the World, INSEAD case study (2020).

Summary and key points

1 A company business strategy is a set of *fundamental choices* which define the company's long-term *objectives*, its *value proposition* to the market, how it intends to build and sustain a competitive *business system* and how it organizes itself

2 There are different levels of strategy:

a *Business strategy* applies at the level of an industry

b *Corporate strategy* applies at the level of a multi-business corporation

c *Global strategy* applies at the level of world operations

3 A global strategy consists of:

a *Global ambition*: stating the relative importance of regions and countries for a company

b *Global positioning*: choice of countries, customer segments and value proposition

c *Global business system*: investments in resources, assets and competencies to create a global value chain and global capabilities through alliances and acquisitions

d *Global organization*: global structure, processes, coordination and HRM

4 Global ambition

a Expresses the role a company wants to play in the world marketplace and how it views the future distribution of its sales and assets in the key regional clusters of the world:

- *Global player*: present in all regions of the world
- *Regional player*: dominant in one region, low or no presence in others
- *Regional dominant*: global player that is particularly strong in one region, but still active in others
- *Global exporter*: sells only, no or limited production investments
- *Global sourcer*: manufactures or buys internationally but sells domestically

b Ambition can be measured by using global indices:

- *Global Revenue Index (GRI)* is the ratio of the company's distribution of sales in the major world regions to the industry distribution of demand in the same region
- *Global Capability Index (GCI)* is the ratio of the company's distribution of assets or personnel in the major world regions to the industry distribution in the same region
- The *customer segments* are the particular groups of customers who request similar value attributes (shared value curve)
- *Degree of world standardization* of products/services:
  - A *standardized value proposition* offers a similar or standard value attribute to the same type of customer segment across the world
  - An *adaptive value proposition* tailors the value proposition to different regions

c The choice of global positioning depends on the company's decisions on the:

- *Scope* of targeted customer segments (broad/focused player)
- *Approach* of making a value proposition in different countries (standardized/adaptive)
- Choice of *generic strategies* adopted (differentiation or cost leadership)

5 A global business system distributes the company value chain across the world. It involves the building and developing of capabilities to compete successfully in the global market space:

a *Value chain*: there are three major generic components of a value chain: *innovative* activities, *productive* activities, *customer relationship* activities

b *Capabilities*: there are three types of capabilities: differentiation, cost leadership and innovation. Capabilities that are unique to a company and non-replicable by competitors constitute a company's *competitive advantage*

6 Competitive advantages: proprietary ownership or access to valuable assets, resources or competencies

a Competitive advantages are sustainable if they provide:

- *Customer loyalty*, which can be built on brand or where there are high switching costs involved
- *Positive feedback* such as network externalities and experience effects
- *Pre-emption of key resources* such as location or key personnel
- *Barriers to imitation*: appropriation by one company of key capabilities that competitors will find difficult to access or to replicate

b Modes of building competitive advantage:

- *First-mover advantages*: being among the first competitors to enter a given market
- *Leveraging advantages*: exploiting capabilities already built in other countries

7 Evolution of firms in the globalization process

a There are three stages of progress:

- *Export*: Sales is the only element in the value chain which is set up in foreign countries. As the company progresses through the export stage, it invests in marketing subsidiaries to actively manage the marketing mix
- *Multinational*: The company manages a portfolio of relatively independent worldwide wholly owned subsidiaries or joint ventures
- *Global*: A global company integrates and coordinates its worldwide operations to take advantage of economies of scale, transfer of know-how and resource optimization; this leads to an interlocked set of value chain activities which falls broadly into three categories: global, regional and local

b *Liability of foreignness* for global firms is the cost of being unfamiliar with the new environment as well as the cost of not having a local network, and the cost of having to manage operations from a distance. It needs to be compensated by a superior competitive advantage

8 The transferability of capabilities:

In the process of globalization, companies need to identify which capabilities can be:

a easily transferred internationally into new territories without any change (*transfer*)

b can be transferred with some adaptation to local conditions (*adapt*)

c or have to be created from scratch when entering new countries (*create*)

9 Strategic alliances:

a Companies usually need to acquire and complement their capabilities by setting up alliances

b Global strategic partnerships are often critical for achieving a global presence and building global competitive advantage

c Forms of strategic alliance include:

- Global alliances to pool complementing capabilities to reach world markets or achieve a critical mass in R&D
- Local partnerships – joint ventures, franchises or licensing for market entry
- Acquisitions

10 Global organization (see Chapter 15):

a Organization *choice* is dependent on the phases of global development:

- Early export
- Early multinational subsidiaries
- Full multinational
- Global
- Global multi-business

b Three types of global organization can be distinguished:

- Centralized hub
- Decentralized federation
- Matrix

c Organizational *dimensions* cover:

- Structure
- System/processes
- Culture

11 Small and medium-sized enterprises (SMEs):

- Only a small proportion of SMEs are engaged in global operations
- Their international exposure is essentially export or sourcing
- Only 5–10 per cent of SMEs are truly international
- SMEs face many barriers to internationalization
- Two major sources to overcome the barriers: government-led and company-led

12 Born global and born digital:

a Born global companies are firms that succeed in world markets without an established domestic base

b Born digital companies are firms that from the start base their business model on internet-based transactions

Learning assignments

1 In 2020 the global distribution of sales in the industrial gas industry was as follows:

Global industrial gas industry €82 billion	Americas	Europe	Asia and Rest of the World
	42%	30%	28%

The 2020 global distribution of sales and assets of the insurance company Air Liquide is shown below:

	Europe	US and Latin America	Asia and Rest of the World
Revenue (million €)	6,800	7,800	5,000
Assets	10,500	18,400	2,000

1 What is Air Liquide's position on a GCI/GRI mapping?

2 In your opinion, in which industries could the UK, Italy and Australia be considered 'key' countries?

3 What could be the benefits of positioning oneself as a standardized global niche differentiator (see Table 5.4)? What kind of competitive advantages does this require?

4 What are the capabilities needed to be a broad adaptive cost leader?

5 What are the ways to sustain competitive advantage?

6 What types of competitive advantage does being a first mover provide?

7 Sketch the mapping of the value chain for:

   a A consulting firm

   b An airline

   c A trading firm

   d A corporate and investment bank

   e An internet-based platform (e.g. Airbnb, Netflix)?

8 For each of the entities in Question 7, can you represent a possible global distribution of their value chain, as illustrated in Figure 5.11?

Key words

- Born digital
- Born global
- Business strategy
- Corporate strategy
- Cost leadership
- Differentiation
- Global business strategy
- Global Capability Index
- Global corporate strategy
- Global positioning
- Global Revenue Index
- Piggybacking
- Value chain
- Value curve
- Value proposition

Web resources

Business Week – Global business:
https://www.bloomberg.com/businessweek
Forbes Global Magazine online, with a section on companies and strategies:
http://www.forbes.com/forbesglobal/
Harvard cases and *Harvard Business Review* reprints:
http://www.harvardbusiness.org/
McKinsey consulting business review:
https://www.mckinsey.com/quarterly/overview
Ernst & Young Consulting:
http://www.ey.com/home
Kearney Consulting:
http://www.kearney.com/
BCG Consulting:
https://www.bcg.com/featured-insights/thought-leadership-ideas

Companion website

Visit the companion website at bloomsbury.pub/global-strategic-management-5e for a multitude of weblinks and resources, self-test questions for revision and appendices.

Notes

1 *Sogo Shoshas* are large Japanese trading companies.
2 Dunning (1993).
3 Rugman (2005).
4 A similar calculation could be done by taking the major countries, but it becomes more complicated. However, it is perfectly possible to apply a similar methodology by taking the ten major world markets, for instance, or applying it at the level of a region (such as the distribution of sales in Asia Pacific among the key countries of the region).
5 Porter (1980).
6 This concept of the value chain was developed by Porter (1985, 1986).
7 Doz and Mikko (2008).
8 Stalk (1988).
9 Kim and Mauborgne (2007).
10 Jeffrey (1992).
11 *Network effects* exist when the customer base of a product or service is such that it induces other products or services providers to adopt it in their own value proposition, which in turn encour- ages new customers to buy the original product or service. *This virtuous circle* creates a positive loop that reinforces the company's competitive position. The classic example of a network effect is Microsoft Windows operating system. Windows is an open system, which encourages various PC makers to make Windows-based machines, which in turn encourages software makers to produce Windows-based software. Thus more Windows-based software is available to customers who buy more Windows-based machines.
12 Ghemawat (2005); Rugman (2005).
13 Zaheer (1995).
14 Some authors have argued that the liability of foreignness does not mean that a firm will possess particularly different competitive advantages from the ones it has developed at home. See Niron and Buckley (2014).
15 Stopford and Wells (1972); Heenan and Perlmutter (1979); Prahalad and Doz (1987); Bartlett and Ghoshal (1989, 2000).
16 Goold et al. (1994).
17 OECD (2019).
18 Ibid., p. 57.

19 European Commission (2010).
20 OECD (201. Op Cit).
21 Lloyd-Reason and Mughan (2003). 30 OECD (2007).
22 Lloyd-Reason and Mughan (2003). 30 OECD (2007).
23 OECD (2009).
24 Zaheer (1995).
25 European Commission (2004).
26 Johanson and Vahlne (1990).
27 Monaghan et al. (2020).
28 Welch and Luostarinen (1988).
29 Rennie (1993).
30 McDougall and Oviatt (2000).
31 Knight (2015).
32 Stoyan (2012).

References and further reading

Anderson, K. and Pinilla, V. (2018) *Wine Globalization A New Comparative History* (Cambridge: Cambridge University Press).

Ansoff, H. L. (1965) *Corporate Strategy* (New York, NY: McGraw-Hill).

Bader, T. and Mazzarol, T. (2009) 'Defining the born global firm: a review of the literature', Paper ANZAM 2009-025.R1, presented at the Annual Australian and New Zealand Academy of Management Conference, 2–4 December.

Banalieva, E. R. and Dhanaraj, C. (2019) 'Internalization theory for the digital economy', *Journal of International Business Studies*, 50 (8): 1372–87.

Bartlett, C. A. and Ghoshal, S. (1989) *Managing Across Borders: The Transnational Solution* (Boston, MA: Harvard Business School Press).

Bartlett, C. A. and Ghoshal, S. (2000) 'Going global: lessons from late movers', *Harvard Business Review*, 78 (2): 132–42.

Besanko, D., Dranove, D., Shanley, M. and Schaefer, S. (2007) *The Economics of Strategy* (New York, NY: John Wiley).

Carr, C. (2020), *Global Oligopolies: A Key Idea for Business and Society* (Milton Park, UK: Routledge, Taylor & Francis Group).

Collis, D. J. and Carr, C. (2011) *Should You have a Global Strategy?*, MIT Management Review, Fall.

Davidson, W. H. (1982) *Global Strategic Management* (New York, NY: John Wiley).

Djärf, T. and Engström, J. (2003) Piggybacking as a method of international market entry, Department of Business Administration and Social Sciences Division of Industrial Marketing, Lulea University of Technology: 141SHU.

Doremus, P. N., Pauly, L. W., Reich, S. and Keller, W. W. (1999) *The Myth of the Global Corporation* (Princeton, NJ: Princeton University Press).

Doz, Y. L. and Mikko, K. (2008) *Fast Strategy: How Strategic Agility Will Help You to Stay Ahead of the Game* (Philadelphia, PA: Pearson Education, Wharton School Publishing).

Dunning, J. H. (1993) *Multinational Enterprises and the Global Economy* (Harlow: Addison-Wesley).

European Commission (2004) *Internationalisation of SMEs* (Luxembourg: Office for Official Publications of the European Communities).

European Commission (2010) *Internationalisation of European SMEs. Final Report* (Luxembourg: Office for Official Publications of the European Communities).

Faulkner, D. O. and Campbell, A. (2003) *The Oxford Handbook of Strategy, I and II* (Oxford: Oxford University Press).

Freeman, S., Edwards, R. and Schroder, B. (2006) 'How smaller born-global firms use networks and alliances to overcome constraints to rapid internationalization', *Journal of International Marketing*, 14 (3): 33–63.

Ghemawat, P. (2005) 'Regional strategies for global leadership', *Harvard Business Review*, 83 (12): 98–108.

Ghemawat, P. (2007) *Redefining Global Strategy, Crossing Borders in a World Where Differences*

Still Matter (Boston, MA: Harvard Business School Press).

Ghemawat, P. (2018) *The New Global Road Map Enduring Strategies for Turbulent Times* (Boston, MA: Harvard Business School Press).

Goold, M., Campbell, A. and Alexander, M. (1994) *Corporate-Level Strategy* (New York, NY: John Wiley).

Hamel, G. and Prahalad, C. K. (1985) 'Do you really have a global strategy?', *Harvard Business Review*, 63: 139–48.

Heenan, D. and Perlmutter, H. (1979) *Multinational Organization Development* (Boston, MA: Addison-Wesley).

Hennart, J. F. (2019) 'Digitalized service multinationals and international business theory', *Journal of International Business Studies*, 50 (8): 1388–400.

International Finance Corporation (2014) *MSME Country Indicators 2014: Toward a Better Understanding of Micro, Small and Medium Enterprises*. https://smefinanceforum.org/data-sites/msme-country-indicators (accessed 9 June 2017).

Jeffrey, W. (1992) 'How sustainable is your competitive advantage', *Californian Management Review*, 34 (3): 29–51.

Johanson, J. and Vahlne, J. E. (1990) 'The mechanisms of internationalization', *International Marketing Review*, 7 (4): 11–24.

Kelly, N. (2020) 'Looking for new global markets? Bigger isn't always better', *Harvard Business Review*. https://hbr.org/2020/11/looking-for-new-global-markets-bigger-isnt-always-better (accessed 1 February 2022) .

Kessler, B. (2020) *Global Strategy for a De-globalising World*, INSEAD Knowledge. https://knowledge.insead.edu/blog/insead-blog/global-strategy-for-a-de-globalising-world-14781 (accessed 1 February 2022).

Kim, W. C. and Mauborgne, R. (2007) *Blue Ocean Strategy: How to Create Uncontested Market Space and Make the Competition Irrelevant* (Boston, MA: Harvard Business School Press).

Kim, W. C. and Mauborgne, R. (2017), *Blue Ocean Shift* (Boston, MA: Harvard Business School Press).

Knight, G. (2015) 'Born global firms: evolution of a contemporary phenomenon', in S. Zou, H. Xu and L. H. Shi (eds), *Entrepreneurship in International Marketing (Advances in International Marketing)*, 25, 3–20 (Bingley: Emerald).

Liesch, P., Steen, M., Middleton, S. and Weerawardena, J. (2007) *Born to Be Global: A Closer Look at the International Venturing of Australian Born Global Firms* (Australian Business Foundation).

Lloyd-Reason, L. and Mughan, T. (2003) 'Competing effectively in international markets: identifying need, sharing best practice and adding value to the Eastern Region through skills and knowledge transfer', Final Report for the East of England Development Agency, web.anglia.ac.uk/anet/faculties/laibs/Research/docs/CEIM_FINAL_REPORT_Anglia.doc (accessed 16 June 2017).

McDougall, P. and Oviatt, B. M. (2000) 'International entrepreneurship: the intersection of two research paths', *Academy of Management Journal*, 43 (5): 902–6.

Mellahi, K., Meyer, K., Narula, R., Isurdu, I. and Verbeke, A. (2021) *The Oxford Handbook of International Business Strategy* (Oxford: Oxford University Press).

Monaghan, S., Tippman, E. and Coviello, N. (2020) 'Born digitals: thoughts on their internationalization and a research agenda', *Journal of International Business Studies*, 51: 11–22.

Monteiro, L. F., Pimentel, M. and Carrick, A. M. (2020) *Quinta do Vallado: From Douro to the World*, INSEAD Case Study. https://publishing.insead.edu/case/quinta-do-vallado (accessed 1 February 2022).

Narula, R., Asmussen, C. G., Chi, T. and Kundu, S. K. (2019) 'Applying and advancing internalization theory: the multinational enterprise in the twenty-first century', *Journal of International Business Studies*, 50: 1231–52.

Niron, H. and Buckley, P. J. (2014) 'Is competitive advantage a necessary condition for the emergence of the multinational enterprise?', *Global Strategy Journal*, 4: 35–48.

OECD (Organisation for Economic Co-operation and Development) (2007) *Enhancing the Role of SMEs in Global Value Chains*, OECD Background Report (Paris: OECD).

OECD (Organisation for Economic Co-operation and Development) (2008) *Removing Barriers to SME Access to International Markets* (Paris: OECD Publishing). http://dx.doi.org/10.1787/9789264045866-en (accessed 8 June 2017).

OECD (Organisation for Economic Co-operation and Development) (2009) *Top Barriers and Drivers to SME Internationalisation*, Report by the OECD Working Party on SMEs and Entrepreneurship (Paris: OECD).

OECD (Organisation for Economic Co-operation and Development) (2012) *Fostering SMEs' Participation in Global Markets: Final Report*, Centre For Entrepreneurship, SMEs and Local Development, Fe/Sme(2012)6/Final (Paris: OECD).

OECD (Organisation for Economic Co-operation and Development) (2019) *OECD SME and Entrepreneurship Outlook 2019* (Paris: OECD). https://doi.org/10.1787/34907e9c-en (accessed 1 February 2022).

Ohmae, K. (1985) *Becoming a Triad Power* (New York, NY: McKinsey).

Porter, M. E. (1980) *Competitive Strategy: Techniques for Analyzing Industries and Competitors* (New York, NY: Free Press).

Porter, M. E. (1985) *Competitive Advantage. Creating and Sustaining Superior Performance* (New York, NY: Free Press).

Porter, M. E. (1986) *Competition in Global Industries* (Boston, MA: Harvard Business School Press).

Prahalad, C. K. and Doz, Y. L. (1987) *The Multinational Mission: Balancing Local Demands and Global Vision* (New York, NY: Free Press).

Rennie, M. W. (1993) 'Global competitiveness: born global', *McKinsey Quarterly*, 4: 45–52.

Rugman, A. M. (2005) *The Regional Multinationals: MNEs and Global Strategic Management* (Cambridge: Cambridge University Press).

Rugman, A. M. and Almodóvar, P. (2011) 'The born global illusion and the regional nature of international business', in R. Ramamurti and N. Hashai (eds), *The Future of Foreign Direct Investment and the Multinational Enterprise* (*Research in Global Strategic Management*, 15 (Bingley: Emerald), 251–69.

Russ, M. and Jones, J. K. (2012) 'International virtual industry clusters and SMEs: early process policy recommendations', in K. I. Westeren (ed.), *Foundations of the Knowledge Economy: Innovation, Learning and Clusters*, 214–33 (Cheltenham: Edward Elgar).

Stalk, G. (1988) 'Time – the next source of competitive advantage', *Harvard Business Review*, 66: 41–51.

Stopford, J. and Wells, L. (1972) *Strategy and Structure of Multinational Enterprises* (New York, NY: Basic Books).

Stoyan, T. (2012) 'Global from the start: the characteristics of born-global firms in the technology sector', *Technology Innovation Management Review*, 2 (3): 5.

Terpstra, V. and Chwo-Ming, J. (1990) 'Piggybacking: a quick road to internationalisation', *International Marketing Review*, 7 (4).

Welch, L. S. and Luostarinen, R. (1988) 'Internationalization: evolution of a concept', *Journal of general management*, 14 (2): 34–55.

Zaheer, S. (1995) 'Overcoming the liability of foreignness', *Academy of Management Journal*, 38 (2): 341–63.

Chapter 6

Assessing countries' attractiveness

At the end of the chapter you will be able to:

- Organize a complete assessment of market opportunities and industry structure in a country
- Understand and value various types of risks involved in operating in a country
- Compare different countries as investment opportunities

Introduction

Within the overall framework of their global strategy firms have to choose the geographical locations where they will set up operational assets. This kind of decision, known as the 'entry' decision, demands that firms take into consideration several factors (Figure 6.1):

- First, there is the need to assess the *attractiveness* of the country, either in absolute terms or relative to another country. This is generally known as **'country attractiveness analysis'**.
- Second, there is the need to decide on the *form of entry*. This is generally known as **'entry strategy'**.

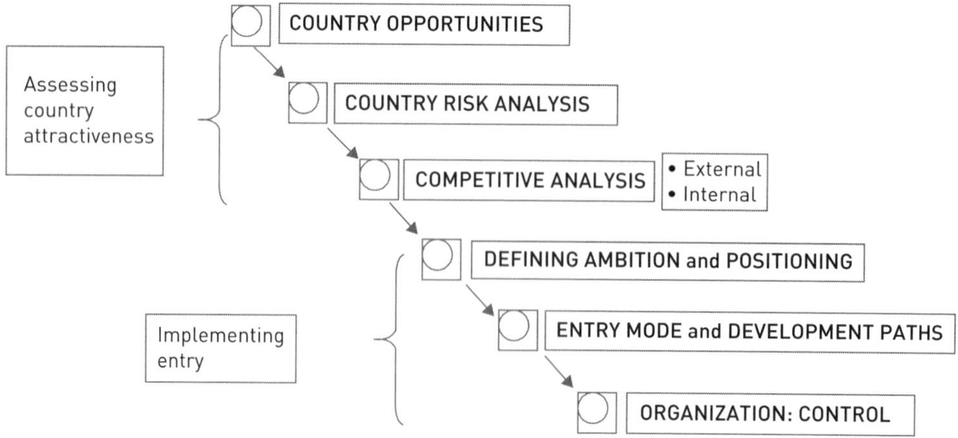

Figure 6.1 The foreign market entry decision

In this chapter, we will concentrate on assessing a country's attractiveness, while in Chapter 7 we will discuss entry strategies.

Country attractiveness is a function of the *market and resources prospects,* the *competitive context* and the *risks of operating* in a country.

This chapter presents a framework for assessing market attractiveness as well as a country's risks.

Why is a country attractive?

Theoretically, a country will be attractive to foreign investors if, by investing in that country, they get a return that is equal to or higher than their *risk adjusted weighted cost of capital.* In fact, the foreign investment decision is fundamentally the same as any investment decision. If we apply the concept to a business investment (as opposed to a financial portfolio investment of securities), the basis behind the decision to invest (or not) is embodied in three key questions:

1. Are the market and resources prospects, and the competitive conditions, in a particular country such that given that company's pre-existing competitive advantages, the business is likely to generate a return *equal to or higher than the cost of capital*?
2. What are the favourable or problematic characteristics of the *socioeconomic and political context within that country* for achieving an economic return?
3. Are the risks of operating in this country *acceptable for the shareholders and employees*?

The fundamental question of a foreign investment thus falls into the general framework of opportunities and risks analysis, as shown in Figure 6.2.

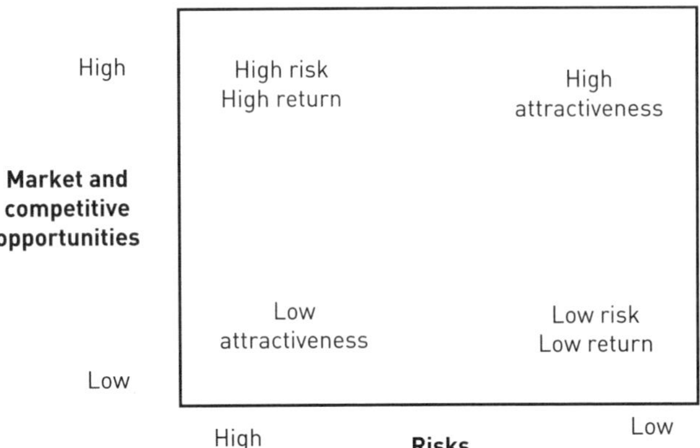

Figure 6.2 General investment framework

Although foreign investments fall into the general category of an opportunities/risks trade-off, the assessment of the international context raises some challenging issues. Many scholars, consultants and practitioners have proposed methodologies for country assessments. Online Appendix 6.1 summarizes the most prominent approaches, which give relative rankings or scores to countries according to different economic, political and social criteria. What we propose here is an analysis of the various dimensions that contribute to country attractiveness. Insert 6.1 gives a short description of an alternative model of dimensions frequently used.

In this chapter we will use the following four broad categories:

- Market and resources opportunities
- Competitive context
- Socioeconomic, political, environmental and cultural distances
- Country risks.

One has to bear in mind first that market and competitive opportunities vary according to the *type of industry,* and risks affect them differently. For instance, a heavy industry demanding a large investment in fixed assets will be more vulnerable to political risks while a service business with a low financial exposure will be less affected. Generalizations are thus difficult to make. Secondly, the merit of a country is first evaluated in *absolute terms* to check whether it meets minimum requirements for opportunities versus risks, and then it is generally compared with other countries having *similar features.* For instance, a company may evaluate investing in Chile, and then compare Chile with Argentina; Thailand may be compared with the Philippines, France with the UK or Germany, and India with China.

Insert 6.1 Pestel: An alternative model of analysis

Introduced initially as ETPS by Professor Aguilar in his book 'Scanning the Business Environment' (Aguilar 1967), the PEST, which later on became PESTEL, is an analytical framework used to analyse environments before making strategic decisions. The components of this framework are:

1. Political
2. Economical
3. Social
4. Technological
5. Environmental
6. Legal

In the present chapter those elements are presented in a different format.

Market, resources and industry opportunities

When looking at a country's attractiveness, businesses need to consider its market, resources and industry opportunities, as shown in Figure 6.3.

Market opportunities assessment measures the *potential demand* in the country for the products or services of the firm:

- Market *size*
- Market *growth*
- Quality of *demand.*

Resources opportunities:

- *Natural* resources
- *Human* resources
- *Infrastructure and support industries* resources.
- *Technology resources*.

Industry opportunities assessment measures how easy it is to *compete* in the country:

- The nature of the *competitive* climate
- The nature of the *industry's competitive structure*
- Any *investment incentives* granted by governments.

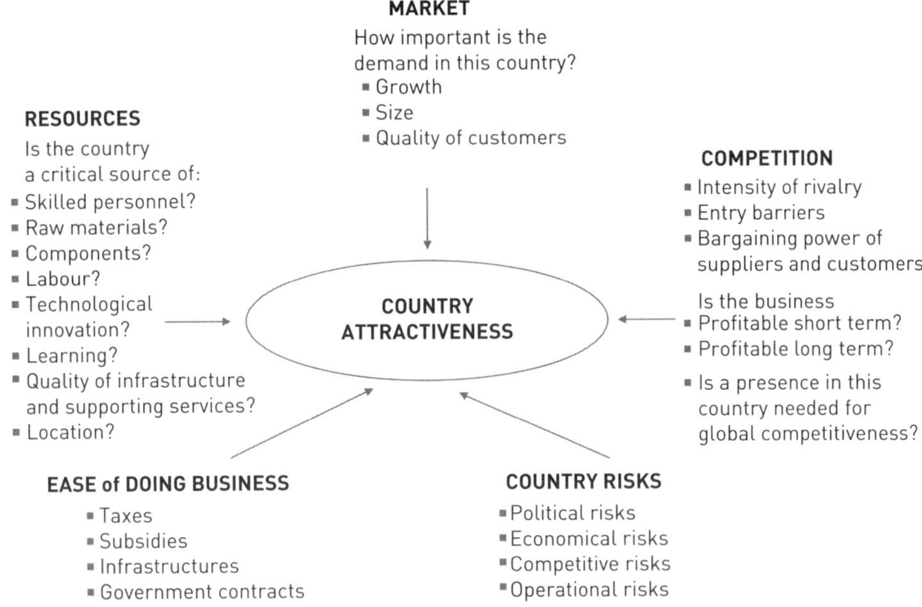

Figure 6.3 Framework for assessment of a country's market, resources and industry attractiveness

Assessing market opportunities

The classic tools of market forecasting and analysis are presented here, in a logical sequence.

Broad assessment of the overall demand, given macroeconomic data

In many instances, this broad assessment uses some sort of correlation between macroeconomic social or institutional indicators, such as GDP *per capita,* with some measure of consumption of certain products. Table 6.1 gives some of the most frequently used **macroeconomic indicators.** Applying forecast GDP growth figures given by international financial organizations such as the World Bank, IMF or OECD gives a crude estimate of the anticipated size of the market.

Figure 6.4 gives a graphical representation of mobile subscriptions as a function of GDP per capita and Figure 6.5 shows the production of cement. In the case of smartphones, the correlation between the two indicators is 0.85 for mobile subscription, indicating that the overall economic standard of the country 'drives' smartphone ownership and utilization. However, we can observe some variations between countries. This may be explained by differences in government policies and social behaviour. In the case of cement the correlation is 0.36 and the relationship is not linear. Emerging countries generate a high level of demand for cement due to their need to build infrastructure. After a peak in economic development, new infrastructure is needed less.

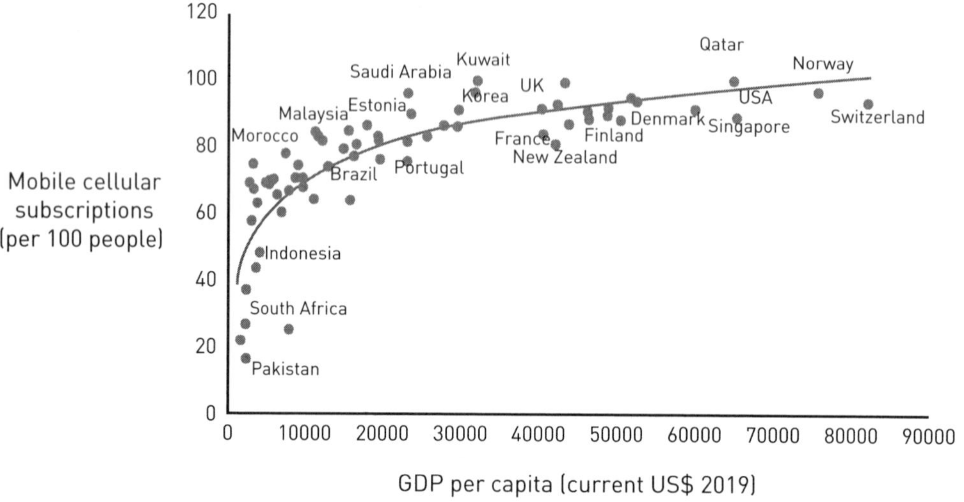

Figure 6.4 Relationship between GDP per capita and mobile subscriptions per 100 people, 2019 (R = 0.85)
Source: Authors' own construction using data from World Bank: World Development Indicators 2019.

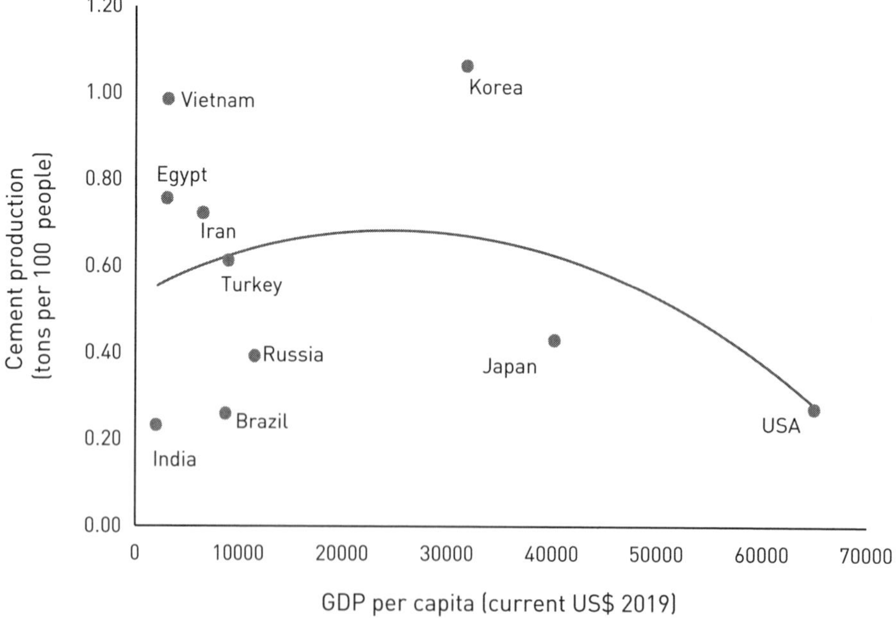

Figure 6.5 Relationship between GDP per capita and the production of cement, 2019 (R = 0.36)
Source: Authors' own, based on data from World Bank, World Development Indicators and United States Geological Survey at https://pubs.usgs.gov/periodicals/mcs2020/mcs2020.pdf.

Table 6.1 Macro indicators used in international market assessments

Economic	Sociological	Demographic	Institutional
• GDP size • GDP size (PPP)* • GDP per capita • GDP per capita (PPP)* • Income distribution • Disposable income • Saving rate • Exports/imports • Investment rates	• Urbanization (percentage of urban population) • Socioeconomic distribution – by income groups – by regions/cities – by education level	• Population • Population growth • Age distribution	• Government spending • Infrastructure: – Power – Telecom – Internet – Roads • Education levels • Number of scientists • R&D expenditure

Note: * *PPP (purchasing power parity) calculations take into account differences in prices and cost of living. Generally, developing countries can buy many more goods and services with one $ than in the United States and therefore have a much higher GDP calculated with PPP than with market exchange rates.*

Plotting trends

As a first indicator, the macroeconomic correlation approach may give some interesting insights into the potential size of a market. When a country is vast and diverse it may be useful to refine the assessment at regional or even urban centre level. When it is used in combination with other factors, such as the degree of urbanization, climatic conditions, income distribution, lifestyles and saving rates, it may give a more precise model. Plotting trends for comparable countries (in terms of economic conditions, economic factors and so on) also gives an insight into the potential future demand, on a per capita basis as well as in absolute value.

The middle-class effect

The demand for most of the mass consumer goods and their related inputs is often triggered by the presence of an affluent middle class. In Chapter 2 the importance of an economically strong middle class in emerging markets was described. Figure 6.6 illustrates the 'middle-class effect', showing that there is strong demand elasticity compared to population and GDP growth for durable consumer goods. The middle-class effect is due to the skewed nature of the income distribution in emerging countries. According to a joint World Bank and Australian Government Report about Indonesia, the 39 million (18 per cent of the total population) middle-class households in 2002 grew to 54 million (20 per cent of the total) in 2019. Figure 6.7 illustrates the middle-class effect in this country, showing that the share of household consumption by the middle class grew from 20 per cent to 42 per cent.

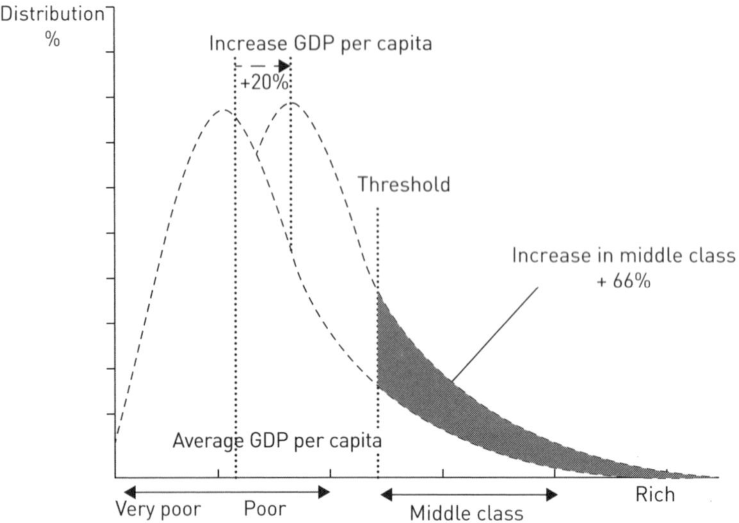

Figure 6.6 The 'middle-class effect'

Note: *With an increase of 20 per cent of GDP, the middle class increases by 66 per cent.*

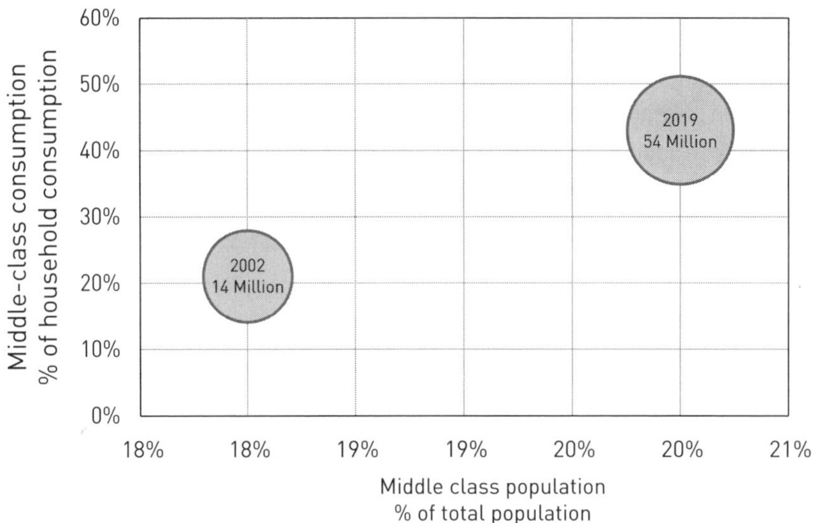

Figure 6.7 Illustration of the middle-class effect in Indonesia between 2002 and 2019

Sources: Authors' own figure, using data from various World Bank Development Indicators (2019); World Bank and 'Aspiring Indonesian: the Expanding Middle Class', September 2019, https://www.worldbank.org/en/country/indonesia/publication/aspiring-indonesia-expanding-the-middle-class (accessed 1 February 2022).

Quality of demand

Quality of demand describes the nature and diversity of **market segmentation** prevalent in a country, and the profile of the customer value curve (as defined in Chapter 5) in each segment. Marketers and strategists generally distinguish two generic segments: 'low end' and 'high end' (Figure 6.8).

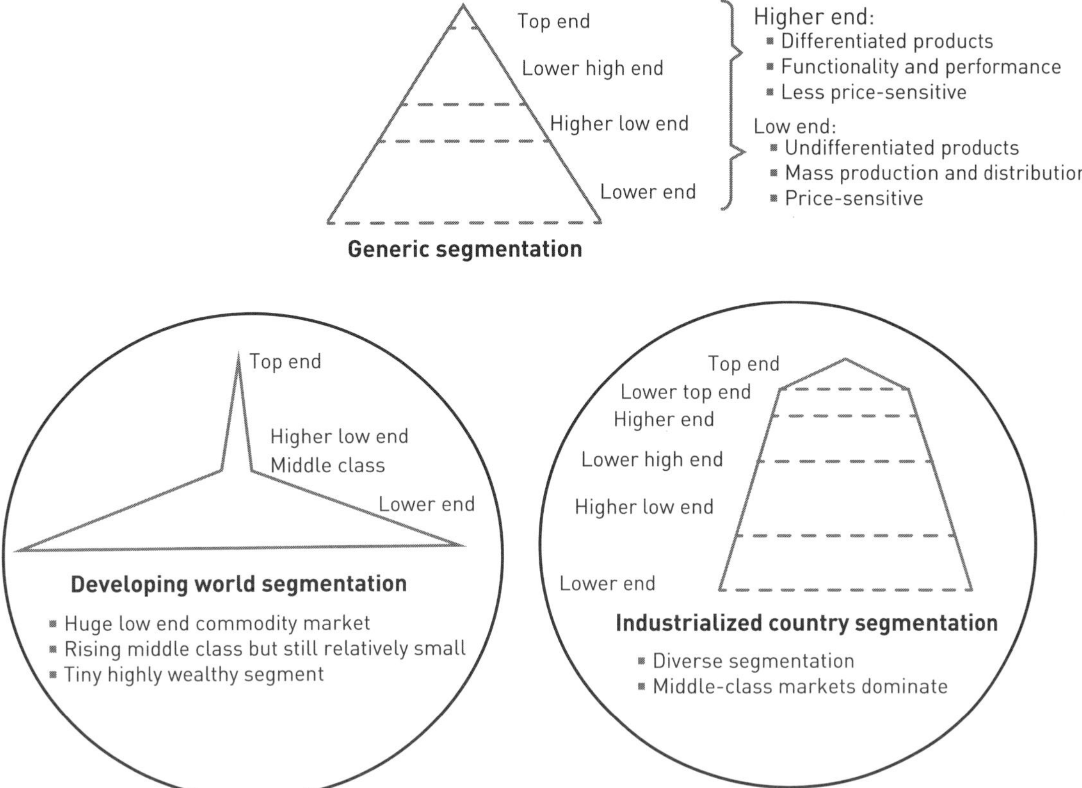

Figure 6.8 Market segmentations

In developing countries (bottom left part of Figure 6.8), the bulk of the market comprises a large undifferentiated, price-sensitive segment, co-existing with a growing, more differentiated middle-class segment. In mature, advanced economies, segmentation is more diverse in societies that are essentially middle class (bottom right of Figure 6.8). However, in practice, as economies develop, markets become more sophisticated than this simple dual segmentation implies.

On the basis of demand characteristics countries can generally be grouped into four major clusters:

1. *Developing countries,* characterized by low income per capita and low growth: most sub-Saharan nations (except Nigeria and South Africa), e.g. Mauritania, Haiti, Yemen.
2. *Emerging countries* such as Indonesia, Thailand, Nigeria, with high growth rate and still relatively low income per capita, but growing fast.
3. *Fast industrializing economies*, characterized by high growth and moderate to high wealth: China, Brazil, Mexico, South Africa.
4. Relatively low-growth/high-wealth *industrialized OECD countries* such as North America, Western Europe and Japan.

The market characteristics of these clusters are described in Table 6.2.

Table 6.2 Characteristics of demand according to country life cycle clusters

Demand characteristics	Developing countries	Emerging countries	Fast industrializing economies	Industrialized countries
Growth	Low	High	High	Low
Size	Small	Small to high	Small to high	High
Segmentation	Dominant subsistence sector Large low-end segment	Fast-growing middle class Large low-end segment	Established middle class Increased diversity of segments	Established middle class Diverse and sophisticated segmentation
Customer value curve	Price Availability	Price Distribution Emerging advertising	Product functionality Performance Services	Product functionality Performance Services
Distribution	Push logistics	Push logistics Beginning of pull	Pull Beginning of mass retailing	Diversity Mass retail important
Competition	Regulated	Beginning of deregulation New entrants	Mainly deregulated Active Increasingly diverse	Deregulated Active Diverse

Assessing resource opportunities

The resources that attract foreign investors fall into three broad categories:

1 *Natural* resources

2 *Human* resources

3 *Infrastructure and support industries* resources.

Natural resources

Countries that do not use their production for national consumption tend to export raw materials, to promote processing by domestic companies or to invite foreign firms to invest in processing and export. Governments are very sensitive about the protection of their natural resources and very often require controls on foreign activities in this domain by negotiating production-sharing agreements as well as joint ventures. Oil and gas are probably the most globally sensitive industries, given the highly strategic nature of the commodity, the inherent risks of exploration, the capital intensity of the investments and the geographical location of the reserves. It is not by chance that the most sophisticated country risks methodologies have been developed in this industry.[1] Figure 6.9 represents selected resource-rich countries in graphical format.

A particular type of natural resource is *geographical location* which, combined with good infrastructure and support services and industry, may give to certain countries or regions within a country the role of a 'hub' or a regional centre. Singapore, located at the end of the Strait of Malacca; Hong Kong, located at the door to continental China; Brussels for the EU; and Miami for Latin America have all developed as hubs based on their geographical location.

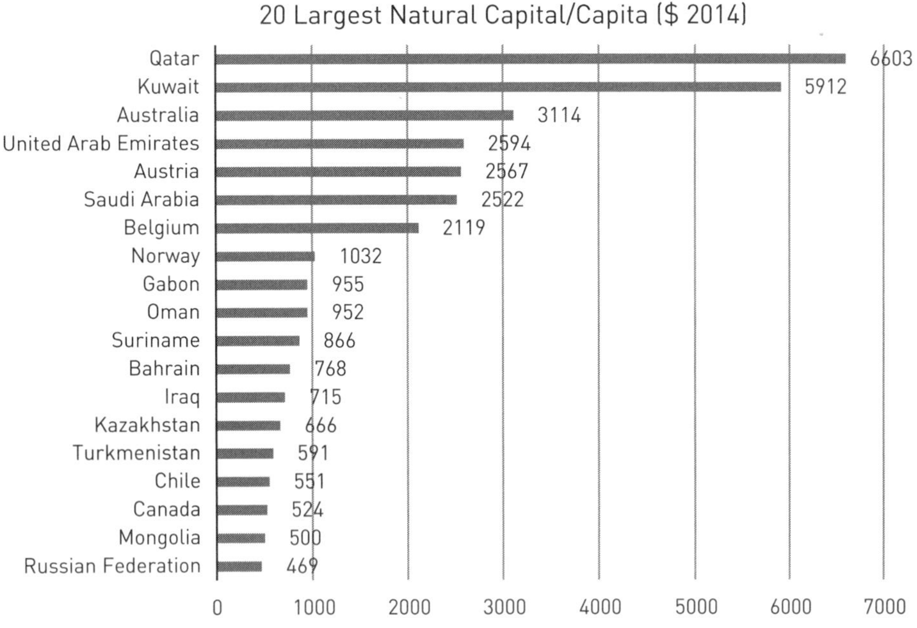

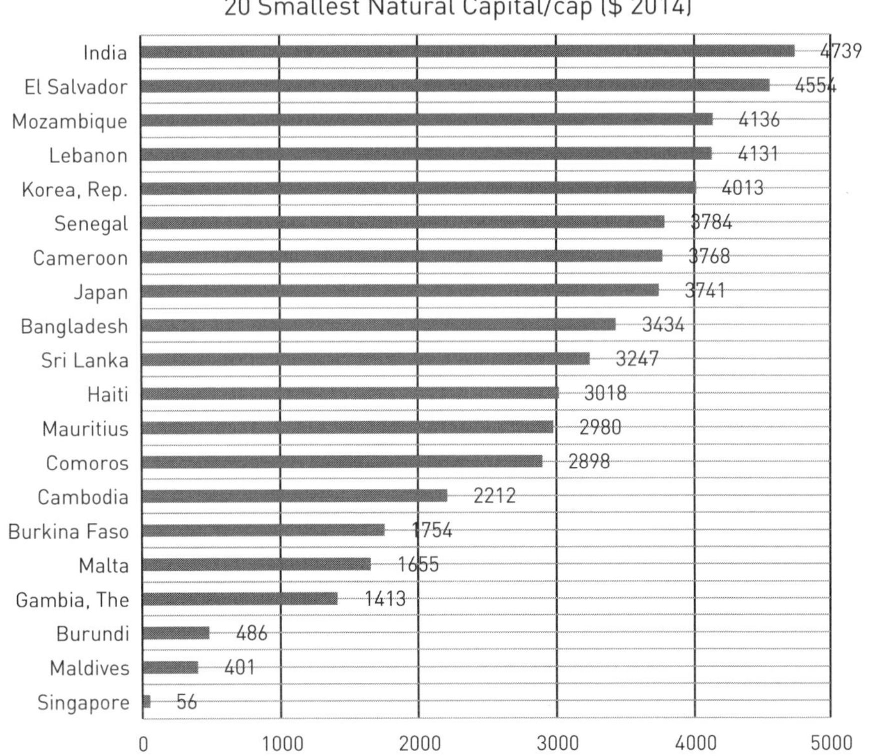

Figure 6.9 Natural resource per capita

Note: *Natural capital is the sum of agricultural, mineral and energy resources calculated as the present value generated by the resources.*

Source: Lange, Wodon and Carey (2018). License: Creative Commons Attribution CC BY 3.0 IGO.

Human resources

The quality and cost of labour was the cause of the migration of international investments that took place in the 1950s and 1960s. Offshore factories in Southeast Asia and Latin America were set up in Export-Processing Zones (EPZs) for the production and assembly of labour-intensive products. International sourcing under the form of original equipment manufacturing (OEM) or straight procurement gave an opportunity for local companies in Japan in the 1950s, in Korea, Taiwan and Brazil in the 1960s, Singapore, Hong Kong and Tunisia in the 1970s, and China, Vietnam and India in the 1980s to develop manufacturing volume and competencies and to establish their international presence.

In practice, two human resource elements are attractive: the *skills of the workforce* and the *unit cost of labour.* Figure 6.10 shows that there is some correlation between those two attributes ($R = 0.84$), but one

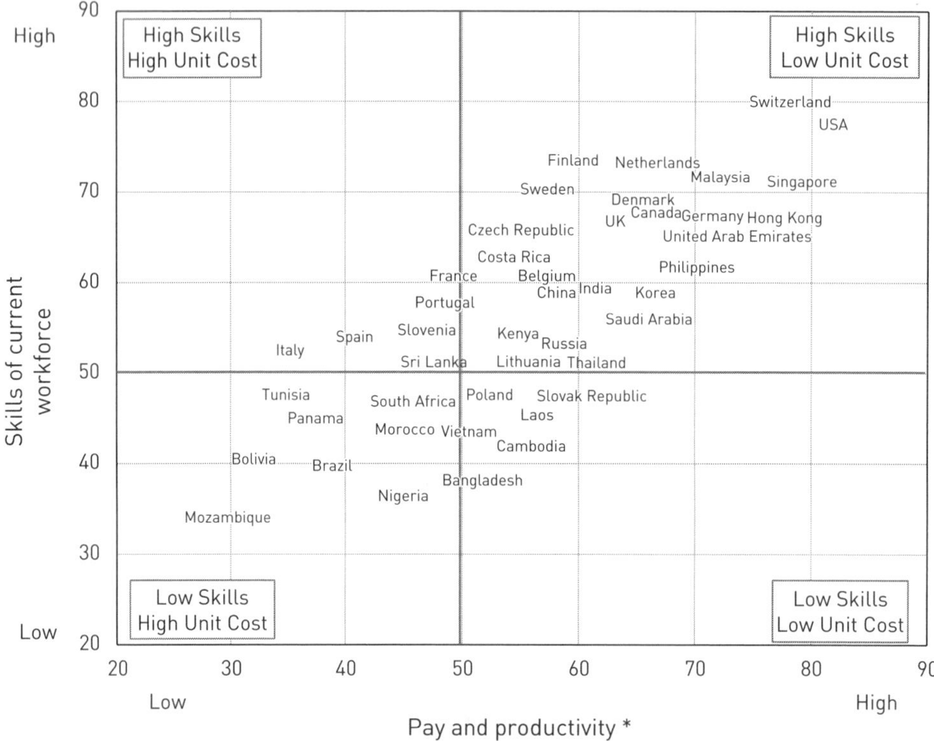

	High pay and productivity/high skills	High pay and productivity/ low skills	Low pay and productivity/ high skills	Low pay and productivity/ low skills
Average GDP/CAP (2019)	35,601	10,981	15,935	6,303
Average inward flow of FDI/ CAP (2000–2019)	36,053	5,111	5,266	2,988

Figure 6.10 Pay and productivity and skills of current workforce

Note: * *This measure (score from 0 to 100), computed by the World Economic Forum, assesses the extent to which pay is related to productivity. It is a proxy for assessing the unit cost of production. High pay with poor productivity would result in a high cost per unit (as seen in the top-left part of the graph). Conversely, low pay with high productivity would indicate a low cost per unit (in the bottom-right quarter). The vertical axis measuring the quality of education is a measure of the quality of work.*

Sources: Authors' own, based on World Economic Forum (2015–2019) for rankings; UNCTAD (2016) for statistics.

can see that countries in the upper-right-hand quadrant that benefit from the highest level of education and the best combination of productivity related to pay have received the highest foreign investment per capita. This indicates that the countries that have been able to combine the best mix of productivity and quality of labour have been seen as attractive for foreign investors.

Countries like China or India that were relying on low labour cost in the 1980s have increased their productivity and their educational system to move to the upper-right quadrant to high value-added production. Since the mid-1980s, India, the Philippines and to a certain extent China have tried successfully to strengthen the production of computer software, particularly in the data capture segments. India, for instance, has focused its attractiveness on offering international companies a combination of low labour costs but highly skilled computer software personnel. Please also see section on the Global Talent Competitiveness Index (GTCI) in Chapter 13.

Infrastructure and support industry resources

The third type of resource that can be of interest to foreign investors is the quality of *communication and logistics infrastructures,* as well as the availability of supporting industries and services. Table 6.3 shows the ten highest and ten lowest countries in terms of quality of various types of infrastructure, as reported by the World Economic Forum.

Table 6.3 Quality of infrastructures

Quality of transport infrastructure	Efficiency of air transport services	Efficiency of seaport services	Quality of utility infrastructure	ICT adoption
10 Highest	**10 Highest**	**10 Highest**	**10 Highest**	**10 Highest**
Singapore	Singapore	Singapore	Iceland	Korea, Rep.
Netherlands	Hong Kong SAR	Netherlands	Finland	United Arab Emirates
Hong Kong	Netherlands	Finland	Netherlands	Hong Kong
Japan	Finland	Hong Kong	Austria	Sweden
Korea, Rep.	Japan	Japan	Singapore	Singapore
Switzerland	Switzerland	Denmark	Hong Kong	Japan
Germany	United Arab Emirates	Panama	Belgium	Iceland
United Arab Emirates	Korea, Rep.	Estonia	Sweden	Qatar
Spain	Panama	Belgium	Switzerland	Denmark
France	United States	United States	Luxembourg	Norway
10 Lowest	**10 Lowest**	**5 Lowest**	**10 Lowest**	**10 Lowest**
Chad	Nepal	Malawi	Mali	Pakistan
Cameroon	Iran, Islamic Rep.	Yemen	Mauritania	Cameroon
Mozambique	Kyrgyz Republic	Haiti	Mozambique	Tanzania

Table 6.3 (Continued)

Gabon	Mozambique	Venezuela	Guinea	Benin
Haiti	Haiti	Bosnia and Herzegovina	Burundi	Mozambique
Venezuela	Congo		Madagascar	Madagascar
Madagascar	Chad		Malawi	Ethiopia
Congo	Mauritania		Burkina Faso	Congo
Lesotho	Yemen		Congo	Yemen
Mauritania	Venezuela		Chad	Burundi
Yemen	Lesotho		Haiti	Chad

Source: Author's own, based on data from World Economic Forum (2020).

Competitive context

The objective of this section is to determine the *profitability potential* of a presence in a country given its *industry and competitive structure* and the incentives provided by government to encourage foreign investments.

Industry and competitive structure

Professor Michael Porter proposed the concepts and techniques of industry analysis for strategic decision making in his seminal book *Competitive Strategy* (1980). According to Porter there are five forces that determine the *long-term profitability potential* of an industry. It is beyond the scope of this chapter to describe in detail the various forces that are presented in Porter's original work, as well as in other classic textbooks on business strategy, but in Table 6.4 we summarize Porter's five forces and their implications for international business entry. We have also added a *sixth force* – government intervention.

Table 6.4 Porter's industry analysis as applied to international business entry

Porter's five forces [plus one]	Relevance for international business entry
Intensity of rivalry When competition is 'cut-throat' due to overcapacity and lack of differentiation of barriers to exit	*Rivalry* increases when market growth is starting to slow down, and windows of opportunity are closing. This phenomenon is visible in countries such as China where overcapacity is present in many industries
Entry barriers Those elements that make it costly, difficult or sometimes impossible to enter an industry	*Entry barriers* can be increased by licensing policy or government actions. Distribution networks, location issues, incumbent competitive positions, as well as cultural specificities are all likely to affect entry costs

Suppliers' bargaining power The negotiating power of suppliers to impose their price and conditions over an industry's incumbents	*Suppliers' bargaining power* is somewhat bigger in protected economies where raw materials are in the hands of state monopolies or when there is a scarcity of skilled labour or of intermediate suppliers of goods and services. Suppliers' bargaining power is also greater when governments adopt a 'local content' policy
Buyers' bargaining power The negotiating power of buyers to deny any price increase from industry's incumbents and to shift easily from one supplier to another	*Buyers' bargaining powers* may also be stronger when distribution networks are tightly controlled, as in the case of Japan
Substitutes New technologies or new business models generate alternatives to existing markets. This may create market disruption of demand for existing incumbents and induce higher rivalry. Ultimately, incumbents may disappear	In international markets substitution may come from new global competitors developing new technologies or business models that disrupt traditional competition
Government policies Governments may introduce *artificial entry barriers* by putting special constraints on foreign investors. Alternatively, governments may lower entry barriers by deregulating or subsidizing factory costs	Government policies may influence profitability and competitiveness through *preferential treatment*, *price control*, *taxation* and so on

Source: Authors' own, based on arguments in Porter (1980).

The country 'diamond'

Porter also argued that countries or regions within countries (what he calls 'clusters') can build competitive advantages that make them attractive for business development in certain industries.[2] He distinguishes four major drivers of national competitive advantage which constitute the country or regional 'diamond':

1. The *natural* endowment such as natural, human, capital, physical, technological and administrative or scientific resources.
2. The quality of the *demand*: whether customers are demanding on quality, fostering the competitiveness of the firm serving them.
3. Vigorous *competition*: whether competitors stimulate each other.
4. The presence of *supporting industries*: whether there is a pool of qualified product and service suppliers that enhance the quality and competitiveness of firms operating in this country. Also, whether there are clusters of successful firms in a particular industry. Porter's examples of successful clusters were the German printing press industry, the US patient monitoring industry, the Italian ceramic tile industry, the Japanese robotics industry, the French aerospace industry or the Taiwanese micro-computer industry. The following Mini-case about TAG Heuer illustrates the fact that Switzerland was a 'country diamond' for the watch industry, hence why TAG Heuer has been historically located there. TAG Heuer developed a presence in California, a 'country diamond' cluster for the digital industry in the Silicon Valley, for its connected watch, forming a cross-cluster collaboration.

MINI-CASE 6.1

TAG Heuer

In 2014, TAG Heuer, a Swiss luxury watchmaker and part of the LVMH group (Louis Vuitton Moët Hennessy) entered into the connected watch market driven by its CEO Jean-Claude Biver and the Head of Product Development, Guy Sémon. With no market research or help from external consultants they surged ahead in the new watch development. This was in response to the introduction of connected devices, in particular the Apple Watch. Based in La Chaux-de-Fonds, the cradle of Swiss watchmaking and a UNESCO World Heritage Site, TAG Heuer was located amid Alpine pastures at an altitude of 1,000 metres. With sales of approximately 600,000 watches and revenues of approximately €750 million in 2015, Biver was enthusiastic about entering a high-growth market that could bring new customers and rejuvenate the brand. However, embracing digital was potentially a paradigm change for TAG Heuer and for the Swiss watch industry more broadly.

Biver had helped save the Swiss watch industry when quartz watches largely replaced mechanical watches in the 1970s and 1980s. In 2004, he became CEO of Hublot, a niche brand which turned into a 100 million Swiss franc business within two years and was bought by LVMH in 2008. When he was made president of TAG Heuer in 2014, he immediately replaced the 'old guard' with a new era of management. He had a start-up mentality, recognizing the need for agility and speed. While the Swiss watch industry was divided as to how the market would react to the launch of the Apple iWatch, at TAG Heuer, Sémon, a R&D guru in the watch industry, recognized that TAG Heuer lacked the technology to fully develop the connected watch and would have to find external partners. He was also convinced it would be a transformational project for the company. Biver saw the onset of smartwatches as both an opportunity and a threat. They sought help from Silicon Valley and after a couple of visits partnered with Intel for the microprocessor and Google for the operating system. In March 2015 the partnership was announced at the Baselworld watch and jewellery show which attracted huge media attention and speculation.

Breaking into the luxury markets

Technical giants like Apple had been trying to break into the luxury sector to understand more about the intangible value of brands such as TAG Heuer. Digital autocrats concentrated on technical features of an object whilst purveyors of luxury preferred the art and emotion of a product. Apple had tried to move into the high-value sector by creating the illusion of scarcity to increase demand. But, despite its best efforts, including attempts to 'poach' employees from high-end Swiss watchmakers and successfully luring TAG Heuer's sales director onto its iWatch launch team, its products remained at a lower price point than its luxury competitors.

Silicon Valley and TAG Heuer

Swiss watchmakers produced watches that were art. They cultivated their image as organizations capable of producing quality at the highest level over generations. Value came from superior workmanship, artistic technique and other intangibles inherent to luxury brands. When TAG Heuer approached Silicon Valley it brought with it an ability to capture these intangible qualities and charge more than $100,000 for a device that tells the time. From TAG Heuer, companies in the Valley could learn about brand positioning and gain an understanding of how consumers value luxury – a mutually beneficial partnership. When the partnership between Intel and Google, the Silicon Valley giants, and TAG Heuer was announced in March 2015, industry experts noted the mutual benefits of this union between the luxury and digital segments. The launch of the TAG Heuer Connected watch – the first 'Luxury Android wear' – later that year attracted massive media coverage. The product sold out in the United States within forty-eight hours, with a price tag of $1,500 per piece. Biver noted in a presentation in May 2017 that 'These customers told us they were buying not just the technology but the exclusivity, status and prestige.'

Questions:

1. Does TAG Heuer have the capabilities to develop a connected watch? If yes, list these elements.
2. Should other Swiss brands compete in the connected watch market? List reasons why and why not.
3. What is the importance of the 'Swiss Made' label for the connected watch segment?

Note: This Mini-case is based on the INSEAD case studies: L. F. Monteiro and A-M. Carrick, 'The TAG Heuer Carrera Connected Watch (A) and (B): Swiss Avant-Garde for the Digital Age', INSEAD Case Study No. 6291, https://publishing.insead.edu/case/tag-heuer-a>, https://publishing.insead.edu/case/tag-heuer-carrera-connected-watch-b-swiss-avant-garde-digital-age (accessed 1 February 2022).

Government incentives

In order to attract foreign investors, governments have designed and implemented a series of *incentives*: fiscal, financial, competitive and operational.[3] These incentives are summarized in Table 6.5.

Table 6.5 Major types of incentive for foreign investments

Type of fiscal incentive	Nature of incentive
Tax reduction	• Tax amnesty for a limited period • Ability to write off losses against profits after the end of the tax amnesty period • Reduced tax rate • Accelerated depreciation • Reduction in social security contributions • Special deductions from taxable incomes for certain types of activities (social, R&D, etc.) • Exemption from property taxes or other special taxes • Reduction of tax base on local content or employment levels • Income tax exemption/reduction for expatriate personnel
Imports and exports	• Exemption from import duties and value added taxes for raw materials, essential equipment and parts • Exemption from export duties • Tax credits on domestic sales based on export performance
Financial incentives	• Subsidies of all kinds • 'Sweetener loans' • Guaranteed loans • Export credits • Equity participation • Risk insurance (exports, exchange rates)

Table 6.5 (Continued)

Competitive incentives	• Protection against imports • Capacity regulation • Monopolistic position • Preferential purchases
Operational incentives	• Preferential rates: rents, land, power, telecoms, etc. • Assistance for market studies • Utilization of public services or government agencies for company operations • Secondment of personnel • Training centres • Access to infrastructure programmes: roads, ports, airports, etc. • Access to public–private partnerships • Access to science parks

Source: Authors' own, based on a framework in the text of UNCTAD (1996) with additions.

Impact of incentives on foreign investor behaviour

A series of research studies on the role of incentives in foreign investment decisions has shown that their role is limited.[4] Market attractiveness, competitive conditions and resource endowments are more important than incentives, but if those conditions are comparable in several locations, incentives may play a positive role in the decision to invest in one country in particular.

Environmental and sustainable issues

As mentioned in Chapter 4, sustainable and environmental issues are becoming strategically important for firms. As a consequence, in assessing the attractiveness of a country multinational firms should consider whether the business under consideration will affect their sustainable development strategies. The elements under consideration are for instance:

- Should a pulp and paper company invest in a country being lenient or encouraging deforestation without reforestation?
- Should one invest in a country favouring child employment?
- Should one invest in a country practising ethnic discrimination?
- Should an agriculture company invest in a country where agriculture is using vast numbers of pesticides?
- Should an industrial company invest in a country where the power generation is still encouraging the use of CO_2 emitting processes?

Socioeconomic, political and cultural distance

One of the main challenges of operating internationally is to maintain a coherent strategy that reflects the fundamental competitive advantages of the global firm, on one hand, and on the other, still to be able to adapt to the specific environments in which the firm operates. Therefore, it is of prime importance to assess how 'distant' the environment of the country under consideration is from environments in which the firm already operates. In the previous sections we have analysed the differences in terms of market, resources and competition, but it is useful to look at the institutional, political, social and cultural differences.

Two models can be used:

- Business system analysis
- CAGE Distance Framework model.

Business system analysis

In Chapter 3 the model of business system analysis was presented.[5] This model can be invaluable in assessing how the various dimensions of governance, institutional fabric and social culture impact upon how much a potential investor has to adopt a different way of doing business in the targeted country.

The CAGE Distance Framework model

The CAGE Framework developed by Professor Pankaj Ghemawat[6] aims at understanding and assessing the differences between two countries (bilateral differences) or between a country and the rest of the world (multilateral differences). Those differences are assessed in terms of four distances: cultural, administrative, geographical and economic. They are summarized in Figure 6.11.

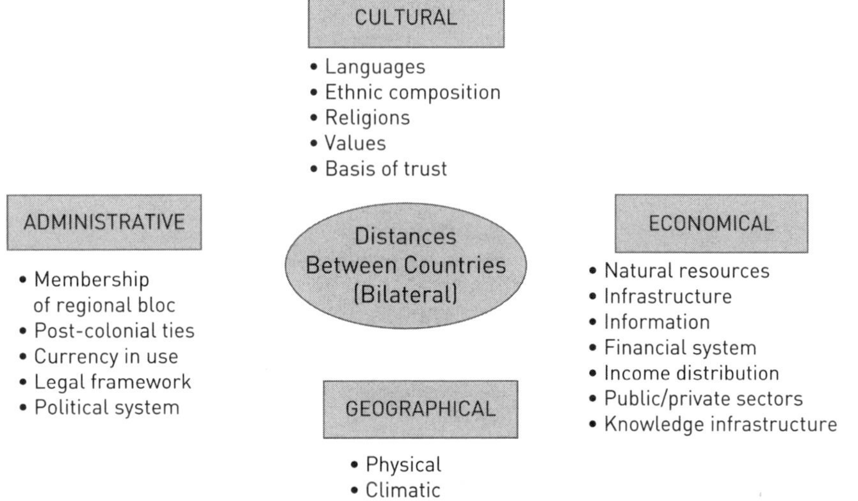

Figure 6.11 Summary of the CAGE Distance Framework model
Source: Adapted from Ghemawat (2007).

Country risk analysis

The purpose of country risk analysis is to assess the probability that adverse circumstances owing to political, economic or social actions will negatively affect business performance.[7] Country risks can be grouped into four categories (see Figure 6.12):

1 Political
2 Economic
3 Competitive
4 Operational.

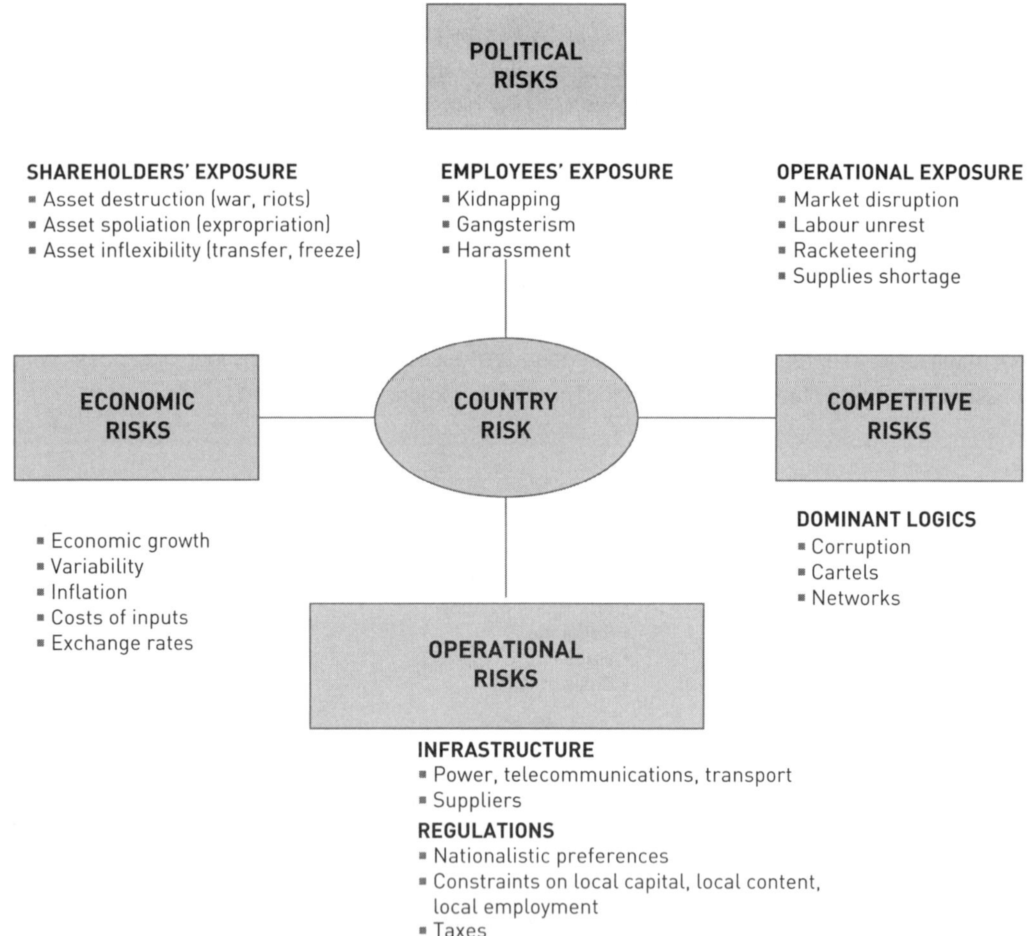

Figure 6.12 Framework for country risk analysis

- *Political risks* are possible disruptions owing to internal or external events, or regulations resulting from the political action of governments or societal crisis and unrest. Political risks may affect business performance in various ways:

- One type of risk exposes *shareholders' value* in terms of loss of capital or loss through the inability to repatriate dividends. This type of risk is associated with asset destruction linked to external or civil wars or riots, asset spoliation owing to expropriation or asset lock-in through funds being frozen or interdiction on capital transfer.
- Another type of political risk lies in *employees' exposure* linked to gangsterism, crime and kidnapping, as well as *operational exposure* linked to labour unrest, and racketeering or market disruptions, or supplies shortages linked to criminal activities.

- *Economic risks* expose business performance to the extent that the economic business drivers can vary and therefore put profitability at risk. As an example, Figure 6.13 shows the growth rate of Hungary as compared to Czech Republic from 2000 to 2019. While the two countries had a similar annual growth rate (2.9 per cent against 2.6 per cent), Hungary had more variability than Czech Republic (coefficient of variation of 1.04 against 0.89) and therefore *ceteris paribus* exhibited a higher economic risk.

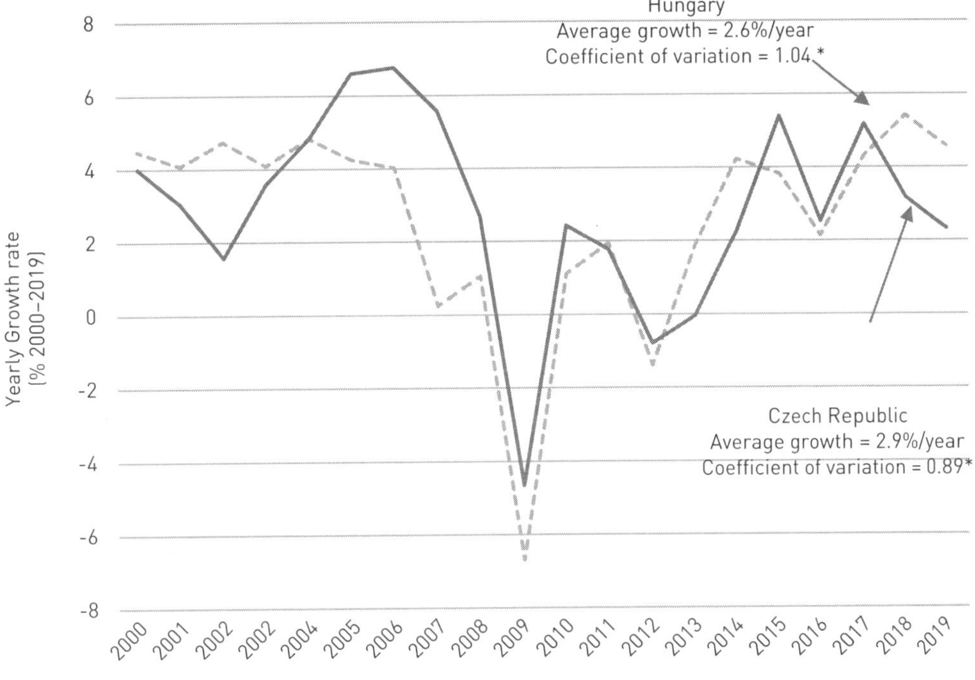

Figure 6.13 Variability of economic growth, Hungary versus Czech Republic, 2000–2019

Source: Authors' own figure using data from World Bank Economic Development Indicators, https://databank.worldbank.org/home.aspx (accessed 1 February 2022).

- *Competitive risks* are related to the non-economic distortion of the competitive context owing to cartels and networks as well as corrupt practices. This makes the competitive battlefield uneven and investors who base their competitive advantage on product quality and economics are at a disadvantage. Competitive risks are managed by the dominant general logic, which was defined by Prahalad and Bettis as 'the way in which managers conceptualize the business and make critical resource decisions – be it in technologies, product development, distribution, advertising, or in human resource management'.[8]

- *Operational risks* are those that directly affect the bottom line, either because government regulations and bureaucracies add costly taxation or constraints to foreign investors or because the infrastructure is unreliable.

Figure 6.14 shows various countries' scores in term of political and economic risks. Both dimensions are clearly correlated.

The impact of country risks on investment decisions is not straightforward. Whilst we can see in Figure 6.14 that foreign direct investments are heavier in countries with lower levels of risk, some countries such as China or Brazil, although perceived as relatively risky, receive a significant amount of investment. This demonstrates that companies are likely to accept a certain level of risk if other aspects of attractiveness are present.

Putting it all together

The various factors presented in this chapter constitute the basic raw materials for assessing whether a particular country is likely to offer opportunities to conduct business safely and profitably. Such assessments first require the collection of a large amount of *information* and second, the capacity to *collate* information in a meaningful fashion.

As an example of this analysis, Appendix 6.2 gives a short summary of the differences between Turkey and Egypt for several indicators.

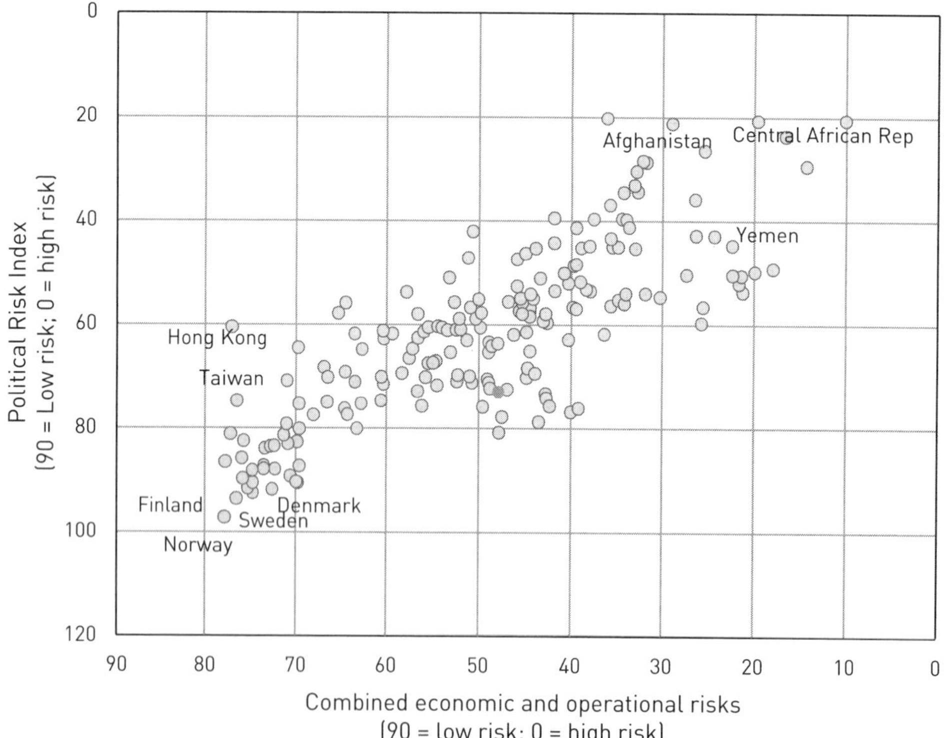

Figure 6.14 Political and economic risks in selected countries

Source: Data from Country Risk Index, Fitch Connect (2019). Reproduced with permission of BMI.

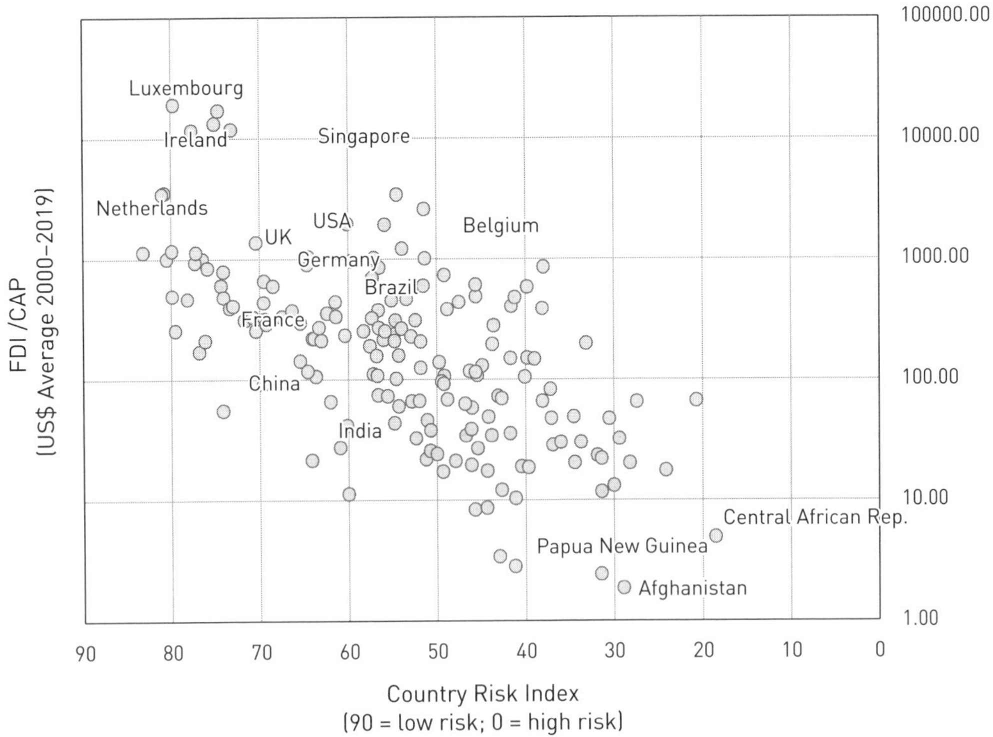

Figure 6.15 Foreign direct investment and country risks, 2000–2019

Note: *The coefficient of correlation between risk and FDI is 0.31, which is significant but not high.*

Source: Authors' own figure, based on data from UNCTAD (2019) and Fitch Connect (2019).

Data collection

Despite the fact that various databases and consultancy firms propose statistical information and analyses, managers are often confronted with problems of the relevance, quality and accessibility of strategic and marketing intelligence specific to their industry. Macroeconomic data are too broad, and managers need to complement them with their own investigations. Various methods exist to assess country opportunities and risks.

The most traditional mode of collecting information is the *Grand Tour* approach. This consists of sending a mission of several executives to visit countries and meet government officials, bankers, journalists, academics and other opinion makers or analysts. At the end of this exercise, managers exchange notes and prepare a report comparing the relative merits of countries. The advantage of the Grand Tour is that company executives get a real feel for the local context and the opportunity to focus on issues that are specific to the company's products or services. The disadvantages are the inherent superficiality of the exercise, as well as the difficulty of *cross-validation* of information owing to time pressures. For the information to be valuable and credible, companies need to organize several Grand Tours and to complement them with other forms of data collection and analysis. The exercise then becomes quite costly, and for that reason many SMEs cannot afford it.

The second method is to rely on *diplomatic sources*, *commercial attachés*, *professional organizations* and *foreign banking institutions*. Although less costly, this type of data-gathering lacks specificity and depth. Information collected this way may suffer from lack of objectivity since diplomats and bankers often have a vested interest in pushing investments in the territories where they operate.

The third method is to call on *consultancy firms* which specialize in country risk and market analysis. The quality of the results depends upon the quality of the relationship between the *client* (the firm) and the *service provider* (the consultancy firm). It is important to ask specific questions, otherwise the firm may be flooded with masses of irrelevant data.

Each approach has its own merit and they complement each other. The Grand Tour approach is necessary to have a feeling about the country, particularly if the company is not exposed at all to the country through a distributor or an agent. The second approach is necessary keeping in mind the bias described earlier. The third approach, the use of a consultant, is often necessary when the investment involved is complex and needs to be preceded by a preliminary investigation made by the company either via a Grand Tour or by desktop research. The company is then in a position to correctly specify the mandate given to the consultant.

Consolidating the data

As the previous paragraphs have illustrated, several parameters shape the opportunities and risks associated with countries. The combination of these parameters generates various *profiles* that distinguish types of country according to the attractiveness factors that interest foreign investors. Countries under consideration can be grouped into clusters that share similarities and in which the ultimate choice will depend on the *strategic ambition* of the global firm and the relative importance attached to the various factors.

The criteria used for clustering countries according to demand characteristics have been described earlier in this chapter, but demand is not the only factor. Dimensions that can be used for clustering are:

- *Regional:* Middle East, East Asia, South America, Southern Africa and so on
- *Demand characteristics* (Table 6.2): growth, GDP/capita, quality of demand
- *Resources*: natural, human, technological (Figures 6.9, 6.18 and Table 6.3)
- *Cultural and socio-political distance relative to the investor's viewpoint* (Table 6.6)
- *Risks*: political, economic, competitive (Figure 6.3)
- *Ease of doing business and government support* (Figure 2.10 and Table 6.5)

After completing this process, one will come up with different clusters organized regionally, and within regions one may distinguish countries fulfilling various types of strategic profile, as described earlier:

- *Hubs*: countries that can serve as regional entry points and regional centres
- *Emerging giants:* countries who by their size are of high strategic importance for investors
- *Fast-growing industrializing:* countries that are offering a high potential for growth
- *Industrialized OECD*
- *Resource-rich countries in terms of natural, human or technological resources, which can also be part of the other categories.*

Table 6.6 gives a clustering for the Asia Pacific region.

Table 6.6 Cluster characteristics, Asia Pacific

Characteristics	Hubs	Emerging giants	Fast-growing industrializing	Developing	OECD	Resource rich*
Population	L	H	M/H	M/H	M/H	Variable
GDP	L	H	M	M/L	H	Variable
GDP/cap	H	M/L	M/L	L	H	Variable
Infrastructure	H	M/L	M/L	M/L	H	Variable
Skills	H	M	M/L	L	H	Variable
Productivity	H	M/L	M/L	L	H	Variable
Natural resources	L	L	M/H	M/H	Variable	H
Risk	L	M	M	M/H	L	Variable
Ease of doing business	H	L	M/L	L	H	Variable
Examples	Singapore Hong Kong	China India	Indonesia Malaysia Thailand	Philippines Vietnam Cambodia Myanmar Papua New Guinea	Australia New Zealand Japan Korea	Australia Indonesia Myanmar

Notes: *L = Low, M = Medium, H = High.* * These countries may also qualify for other categories.

MINI-CASE 6.2

Izmir Industrial Electric: Exercise

Izmir Industrial Electric (IZIEC) is a (fictional) Turkish medium-sized manufacturer of electronic data processing and office equipment including fibre optic data centre products, rack cabinets and power distribution. Its products are sold to industrial customers in more than fifty countries. Headquartered in Istanbul it employs 500 associates including eighty engineers. As part of its strategic development plan the management decided to investigate the setting up of an assembly plant in Africa. Five countries were considered: Angola, Ghana, Kenya, Nigeria and South Africa. The following data was produced to feed the discussion of the management committee.

Angola is a vast country; its capital is Luanda and it has maintained political stability since the end of the twenty-seven-year civil war in 2002. In 2010, a constitution established a presidential parliamentary system. Despite significant progress on macroeconomic stability and structural reforms, Angola is still suffering the effects of lower oil prices and production levels. The transformation of a state-led oil economy to a private-sector-led growth model is a complex and long-term process and the oil sector will continue to play an important role during this transition period.

Kenya has the potential to be one of Africa's success stories due to its growing youthful population, a dynamic private sector, highly skilled workforce, improved infrastructure, a new constitution and its pivotal role in East Africa. Kenya has made significant political, structural and economic reforms that have largely driven sustained economic growth, social development and political gains over the past decade.

A former territory of the British Empire, **Ghana** is the result of the unification of four territories along the Gulf of Guinea and the Atlantic Ocean. Ghana's population is made up of a variety of ethnic, linguistic and religious groups. It consistently ranks in the top three countries in Africa for freedom of speech and press freedom, with strong broadcast media; radio being the medium with the greatest reach. Factors such as these provide Ghana with solid social capital.

Nigeria obtained independence from Britain in 1960. After a series of *coups d'état* a formal democracy was established and stabilized in the early 2000s. Nigeria is facing an Islamist rebellion in the north of the country. Located in central Africa, its 181 million people are composed of myriad ethnic groups. English is the official language, and 50 per cent of the population belong to the Muslim community while 40 per cent are considered as Christian.

South Africa's political transition is known as one of the most remarkable political feats of the past century. Formed in 1910 from separate states as an independent British dominion, it became a republic in 1961, dominated by former British and Dutch settlers known as *Afrikaners*. From 1948 to 1994 a policy of segregating the population according to ethnic origin (apartheid) was strictly enforced, in the face of growing international condemnation. A new constitution was established in 1997, creating a multi-racial parliamentary republic. Black Africans are the ethnic majority followed by white Afrikaners and Asians. Christianity in various forms is the dominant religion. There are eleven constitutionally recognized official languages including English, Zulu, Xhosa and Afrikaans.

Table 6.7 Country profiles

	Angola	Ghana	Kenya	Nigeria	South Africa	Turkey
GDP (US$ bn, 2019)	88.8	67.0	95.5	448.1	351.4	761.4
GDP/Cap (U$, 2019)	2,791	2,202	1,817	2,230	6,001	9,127
Population (million)	32	30	53	201	59	83
Country Risk Index (0 = high risk to 100 = low risk)	43	55	51	45	56	57
Ease of doing business score (0 = lowest to 100 = best)	41	60	73	57	67	77
Starting a business score (0 = most difficult to 100+ = easiest)	73	84	82	83	81	88
Control of corruption (–2.5 = lowest to 2.5 = highest)	–1.05	–0.08	–0.78	–1.09	0.08	–0.29
Government effectiveness (–2.5 = lowest to 2.5 = highest)	–1.12	–0.21	–0.38	–1.09	0.37	0.05
Political stability and absence of violence (–2.5 = lowest to 2.5 = highest)	–0.31	0.10	–1.12	–1.93	–0.22	–1.34
Regulatory quality: estimate (–2.5 = lowest to 2.5 = highest)	–0.89	–0.11	–0.28	–0.86	0.16	–0.01

Imports of integrated circuits and electronic components (US$ m)	417	15	39	286	666	3,559
Exports of integrated circuits and electronic components (US$ m)	1	1	5	0	82	281
Imports of electronic data processing and office equipment	154	99	208	1,778	3,460	3,559
Exports of electronic data processing and office equipment	1	1	9	0	426	1,611
Industry value added (% of GDP)	46	30	17	28	23	28

Questions:

1 On a first basic evaluation, which of these African countries do you think ZIEC is considering for investment?

2 In particular, can you evaluate the differences between Turkey and those countries as well as the opportunities and risks?

Sources: This exercise was written by the authors. The data is from World Bank Enterprise Survey, World Bank Development Indicators, World Bank World Governace Indicators, World Trade Statistics, Fitch Solutions Country Risks Index.

Summary and key points

1 Foreign investment decisions take into account:

- **a** Country attractiveness
- **b** Entry strategy (to be discussed further in Chapter 7)

2 A country's attractiveness assessment is based on three dimensions:

- **a** Market, resources and competition
- **b** Socioeconomic, political and cultural distance
- **c** Country risks

3 A market opportunities assessment measures the potential demand in the country for a firm's products or services based on:

- **a** Market size and growth: function of macroeconomic, income distribution, lifestyle and government policy factors
- **b** Quality of demand: function of diversity of market segments and size of middle class

4 Demand characteristics of a country:

- **a** Depend on the *life cycle cluster* to which the country belongs
- **b** Four types of country cluster:
  - Developing countries
  - Emerging countries

- Fast industrializing economies
- Industrialized countries

5 Resource availability:

a Natural resources: includes raw materials, mining, agricultural and geographical location

b Infrastructure and support industries resources

c Human resources: cost, productivity and quality of workforce

6 The competitive context determines the profitability potential of a company's presence in a country given the characteristics of the industry competitive structure (Porter's five forces of industry analysis framework plus government factors):

a Intensity of rivalry

b New entrants and entry barriers

c Bargaining power of suppliers

d Bargaining power of customers

e Threat of substitutes

f Government regulations and incentives

7 Socioeconomic, political and cultural distance analyses assess how much a country is different from the investor's country's presence

Two types of distance assessment:

- Business system analysis (see Chapter 3)
- The CAGE Distance Framework assessing cultural, administrative, geographical and economic distances

8 Country risk analysis assesses how adverse conditions may affect business performances

Four types of risk:

- *Political* risks:
  - Employees' exposure, gangsterism, kidnapping
    - Shareholders' exposure
    - Market disruption
- *Economic* risks: variability of economic factors
- *Competitive* risks: corruption, cartels
- *Operational* risks: infrastructure instability, availability of suppliers, constraints on local capital, local content or local employment

9 Data collection

Three methods: Grand Tour, diplomatic, professional and consulting sources

10 Assessment is done by clusters of countries

Learning assignments

1 Take two countries of your choice and compare their country risk profiles.

2 What is the 'middle-class effect'?

3 What determines the quality of demand?

4 What are the tools used by governments to promote foreign investments?

5 Can you give examples of a hub in Africa, an emerging giant in Latin America and a resource-rich country in Eastern Europe?

6 Make a CAGE analysis of Morocco, Romania and South Korea. What conclusions do you draw from the point of view of a South Korean firm willing to invest in an assembly plant in one of these two territories?

Key words

- CAGE Distance Framework
- Clusters
- Country 'diamond'
- Country life cycle
- Country risk analysis
- 'Grand Tour'
- Hub
- Incentives
- Industry analysis
- Macroeconomic indicators
- Market opportunities
- Market segmentation
- 'Middle-class effect'

Web resources

CIA factbook:
https://www.cia.gov/the-world-factbook/
Doing Business Data base:
https://www.doingbusiness.org/en/doingbusiness
Euromonitor Country Profiles:
https://www.euromonitor.com/countries
Fitch Solutions Country Risk:
https://www.fitchsolutions.com/products/country-risk
OECD Country Profiles:
https://www.oecd.org/regional/regional-policy/country-profiles.htm
UNCTAD Country Profiles:
https://unctadstat.unctad.org/countryprofile/en-gb/index.html
UNCTAD Statistics:
https://unctad.org/statistics
United Nations Human Development Programme:
http://hdr.undp.org/en/countries
World Bank country data:
https://data.worldbank.org/country
World Bank Development Indicators:
https://databank.worldbank.org/source/world-development-indicators

World Bank Enterprise survey:
https://www.enterprisesurveys.org/en/enterprisesurveys

World Economic Forum:
https://www.weforum.org

World Resources Institute:
https://www.wri.org

Notes

1 See countries' petroleum risk environment: http://www.riskworld.com (accessed 12 June 2017).
2 Porter (1998).
3 UNCTAD (1996).
4 Guisinger (1985, 1992).
5 Witt and Redding (2014); see Chapter 3.
6 Ghemawat (2007).
7 Literature is abundant on country risk: Brewer (1985); Howell and Chaddick (1994: 70–90); Rogers (1997).
8 Prahalad and Bettis (1986, 1995).

References and further reading

Aguilar, F. (1967) *Scanning the Business Environment* (New York, NY: Macmillan).

Austin, J. E. (1990) *Managing in Developing Countries: Strategic Analysis and Operating Techniques* (New York, NY : Free Press).

Berry, H., Guillén, M. F. and Zhou, N. (2010) 'An institutional approach to cross-national distance', *Journal of international business studies*, 41 (9): 1460–80.

Beugelsdijk, S., Ambos, B. and Nell, P. C. (2020) 'Conceptualizing and measuring distance in international business research: Recurring questions and best practice guidelines', in *Research methods in international business*, 449–98 (Basingstoke: Palgrave Macmillan, Cham).

Beugelsdijk, S., Kostova, T., Kunst, V. E., Spadafora, E. and Van Essen, M. (2018) 'Cultural distance and firm internationalization: A meta-analytical review and theoretical implications', *Journal of Management*, 44 (1): 89–130.

Brewer, T. L. (ed.) (1985) *Political Risks in International Business: New Directions for Research, Management and Public Policies* (New York, NY: Praeger).

Cunha, O., Chenh, S. and Abida, R. (2013) *Redefining Brazil's Emerging Middle Class: How to Prepare for the Next Wave of Consumption Growth* (Boston Consulting Group, BCG Perspectives). https://www.bcgperspectives.com/ (accessed 11 June 2017).

Farrell, D., Gerch, U. A. and Stephenson, E. (2006) 'The value of China's emerging middle class', *McKinsey Quarterly*, Special edition: Serving the New Chinese Consumer, June.

Fitch Connect (2019), Country Risks & Industry Research. https://www.fitchsolutions.com/products/country-risk-and-industry-research (accessed 20 October 2021).

Fitch Solutions (2021) *Global Pharmaceutical & Healthcare Report Q2*. Available from fitchsolution.com

Ghemawat, P. (2007) *Differences across Countries: The Cage Distance Framework* (Boston, MA: Harvard Business School Press).

Guisinger, S. (1985) *Investment Incentives and Performance Requirements* (New York, NY: Praeger).

Guisinger, S. (1992) 'Rhetoric and reality in international business: note on the effectiveness of incentives', *Transnational Corporations*, 1: 111–23.

Guisinger, S. (2001) 'From OLI to OLMA: incorporating higher levels of environmental and structural complexity into the eclectic paradigm', *International Journal of the Economics of Business*, 8 (2): 257–72.

Howell, L. D. and Chaddick, B. (1994) 'Models of political risk for foreign investment and trade: an assessment of three approaches', *Columbia Journal of World Business*, Fall: 70–90.

James, M. and Koller, T. M. (2000) 'Valuation in emerging markets', *McKinsey Quarterly*, 4.

Kelly, N. (2020): Looking for New Global Markets? Bigger Isn't Always Better, Harvard University. https://hbr.org/2020/11/looking-for-new-global-markets-bigger-isnt-always-better (accessed 1 February 2022) .

Lange, G. M., Wodon, Q. and Carey, K. (eds) (2018) *The Changing Wealth of Nations 2018: Building a Sustainable Future* (Washington, DC: World Bank), doi:10.1596/978-1-4648-1046-6.

Lasserre, P. and Schütte, H. (1999) *Strategies for Asia Pacific: Beyond the Crisis* (Basingstoke: Palgrave Macmillan).

Monteiro, L. F. (2018) *The Consummate Opportunities of Cross-Cluster Collaboration*, INSEAD Knowledge.. https://knowledge.insead.edu/strategy/the-consummate-opportunities-of-cross-cluster-collaboration-7336 (accessed 1 February 2022).

Monteiro, L. F. and Carrick, A. M. (2017) 'The TAG Heuer Carrera Connected Watch (A): Swiss Avant-Garde for the Digital Age', INSEAD Case Study. https://publishing.insead.edu/case/tag-heuer-a (accessed 1 February 2022).

Monteiro, L. F. and Carrick, A. M. (2017) *The TAG Heuer Carrera Connected Watch (B): Swiss Avant-Garde for the Digital*, INSEAD Case Study. https://publishing.insead.edu/case/tag-heuer-carrera-connected-watch-b-swiss-avant-garde-digital-age (accessed 1 February 2022).

Porter, M. (1980) *Competitive Strategy: Techniques for Analysing Industries and Competitors* (New York, NY: Free Press).

Porter, M. (1998) *The Competitive Advantage of Nations* (New York, NY: Free Press).

Prahalad, C. K. and Bettis, R. A. (1986) 'The dominant logic: a new linkage between diversity and performance', *Strategic Management Journal*, 7 (6): 485–501.

Prahalad, C. K. and Bettis, R. A. (1995) 'The dominant logic: retrospective and extension', *Strategic Management Journal*, 16 (1): 5–14.

Rogers, J. (ed.) (1997) *Global Risk Assessments: Issues, Concepts and Applications* (Riverside, CA: Global Risk Assessment).

UNCTAD (United Nations Conference on Trade and Development) (2016), *World Investment Report 2016: Investor Nationality: Policy Challenges* (Geneva: United Nations Publications).

UNCTAD (United Nations Conference on Trade and Development) (2019), *World Investment Report 2019: Special Economic Zones* (Geneva: United Nations Publications).

UNCTAD (United Nations Conference on Trade and Development) (1996) *Incentives and Foreign Direct Investment* (Geneva: United Nations Publications).

UNCTAD (United Nations Conference on Trade and Development) (1996–2020) *World Investment Reports* (Geneva: United Nations Publications).

Witt, M. A. and Redding, G. (eds) (2014) *The Oxford Handbook of Asian Business Systems* (Oxford: Oxford University Press).

World Bank (2019) *Aspiring Indonesian – the Expanding Middle Class*. https://www.worldbank.org/en/country/indonesia/publication/aspiring-indonesia-expanding-the-middle-class (accessed 1 February 2022).

World Economic Forum (2015–2020) *Global Competitiveness Report 2019*. http://www3.weforum.org/docs/WEF_TheGlobalCompetitivenessReport2019.pdf (accessed 13 April 2021).

https://www3.weforum.org/docs/GCR2018/05FullReport/TheGlobalCompetitivenessReport2018.pdf;

https://www3.weforum.org/docs/GCR2016-2017/05FullReport/TheGlobalCompetitivenessReport2016-2017_FINAL.pdf;

https://www3.weforum.org/docs/gcr/2015-2016/Global_Competitiveness_Report_2015-2016.pdf;

https://www3.weforum.org/docs/WEF_TheGlobalCompetitivenessReport2020.pdf (accessed 1 February 2022).

Journals

McKinsey Quarterly: https://www.mckinsey.com/quarterly/overview

Transnational Corporations: https://unctad.org/Topic/Investment/Transnational-Corporations-Journal

The World Bank Economic Review: https://academic.oup.com/wber/article-abstract/35/2/287/5607661?redirectedFrom=fulltext

Chapter 7

Entry strategies

At the end of the chapter you will be able to:

- Complete a full analysis of various entry alternatives
- Assess the advantages and disadvantages of alternative entry strategies in a real-life situation
- Conduct a financial analysis of alternatives

Introduction

Having performed the analysis of a country's attractiveness and decided to enter, a company has to work out an *entry strategy*. This is determined by four factors:

- *Entry objectives* (what the company is looking for in that country)
- *Timing* of entry (when to enter)
- *Mode* of entry (what kind of operations and under which legal form to operate)
- *Pace of entry* (*degree of progressive commitment of resources in the country*).

There may be four categories of *objectives*:

- to develop the market
- to access critical resources
- to capture knowledge available in the country
- to set up a regional or global centre for coordinating various activities.

The *timing* of entry can be critical for building sustainable competitive advantage. First movers can capture initial advantages over competitors, but run a variety of risks.

The choice of a *legal structure* is contingent upon many external and internal factors. There are six legal forms of entry:

- wholly owned operations built from scratch
- acquisitions
- joint ventures
- licensing or franchising
- distributors' agreements
- representative office.

The advantages and disadvantages of each of these forms are discussed.

In addition to the timing of entry one may consider the sequence and pace of entry. Entry into a foreign market can be assimilated to a learning process (Johanson and Vahine 1977) by which the incumbent firm accumulates knowledge about the country and increases progressively its commitment of resources and adopts different modes of entry over time depending upon the degree of familiarity with the rules of business in the particular country.

The chapter ends by looking at entry strategy as a 'real option', and a numerical example is examined.

EXAMPLE 7.1 IKEA's market-seeking entry strategy in India

IKEA, created in 1943 in Sweden as a mail order furniture retailer, opened its first physical IKEA store in 1960. Customers could buy packed Scandinavian style furniture which appealed to young couples. Customers transported and assembled the furniture themselves. The furniture was produced by external suppliers' factories.

Internationalization started with the opening in 1973 of the first store in Zurich. It expanded progressively in Europe and Australia throughout the 1970s and in the 1980s throughout North America and Asia. By 2015, with sales of €32.7 billion, IKEA had operations in 43 countries with 328 stores in 28 countries, 33 distribution centres in 17 countries and 43 production units in 11 countries. IKEA kept its basic concept store design but had to make some adaptations such as the need to provide delivery and installation. In 1974, it closed the first store it had opened in Japan only to re-enter the country in 2006. The IKEA internationalization policy was to enter countries as wholly owned subsidiaries, resisting the idea of entering into joint ventures.

India

From the late 1980s IKEA had been sourcing furniture components in India from around fifty suppliers. By 2006, the company considered entering the country as a retailer and implanting several of its famous blue-coloured IKEA stores. The main motivation was to take advantage of the growing urban middle-class of Asian emerging countries.

One of the first hurdles in India was the regulation that limited the implantation of foreign retailers. Single-brand retailers, such as IKEA, could only set up a store if they entered a joint venture with a local partner in which they were allowed a maximum of 50 per cent share. In addition, there was a requirement to source at least 30 per cent of the goods sold in a store locally. Given IKEA's foreign investment policy, the company backed off. Hoping for a future change of government policy, the company undertook in-depth market research in various cities including Mumbai, Delhi, Hyderabad and Bangalore. The goal was to capture the key characteristics of living styles as well as logistical systems.

In 2012, the Indian government changed the joint venture requirement and allowed 100 per cent ownership. This was followed in 2018 when it softened the 30 per cent local sourcing requirement. This paved the way for the first IKEA store to open. Contrary to industry observers' beliefs, the city chosen was Hyderabad, the capital of the state of Andrah Pradesh. With a metropolitan population of nearly 10 million people, it is the fifth largest urban economy in India with a significant 30 per cent minority of Muslims.

The year before the store's opening, a cohort of seventy-five Indian IKEA's employees (called *co-workers*) were sent to Sheffield in the UK to experience a new store opening. They also trained employees and external artisans to assemble IKEA furniture ('Do It Yourself').

The first store opening took place on 9 August 2018.

Why enter? Defining strategic objectives for a country presence

There are four major types of strategic objectives, and they are not necessarily independent of each other:

- Market development
- Access to resources
- Learning
- Coordination.

EXAMPLE 7.2 Cargill's market- and resource-seeking entry strategies

Cargill is a US privately owned global firm specializing in foodstuffs and agricultural products. It operates in seventy countries with 150,000 employees. Its global investment is a combination of resource-seeking and market-entry strategies. Major resource-seeking investments can be found in Brazil (for cocoa and sugar), Indonesia and Malaysia (for palm oil), Turkey (for cotton), Thailand (for poultry) and Norway (for salmon), amongst many others. One example of strong combination of market- and resource-seeking strategy is provided by Cargill India where the company sells locally produced foods and cooking oil, and exports corn, soybeans and cotton.

A company's entry strategy involves answering three questions:

- Why does the company *want to enter* the country?
- When is it *appropriate* to enter?
- *How* can it enter?

Market development objectives apply to those countries offering size and growth opportunities. To a certain extent, all countries in the world offer some kind of market opportunity as a function of their population and income. Some countries, however, are more important than others, owing to their size or the quality of their customer base. Those countries are often called *key countries*; that is, countries in which a presence is needed for long-term global competitiveness. For that reason, China, the United States, Japan, Germany, France and the UK are often considered to be key countries. Market development objectives constitute the most common entry objectives.

Objectives relating to access to resources are based on the presence of a key resource – mineral, agricultural or human – that contributes to competitive advantage. An investment in a resource-rich country will essentially be made to exploit the resource by setting up the appropriate operational asset – a mine, an exploration field, a plantation, an assembly plant or a software centre.

Learning objectives are the basis of investments in countries where the industry is state of the art and in which a foreign investor gains knowledge and competencies by being present, even if the long-term market prospect is not favourable. Automobile companies set up operations in Japan in the 1980s to be close to the network of car manufacturers and component suppliers and to learn about their mode of relationships. California, Washington State or Texas may similarly be considered as learning grounds for the internet-based 'new economy' (see Chapter 14), while companies dealing with fashion and perfume may consider Paris or Milan as an investment site.

Coordination objectives apply to hub countries where a presence is justified for the regional coordination of activities thanks to their location and infrastructure advantages. Clear examples are Singapore in Southeast Asia and Hong Kong in the Far East where a large number of global firms have set up their regional headquarters (see Chapter 14 for the role of regional headquarters).

Table 7.1 gives a summary of the four types of objectives and the expectations of foreign investors in each category.

Table 7.1 Entry strategy objectives

	Market	Resources	Learning	Coordination
Expectations	Market penetration and development Capture a share of market	Access to natural resources Access to skilled low-cost labour Access to suppliers	Understand state-of-the-art technology Close to best practices Learn to compete in difficult and sophisticated markets	Set up base for global or regional development Establish logistic centres close to financing institutions
Key performance indicators (KPIs)	Growth Market share Gross margin	Costs Quality Supply access	Know-how Process improvement	Speed Control Synergies
Timing	Window of opportunity First mover versus follower	First mover in order to pre-empt resources	As soon as country is recognized as 'competency' centre	Three stages: – Initiation – Growth – Coordination

	Market	Resources	Learning	Coordination
Types of country	All types prioritized as a function of market potential, quality and competitive context	Resource-rich countries	Countries with strong technological and know-how infrastructure	Hubs
Mode of entry	Depending upon risks, opportunities, timing and skills, all modes of entry may apply	Wholly owned (if allowed and if low risk) Joint venture (if requested) Long-term sourcing contracts	Joint venture R&D centre Observatory	Representative office Global headquarters Regional headquarters Logistic centre Training centre Financial centre

When to enter? First mover, follower, or acquirer?

The timing of entry is contingent upon the window of opportunity as well as the type of risk the company is willing to take.

For market-based objectives, a window of opportunity is open when the demand starts to become significant and the competitive context is not yet well established. For resource-based objectives, the window is open when rights of access are available and closed when competitors have established a strong market presence or pre-empted available resources. In such cases, only acquisitions or innovation can allow entrants to open the window. The concept of a window of opportunity is not unique to international entry. It applies also to new product or service development. In the entry context, four phases can be distinguished:

- The *premature phase*, during which a significant investment in the country would not generate enough long-term revenues because of a lack of purchasing power or the absence of demand for the product or service. This phase is characteristic of developing countries at an early stage or of a product that does not fit the demand in a particular country. Although in the United States the credit card business is very lucrative, smartcard manufacturers have found it difficult to penetrate the market because of the lack of support from the banking industry. A significant investment in smartcards in the 1980s or 1990s would not have been appropriate until the window of opportunity was open. It is not suggested that no investment is required at this stage, but it should be limited to representative offices, listening posts and distribution agreements.
- The *window phase*, during which the market takes off but the competitive landscape is not yet well established. At this stage, the choice is to take a *first-mover view* or a *follower view*. The advantages and disadvantages of being a first mover have been widely discussed[1] and there is empirical evidence that to be the first to enter in a country can lead to a strong competitive advantage[2] in emerging markets. Table 7.2 lists the arguments for and against being a first mover.

- The *competitive growth phase*, when various competitors have taken advantage of the window of opportunity and are jockeying for market share in a high-growth situation. New entry at this stage is hazardous and requires either massive resources or a highly differentiated competitive strategy. One way to circumvent the handicap of being a latecomer is by an acquisition or joint venture.
- The *mature phase*. At this stage, the competition is well established and acquisition or direct investment with an innovative product is generally the only way to enter successfully.

Table 7.2 Advantages and disadvantages of being a first mover

Advantages	Disadvantages
• Monopolize resources: – Distribution – Location – People – Contacts – Suppliers • Establish brands • Establish standards • Learn about customers	• Taking a risk: – Market immaturity – Product fit to market uncertain – Lack of infrastructure • Struggle now for the benefit of others later (do all the ground work)

The pace of entry

Pace of entry combines the speed of entry and the progressive adoption of low risk/low commitment mode of entry to higher risk/higher commitment of resources (from export agent to wholly owned subsidiary). This will depend on various factors:

- The degree of past experience in similar countries
- The cultural distance (the CAGE model discussed in Chapter 6) of the country
- The country risk (see Chapter 6)
- The resources available to commit to the country
- The dispersion of entries into different countries at the same time
- The number of resources at stake.

It has been argued that too many hasty entries into many countries within a similar time frame may have a negative effect on a firm's performance.[3] An example of this hasty pace can be found in Whirlpool's entry into China. After having decided to develop a presence in China in 1994, Whirlpool established in the same year four joint ventures: one in Beijing for refrigerators (Snowflake), one in Shanghai for washers (Whirlpool Narcissus), another in Shendu for microwaves (MCV) and a further one in Shenzhen for air conditioners (Whirlpool Raybo), coordinated by a regional headquarters in Hong Kong plus a technical centre in Singapore. This concentrated effort put a great strain on the company's resources to be able to fight against strong local competition. In 1997 Whirlpool's focus moved from refrigerators and air-conditioning ventures to the production of compressors in Beijing, microwaves in Shunde and washers in Shanghai. By 2021 Whirlpool had two factories in China (Heife and Shunde) and one technology centre (Shenzen).

Entry modes: How to enter?[4]

From the point of view of a foreign investor, the typical choice on entering a country is based on a combination of two major dimensions:

- The *control* dimension: going it alone with wholly owned operations in which the foreigner investor has full control and ownership, or entering into partnerships.
- The *investment intensity* dimension: investing in assets and competencies for value-adding activities, or limiting operations to commercial, development and administrative activities.

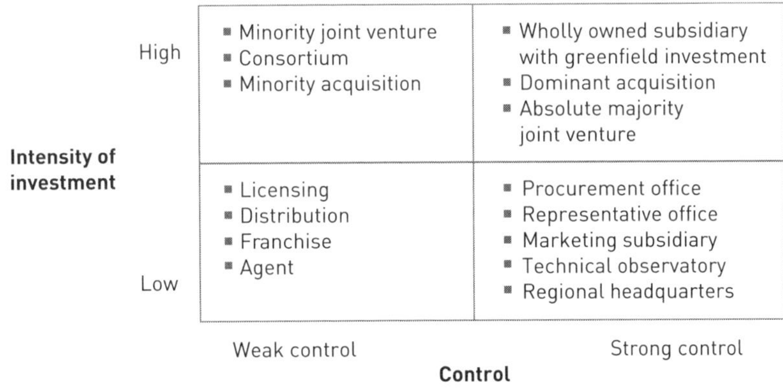

Figure 7.1 Entry modes

This leads to the various types of entry mode represented in Figure 7.1. Those choices should generally be determined by the following factors (Figure 7.2):

- The *overall attractiveness* of the market (as discussed in Chapter 6)
- The *political and operational risks* involved
- The *government requirements*
- The *time pressures*
- The *internal capabilities* of the firm to enter and develop local resources, assets and competencies in order to gain and sustain competitive advantage
- The *strategic objectives* and the expected *return on investment* (ROI).

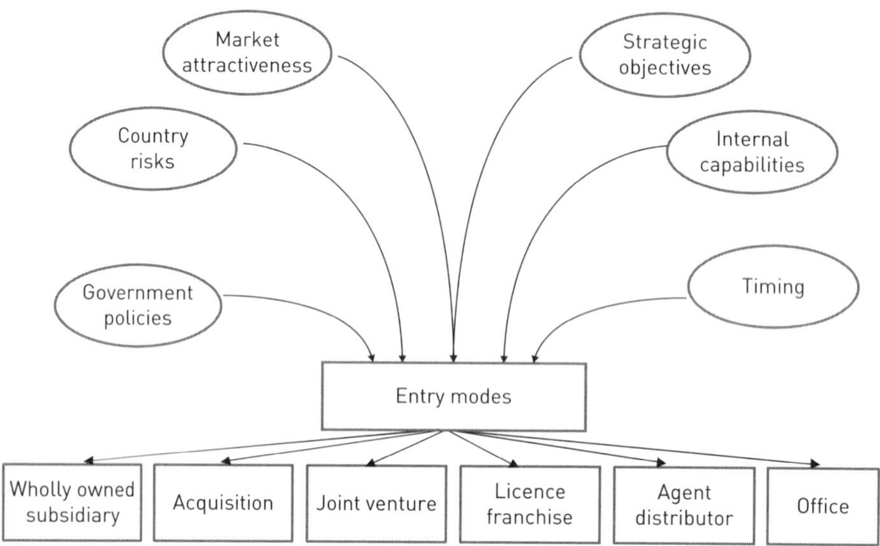

Figure 7.2 Factors influencing entry modes

The next part of the chapter is devoted to analysing the main forms of entry along these dimensions. As far as the *joint venture mode* and *acquisition mode* examined in Chapter 9 are concerned, the factors discussed will also apply there.

Entering a country through wholly owned subsidiaries

This entry mode is the one that gives the most control over operations, but also involves the highest mobilization of resources and competencies and bears the highest risks. Creating a subsidiary in a country calls for the following requirements:

- Assuming that a proper country attractiveness and risk analysis has been done prior to the investment, one needs to first familiarize oneself with the *legal*, *institutional*, *commercial* and *relational* environment. Although the firm has done sufficient analysis to make the investment decision, another level of research and analysis is needed to fully understand the concrete operational realities of local investment. This is the role of the *feasibility study*: to analyse the various aspects of an investment dealing with real estate, construction, project management, sourcing, recruitment, incorporation, registrations, financing, fiscal and legal matters. Feasibility studies should be supported by a full financial plan projecting future cash flow calculations and financial needs. Feasibility studies as well as project management can be contracted out to locally based consultants or engineering firms, but the overall control and responsibility fall upon the foreign investor.
- Managing a construction project in a foreign country involves a series of practical and sometimes difficult impediments, such as the norms and standards of construction, the professionalism of

local contractors and their commercial practices, the availability of supplies, customs clearance of imported materials and components, the behaviour and attitude of project workforces and local bureaucratic hassles. When an investor is investing in a greenfield operation for the first time in a country, it is advisable that they rely on a *locally based project manager*.

- A further impediment of a greenfield operation is the need for *recruitment*, *training* and *management* of a local workforce and the capacity of expatriate personnel to quickly get culturally acclimatized and able to *transfer technology*. This determines the timing and the cost of the investment, which will ultimately affect the cash flow and overall profitability of the project.
- On the positive side, a greenfield, wholly owned investment gives the investor full control over operations and access to the *full profitability* of the investment. Sometimes the feeling of 'full control' may be illusory if the company has sent expatriates with a superficial knowledge of the country and a lack of cultural understanding. In such cases, expatriate top managers will end up isolated in an ivory tower while local personnel manage operations in their own way, hiding behind apparent obedience and respect.
- On the financial front, a wholly owned investment demands that foreign investors bear the full risk of *equity and debt financing*, sometimes facilitated by export credit insurance granted by the home country government or insurance community.

Entering a country through acquisitions

Chapter 8 will deal with international acquisitions so there is no need to discuss in detail here what will be examined there. Overall, the advantage of acquisitions as an entry mode is the immediate availability of resources, assets and competencies that saves time for the foreign investor. Another advantage is the access provided to a market of resources when the competitive arena is already well occupied and the window of opportunity is closed. On the less positive side, acquisitions in foreign environments demand *cross-cultural integration skills* that may not be the prime talent of investors. Acquisitions of local firms by foreigners can also be seen in certain cases as an intrusion that bruises national pride. Finally, acquisitions are often made with high acquisition premiums that make this mode of entry more costly than other alternatives.

Entering a country through joint ventures[5]

Local joint ventures will also be discussed more fully in the next chapter. What needs emphasizing here is that there are several considerations to joint ventures, as briefly outlined below:

- *Partner selection:* Several choices are open to a foreign investor. Table 7.3 gives an overview of the different types of partners to be found in host countries alongside the advantages and disadvantages of each. Selecting the right local partner is probably the most critical decision for a good joint venture. Multiple sources of information need to be used; track records of the partner need to be carefully scrutinized and if possible several alternatives should be considered. Ideally, a company should select a local partner with whom it has experienced previous business dealings during which it had the opportunity to appreciate the capabilities and the business practices of the local firm. *Fit analysis* (see Chapter 8) should be performed rigorously as due diligence.

- A *joint feasibility* study has to be carried out jointly between the two partners as a real business plan, and not just considered as an administrative constraint. This joint work fosters a mutual understanding between the partners before they commit themselves to the relationship. This study should be executed in parallel with the financial and legal negotiations.
- Particular attention has to be given to the *selection of personnel* detached to the joint venture. Cultural, interpersonal and teaching skills should be given as much priority as technical skills.
- *Operational personnel* should be part of the negotiation process, at least partially, because only operational people can identify the day-to-day technical and logistical problems that may occur during the running of the business.
- *Integration teams* (discussed in Chapter 8) should be organized as early as possible.
- *Training programmes* are an important part of foreign investment, mainly when technology transfer is needed. They are particularly important when the joint venture is set up in an emerging country.
- Building and maintaining *trust* is an essential source of success in a joint venture. Below are the main actions and behaviours that are conducive to trust:
  - Demonstrate commitment to the joint venture, by detaching the right personnel, the right technology and the appropriate financing.
  - Keep personal communications running, even (or especially) when times are difficult and possible conflicts arise.
  - Provide advance warning of any changes that you plan to introduce.
  - Make sure that you and your personnel show respect toward the other party. Cultural sense is a key ingredient of trust.
- When *ending* a joint venture make sure that a *win–win* (or at least a *no-blame*) solution is found. Even when the joint venture dissolves because of conflicts or bad results it is important to make sure that nobody loses face in the process.

Entering a country through 'arm's-length' agreements: licensing, franchising, agents and distributors

When a direct investment is not justified, foreign companies can still establish a presence in a particular country by contracting an agreement in the form of a licence, a franchise, an agency or a distribution contract.

Table 7.3 Advantages and disadvantages of country-based joint venture partnerships

	Types of local partners					
	Suppliers	**Customers/ distributors**	**Competitors**	**Diversifiers**	**Investors**	**Government**
Prime motives or advantages for local partner	• Secure sales of raw materials • Learn about downstream technology and processes • Pre-empt competitors • Control price	• Access to product/process technology • Pre-empt competitors • Control price of raw material or components	• Market control • Access to technology • Product complementation • Access to best practices	• Additional source of profit • Capture new opportunities • Risk spreading • Learning new technology	• Return • Shareholder value • Financial diversification	• National development • Technology • Employment • Political payoff
Disadvantages for local partner	• Lack of flexibility: being stuck with one customer	• Lack of flexibility: being stuck with one technology	• Lack of flexibility: being stuck with one technology	• Lack of flexibility: being stuck with one technology	• Risk of poor performances	• Risk of poor performances
Prime motives of foreign partner	• Secure raw material resources	• Market access • Learn about market	• Market access • Learn about market • Resources: assets and people • Market control	• Power/contacts • Possible high profile and reputation • No or little interference in operations • Flexibility	• Contacts • Possible high profile and reputation • Satisfy legal requirements • Capital	• Satisfy legal requirements • Favourable preferences
Disadvantages for foreign investor	• Lack of flexibility: being stuck with one supplier • Being stuck with a non-optimal quality • Pressure for vertical acquisition by partner	• Lack of overall industrial competencies • Short-term mindset of partner • Dependency • Pressure for vertical acquisition by partner	• Copying and technology leakage • Conflicts with other products	• Thin resources from partner • No 'learning' from partner • Possible opportunism	• No 'learning' from partner • Opportunism • No operational support	• Bureaucracy • Politics: being involved in political struggles

These contractual arrangements are made when one or more of the following characteristics are present:

- The market is *too small* for the company to justify a full investment
- The country is perceived as *too risky*
- There is already a direct investment in a nearby country and an additional one would be redundant
- The *government does not allow any other form* of presence
- The company wants to *test the market*.

Licensing agreements and franchises

Licensing agreements[6] are contractual arrangements by which a company (the *licensor*) transfers to another company (the *licensee*) its product and/or process technology with the right to exploit it commercially. The brand name of the licensor may or may not be part of the licensing agreement. The licensor receives financial compensation in the form of royalties and an up-front lump sum payment. Royalties can be calculated as a percentage of sales or as a fixed amount per unit sold. In addition to the transfer of technology, the licensor may send its engineers to help with technology transfer and support. It may also receive some form of technological licence fee. Finally, within a licensing agreement, a licensor can contractually force the licensee to buy intermediate products or components. In that case, the licensor also gets the benefits and profits associated with those sales.

The benefit of licensing is the low commitment in terms of personnel and capital involved. It is an economic way to enter a market. However, the disadvantages are manifold. First, there is a risk of *technological appropriation* by the licensee, who may become a future competitor. This has been the case in the past with Framatome of France, which licensed the technology of high-pressure nuclear reactors from Westinghouse and progressively became more advanced and more competitive than the licensor. Another risk involves *quality control*, particularly when the licence includes the right to use the brand name of the licensor. The good name of the licensor may be ruined if the licensee is not quality conscious. The main strategic disadvantage of licensing is that the licensors are very distant from the market and have no direct control over the company's destiny in the licensee country.

Franchises[7] are another form of indirect contractual arrangement through which the *franchiser* grants the *franchisee* the right to use its name and receive financial compensation in a similar way to the licensing agreement (fixed plus royalties). The franchiser generally forces the franchisee to adopt a certain number of operating policies so that it can maintain a standard level of quality associated with its brand name. Examples of international franchises can be found in the hospitality industry (Hilton, Accor), beverages (Coca-Cola bottling), fast food (McDonald's) and distribution (retail) (Benetton, Gap).

The advantages and disadvantages of franchises are very similar to those of licensing.

Local agents and distributors

The appointment of a local agent or distributor is probably the most frequent mode of entry for the thousands of SMEs that want to reach international markets. For the most established large multinational enterprises, this is also a means to reach countries that are either risky or whose size does not justify a major investment. It can also be an economic way to test markets without committing too many resources up-front. The distinction between an *agent* and a *distributor* is that the latter carries out the logistical tasks of stocking, transporting and billing, while the former is simply a salesperson and an order taker. In emerging markets one often finds three categories of agents and distributors: domestic companies (most often medium-sized firms or large multi-business family conglomerates), government monopolies in planned economies or large international trading companies such as Jardine Matheson, Diethelm Keller and Swire in the Asia Pacific region.

The main advantage of distribution agreements is that they require a limited amount of resource from the global firm; the main disadvantages are the lack of contact with the market and the conflict of interest that can emerge when sales reach a certain level.[8] The economic reason for this conflict is the fact that distributors are generally remunerated by a commission as a percentage of sales. When sales grow, the total commission may reach a point where it is bigger than the fixed costs required to set up a wholly owned marketing subsidiary. The multinational firms then try to get rid of the local distributor, as was seen in Europe with the Japanese car makers who progressively replaced their distributors with their own organizations in major countries. Knowing this, the local distributor is disincentivized to push sales once it becomes obvious that the substitution point is approaching. Instead of fighting a lost cause, international distributors have often adopted a strategy of becoming 'partners' rather than pure distributors and raising the added value of their services to both customers and principals in order to raise 'switching costs'. However, when that country is contributing a significant portion of the turnover and has thus become 'key', the global firm will generally shift to another, more direct mode of entry.

Entering a country through a representative, technical or procurement office

The **representative office** is another very frequent entry mode, considered as a stepping stone or a beachhead. In countries where a company is entering for the first time this type of entry consists of sending an expatriate manager (sometimes using a locally recruited person) to collect information, establish contacts, organize direct sales, lobby for licences, negotiate distribution or joint venture agreements and recruit local personnel. This entry mode is frugal in resource consumption and beneficial in building competencies, but it reaches its limit when it comes to actually running a business. It suits corporations that are selling big projects (railways systems, airport or defence contracts, turnkey plants) at the pre-bidding phase. In these cases, representative offices complement and control the local agents who are lobbying for information and access to decision makers.

Technical offices are another form of entry. Technical offices are most relevant when the country is considered to be a source of technological innovation and a presence can give access to useful contacts and information.

Procurement or **purchasing offices** are most appropriate for large retailers or big commodity buyers who set up an office in order to be close to suppliers, to negotiate contracts and to control their execution. Some companies specialize in buying for third parties and are used by firms that do not want to commit resources to establishing their own office.

Entry modes seen as 'real options'

The concept of the '**real option**' has been proposed in business strategy literature to explain some investment decisions, including foreign investment decisions.[9] The theory of the real option is directly derived from the financial theory of options. According to real option proponents, some investments can be assimilated to a 'call option', that is, a preliminary investment to observe the future development of the business, and at the end of a trial period, the company has the possibility of expanding or retreating. The cost of making the preliminary investment is equivalent to the price of an option. If the company sees that the foreign investment is creating future value then it can exercise its option and expand – that is, increase its stake in a joint venture, transform a licence into an acquisition or replace a distributor with a full investment. If the business does not seem to be developing, it stops the investment, sells its share in the joint venture and continues under licence or as a distributor, or sells the business.

Comparing entry modes

Each mode of entry has its advantages and disadvantages. Table 7.4 summarizes the positives and negatives of each based on various criteria.

Table 7.4 shows that *wholly owned approaches* and *acquisitions* have the most significant market impact and subsequent payout. The return on investment is high to moderate and, at least, close to the cost of capital. The reason is that in the case of a wholly owned investment, it takes time to build a market presence and in the case of an acquisition, the original investment requires an up-front premium. The residual value in these two cases provides most of the return, indicating that these two kinds of investment are valid from a long-term perspective and should be used only when country risks are limited. Licensing is highly profitable from a return viewpoint. This is owing to a minimal up-front investment and a constant flow of royalties, but the absolute value is small. This fits a situation of high risks and low commitment. The long-term exposure in a licensing agreement is negligible. Joint ventures are middle of the road and the example in Mini-case 7.1 shows that they give a higher return than either the wholly owned or acquisition modes. However, joint ventures, as mentioned earlier, do not have a brilliant performance record, showing that the theoretical value of this mode of entry is often hampered by poor implementation.

See Mini-case 7.1 for details of how this works in practice. The cash flows are the cumulative flow of investments paid by the foreign firm and the dividends or royalties received plus the terminal value at the end of the period.

Choosing an entry mode

The choice of entry mode is a function of the factors described at the beginning of the chapter and illustrated in Figure 7.2. There is no ideal solution and the choice is up to each company, according to the weighting given to corporate global strategy, country risks and opportunities, capabilities, timing and government constraints. Figure 7.3 gives a mapping of possible choices as a function of some of

Table 7.4 Comparing various entry modes

	Wholly owned	Acquisition	Joint venture	Licensing	Representative office	Agent/ distributor
Up-front investment, financial and managerial	High	High	Medium	Low	Low/Medium	Low
Speed of entry	Slow	Quick	Quick	Medium	Low	Possibly quick
Market penetration	Medium	High	Medium/High	Medium/ Low	Low	Medium/ Low
Control of market (customer knowledge)	High	High	Medium	Nil	Low	Low/Nil
Political risk exposure	High	High	Medium	Low	Low	Low
Technological leakage	Low	Low	High/Medium	High	Low	Low
Managerial complexity	High	High	High	Low	Medium	Low
Potential financial return	High risk High/ Medium return High payout	High risk High/Medium return High payout	Medium/High risk High/Medium return Medium payout	Low risk High return Low payout	Low risk Variable return	Low risk Variable return

these factors, but in the end, the final decision is a multidimensional one that resists a simplistic 3 × 3 representation.

Over time, with economic growth and increased internal capabilities, foreign investors may shift from predominantly choosing one mode to favouring another. In China, for instance, wholly owned foreign enterprises overtook equity joint ventures in 1997.[10]

Entry strategies in the digital space

As mentioned earlier in Chapter 1, digital companies are more likely to be 'born global' than traditional firms. This is mainly due to lower transaction costs of entering foreign markets. As indicated by Watson et al. (2017) there are three models of market entry:

1. The *Relational model*, implying the building of contracts with local entities: distributors, subcontractors, partners

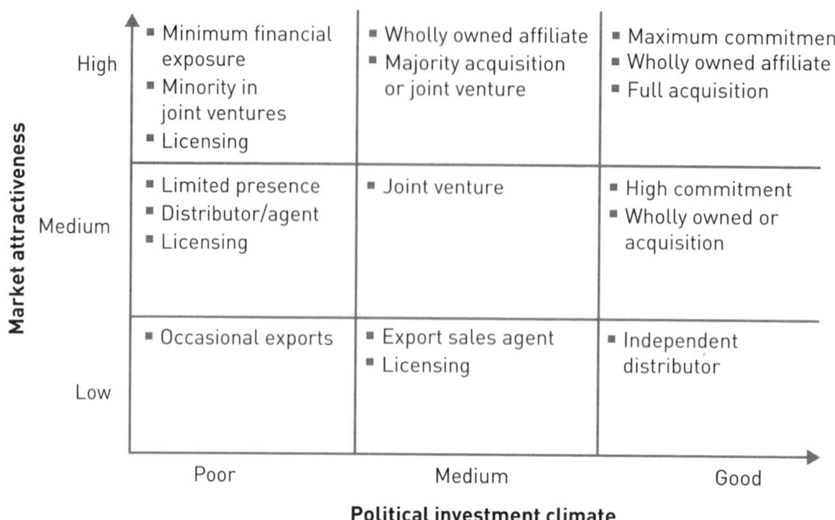

Figure 7.3 Mapping of entry mode choices

2 The *Digital model* that relies only on the deployment of platforms

3 The *Hybrid model* which is a combination of both.

In the case of digital and hybrid models 'Internet communication technologies enable businesses to identify and exploit market opportunities faster and across wider geographic areas than was previously possible'.[11] This is true when the delivery is purely digital (Facebook, Alphabet, Microsoft, PayPal) as those firms can deploy their internet infrastructure with the only constraint of foreign language and legal adaptation. When digital companies are also involved with the distribution of tangible products or services, they may adopt a hybrid type of market entry. Table 7.5 summarizes the differences among the three models of entry.

Table 7.5 Three models of entry

Traditional relational	Digital	Hybrid
Based on contracts with local authorities and partners: • Distributors • Local partners • Logistics • Local personnel • Productive investments	Based on internet infrastructure developed internally • Pure digital delivery • Drop shipping and/or downloading • Cloud computing	Combined relational and digital • B2B and B2C platforms • Physical presence • Customer service platforms • Local personnel • Alliances • Local partners

Sources: Authors' own construction from Watson, Weaven and Perkins (2017).

MINI-CASE 7.1

Schneider Electric and the power backup market in India

Schneider Electric calls itself 'The Global Specialist in Energy Management'. With a turnover of €250 billion and employing 135,000 people in more than 100 countries in 2019, Schneider Electric provides products and services five energy markets: infrastructure, data centres and networks, industry, residential and buildings.

The company entered India in 1993 through a series of partnerships and established its own subsidiary in the same year. India rapidly became an important market. Schneider focused on the premium market segments with a distribution strategy that was based on direct selling, and was not very familiar with the retail indirect selling markets. It developed a strategy of creating and locally manufacturing products specifically for India, the 'in India for India push'. By the end of 2010, Schneider Electric Corporation had about 15,000 employees, 31 manufacturing plants and 2,000 channel partners. In 2011, the company faced a decision regarding Schneider Electric's power backup products.

Electrical backup devices are designed to ensure a continuous supply of power to a site. The market for backup products in India is made of two major segments:

1. The UPS (uninterruptible power supply) segment needs devices with an in-built battery and/or electronic devices to briefly provide emergency power to computers and other critical equipment before backup generators kick in. Large-scale UPS devices were sold directly to corporate customers. The market for small UPS devices was price sensitive, fragmented and sales were made through distributors. The large-scale UPS market in India, worth $530 million and growing at 7 per cent annually, was dominated by large global firms. Schneider, with 9.4 per cent of market share, was one of the big players in this segment. It had developed products as part of the 'in India for India' programme with its own R&D team, its devoted manufacturing and both direct and indirect distribution channels. Schneider revenue from the UPS segment was about $50 million.
2. The inverter segment was made up of devices serving non-critical applications such as lights, fans and TVs for several hours to a day. While backup power in large apartment or office complexes was met by diesel generators, this was not the case for individual homes or small businesses. Unlike the UPS devices, the inverter's battery, which could be bought separately, was a critical element of the device since it had to provide longer hours of use. Batteries had to be changed frequently and cost up to three times that of the inverter device itself. This technology was less advanced and the market, although less lucrative, was bigger in terms of units sold than the UPS market. The know-how and components were widely available and the market, worth $430 million and growing 20 per cent annually, was dominated by Indian producers. Foreign multinational attempts to break into this market had met with limited success.

For Schneider, these Indian backup products were part of the data centres and networks business. Considering the success of the division in the UPS segment, Schneider decided to enter the inverter market, playing on its technological superiority. The Schneider products cost about 20 per cent more than competitive products and Indian customers found the price too high despite impressive technological features. It was difficult for the company to lower its costs given the global standards of the company. Inside the company three differing points of view were expressed: to leave the product as it was, to develop a new low-cost product or to consider acquiring or allying with a local firm.

The third position was supported by the fact that the company had entered discussions with Luminous Company, a local Indian family group. Luminous had 3,000 employees, 9 manufacturing plants, 25 sales offices and a network of 25,000 dealers. Luminous had a presence in power backup products such as inverters, batteries, home electrical devices, renewable energy and services. Inverters made by Luminous featured an integrated battery. In the inverter segment Luminous' revenues were about $65 million. The company was looking for diversification areas such as diesel engines, solar energy and expansion into UPS and the overall energy management segment.

Questions:

1 What are the pros and cons of all three alternatives open to Schneider?

2 Considering the third alternative, what method do you recommend: ally or acquire?

3 Once you have selected one alternative, how do you recommend this be implemented?

Source: Modified with permission from Singh (2012).

MINI-CASE 7.2

Entry and development of Transsion in Africa

Founded in 2006 by Zhu Zhaojiang in Shenzhen, Transsion Holdings manufactures and sells mobile phones. In 2008 the company decided to enter Africa with the opening of its first subsidiary in Nigeria, extended later into Ethiopia, Kenya, Cameroon, Morocco, Egypt and Tanzania.

Zhu saw a strategic opportunity to focus on the African market where the potential demand was high with an existing penetration of mobile phones of 18 phones per 100 inhabitants compared with 101 per 100 inhabitants in Europe. In 2008 the leaders in Africa were Samsung and Nokia who provided standardized products at a relatively high price. Zhu's idea was to take on this opportunity by designing a specifically tailored strategy to Africa based on customers' market surveys.

- Low pricing as compared to existing dominant brands.
- Two or four SIM cards slots to take care of the expensive call charges between telecom operators.
- Local languages phones: Amharic in Ethiopia, Tigrinya and Oromo in Eritrea, Swahili in Kenya and Tanzania, Hausa in Nigeria.
- Louder and clearer speakers for music and phone calls.
- Long-lasting battery and low-cost quick-charge technology to overcome the problem of insufficient, unreliable electric power supply in some countries.
- An anti-corrosion coating technology tailored to hot and humid climates.
- A camera that allowed selfies to be taken in low light.
- A database based on millions of pictures of dark-skinned people, optimized the photo beautification algorithm to take good quality photos using big data and machine learning, and develop other technologies to enhance photography and face recognition accuracy in low light.
- Sales network starting in rural areas with a strategy called 'countryside surrounding city' relying on phone distributors using the prepaid mode.
- Partnerships with other distributors.

By 2019 Transsion brands (Tecno, Itel, and Infinix) had captured a 38 per cent market unit share in Africa ahead of Samsung's 19 per cent and Huawei's 10 per cent.

Source: Modified with permission from Chen and Zhuang (2020). Copyright © 2020.

MINI-CASE 7.3

Lubricador SA

Lubricador SA is an Italian specialist chemical company with a wide range of products serving various industrial applications., The car division of the company specializes in lubricants for brake and air-conditioning systems. In late 2020, the company sent a mission to China to analyse the market and prepare an analysis of various investment alternatives. China had become the second largest car market in the world and was on the way to full recovery after the pandemic crisis of 2020. The Chinese car industry was extremely competitive, with local as well as international players fighting for market share. The study team had concentrated on one particular type of product: brake fluid additive. It estimated that the current domestic market of 50 million litres a year would grow at a rate of 8 per cent a year over the decade from 2020 to 2030. The competition was made up of two domestic firms which controlled 70 per cent of the market and one Japanese joint venture which controlled 30 per cent. The study team concluded that there were four major alternatives for market entry:

- *Set up a greenfield operation and operate as a 100 per cent subsidiary.* The minimum economic capacity was 20 million litres for a total investment of $20 million. The financing of the investment would be done entirely by the mother company and it could expect to repatriate a dividend of 80 per cent of net profit when this became positive. The subsidiary could not expect to capture more than 10 per cent of market share in the first year, growing progressively by 5 per cent a year and stabilizing at 20 per cent after the fifth year of operations. Export output would be around 5 million litres in the first year, increasing by 0.5 litres per year up to 8 million litres.
- The second alternative was to *buy the Japanese competitors*. The acquisition price would be $70 million but Lubricador could expect to capture the 30 per cent market share right away. The yearly growth and export output, as compared with the first alternative, would be the same. An additional investment of $10 million might be needed for an additional 10 million litres. Dividends would be 90 per cent of net profit.
- A third option would be to *form a joint venture with one existing Chinese firm*. The immediate market share would be 30 per cent, rising to 50 per cent in the third year owing to the improved technology of the Italian firm. The total investment cost would be $30 million. The financing of the joint venture would be one-third equity to be shared 50/50 with the local partner and two-thirds debts to be serviced over seven years. The maximum exports in that case would only be 6 million litres per year. All other hypotheticals would remain the same.
- Finally, it was possible to conclude a *licensing agreement with a local firm* which could use and transform its existing facilities and obtain, at best, a 20 per cent market share. In such a case, Lubricador SA would have to invest $600,000 over the next three years to transfer its technology and receive a royalty of 3 yuan/Ltrs after three years.

Other factors to consider were:

- *Exchange rate:* US$1 = 6.58 yuan (the study considered that the yuan might appreciate against the US dollar by 20 per cent)
- *Prices/costs:*
  - Selling price (domestic) = 3.5 yuan/kg
  - Selling price (export) = 4.5 US$/kg
  - Production costs = declining function with cumulated volume = $2500 - 0.025 * 10^{\log \text{(cumulative volume)}}$

    - Administrative/marketing costs = 1,200 million yuan, increasing to 1,600 million yuan
- *Working capital requirement* = 33 per cent of production costs
- *Tax rate on profit* = 30 per cent
- *Weighted average cost of capital* (WACC) = 15 per cent
- *Domestic loans interest rate*: 10 per cent
- *Net present value (NPV) assumes capital costs* = 15 per cent
- *Debt servicing*: 7 years.

Questions:

1. What are the economic benefits for Lubricador in each option?
2. Beyond the return, what are the advantages and disadvantages of each option?
3. Which option would you select and why?

Summary and key points

1. Entry strategy concerns three aspects:
    - **a** Entry *objectives* (*why*)
    - **b** *Timing* of entry (*when*)
    - **c** *Mode* of entry (*how*)
2. Entry objectives:
    - **a** *Market development* objectives to enter a market are:
        - Size and growth opportunity – depends on income and population of a country
        - Criticality of countries – there are key countries in which a presence is needed for global long-term competitiveness owing to size and/or quality of customer base
    - **b** *Resource access* objectives – extracting key resources such as natural or human resources which contribute to competitive advantage
    - **c** *Learning* objectives – gains in knowledge/competency in countries where industry is state of the art
    - **d** *Coordination* objectives – coordination hub for regional activities owing to favourable location and infrastructure advantages
3. Timing of international entry – there are four phases:
    - **a** *Premature* phase:
        - Absence of demand
        - Common in developing countries at an early stage or for a product that does not fit demand in a particular country

- Appropriate investment at this stage is the establishment of any of:
  - Representative offices
  - Listening posts
  - Distribution agreements

b *Window* phase ('window of opportunity'):

- Market is now taking off with relatively little competition
- Potential strategies include:
  - Follower
  - First mover:
    - Advantages – pre-empt run on resources; establish brands; establish standards; learning about customers
    - Disadvantages – taking all the risks; others can take a 'free ride' on the back of your groundwork

c *Competitive growth* phase:

- High market growth but competitors have received first-mover advantages
- Potential strategies:
  - Hazardous entry except with massive resources or a highly differentiated strategy
  - Acquisition or joint venture arrangement

d *Mature* phase:

- Well-established market
- Potential strategies:
  - Acquisition
  - Direct investment with an innovative product

e Pace of entry

Combines the speed of entry and the progressive adoption of low risk/low commitment mode of entry to higher risk/higher commitment of resources

4 Mode of entry:

a Factors influencing entry mode:

- Strategic objectives
- Country risks (political and operational risks)
- Opportunities
- Company's internal capabilities
- Time pressure
- Government requirements

b *Types* of entry mode:

- *Wholly owned subsidiaries:*
  - Advantages – gives most control over operations; low technological leakage
  - Disadvantages – requires the highest mobilization of resources and competencies; highest risk; high up-front investment; slow entry
- *Acquisition*:
  - Advantages – immediate availability of resources, assets and competencies; enables access to market when window of opportunity is closed; high market penetration; high control of market; low technological leakage
  - Disadvantages – requires cross-cultural integration skills that acquiring company may not possess; some nationalities may view acquisition by foreigners unfavourably; costly, as often associated with high acquisition premiums; high political risk exposure
- *Joint venture:*
  - Advantages – quick entry; medium to high market penetration
  - Disadvantages – medium to high technological leakage; high managerial complexity
  - Partner selection – depends on the combination of legal requirements and internal capabilities the firm possesses
  - Partner categories:
    - Sleeping
    - Complementing
    - Investor
    - 'Teaching'
    - Acquisition
  - Partner types – each has their own advantages and disadvantages:
    - Supplier
    - Customer/distributor
    - Competitor
    - Diversifier
    - Investor
    - Government
  - Partner evaluation uses the same criteria as assessing an alliance partner: strategic fit, capability fit, cultural fit and organizational fit
  - Management:
    - Staffing – foreign managers should possess political and cultural skills; local staff should ideally be loyal to the joint venture, not to the local partner

    - Control – can be obtained through shareholding ownership or responsibility over operational functions
  - Termination, problems and renewal:
    - Termination – potential problems are the '*death valley*' issue (development of a vicious cycle in which partners' communications shut off) and joint venture decay (drop in mutual interest and loss of impetus for further collaboration)
    - Failures/problems – absence of strategic vision; 'believing without seeing'; failure to understand local partner's strategic logic; haste in negotiation; insufficiently prepared staff or lack of organizational support
    - Renewal – revitalize the joint venture by increasing range or broadening the scope of its activities
- *Licence or franchise:*
  - Advantages – low economic risk (minimal commitment of personnel and capital); low political risk exposure
  - Disadvantages – risk of technological appropriation by licensee who may become future competitor; damage to brand name if licensee is not quality conscious; licensor's lack of control over licence destiny in the licensee country
- *Agent or distributor:*
  - Frequently used by SMEs for reaching international markets
  - Entry mode for reaching countries that are either risky or whose size does not justify a major investment
  - There are three categories of agent or distributor in emerging countries:
    - Multi-business family conglomerates
    - Government monopolies
    - Large international trading companies
  - Advantages:
    - Economic (low resource commitment)
    - Possible quick entry
    - Low political risk exposure
    - Low technological leakage
  - Disadvantages:
    - Lack of contact with market
    - Conflict of interest when the sales reach a certain level

- *Office* (representative office/procurement office/technical office):
  - Representative office
    - Advantages – frugal in resource consumption; beneficial in building competency; appropriate when corporations are selling big projects at the pre-bidding phase; low political risk exposure; low technological leakage
    - Disadvantages – slow entry; low market penetration; low control of market
  - Technical or procurement offices:
    - Useful when country is source of technological innovation and company presence gives access to useful contacts and information
    - Procurement offices most appropriate for large retailers or big commodity buyers who want to be close to suppliers and control contract execution

c *Choice* of entry mode – dependent on weighting a company assigns to various factors influencing entry modes

d A 'real option' (a call option)

- Price of option is the cost of making the preliminary investment
- Choices from real option are:
  - Expand investment if foreign investment is creating future value
  - Terminate investment if foreign investment does not seem to develop

Learning assignments

1. What are the relative advantages and disadvantages of setting up a wholly owned subsidiary instead of a joint venture?
2. What is a 'window of opportunity'?
3. Under which conditions does being a first mover give sustainable competitive advantage?
4. What are the major problems associated with licensing?
5. What potential problems does a foreign investor experience in an industrial joint venture with an ex-local agent or distributor?
6. Why do joint ventures often fail?

Key words

- Entry modes
- First mover
- Franchise
- Joint venture
- Licensing
- Pace of entry
- Real option
- Representative offices
- Wholly owned operations
- Window of opportunity

Web resources

Academia:
https://www.academia.edu
UNCTAD Publications:
https://unctad.org/publications
UNCTAD World Investments Reports:
https://unctad.org/topic/investment/world-investment-report

WTO (World Trade Organization) *International Trade Statistics*:
https://data.wto.org/en

Companion website

Visit the companion website at bloomsbury.pub/global-strategic-management-5e for a multitude of weblinks and resources, self-test questions for revision and appendices.

Notes

1 Lieberman and Montgomery (1988).
2 Luo and Peng (1998).
3 Vermeulen and Barkema (2002).
4 On entry modes, see Anderson and Gatignon (1986); Kim and Hwang (1992).
5 Beamish and Bank (1987).
6 See Contractor (1981); Beamish (1996).
7 Gompers and Connely (1997).
8 Arnold (2000).
9 Kogut and Kulatilaka (1994); Luermann (1997); Williamson (1999).
10 Vanhonacker (1997).
11 Watson et al. (2017).

References and further reading

Adarkar, A., Adil, A., Ernst, D. and Vaish, P. (1997) 'Emerging market alliances: must they be win–lose?', *McKinsey Quarterly*, 4: 120–37.

Anderson, E. and Gatignon, H. (1986) 'Modes of foreign entry: a transaction costs analysis and propositions', *Journal of International Business Studies*, 17 (3): 1–26.

Arnold, D. (2000) 'Seven rules of international distribution', *Harvard Business Review*, 78 (6):131–7.

Beamish, P. (1996) 'Note on international licensing', Richard Ivey School of Business, University of Western Ontario, Note 9A96G008.

Beamish, P. and Bank, J. (1987) 'Equity joint ventures and the theory of the multinational enterprise', *Journal of International Business Studies*, 18 (3): 1–16.

Cavusgil, S. T. and Ghauri, P. N. (1991) *Doing Business in Developing Countries: Entry and Negotiation Strategies* (London: Routledge).

Chen, G. and Zhuang, X. (2020) 'Transsion Mobile: Deep Blue Ocean in Africa'. https://publishing.insead.edu/case/transsion-mobile-deep-blue-ocean-africa (accessed 1 February 2022).

Contractor, F. (1981) *International Technology Licensing: Compensation, Costs and Negotiation* (Lexington, MA: D.C. Heath).

Decarli, M. and Neubert, M. (2021) 'Internationalisation Patterns of European Mobile Network Operators', Working Paper No. 004, UIBS United International Business Schools.. https://papers.ssrn.com/sol3/papers.cfm?abstract_id=3781542 (accessed 1 February 2022).

Gompers, P. and Connely, C. (1997) 'A note on franchising', *Harvard Business School*, Note 9297108.

Hopkins, R. (2017) *Grow Your Global Markets A Handbook for Successful Market Entry* (New York, NY: Springer).

Johanson, J. and Vahine, L-E. (1977) 'The internationalization process of the firm: a model of knowledge development and increasing market commitment', *Journal of International Business Studies*, 8 (1): 23–32.

Kaha, H. (2014) 'Strategic motives of Turkish foreign direct investment firms: an empirical study on manufacturing sector', *İstanbul Üniversitesi İşletme Fakültesi Dergisi Istanbul University Journal of the School of Business Cilt*, 43 (2): 368–90.

Kim, C. and Hwang, P. (1992) 'Global strategies and multinational entry mode choice', *Journal of International Business Studies*, 23 (1): 29–53.

Kogut, B. (1989) 'The stability of joint ventures: reciprocity and competitive rivalry', *Journal of Industrial Economics*, 38 (2): 183–98.

Kogut, B. and Kulatilaka, N. (1994) 'Options thinking and platform investments: investing in opportunity', *California Management Review*, Winter: 52–71.

Lieberman, M. and Montgomery, D. (1988) 'First mover advantages', *Strategic Management Journal*, 9: 41–58.

Luermann, T. (1997) 'Investment opportunities as real options: getting started on the numbers', *Harvard Business Review*, 76 (4): 51–67.

Luo, Y. and Peng, M. (1998) 'First mover advantages in investing in transitional economies', *Thunderbird International Business Review*, 40: 141–63.

Miller, R., Glen, J. D., Jasperen, F. and Karmokolias, Y. (1996) 'International joint ventures in developing countries: happy marriages?', International Finance Corporation, Discussion Paper, 29.

Mowla, M., Hoque, N., Mamun, A. and Uddin, M. A. (2014) 'Entry mode selection, location choice and the sequence of internationalization: a case study on Ranbaxy Laboratories Ltd.', *Asian Social Science* 10 (6): 145–54.

Mudambi, R. and Zahra, S. A. (2018) 'The survival of international new ventures', *International Entrepreneurship*, 85–130.

Rigman, T. (1996) 'Window of opportunity: timing and entry strategies', *Industrial Management and Data Systems*, 96 (5).

Root, F. (1994) *Entry Strategies for International Markets* (San Francisco, CA: Jossey Bass).

Singh, J. (2012) 'Schneider Electric in India: power backup products', INSEAD case no. 004/2013-5882.

Tang, J. and Liu, B. S. (2011) 'A network based theory of foreign market entry mode and post-entry performance', *International Journal of Business and Social Science*, 2 (23) Special Issue: 50–9.

Vanhonacker, W. (1997) 'Entering China: an unconventional approach', *Harvard Business Review*, 75 (2): 130–41.

Vermeulen, F. and Barkema, H. (2002) 'Pace, rhythm, and scope: process dependence in building a profitable multinational corporation', *Strategic Management Journal*, 23, 637–53. http://dx.doi.org/10.1002/smj.243 (accessed 1 February 2022).

Watson G. F., IV, Weaven, S. and Perkins, H. (2017) 'International market entry strategies: relational, digital, and hybrid approaches', *Journal of International Marketing*, December, doi: 10.1509/jim.17.0034.

Williamson, P. J. (1999) 'Strategy as options on the future', *Sloan Management Review*, Spring: 117–26.

Williamson, P. J. and Qionghua, H. (1994) *Managing the Global Frontier: Strategies for Developing Markets* (London: Pitman).

Zhao, H., Ma, J. and Yang, J. (2017) '30 years of research on entry mode and performance relationship: a meta-analytical review', *Management International Review*, 57 (5): 653–82.

Journals

Global Strategy Journal: https://onlinelibrary.wiley.com/journal/20425805

Journal of International Marketing: https://journals.sagepub.com/home/jig

Journal of World Business: https://www.journals.elsevier.com/journal-of-world-business

Sloan Management Review: https://sloanreview.mit.edu

Chapter 8

Global mergers, acquisitions and strategic alliances

At the end of the chapter you will be able to:

- Understand the strategic value of various forms of combining capabilities through mergers, acquisitions and strategic alliances
- Identify the critical elements of value creation in an acquisition plan and implement integration
- Understand the various phases of post-merger integration and explain the different modes of integration
- Explain the different types of strategic alliances in a global context
- Analyse the various fits among parties involved
- Structure a negotiation for reaching an agreement
- Anticipate potential issues in the management of the alliances and understand how to set up the proper mechanisms to solve them
- Discuss the specific aspects of joint ventures for market entry

Introduction

As part of their strategic vision to globalize, firms can use three methods: building their own capabilities abroad by investing their own resources, borrowing capability from a partner by setting up an alliance or buying those capabilities by acquiring or merging with a company: the build, borrow or buy paradigm.[1]

In this chapter we will look at the strategic and managerial issues involved in the combination of mergers, acquisitions or alliances capabilities between firms from different countries of origin.

In the first part of the chapter we will focus on mergers and acquisitions and will look at the two phases of mergers and acquisitions (M&As): the pre-acquisition phase and the post-acquisition phase. The pre-acquisition phase deals with the decision-making process: how companies make the M&A decision, calculate the potential value of the acquired company and negotiate the deal. The post-acquisition phase refers to the managerial processes involved in the integration of the merged companies. This phase is considered by consultants and academics to be the most important source of success or failure.

In the second part we will deal with the different forms of alliances and discuss the various types of potential alliance whether global alliances or joint venture for market entry.

We will study aspects of forming, analysing, negotiating and implementing global strategic alliances.

In both parts we will present a framework for studying the various stages of mergers, acquisitions and alliance formation made of four main steps:

- Understanding the strategic value of a merger, acquisition or alliance.
- Analysis of partner(s) or target: strategic fit, capabilities fit, cultural fit and organizational fit.
- Negotiation and design of the structure.
- Implementation: making the arrangement work thanks to a properly managed integration.

At the end of the chapter we shall present some criteria for successful mergers, acquisitions or alliances.

Global mergers and acquisitions

The rationale for cross-border M&AS

Since 1985 there has been an average increase of 12 per cent per year[2] in the value of cross-border M&As. M&As are instruments used by companies to increase their global reach and competitiveness. Even in the Asia Pacific region, traditionally allergic to M&As, the financial crisis that struck the region in 1997 opened the door to an acquisition spree.

Cross-border M&As have been a means of international expansion since the 1970s. The acquisition policy of Getinge, a Swedish medical equipment firm, illustrates this point in the following example.

EXAMPLE 8.1 Getinge's growth via international acquisitions

Getinge, a Swedish-based company specializing in healthcare equipment, employs 15,000 people in forty countries with revenues of 30 billion SEK (US$ 3.4 billion). Getinge was created in 1904 as a manufacturer of agricultural machinery. In 1932 it entered the medical equipment business (sterilizers) and in the 1970s engaged in an internationalization strategy mainly based on the acquisitions of companies outside Sweden. Below is the record of this acquisition drive.

Year	Acquired company	Speciality	Country
1973	Vaxjo Rostfritt	Disinfection equipment	UK
1975	Sterilizing Equipment Co.	Sterilizing equipment	UK
1981	Lequeux	"	France
1983	Fred Clarke	"	Australia
1985	ZK Hospital	"	Germany

Year	Acquired company	Speciality	Country
1990	Scott	Disinfection equipment	UK
1993	British Sterilizer	Sterilizing equipment	UK
"	Stirn Industries	Disinfection equipment	UK
1994	Lancer	"	France
"	D.S.E.	Distribution company	France
1995	Merger with Arlo	Patient care	Netherlands/Belgium
"	Persitel	Sterilizing equipment	Sweden
"	Anzy	"	France
1996	MDT	Infection control	South Africa
1998	Kemiterm	"	USA
"	Omasa	"	Denmark
"	Royal Linden	"	Italy
"	SM/BBC	"	Netherlands
"	Pegasus and Egerton	Extended care	France
"	Medibol	"	UK
1999	Lunatronics (25%)	IT	Netherlands
2000	Parker Bath	Extended care	Denmark
"	Lenken Healthcare	"	UK
"	Gestion Techno-Médic	"	Ireland
"	Maquet	Surgical tables	Canada
2001	ALM	Surgical lights	Germany
2003	LSS	Ventilators	France
2004	BHM	Patient handling	Germany
2005	La Calhene	Sterilized products	Canada
2006	OTY GmbH	Telemedical equipment	France
"	Medical System Comecio	Cardiopulmonary products	Germany
2007	Huntleigh Technology	Extended care equipment	Brazil
2008	Cardiac and Vascular	Cardiac surgery	UK
"	Division of Boston Scientific	Cardiovascular products	USA
2009	Corporation	Infection control	USA
"	Datascope Corp	Cardiovascular products	UK
2010	Numac	Medical equipment	USA
"	STS	Vascular devices	Austria
2011	Odelga	Catheters	USA
2012	Atrium Medical	Therapeutic furniture	China
"	Acare Medical Services	Implants	Japan
"	USCI	Medical services	USA
"	Avalon Elite	Autoclaves and disinfectors	USA
2013	Kinetic Concepts	Monitoring	USA
"	Laax	IT systems	USA
"	STS East	Infection control	Turkey
2014	Trans Medikal Devices	"	Germany
"	Pulsion Medical Systems	"	Denmark
	(75%)	Cell and gene therapy	Thailand
	Cetrea	Clinical logistics solutions	Denmark
2019	Applikon biotechnology	Bioreactor systems	Netherlands

Cross-border M&As grew in prominence during the 1990s, mostly fuelled by the globalization of markets and competition. Three particular events accelerated the movement: the Single European Market (SEM), followed by the advent of the euro; the 1997 Asian crisis; and the use of the shareholder value model of corporate governance. The SEM and the euro created the economic conditions for the consolidation of European companies, the Asian crisis gave an opportunity to Western corporations to buy Asian assets and finally the shareholder value model forced companies not only to de-diversify but also to concentrate on core activities. The example of Aventis illustrates this last point. Aventis was the result of the merger of the life-sciences activities of Rhône Poulenc Rorer (France and United States) and Hoechst (Germany). Before merging, Hoechst and Rhône Poulenc spun off their chemical businesses. Ultimately, Aventis became part of the French pharma giant Sanofi.

The collapse of the internet bubble in the early 2000s, the subprime crisis in 2008 and the Covid-19 pandemic which started in early 2020 slowed down the growth trend (see Figure 8.1).

Insert 8.1 gives some examples of significant global mergers and acquisition since 2000.

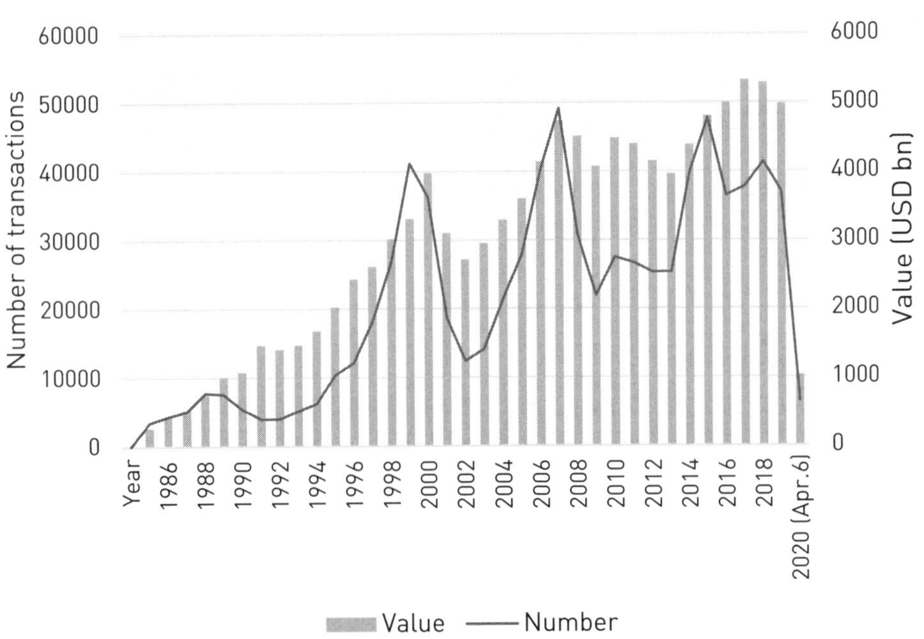

Figure 8.1 Number and value of global mergers and acquisitions from 1985 to 2020

Source: Institute for Mergers, Acquisitions and Alliances (IMAA) research, Thomson Financial.

The effect of Covid-19 on global M&As

Global M&As declined in volume and value during the first two quarters of 2020 but experienced a rebound in the last two quarters, mainly driven by digitalization. According to a report from PricewaterhouseCoopers, the technology and telecom sectors experienced the highest growth; 'the acceleration of deals in digital and technology, and increasing attention to environmental, social and governance (ESG) matters'.[3]

Insert 8.1 Examples of some global acquisitions and mergers since 2010

Mega mergers in the beer industry

From 2000 to 2016, the global beer industry experienced a series of mega mergers that crossed three continents. In 2002 SAB (South African Brewery) acquired Miller, the second largest US brewer. Two years later in 2004, the Belgian group Interbrew merged with AmBEV from Brazil to form InBev and become the largest global beer producer; InBev in 2008 then merged with the US firm Anheuser Busch to form AB InBev, registered in Belgium. In 2014 AB InBev acquired SAB Miller, consolidating its leading global position.

Bayer Monsanto

On September 2016, German pharmaceutical and chemicals giant Bayer bought US seed and agricultural chemical company Monsanto. The combined company would control over a quarter of the global supply of seeds and pesticides.

ChemChina Syngenta

In May 2017 the Chinese giant ChemChina acquired the Swiss agrochemical company Syngenta for $43 billion, one of the largest Chinese foreign acquisitions.

Holcim-Lafarge

In July 2015, Lafarge, a global French cement company, and its Swiss competitor Holcim agreed to merge through an exchange of shares with a view to achieving leadership in the global cement industry.

EssilorLuxottica

In January 2017 the French specialist of corrective glasses merge with the Italian Luxottica specialist of eye glasses to create an integrated global leader in the vision industry.

Qualcomm and NXP Semiconductors

In October 2016, US Qualcomm acquired the Dutch manufacturer NXP Semiconductors. This purchase offers Qualcomm better access to technology and a wider world market in the automobile semiconductor and security sectors.

Teva-Allergan

In July 2015, Israeli firm Teva bought US Allergan's generics unit. It is expected that this acquisition will increase Teva's competitiveness in generic pharmaceuticals.

Nokia-Alcatel-Lucent

Nokia from Finland announced in April 2015 that it would acquire the French-US telecom equipment manufacturer Alcatel-Lucent.

Haier-GE Appliances

On June 2016, Qingdao Haier Co., part of the Chinese electro-mechanical group Haier, announced the acquisition of US General Electric's appliance division. With this purchase, Haier, which had held only 1.1 per cent of the US appliance market, increased its market share in the USA to 15 per cent, and became the world's leading appliance manufacturer.

Alfa-Campoformio

In November 2013, Mexico's largest processed-meats producer, Sigma Alimentos (part of the Alfa SAB group) acquired the Spanish sausage maker Campofrio Food Group as part of its strategy to expand its presence in Europe.

Bharti Airtel-Zain

In July 2010 Airtel, a subsidiary of the Indian conglomerate Barthi Enterprises, acquired the African business of the Kuwaiti company Zain Telecom, with a view to accessing the African and Middle Eastern markets. Following this $10.7 billion deal, the chairman of Barthi said that this acquisition would make Barthi Airtel a truly global telecom company with operations across eighteen countries.

Blackstone-Thomson Reuters

On October 2018 the US private equity firm Blackstone acquired a 55 per cent stake in the Financial & Risks division of the British firm Thomson Reuters for about $20 billion.

Advent, Cinven, Rag-Thyssen Group

On February 2020 the elevator division of the German Thyssen Group was sold for $19 billion to a consortium of companies: Advent (USA), Cinven (UK) and Rag Foundation (Germany).

Cross-border acquisitions performance

It is difficult when evaluating the performance of M&As to differentiate which results are due to its international aspects and which are due to good or bad management practices. Several studies have tried to assess the value created by M&As; some have analysed M&A deals and their results without differentiating between domestic acquisitions and international ones. Overall, these studies showed that 45–75 per cent of acquisitions fail to deliver the value that was expected by their initiators.[4] John Kitching,[5] looking at cross-border acquisitions in Europe in the 1970s, found that overall 25 per cent were straight failures and 25 per cent were not worth doing, giving a success score of 50 per cent. A more recent study concluded that 'M&A is a mug's game: typically 70–80% of acquisitions are abysmal failures'.[6] The conclusion that can be derived is that international M&As are no worse than domestic ones. One of the reasons for this is that most cross-border acquisitions are horizontal (i.e. in core business) and all the studies found that horizontal acquisitions tended to be more successful than others. A 1990 McKinsey study[7] found that cross-border acquisitions were essentially done in core businesses, while this was less the case in domestic ones. Since no research has tried to compare performances of horizontal international and horizontal domestic M&As, it is difficult to discover the specific success/failure factors of international acquisitions. The intuitive conclusion that can be drawn is that, on top of all other management factors, cultural differences can be a specific challenge in cross-border deals, as the case of Sony's acquisition of Columbia Pictures demonstrates.

Academics and consultants who have analysed M&As generally come to the same conclusions.[8] Success or failure comes from two key issues: the quality of the pre-acquisition process – how companies make the M&A decision; and the quality of the post-acquisition process – how the integration is managed. This process is considered the most important cause of success or failure.

The process of mergers and acquisitions

The sequence of planning and achieving a merger or an acquisition involves two processes (Figure 8.2):

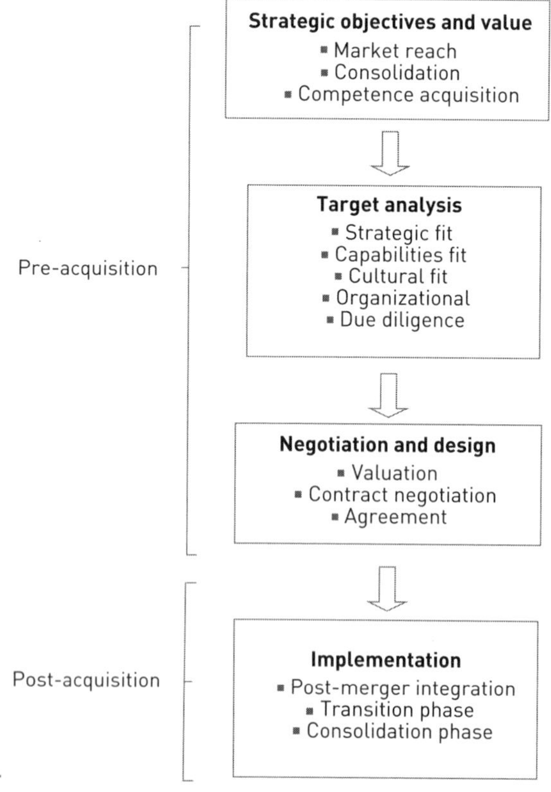

Figure 8.2 The process of mergers and acquisitions

- The pre-acquisition process involving: a) defining the strategic objectives and the strategic value of a deal; b) analysis of the potential acquisition target or merger partner; c) valuation and negotiation.
- The post-acquisition process involving the implementation of the integration of the two companies in the transition and the consolidation phases.

Pre-acquisition

1 Strategic objectives and potential for value creation

Theoretically, M&As contribute to enhancing the economic value of the companies involved. The economics of M&As are simple: a merger or an acquisition is justified if, and only if, the value of the new merged or combined entity is bigger than the sum of the value of the independent entities prior to the merger.

The three main value-creation objectives behind cross-border M&As are:

- Market reach:
  - Gaining market power globally by extension of global presence (global M&A): Holcim-Lafarge in the cement industry.
  - Developing a presence in local markets (acquisition for market entry): Airtel's acquisition of Zain Telecom Company in Africa and Middle East.
  - Diversifying into a new domain (diversification acquisition): Sony's acquisition of Columbia Pictures in the USA.
- Consolidation: search for economies of scale:
  - Merger of two companies in the same business (horizontal M&A): British American Tobacco or AB InBev and SAB Miller Anheuser Bush inBev in the beer industry.
  - Merger of two companies which are buyers or suppliers of each other's products (vertical integration M&A): Bayer and Monsanto in the chemical and seeds industries.
- Competencies acquisitions:
  - Merger in related or new technologies
  - Options or the acquisition of a firm in a new technology or market to monitor its evolution. These categories include the acquisition by the Swiss pharmaceutical group Ciba-Geigy in the early 1980s of the Californian company Alza in order to get access to advanced drug delivery systems technologies; and more recently the acquisition of US Allergan Generics by Teva from Israel.

International M&As usually belong to the first or second type, but the rush toward the internet-generated 'new economy' has triggered the development of diversification and options M&As.

Whatever the type of M&A, value is created through two modalities:

- Short-term one-off value
- Long-term strategic value.

Short-term value comes from the one-off post-merger realization of cash benefits coming from a tax shield, asset disposals and immediate cost savings or debts leverage.

Long-term value comes from the competitive advantage gained from the merger: either it provides enhanced differentiation capabilities, a larger market, new growth opportunities, enhanced competencies or cost advantages through economies of scale or scope. These advantages are often referred as the 'synergistic' effects of a merger (see Table 8.1).

Table 8.1 Value creation in M&As

Types of value creation	Benefits
Short-term value creation	
• Tax shield	• Diminution of tax bill (cost benefits)
• Asset disposals	• Lower capital invested (higher return, lower cost)
• Financial engineering: – Debt leverage – Price/earnings (P/E) ratio leverage	• Lower cost of capital (assuming cost of debts lower than cost of equity) • Total market value increased after the merger (assuming a P/E differential between buyer and seller and a positive market reaction)
Long-term value creation	
• Pooling and sharing resources and assets – Joint purchasing – Manufacturing rationalization – Joint distribution and logistics – Common IT and central services – Common treasury	Economies of scale and scope (cost benefits)
• Enlarged market – Geography – Products • Transfer of competencies – Technology – Best practices	• Growth potential enhanced • Richer value proposition (higher reach and possibly higher differentiation) • Higher differentiation • Processes more effective • Innovation (higher differentiation and lower costs)

2 Fit analysis

In international mergers and acquisitions one will find generally three types of potential target: a) consolidation targets, companies in the same industry (mainstream); b) vertical integration targets, either upstream (on the supplier side) or downstream (on the customer side); and c) diversification targets, firms in a different industry. Most of the time, targets will be found among companies already known to the firm, either as competitor, supplier, customer or partner in an existing alliance.

Fit analysis consists of determining the extent to which the addition of the two entities involved in the merger or acquisition will add more value than the separate value of each separate entity. A fit analysis consists of four assessments (Figure 8.3):

- Strategic fit
- Capabilities fit
- Cultural fit
- Organizational fit.

Figure 8.3 Fit analysis in mergers and acquisitions

Strategic fit

The purpose of strategic fit analysis is to assess to what extent the strategic positioning of the two entities involved in the deal reinforce each other. It consists of answering two very simple questions:

- To what extent does the addition of the two entities consolidate the strategic positioning of the merged entities? A good example of a critical deal can be found in the recent acquisitions of Fiat-Chrysler by the French Peugeot group. It allows Peugeot to reinforce its presence in the US and China and gives the company a global profile instead of a European one.
- Is there a risk of dilution of image if the competitive positioning of the two firms are too distant? As an example the difficulties encountered in the acquisition by Daimler Benz of the US-based Chrysler can be attributed to the positioning distance between Chrysler's middle-range class type of vehicle and Daimler's top of the line.

Capabilities fit

The objective of a capabilities fit analysis is to assess the extent to which the entities' assets and competences complement or supplement the competitive capabilities of the merged businesses.

The framework for this analysis is straightforward. It consists, first, in determining the required resources, assets and competencies needed in the value chain of the business. Then to assess the specific contribution the merger or the acquisition can make to each element of the value chain either by supplementing or complementing capabilities. In other terms the capabilities fit determine the amount of synergies the deal is likely to generate.

This logical analysis is described in Figure 8.4.

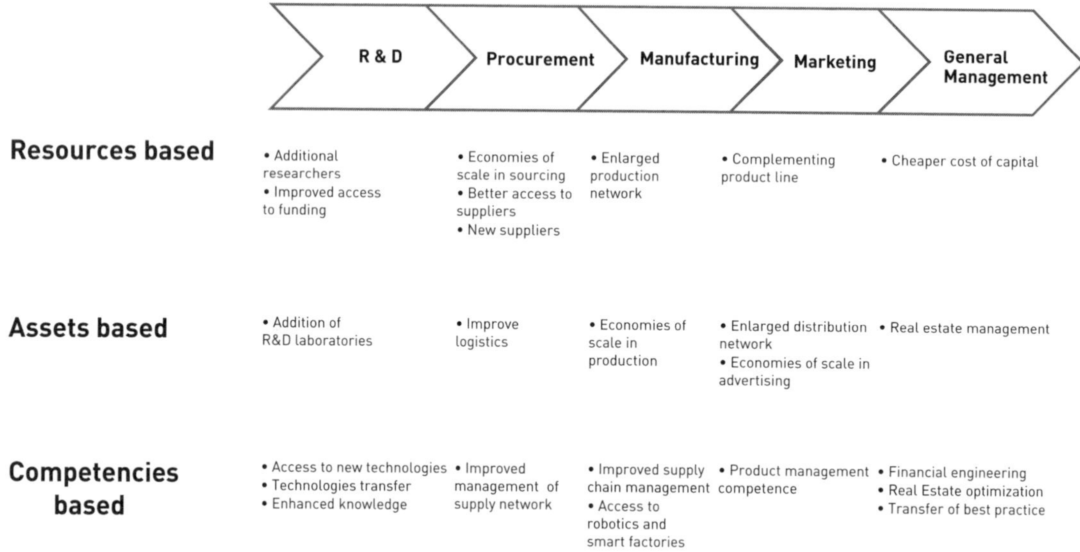

Figure 8.4 Framework for capabilities analysis in mergers and acquisitions

Cultural fit

Three types of cultural difference can be distinguished in global mergers and acquisitions – corporate, industrial and national – each of them likely to create a gap that may affect the future functioning of the merged entity. The role of cultural fit analysis is to understand the nature of these differences, to anticipate their possible impact on the functioning of the post-merger situations and to take action in order to prevent negative consequences.

In organizations such as companies, culture is the set of beliefs – values, assumptions and causal models – that influences the way individuals in that organization think and behave. As mentioned earlier, three types of difference in organizational cultures can be identified:

- Differences in corporate cultures
- Differences in industry cultures
- Differences in national cultures.

Corporate culture differences come from the history of the company (start-up versus well-established firm), its ownership structure (family-owned versus public company versus government-owned), its managerial style (entrepreneurial versus bureaucratic), as well as the personality of its leaders. Good or bad past experiences with strategies and alliances also have a strong influence on corporate cultures.

Industry cultures are the norms encountered in the type of business in which firms are engaged: fast-moving consumer goods (FMCG) companies share a marketing mindset that would not fit particularly with a specialist chemical company, for instance.

National or ethnic cultures are the product of the history, educational systems, religions and social codes that each nation has woven over the centuries. In Chapter 3, we analysed national cultures in some detail, but as far as alliances are concerned, we will take for granted the fact that firms are influenced by the national culture of their country of origin and the citizenship of their key executives.

All three differences can be present in global mergers and acquisitions. These differences may impact the post-merger management in five main ways:

- On the difference in the existing strategic trajectory of the companies: growth versus profit optimization, short-term versus long-term objectives are the major conflicts that cultural differences may exacerbate.
- On competing and doing business: price competition versus differentiation.
- On the way communication is organized: formal versus informal, hierarchical versus horizontal, degree of openness, emphasis on interpersonal communications.
- On financing and reinvesting: distribution of dividend versus reinvestment of profits, and debt policy.
- On human resources management (HRM): criteria for recruiting, degree of autonomy and criteria for performance evaluation.

All of these will considerably affect the post-acquisition management process.

Organizational fit

Organizational fit is strongly correlated with cultural fit. The objective is to assess whether the merged organizational structure systems and procedures differ significantly to the extent that the post-merger organization is affected.

The main dimensions included in organizational fit analysis are:

- The degree of decentralization of decision making
- The degree of documentation of policies and rules

- The accounting and reporting methods and systems
- The degree of formalization of decision making
- The kind of incentives used to motivate personnel.

Altogether the analysis of the four fits will reveal the amount of reconciliation and reconfiguration of the strategic, organizational, capabilities and cultural differences to be taken into account when the integration phase will take place.

Due diligence

One particular aspect that deserves attention in the case of international M&As is related to the conduct of due diligence leading to valuation, that is, the evaluation of the target's real capabilities and financial standing. It involves four types of due diligence: financial, operational, legal and human resources.

Due diligence and subsequently valuation are among the main handicaps to global acquisitions, particularly in emerging markets. There are three main reasons for this. First, marketing and strategic information is often less accurate and reliable, or at least less accessible, than in the home country of the buyer. Second, political or nationalistic attitudes may hamper fair assessment. Third, local accounting standards are not necessarily in line with international standards. In Korea, for instance, *chaebols* ('conglomerates') do not usually consolidate their accounts, and do not eliminate inter-company transactions within the same group, which can lead to inflated revenues. In Southeast Asia accounting ledgers are kept for tax purposes and the figures have very little relevance for asset valuation. Other major inaccuracies to be wary of include:

- Inventories may be overvalued
- Employees' retirement benefits may not appear or may be underfunded, meaning provisions have to be added for future liabilities
- In certain cases, accruals are ignored and have to be restated
- Real estate has to be (re)valued at market prices, and necessary tax adjustments made
- Hidden liabilities such as legal actions may be uncovered.

These adjustments are the most frequent. In the event of the acquisition of a company that is part of a conglomerate, adjustments might have to be made for any cross-subsidiary transfers which may have distorted the announced profitability, and checks made as to whether any licences, distributors or contractual arrangements will still apply after an acquisition. If such contractual assets had originally been granted to the mother company, adequate transfers have to be included in the acquisition agreement. More time and effort is required to validate data than normal: detailed interviews with customers, suppliers and bankers all have to be part of due diligence.

3 Valuation

Economic valuation is necessary in order for a potential buyer to decide at what price it is willing to conclude the deal – or, in the case of a merger, the relative proportions of shares to be exchanged.

Three main methods are used for such valuations.[9]

Asset-based valuation

This method determines the actual value of assets minus liabilities, using a replacement price for physical assets and adjusting for inventories or debtors' book value. Intangible assets and goodwill are estimated using a comparable value for similar businesses or using formulas such as dollars per customer. If the company's assets are predominantly physical, this approach may give a fair estimation of its value. When, on the other hand, the company's profitability relies on intangible resources and capabilities such as employees' commitment, knowledge and competencies, this method fails to give a good economic price.

Market-based valuation

This approach relies on direct market valuation if the company is listed on a stock exchange or otherwise on market equivalent valuation. When using stock exchange market value, the transaction will require that the bidder puts a premium on the deal. Premiums are based on an anticipation of value added from the merger, either short or long term through synergies. Research has found that premiums 30–100 per cent over market value are not unusual in cross-border acquisitions. In order to calculate how much premium the company is ready to accept, one is forced to turn to a cash-flow method of valuation since the future profit coming from the merger will accrue over the years and no other method is available to calculate a premium. Stock market prices may not always reflect economic reality in countries where stock exchanges are not efficient owing to lack of liquidity, partial listing, lack of proper regulations or insider trading.

When the target company is not listed on the stock market, you can use market equivalent measurements such as P/E ratio, price/cash flow ratio or price/revenues ratio calculated from similar deals or comparable companies listed on the stock exchange. Such a measurement is crude, and should be used only as a reference since no deal and no company, even in the same industry, is exactly the same. In addition, particular deals may have been done on the basis of unsound calculations and there is no reason to replicate them.

Cash-flow-based valuation

Economic theory would say that this is the only valid method, apart from the actual market price put on the stock market when the market is efficient.[10]

With this method, the value of a firm's equity is equal to the net present value of future free cash flows (FCF) discounted by the weighted average cost of capital (WACC), minus debts. In practice, this method implies:

- A calculation of future cash flows: revenues – cash costs – increase in required working capital – future investments – taxes
- A determination of the WACC, taking into account the risks of the deal; the WACC is the weighted average of the cost of equity and cost of debts.

In order to calculate future cash flows, it is necessary to forecast revenues based on demand, price and market share assumptions as well as costs over a period that reflect a sound strategic horizon. As mentioned earlier, this can represent a big challenge in cross-border acquisitions in emerging countries or emerging industries where forecasting is more a matter of guesswork than hard computation. Another issue that can arise is the estimation of the WACC, which could be risk adjusted to take into consideration different risk profiles in different countries.[11] Another method is to adjust the cash flows for potential risks (see Chapter 13 for more details).

Two kinds of future cash flow need to be valued in M&As:

- The future free cash flow (FCF) of the merging or of the acquired company calculated as if the company continued its activities without the merger. This is the stand-alone value. Normally, if the company is listed on the stock market its market capitalization should reflect its stand-alone value, otherwise forecasting and discounting are needed.
- The future value of the added value brought in the short term and the long term by the merger of the two companies (see Table 8.1 above). This is the synergies value.

These two streams of cash flow give a present value that reflects the bargaining range of the price negotiation. Below the stand-alone value no seller would sell (unless as a fire sale or because of extreme non-economic pressure) since they could achieve this value without being acquired. Above the stand-alone plus synergies value, the buyer company should not buy since, if the calculation is correct, it would transfer the value to the seller and the buyer would not get anything for itself (Figure 8.5).

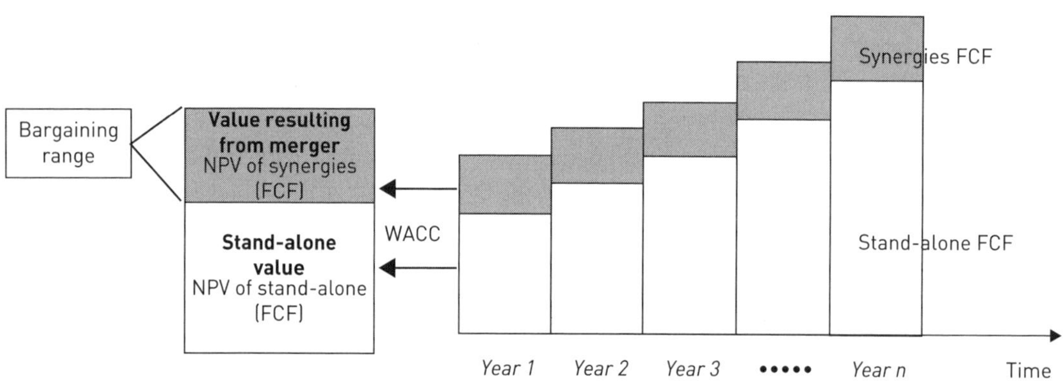

Figure 8.5 Cash-flow-based valuation for M&As

4 Negotiation and design

Most of the legal terms of agreements negotiated in domestic M&As apply when the deal involves two companies from different countries. The main points of difference relate to the choice of applicable legal system, generally that of the seller's country, and of the arbitration chamber for dealing with conflicts. All other items such as the mode and currency of payment (cash or shares), no-competition clause or retention of personnel are similar to those for a domestic M&A. As far as the design is concerned, the choice is either to maintain the acquired company's existing name and organization or to integrate it within the organization of the acquirer. Another aspect of design is the degree of autonomy that the acquired company will enjoy within the new owner.

5 Implementation: the integration phase

The integration phase starts once deals have been negotiated and the acquisition or merger decided. All researchers consider this phase of M&As as the most important, and the major source of failure when not handled properly. Table 8.2 summarizes the main sources of failure and their effects.

Table 8.2 Failures in the integration process

Source of failure in integration process	Effects
Lack of strategic direction	Actions and decisions not understood Resistance to change Uncoordinated decisions
Lack of integration plan	Improvisation Time lost Anxiety not reduced Slow response to events
Leadership vacuum	Anxiety not reduced Bureaucratic wrangles Political in-fighting
Determinism (stubborn implementation of the integration plan)	Trying to impose 'pre-fabricated' solutions Lack of flexibility to solve unexpected problems Arrogant behaviour from acquirers' employees Discouragement of front-line staff
Lack of communication	Anxiety not reduced Fears and rumours
Cultural mishandling	Stereotyping clashes, 'them and us' syndrome Politicking Disengagement
Lack of operational focus	Too much talk, not enough action Lack of concrete results No 'quick wins' to boost morale and speed process
Loss of key management talent	Less productive workforce Negative signal to internal and external stakeholders
Wrong synergies	Loss of efficiency Dysfunctional operations
Waste of financial resources, lack of buy-in	No motivation, passivity Politicking

Sources: Authors' own from text in Haspeslagh and Jemison (1991); Mitchell and Holmes (1996); Viscio et al. (1999); Habeck et al. (2000).

Ultimately, the factors shown in Table 8.2 lead to value destruction instead of value creation. This is the reason why a proper integration process needs to be put in place, as we shall explore in the next section.

Integration framework

The integration process is structured in three phases:

- An integration framework leading to an integration plan
- Transition management
- Strategic consolidation.

An integration framework is needed as a road map for implementing a merger. Since the post-merger phase is a period of intense anxiety and uncertainty for the employees, suppliers and distributors of the companies involved, it is important that a framework guides the management of the process. Various frameworks have been offered by academics and consultants and they belong to two broad categories:

- Linear frameworks are step-by-step or checklist approaches to integration that apply to all M&As. Figure 8.6 illustrates one such framework.

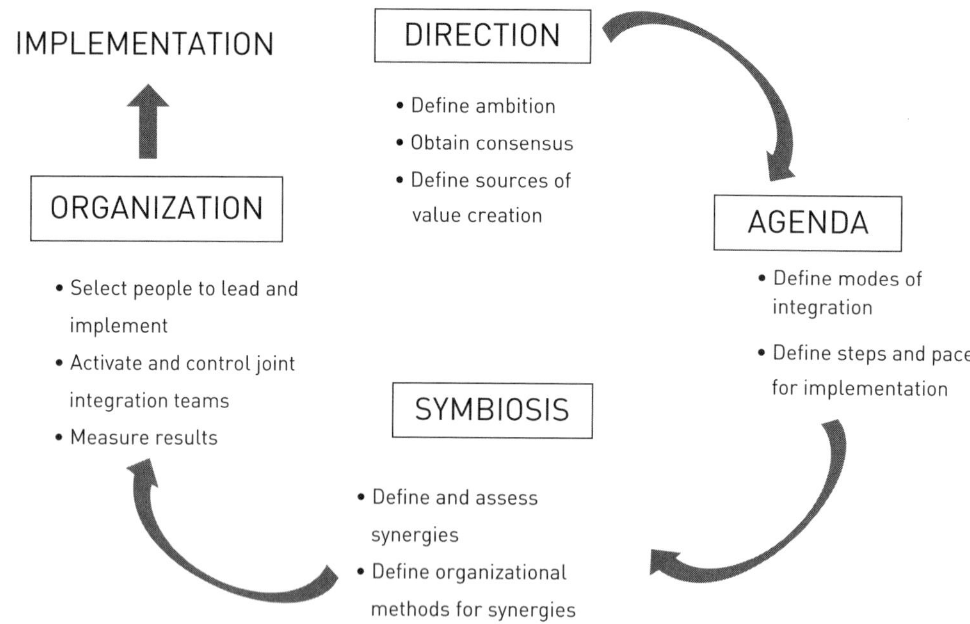

Figure 8.6 A model of a step-by-step integration framework
Source: Authors' adapted from Viscio et al. (1999).

- Contingent frameworks that differentiate integration processes according to environmental and strategic factors. This type of framework does not assume a unique approach to integration. We present here the contingent framework developed by Philippe Haspeslagh and William Jemison (1991).

In their contingent framework, Haspeslagh and Jemison identified three modes of integration, depending on:

- The degree of required operational interdependencies between the two companies that are needed to achieve synergies. For instance, the rationalization of manufacturing or the transfer of competencies between companies.
- The degree of required organizational autonomy that the acquired company would need because of the difference in market and environment conditions with the acquirer; for instance, an acquisition in a different business or country.

The three integration modes that Haspeslagh and Jemison identified (see Figure 8.7)[12] are:

- The preservation mode of integration
- The absorption mode of integration
- The symbiotic mode of integration.

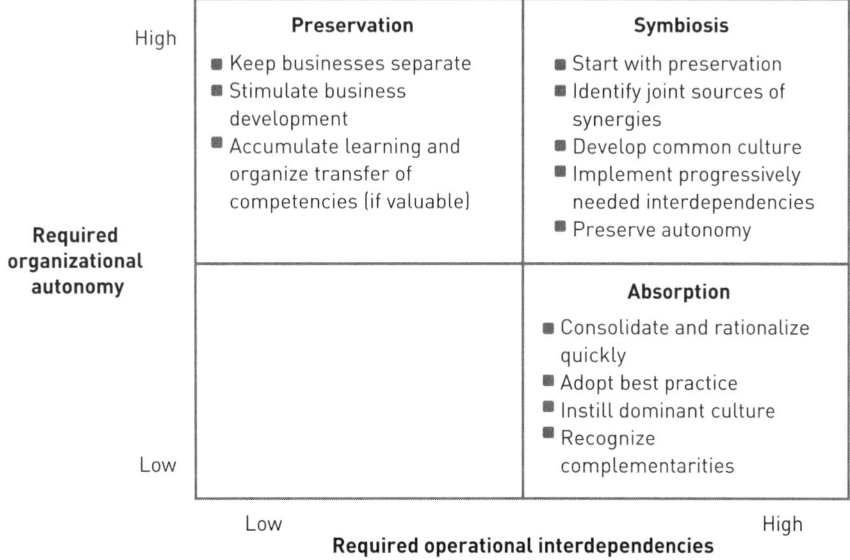

Figure 8.7 Contingent integration modes
Source: Adapted from Haspeslagh and Jemison (1991).

The preservation mode fits with situations in which very few operational synergies can be gained and the business context calls for a large degree of autonomy in decision making, as in the case of diversification or option acquisitions. Since no benefits from interdependencies are to be expected and no major value can be brought in by forcing the integration of processes, assets and decision making, the key objective is first to 'preserve' the identity and autonomy of the acquired company, keeping in place, as far as possible, the existing management and learning progressively the 'rules of the game' of the business. The value here essentially comes from an enlargement of markets and products as well from the transfer of resources or new competencies. In this mode, you should not try to expedite the transfer of new competencies until you have understood their logic and their impact on the organization and culture of the recipient company. Transfer of resources comes essentially from the injection of capital or stimulation of business development by giving access to logistical, IT or distribution facilities to the acquired company. Transfer of people has to be done more for learning than for controlling purposes in such cases. The danger of this mode of integration is being confronted by a 'weak' management team in the acquired company that behaves opportunistically in siphoning off the resources of the acquirer. This was the case in the mid-1980s when the UK's Midland Bank acquired a Californian financial company.[13]

The absorption mode of acquisitions takes place when value is expected from the realization of operational synergies in companies operating in similar business contexts. The objective here is to achieve the necessary consolidation and rationalization as rapidly as possible. Since the businesses are very similar, the top management of the acquirer and of the merging firm is competent to rapidly find sources of savings and to understand which best practices to adopt. As mentioned earlier, this rationalization may raise some practical difficulties in the case of 'equal mergers' when duplicated functions have to be eliminated. The ultimate objective, as the case of SmithKline Beecham illustrates, is to back up the 'Now we are one' credo by rapidly creating a common culture.[14]

Finally the symbiotic mode of acquisitions seeks to balance interdependencies and autonomy. This is often the case in cross-border horizontal acquisitions where a lot of value could be gained from the achievement of synergies but the differences in contexts require a high degree of autonomy. In this mode, the starting point is to use a preservation mode and to find jointly the real sources of synergies and their practicalities. This approach was used when Air France acquired the majority shareholding of the Dutch airline KLM but kept the entities separated from the marketing and legal point of view, organizing synergies only for the procurement of certain items (fuel), rationalization of routes and frequent flyer programmes.

Integrating the companies: the transition phase

Whatever the mode of integration, the critical phase in any merger or acquisition is the transition phase. Immediately after a merger or acquisition, the various stakeholders of the acquired or merged firms are in a state of shock, or at least anxiety, and operations may suffer from uncertainties that grew during the pre-acquisition phase. In Asia Pacific, for instance, during the late 1990s, when Western firms made a lot of acquisitions of financially strapped companies, the situation required a fast turnaround. The transition period is the time for the acquirer or the merging partners to establish their credibility and demonstrate their ability to manage the new concern.

Eight main issues need to be solved at this stage:

- The appointment of an executive team that is capable of leading the integration process and managing the interface between the two companies.

- The expression of a clear sense of purpose, demonstrating to stakeholders that the acquisition or the merger was well planned.
- The focus on concrete operational results that motivate employees and distract them from destructive rumours.
- The development of a mutual understanding, bridging or palliating the cultural gap.
- The demonstration of respect for the acquired company personnel, avoiding arrogant behaviour and preventing the 'brain drain' of valuable employees.
- The installation of measurement tools to measure and control progress.
- The creation of a winning spiral that reinforces a sense of success and achievement.
- The demonstration of credibility that reassures stakeholders and reduces anxiety.

Appointment of an executive team and interface management

In the case of a merger, the critical issue is to install a management team that is capable of understanding the cultures of both parties and transforming them into a new culture. Most of the time this change will be demonstrated by a new brand that may or may not combine the two names of the founding companies: Aventis in the case of Rhône-Poulenc and Hoechst, or SmithKline Beecham. Personnel problems (who is in charge?) need to be sorted out before the beginning of the transition phase, at least for the key roles, to avoid confusion. The projected merger between SKB and Glaxo Wellcome could not be carried through because of disagreements over choosing the CEO of the new entity. This problem did not arise when SmithKline and Beecham merged.

In acquisitions, the critical issue is to trade off the need to control against the need to preserve the key contacts and knowledge of the previous management team. There is also the need to make sure that the appointed management team will be an efficient interface between the acquired company and the foreign acquirer. The best way to achieve an efficient interface is to appoint, as managing director, an executive or a team of executives having the capabilities to understand the cultures of both the seller and the buyer organization, and to serve as a bridge between the newly acquired entity and the new owners.

Clear sense of purpose

Anxiety and resistance reduction can best be achieved if the new management communicates credible goals, demonstrating to stakeholders that the merger or the acquisition was well planned, thus reassuring them of a determination to lead the company to success. Systematic and structured communication campaigns need to be organized. Through meetings with managers and employees, publications or social events, the new management can disseminate the main messages: what are the objectives? What direction is the company going to take?

Operational focus

Focusing the attention on concrete operational details and performance targets has two major advantages. Firstly, it is likely to ease the uncertainty created by the takeover by demonstrating that the acquired or newly created company is still in business. As in the case of alliances, discussed earlier, one of the most powerful methods is to create integration teams. Task forces are appointed, combining personnel from the acquirer and acquired companies for each of the key operational activities (accounting, purchasing, quality and so on). The working party is asked to discuss and propose concrete solutions to operational aspects: what software to use for inventory control, what methods to adopt in order to recover ongoing receivables, how to deal with distributors, what the possibilities are of cost reduction in logistics and so on. The advantage of such an approach is that it gives people a tangible sense of participation in the integration process. It also helps to develop mutual understanding among the employees of both organizations.

Secondly, such teams can also rapidly detect and correct any intrinsic weaknesses in the acquired organization. Rapid turnaround is vital, and this is a means of establishing confidence in, and demonstrating the visible benefits of, the acquisition. Effectiveness is more important than optimized efficiency: a quick minor gain is more important at this stage than a slow major one. This is the reason why the use of integration teams to put in place practical solutions to practical problems is so useful. The involvement of technical and administrative or commercial middle management is critical here, because their technical expertise, if properly combined, can bring quick results.

Mutual understanding and respect

Cross-cultural issues are likely to arise, especially in cross-border mergers. The ability of the two entities to understand each other is critical for the success of any integration. The objective at the transition phase is not so much to merge the two cultures as to create a climate of mutual understanding. The kind of culture that will surface from the merger is contingent upon the mode of acquisition. A preservation mode will not attempt to blend the two cultures but on the contrary will keep them separate, while absorption would seek to create a common culture.[15] Mutual understanding is enhanced when the acquiring company's staff and executives show respect for the employees of the acquired company and are sensitive to cultural differences and avoid behaving like the 'conquerors' of a besieged city. The risks are high if the acquirers come and impose their viewpoints, their methodologies and work processes, as if the merged company's practices were not worth considering. Acquirers should instill a climate of mutual understanding by studying carefully the existing practices of the acquired company, and seeking opinions from its employees before introducing change.

Measurement and control

Talking with facts and figures helps communication, allows a measure of improvement and reduces the scope for 'cultural excuses'. These cultural excuses are used to cover up difficulties or disagreements, and are based on impressionistic or stereotypical judgements. The collation of marketing, operational and financial hard facts and figures is a necessary condition for an efficient and productive dialogue.

In the case of the merger between SmithKline and Beecham, a specific methodology was introduced in the integration team to guide the process and to measure its progress.

Winning spiral

The search for tangible and immediate performance improvement should also be on the agenda of the transition-period management. 'Quick wins' usually derive from the joint efforts of the integration teams, as illustrated in the case of Renault–Nissan (see Chapter 8). Rapid performance improvements in quality, costs and market success give people a sense of achievement and enhance confidence in the whole acquisition process.

Credibility

Confidence is not likely to be established if the various stakeholders do not perceive that what the new owners say, and do, is credible. Credibility relies essentially on the quality of the people who are put in place to run the company, and the perception of their real power within the mother organization. It is essential that managers appointed to the acquired company work closely with central headquarters to make sure that the acquisition is well supported from the top, and that sufficient resources are devoted to making it work.

Integrating the companies: the consolidation phase

The consolidation phase sees the final integration of the two companies and the definition of respective strategic roles within the merged company. In the case of a merger, it consists of creating and finalizing a new organizational structure in which the merging firms dissolve themselves into the new design. SmithKline and Beecham, with the programme of a 'Simply Better' way and a strategic vision of the new company under the umbrella of 'global healthcare', achieved this after one year.

In the case of a cross-border acquisition, the consolidation phase consists of providing the acquired company with a strategic identity and making sure that it has a clearly defined role in the overall regional or global strategy of the acquirer. Employees, governments and the local community may see the acquisition generally as a foreign intrusion, perhaps even reminiscent of an old colonial past. During the transition phase described earlier, the purpose was to instill confidence in the various stakeholders about the will and capabilities of the acquirer to contribute to the development of the firm. At the consolidation phase, there is a need to confirm that the acquisition is not only a trading of assets or a good bargain, but also a real strategic move in which the acquired firm has a role to play. This gives employees a sense of direction and self-esteem. The acquired firm's employees must feel that they are not pawns, but strategic partners, who are part of a strategic vision and essential in achieving it. One of the best methods is to give the firm some responsibilities in leading strategic initiatives in terms of business or product developments. In the case of Lenovo's acquisition of the computer arm of IBM, IBM was given strategic leadership for the global development of PCs.

The second challenge is to make the acquired company part of the family by plugging it into the existing network of knowledge and competencies. This is achieved through secondment of personnel to other subsidiaries, participation in conferences and seminars, and by teamwork in various operational areas where transfer of competencies can add real value. Control has to be exercised without stifling entrepreneurial benefits. The ideal situation is to rely on most of the existing senior and middle-management talent already existing in the acquired company and to support it with adequate training and reward. An important consideration is the practice of 'fair process'[16] that gains the loyalty and commitment of managers. Fair process is a management practice based on combining those integration principles that are advantageous to both efficiency and local entrepreneurship. This has also the tremendous benefit of buying in the loyalty of the employees, and the goodwill of governments and local communities. In this way the acquirer positions itself as neither an intruder nor an invader, but an insider.

MINI-CASE 8.1

The long road of global mergers in the telecoms equipment industry

On 16 April 2015 Nokia announced that it would buy Alcatel-Lucent for $16.6 billion. This announcement marked the latest in a swirl of global mergers and acquisitions in the fast-evolving telecoms equipment industry.

The telecommunications equipment industry produces products and services that are used to support telecommunication services: wireless and landline infrastructure equipment (such as cables, routers, exchanges), as well as handsets and mobile phones. Since the invention of the telephone by Alexander Graham Bell the telecommunication industry has been divided into two segments: the equipment and the services. Originally, in many countries, the services operators were national government-owned companies. In the USA, the American Telegraph and Telephone Company was involved in both segments. In other parts of the world, national operators bought equipment from national or nationally based producers. Hence the development of strong national equipment producers: Ericsson in Sweden, Alcatel in France, Nortel in Canada, NEC in Japan and Nokia in Finland. The 1960s saw a series of developments that transformed the industry, and still affect it today.

First, technological development such as digitalization, the opening of trade barriers and deregulation created the full or partial denationalization of operators, while economies of scale pushed firms toward concentration of competition.

Second, the internet revolution introduced new technologies and products such as routers, giving rise to crucial new markets that were captured by new players such as Cisco in the USA or Huawei in China.

Third, mobile technology saw the creation of a new type of internet-based technology: the smartphone, as initiated by Apple and Samsung, modified the competitive landscape.

This is the rapidly evolving background against which the acquisition of Alcatel-Lucent by Nokia took place.

Alcatel, created in 1879, was originally a giant French conglomerate involved in power generation, transportation equipment, and shipbuilding and telecommunications equipment. In 1992, the non-telecoms businesses were divested and Alcatel concentrated on telecommunications.

In the USA, Lucent was spun off from American Telegraph and Telephone (ATT), which itself had been created in 1876 under the name of the Bell Company.

Both Alcatel and Lucent were affected by the bursting of the internet bubble in 2001, seeing revenues and profit decline as telephone operators cut costs. In 2006 Alcatel and Lucent merged. The two companies had very different cultures and neither Alcatel nor Lucent had strong products in wireless technologies. Changes in management and reorganizations were not sufficient to keep a strong position in the telecoms equipment industry dominated by Cisco, Huawei, Apple and Samsung.

Nokia, founded in 1865 as a pulp and paper company, developed as an industrial conglomerate involved in rubber and cables. The mobile phone business, created in 1979, achieved global predominance in the 1990s with its digital cellular handsets, overtaking Motorola as the world number one producer of mobile phones. In 2007 its global market share was 30 per cent. However, Nokia did not manage to break into the smartphone industry dominated by Apple's iPhones and Samsung's Android. By 2011, Nokia's market share in mobile phones had declined from 30 per cent to 14 per cent. Despite cost cutting, Nokia was unable to make its mobile phone business profitable again. The company decided to sell this division to Microsoft and concentrate on the supporting equipment business. Hence the decision to acquire Alcatel-Lucent. However the integration of the two companies proved to be difficult, hence the decision to cut 1,233 jobs in French in 2020, creating an uproar in French political circles.

Questions:

1 What pushed those giant companies to join forces?

2 Did Nokia made a good decision in acquiring Alcatel-Lucent?

Global alliances and joint ventures

Strategic alliances in a global context

An alliance can be defined as the sharing of capabilities between two or more firms with a view to enhancing their competitive advantages and/or creating new business without losing their respective strategic autonomy. What makes an alliance strategic is that the sharing of capabilities, such as R&D, manufacturing or marketing, affects the long-term competitiveness of the firms involved and implies a relatively long-term commitment of resources by partners.

According to economists, a joint effort involving the contributions of separate firms can be organized either through a market contract, such as a buyer–supplier contract, or through the merger of capabilities under a single management control, as in the case of a merger, an acquisition or an internal development. An alliance falls somewhere in between, when either full control by one partner is not feasible for legal or practical reasons, or when a contract is difficult to draw up because of the uncertainties involved. As a consequence, a strategic alliance has been sometimes defined as 'a governance structure involving an incomplete contract between separate firms and in which each partner has limited control'.[17] An alliance represents an incomplete contract to the extent that 'it cannot specify fully what each party should do under every conceivable condition' and, therefore, requires that both parties engage in some form of trusting, open-ended relationship in which decision making is shared in order to best allocate resources and distribute the outcome of the joint activity according to the prevailing business conditions.

International business and the pressure for globalization often make alliances necessary. In the global context, four types of alliance can be distinguished, which depend on the scope (global or local) and the object (market access or capabilities enhancing), as in Figure 8.8.

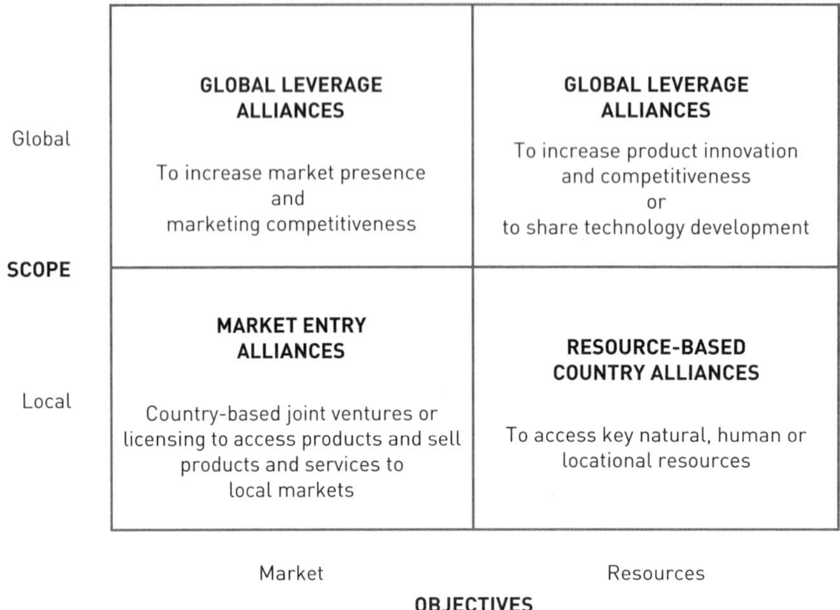

Figure 8.8 Various types of alliance in a global context

A global alliance would be one in which the objective is either to develop a global market presence (global reach alliance) or to enhance the worldwide competitive capabilities of the firms (global leverage alliance).

A local alliance would be one in which the objective for a foreign company is either to penetrate a local market (alliance for market entry) or to have access to a set of resources available in a particular country (resource-based country alliance).

Global and local alliances can take the form of joint ventures in which the partners share the capital of a legal business entity or of long-term contractual agreements.

Global alliances versus local alliances

Global alliances are much more complex and subtle in their strategic and economic scope than traditional local alliances or local joint ventures. Doz and Hamel (1998) distinguish three broad types of strategic alliance:[18]

- Market reach (what Doz and Hamel call 'co-option') are alliances of competitors, distributors and suppliers in the same industry pooling their capabilities with a view to spanning world markets (the search for 'global reach'), to establish a common standard, or to share some capabilities in order to increase marketing effectiveness. Airline alliances such as ONEWORLD, SKYTEAM or STAR represent good examples of such alliances.

- Global leverage alliances are alliances of firms that join their respective unique but complementary capabilities to create a business or develop new products or technology. What characterizes this type of alliance is that each partner contributes a unique asset, resource or competency. Combined together, the partners can realize all the capabilities needed for business development. Airbus and GE-SNECMA in the aerospace industry are examples of such alliances.
- The third form of alliance, learning alliances, is a particular form of agreement that serves as a vehicle for know-how transfer between partners. A classic example is the (now-defunct) alliance formed between Toyota and General Motors (GM), called the NUMMI project, in which the fundamental purpose for GM was to learn 'lean' manufacturing processes and for Toyota to learn how to operate in the highly unionized North American environment. Learning alliances can also be found in the multiple partnerships developed between pharmaceutical firms and biotech companies or in the telecom/internet industries.

Global strategic alliances differ from local joint ventures in four main aspects:

- First, they differ not only in their geographical scope – local versus global – but also in the complexity of their strategic objectives. While in the case of country-based joint ventures the objectives are straightforward, these are less obvious in the case of strategic alliances. Very often, market objectives are combined with technological learning or strategic options. Hidden agendas are more often present in strategic alliances than in joint ventures.
- Local joint ventures are based on a simple complementary scheme – market access against technology transfer – while strategic alliances have a more complicated strategic architecture. Often there is a mixture of complementary capabilities, consolidation of certain activities as well as technology transfer from both sides.
- The valuation of strategic alliances is more difficult than for local joint ventures since they frequently involve contributions in intangible assets and know-how, and in most situations they take place in new and volatile products or processes.
- Finally, in local joint ventures the value is created by the venture and distributed to the partner under the form of dividends or transfer pricing. In a strategic alliance value is created not only in the alliance but also outside the alliance through the applied learning that partners can utilize in other products of their own.

Local alliances (often referred to as joint ventures) have been traditional vehicles for market entry since 1945 in countries that aimed to welcome value-adding productive activities to their economy, while still protecting their natural resources and promoting the strategic development of national firms. Japan in the 1950s, and South Korea, China, Indonesia and India in the 1960s are among the countries that have systematically encouraged the formation of international joint ventures between foreign investors and local firms. Although in these countries the legal requirements for joint ventures have been relaxed somewhat, a joint venture mindset remains. The logic of these joint ventures is simple: it consists of an exchange of a market or resources for technology. Foreign investors are invited to import their products, processes and management technologies alongside their capital in exchange for entry into the domestic market or access to key natural resources. The value created by these local alliances is straightforward: the value for the foreign partner is an increase in market penetration and a set of profits coming from various sources – dividends, transfer prices, management fees. The value for the local partner is an increase in know-how, a flow of dividends and other indirect cash flow such as rental fees, local procurement and so on.

A joint venture is an ambiguous concept because it embraces several forms of partnership, although most of the time a joint venture is a separate legal entity in which two or more partners invest tangible and intangible capital. Some countries, such as China, have set up the concept of 'contractual joint ventures' that are a hybrid form of equity and project partnership agreement, but these are relatively limited and in practice the implications of their management are very similar to equity joint ventures. In emerging markets, joint ventures have in the past been the main form of foreign direct investment (FDI) and this remains the case in some countries such as India.

Understanding the strategic context and spelling out the strategic value of an alliance

Framework for analysis

The study of strategic alliances can be divided into four major steps, as shown in Figure 8.9:

- Understanding the strategic context and spelling out the strategic value of an alliance
- Partner or target analysis
- Negotiation and design
- Implementation.

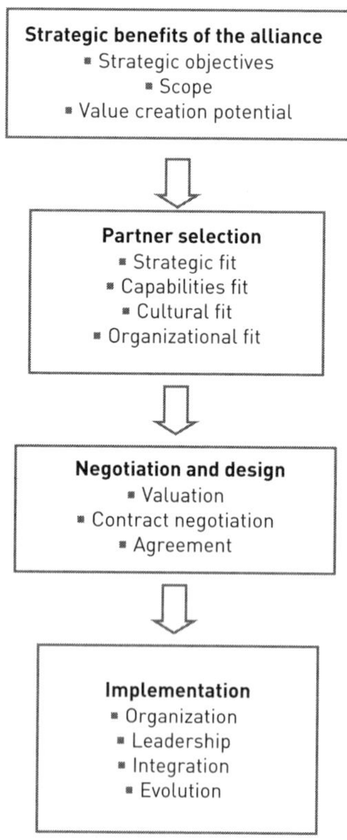

Figure 8.9 Framework for the analysis of strategic alliances

In order to discuss in detail these different steps, we will take the example of the long-lasting strategic alliance between the Japanese company, Nissan, and the French company, Renault.

Strategic context

The starting point of any alliance analysis is a deep understanding of the industry drivers and competitive forces that shape the prevailing position of the partners and the challenges they confront. In the case of Renault and Nissan, both companies had a strong strategic reason to enter into an alliance and neither of them was capable of doing it alone. Renault was a regional player that wanted to reach a global scope while Nissan was on the verge of bankruptcy and needed a solvent partner.

From there the second step consists of determining a) the strategic objectives of the alliance, that is, what the partnership is expected to achieve; and b) setting the value expected from the alliance and calculating the sources of value creation potential.

Table 8.3 describes the main strategic objectives pursued in various types of alliances.

Table 8.3 Main strategic objectives pursued in various types of alliance

	Market reach alliances	Global leverage alliances	Learning alliances
Objectives	• Market reach or access • Increase marketing competitiveness through pooling of capabilities	• Develop new products • Specialization of capabilities • Complementary capabilities	• Development of new technology and learning from partner
Economic value	• Economies of scale • Economies of scope • Increased revenues • Increased customer responsiveness • Increased quality	• Maximization of asset utilization by each partner • Faster to market • Product development (new revenue streams)	• Skills development

Value potential

The value potential of the alliance is calculated on the basis of the potential benefits it brings to the alliance partners involved. In theory, it is a straightforward calculation consisting of two steps (see Figure 8.10 and numerical worked example shown in Insert 8.2):

- Step one: value created by the alliance
- Step two: value captured by each partner.

The value created by the alliance is driven by four factors:

- Revenues generated by the alliance through volume of sales
- Revenues generated by the alliance through the ability to command a high differentiated price
- Future revenues or cost benefits coming from joint R&D products or processes
- Cost benefits resulting from economies of scale and scope.

The value captured by partners comes from:

- Distribution of the alliance profits when the alliance is structured as an autonomous economic entity
- Profit generated by the sales of intermediary products, components or services by the alliance
- Profits derived from products or processes developed thanks to the alliance – increased revenues or cost reductions coming from the alliance because of increased market reach or economies of scale or scope
- Profits coming from other products whose sales are boosted because of the alliance.

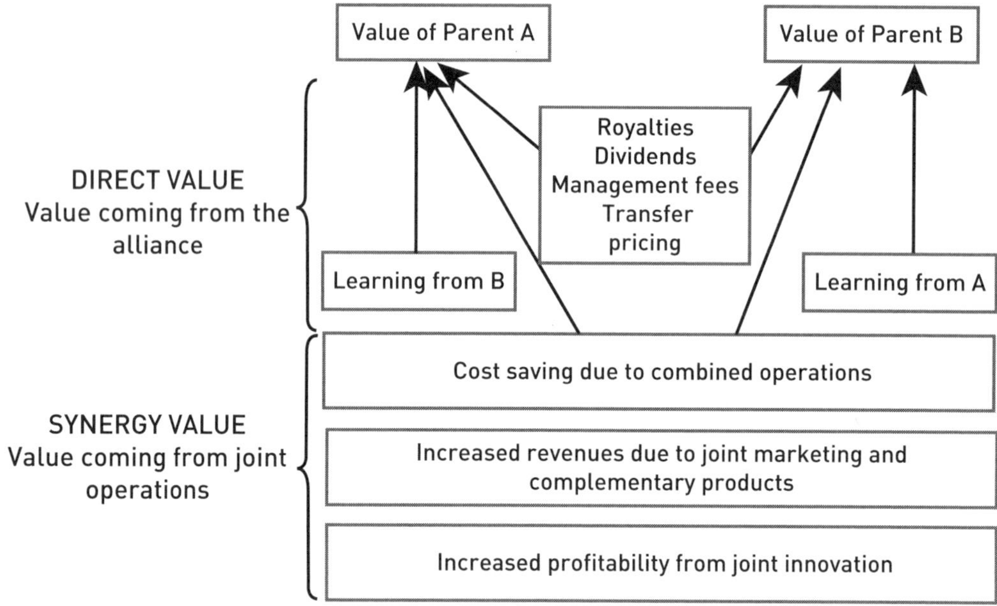

Figure 8.10 Economic value potential for each partner in an alliance

Insert 8.2 Numerical example of value creation and distribution in a joint venture

Company AB is a country-based joint venture between A (the foreign investor) and B (a local partner). The joint venture agreement states that:

- The invested capital is $2,000,000 and the shareholding is divided 60 per cent for A and 40 per cent for B
- A is to receive 7 per cent royalties on sales of AB for technology transfer
- A is to be compensated $50,000/year for detachment of personnel costed at $20,000
- A also sells its own products via the joint venture, on which it makes 1 per cent net profit
- B is to lease out its land and factory for a net contribution of $30,000/year
- B uses its distribution network for selling A and AB products. For this it takes a 10 per cent commission

- Thanks to technology transfer B is able to improve its productivity and to reduce the costs of its own products by 10 per cent

What is the value created and the distribution of this value in Year One of AB's operations? Assume that the distributed profits of the joint venture are 20 per cent on $2,000,000 sales of AB products plus $800,000 sales of A's own products distributed by AB. Separately B sells $1,000,000 of its own product.

Table 8.4 Value creation and distribution

Value created ($000) and Distribution of Value	A	B	Total
Distributed profit (20% of 200000)	240	160	400
Royalties on sales for technology transfer (7% of 2000000)	140		140
Detachment of personnel	50		50
Profit for A from products sold through joint venture (12% of A product sales)	96		96
Profits made on sales of A own products via the joint-venture (1% of 800000)	80		80
Rental of land/factory by B ($30000/year)		30	30
Commission on total sales for B (10% of 2000000)		280	280
Productivity improvement on B's own products (10%)		100	100
TOTAL VALUE	606	570	1080

This example shows that the value extracted by partners in a joint venture goes far beyond the simple distribution of dividends.

However, whatever the type of alliance, the value created by global alliances is more difficult to assess than for a traditional joint venture for market entry or natural resource access. According to Doz and Hamel (1998), the reasons for this are:

- Partners bring hard-to-value non-traded or intangible resources, assets or competencies
- The breakdown of relative contributions is often hard to assess
- Most of the time, much of the value accrues outside the alliance
- The relative value to each partner may shift over time
- Partners may not declare what real value they seek or receive from the alliance.[19]

Despite these difficulties, it is advisable to try to measure the value expected from the alliance since it can serve as a yardstick to assess its success or failure.

In the case of Renault–Nissan, the value of the alliance came from the synergies generated by common purchasing, common platforms, joint development and cross-manufacturing.

Partner analysis

Partner analysis consists of determining the extent to which the relationship with the proposed partner is viable and valuable. In a similar fashion as the fit analysis described earlier for mergers and acquisitions

(Figure 8.3), partner analysis consists in determining whether there is a fit between the company and its potential partner in four domains (Figure 8.11):

- Strategic fit
- Capabilities fit
- Cultural fit
- Organizational fit.

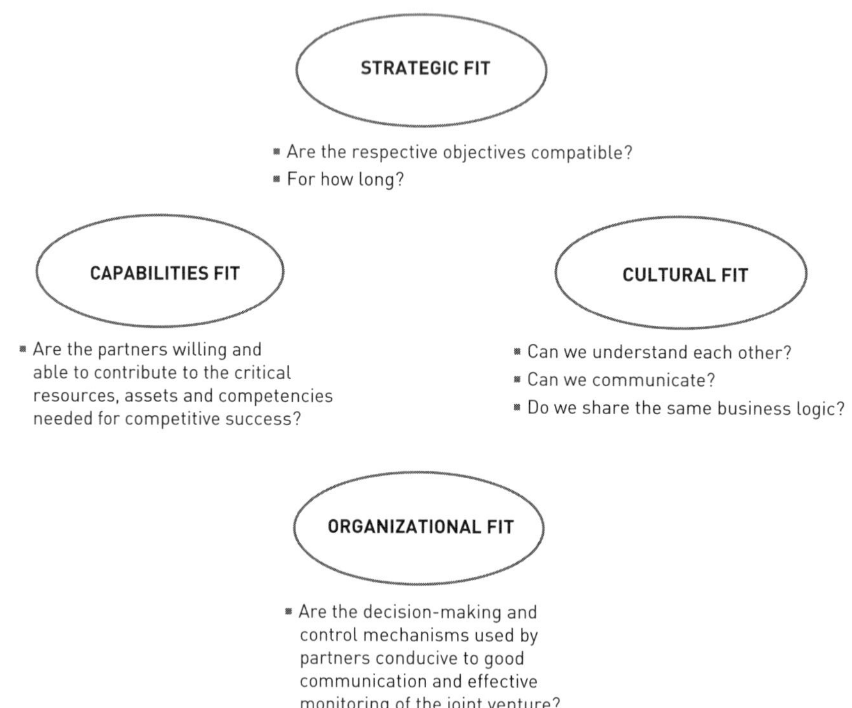

Figure 8.11 Partner's fit analysis in strategic alliances

Strategic fit

The purpose of strategic fit analysis is to assess the degree of compatibility among the partners, given their respective explicit or implicit strategic objectives. When stated objectives are explicit the analysis is simple, but when there are implicit objectives (a hidden agenda) behind the stated objectives, the analysis requires an in-depth study of the partner's strategic context – their competitive position and managerial power structure – to unravel the 'real' expectations of the other party. An analysis of strategic fit implies the following assessments:

- Criticality of the alliance for the partners
- The relative competitive position of partners
- The compatibility in strategic agendas.

Answering two very simple questions will evaluate the criticality of the alliance for each partner:

- How important is the alliance for the partners?
- Do they need an alliance to achieve their objectives?

The answers to these two questions can be represented by two different matrices, as in Figure 8.12, where we can assess the degree of commitment expected from partners to the alliance.

The importance of the alliance for partners is determined on the basis of the contextual analysis done earlier. If both partners have a strong strategic stake in the business, you can expect a high commitment that is favourable to a good fit. If the strategic importance is unbalanced (it is important for one partner but not for the other), there will be a divergence in commitment and the fit will be more questionable. When both partners have a low strategic stake, you may not expect a high degree of commitment from either partner, which by itself represents a fit, but not a favourable one for the future of the alliance. We may wonder, under such conditions, why they should even consider a strategic partnership. The answer to that question can be found in the theory of real options.[20] Partners may consider the alliance as a forward option for a future decision. In such a case, the degree of commitment may be positive although there is a question mark over what will happen when the option has to be called in or forfeited.

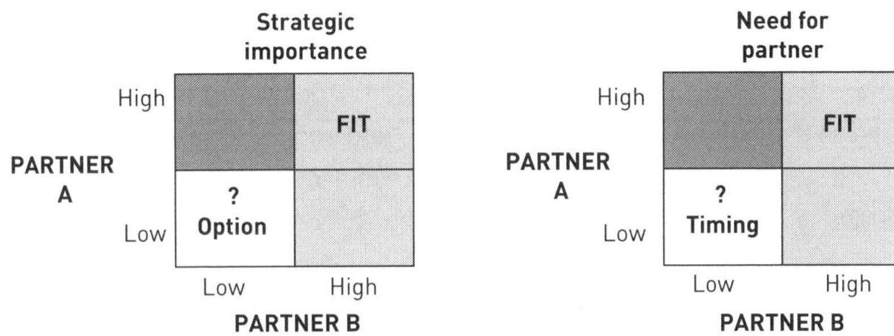

Figure 8.12 Assessing the strategic fit based on the criticality of the alliance for partners

The ability to go it alone depends on the existing resources – assets and competencies – that each partner possesses at the time, and the degree of time pressure on them. Again, when both parties do not have the necessary capability to venture alone, there is a strong incentive for and commitment to the alliance provided that the capability fit is favourable, as we shall see. Otherwise, an unbalanced situation will create the conditions for a poor fit. When both partners have the capability to proceed alone, the only condition under which the commitment would be favourable is if time pressure obliged them to share the tasks in order to accelerate their business entry. Renault had developed strong capabilities in car design and in an efficient supply chain while Nissan was excellent in engineering and quality management. The car models complemented each other somewhat, and in terms of geographical presence Renault was strong in Europe and Nissan in Asia and the USA.

The relative competitive position of partners is a second important parameter to investigate when assessing a strategic fit. Doz and Hamel (1998: ch. 4) have developed a typology of competitive positions and postulated their mutual degree of fitness depending upon the type of alliance.

They class competitors in three broad categories: leaders (dominant firms in the industry), challengers (second-tier firms in the industry) and laggards (firms which need to catch up). They conclude that alliances among leaders are plagued with problems.

The last part of strategic assessment is the confrontation of the strategic agendas and their resulting expectations. There are four kinds of strategic agenda:

- Venturing agendas
- Extractive agendas
- Sharing agendas
- Options agendas.

In venturing agendas partners have a deliberate desire to engage in collaboration to create a business. Their prime motivation is to see the alliance grow and flourish, and they get their reward from the continuation of a successful partnership.

Extractive agendas have a different logic: the objective is to 'learn' or to 'acquire' capabilities from the partner or from the alliance. The prospects of a fit in such a case are short term: as long as the partners get the necessary capabilities they stick to the alliance, but as soon as the learning or acquisition goal is achieved, the strategic value of the alliance vanishes.

Sharing agendas are limited ones, their prime objective being to maximize efficiency in certain elements of the value chain through economies of scale and scope. Airline alliances are of that nature: they share flight codes, lounges, frequent flyer programmes and sometimes aircraft maintenance.

Options agendas, as noted earlier, are based on the desire for partners to 'have a look' without committing vast amounts of resources, using the alliance as an experimental platform for monitoring the business. As in any option, such an agenda has a time limit, at the end of which partners have to make up their mind: break the alliance and continue alone or continue and expand the alliance.

Figure 8.13 gives a graphical representation of those various types of strategic agendas and their combinations.

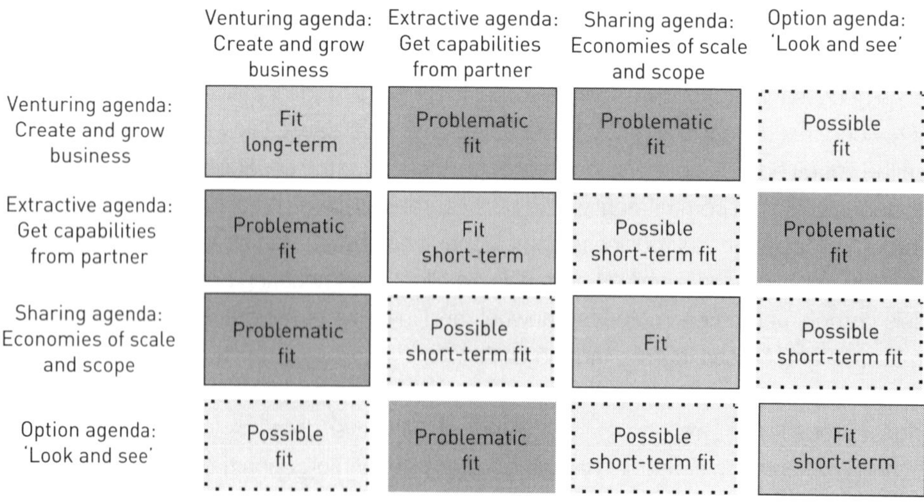

Figure 8.13 Strategic fit against partners' strategic agendas

Capabilities fit

The objective of a capabilities fit analysis is to assess the extent to which partners are capable of contributing to the necessary competitive capabilities of the business. Capabilities fit analysis in the case of strategic alliances and joint ventures is similar to the one described earlier for mergers and acquisitions (see Figure 8.4).

The framework for this analysis is straightforward. It consists of determining the specific contribution that each partner can make to each element of the value chain, based on declared or supposed resource assets and competencies. The last phase of the analysis determines the potential gap to be filled by joint investment before finally making an evaluation of whether the mutual contributions plus the additional investments make the future alliance effective.

Cultural and organizational fits

The assessment of cultural and organizational differences as in the case of mergers and acquisitions are an important part of partner's analysis in strategic alliances. Given the fact that each partner in an alliance keeps its strategic and organizational autonomy, cultural and organizational clashes can affect the long standing of the deal. From a methodological point of view the analysis is similar to the ones described earlier for mergers and acquisitions.

Negotiation and design

Operational scope

One of the first essentials is to agree on the organizational design and the operational content of the alliance. When deciding on the organizational design, the parties have to choose between two approaches according to the degree of operational capabilities they want to give to the alliance structure. There are four generic types of alliance design, depending on whether the structure has full operating capabilities or acts as a broker and also whether it is a market reach, global leverage or a learning alliance (Figure 8.14).

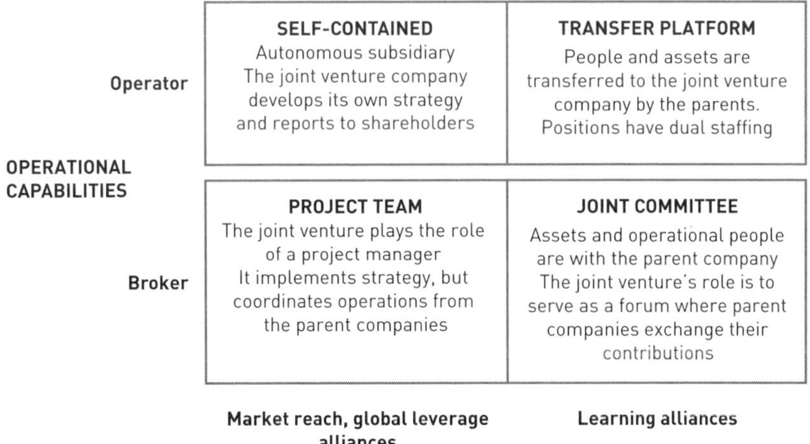

Figure 8.14 Organizational designs in alliances

In broker designs, the alliance structure acts as an intermediary between the partners, which retain their own operational capabilities (resources, assets and competencies). Broker structures can be either in the form of a project management or coordination structure, or alternatively can consist of a series of joint committees. When the alliance is a coalition or a co-specialization, the alliance structure is generally similar to a project team or a coordination structure. Renault–Nissan adopted this design. The partners formed an independent legal entity named Renault–Nissan BV incorporated in Holland, in which each company owned 50 per cent. The role of this joint venture would be to coordinate activities between the two parties. Each company worked on its own R&D, manufacturing and servicing on the basis of a strategic plan decided upfront. This structure owns no assets and the people working in it are essentially relationship managers. In the case of learning alliances, broker designs will consist generally of joint committees. For instance, in the case of the Alza–Ciba-Geigy alliance for advanced drug delivery systems, the design of the partnership was based on the regular meeting of three committees: an audit committee, a joint research board and the board of a series of joint research conferences.[21]

The operator alliance structure owns and operates its own operational capabilities, which are either transferred to it by the parent companies or built and developed by the alliance with capital injected by the parents. Again, an operator design can take two different forms: self-contained or transfer platform.

In self-contained designs, the alliance structure creates economic value by itself and distributes it to the parent shareholders, as in any company. An example of a highly successful alliance of this type can be found with Fuji Xerox, which develops, manufactures and markets products with a high degree of autonomy from the parents.

Transfer platform designs are structures in which the joint venture controls its own resources, assets and competencies and therefore is fully responsible for creating the value. But in such designs, partners allocate engineers and staff to the joint venture with the view of 'learning' from the other partner and from the alliance. As discussed previously, a good example is the NUMMI 50/50 joint venture between Toyota and General Motors. General Motors allocated a factory at Fremont, California, and transferred 2,500 workers plus around 25 engineers to the joint venture. Toyota brought managers and specialists in 'lean' manufacturing systems. NUMMI could be considered as a transfer platform for Toyota to learn how to operate in an American unionized environment, while GM learnt how to implement 'lean' manufacturing systems.

Interface and governance

Deciding on the interface and governance mechanisms for the alliance is probably the most difficult part of the negotiation between partners. Six domains have to be agreed:

- The legal structure and the decision-making mechanisms
- The degree of task integration
- The appointment of executives
- The distribution of value
- The reporting and communication processes
- The conflict resolution mechanisms.

As far as the legal structure is concerned, the majority of alliances will be created under the form of a joint venture company, in which the respective equity shares will be clearly defined and valuations of contributions and results isolated from the parent companies' own accounts. In joint ventures, executive power is granted to a board of directors where each partner has seats corresponding to their equity share. Boards appoint operating executives, who in turn are responsible for producing results with the collaboration of personnel directly recruited by them or 'transferred' by the parent companies. Minority partners may negotiate some 'concurrence' clauses for certain key decisions that give them the right of veto (see below). The articles of association will determine the various elements of the agreement. Figure 8.15 shows the various items that would typically be negotiated and included in a joint venture.

Joint ventures are not the only legal form that alliances can take. Four other types of legal mechanism that are commonly found in global alliances are:

1 Equity participation by one partner in the capital of the other. This type of legal structure is very close to an acquisition, but, in reality, as long as the equity partner does not get full control of the operation, it is still considered to be an alliance.
2 Joint equity participation, in which one partner takes a shareholding in the other partner's capital. This kind of agreement has to be complemented by contractual arrangements that define the scope of the joint activities and their respective valuations. This was the case with the now-defunct alliance between Renault and Volvo. In that case, the joint equity was supposed to be the prelude to a merger that was ultimately refused by Volvo's shareholders.

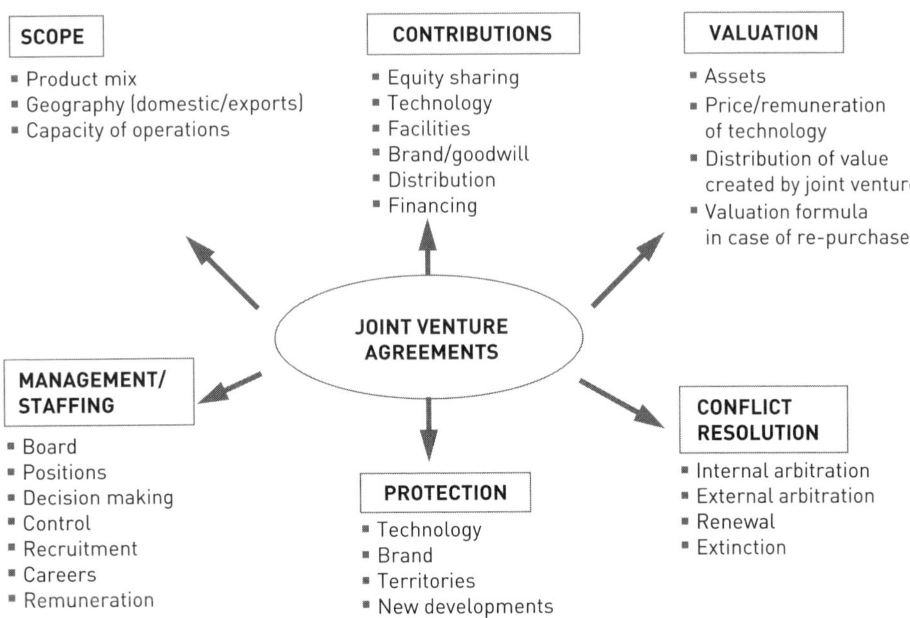

Figure 8.15 Typical items in a joint venture agreement

3 Long-term contract agreements, such as distribution agreements or manufacturing agreements. Cisco, for instance, manufactures 75 per cent of its products with external suppliers with whom it has long-term relationships.

4 R&D joint projects.

Legal structure and decision-making mechanism

When negotiating an alliance agreement, the majority of executives insist on having 'control', meaning that they want to obtain the majority shareholding in a joint venture. Many academic studies have found that this is one of the requirements stated by most managers surveyed. However, research has also found that 'control' is not correlated with 'success'.[22] In fact, a legal majority control only guarantees a fraction of the total control over a company or a set of operations. First, there is the possibility for a minority partner to activate 'concurrence' clauses that may limit the power of the majority and ultimately block decisions. You can perceive intuitively that control is real if, and only if, a person or a group of persons is able positively and negatively to influence behaviour. A majority shareholding does not guarantee that. Some authors have even argued that a 50/50 joint venture arrangement is even better than a majority arrangement because it forces partners to make every necessary effort to make the alliance work.[23]

The degree of task integration

Task integration defines which activities are carried out by the alliance, which ones are carried out separately, and the extent to which activities carried out by each partner need to be integrated. For instance, when the task is to jointly develop a new product, R&D departments often need to be merged, at least partially, while if the alliance is only a sharing of distribution networks, the amount of interdependency between the two networks may be limited. Integration requires coordination and joint work and therefore is likely to demand complex management approaches. Alternatively, if integration is limited, each party fulfils its obligations separately, making coordination straightforward and simple. Limited integration is possible if tasks are defined precisely upfront and the joint output is obtained by 'assembling' the separate outputs with limited interactions. This is a 'plug-in' operation. The synergies are structured only for a certain number of tasks and, except for the procurement of components, most of the other interactions are organized according to a mode of technology transfer. When the task complexity is such that clear separation of job distribution is not possible, then a self-contained joint venture, in which teams are temporarily merged, is the best solution. Otherwise, coordination of interdependencies could prove to be a hurdle.

Appointment of executives

Who to appoint as the alliance leader is often a major factor in the success of the venture, as well as a subject of contention between partners as they negotiate the agreement. Two key issues arise: the amount of parents' transfers and the skills of alliance managers.

Strategist	Initiator	Negotiator	Integrator	Co-ordinator
				▪ Maintain communication among partners
			▪ Lead the post-acquisition integration	
			▪ Create and monitor joint-company teams	
		▪ Organize negotiation process	▪ Inspire confidence	▪ Address potential conflicts
	▪ Form a team	▪ Lead negotiations	▪ Communicate to all parties	
▪ Formulate rationale and need for alliance	▪ Engage in conversations with potential partners	▪ Contribute to planning for the alliance	▪ Focus on short visible wins to maintain momentum	▪ Initiate any necessary changes to own company culture
▪ Draw up a plan	▪ Initiate partner selection	▪ Coordinate the evaluation of business synergies	▪ Show respect (and no arrogance) towards partner employees	
▪ Identify potential partners	▪ Evaluate candidate risks/benefits	▪ Maintain communications with partner	▪ Lead the achievement of operational synergies	▪ Make sure that both parties get expected value from the alliance
▪ Promote alliance internally	▪ Present and defend a partnership plan	▪ Finalize and defend the alliance agreement internally	▪ Build trust	▪ Maintain communication among partners

Figure 8.16 Management skills needed in alliances
Source: Authors' own figure based on personal experience and inspired by Spekeman and Lynn (2000); Yoshino and Rangan (1995); Greve et al. (2013).

Parents' transfer refers to the allocation of managers and staff from each parent to the venture, as opposed to the independent staffing of the alliance structure. When the alliance is a co-specialization or one of reciprocal learning, partners' transfer is expected to be high since the whole purpose is to activate the unique capabilities of partners. Alternatively, when the alliance is a coalition or co-learning (both partners want to learn from the alliance but not necessarily from each other), people transfer is less of an issue.

In the case of transfer, the problem arises of the distribution of functions and roles. One technique, known as the 'shadow' organization, consists of putting a manager from one partner in charge of a function with a manager from the other partner as their deputy. This technique seems appealing because of its apparent fairness, but it is not necessarily effective, since it can reinforce a 'them and us' attitude and leads to a longer decision-making process and possibly more conflicts. In the case of Renault and Nissan, twenty-one Renault managers were transferred to Nissan in order to participate in the Nissan Revival Plan. In addition, French personnel were temporarily detached to the CCTs or the CFTs.

The second important consideration is to select managers with the appropriate skills to manage the alliance.

Several authors have identified the leadership skills needed to manage an alliance.[24] Figure 8.16 gives a summary of their findings. Of particular importance are the communication and negotiation skills of managers in the alliances.

Distribution of value

As mentioned earlier, an alliance creates value and this value has to be distributed to the partners according to an agreed scheme. Owing to the fact that valuation is complex, alliance negotiators often have difficulty in finding a 'fair' mechanism that takes into consideration all the elements that contribute to value. The simplest form is the distribution of profits in a joint venture. This works only if the entire profit is created by the joint venture without any significant input apart from the partners' initial capital. When profit is dependent on inputs provided by the parents, there is a high risk of transfer pricing disputes. In the case of Renault–Nissan there is no issue of value transfer since each company generates its own revenues and profits. As cross-shareholders, each company benefits from the profits generated by the other in proportion to its ownership.

In a revenue-sharing scheme each partner receives the revenues generated by the alliance proportionate to their share of work. Then it is up to each partner to manage its costs and to generate profit. This method implies that there is an upfront agreement on work sharing. If that is the case, the partners are already familiar with the technology involved and have a pretty good awareness of the relative importance of the work to be completed by each party. An example of this type can be found in the case of GE–SNECMA, a long-lasting alliance in the aero-engine industry.[25] Corrective mechanisms were included in case a work discrepancy appeared during the implementation of the alliance.

Reporting and communication processes

Alliance agreements should provide communication platforms so that partners remain informed about the development of the venture. Academic research has stressed the importance of communication at all levels in the success of alliances.[26] The legal forum for communication in a joint venture is the board of directors, but this is not enough. Communication needs to be organized horizontally and vertically among partners and within partners. It is particularly important to involve and engage the people at middle and low levels within each organization. These are the employees who will have to run the operations and, not having been involved in the negotiations, they need to understand the objectives and appreciate the value of making the alliance a success.

In the case of Renault–Nissan, communication is mediated within the CFTs and CCTs under the responsibility of Renault–Nissan BV. A large number of middle-level employees are involved in these committees.

Conflict resolution mechanisms

Friction and conflict are almost inevitable. As will be seen later, disenchantment, frustration and conflict of interests may surface rapidly after the deal is consummated (the 'death valley' problem illustrated in Figure 8.17) or during the life of the alliance.

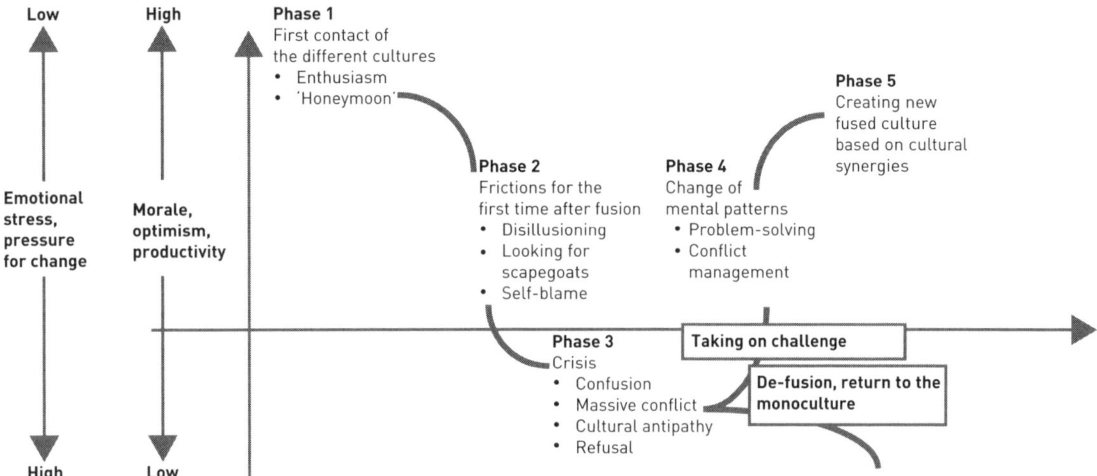

Figure 8.17 The death valley spiral

All contracts include legal provision for conflict management between shareholders in joint ventures by arbitrage clauses. The real problem is not these legal mechanisms – which in many cases are only employed when the two parties have more or less already decided to terminate their agreements – but the difficulty of creating the internal mechanisms for solving problems before they can escalate to the arbitrage stage. In the case of Renault–Nissan, for instance, potential disagreements are dealt with by the joint strategic organization Renault–Nissan BV.

Implementation

The last stage in alliance management, but not the least, is the implementation stage. Two different aspects of implementation have been identified as critical: integration and cooperation, and learning.

Integration and cooperation

Once the alliance has been formed the immediate implementation phase is to put the respective companies and the alliance structure to work so that the teams allocated to the alliance achieve the planned output. This phase is frequently operationalized by 'integration teams'. Integration teams are functional working groups of managers from the different partners who have been assigned the task of identifying and resolving the practical considerations of implementing the alliance. This covers items such as which processes to adopt, which IT platform to install, the kind of measurements to adopt, how to manage relationships with third parties, which accounting system to use and so on. Integration teams are important because they offer the first opportunity to work together in a concrete fashion. Cultural differences are discovered, as well as practical issues that were not anticipated during the negotiation phase. The way these unanticipated issues are handled sets the initial tone for relationships and demonstrates the actual mindset of partners. Since integration teams are staffed with operational people, of whom a large majority did not participate in the alliance negotiations, their attitudes and perspectives have to be 'shaped' by their respective management teams. An 'internal selling job' is often needed to erode fears or misinterpretation of the alliance's value; trade unions have to be convinced that the alliance is not designed to eliminate jobs and cultural stereotypes have to be challenged through internal training sessions.

Despite all these preparatory efforts, what is called the 'death valley' issue often arises. This model was inspired by many global alliances, and is based on the fact that surprises and unanticipated events or behaviour occur frequently during alliance implementation. If not properly prepared, managers may retreat into blaming and stereotyping – particularly cultural stereotyping – instead of coping with the stress and anxiety provoked by any surprises. A vicious spiral then develops (see Figure 8.17) in which communications are shut off and the viability of the alliance is called into question. Since encountering such a 'death valley' scenario is almost inevitable at some point, companies that frequently engage in global alliances should prepare their managers to cope with the situation, to avoid blaming and stereotyping and to look for win–win solutions.

Learning

As we have seen earlier, some types of partnership are specially designed as learning alliances, but all alliances in practice involve some kind of learning. There are two forms of learning:

- Learning from the alliance, or co-learning: what the partners learn within the alliance
- Learning from the partners, or captured learning: what the partners learn *from* each other.

Learning from the alliance[27]

In implementing alliances, partners can learn:

- About the business

- About the tasks
- About partners' expectations and capabilities.

Partners discover jointly the characteristics and trends of markets, the industry and its competitive drivers. This kind of learning is normal in any venture, whether joint or not. The specific issue in the case of a partnership is to put in place the organizational mechanisms for such learning to take place and to be distributed to partners. This is done by setting up and using common databases, and possibly, with the advent of e-business platforms, by integrating the joint venture database with the partner's intranet software. In addition, the alliance structure should organize reflective and analytical forums for joint planning, seminars, conferences and review sessions.

Partners should also be able to redefine their mutual contributions and work processes in the light of new events and changes in business context. Functional committees and operational reviews can facilitate such mutual adjustments. Over time, partners' expectations may change and imbalances in the value distribution may appear. This kind of change is obviously one of the most difficult to handle since a change in expectations may undermine the initial alliance's foundations. Constant monitoring for potential triggers for change in a partner's internal context, such as a new CEO, modification of strategic direction, analyst opinions and so on, helps to predict the likelihood of a shift in expectations. One potential issue in the case of Renault and Nissan would be that one partner becomes highly successful commercially and financially while the other lags behind. Over time that may create an imbalance leading to a reconsideration of the alliance.

Learning from the partner

In 1986 Reich and Mankin published an explosive article titled 'Joint ventures with Japan give away our future'. In a more moderate vein, Doz, Hamel and Prahalad argued in 1989 that Western partners could use alliances to regain competitiveness against Japanese competitors. They gave as an example the case of Thomson Multimedia, which gained expertise in the design and manufacture of video recorders thanks to its alliance with a joint venture company.

In both cases, the arguments were based on 'learning from the partner' in an alliance context. In practice a 'learning from the partner' approach requires two key capabilities: clarity of objectives and organizational receptivity.

Clarity of objectives implies that the company engaged in an alliance for learning should identify clearly what it wants to learn and set up a learning agenda defining the learning sequence. All capabilities cannot be learned at once. Thomson embarked on a step-by-step approach to learning first the assembly of VCR components, and then the ability to design and manufacture next-generation products such as handheld mini video cameras.

Receptivity is the second type of learning capability. It consists of the various internal organization mechanisms that companies engaged in alliances may use to accumulate, retain and transfer knowledge. Table 8.5 gives a list of such weak and strong learning mechanisms.

Table 8.5 Receptivity in learning

Weak learning capabilities	Strong learning capabilities
• No systematic collection of information	• Organized intelligence
• No sharing of information	• Networked internal information exchange
• 'Not invented here' attitudes	• 'Why' attitude, curiosity, search for benchmarking and outside best practices
• No 'organizational memory'	• Planned approach to skill acquisition
• Pressure to achieve only operational/financial results	• Internal training
• Recruitment of people based only on technical professional skills	• Allocation of time and budgets to 'learn' • Recruitment of people based on 'social' as well as professional skills

Global multilateral alliances[28]

Most of the discussions in this chapter have been centred around dyadic alliances involving only two partners. In practice, global companies are often engaged in a multiplicity of alliances, some of them domestic, but the vast majority with 'foreign' partners.

Each product division of multi-business corporations is engaged in multiple alliances, so that if you were to count the total number of strategic partnerships for the whole corporation, you might find several hundred, as in the case of IBM, Motorola or Siemens.

Gomez-Casseres has classed these alliances as 'constellations' in which partners are cooperating in one business segment but possibly competing in another.[29]

Doz and Hamel identify three types of constellation (see Figure 8.18):

- Alliance networks
- Alliance portfolios
- Alliance webs.

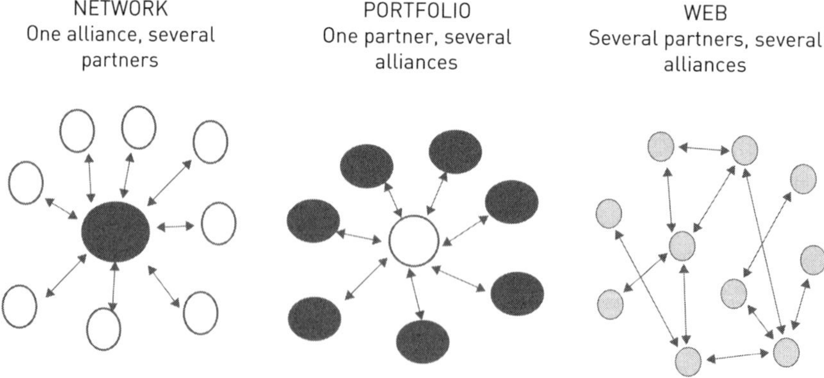

Figure 8.18 Types of alliance constellations

Source: Authors' own figure, based on text of Doz and Hamel (1998).

Alliance networks are those to which partners contribute to increase reach, adopt a common standard or promote a new technology. Visa (credit card), SWIFT (banking) and STAR (airlines) are alliances of this nature. As in a club, several partners contribute and benefit from the alliance provided they subscribe to the rules and discipline of the network. It is a 'one alliance, multiple partners' design.

Alliance portfolios are those in which a company enters a partnership with multiple companies, with different products, technologies or markets. The company deals with its partner as a portfolio, or on a one-to-one basis. There is no interaction among partners, only between partners and the 'core' party. This is a 'one partner, several alliances' design. Nestlé is a good example.

Alliance webs are constellations in which partners contribute and benefit interdependently in a 'several partners, several alliances' design. Since the 1990s, Airbus has functioned as a 'global web'. In an alliance web, you can find some characteristics of alliance networks (a common platform) or of alliance portfolios (one company in the web may have a central nuclear position) but the relationships among partners are more equal and interdependent than in alliance portfolios and even more so than in alliance networks.

Constellations of global partners put a high degree of constraint on companies, because of their complexity and diversity. Managerial challenges can arise at two levels:

- At the alliance level: how to make it work?
- At the partners' level: how to cope with multiple alliances, and in each alliance how to manage the relationships with other parties?

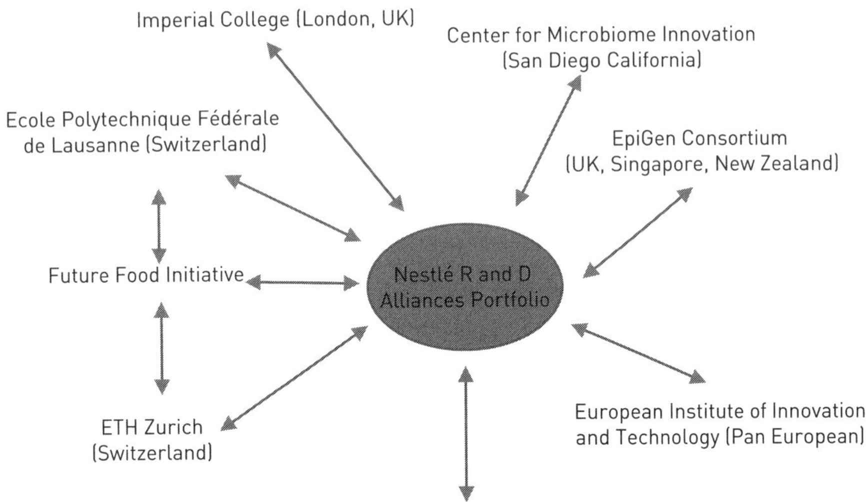

Figure 8.19 Nestlé Alliances Portfolio

Source: https://www.nestle.com/randd/partnerships (accessed 1 August 2020).

Alliance webs are constellations in which partners contribute and benefit interdependently in a 'several partners, several alliances' design. Since the 1990s, Airbus has functioned as a 'global web'. Similarly Arqus, an European universities alliance, is an example of a constellation alliance (Figure 8.20). In an alliance web, you can find some characteristics of alliance networks (a common platform) or of alliance portfolios (one company in the web may have a central nuclear position) but the relationships among partners are more equal and interdependent than in alliance portfolios and even more so than in alliance networks.

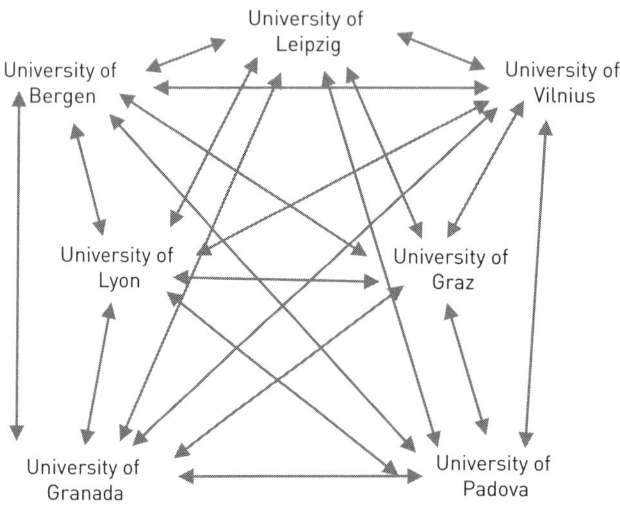

Figure 8.20 Arqus European universities alliances
Source: https://www.arqus-alliance.eu (accessed 1 August 2020).

Constellations of global partners put a high degree of constraint on companies, because of their complexity and diversity. Managerial challenges can arise at two levels:

- At the alliance level: how to make it work?
- At the partners' level: how to cope with multiple alliances, and in each alliance how to manage the relationships with other parties?

Depending upon the type of alliance, the managerial challenges will typically address four kinds of issues: first, alliance creation and mobilization; second, *partners* selection and attraction; third, alliance governance and maintenance; and fourth, partnership leverage and relationships.

1 Alliance creation and mobilization. Both alliance creation and mobilization depend on core companies or on an outsider. This can be a government body or a new technology developer. In the case of a portfolio network the initiative relies on the core company to identify the benefits of those alliances and to 'sell' them to multiple partners on a one-to-one basis. In the case of a platform network the initiative relies on one initial member or a group of members who creates an institutional body

that can be a corporation, as in the case of *Visa*, a cooperative, as in the case of *Skyteam*, or a non-government organization (NGO), as in the case of the *International Olympic Committee*, to which members adhere. When the benefits of the alliance are obvious, as in the case of airline alliances, the task may be relatively easy, although the key element in that case is to make sure that alliance members are sufficiently compatible among themselves. In the case of a web alliance network the initiative takes place though multiple dyadic agreements. Eventually web alliances can create a coordinating organization similar to the one found in platform networks.

2 Partner selection and attraction. In an alliance portfolio, the prime objective for the 'nodal' firm (the portfolio manager) is to utilize a multiplicity of co-specialized, co-allied and learning alliances in order to foster its global competitive capabilities. In selecting partners, the 'nodal' firm will look at firms bringing the necessary complementary capabilities but which are not likely to take advantage of the alliance in order to build their own competing capabilities. Corning, for instance, in its alliances with Siemens to develop, manufacture and sell optic fibers for communication, selected a partner that was not interested in building a competitive position in the design and production of fibers, but only in their utilization. In the case of platform alliances members apply to the governing institutions who decide on their admittance. In web alliances members are co-opted on a one-to-one basis with the possible agreement of the institutionalized coordinating body.

3 Alliance governance and maintenance. There are multiple forms of governance as there are multiple forms of alliances (Doz 2019). As far as portfolio networks and platform networks are concerned, Lorenzoni and Baden-Fuller (1997) suggest alliance networks must establish a centre or a 'network manager', whose role is to make sure the partners contribute fairly to the partnership and respect the common rules. Alliance managers also serve as an information exchange and clearing house for mutual transaction. As mentioned earlier, alliance managers work in an appropriate organizational structure that has been created. As in the case of a web alliance network the maintenance of an alliance relies on the multiple alliance managers in the members' companies, with frequent meetings of members organized by a supporting 'governing body'.

4 Managing partner leverage and relationships. The 'nodal' organization, when there is one, in the case of portfolio networks and platform networks, will make sure that the 'relevant' capabilities are obtained from the alliance, but also that it contributes positively and significantly to the partners' expectations. By keeping a partnership as a one-to-one relationship, the 'nodal' firm builds a set of converging capabilities that are not shared by the whole constellation of partners. In alliance webs, in contrast, the task of the 'nodal' firm is to build an interdependent set of mutual relationships to which each participant contributes but gains from all the others. Pixtech, for instance, has built a web of partners for the development of field emission display (FED) technology for flat panel displays to be used in a variety of applications. Partners entering the alliance have to demonstrate their commitment by opening their R&D labs (the FED-related technology) to other partners. Each party has to host meetings in its own facilities for alliance members to exchange their research progress. Reciprocal patent licensing is also involved in this type of alliance.

Insert 8.3 GAVI global vaccine alliance

In 2000, the Bill and Melinda Gates Foundation, Nelson Mandela and the World Health Organization created an international organization – Global Vaccination Alliance (GAVI). Its long-term mission was to eradicate infectious diseases through the vaccination of children. The idea was to bring together public and private sectors with the shared goal of creating equal access to new and underused vaccines for children living in the world's poorest countries.

In June 2019, the Gavi Board approved a new five-year strategy ('Gavi 5.0') with a vision to 'leave no-one behind with immunisation' and a mission to save lives and protect people's health by increasing equitable and sustainable use of vaccines.

By 2020 GAVI has helped to vaccinate more than 760 million children in fifteen of the world's poorest countries, preventing more than 13 million deaths.

The alliance partners are represented below.

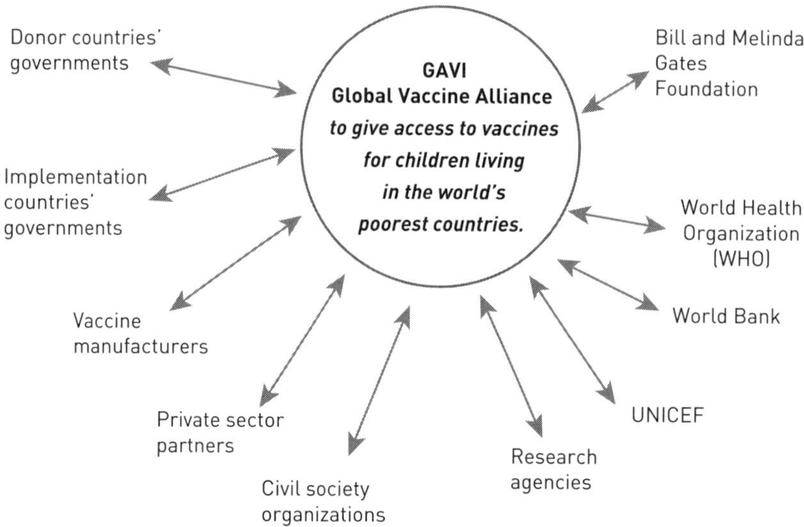

Figure 8.21 Alliance partners in GAVI

Governance

The Gavi Alliance has international institution status in Switzerland and public charity status in the United States.

While the Gavi Secretariat oversees the day-to-day operations of the Vaccine Alliance, the Board is responsible for giving strategic direction and policy-making. These are the people, policies and processes that govern Gavi.

Some of the partners have a financing role, while others have an operational role in vaccine research, production, logistics and delivery.

Source: https://www.gavi.org; Doz (2019).

Global industrial ecosystems

The biological concept of the ecosystem has been used in industrial economics.[30] There are many definitions of industrial ecosystems. We will retain the following definition: 'An industrial ecosystem is group of interacting firms that depend on each other's activities.'[31] It can be considered as a quasi-alliance to the extent to which there is a mutual destiny of all members, although contrary to multilateral alliances described earlier, there is no formal organizational architecture and no overreaching contractual legal arrangement that governs the organization and the strategy and relationships among members. In most ecosystems there may be some clusters that are regulated by commercial suppliers–buyers contracts, however, this is not the case for all members of the ecosystem. What is important for a firm is to define the relevant ecosystem to which it belongs – that is to say, the one it can influence.

One may identify three types of industrial ecosystem:

1. The *Lead firm*:[32] ecosytem in which a company plays a central role the regulates the system. For instance Apple (Figure 8.23), Airbus, Amazon.
2. The *Value-proposition*: ecosytem in which the dominant factor are the consumers. For instance the long-distance air travel ecosystem (Figure 8.24),
3. The *Technology-centred* ecosystem: for instance the electric car (see Figure 8.25 on page 338), cancer treatment, 5G.

Some ecosystems may be purely national (American football) while the large majority have an international or global participation.

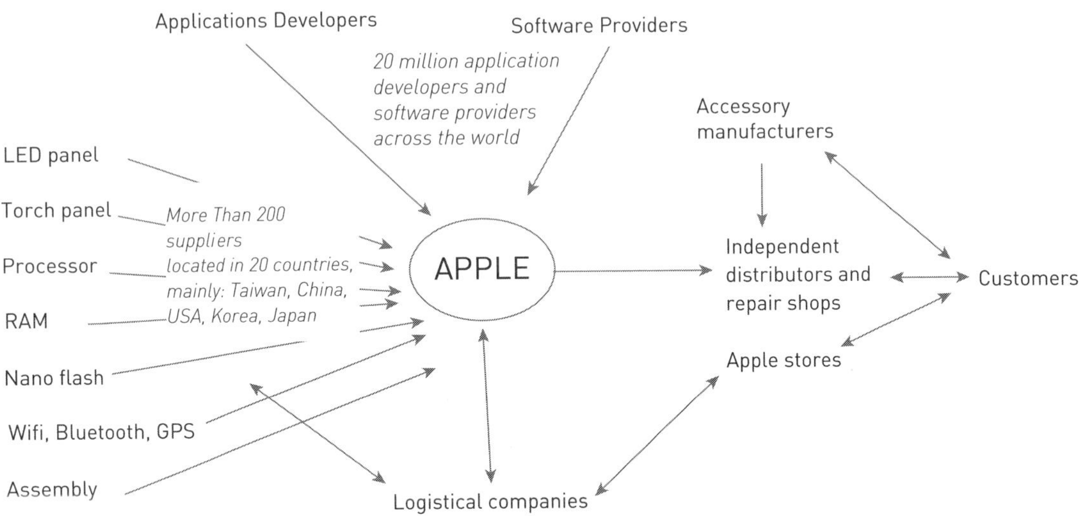

Figure 8.22 Lead firm ecosystem: a simplified view of Apple iPhone ecosytem

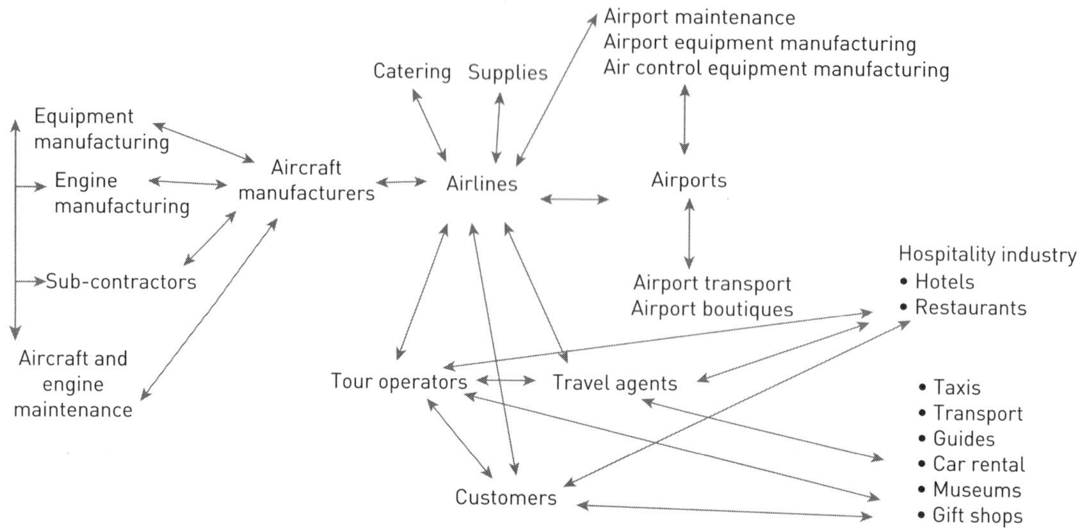

Figure 8.23 Simplified example of a value proposition ecosystem: long-distance travel ecosytem

Ecosystems *per se* do not elaborate on strategies except possibly in the case of a 'Lead firm ecosystem in which the lead firm can influence the system in order to foster it competitive advantage as advocated by Williamson and Meyer'.[33] Another case of potential strategy formulation for an ecosystem can be found in government effort to develop some sort of state planification at the industry level. For

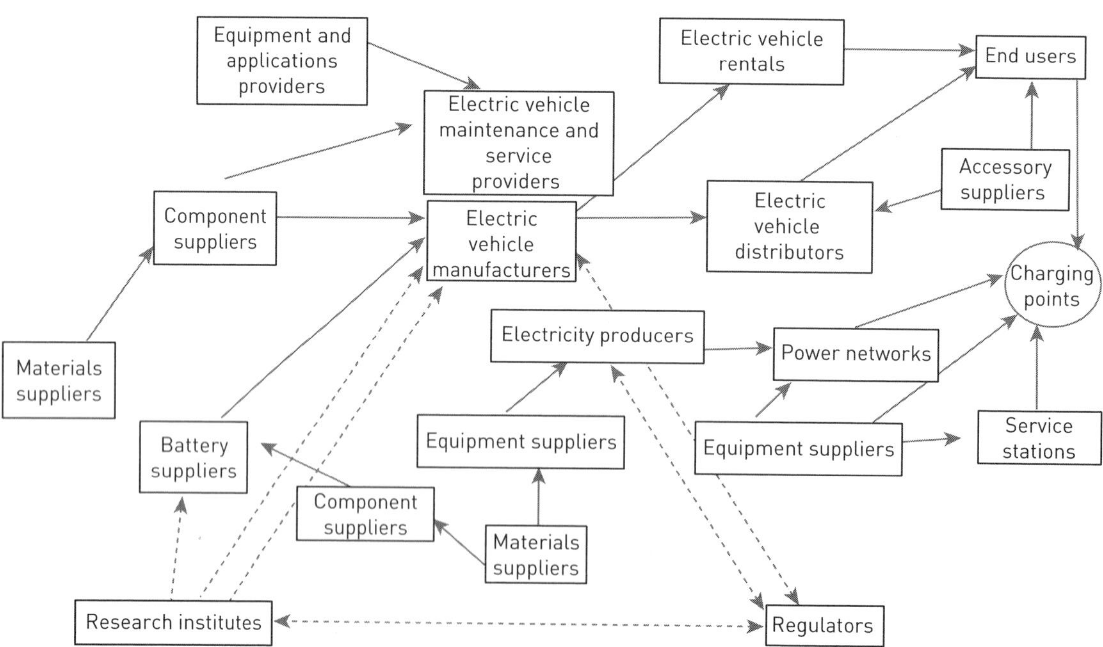

Figure 8.24 Example of a technology-centred ecosytem: electrical vehicle ecosytem
Source: Zulkarnain et al. (2014).

instance the French government in 2020 organized a 'National Council for Industries for 18 Sectors' ecosystem which grouped government experts, industrialists, and trade unionists together for the elaboration of policies in each sector such as construction, marine industries or health industries.[34]

Joint ventures for local market entry

This section examines joint ventures for market entry in particular. This type of alliance has a local focus: typically, as seen in Chapter 7, a global firm teams up with a local partner to form a joint venture company. It is a way for a global firm to enter a local market either as required by the government or by the desire to acquire operational capabilities. Most of the issues described earlier in the case of global alliances will apply in the case of local joint ventures. Below we focus on the issue of partner selection.

Local partners

The type of partner to be selected is a function of the strategic dimensions mentioned earlier. One distinguishes several types of partners:

- Complementing partner: a partner who brings operational capabilities to the venture.
- Investor: a partner who only plays the role of shareholder without engaging in operations. This type of partner is considered when one party believes that it possesses sufficient operational capabilities by itself.
- Diversifier: a partner who engages in an alliance with a view to entering a new business and using the other partner's product and knowledge.
- Political partner: in the case of a joint venture for market entry if the local government requires or imposes a local partner whose contribution is to offer its political presence.

Investors, political partners and sometimes diversifiers may not interfere in the management of the alliances; they are often referred to as dormant or sleeping partners. Table 8.6 shows the various types of partners' contributions, advantages and disadvantages.

Table 8.6 Types of local partner for market entry joint ventures

Partners contributing to operational capabilities	Partners contributing to non-operational resources
• **Partner in the same industry: brings full capabilities**	• **Diversifier: brings business reputation and country knowledge and looks to enter into a new business**
• **Supplier**: secures supplies	• **Investor**: brings finance, looks for return
• **Distributor**: secures market coverage	• **Central or local government**: looks for development and jobs and brings authority
• **Customer**: secures market	• **Political partner**: brings contacts and looks for remuneration

Table 8.6 *(Continued)*

Partners contributing to operational capabilities	Partners contributing to non-operational resources
• **Advantages**: enhances competitive capabilities and speeds up entry	• **Advantages**: speeds up entry, brings knowledge, contacts
• **Disadvantages**: risks of copying and reinforcing/ creating a local competitor	• **Disadvantages**: does not provide operational capabilities; political risks exposure when the partner is a government body or a political partner

In any case the selection of a potential partner has crucial, long-term consequences. It is important to find a partner with compatible objectives, and with whom it is possible to communicate and build a stable, lasting partnership. The foreign firm's success will depend on the partner's capabilities and willingness to cooperate, and the climate of mutual trust. Often, firms conduct far too little advance planning. In Asia Pacific (see Lasserre 1984: 43–9) for instance, where joint venture had been a predominant entry mode, Western foreign firms conducted little or no screening and, in many cases, ended up choosing a long-term local agent or distributor without researching alternatives.

To investigate potential partners thoroughly, foreign firms should:

- Request information
- Interview in depth the owner, top managers and operating staff in manufacturing and sales
- Ask for financial data (although these may be of limited value, and possibly selectively presented to look as attractive as possible)
- Interview the local firm's other joint venture partners, bankers, suppliers, customers and competitors, as well as diplomats and established foreign investors.

Selection criteria

As already described for global alliances, the assessment of fit is an important selection criterion (see Figure 8.11).

1 A strategic fit exists when the two partners have compatible long-term objectives. They will pool some of their resources to reach goals that they cannot attain alone. Assessing strategic fit involves analysing the partners' implicit or explicit motives for joining forces, as well as the benefits they expect to gain. In joint ventures for market entry, you typically find three main types of agenda behind the strategic objectives for engaging in joint ventures:

    - The venturing agenda, in which the two partners want to develop the potential of a given market by creating a new business activity. In this case, the primary intention is to join forces rather than to take advantage of the other partner.
    - The extractive agenda, in which one partner wants to acquire a key resource, asset or competency from the other. Local partners typically seek product or process technology, hardware and software from foreign joint ventures. They may also want to gain access to international

markets. Foreign partners often use joint ventures to build relationships and win market access, or to make upfront profits through high transfer pricing on equipment, components or management services. Sometimes they are more interested in access to raw materials or low-cost labour rather than in promoting the business of the joint venture itself.

- The opportunistic agenda, in which the local partner may want to capitalize on citizenship and political contacts, or seek a financial return. The foreign partner may be complying with regulations, or want to enter into a short-term deal.

A classic example of conflicting goals would be a foreign partner that wants to acquire marketing expertise and a local partner looking for technological expertise.

The degree of commitment to the joint venture is particularly important: the moment of truth comes when unexpected problems arise in day-to-day operations. Even if individual managers assigned to a joint venture are committed, the two parents may give it relatively low priority. When a cooperative agreement is purely opportunistic, commitment is problematic, which is why many opportunistic partnerships end in failure.

2 A good capabilities fit means that both partners must be able to contribute to the resources and competencies needed; they must identify and solve potential gaps in contribution. The same methodology for assessment of capabilities fit that was developed earlier applies to joint ventures for market entry. What is particularly significant in emerging countries is the fact that, due to poor information, a good capability fit analysis is difficult. A classic mistake is to overestimate your partner's contribution to the joint venture. Problems also arise when initial resources, assets and competencies become insufficient to sustain competitiveness over time. New funding will be needed; profits will have to be reinvested into the business. A short-term orientation, opportunism or simply the inconsistency of one or both partners may aggravate a potential resource gap.

Valuing contributions that do not have a market price, because they are either not traded or intangible, can cause conflict. Intangibles and technology are often the most valuable contributions brought to a joint venture, and can become a key element in the negotiation.

3 Cultural dissimilarity emanating from corporate, industry or national and ethnic differences is always present in international joint ventures, and can create many problems and conflicts when it comes to the practical operations of the venture. As already indicated, cultural differences often lead to a difficult period of adaptation, called the 'death valley', that requires patience and flexibility on the part of managers to successfully get through. It is therefore important that prior to any agreement a cultural fit assessment be made to address questions such as: can we understand each other? Do we speak the same business language? Do we share a common logic? Can we communicate with each other?

4 Finally, the result of an organizational fit analysis reveals profound differences in management practices. Most often in emerging countries a local entrepreneurial firm with no set procedures may have trouble cooperating with a big, bureaucratic multinational corporation. Organizational fit is hard to achieve when it comes to integrating the local joint venture into the parent company's network of subsidiaries.

Staffing joint ventures

Joint ventures require managers with political and cultural skills as well as technical competencies. Foreign managers unprepared for cultural complexity will not handle critical situations properly and will jeopardize their parent company's ability to learn. The most important task of managers assigned to joint ventures, particularly when the strategic intent is to extract knowledge from the local environment, is to synthesize and transmit learning experiences back to each relevant department in their parent company. It would be a mistake to assign managers lacking clout or prestige to a foreign joint venture; the local partner may interpret this as a lack of commitment to the partnership. The worst attitude is to consider such postings as a form of exile for undesirable personnel.

When recruiting local employees, identity and loyalty are critical. Do they feel that they belong to their parent company, or to the joint venture? Most of the time, the local partner will recruit local staff; foreign partners should carefully monitor hiring to ensure that the new employees are loyal to the joint venture, not just to the local partner.

Control

Joint ventures are controlled by a board of directors consisting largely of executives, as well as a few non-executive directors; these are usually local personalities who can play a useful role as go-betweens in cases of conflict with the local partners. Western companies tend to prefer having a majority stake in a joint venture, although there is no evidence that this allows them to exert real control. When a firm controls more than 70 per cent of capital, the joint venture can be considered a 'quasi-acquisition', in which case the majority partner is in command. Below 70 per cent, this is not necessarily the case. Several studies have failed to demonstrate a significant correlation between shareholding and control: some companies that are in charge of key operational functions can be in control even with a minority stake.

Joint venture decay and failure

It is common for joint ventures to experience a rapid deterioration immediately after start-up as the partners find out more about each other and make efforts to adapt. After this 'death valley' period, relative stability follows, and can last for three to six years. After that, mutual interest suddenly drops. The resulting crisis can lead to a split, and this phenomenon, known as joint venture decay, happens when both partners feel that they have acquired whatever advantage they sought from their association. At this moment the impetus for further collaboration can vanish. If both partners want to avert a divorce, they must revitalize their association by increasing the range or broadening the scope of the joint venture's activities.

The experience of foreign companies in joint ventures has not always been a happy one. Empirical evidence on international joint ventures indicates that at most 40–50 per cent end up producing the expected return. Most companies become disillusioned because of unforeseen problems in setting up and operating their partnerships. There are many causes of failure or difficulty. Below are the most prevalent:

1 Absence of strategic vision. When a joint venture is launched hastily, or for purely defensive or opportunistic reasons, the foreign firm often fails to evaluate the intentions and capabilities of the local

partner. A classic error in an industrial partnership is to choose a distributor whose corporate culture is likely to be inappropriate to a slow cash flow cycle, and who will probably prioritize a few rapid cash flow deals instead of investing for the long term.

2 Believing without seeing. The art of appearances can be highly refined in some countries and many a foreign investor has been led into mistaking elaborate ceremony for a real commitment.

3 Failing to understand the local partner's strategic logic. In most cases, a thorough investigation would reveal the real intent – for example, to achieve vertical integration to appropriate technology, or simply to enter into an opportunistic deal.

4 Haste in negotiation. The desire to conclude a deal rapidly often leads the negotiators to concentrate on financial or legal clauses and neglect technological or operational issues. In Asian countries, for instance, the contractual stage must be preceded by an overall planning session for the project, during which the partners will agree on objectives and strategies. This implies a minimum investment in understanding the partner's logic. It is a good idea to advance step by step: a licensing contract, for example, can be a good way of testing the capacities of the other party before making a longer-term commitment.

5 Insufficiently prepared staff and lack of organizational support. Unprepared expatriate managers who fail to understand their partner's and employees' logic can exacerbate tensions, and damage the reputation of both the joint venture and the foreign parent. Local partners in emerging countries are often highly respected professionals, and when they suffer what they see as inappropriate treatment at the hands of unsophisticated foreign staff, they quickly become disillusioned. Besides, the joint venture is often poorly served by headquarters (delays in technical assistance, delivery of poorly adapted products, exorbitant transfer pricing, exaggerated administrative rules or constraints that ignore local conditions).

6 'Control' mindset on the part of executives who have difficulty shedding the hierarchical model of management inherited from vertically integrated business activities. Partnership requires the use of a selection of skills and mindsets on the part of the manager involved, giving them the capacity to work in a network.[35]

7 Difficulty in building trust between organizations from different cultures: mistrust is probably the leading single factor that explains partnership failure.[36] Building trust requires competencies that are not necessarily taught in engineering and business schools; it requires the mastery of techniques belonging to the social sciences such as 'negotiation analysis', the art of 'signalling' and the practice of 'credible commitment'.

These causes of failure are often interrelated, contributing to a vicious circle of misunderstanding which can degenerate into open conflict and end in frustration, loss of market share and sometimes legal action. Studies on joint ventures have shown that good cultural and strategic fit, leading to trust between partners, are the crucial factors for success. Foreign enterprises that seriously consider setting up through joint ventures should devote enough resources and effort to carefully preparing and monitoring the selection of a partner and management of the venture as well as management of the continuous flow of communication with their local partners.

EXAMPLE 8.2 An ongoing global alliance: the Renault–Nissan alliance

With the globalization and consolidation of the automotive industry, the only means of ensuring long-term sustainability is by forming a large group to leverage market power. For Renault, a European player, alliance was essential for long-term sustainable growth and expansion. Finding a partner in Asia was therefore a critical mission for Renault. For Nissan, which was a financially troubled company in the late 1990s, finding a partner was the only means of survival in the increasingly competitive global auto industry. In 1998, Nissan's debts were estimated at $21 billion, or 2.5 times its equity.

After a period of fact-finding and a joint evaluation of potential synergies, on 27 March 1999 Mr Louis Schweitzer, CEO of Renault, and Mr Yoshikazu Hanawa, CEO of Nissan Motor Co., announced that they had signed an agreement for a total partnership 'which will create the fourth [largest] automobile manufacturer in the world, while providing growth and profitability to the two partners'.

The agreement was as follows:

- Renault was to invest 605 billion yen ($5.1 billion) to acquire 36.8 per cent of the shares of Nissan Motor Co. with an option to acquire an additional 8 per cent in the future.
- Nissan would have the possibility of becoming a shareholder of Renault.
- An executive from Renault would become the new COO of Nissan and join its board of directors.
- The CEO of Nissan Motor Co. was offered a place on the Renault board of directors.

The Renault team appointed to Nissan initiated the Nissan Revival Plan. They made three commitments:

- Return to profitability by the financial year (FY) 2000
- Achieve consolidated operating profit of 4.5 per cent of sales by FY2002
- Reduce net debt from 1.4 trillion yen to less than 700 billion yen by FY2002.

It was also promised that, should any of these commitments not be achieved, the executive committee would resign.

A Global Alliance Committee (GAC) was created as the governing body of the alliance to promote joint strategy and synergies between the two companies. Cross-company teams (CCTs) and cross-functional teams (CFTs) were created to organize synergies (see Figure 8.26).

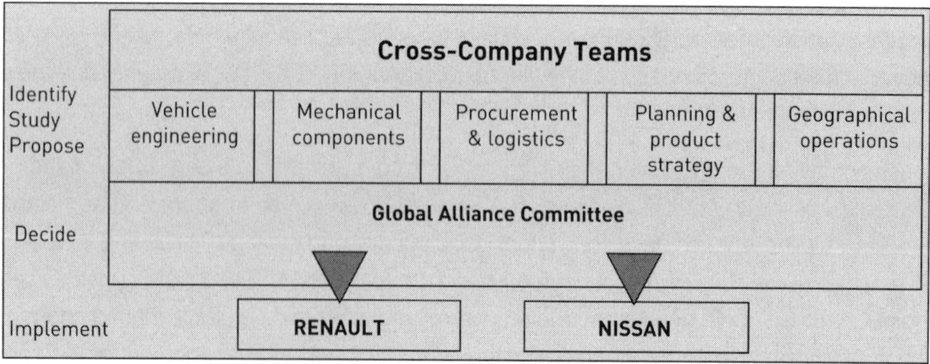

Figure 8.25 Organization of the cross-company teams and global alliance committee in the Renault–Nissan Alliance

The CFTs and CCTs generated more than 2,000 new ideas (see Figure 8.26).

Business development Shift resources from cost reduction to product development. Nissan plans: • to introduce 22 products by 2002 • Increase capital expeditures by 25 up to 5% of net sales	**Purchasing** Reduce procurement costs by promoting concentrated and global purchasing Nissan plans: • to reduce by 20% purchasing costs which ccount for 60% of total costs by 2002
Manufacturing Reduce excess domestic production capacity to achieve maximum efficiency and cost competitiveness on a global scale Nissan plans: • to terminate production of vehicles and powertrains in five factories • improve productivity in the remaining plants	**Research and development** Concentrate resources and use them by selecting the areas of R&D that is the core competence of the company and sharing with Renault **Financial cost** Concentrating on the core automotive business and reducing debt by selling non-core assets. • Sales of shareholdings
Sales, general and administrative costs Reduce inefficiencies and increase efficiencies by organizational changes and headcount reduction Nissan plans: • reduce cost of sales and general administration by 20% • overhaul organization of domestic R&D and sales operations • Streamline operations in North America and reorganize marketing in Europe • Reduce global workforce by 21,000	**Organization and decision-making process** Making its organization global and promote efficiency of decision making Nissan plans: • establish management committee in Europe and the USA as a strategic decision-making organisation • Strengthen the capacity to develop global strategies and empower regional operations to implement the Nissan Revival Plan • Sales of non-core assets • Decrease inventory-to-sales by 30%

Figure 8.26 The Nissan Revival Plan and the cross-functional teams
Source: Adapted with permission from Nissan Motor Facts File, 2000, http://www.nissan-global.com/GCC/Japan/FACTFILE/ff00e.pdf (accessed 2001).

A year and a half later, in 2000, Nissan returned to profitability and the Nissan Revival Plan objectives were fully achieved by 2001, one year ahead of schedule. Since then the alliance has evolved into the organizational structure shown in Figure 8.27.

In 2010, the global sales amounted to 6.3 million vehicles and represented 9 per cent of the worldwide market. While the two companies are still operating independently, their strategic orientation and the organization of synergies is supervised by a joint management company, Renault–Nissan BV (RNBV).

The main synergies are:

- Renault–Nissan Purchasing Organization (RNPO) that sources 7 per cent of the Alliance's 2006 worldwide purchases
- Common platforms are being developed
- Cross-manufacturing operation
- Common distribution in Europe

43.4%
RNVB DIRECTORS
RENAULT
50%
RENAULT–NISSAN BV
ALLIANCE BOARD
50%
NISSAN
STEERING COMMITTEES
15%

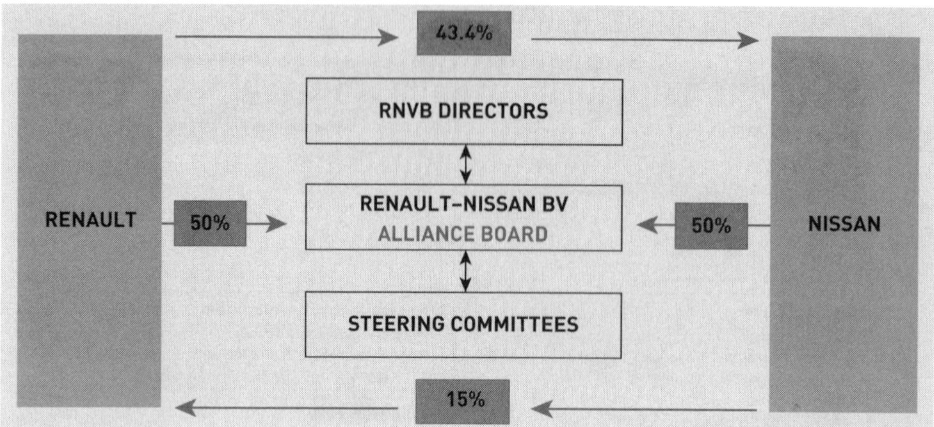

Figure 8.27 New organization of the Renault–Nissan Alliance

Source: Reproduced with permission from Renault: https://group.renault.com/en/our-company/a-group-an-alliance-and-partnerships/our-alliance-with-nissan/ (accessed 2001).

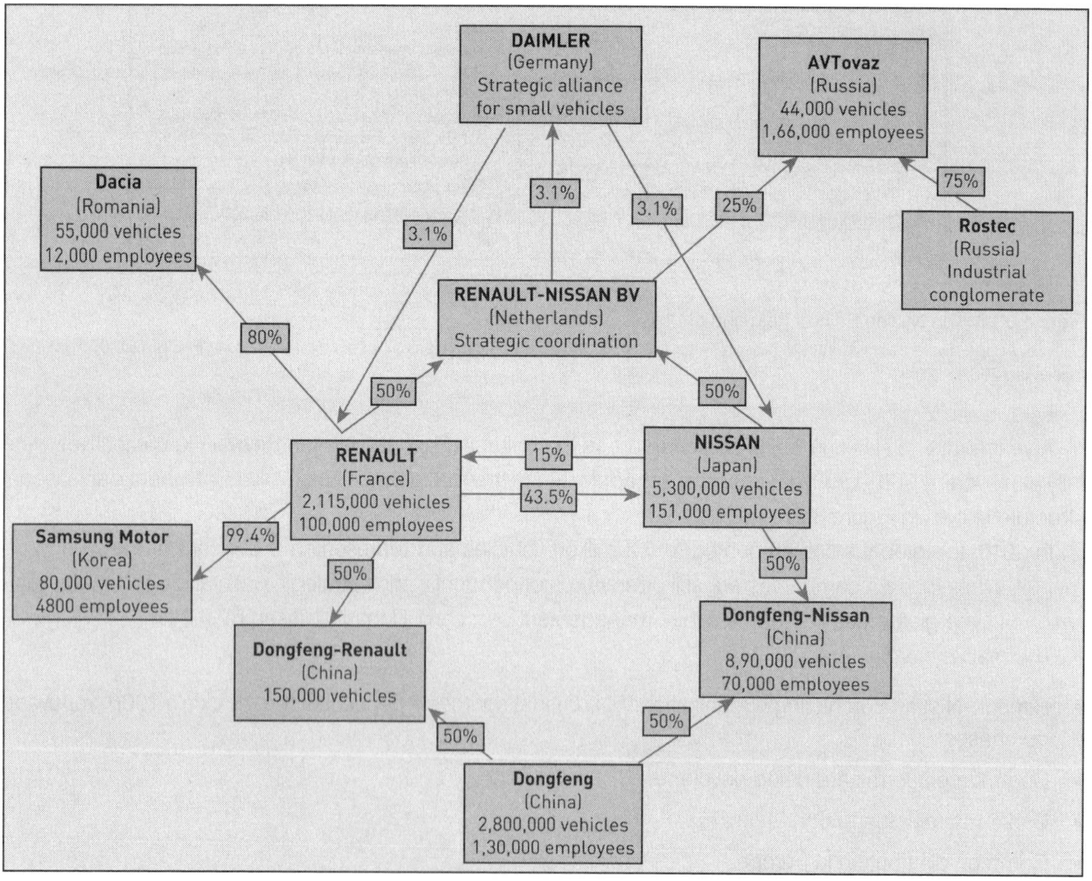

DAIMLER
(Germany)
Strategic alliance
for small vehicles
AVTovaz
(Russia)
44,000 vehicles
1,66,000 employees
Dacia
(Romania)
55,000 vehicles
12,000 employees
3.1%
3.1%
3.1%
25%
75%
Rostec
(Russia)
Industrial
conglomerate
RENAULT-NISSAN BV
(Netherlands)
Strategic coordination
80%
50%
50%
RENAULT
(France)
2,115,000 vehicles
100,000 employees
15%
43.5%
NISSAN
(Japan)
5,300,000 vehicles
151,000 employees
99.4%
Samsung Motor
(Korea)
80,000 vehicles
4800 employees
50%
50%
Dongfeng-Renault
(China)
150,000 vehicles
Dongfeng-Nissan
(China)
8,90,000 vehicles
70,000 employees
50%
50%
Dongfeng
(China)
2,800,000 vehicles
1,30,000 employees

Figure 8.28 Renault's alliances and global acquisition network

- Common information systems
- Exchange of best practices, especially in the manufacturing sector
- Joint development in hybrid and fuel-efficient vehicles.

By 2016 Renault had engaged in a network of alliances and acquisitions producing around 8.5 million cars (Figure 8.28). Also in 2016 it was announced that discussions were under way with Mitsubishi about joining the alliance. That would bring the total volume to around 10 million cars per year. The alliance faced a crisis in 2019 when the Renault-appointed COO was accused of fiscal under-reporting. He was replaced but the alliance continued even when in 2020 the Covid-19 pandemic plunged the automobile sector into crisis.

MINI-CASE 8.2

General Motors' global alliances: a Sisyphean task

General Motors (GM) is a global US car company which produced 9.8 million vehicles in 2015, sold in 125 countries, split between ten brands: Chevrolet, Buick, GMC, Cadillac, Opel, Vauxhall, Holden, Baojun, Wuling and Jiefang. Since the early 1980s GM has built its global strategy on a series of wholly owned overseas investments as well as international strategic alliances. One GM chief executive called the policy of alliances 'a faster and more capital-efficient way to grow'. Over the years many partnerships have been created and some terminated. Some of them were local joint ventures established with a view to assembling cars. Some others were tie-ins with component manufacturers and finally some others were global strategic alliances, mainly in Europe and Asia. The following text describes their most well-known strategic partnerships.

Europe

Italy: GM Fiat

In 2000 GM took a stake of 20 per cent in the Italian company Fiat Auto for which Fiat Auto would receive 5.6 per cent of GM capital. GM also had an option between 2005 and 2010 to buy the remaining 80 per cent of Fiat. The objective of the alliance was to create synergies in component manufacturing, platform exchanges, joint purchasing and sales in Europe and Latin America. Poor performances at Fiat and GM led GM to decline to exercise the option, and led to the dissolution of the alliance. In 2014 Fiat acquired the American automobile manufacturer Chrysler and the merged group was renamed Fiat Chrysler. Fiat Chrysler attempted to recreate an alliance with GM in 2015 but this attempt failed.

France: GM Peugeot

In 2012 GM and PSA Peugeot of France announced the creation of a strategic alliance with a stake of 7 per cent in the capital of PSA. The alliance concerned the sharing of vehicle platforms, components and modules; and the creation of a global purchasing joint venture for the sourcing of commodities, components and other items. However, in 2013 GM sold its share in the company although it maintained its desire to collaborate with PSA.

ASIA

Japan: GM Toyota

The New United Motor Manufacturing Incorporated (NUMMI) alliance was created in 1983 as a 50/50 joint venture between General Motors and Toyota in order to manufacture a compact car in Fremont, California. GM's main motive for participating in this alliance was to benefit from Toyota's know-how and expertise in small cars, and learn about Toyota's highly productive lean manufacturing system. Toyota's motivations were to get around potential US protectionist policies as well as to learn about the management of the highly syndicated American automobile workers. The joint venture continued until it was terminated in 2010 in light of GM's financial difficulties, and the Fremont plant was closed.

GM Fanuc

In 1982 GM created a joint venture with the Japanese robotics company Fanuc with a view to producing industrial robots for the automotive industry. This type of investment was considered as non-core by GM and the venture was terminated in 1992.

GM Suzuki

In 1981 GM took 5.3 per cent of the capital of the car maker Suzuki. They jointly developed a small car that was sold both in the USA and Japan. In 1986 they created a 50/50 joint venture named CAMI, to jointly build a plant in Canada to assemble some Suzuki models. In 2000 GM increased its share of Suzuki to 20 per cent, then sold it back to Suzuki in 2008. In 2010 Suzuki stopped the joint development of a hybrid car with GM and in 2012 sold its share in CAMI to GM. It left the US market the same year, and went on to develop a strategic partnership with Volkswagen in 2016.

GM Isuzu

In 1971 GM acquired a 34 per cent share of Isuzu, a small Japanese car maker. GM's aim was to work with and support Isuzu in developing and marketing small cars for the GM network. The management was completely in the hands of Isuzu managers. Over the years the alliance took many forms of collaboration. In 1999 GM increased its share to 49 per cent but in 2002 due to GM's financial difficulties Isuzu repurchased 37 per cent of the shares owned by GM and the alliance was put on hold. The collaboration was reactivated in 2014 with a proposed alliance for the development of mid-sized trucks but in 2016 Isuzu and GM announced the end of their collaboration in this area.

South Korea

GM Daewoo

In 1972 GM acquired 50 per cent of the shares of a Korean car maker and in 1978 that Korean partner was bought by Daewoo, a Korean conglomerate. In 1982 the management of the joint venture was handed to Daewoo and the active participation of GM was minimized. Following the Asian financial crisis of 1996 Daewoo sold its shares to GM. The company is now a wholly owned GM subsidiary, under the new name of GM Korea.

China

In China GM has eleven joint ventures and two wholly owned subsidiaries. The major joint ventures are with the Shanghai Automobile Industrial Corporation (SAIC) and First Automotive Work (FAW).

The SAIC-GM joint venture, launched in 1997, has four major manufacturing bases – Jinqiao in Shanghai, Dong Yue in Yantai, Norsom in Shenyang and Wuhan – with eight vehicle plants and four powertrain plants. SAIC-GM offers more than twenty product lines under the Buick, Chevrolet and Cadillac brands.

The 50/50 joint venture between GM China and China FAW, launched on 30 August 2009, is based in Changchun and is focused on the production and sale of light-duty trucks and vans. It also engages in R&D, exports and after-sales support. The joint venture has facilities in Changchun, Harbin in Heilongjiang and Qujing in Yunnan. Its products include luxury vehicles, economy and premium sedans, MPVs and SUVs, and hybrid and electric vehicles.

Questions:

1 Why in your opinion were some of those partnerships terminated?

2 Do you think that GM has benefited from those?

Sources: This text is the authors' own, derived from internet-based research. Some data are drawn from *Harvard Business Review* case no. 9-388-094, 'General Motors' Asian Alliances' and from INSEAD case 305-300-1, 'GM Alliances fifteen years later'.

Summary and key points

1 There are three motives for cross-border mergers and acquisitions:

   a Market reach

   b Consolidation

   c Competencies acquisition

2 *Due diligence* and *valuation* are among the main handicaps to global acquisitions, particularly in emerging markets

3 Three main methods are used for valuations:

   a Asset-based

   b Market-based

   c Cash-flow-based

4 The *integration phase* is considered to be the most important source of success or failure in M&As. The integration process consists of:

   a The integration plan

   b Transition management

   c Strategic consolidation

5 There are three integration models:

   a Preservation

   b Absorption

   c Symbiotic

6 There are eight main issues for successful integration:

   a leadership

b clear sense of purpose

c concrete operational results

d mutual understanding

e showing respect to acquired company's personnel

f measurement tools

g winning spiral

h credibility

7 An alliance:

a is the sharing of capabilities between two or several firms

b with a view to enhancing their competitive advantages and/or creating new business

c without losing their respective strategic autonomy

8 A global alliance aims at developing a global market presence or enhancing global competitiveness

A *local alliance* or *local joint venture* aims at facilitating market entry or access to resources and is driven by three forces:

- Administrative requirements
- Capabilities
- Risk hedging

9 There are three broad types of global strategic alliance:

a Market reach alliance

b Global leverage alliance

c Learning alliance

10 There are four major steps in the analysis of strategic alliances, mergers and acquisitions:

a Understanding the strategic context and spelling out the strategic value of an alliance or an acquisition or merger

b Analysis of partner(s) or targets

c Negotiation and design

d Implementation

11 The value potential of an alliance is calculated on the basis of the potential benefits it brings to the alliance partners: the revenues and cost benefits generated by the alliances

12 Partner analysis consists of four assessments:

a Strategic fit

b Capabilities fit

   - **c** Cultural fit
   - **d** Organizational fit

13 There are two major types of alliance design: broker or operator

14 There are two critical phases of implementation of alliances: integration and learning

15 There are three types of global multilateral alliance: alliance networks, alliance portfolios, alliance webs

16 An industrial ecosystem is group of interacting firms that depend on each other's activities

17 In joint ventures for market entry there are several types of partner: complementing partners, investors, diversifiers, political partners

18 Failures/problems: there are five main reasons why joint ventures fail:

   - **a** Absence of strategic vision
   - **b** 'Believing without seeing' (failure to carry out diligent research)
   - **c** Failure to understand local partner's strategic logic
   - **d** Haste in negotiation
   - **e** Insufficiently prepared staff or lack of organizational support

Learning assignments

1 The chapter describes six examples of cross-border mergers: can you identify the source of long-term value creation in each case?

2 What are the problems in conducting due diligence in a global context?

3 What determines the bargaining range of a negotiation?

4 What are the critical issues in the post-acquisition transition phase?

5 In what circumstances is the symbiotic mode of integration appropriate?

6 What are the most frequent sources of failure in M&As?

7 The text distinguishes between market reach, global leverage and learning alliances. In which category would you place the alliance in vaccines between Pfizer (USA) and BioNtech (Germany)? What do such partners look for?

8 What are the sources of value creation in an alliance?

9 What are the criteria to be assessed in order to determine the strategic fit between partners?

10 What is an extractive agenda in an alliance?

11 What distinguishes an ecosystem from a multilateral alliance?

12 When looking at Figure 8.24 can you explain why in 2021 the main electric vehicle companies were obliged to reduce their production?

13 What impact may cultural differences between partners have on global alliances?

14 What are the six domains that need to be negotiated in relation to the interface and governance of an alliance?

15 What are the different types of local partner in joint ventures for market entry?

Key words

- Absorption mode of integration
- Alliance
- Capabilities fit
- Constellations
- Cultural fit
- 'Death valley'
- Due diligence
- Ecosystem
- Extractive agenda
- 'Fair process'
- Integration process
- Interface management
- Joint venture decay
- Joint venture for market entry
- Learning alliances
- Organizational fit
- Political partner
- Post-acquisition process
- Pre-acquisition process
- Preservation mode of integration
- Sharing agenda
- Stand-alone value
- Strategic fit
- Symbiotic mode of integration
- Synergies value
- Valuation
- Venturing agenda

Web resources

Institute for Mergers, Acquisitions and Alliances (IMAA) research, Thomson Financial:
https://imaa-institute.org
Pitchbook for Mergers and Acquisitions:
https://get.pitchbook.com/mergers-and-acquisitions-data
PwC Global:
https://www.pwc.com
Thomson Research:
http://mergers.thomsonib.com/NASApp/DealSearch/MAOverview.htm?ExpressCode=DELOITTEDEALS

Companion website

Visit the companion website at bloomsbury.pub/global-strategic-management-5e for a multitude of weblinks and resources, self-test questions for revision and appendices.

Notes

1 Capron and Mitchell (2012).

2 Institute for Mergers, Acquisitions and Alliances (IMAA) research, Thomson Financial, https://imaa-institute.org/. (Accessed 1 February 2022) and PWC https://www.pwc.com/gx/en/services/deals/trends.html (Accessed 1 February 2022).

3 A series of studies by consulting firms Mercer, McKinsey and Bain & Co. show a rate of unsuccessful acquisitions ranging from 50 per cent to 75 per cent. These aggregate figures do not differentiate between domestic and international acquisitions.

4 Kitching (1973).

5 Martin (2018).

6 Bleeke et al. (1990).

7 The following literature covers both domestic and cross-border acquisition processes: Haspeslagh and Jemison (1991); Von Krogh et al. (1994); Mitchell and Holmes (1996); Habeck et al. (2000).

8 Eccles et al. (1999); Hawawini and Viallet (1999).

9 Eccles et al. (1999).

10 Financial theory would argue that markets implicitly use the cash-flow method by discounting the flow of future dividends to determine a price: this is the efficient markets theory.

11 Lessard (1996).

12 Haspeslagh and Jemison (1991).

13 Davidson and de la Torre (1989).

14 Hyde and Haspeslagh (1994).

15 Smith (2000).

16 Kim and Mauborgne (1997).

17 Gomez-Casseres (1995: ch. 1), emphasis added.

18 Doz and Hamel (1998: 66).

19 Ibid.

20 Kogut (1991: 19–33); Williamson (1999: 117–26).

21 Akadar et al. (1997).

22 Geringer and Hebert (1989: 235–54).

23 Bleeke and Ernst (1991: 127–35).

24 Spekeman and Lynn (2000); Yoshino and Rangan (1995); Greve et al. (2013).

25 Krishna and Gee (1998).

26 See, for instance, Harrigan (1986), and also Dent (1999).

27 This section is largely based on Doz and Hamel (1998: ch. 7).

28 This section is largely based on Doz and Hamel (1998: ch. 8). See also Gomez-Casseres (1995).

29 Gomez-Casseres (1995).

30 Jacobides et al. (2018).

31 Williamson and Meyer (2012).

32 Greve, Rowley and Shipilov (2013)

33 Williamson and Meyer (Op. cit)

34 https://www.conseil-national-industrie.gouv.fr

35 Gomez-Casseres (1995: ch. 9).

36 Ariño et al. (2001).

References and further reading

Adner, R. (2017) 'Ecosystem as structure: an actionable construct for strategy', *Journal of Management*, 43 (1), January: 39–58.

Aharens, N. (2013) 'China competitiveness, myth, reality and lessons for the United States and Japan: case study: SAICMotor Corporation', Centre for Strategic and International Studies. https://csis-website-prod.s3.amazonaws.com/s3fs-public/legacy_files/files/publication/130215_competitiveness_Huawei_casestudy_Web.pdf (accessed 1 February 2022).

Akadar, A., Adil, A., Ernst, D. and Vaish, P. (1997) 'Emerging market alliances: must they be win–lose?', *McKinsey Quarterly*, 4: 120–37.

Ariño, A., de La Torre, J. and Ring, P. S. (2001) 'Relational quality: managing trust in corporate alliances', *California Management Review*, 44 (1): 109–31.

Ashkenas, R., DeMonaco, L. and Francis, S. C. (1998) 'Making the deal real: how GE capital integrates acquisitions', *Harvard Business Review*, 76 (1): 165–78.

Bleeke, J., Isono, J., Ernst, D. and Weinberg, D. (1990) 'Succeeding at cross-border M&A', *McKinsey Quarterly*, 3: 46–55.

Bleeke, J. A. and Ernst, D. (1991) 'The way to win in cross-border alliances', *Harvard Business Review*, 69 (6): 127–35.

Capron, L. (1999) 'The long-term performance of horizontal acquisitions', *Strategic Management Journal*, 20 (11): 987–1018.

Capron, L. and Mitchell, W. (2012) *Build, Borrow, or Buy: Solving the Growth Dilemma* (Boston, MA: Harvard Business Review Press).

Castañer, X. and Oliveira, N. (2020), 'Collaboration, coordination, and cooperation among organizations: establishing the distinctive meanings of these terms through a systematic literature review', *Journal of Management*, 6 (6): 965–1001.

Cirjevskis, A. (2020) 'Valuing reciprocal synergies in merger and acquisition deals using the real option analysis', *Administrative Sciences*, 10 (27).

Conseil National de l'Industrie (2020) 'Remettre les filières au cœur de la politique industrielle français'. https://www.conseil-national-industrie.gouv.fr/csf-remettre-filieres-au-coeur-de-la-politique-industrielle-francaise (accessed 15 June 2020).

Cunningham, M., under the supervision of R. Angelmar and Y. L. Doz (1994) 'Alza Ciba Geigy advanced drug delivery systems', INSEAD Case Study 2/94-4243.

Cuypers, I. R. P., Cuypers, Y. and Martin, X. (2017) 'When the target may know better: effects of experience and information asymmetries on value from mergers and acquisitions', *Strategic Management Journal*, 38 (3): 609–25.

Davidson, W. H. and de La Torre, J. (1989) *Managing the Global Corporation: Case Studies in Strategy and Management* (New York, NY: McGraw-Hill).

Dent, S. M. (1999) *Partnering Intelligence: Creating Value for Your Business by Building Smart Alliances* (Palo Alto, CA: Davies-Black Publishing).

DePamphilis, D. M. (2010) *Mergers, Acquisitions and Other Restructuring Activities* (Cambridge, MA: Academic Press).

Doherty, R., Ferrer, C. and Rinaudo, E. K. (2016) 'Building the right organization for mergers and acquisitions', *McKinsey Quarterly*. https://www.mckinsey.com/business-functions/strategy-and-corporate-finance/our-insights/building-the-right-organization-for-mergers-and-acquisitions (accessed 1 February 2022).

Doz, Y. L. (2019) 'Governing multilateral alliances', *California Management Review*, 61 (3): 93–114.

Doz, Y. L. and Hamel, G. (1998) *Alliance Advantage* (Boston, MA: Harvard Business School Press).

Dyer, J. H., Singh, H. and Hesterly, W. S. (2018) 'The relational view revisited: a dynamic perspective on value creation and value capture', *Strategic Management Journal*, 39 (12): 3140–62.

Eccles, R. G., Lanes, K. L. and Wilson, T. C. (1999) 'Are you paying too much for that acquisition?', *Harvard Business Review*, 77 (4): 136–46.

Ernst, D. and Halevy, T. (2000) 'When to think alliance', *McKinsey Quarterly*, 4: 47–55.

Ernst, D. and Steinhubl, A. M. J. (1999) 'Petroleum: after the megamergers', *McKinsey Quarterly*, 3: 49–57.

Friedheim, C. F. (1999) 'The battle of the alliances', *Management Review*, September: 46–51.

Geringer, J. M. and Hebert, L. (1989) 'Control and performance of international joint ventures', *Journal of International Business Studies*, Summer: 235–54.

Ghemawat, P. and Ghadar, F. (2000) 'The dubious logic of global megamergers', *Harvard Business Review*, 78 (4): 64–72.

Ghoshal, S. and Haspeslagh, P. (1991) 'Electrolux: the acquisition and integration of Zanussi', INSEAD Case Study 09/90-123.

Ghosn, C. (2002) 'Saving the business without losing the company', *Harvard Business Review*, 80 (1): 37–44.

Goedhart, M., Koller, T. and Wessels, D. (2017) 'The six types of successful acquisitions', *McKinsey Quarterly*. https://www.mckinsey.com/business-functions/strategy-and-corporate-finance/our-insights/the-six-types-of-successful-acquisitions (accessed 1 February 2022).

Gomez-Casseres, B. (1995) *The Alliance Revolution: An Entrepreneurial Approach to Globalization* (Cambridge, MA: Harvard University Press).

Greve, H. R., Rowley, T. and Shipilov, A. (2013) *Network Advantage: How to Unlock Value from your Alliances and Partnerships* (Chichester: John Wiley).

Habeck, M., Kröger, F. and Träm, M. (2000) *After the Merger: Seven Rules for Successful Post Merger Integration* (Englewood Cliffs, NJ: *Financial Times*/Prentice-Hall).

Hamel, G., Prahalad, C. K. and Doz, Y. L. (1989) 'Collaborate with your competitors, and win', *Harvard Business Review*, 67 (1): 133–9.

Harrigan, K. (1986) *Managing for Joint Venture Success* (Lanham, MD: Lexington Books).

Haspeslagh, P. and Jemison, W. (1991) *Managing Acquisitions: Creating Value Through Corporate Renewal* (New York, NY: Free Press).

Hawawini, G. and Viallet, C. (1999) *Finance for Executives* (Cincinnati, OH: South-Western Publishing), ch. 12, 379–428.

Hyde, D. and Haspeslagh, P. (1994) 'The making of the simply better healthcare company: SmithKline and Beecham: the simply better way', INSEAD Case Study 03/95-4449.

Inkpen, A. C. (1998) 'Learning and knowledge acquisition through strategic alliances', *The Academy of Management Executive*, November: 69–80.

Inkpen, A. and Ross, J. (2001) 'Why do some strategic alliances persist beyond their useful life?', *California Management Review*, 44 (1): 132–54.

Jacobides, M. G., Cennamo, C. and Gawer, A. (2018) 'Towards a theory of ecosystems', *Strategic Management Journal*, 39: 2255–76.

Kaetzler, B., Kordestani, K., O'Loughlin, E. and Van Ostende, M. (2019) 'Managing and supporting employees through cultural change in mergers', *McKinsey Quarterly*. https://www.mckinsey.com/business-functions/organization/our-insights/managing-and-supporting-employees-through-cultural-change-in-mergers (accessed 1 February 2022).

Khou, J. and Spar, D. (1994) 'SONY Corporation and Columbia Pictures', Harvard Business School Case 9/795/025.

Kim, C. and Mauborgne, R. (1997) 'Fair process: managing in the knowledge economy', *Harvard Business Review*, 75 (4): 65–75.

Kitching, J. (1973) 'Acquisitions in Europe', *Business International*, Research Report 73-3, Geneva.

Klincewicz, K. (2005) *Strategic Alliances in the High-tech Industry* (Berlin: Logos Verlag). http://citeseerx.ist.psu.edu/viewdoc/download?doi=10.1.1.137.215&rep=rep1&type=pdf (accessed 12 June 2017).

Kogut, B. (1991) 'Joint ventures and the option to expand and acquire', *Management Science*, 137 (1): 19–33.

Krishna, L. N. and Gee, F. (1998) 'General Electric and SNECMA', INSEAD Case Study 11/ 98-3450.

Lasserre, P. (1984) 'Selecting a foreign partner for technology transfer', *Long Range Planning*, 17: 43–9.

Lessard, D. (1996) 'Incorporating country risks in the valuation of offshore projects', *Journal of Applied Corporate Finance*, 9 (3): 52–63.

Li, C. and Reuer, J. (2021), 'The impact of corruption on market reactions to international strategic alliances', *Journal of International Business Studies*: 1–16.

Martin, R. (2016) 'The One Thing You Need to Get Right', *Harvard Business Review*, June: 42–8. https://hbr.org/2016/06/ma-the-one-thing-you-need-to-get-right (accessed 1 February 2022).

McKinsey Collection (2021), 'The future of M&A and post pandemic business priorities'. https://www.mckinsey.com/featured-insights/collections/the-future-of-ma-and-postpandemic-business-priorities (accessed 1 February 2022).

Mitchell, D. and Holmes, G. (1996) *Making Acquisitions Work: Learning from Companies' Successes and Failures* (London: Economic Intelligence Unit).

Moore, J. F. (1993) 'Predators and prey, a new ecology of competition', *Harvard Business Review*, May–June.

J. P. Morgan, *M&A Global outlook, JP Morgan Insights 2016*, https://www.jpmorgan.com/global/insights/maglobaloutlook (accessed 19 June 2017).

Oxley, J. (2019) *Governance of International Strategic Alliances (RLE International Business) Technology and Transaction Costs* (London: Routledge).

Probert, J. and De Meyer, A. (1998) 'Francolor Pigments: a Toyo Ink acquisition', INSEAD Case Study 05/ 98-4756.

Purshe, W. (1996) 'Pharmaceuticals: the consolidation is not over', *McKinsey Quarterly*, 2: 110–19.

PwC Global (2020) 'Global M&A industry trends'. https://www.pwc.com/gx/en/services/deals/trends.html (accessed 1 February 2022).

Rudnicki, J. and Thorpe, R. (2017) 'The artful synergist or how to get more value from mergers and acquisitions', *McKinsey Quarterly*. https://www.mckinsey.com/business-functions/strategy-and-corporate-finance/our-insights/the-artful-synergist-or-how-to-get-more-value-from-mergers-and-acquisitions (accessed 1 February 2022).

Sarala, M., Vaara, E. and Junni, P. (2019) 'Beyond merger syndrome and cultural differences: new avenues for research on the "human side" of global mergers and acquisitions (M&As)', *Journal of World Business*, 54: 307–21.

Shipilov, A. (2021) 'Don't confuse platforms with ecosystems', INSEAD knowledge. https://knowledge.insead.edu/blog/insead-blog/dont-confuse-platforms-with-ecosystems-15801 (accessed 1 February 2022).

Shipilov, A. and Gawer, A. (2020) 'Integrating research on interorganizational networks and ecosystems', *Academy of Management Annals*, 14 (1): 92–121. https://doi.org/10.5465/annals.2018.0121 (accessed 1 February 2022).

Smith, K. (2000) 'A brand new culture for the merged firm', *Mergers & Acquisitions*, June: 45–50.

Spekeman, R. E. and Lynn, I. (2000) *Alliance Competence: Maximizing the Value of Your Partnerships* (New York, NY: John Wiley).

Tao, Z. (2004) *Anheuser-Busch versus SABMiller: Bidding War in China's Beer Industry*, Asia Case Research Centre and Fudan University, Case HKU411.

Viscio, A., Harbison, J., Asin, A. and Vitaro, R. (1999) 'Post-merger integration: what makes mergers work?', *Strategy+Business*, fourth quarter, 17: 26–33. http://www.strategy-business.com (accessed 19 June 2017).

Von Krogh, G., Sinatra, A. and Singh, H. (eds) (1994) *The Management of Corporate Acquisitions: International Perspectives* (London: Macmillan).

Williamson, P. (1999) 'Strategy as options for the future', *Sloan Management Review*, Spring: 117–26.

Williamson, P. and De Meyer, A. (2012) 'Ecosystem advantage: how to successfully harness the power of partners', *California Management Review*, 55 (1), Fall.

Yoshino, M. Y. and Rangan, U. (1995) *Strategic Alliances: An Entrepreneurial Approach to Globalization* (Boston, MA: Harvard Business School Press).

Zulkarnain, Z., Kinnumen, T., Leviagängas, P. and Kess, P. (2014) *The Electrical Electric Ecosystem Model – Construct, Analysis and Identification of Key Challenges*, Technical Research Centre of Finland, Finland. http://www.fm-kp.si/zalozba/ISSN/1581-6311/12_253-277.pdf (accessed 1 February 2022).

Journals

Academy of Management Journal: https://aom.org/research/journals/journal

Advances in Mergers and Acquisitions: https://www.emerald.com/insight/publication/issn/1479-361X

Journal of Applied Corporate Finance: https://onlinelibrary.wiley.com/journal/17456622

Journal of Financial Economics: https://www.journals.elsevier.com/journal-of-financial-economics

Journal of Management: https://journals.sagepub.com/home/jom

Part III

Managing globally

Chapter 9 Global marketing | This chapter starts by discussing the theory of customer convergence and then analyses the practical approach to global marketing as it affects the various elements of the marketing mix: branding, pricing, global account management, global solution selling and global distribution.

Chapter 10 Global operations and digital networks | Chapter 10 deals first with the classic issues of the localization of operational facilities: the role and location of manufacturing plants in a global production network, global procurement and the management of the supply chain. It then describes the management of international infrastructure projects. In the final section it discusses at length the role of the internet in the globalization of operations and how digital networks impact the way strategies are formulated and implemented.

Chapter 11 Global innovation | Chapter 11 deals with the management of research and development (R&D) in global companies as well as knowledge management, transfer of best practices, global open innovation and the issues of technology transfer and protection of intellectual property rights (IPR).

Chapter 12 Global financial management | Chapter 12 addresses some of the contemporary issues that global corporations face in managing their financial resources. The first section deals with the risks associated with foreign exchange fluctuations and the hedging techniques used to cover those risks. The second part looks at project financing. The third part discusses the sources of global financing – both equity and debt. Finally cryptocurrencies and trade financing are described.

Chapter 13 Global human resource management | Chapter 13 addresses the practical managerial aspects of dealing with human resources in global firms. Besides the classic problems of expatriation, it looks at the means of developing local talent in the various countries in which the firms operate and creating a truly global organizational culture. In the final section, it discusses the challenges and opportunities of working from anywhere (WFA).

Chapter 14 Designing a global organization | Chapter 14 describes the advantages and disadvantages of the various forms of global organizational designs, from pure geographical to global and matrix models. It ends by presenting the transnational organizational culture that is considered necessary to support the structure, processes and system of the global organization. It ends by looking at key recent trends in the management of global companies.

Chapter 9

Global marketing

At the end of the chapter you will be able to:

- Understand customer behaviour; its divergence and convergence across countries
- Understand differences in segmentation
- Design a product policy toward standardization or adaptation
- Decide whether the company will push global or local brands
- Decide whether the company should have a global pricing policy
- Design an appropriate global distribution system
- Develop a global account and global solution selling policy

Introduction

In 1983 Theodore Levitt, in a far-sighted article, predicted the 'globalization of markets'. His arguments were based on the *convergence of consumer needs and behaviours* that would erase national differences and would lead to the standardization of marketing policies.

In Chapter 1 we showed that since 1980, globalization had definitely gained ground and that many companies had designed, launched, promoted, priced and sometimes distributed products and services globally. Brands such as Coca-Cola, Apple, Mercedes and Windows are known in nearly all cities and through YouTube, TikTok and Instagram they reach users all over the globe. Newspapers and magazines such as the *Financial Times*, the *Wall Street Journal* and *The Economist* are distributed simultaneously all over the world. This chapter discusses the practical implications of globalization for marketing, as well as its limitations. It starts by examining the validity of the theory of customer convergence and then looks at the practical approach to global marketing in the various elements of the marketing mix.

Customer behaviour, convergence and global segmentation

The prime task of any marketing manager is to understand customers' needs, embodied in customer value curves. Customer needs are driven by a series of factors, as summarized in Table 9.1.

It can be seen from Table 9.1 that several of the factors shaping customer needs are linked to *culture and geography*. For instance, Schütte (1998) argued that Asian customers have a different hierarchy of needs and consequently exhibit value curves that differ from Western ones[1] (Figure 9.1) and Parker (2000) showed that bioclimatic conditions change customer preferences.[2]

Beside Levitt, Kenichi Ohmae[3] and George Yip[4] are defenders of global convergence, arguing that an increasing percentage of the population, at least in the market-led economies, share the same tastes and needs for larger quantities of products and services. Ohmae has proposed the term *Californization* to describe this convergence.

Table 9.1 Customer needs and value curves

Factors shaping customer needs	
Consumer markets	**Business-to-business markets**
• Income	• Industry type
• Psychology	• Usage
• Social habits	• Cost/benefit
• Social status	• Technological requirements
• Climatic conditions	• Time availability
• Time availability	
Typical customer value curve elements	
• Product/service functionalities (comfort, design, appeal, etc.)	• Product/service functionalities
• Product/service quality	• Product/service performance
• Image	• Reputation
• Price	• Relationships
• Availability	• Price and associated costs
• Convenience	• Associated services
• Associated services	• Financing
• Financing	• Network effects

There is no conclusive evidence of full convergence for consumer goods except in the case of a few products or services that are highly publicized (portable computers, mobile phones, luxury goods). However, in business-to-business (B2B) sectors convergence is gaining ground, since purchasing motives are essentially technical and economic. Each industry market can be divided into different broad segments, as illustrated in Figure 9.2.

Another consideration, in particular for expanding companies that originate from emerging or developing markets, is to assess and manage foreign market perception, not only of their brand, but of the original headquarters country itself.

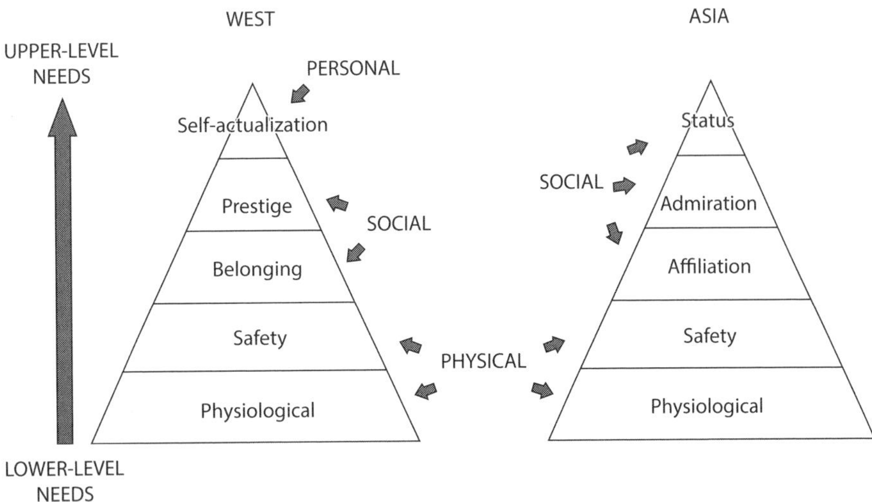

Figure 9.1 Western versus Asian hierarchy of needs
Source: Schütte and Ciarlante (1998). Reproduced with permission from Palgrave Macmillan.

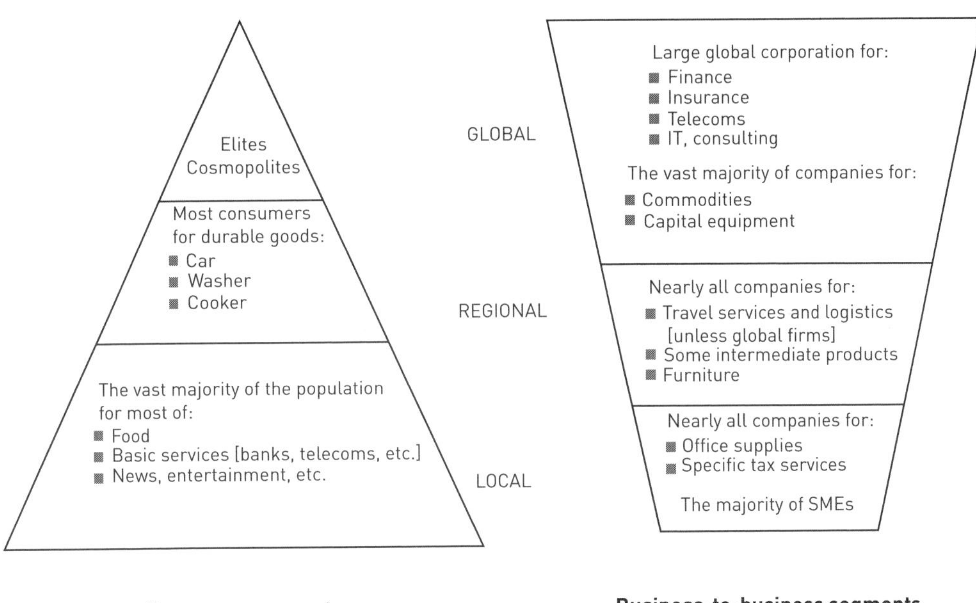

Figure 9.2 Customer segmentation

Product standardization

The standardization of products and services is a function of two main factors. First, *customer value curves*: the more similar customer needs are across the world, the more the product can be standardized. Second, the *minimum economic size of production*: the higher the volume required, the more standardization. Figure 9.3 shows four categories of product and the importance to them of those two factors.

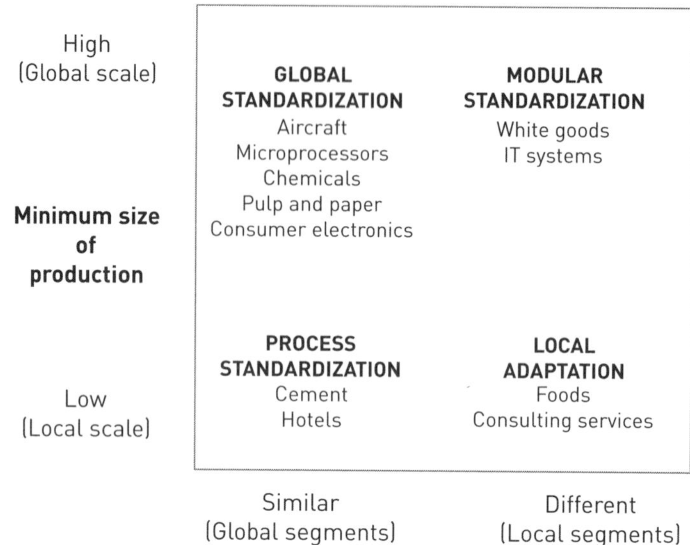

Figure 9.3 Global product standardization types

The first category, *global standardization*, corresponds to products or services that target global customer segments and require a high volume of concentrated production to be cost competitive. This is the case with chemicals, aircraft, microprocessors and consumer electronics.

The second category, *process standardization*, refers to products or services that serve similar needs but do not require a high volume. Their production is localized, the production process standardized and, as a result, the final product is also standardized. Cement production is local in production and factories apply the same processes across the globe for delivering standard products.

The third category, *local adaptation*, includes products or services that are fully tailored to local needs, such as foods or consultancy services.

The last category, *modular standardization*, is needed when economies of scale are important, but customers demand product differentiation. Modularization is achieved by producing standard components in global production or service centres and differentiating the product at the assembly stage. This is the case with white goods (refrigerators, washing machines and so on) or IT systems.

In some cases companies combine different categories. Fast-food restaurants are an example of a mix of process standardization together with local adaptation. McDonald's hamburgers for example are produced the same way everywhere. However, over the years, McDonald's has adapted its product offering to cater for national differences (in India, chicken is used rather than beef, rice wraps are used in China and in the UK bacon rolls are offered), but the processes follow strict global rules.

Global branding[5]

A brand is *global* when the product or service it represents is marketed across the world under its name. Every year various organizations publish a list of the most famous or valuable global brands. Table 9.2 lists the five brands that topped the leading classifications.

Table 9.2 Top five leading global brands comparison between 2020 and 2000

2020	2000
Amazon, Apple, Google, Microsoft, Facebook	Coca Cola, Microsoft, IBM, GE, Intel

Sources: https://brandirectory.com/rankings/global/table; https://interbrand.com/best-brands/; https://www.forbes.com/the-worlds-most-valuable-brands/#fd94efd119c0; https://www.kantar.com/inspiration/brands/what-are-the-most-valuable-global-brands-in-2021; https://app.flourish.studio/visualisation/1163270/ (all accessed 1 February 2022).

Global brands may be the name of individual products or services (Pampers, Diet Coke, Playstation) or the name of the corporation that produces them (Proctor & Gamble, Coca-Cola, Sony). In the latter case, the brand is the symbol of *corporate identity* and it is encapsulated in a logo that is present on all the firm's documents and associated with all of the company's individual products or services even if they have a separate individual trademark. Global branding is a combination of both types: global firms develop a corporate name that will apply to all subsidiaries in the world and they also market products under different names. For instance, Intel is the corporate brand and Core is the trademark of a family of microprocessors; Nestlé is the corporate name and Nescafé or Perrier are the global names of individual products. The same would apply to Microsoft and Windows, Explorer or Office. It does not mean that all the products of a global firm will make use of the same name, either corporate or product. Coca-Cola, Heineken or Electrolux use the corporate name for some of their products (global products or services) and market other products locally under a local or regional name (Table 9.3). Companies will try to limit the number of individual product names and market products under a global name. In 2020 Unilever, one of the oldest multinational corporations, owned over 400 brands in 190 countries.[6] Procter and Gamble owned 65 brands in 10 product categories and was present in 180 countries.[7]

Table 9.3 Examples of corporations using global and local brands

Global corporate	Global brand	Sample of local/regional brand name
Coca-Cola Around 500 brands[8]	Coke Sprite Fanta Dasani Smartwater	• Del Valle (Latin America) • Fuzze (India) • Maaza (India) • Ciel (Latin America) • Vitamin Water (USA)
Heineken 300 brands in 190 countries[9]	Heineken Amstel Sol Desperados Affligem Strongbow cider	Some local brands: • Tiger (Asia Pacific) • Anchor (Asia Pacific) • Bintang (Indonesia) • Feyrouz (Morocco) • Goldberg (Nigeria) • 33 Export (France) • Moretti (Austria) • Kruzovice (Czech Rep.) • Zywieck (Poland)

Global corporate	Global brand	Sample of local/regional brand name
Electrolux 8 strategic brands, 3 of which are global More than 30 national brands 50 licensing brands (http://www.electroluxgroup.com/annualreports/2015/en/strategic-development/brand-and-design/ (accessed 22 January 2022))	Electrolux Grand Cuisine Molteni AEG	Regional strategic brands: • Frigidaire (North and Latin America) • Zanussi (Europe) • Eureka (North America) • Westinghouse (Asia Pacific) Regional or national brands (examples): • Arthur Martin (France) • Castor (Italy) • Chef (Australia) • Juno (Germany)

According to Professor John Quelch (1999), the common features of global brands are that they are:

- Strong in their home market
- Consistent in product positioning
- Present geographically in a balanced way across regions
- Address similar consumer needs worldwide
- Easy to pronounce.

As mentioned earlier, many global brands are now dissociated from the corporate name (Nestlé and Perrier, Unilever and Lipton Tea, Apple and iPhone) and many global names are used in many product categories (Sony, Samsung).

For Hankinson and Cowking (1996), global brands can be categorized in a 2 × 2 matrix according to the degree of consistency in brand positioning (whether they convey the same message to the same segments across the world) and according to the standardization of the products or services they represent (see Figure 9.4). Volvo is an example of a brand representing a standardized product with different country segmentation. Nescafé has the same brand positioning with products adapted to customer tastes. McDonald's started initially with a standardized product and the same positioning across the world but, as already mentioned, has been obliged to adapt products to local conditions.

This classification shows that the meaning of global branding can be quite diverse and obliges companies to define a 'global branding' strategy by which they articulate what they are striving for.

Advantages of global branding

There are three main advantages of global branding: strategic, economic and organizational.

From a *strategic* point of view, global branding is likely to reinforce market power thanks to a concentration of marketing effort on a single name, as well as the ability to benefit from a spillover

		Degree of global consistency in brand message and segment	
		Adapted to country specificities	Highly consistent across the world
Degree of product/service standardization	Standardized	**Positioning adaptive global brand** *Volvo*	**Pure global brand** *Intel* *Apple*
	Adapted to country specificities	**Fully adaptive global brand** *Nescafé*	**Product adaptive global brand** *McDonald's*

Figure 9.4 Global brand positioning
Source: Authors' own figure, adapted with author's permission from Hankinson and Cowking (1996).

effect from country to country. It also saves time in launching new products because, if the product comes under the umbrella of an already-established global name, it facilitates customer awareness and benefits from a more efficient promotion roll-out.

From an *economic* point of view, global branding brings savings in external communication with customers (advertising, promotion, direct selling), as well as internal costs because it reduces inventories, product administration and accounting, as well as training and internal communication costs.

Finally, from an *organizational* point of view, it reinforces corporate identity, and facilitates the transfer of personnel and best practices across the organization.

Disadvantages of global branding

The detractors of global brands argue that they ignore national differences in terms of culture, customer behaviour and stages of economic development, and lead to over-standardization and heavy corporate headquarters centralization, thereby stifling entrepreneurship. There are abundant anecdotes of so-called global names that have negative or aggressive connotations in certain cultures. The whole argument usually boils down to opportunity costs, so the company relying on global brand alone only skims the market and forgoes the main sources of growth that lie untapped in the masses of customers who are still culturally centred.

The argument against over-reliance on the global brand has proven to be true on many occasions. In the case of the beer industry in China, for instance, global marketers have been suffering from relying too much on their global brand to conquer the second largest (soon to be leading) market in the world. Foster's, Asahi and Budweiser accumulated losses for not pushing local brands in the way that

South African Brewery did successfully, by building its presence with local brands such as Snowflake or Keller.[10] In practice, global firms adopt a multiple branding strategy by offering local markets both global and local brands when there are significant opportunities to do so (as shown by the example of L'Oréal).

Examples of global brand failures

KFC's slogan 'finger licking good' was translated as 'eat your fingers off' when they entered the Chinese market in the 1980s.

The American beer company Coors translated its slogan, 'Turn It Loose', into Spanish, where it is a colloquial term for having diarrhoea.

Nike had to recall its products when a decoration intended to resemble fire on the back of the shoes resembled the Arabic word for Allah.

Pepsi's slogan 'Pepsi Brings You Back to Life' in China was translated to 'Pepsi Brings You Back from the Grave'.

HSBC Bank had to rebrand its entire global private banking operations after the US campaign expanded internationally in 2009. Its 'Assume Nothing' message was translated in many countries as 'Do Nothing'.

Car manufacturer, Ford, made two translation errors. The first when marketing the Ford Pinto in Brazil. Ford had no idea that the term 'Pinto' means 'tiny male genitals' in Brazilian Portuguese. In Belgium, Ford's message 'Every car has a high-quality body' was translated into 'Every car has a high-quality corpse'.

Source: Authors' creation based on: https://www.linkedin.com/pulse/17-global-brand-failures-some-hilarious-examples-stefan-weynfeldt/; https://www.foxbusiness.com/features/lost-in-translation-9-international-marketing-fails; https://www.inc.com/geoffrey-james/the-20-worst-brand-translations-of-all-time.html (accessed 1 February 2022).

EXAMPLE 9.1 Global/local branding – L'Oréal in China

L'Oréal, which defines itself as 'The Beauty Company', is present in 150 countries in the world with sales of $29.8 billion in 2019.[11] Its brands fall into two broad categories: luxury products and (mass) consumer products including cosmetics, skin care, perfume and hair care. L'Oréal has been present in China since 1997, and it is now their second largest market after the USA. L'Oréal's brand offerings in China straddle both the global and local. In the luxury segment its global brands are Lancôme, Giorgio Armani, YSL, Kiehl's and Helena Rubeinstein. Local high-end brands are Yue Sai and Shu Urmonea. In the consumer market the global brands are Maybelline and Garnier, and the local brands are Hydofresy and Magic. Its market share is estimated in total at 20 per cent. The company has created an R&D centre in Shanghai for developing and adapting products to fit with Asian consumers' characteristics.

Building a global brand

Riesenbeck and Freeling (1991) have identified two approaches to building global brands: the waterfall model and the sprinkler model.

In the *waterfall model* the brand is developed in one country at a time, while in the sprinkler model it is developed simultaneously in all key countries. The *sprinkler model* is currently favoured by global marketers, as seen in the launch of new computers (iMac) and software (each new Windows Office suite). However, one of the main issues that major global companies are facing is the need to 'globalize' under a single name a large variety of existing local subsidiaries' names and acquisitions. Allianz, the German insurance company, was confronted with multiple subsidiaries' names after its acquisitions of the French Assurances Générales de France, the US Fireman's Fund and the UK's Cornhill,[12] and had to cope with the difficulties of adopting Allianz as a global corporate brand.

Brand relevance

Branding is valuable but its success is difficult to measure. Traditionally it has been limited to criteria including sales, recognition and image. The digital revolution has meant that brand relevance is more salient than brand recognition, some experts argue.[13] Brand loyalty has a different meaning in the digital ecosystem with a successful brand being one that comes up spontaneously whilst ordering products through digital means, be it searching on Google or using devices such as Alexa or Amazon digital assistant. These relevant brands are embedded in customers' lives, therefore, unlike brand recognition, brand relevance cannot be bought with marketing budgets. The Brand Relevance Index (BRI) ranks hundreds of the world's largest brands according to how important/meaningful they are to 'real' consumers. Brand relevance in the index is measured through qualitative research: a list of fifty attributes describing how consumers perceive relevant brands was drawn up. It was reduced to sixteen attributes driving brand relevance under four pillars: *customer obsessed* (brands that work tirelessly to entrench themselves in consumers' lifestyles); *ruthlessly pragmatic* (brands that do whatever it takes to be there for their customers); *pervasively innovative* (brands that are constantly shape-shifting to stay ahead of technological changes and consumer trends); *distinctively inspired* (brands with a talismanic, aspirational quality which dovetails with consumers' dreams).[14]

Together, these four pillars comprise what the BRI terms 'relentless relevance'. The BRI asserts that relentlessly relevant brands are best equipped to thrive in an increasingly fast-paced future. BRI results can be compared to best global brands rankings which emphasize brand value: brands that are relevant to consumers such as Pinterest, Spotify and Netflix score lower on the brand value index. This can be explained by the nature of the brands: they are young digital players with many loyal users. Similarly there are high-value brands such as Coca-Cola that do not appear in the BRI top 50. Brands need to win at both value and relevance to survive, for brands that rank highly in either relevance or value might benefit from collaboration with an opposite. Apple is an example of one such entity that is high in BRI and Best Global Brands.

Source: https://knowledge.insead.edu/blog/insead-blog/how-brands-can-stay-relevant-in-the-digital-age-10231

Table 9.4 Top ten relevant brands, 2019

	CHINA	USA	UK
1	Alipay	Apple	NHS
2	Huawei	Spotify	Spotify
3	Android	Android	Netflix
4	DJI	Bose	PlayStation
5	WeChat	Disney	Apple
6	Bilibili	KitchenAid	LEGO
7	Xiaomi	Amazon	Fitbit
8	China CITIC Bank	Netflix	Lush
9	Intel	PIXAR	Samsung
10	Audi	Pinterest	Google

Source: https://www.prophet.com/relevantbrands-2019/ (accessed 1 February 2022).

Advertising

The issue of conveying the brand's image to the public is related to global branding. These are the issues facing advertising:

- Should the company use a *single* advertising agency for the world or local agencies?
- Should the *advertising* content be the same or differentiated?

The trend today for global companies is to deal with a single agency across the world. This trend leads the industry to consolidate and globalize (Table 9.5). There are four main advantages of working with a single agency:[15]

- *Simplicity* of relationship
- Easier to retain *control*
- *Buying power* over global media and global support (brochures, promotional material)
- *Economies of scale* in production.

Table 9.5 Major global advertising agencies, 2019

Company	Short profile
WPP http://www.wpp.com UK	3,000 agencies over the world. Ogilvy, Wundeman Thompson, AKQA are part of the group. Revenues in 2019: £13.2 billion; 107,000 employees
Omnicom www.omnicomgroup.com/ USA	1,500 agencies over the world. BBDO, DDB and TBW are part of the group. Revenues in 2019: $15.1 billion; 70,000 employees

Company	Short profile
Publicis http://www.publicisgroupe.com/ France	Present in 100 countries. Saatchi & Saatchi, Leo Burnett, BBH are part of the group. Revenues in 2019: €9.8 billion; 80,000 employees
The Interpublic Group of Companies (IPG) http://www.interpublic.com/ USA	100 offices in the world. McCANN, MULLEN LOWE, FCB are part of the group. Revenues in 2019: $2.9 billion; 52,000 employees

Source: Websites of above-mentioned companies.

Concerning content, global firms must be careful not to offend local cultures and to adapt their advertisements while retaining the same message. In 2000, the advertisement of a French perfume in Europe represented a young naked woman. In the United States the same woman was dressed. Benetton and Swatch are the 'avant-garde' of global advertising, using the same content and message everywhere, sometimes with unfortunate results.[16] In 2018 Dolce & Gabbana launched an advertising campaign on social media ahead of its fashion show in Shanghai. It depicted a Chinese woman, adorned in D&G jewellery, using chopsticks to eat pizza, spaghetti and an oversized pastry called cannoli. Dolce & Gabbana labelled the series 'Eating with Chopsticks', and tagged each of the ads with #DGLovesChina. It caused outrage in China, resulting in the show being cancelled.

Online global advertising

Until 2020, when Covid-19 put a halt on many industries, spending on advertising worldwide had increased steadily and was expected to return to its growth track starting in 2021, and surpass $630 billion in 2024. American consumer goods corporation Procter & Gamble was the largest advertiser worldwide in 2018, having spent more than $10 billion on ads. Other big advertisers include South Korean Samsung, French L'Oréal and Dutch-British Unilever, respectively second, third and fourth in the ranking.

Digital advertising spending worldwide amounted to $325 billion in 2019. There was a drop in 2020 due to the coronavirus-related market issues but it was estimated to grow to $389 billion in 2021 with a year on year growth of 12.2 per cent. Mobile internet advertising was the fastest growing medium in the global ad market. In 2019, mobile ad spend worldwide amounted to roughly $189 billion and it was expected to grow further to $247 billion by 2022.[17] Digital advertising can take several forms: banner advertisements, pre-video clips, search engine advertising and pop-ups. Because of its global accessibility and its data-mining capability, the internet offers opportunities to advertisers to launch global advertising campaigns with local content (Coca-Cola's 'Taste the Feeling' campaign for Chinese New Year, Nike's 'Just Do it' slogan with the Brazilian soccer team).[18]

Online advertising and social media is a means for small players and start-ups to reach a global audience quickly with little cost. It also allows these smaller ventures to expand rapidly internationally adapting their marketing where necessary to local markets without incurring large traditional marketing budgets (the Mini-cases below are examples of how this has been applied in the beverage and ice cream markets).

Global pricing

Global pricing consists of setting a *consistent pricing policy* across borders. The only differences in prices are due to taxation or regulatory reasons. Basic Swatch watches are sold at a price that varies little from the equivalent of $65.

There are three main advantages to global pricing:

- It avoids *arbitrage*. When countries are not isolated geographically and when there are no barriers to trade, consumers can shop at the lowest-priced place. In the 1980s, French car dealers were buying French cars in Belgium, where prices were lower, to resell them. The price differences were due in part to differences in taxes (VAT) but also to the policies of the car manufacturers who priced differently depending upon the country's competitive climate. With the development of the EU and the arrival of the euro, prices tended to converge.
- It protects the *brand integrity*. Customers who discover that the product they buy in one country is sold at a discount in another may question the reason why it is so, and may attribute the price difference to an overall lower quality.
- It facilitates the servicing of *global customers*.

The disadvantages are that global pricing does not account for differences in customer utility curves and leads to *sub-optimization* (see Insert 9.1).

In practice, global pricing can be implemented in one or several of the following cases:

- When the product or service is targeted at customers who have *similar profiles* and have the same or similar value curves, the so-called 'global segments'. In the case of consumer goods we find luxury goods (Dom Perignon, Louis Vuitton, Gucci etc.), fashion items (Swatch, Benetton, Esprit etc.), personal computers and software (iMac, IBM, Microsoft Office etc.). In the case of B2B marketing the similarity applies to products or services sold to subsidiaries of multinational companies (global accounts)
- When the product or service is sold under a strong '*global brand*'
- When there are strong possibilities of *arbitrage*
- When the company deploys a *multi-brand policy* of global and local products and wants to clearly differentiate the global brand from the rest
- When the product or service has *standardized* functionalities, qualities and features.

Insert 9.1 Sub-optimization

Suppose that for a particular product the customer's utility curve generates a *demand function*:

In country *A*: volume sold (V_A) = 204 − 6 × Price (P_A)
In country *B*: volume sold (V_B) = 160 − 4 × Price (P_B)

The *cost* function of the product is:
Total cost (C) = 600 + 10*V* (10 is the variable cost of the product)

The *total revenue* function is:
Total sales (S) = $P \times V$
Then the profit is $R = S - C = P \times V - C$

In the case of country *A*:
Profit is $R_A = -6P_A^2 + 264P_A - 2{,}640$
Profit is maximized when $264 - 12P_A = 0$ or $P_A = 264/12 = 22$

In the case of country *B*:
Profit is $R_B = -4P_B^2 + 200P_B - 2{,}200$
Profit is maximized when $200 - 8P_B = 0$ or $P_B = 200/8 = 25$

It can be seen that profit is maximized when prices are differentiated and not global. The maximum profit is 564 when prices are set at 22 in country *A* and 25 in country *B*. If you adopt a global pricing strategy, the profit will be lower:

- If price is 22, profit is 548
- If price is 23, profit is 542
- If price is 24, profit is 536
- If price is 25, profit is 510

Global account management

When the customers of a global firm are themselves global, and find they need similar products or services across their operations (for instance, computer equipment), it may be economically and strategically beneficial for both supplier and customer to coordinate their transactions globally. For that reason, in many sectors global firms have created what is known as global account management (GAM) to serve their global customers (global accounts).

The principle of global account management is illustrated in Figure 9.5.

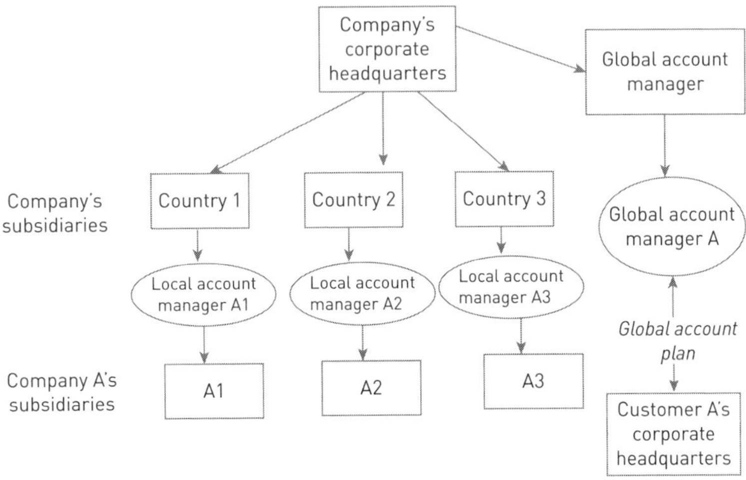

Figure 9.5 Principle of global account management

At the firm's corporate headquarters a central function of global account management is the supervision of the activities of the global account managers who reside close to the customer's corporate headquarters. (Global accounts are those customers who generate a significant flow of sales.) The global account manager negotiates with the corporate client a global account plan for the year, specifying the price and quantity of products or services to be delivered. In each of the subsidiaries of the firms a local account manager deals with the customer's local subsidiary for the implementation of the agreed deal.

Global accounts are primarily used in the following industries:

- *Financial services:* catering for the varied financial needs of the subsidiaries of multinational companies. Citibank, for instance, created the World Corporate Group in 1974 in order to serve the cross-border financial needs of 450 major companies.[19]
- *Advertising:* developing and implementing campaigns worldwide. Saatchi & Saatchi initiated the concept of global supermarkets in the late 1970s.
- *Telecoms equipment manufacturers:* catering for the equipment and associated services needs of globalizing telecoms operators. Ericsson set up a global account management organization in 1994 serving thirty clients located in ten home countries, such as AT&T, Vodafone and BT.[20]
- *Telecoms services operators:* providing seamless communication data and voice services; BT, Orange, set up global accounts in the 1990s.
- *Computer equipment manufacturers or software companies:* providing IT equipment and services. Hewlett-Packard (HP) led the way, followed by IBM for global IT delivery. Cap Gemini, EDS and Oracle in the service sectors have set up account management.
- *Accounting firms:* PricewaterhouseCoopers, and so on.
- *Industrial equipment:* Siemens, Schneider Electric.
- *Aerospace manufacturers:* Airbus, Boeing to support airline operations.

A fictitious example of global account management in banking is illustrated in Figure 9.6. The bank's corporate headquarters is in London, but the client is a big chemical firm in Munich. The bank's Parent Account Manager (PAM), who is located at the branch closest to the client's corporate headquarters, negotiates with the client's Chief Financial Officer a global financing plan for financial deals or services in various parts of the world. The Subsidiaries' Account Managers (SAMs), located in the bank's international branches, deliver the services under terms negotiated centrally. In such a system, trade-off and arbitrage are done centrally. It may well happen that a 'good discount' is granted to the Brazilian investment but, as a counterpart, the bank will get a profitable deal regarding a Hong Kong syndication.

The four main advantages of global account management are:

- The ability to provide *full and consistent services* to customers, reducing the hassle of negotiating deal after deal
- A *lower overall cost* for the customer, partly owing to volume purchases
- The ability for customers to *optimize their procurement strategy* (in the case of banking, their financing strategy)
- For the product and service provider, to *increase overall sales and optimize profitability.*

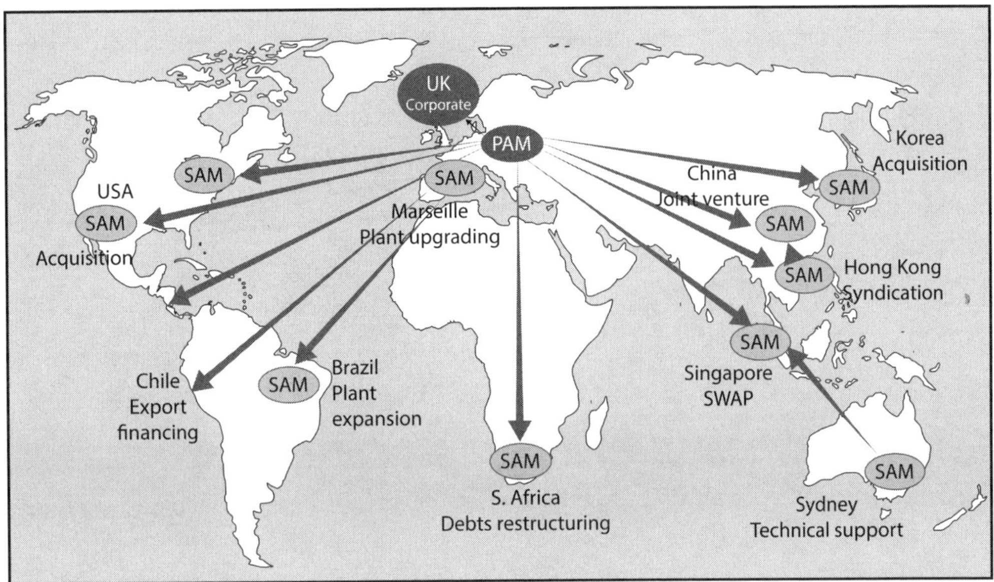

Figure 9.6 A financial global account management network servicing a leading European manufacturer
Source: Authors' own figure, based on text in Malnight (1995).

In the implementation of a global account management system, three main issues arise:

- Customer subsidiaries may be reluctant to accept global procurement. Local operations may find that it is cheaper or better to source locally.
- Supplier subsidiaries may be reluctant to abandon potential sources of local income for the benefit of the global account if they could have got a better deal by negotiating separately.
- A complex internal accounting system may be required for reallocating income among subsidiaries.

Global account systems have proven to be beneficial to companies that have been the first to implement them in their industries, setting the standards for others. In the sectors mentioned earlier the question is not whether to implement a GAM, but how to do it properly.[21]

Global solution selling

Global solution selling is a mirror image of global account management. It consists of mobilizing the resources and competencies of several subsidiaries across the world in order to offer a valuable solution to a client located in a particular country. In the example shown in Figure 9.7, the company, a large power generation corporation headquartered in Europe, has to make an international bid for a turnkey project in Tianjin, China. The offer has to be complete and requires not only the sale of equipment but also the training of personnel and the management of the plant for five years under a Build, Operate and Transfer (BOT) contract. In order to give the best solution at the best price, the company has to mobilize the expertise of its US, French, German and Australian subsidiaries.

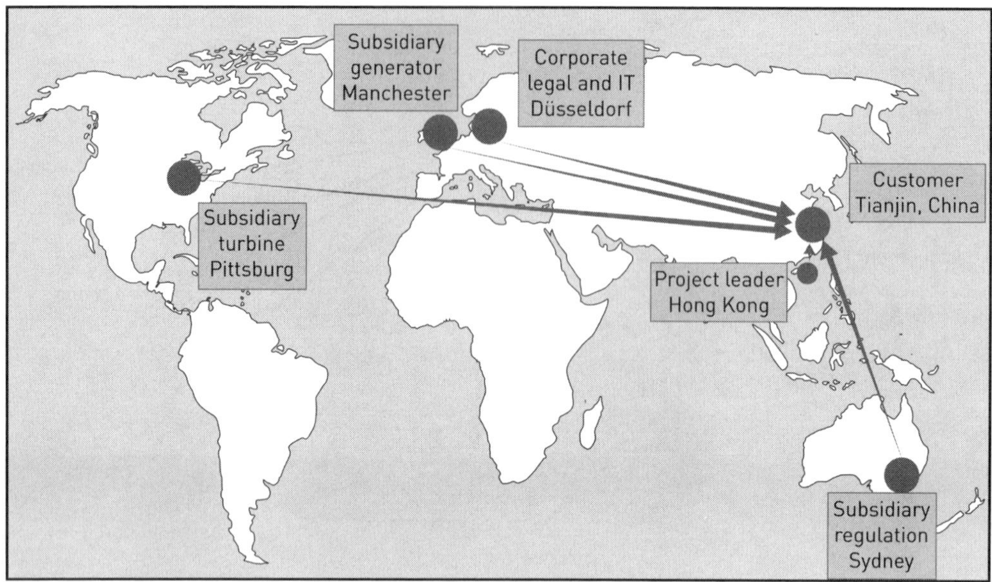

Figure 9.7 Global solution selling: an international bid for a power plant in China

The lead officer, who is in charge of preparing the bid, is located in Hong Kong; she is also in charge of negotiating the financing of the deal with a global consortium of banks with branches in Hong Kong.

This type of global solution selling is frequent in industries such as:

- *Banking:* to mount a complex financing package (all major global banks)
- *Consultancy:* to offer a complete business solution including strategy, IT, organization and change management (Accenture, McKinsey, BCG etc.)
- *Information technology:* to offer a complete seamless IT solution (AWS, IBM, Cap Gemini, Microsoft, SAP etc.)
- *Telecoms operators:* to bid for a UMTS (Universal Mobile Telecommunications System) licence, or a complete mobile infrastructure and operational network (all major operators)
- *Engineering:* turnkey projects or BOT contracts (ABB, Enron, Alstom, GE, all major international engineering firms).

The issues are quite similar to those in global account management. Global solution selling draws on the resources, experience and expertise of the international business units. What matters is the speed and the coherence of the solution package, as well as the leadership of the solution-selling team. It requires the cooperation of local subsidiaries and an appropriate mechanism to divide the revenues among them. There is a temptation for local business units to charge their normal rates for their respective contributions; if this happens, the overall proposal will be uncompetitive. Therefore, there needs to be a central global leader who decides on the overall price/content of the solution. Another issue is the allocation of resources to global projects when those resources may be more fruitfully allocated to domestic projects for which the local subsidiary would obtain full credit. Table 9.6 describes the capabilities needed to implement a global solution-selling system.

Table 9.6 Capabilities required for global solution selling

Capabilities	
• Ability to understand customers' problems • Ability to interpret customers' problems and to design solutions • Ability to formulate solution package • Ability to cultivate relationships and support • Ability to transfer solutions to customers' subsidiaries across the world	• Ability to provide consistent services across the world • Ability to identify internal and external resources and competencies • Ability to mobilize resources • Ability to coordinate the use of resources • Ability to maintain cost and price at competitive levels

Global sales and distribution

Sales and distribution are probably the elements of the marketing mix that are the most difficult to standardize globally. There are many reasons:

- Language
- Social codes in supplier/buyer relationships
- Negotiation cultures
- Spatial dispersion of customers
- Local regulations
- Existing distribution structures.

However, the desirability of being able to sell and distribute globally, as opposed to the use of localized sales forces and distribution channels, depends upon the frequency of purchase and the dispersion of customers (Figure 9.8). The more limited the number of customers for the product or service, especially if sales are infrequent (for instance selling aircraft to airlines), the less the need for a local sales force.

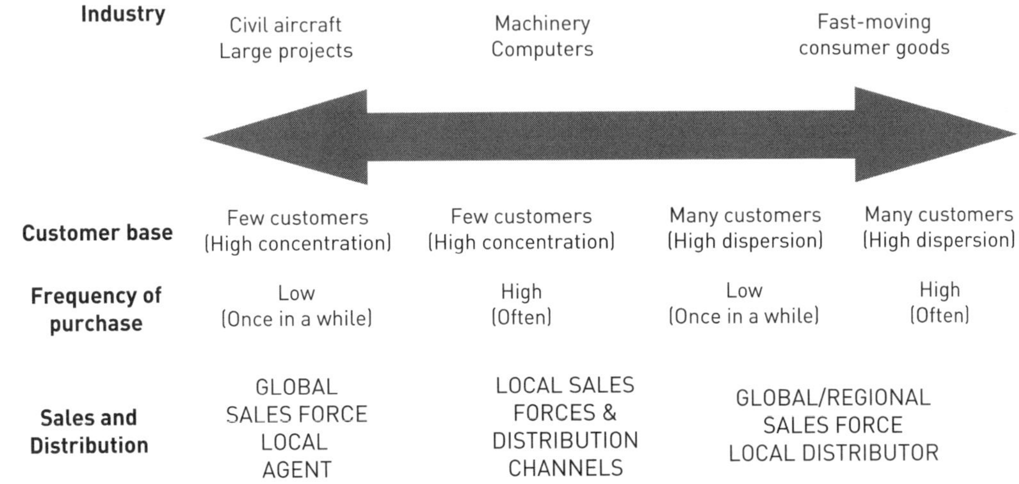

Figure 9.8 Sales and distribution

Salespersons located at corporate or regional headquarters can handle negotiations with the help of a local agent or representative.

At the other extreme, frequent purchases from numerous, widely spread customers call for local sales forces and distribution, either through subsidiaries or through local or international distribution companies.

Global marketing positioning

Global marketing can take several forms. For each element of the marketing mix a trade-off has to be made between a fully fledged standard global approach and a complete local adaptation. The combination of choices leads to a variety of marketing strategies and policies, as illustrated in Table 9.7. The final choice, as seen in this chapter, is a function of many parameters:

- Customers' needs and value curve
- Customers' dispersion
- Frequency of purchase
- Importance of solution selling and account for globally dispersed customers
- Economies of scale.

The ultimate choice will have to be made with regard to the global strategic positioning issues discussed in Chapter 2.

Table 9.7 Various global marketing positions

	Global usage and product	Local usage, global product	Global usage, local product	Local usage and product
Product	Similar	Similar	Different	Different
Message	Similar	Different	Similar	Different
Customer group	Similar	Different	Similar	Different
Usage	Similar	Different	Similar	Different
Distribution	Similar	Different	Similar	Different
Brand	Similar	Different	Similar	Different
Price	Similar	Different	Similar	Different
Examples	***Swatch iPhone iPad Coca-Cola***	***Tiger Balm***	***Danone McDonald's***	***Coca-Cola's or Unilever's local brands***

Fair trade marketing

Fair trade is a form of international trade promoting rules and practices that provide better terms of trade for small and medium-sized producers from the developing world.[22]

According to the World Fair Trade Organization, fair trade enterprises impacted 965,700 livelihoods globally, with over a million producers located in 76 countries generating $9.8 billion of fair trade sales in 2018.[23] Most of the products are agriculturally derived (coffee, cocoa, cotton ware, spices, wine etc.)

Fair trade (or *equitable* trade) relies on the application of ten principles:[24]

1. It supports economically disadvantaged producers (family businesses, or cooperatives). It recognizes, promotes and protects the cultural identity and traditional skills of small producers as reflected in their craft designs, food products and other related services.
2. All relevant information is provided to all its trading partners.
3. It respects contractual fair trading practices and ensures that orders are paid on time and that pre-payments are passed on to producers.
4. A fair price is one which provides fair pay to the producers.
5. It ensures that no child- or forced-labour policies are practised.
6. It does not discriminate against employees based on race, caste, national origin, religion, disability, gender, sexual orientation, union membership or political affiliation, and respects the right of all employees to form and join trade unions of their choice.
7. It provides a safe and healthy working environment for employees and/or members.
8. Firms working directly with small producers develop specific activities to help these producers improve their management skills, production capabilities and access to markets – local, regional and international.
9. Honest advertising and marketing techniques are always used.
10. Firms which produce fair trade products use raw materials from sustainable sources and minimize their environmental impact by using organic or low pesticide use production methods wherever possible.

Global marketing and its limits

In this chapter we have looked at the many aspects of the marketing mix from a global viewpoint. Overall, we have argued that the success of global marketing is contingent upon the characteristics of the products (technical products tend to be more suited to a global approach despite the differences in norms and specifications) and of the customers' value differences. Global marketing has advantages of economies of scale in product and services development, production, promotion and distribution. However, global marketing shows its limitations in a variety of cases. A 2015 *Harvard Business Review*[25] article identified six major mistakes in implementing global marketing:

- Not addressing the specific realities of different country markets
- Not paying enough attention to internal data
- Not adapting the sales and marketing channel
- Not adapting product offerings
- Not letting local teams lead the way
- Not thinking through the global logistics.

MINI-CASE 9.1

waterdrop®

The global beverage industry was expected to reach $1.9 trillion by 2021, based on projected growth of 3.0 per cent (CAGR) from 2016 to 2021, with the non-alcoholic segment identified as a key driver.[26] It is competitive and dominated by a few large international players that own hundreds of brands, leverage supply chains and hold critical retail space with significant marketing budgets. Profitability requires massive scale, millions of dollars in marketing spend and a strong brand to maintain loyalty amidst thousands of players. Barriers are low for entering the industry as the production of drinks is relatively easy. Despite the thousands of new drinks flooding the market and mass marketing by established players, the non-alcoholic segment provided fertile ground for innovative start-ups, where branding is key. Martin Donald Murray created one such business – waterdrop® – a small cube made up of natural aromas, superfood extracts and vitamins that is placed in water, designed to encourage healthier consumption. Martin built the business on a lean budget creating a unique brand that is key for the success of his innovative, sustainable product – what he created is an entirely new category that he calls 'a micro drink'. As it is a cube, it is easily sold online which makes it the most sustainable drink on the market as CO_2 is drastically reduced compared to bottled waters and the use of plastic is reduced by 98 per cent.

Martin's initial idea was prompted by the limited drinks available onboard a flight to Singapore in 2016. The company took three steps crucial to entering or disrupting a competitive market: challenging the rules of the game, changing the winning team and understanding customer pain points and the importance of the unique selling proposition (USP).

Rather than producing another water, carbonated soft drink or juice, the waterdrop® concept captures health and hydration trends by creating a micro drink using water as its platform. waterdrop® has shown customer-focus, with choice, convenience and awareness of the consumer trend towards self-improvement and well-being. From the start the customers were part of the development process with pop-up shops used for research.

waterdrop® soft-launched in the B2B sector and began selling to consumers in 2017 with smaller 'on-the-go' cases and customized subscription models – the theory was that people consume most of their drinks at work and it seemed simple to get something small and innovative into companies. It would act as a platform to connect with and communicate to consumers, generating product demand through many touchpoints. The idea was to put boxes into meeting rooms and canteens where they would spread the buzz. Coming from a corporate setting, Martin believed that firms would be interested in the health of their employees and could use their clients and visitors to create awareness – 'word of mouth'. They also used viral email campaigns using friends to market the digital drink: The founder explains:

> We did not use traditional marketing tools as they were too expensive and not trackable. The real deal is to make a product that creates interest and invest all your money into social where you by far have the highest return on your marketing dollar. We created a link called 'waterdrop is coming' where you could share with a friend, sign up and get free product. The more friends you shared with, the more product you get. We collected thousands of email addresses in no time with this.

Despite being a 'digital' drink, waterdrop® also needed to create buzz offline. As it was a novel concept for the Austrian market, traditional mediums including PR, sampling opportunities and brick-and-mortar presence were also employed. While the initial communication and POS was purely online, the need for offline touchpoints and sampling was evident – the wave of early adopters in Austria was quickly swamped by more hesitant but curious potential consumers. Through online and offline activations the waterdrop® brand grew.

The development of community was an important aspect of waterdrop®'s marketing funnel but it required time, money, effort and a dedicated team. Martin initially considered outsourcing content development, social media marketing and interaction. Finally it was kept in-house which meant a shift in how the team spent their time. The marketing director was adamant that it was integral to developing waterdrop®'s brand identity and organizational culture.

By 2020 the company had saved up to 30 million plastic bottles, opened 15 waterdrop® stores, had a staff of 120, 500,000 customers online and were also available in 3,000 retail stores.[27] It was valued at €300 million and had expanded internationally.

Source: This Mini-case is based on the INSEAD case study, Niessing, Baumer and Carrick (2019).

MINI-CASE 9.2

Halo Top – using digital marketing to disrupt the global ice cream giants

Halo Top is an ice cream brand founded in 2011 by former corporate lawyer, Justin Woolverton, who began making ice cream in his kitchen in Los Angeles, in an attempt to reduce his carbohydrates and refined sugars intake, without losing the pleasure of ice cream consumption. Through its innovative product and digital marketing, the company soon challenged the well-established ice cream giants. With slogans such as 'guilt-free zone' and 'no bowl, no regrets' with the number of calories displayed in large numbers on the tub, the company focused on digital channels to generate brand and product awareness. It chose to invest in targeted ads on social media platforms like Facebook and Instagram rather than traditional media. Justin and his team also used influencer marketing to reach its target market of millennial, health-conscious individuals. Initially Justin contacted relatively small and medium-sized fitness influencers asking them to try the ice cream or offer a discount code to their followers.

By 2017, Halo Top was the fastest-selling brand in the US and number one in the sale of pints of ice cream in the country.[28] With its success came its imitators, from new brands and well-established companies like Ben & Jerry's who launched its 'Moo-phoria' range and Unilever with its Culture Republik, a 'better for you' alternative that was lower in calories and contained probiotic cultures.[29]

Justin Woolverton first experimented with freezing Chobani, a thick, high-protein Greek-style yoghurt, by adding fruit and sugar substitutes. He moved on to making ice cream using stevia, a leafy shrub from Paraguay that was a sugar substitute. He combined this with a no-calorie sugar alcohol found in certain fruits, erythritol, milk, cream and air to make the ice cream. The result was an ice cream that had all the attributes and taste of the premium brands but with less calories. A 473ml tub of Halo Top's Chocolate Chip Cookie Dough was 360 calories, compared to 1,120 for the Ben & Jerry's equivalent.[30]

To scale his operation, Woolverton signed a deal with a 'copacker' – a manufacturer that produces packaged foods under contract – a California-based manufacturer. He paid a designer to create the packaging and logo, and persuaded a local gourmet store to stock the ice cream. Doug Bouton, another former lawyer, joined Justin and they built the Halo Top brand using targeted Google search ads, marketing on Facebook and more importantly the photo app Instagram – avoiding TV advertisements that were beyond their budget. Free samples were given to thousands of 'influencers' including athletes, sports trainers and healthy-living gurus. In 2016, a journalist for *GQ* magazine ate nothing but

Halo Top for ten days and lost four kgs in weight. This was the catalyst for the brand and sales soared.

Following Halo Top's success imitators and competing products pushed Halo Top to expand abroad or risk losing the first-to-market advantage that was crucial to its local success. They knew that the food consumer giants would soon roll out healthier ice creams internationally quicker than they could. In mid-2017, Matt Fulbrook, a former sales director for Ben & Jerry's in the UK, contacted the duo and suggested they expand to the UK. With the help of Fulbrook and his company Brand of Brothers, Halo Top expanded to Europe in exchange for commission on sales, securing UK distribution speedily in top supermarkets Tesco, Sainsbury's, Morrisons and Asda among others.

Halo Top needed to tailor its advertising and marketing for the UK audience with a brand voice that was authentic and genuine. They hired local staff and ad agencies. They produced an ice cream flavour called Lemon Wedding Cake in homage to Meghan Markle and Prince Harry's wedding cake. The company recorded sales of £20.2m, according to IRI, and by 2018 they were outselling Häagen-Dazs in Tesco. This was followed by expansion into Germany where they contracted an ice cream manufacturer that could supply continental Europe rather than shipping over supplies. Within a few years, Halo Top had become a poster child for shaking up the consumer goods industry. They also sold directly to consumers online, using social media to build a following and attract attention. The people who bought the ice cream were no longer customers but fans – social media provided loyal customers that promoted the brand. By keeping the marketing activities in-house through digital channels they also developed an authentic personality for the brand of a healthier option to mainstream ice cream brands.

Its aggressive digital marketing strategy paid off with Twitter followers increasing by 2,233 per cent and Facebook fans 59,282 per cent from 2018 to 2020.[31] It had Facebook and Instagram pages in different geographies including the US, France, Canada and UK. Following Halo Top's success with pints of ice cream available in dairy, non-dairy and Keto-diet friendly versions the company introduced ice cream pops. By 2020 Halo Top was available in the United States, Australia, Mexico, Canada, Ireland, New Zealand, France, the Netherlands, Germany, South Korea, Taiwan, Austria, Norway, Bahrain, Denmark and the United Kingdom. It is now ranked consistently in the top three best-selling brands with Ben & Jerry's and Häagen-Dazs.[32] Notably Halo Top's competitors also adopted digital channels to reach their customers. In 2020, Häagen-Dazs reduced its traditional advertising budget in response to the Covid-19 pandemic and increased its efforts in digital marketing.[33]

By 2020 Halo Top was the brand with the largest market share in the ice cream and frozen dessert market with a 6.4 per cent share globally according to Euromonitor (2021). Through its strategy of digital marketing it had topped the consumer giants in just ten years.

Summary and key points

1 Convergence of customer needs:

- **a** No conclusive evidence of convergence of all consumer goods but gaining ground in B2B sector
- **b** *Product standardization is* appropriate when there are *similar* customer needs across the world and when there is high minimum size of production
- **c** *Local adaptation* is appropriate when customer needs are different and the minimum size of production is low

  d *Modular standardization* applies if customer needs are different and minimum size of production is high

  e *Customer value curves* describe the various elements of customers' needs

2 Global branding:

  a *A global brand* applies to all products or services across the world, and includes the following features:

  - Strong in home market
  - Consistent in product positioning
  - Present geographically in a balanced way across regions
  - Addresses similar consumer needs worldwide
  - Easy to pronounce

  b Advantages:

  - Concentration of marketing effort on a single name reinforces market power
  - Cost savings in marketing mix for advertising, promotion, direct selling
  - Reinforces corporate identity

  c Disadvantages:

  - Ignores national differences and hence affects local growth potential

3 Global advertising:

  a Advertising is global advertising when a similar message is conveyed across the world

  b A single agency is commonly used, the advantages are:

  - Simplicity in relationships
  - Easy control
  - Economies of scale in production
  - Buyer power over global media and global support

  c Digital online advertising is increasingly important and favours global advertising

4 Building a global brand

- Two approaches to building global brands:
  - the waterfall model (one country at a time)
  - the sprinkler model (simultaneously in key countries)

5 Global pricing:

  a Involves setting consistent pricing policy across borders

  b *Useful:*

  - When product/service is targeted at 'global segments' (customers with similar value curves)

- When product/service is sold under strong 'global brand'
- When there are strong possibilities of arbitrage
- When company implements a multi-brand policy of global and local products
- When product/service is standardized

c *Advantages:*

- Avoids arbitrage (when customers shop in the lowest-priced country)
- Protects brand integrity
- Facilitates servicing of global customers.

d *Disadvantages* are sub-optimization owing to a lack of consideration for differences in customers' utility curve

6 Global account management:

a The organizational process which serves global accounts (customers present in many countries and requiring products/services as specified in a central buying agreement)

b *Advantages:*

- For the customer:
  - Low overall cost partly owing to volume purchase
  - Ability to optimize procurement strategy
- For the seller:
  - Increases overall sales and optimizes profitability
  - Reduces transaction cost (deal negotiation cost) and enhances ability to provide full and consistent services to customers

c *Disadvantages:*

- Customers' subsidiaries reluctant to accept global procurement
- Suppliers' subsidiaries reluctant to abandon potential source of local income
- Complex internal accounting system required to reallocate income among subsidiaries

7 Global solution selling:

a Involves mobilizing resources and competencies of several *worldwide subsidiaries* to offer a valuable solution to a client in a specific country

b *Key issues:*

- Speed of solution delivery
- Leadership of solution-selling team
- Revenue distribution among parties involved
- Optimization of resource allocation

8 Global sales and distribution:

a Very *difficult to standardize*:

- Languages
- Social codes in supplier/buyer relationships
- Negotiation cultures
- Spatial dispersion of customers
- Local regulations
- Existing distribution structures

b Determinants of need for *local sales force* are:

- Frequency of purchase
- Extent of customer dispersion

9 Global marketing positioning:

Choice of *marketing mix* depends on:

- Company's global strategic positioning
- Customers' needs and value curve
- Customers' dispersion
- Frequency of purchase
- Importance of solution selling and account for globally dispersed customers
- Economies of scale

10 Fair trade marketing

a Supports economically disadvantaged producers

b Mainly in emerging countries

11 Limits of global marketing

Six major mistakes in implementing global marketing:

- Not specific about countries
- Not paying enough attention to internal data
- Not adapting the sales and marketing channel
- Not adapting product offering
- Not letting local teams lead the way
- Not thinking through the global logistics

Learning assignments

1 What are the benefits of global standardization?
2 Can you identify ten 'global' products?
3 In Table 9.4 (p. 362), most of the top global brands are from the United States. Why do you think this is?
4 Why did Unilever announce that it was reducing the number of its brands from 1,600 to 400? What were the risks of doing so?
5 What potential problems will a marketer encounter in having a 'global' advertising campaign?
6 What are the benefits of using a single advertising agency?
7 Why can global pricing lead to sub-optimization?
8 What is the difference between global account management and global solution selling?
9 What are the typical problems associated with global account management?

Key words

- Advertising agency
- Arbitrage
- 'Californization'
- Convergence
- Customer value curve
- Global accounts
- Global solution selling
- Hierarchy of needs
- Marketing positioning
- Modularization
- Segmentation
- Sprinkler model
- Sub-optimization
- Waterfall model

Web resources

EMIS (Emerging Market Research):
https://www.emis.com/
Euromonitor:
https://www.marketresearch.com/Euromonitor-International-v746/
Market Line:
https://www.marketline.com
McKinsey Global Institute:
https://www.mckinsey.com/mgi/overview
Statista:
https://www.statista.com
Warc:
https://www.warc.com/Welcome
World Bank Development Indicators:
https://databank.worldbank.org/source/world-development-indicators

Companion website

Visit the companion website at bloomsbury.pub/global-strategic-management-5e for a multitude of weblinks and resources, self-test questions for revision and appendices.

Notes

1 Schütte (1998).
2 Parker (2000).
3 Ohmae ([1985] 1995).
4 Yip (1994).
5 This section is partly based on Riesenbeck and Freeling (1991) and Quelch (1999).
6 https://www.unilever.com/brands/ (accessed 1 February 2022).
7 https://www.pgcareers.com/ (accessed 1 February 2022).
8 https://www.coca-colacompany.com/ (accessed 1 February 2022).
9 https://www.theheinekencompany.com/ (accessed 1 February 2022).
10 Williamson (1999).
11 https://www.loreal-finance.com/eng/focus/loreal- worldwide (accessed 1 February 2022). and https://www.statista.com/statistics/243986/consolidated-sales-of-loreal-worldwide/#:~:text=Between%202010%20and%202019%2C%20the,in%20global%20sales%20in%202019 (accessed 1 February 2022).
12 Tribewalla (1999).
13 https://knowledge.insead.edu/blog/insead-blog/how-brands-can-stay-relevant-in-the-digital-age-10231(accessed 1 February 2022).
14 Ibid.
15 Quelch (1999: 11).
16 Pinson and Tribewalla (2001).
17 https://www-statista-com.ezproxy.insead.edu/topics/990/global-advertising-market/ (accessed 1 February 2022).
18 https://alphaefficiency.com/digital-ad-spend/ (accessed 1 February 2022).
19 Malnight (1995).
20 Dragonetti and Noda (1999).
21 David et al. (2001).
22 Doherty et al. (2015).
23 World Trade Organization: https://wfto.com (accessed 6 may 2022).
24 https://wfto-europe.org/the-10-principles-of-fair-trade-2/ (accessed 6 may 2022).
25 Kelly (2015).
26 Monitor (2015).
27 https://en.waterdrop.com/ (accessed 1 February 2022).
28 https://econsultancy.com/how-halo-top-is- challenging-the-ice-cream-market-social- marketing-strategy/ (accessed 1 February 2022).
29 Ibid.
30 Financial Times (2019) :https://www.ft.com/content/b5ffbe6e-1360-11e9-a168-d45595ad076d (Accessed on 6 May 2022).
31 https://www.referralcandy.com/blog/halo-top-marketing-strategy/ (accessed 6 May 2022).
32 https://www.goodhousekeeping.com/food-products/g34313693/best-sugar-free-ice-cream/ ((accessed 6 May 2022).
33 https://www.marketingweek.com/haagen-daz-digital-investment-doubles/ (accessed 6 May 2022).

References and further reading

Books and articles

Aaker, D. A. and Joachimsthaler, E. (1999) 'The lure of global branding', *Harvard Business Review*, 77 (6): 137–44.

Abboud, L. (2019) 'Halo Top challenges big brands for scoop of ice-cream market', *Financial Times Special Report – Entrepreneurship*, March 15.

Barth, K., Karch, N. J., McLaughlin, K. and Smith Shi, C. (1996) 'Global retailing: tempting trouble?', *McKinsey Quarterly*, 1: 117–25.

David, A. (2000) 'Seven rules of international distribution', *Harvard Business Review*, 78 (6): 131–7.

David, A., Birkinshaw, J. and Toulan, O. (2001) 'Can selling be globalized? The pitfalls of global account management', *California Management Review*, 44 (1): 8–20.

Doherty, B., Smith, A. and Parker, S. (2015) 'Fair trade market creation and marketing in the global south', *Geoforum*, 67: 158–71.

Dragonetti, N. and Noda, T. (1999) 'Building a customer oriented networked organisation: Ericsson's global account management programme', INSEAD, Case Study 11, 1999–4857.

Geyer, F. and Niessing, J. (2020) *The Definitive Guide to B2B Digital Transformation: How to Drive Uncommon Growth by Prioritizing Customers Over Technology* (Cambridge, MA: B2BDigitalTransformation.com).

Godin, S. (2018) *This is Marketing: You Cant't be Seen Until you Learn to See* (London: Penguin). https://www.penguinrandomhouse.com/books/600458/this-is-marketing-by-seth-godin/ (accessed 1 February 2022).

Hankinson, G. and Cowking, P. (1996) *The Reality of Global Brands* (London: McGraw-Hill).

Katsikeas, C., Leonidou, L. and Zeriti, A. (2019) 'Revisiting international marketing strategy in a digital era: opportunities, challenges, and research directions', *International Marketing Review*, 37 (3): 405–24. https://doi.org/10.1108/IMR-02-2019-0080.

Kelly, N. (2015) 'The most common mistakes companies make with global marketing', *Harvard Business Review*, September.

Kelly, N. (2020) 'Name Your brand with a global audience in mind', *Harvard Business Review*, September.

Levitt, T. (1983) 'The globalization of markets', *Harvard Business Review*, 61 (3): 92–101.

Malnight, T. (1995) 'Citibank: global customer management', Harvard Business School and Wharton School Case Study 9-395-142.

Narayandas, D., Quelch, J. and Schwartz, G. (2000) 'Prepare your company for global pricing', *Sloan Management Review*, Fall: 61–70.

Niessing, J. and El Noshokaty, T. (2018) *How Brands Can Stay Relevant in the Digital Age*, INSEAD Knowledge. https://knowledge.insead.edu/blog/insead-blog/how-brands-can-stay-relevant-in-the-digital-age-10231 (accessed 22 January 2022).

Niessing, J., Carrick, A.M. and Baumer, C. (2019) *waterdrop®: Changing the Paradigms of the Beverage Industry with Limited Resources and Digital Marketing*, INSEAD Case Study 6399. https://publishing.insead.edu/case/waterdrop (accessed 21 January 2022).

Ohmae, K. ([1985] 1995) *Triad Power* (New York, NY: Free Press).

Parker, P. (2000) *Physioeconomics* (Cambridge, MA: MIT Press).

Pinson, C. and Tribewalla, V. (2001) 'Benetton', INSEAD Case Study 4520. https://publishing.insead.edu/search?search=benetton&

Quelch, J. (1999) 'Global branding: taking stock', *Business Strategy Review*, 10 (1): 1–14.

Riesenbeck, H. and Freeling, A. (1991) 'How global are global brands?', *McKinsey Quarterly*, 4: 3–17.

Schütte, H. (1998) *Asian Consumer Behavior* (Basingstoke: Macmillan).

Schütte, H. and Ciarlante, D. (1998) *Consumer Behaviour in Asia* (Paris/London: INSEAD/Macmillan).

Williamson, P. J. (1999) 'China's beer war', INSEAD Euro Asia Centre Case Study 05/ 98-4755.

World Fair Trade Organization (n.d.) *10 Principles of Fair Trade*. http://wfto.com/fair-trade/10-principles-fair-trade (accessed 20 June 2017).

Yip, G. (1994) *Total Global Strategy* (Englewood Cliffs, NJ: Prentice-Hall).

Journals

International Marketing Review (Quarterly), MCB University, UK: https://www.emeraldgrouppublishing.com/journal/imr

Journal of International Marketing (Quarterly), American Marketing Association, USA: https://journals.sagepub.com/home/jig

Journal of Consumer Research: https://consumerresearcher.com/

Journal of Marketing: https://journals.sagepub.com/home/jmx

Chapter 10

Global operations and digital networks

At the end of the chapter you will be able to:

- Understand the various factors contributing to the location decision
- Explain the different roles of international factories and service centres, and their evolution
- Evaluate the advantages and disadvantages of centralized versus decentralized purchasing
- Understand the role played by the internet in the management of global operations
- Discuss the functions of a global logistics system
- Set out the various phases in international infrastructure projects and their management design

Introduction

The internationalization of value chains is a salient and controversial feature of globalization. This phenomenon, known as offshoring, creates a global operational network of integrated production and service centres deployed across the world (Figure 10.1). Global operational management is concerned

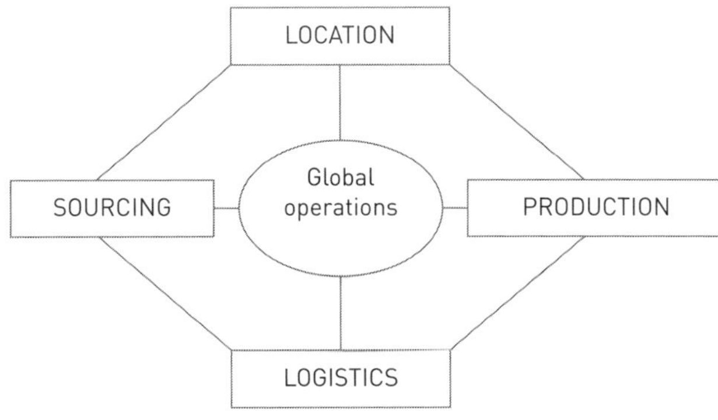

Figure 10.1 The global operations network

with the management of such a network. At the beginning of the chapter different types of offshoring will be discussed. Then various issues of managing global value chains will be discussed. The first issue is to decide where to set up the operational, productive and logistical facilities such as factories, services and distribution centres. This kind of decision is known as the location decision: it requires multiple criteria analysis taking into account regional resources and risk characteristics as well as customer proximity. Second, each element of the network has to be attributed a specific role and the network has to be managed. This chapter presents different categorizations of global manufacturing networks. Third, the procurement function, including electronic purchasing through electronic data interchange (EDI) or through the internet, is considered, as well as the role of the internet in the management of global networks. The fourth domain of operational management is concerned with the managerial issues associated with the physical flow of goods – otherwise known as logistics. The chapter continues with the analysis of the managerial issues associated with the handling of large-scale international infrastructure projects. Finally the impact of the internet on global management will be addressed.

The globalization of value chains: offshore production and outsourcing

Since the 1980s, the globalization of markets and competition have induced companies to internationalize their value chains. Manufacturing as well as service sites have been set up offshore.[1] In 2010 the OECD published an Index of Offshoring Activities in the manufacturing and service sectors. This index showed that in OECD countries offshoring had increased from 21 per cent to 26 per cent in the manufacturing sector during the decade from 1995 to 2005.[2] The study has not been replicated since then. Another source of information is the various studies from consulting firm Kearney to produce a reshoring index measuring the reactive movement – that of the repatriation of activities to the country of origin. Kearney's seventh annual edition showed a reversal of a five-year trend, as domestic US manufacturing in 2019 commanded a significantly greater share versus the fourteen Asian low-cost countries (LCCs) tracked in the study, with manufacturing imports from China registering a particularly sharp decline.[3]

Offshoring can take place internally via the setting up of factories or services in international locations (offshore production) or by the outsourcing of such activities to external suppliers (offshore outsourcing). It can be motivated by the desire to take advantage of a local market (market localization) or by the search for resources and cost advantages that enhance global competitiveness. These four forms of offshoring are represented in Figure 10.2.

Although offshoring for markets is accepted politically and socially in the home countries of the investing firms, the second reason for offshoring – for global competitiveness – is not. When a company invests in a country in search of low wage costs and closes a factory or a service centre in a high-wage country it delocalizes, which creates a loss of jobs that in turn generates demand for sanctions and protectionism.

Over the years a particular offshore centre may see its mission evolving. For instance, in 1970 Hewlett-Packard chose Singapore to build a factory to produce components. Four years later the factory was

Offshoring modes

Offshoring objectives	Offshore production	Offshore outsourcing
For market	**Local for local production** Production of goods or services internal to the company in internationally dispersed sites for serving local markets	**Local for local outsourcing** Sourcing of goods or services with external local domestic suppliers serving local operations
For global competitiveness	**Local for global production** Production of goods or services internal to the company in internationally dispersed sites for serving local markets	**Local for global outsourcing** Sourcing of goods or services with external international suppliers serving global operations

Figure 10.2 Forms of offshoring

making a complete product – a handheld calculator. In the following years more and more products were transferred there, still designed in the USA, but gradually by the mid-1980s the Singaporean operation had started to redesign products and introduce new ones. By the mid-1990s it had developed and produced a wholly new product: the Deskjet SOS.

Hewlett-Packard exemplifies the topic of this chapter: in dealing with the four major decision dimensions of global operations the issues (as represented in Figure 10.2) are:

- Location: where to put facilities?
- Production: what to produce (manufacturing and services) and where?
- Sourcing: from whom to buy, what and how?
- Logistics: how to manage the flow of goods and information?

Selecting operational sites

The first type of decision in the management of a global operations network consists of selecting countries and regions in which to set up operational facilities. Table 10.1 presents the various criteria usually utilized to choose a location for facilities such as a plant, a back office, a distribution facility or a service centre.

The choice is contingent upon the kind of facilities and their role in the network. Procurement offices will be located in places where resources and suppliers are available, while distribution centres will be located close to dense markets. Rotterdam in Europe, Singapore and Hong Kong in Asia play major roles as distribution and logistics centres in their respective regions because of their nodal geographical position and their world-class infrastructures. Bangalore or Manila will be chosen in the field of computer software because of their abundance of skilled and low-cost programmers, while Shenzhen in China or Batam in Indonesia are locations for labour-intensive processing.

Table 10.1 Criteria for facilities location

COSTS	LABOUR COSTS	• Remuneration level • Skill level • Skill availability • Productivity • Social regulations • Flexibility • Unionization
	OPERATIONAL COSTS	• Raw material costs • Telecommunications • Energy, water, transport • Property, rent • Logistics • Services • Financial costs • Environmental costs • Expatriate cost of living
	TAXATION	• Tariffs • Indirect taxes • Income taxes
	INCENTIVES	• Subsidies • Tax relief
PROXIMITY	CUSTOMER PROXIMITY	• Ability to offer fast delivery • Ability to offer fast servicing • Ability to customize
	SUPPLIER PROXIMITY	• Availability of raw materials • Quality of raw materials • Reliability of supplies
	LOGISTICS	• Import/export facilities
ENVIRONMENT	PROFESSIONAL	• Financial institutions • Legal and consultancy services • Training services
	INTELLECTUAL	• Libraries • Information • Universities
	QUALITY OF LIFE	• Government regulation • Freedom of movement • Climate • Housing • Presence of international schools • Crime

LEARNING	LEARNING FROM SUPPLIERS	• Quality of international and domestic suppliers • Supplier innovation
	LEARNING FROM CUSTOMERS	• Variety of segmentation • Variety of customer demands • Customer sophistication
	LEARNING FROM COMPETITORS	• Variety of competitors
	LEARNING FROM INSTITUTIONS	• Innovation context due to universities, technical and design centres

Source: Author's own, based on discussions in Haigh (1990); Ernst & Young (1992); Ferdows (1997); De Meyer and Vereecke (1994).

Global manufacturing networks

Ferdows' strategic roles model

Based on extensive longitudinal research, Kasra Ferdows (1997) proposed a model of classification for manufacturing centres in a global network leading to the definition of various strategic roles. This classification is based on two main variables:

- The primary strategic reason for setting up a plant in a particular country. Ferdows identifies three main reasons:
  - To access low-cost production
  - To access skills and know-how
  - To access markets.
- The **competencies of the plant**, in terms of the various tasks that a given site is capable of doing:
  - The ability to assume responsibility for production
  - The ability to maintain technical processes (maintenance responsibility)
  - The ability to purchase locally (sourcing/logistical responsibility)
  - The ability to make process improvements
  - The ability to develop suppliers
  - The ability to develop processes
  - The ability to make product improvement recommendations
  - The ability to develop products (product development responsibility)
  - The ability to supply global markets
  - The ability to become a global hub for product and process knowledge.

Based on those two main dimensions, Ferdows identifies six types of global plants in a network:

- The offshore factory
- The source factory

- The server factory
- The contributor factory
- The outpost factory
- The lead factory.

Each of these has a precise role, as defined in Table 10.2.

Table 10.2 Ferdow's classification of globally set-up factories

OFFSHORE FACTORY	Local production sites manufacturing low cost global products or components designed globally
SOURCE FACTORY	Autonomous local production sites benefiting from large autonomy manufacturing global and local products or components
SERVER FACTORY	Local production site manufacturing products or components designed globally for local or regional markets
CONTRIBUTOR FACTORY	Local production site manufacturing products or components designed locally for local or regional markets
OUTPOST FACTORY	Local production site manufacturing products competing with technologically dominant local players in view to learn about the technological environment
LEAD FACTORY	Global production center having the full design, sourcing capabilities to produce global products

Source: Author's summary based on Kasra Ferdows, 'Making the most of foreign factories' (Ferdows 1997).

Overall, the combination of the various types of factories constitutes a global manufacturing network in which all production centres are to some extent interrelated. The architecture of the network and the shifting roles of factories evolve according to new opportunities and competitive pressures. Ferdows advocates the design of what he calls a 'robust' network that evolves without resorting to drastic measures, such as plant closures or abrupt shifts of production from one country to another.

De Meyer and Vereecke's network architecture model

De Meyer and Vereecke (1994) emphasize the role of plants as information and knowledge creators in addition to the traditional roles of foreign factories as supply bases. They define four main categories of plants in a network:

- Isolated plants: concentrating on the production of products for specific geographical markets. These plants do not communicate greatly with others. They are installed in import substitution countries that require local production for their domestic markets.
- Blueprint plants: receiving a lot of innovation but not creating any. They produce goods according to blueprints received from elsewhere. Those plants could be located in low-cost countries or Export Processing Zones (EPZs).
- Host plants: network players here are well-established factories serving large markets that have developed a high degree of competency in state-of-the-art manufacturing but are not at the forefront of innovation.
- Innovator plants: network players here play a central role in product and process adaptation and innovation and are a source of inspiration for other factories.

Global services networks

The internationalization of services can take many forms, as represented in Figure 10.3.

One of the key distinctions in respect of services, as opposed to manufacturing, is the relative importance of the front office compared to back office activities.[1]

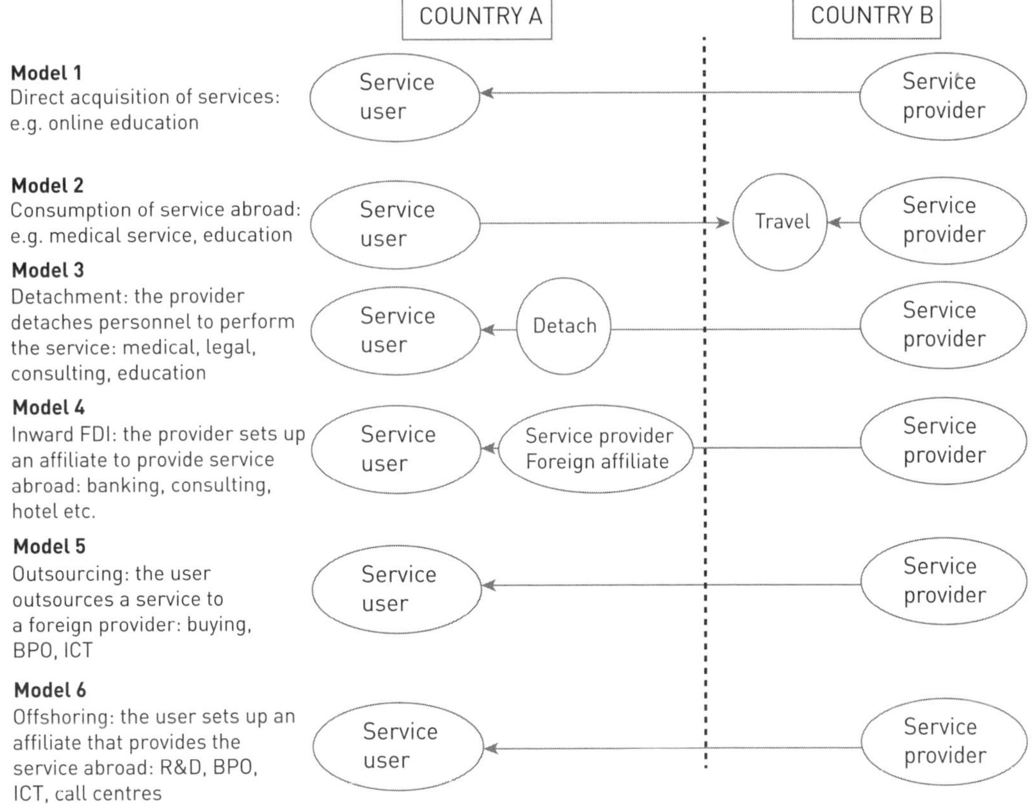

Figure 10.3 Different models of internationalization of services

Source: Authors' own figure, based on Chart 2 in Lindner et al. (2001).

In *front office* activities, consumption and production are concomitant: in a plane the traveller 'consumes' the travel at the same time as it is produced, in a retail store the customer 'consumes' (the act of buying) at the same time as the act of selling is performed. In *back office* activities, goods or support to services (software, insurance policies, bank transfer processing) can be performed separately from their consumption; goods or services support can be stockpiled. In global services, back office activities can be classified in a similar way to manufacturing plants:

- Offshore centres perform isolated acts of production: data entry performed in Guandong for a company headquartered in Europe, for instance
- Source centres produce with a certain degree of autonomy for supporting local markets: catering facilities, distribution centres
- Contributor centres may have a regional role: maintenance centres, regional warehousing
- Dispatch centres
- Outpost centres: market intelligence
- Lead centres: design function.

Front office operations are in immediate contact with the customer and need to be close to the market. There are two main types of front office:

- The physical front office: banking branch, retail store, restaurant, repair centre, hotel
- The remote front office: call centre, reservation office, e-commerce centre.

Front office activities, because of their high degree of interaction with customers, demand particular attention to language, customs and social codes. Adaptations require the localization of facilities and personnel. For instance, medical, educational or legal, as well as home hospitality or consultancy services, will deploy facilities, either directly or through alliances, in order to perform the interface with their customers (models 2, 3, 4 in Figure 10.3). Some online services can be performed with contact only via the internet (e-learning for instance, model 1).

By contrast, many back office activities can be centralized in global or regional centres localized in places selected according to their cost benefit characteristics. For instance, India has been the centre of business process outsourcing (BPO) and IT back office functions (models 5 and 6).

Global sourcing

Global sourcing is the organization of a coordinated approach to the selection of suppliers located across the world and the procurement of goods and services for the global supply chain. Global sourcing can take several forms, depending on the degree of centralization and integration of the procurement function, as illustrated in Figure 10.4.

The outsourced global procurement model

In this model, the global firm delegates the procurement to an **international buying** or **purchasing agent** who is in charge of the whole procurement function. Li & Fung, who set up the concept of a 'virtual factory',[5] provide a good example of such an agent. The example below provides a description of Li & Fung's global sourcing.

Degree of vertical integration of procurement function	Centralized procurement	Decentralized procurement
Outsourced procurement	**Outsourced central procurement** One global purchasing agent takes care of sourcing needs *Li & Fung*	**Outsourced dispersed procurement** Local purchasing agents take care of sourcing needs according to global specifications *Most multinational corporations*
Internal procurement	**Central internal procurement** Central purchasing department sources globally *Major airlines*	**Dispersed internal procurement** Local subsidiaries source locally according to global specifications *McDonald's, Carrefour*

Degree of centralization of procurement decisions

Figure 10.4 Different global sourcing designs

EXAMPLE 10.1 Li & Fung's 'virtual factory' concept

Founded in Guangzhou, Li & Fung began as a traditional exporter of Chinese porcelain. Today, this family-owned group has 42 offices in 20 countries, employing 2,500 employees in Asia, Europe and Africa. It deals with a network of more than 3,000 manufacturers for textiles, toys, sporting goods and furniture. Its main customers are major retail chains in the United States and Europe. The company participates in the design and engineering of products with its customers, selects suppliers, deals with quality control, final assembly and testing as well as logistics issues. A product like a parka, for instance, will be made of various components manufactured in different international locations: Korea (the shell), Taiwan (the lining), Japan (the zip), Hong Kong (the elastic, studs, toggles and string) and China (the filler and final assembly).

The internal central purchasing model

In this model, a central department with its own offices located in the major sourcing country centralizes the purchase of key components, raw materials or products. The purchasing division will act in exactly the same way as an **independent purchasing agent**, dealing with the whole supply chain from requesting quotations, through negotiation, orders, quality control, reception, expedition, logistics and finally to payment. Nike, for instance, operates a central 'virtual' enterprise from its headquarters in Oregon. The product is designed centrally and then sourced from different factories in Korea, Japan, Taiwan, Indonesia and the United States.

The distributed procurement model

In this model, each production centre in charge of a product or component takes care of its own procurement, based on **centrally defined product specifications**. This model applies particularly when there is a local content requirement imposed by a country or when a subsidiary has complete responsibility for a product. It is not unusual for global companies to encourage their major suppliers to locate factories near their own plants, a process known as **piggybacking**.

Electronic sourcing (EDI and e-procurement)

The development of digital IT has enhanced the ability of companies to source globally. Proprietary software, known as **electronic data interchange (EDI)**, links corporations to their suppliers, enabling the exchange of information and the automatic placement and tracking of orders. The internet, thanks to its connectivity and language compatibility, has given birth to **electronic marketplaces** (e-marketplaces) that complement and to some extent replace traditional EDI. There are three main types of procurement marketplaces:

- Horizontal marketplaces (aggregators) specialize in one category of product or service for all types of industry. An example is Jaggaer (https://www.jaggaer.com/), a marketplace for scientific products used mainly by pharmaceutical, chemical, biotechnological and educational organizations as well as R&D laboratories across several industries.
- Vertical marketplaces specialize in one type of industry, offering a one-stop shop for a large variety of products and services within that particular industry sector. There are numerous examples of vertical e-procurement sites ranging from automotive, electronics, heavy equipment construction materials, chemicals, etc. (see a list and references at https://virtocommerce.com/blog/vertical-b2b-marketplaces).
- Exchanges organize spot markets among a large number of suppliers and buyers for certain types of commodities such as steel (http://www.esteel.com) or chemicals (http://www.chemnet.com).

There are also various forms of contracting methods. Transactions can be one-to-one transactions or made in the form of reverse auctions. The example below discusses an auction organized by SAP Ariba (https://www.ariba.com/), a reverse auction market-maker. In theory, electronic procurement enhances the capability to organize global procurement because it can reach a larger number of suppliers than more traditional methods. It also facilitates the valuable interaction between suppliers and buyers. These reach capabilities are at the roots of B2B marketplaces where global sourcing can develop. However, companies need to invest in integrated software called Enterprise Resource Planning (ERP) that is offered by companies such as SAP (http://www.sap.com) or Oracle (http://www.oracle.com).

EXAMPLE 10.2 E-procurement and reverse auctions[6]

Reverse auctions online is a process by which potential buyers of goods or services invite potential sellers to bid online in a given time frame. The initiator of reverse auctions was Freemarkets Online, which organized e-procurement for industrial companies using proprietary competitive bidding software, and connected more than 100 buyers and 11,100 suppliers from 64 countries.

Freemarkets Online has since been sold to SAP Ariba. The process of a reverse auction works as shown in Figure 10.5.

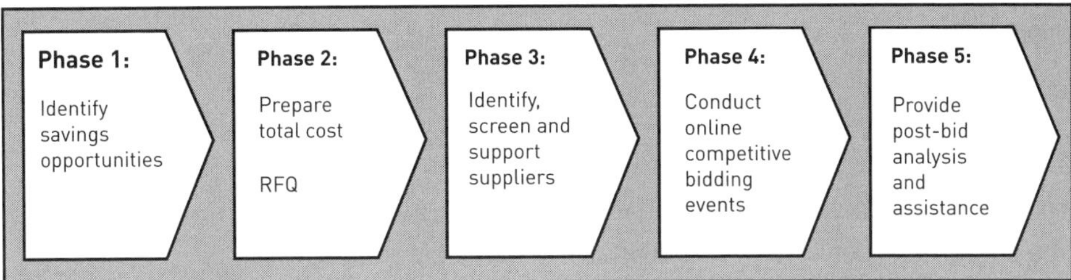

Figure 10.5 Reverse auction process
Note: *RFQ = Request for qualification.*

The actual auction takes place in real time and can achieve 30–40 per cent savings, as illustrated in the following bidding example (Figure 10.6).

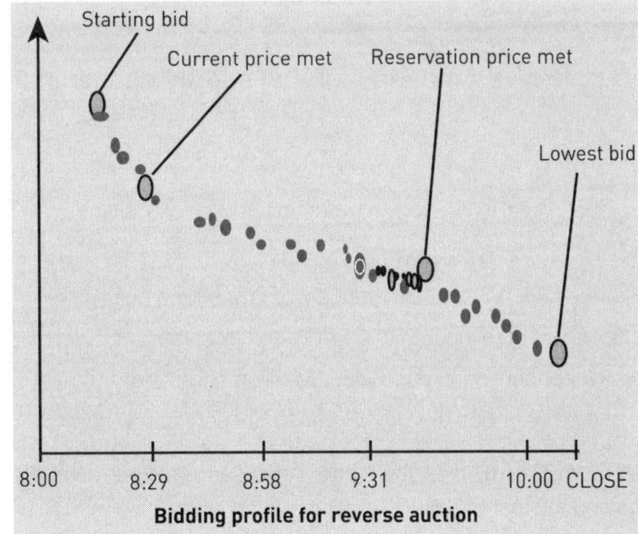

Figure 10.6 Bidding profile for reverse auction

Remember also that e-procurement does not eliminate the need for the physical movement of goods. That still requires attention to good logistics and all the vagaries of international trade such as import barriers, quotas or duties.

Global logistics

An interconnected network of specialized suppliers and production centres scattered across the world requires timely, secure and 'lean' logistics. Logistics are made up of three major functions:

- Allocation
- Distribution
- Transportation.

The allocation function consists of deciding which products, in what quantity and when/where they are going to be sent. These decisions depend upon five major parameters:

- The demand for the product or component in a particular place
- The degree of specialization of the production or procurement unit
- The capacity of the production or procurement unit
- The level of acceptable inventories
- The estimated transportation time.

EXAMPLE 10.3 Apple's vs Amazon's global supply chains in 2015

Apple

Apple is the leading global digital technology firm with a turnover of $365 billion in 2021. Apple's products are grouped into four main categories:

- Smartphones (iPhone): 53.5 per cent of revenue with 232 million units sold
- Tablets (iPad): 8.7 per cent of revenue with 53 million units sold
- Computers (Mac): 9.6 per cent of revenue with 25 million units sold
- Services (iTunes) and other goods (iWatch, iPod): 10 per cent of revenue

Apple's products are distributed all over the world: Americas (41.8 per cent), Europe (21 per cent), China (24.6 per cent), Japan and the rest of Asia (15.1 per cent).

- Apple's global supply chain is made of five components: research and development, parts production, assembly, logistics and retail.
- Apple's R&D centre based in Cupertino, California develops products in-house but works closely with hardware and software suppliers in order to design and test components.
- Part-production is allocated to 225 suppliers scattered in 27 countries mainly across Asia (Taiwan, Singapore, Malaysia, China), USA and Europe under the coordination of a global procurement team.
- One single assembly plant, Foxconn located in China, handled 80 per cent of the production of the 232 million iPhones sold in 2015.

- Logistics is supplied by a series of warehouses and distribution centres: Apple's facility in Elk Grove, California, plus UPS and Fedex facilities in Australia, China, the Czech Republic, Japan, Singapore, the UK and the USA.
- Finally, retailing is provided via 519 Apple stores (located in 25 countries), third-party retailers and online country-centred websites. Retailing is completed by a reverse logistics system to manage product returns.

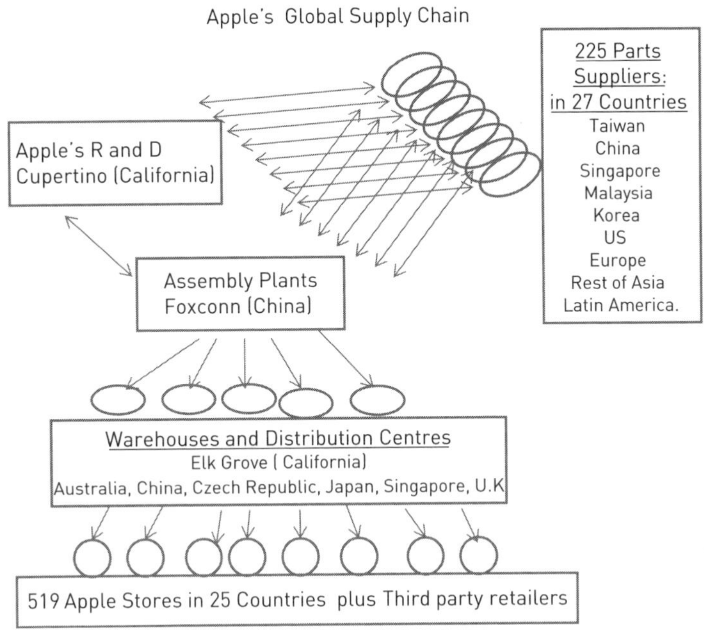

Figure 10.7 Apple's global supply chain

Amazon

Amazon, created in 1994, is the world's leading internet-based retailer. Consumers browse and shop on the Amazon website for a large variety of goods ranging from books, electronics, home and kitchen, and beauty products. It is estimated that Amazon offers customers more than 12 million products via 13 different devoted country websites. In addition around 350,000 suppliers worldwide serve customers through Amazon Marketplace. Some of the suppliers are direct, their products being stocked in Amazon's fulfilment centres, and some are third parties for whom Amazon process the orders.

In each country the Amazon website receives orders that are transferred electronically to the fulfilment centres or the third-party suppliers. All products transit through around 285 fulfilment centres. where Amazon stores, packs, ships, and handles customer service. In 2021 Amazon's turnover was \$1470 billion of which the USA provided 60 per cent. In addition to the fulfilment centres, Amazon has invested in transportation equipment to support air carriers such as UBS and Fedex, and ocean shipping freight contractors. The following picture sketches the Amazon global supply chain.

In 2016 Amazon unveiled an ambitious plan, called 'Dragon Boat', to upgrade its global delivery system. Its ambition is to control the global flow of goods, and as part of the plan, the company bought delivery companies and bought 11 Boeing planes in 2021 in addition to using leased aircraft.

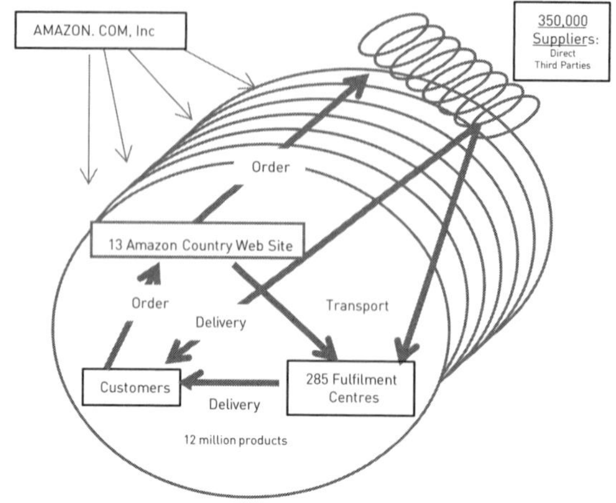

Figure 10.8 Amazon's global logistics

Another example of a cross-border logistics network is given in Figure 10.9, showing how Airbus Industries organizes the flow of aircraft components to their final assembly in either Hamburg or Toulouse.

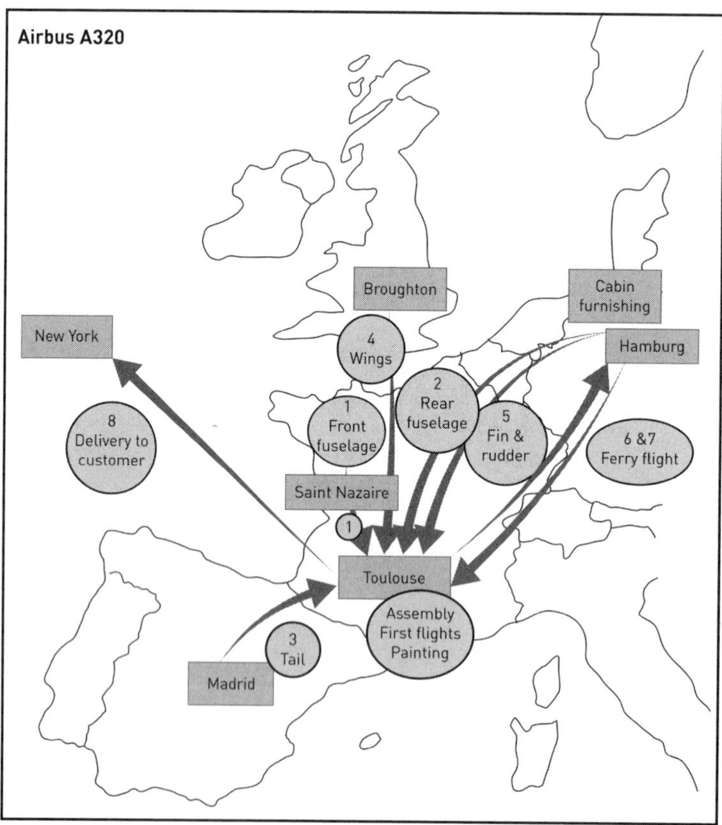

Figure 10.9 Airbus logistics

The global management of infrastructure projects

Large infrastructure projects such as airports, power plants, petrochemical plants, pulp and paper mills, railway systems, bridges, toll roads, real estate developments and so on constitute a particular category of global operation. These projects involve various players, as described in Figure 10.10.

The various phases of international project management are described in Table 10.3. There are many configurations of project management, but they can be grouped into three main categories:

- The direct project management configuration, in which the customer fulfils the role of project manager. For instance, when the Republic of Singapore decided to build a mass-transportation system, it created a special organization, the Mass Railways Transit (MRT), to take charge of managing the project to completion. The customer can call upon engineering firms to supervise the work and actually manage the project, but the engineering project team acts on behalf of the customer to coordinate these firms and is financially responsible only for the amount of its fees.
- The turnkey project configuration, in which the customer contracts out the whole project to a specialized engineering firm or to a consortium of equipment suppliers. The project manager ensures completion at a fixed price and delivery time and hands over the project to the customer after the start-up phase. The project manager has control of and responsibility for the whole amount of the contract.
- The Build, Operate and Transfer (BOT) configuration and its derivatives, in which the project manager is not only in charge of the construction, but also of the operation. At the end of a pre-arranged period, the infrastructure and operational responsibility is handed over to the customer. The project manager is responsible for the output and is paid on the basis of a predetermined price per unit of output ($ per kilowatt/hour, $ per toll fee, $ per cubic metre of water etc.). There are three main derivatives:
    - BOO (Build, Operate and Own): the project manager keeps ownership
    - BOOT (Build, Own, Operate and Transfer): the project manager has full ownership of the infrastructure during the period of operation
    - ROT (Refurbish, Operate and Transfer): similar to BOT but involving refurbishment of old installations.

More and more infrastructure projects in emerging countries are now made on the basis of BOT contracts. BOT projects have an intrinsic risk that can be analysed as a 'hostage risk'.[7] Before completion of the project, the customer is willing to accept favourable conditions because they need the infrastructure. Once the infrastructure is set up, the supplier has no more bargaining power and its investment is sunk in the project. Customers may argue that contracted fees for the supply of the final output are too high. This hostage problem has been described by Wells and Gleason (1995) and is well illustrated by the Enron Power Plant at Dabhol in the state of Maharashtra in India (see the example that follows).

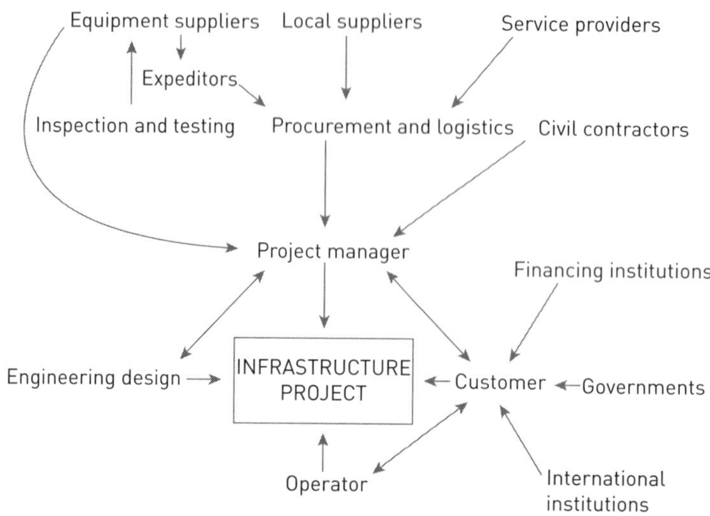

Figure 10.10 Players in an international infrastructure project

Table 10.3 Phases in international infrastructure projects

Phases	Content
Pre-feasibility	• Project concept • Need/market assessment • Strategic plan • Approach international financial institutions • Approach engineering consultants and major industrial specialists • Set overall financial budgets
Feasibility	• Assign consultant for feasibility study • Sketch broad project characteristics, including cash flows and computation of financial returns • Arrange financing • Choose project organization • Select engineering firm
Basic engineering	• Define basic technical parameters • Infrastructure blueprints • Project breakdown into various technical areas (civil engineering, electrical, chemical, power generation, IT, regulations to satisfy etc.)
Detailed engineering/tendering	• Prepare documents for tendering • Tenders, negotiation/selection of equipment and contracting suppliers • All detailed parameters in each project part defined
Expediting/site construction	• Preparation of construction site • Civil engineering and construction (piling, infrastructure – roads, ports, pipelines, transmission, power, building contractors) • Reception of equipment • Erection/assembly of machinery • Layout of pipes, electrical cables, water etc. • Final assembly

Training	• Recruitment of personnel • On-the-job training at suppliers' sites • Mock-up training
Start-up	• First operations
Operation	• Verification of technical parameters • Reception by client • Managing the operation

EXAMPLE 10.4 Enron in India: the Dabhol Power Plant[8]

The Dabhol Power Company (DPC) was a consortium of Enron Power, Bechtel Enterprises and General Electric, led by Enron. In 1995, DPC signed a contract with the Maharashtra State Electricity Board for the construction and operation of a 625 megawatt power plant costing $922 million. According to the contract, the state committed to buy the output at a level of tariff structure that would provide DPC with a 25.22 per cent return on investment. During the same year, general elections brought to power a new state government which cancelled the project, invoking a lack of transparency and too high a proposed tariff payable to DPC. After negotiations, the project was redesigned and finally accepted under different terms. The first phase of the project was completed and the financing of a second phase was finalized in 1999. However, by April 2001 Enron was threatening to withdraw from India because the local utility company was not complying with its obligations. Following Enron's financial debacle, the Dabhol Power Plant went up for sale in early 2002.

The internet and global operations

The combination of broadband capabilities, connectivity, standard languages (HTML, XML), wireless communication and portability have given birth to the digital age and its most pervasive manifestation: the internet. The internet is a global network connecting billions of devices across the world, exchanging data, opinions, information and news using a common architecture, the Internet Protocol (IP). In essence, the internet is a global tool since it has abolished physical distance barriers to the transmission of data, images and sounds and it has standardized the transmission protocol as well as the machine software, making it possible for any computer in the world to be part of the network and to 'talk' to other computers. Estimates show that e-commerce reached around $13 trillion in 2021. Internet usage is spreading and growing all over the world (see Figure 10.11). The internet was at the root of the so-called 'new economy' that flourished from 1995 to 2000 and is still growing quickly today despite slumping in 2001 as the 'dotcom bubble' burst. According to the McKinsey Research Institute, 'the internet is, and will remain over coming decades, one of the biggest drivers of global economic growth'.[9]

The Digital Revolution

Digital affects all sectors of business and society. It was estimated that over 2.14 billion people worldwide bought goods and services online in 2021, an increase from 1.66 billion global digital buyers in 2016.

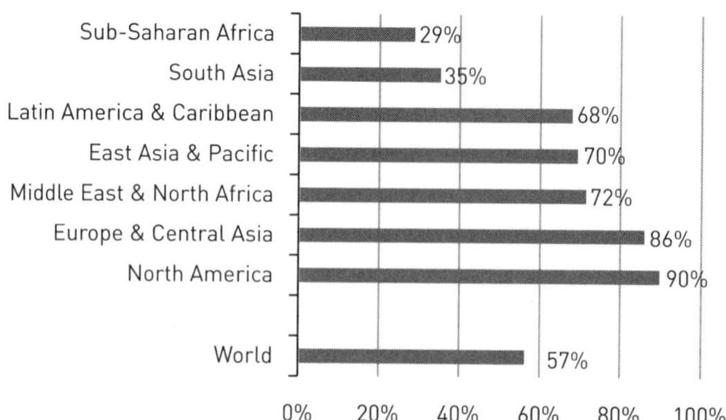

Figure 10.11 Global use of the internet, April 2020
Source: World Development Indicators, The World Bank, http://wdi.worldbank.org/table/5.12# (accessed 1 February 2022).

As noted by Monteiro and Carrick in their report 'Digital transformation in Latin America: leapfrogging and social impact,'[10] during 2018, global e-retail sales amounted to $2.8 trillion and projections show a growth of up to $4.8 trillion by 2021.[11] The number of smartphone users by August 2020 surpassed 3 billion and is forecast to grow further by several hundred million in the next few years.[12] New business models were disrupting traditional ways of doing business – be it Uber, Facebook, Google, Amazon, PayPal, Skype, Spotify or WeChat. AI and sophisticated analytical software signalled that the digital revolution was in full flight. In response, incumbents reinvented their businesses – for example IBM's supercomputer Watson combined AI and sophisticated analytics software.

Significant landmarks in the history of digital included the arrival of mass-market personal computers (PCs) in the mid-1980s. In the 1990s, organizations and businesses computerized processes with the maturing of digital design tools and robotized manufacturing equipment. The 2000s witnessed the arrival of outsourcing and 'offshoring' operations and services. Henceforth, multinational enterprises could exploit once-incongruent corporate IT systems to improve coordination.

There were two fundamental dimensions to digital transformation for all businesses: 1) cutting costs and 2) getting closer to the customer.[13] Connectivity was key. Analysts estimated that 63 per cent of the world's population would have access to internet by 2021 and 50.5 per cent by mobile.[14] In 2020, smartphone sales reached 1.57 billion. People spent more time on mobile devices as the number of apps grew. Cisco estimated that there would be a sevenfold increase in global mobile data traffic by 2021.

Connectivity to customers, suppliers and other stakeholders allowed organizations to turn processes and devices into networks to capture the vast amounts of information they received. Businesses used digital platforms that connected all players rather than doing business through intermediaries. Platforms were an integral part of the digital economy, used for making payments and ecommerce (see Table 10.4). Businesses often used third-party platforms for new projects rather than building them in house.

Most digital initiatives were built on 'third platform technologies' including mobile, cloud computing, big data/analytics and social technologies. Innovation accelerators such as IoT, robotics, 3D printing and security all depended on these platforms and were considered key growth factors for many businesses.

Another dimension was the advent of social media, and new tools for data analysis. Facebook monthly users increased from 1 million at the end of 2004 when it was launched, to 600 million at the end of 2010, and 2.7 billion by the second quarter of 2020.[15] By August 2020, there were 3.8 billion social media users globally.[16]

The players

As with many innovations, the internet was originally created in the 1960s out of the Advanced Research Projects Agency (ARPA) in the USA. It became a really widespread tool in the late 1990s and grew at a tremendous pace during the first decade of the twenty-first century. The internet is mainly known for its main application, the World Wide Web, or the Web. Today Web technology has evolved into what is commonly known as Web 2.0, which allows for intercommunication among internet users. In 2022, already a third internet generation (Web 3.0), more decentralized, using artificial intelligence and machine learning was gaining importance. The internet is no longer a passive tool but a real exchange platform.

Usage of the Web is divided broadly into two categories:

- The individual users' space for persons or organizations who use the Web for emailing, browsing for information, downloading documents or videos, playing games, listening to music, watching movies, chatting on social networks such as Instagram, Twitter, WeChat and possibly buying goods and services
- The commercial space or e-business, consisting of three major categories of players:

  1. The traditional companies of the so-called 'old economy', also called *'bricks and mortar'*, that offer physically produced products and services with 'real' assets. These companies use the technology for selling, buying, partnering and internal management through their internet (open to the general public) or intranet (secure site internal to the company) websites or extranet (secure websites external to the company).
  2. The 'pure players' or '*dotcom*' companies that have been created to enable Web transactions and whose products and services essentially organize transactions, serve as e-commerce intermediaries and provide software platforms. Among those players you can find:
     - *E-commerce* companies selling or organizing sales to customers (B2C: business-to-consumer), trade among companies (B2B: business-to-business) or among customers (C2C: customer-to-customer). Well-known examples are Amazon (B2C retailer), eBay (C2C auctioneer), E*Trade (B2C investment), SAP Ariba (B2B procurement) and Alibaba (B2B and B2C commerce).
     - *Intermediaries* providing tools for transactions: e-payment, security, domain names, search engines and so on (e.g. Paypal for payment, Skype for telephony).
     - *Search engines* or *browsers* such as Google or Yahoo!
     - *Social networks* such as Facebook, Twitter, LinkedIn, Instagram.
  3. The companies providing physical products or services to the two previous types of players:
     - Internet Service Providers (ISPs) providing access to the Web: ATT, BT, Orange, Deutsche Telecom and most of the traditional telecom operators.

- Traditional software vendors and application service providers (ASPS), selling or supporting software: Oracle, SAP, IBM.
- Web hosting and maintenance: companies that provide space on servers and various services for data management including cloud storage.
- Consulting firms advising companies about internet applications and development: Accenture, Gartner, Forrester.
- Content providers: Reuters, Netflix, Apple, Walt Disney, media companies.
- Equipment providers: CISCO, Nortel, Nokia, Huawei.

Figure 10.12 gives a pictorial representation of the internet space.

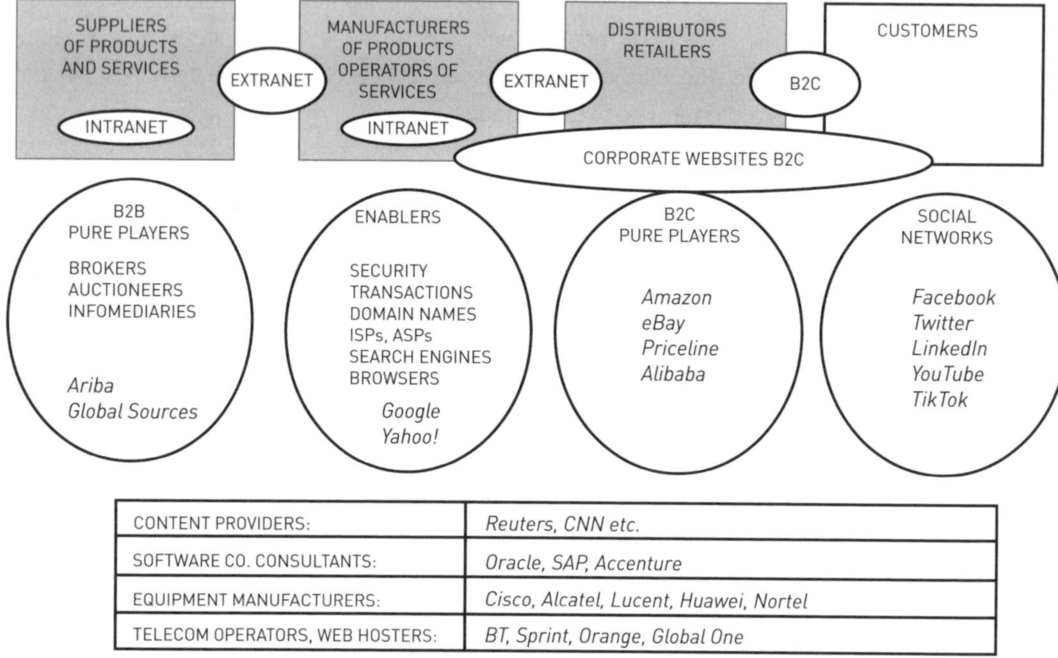

Figure 10.12 Players in the internet space

Table 10.4 below provides a summary of the different types of digital platforms.

Table 10.4 Digital platforms

Non-profit-oriented digital platforms and examples	Profit-oriented digital platforms and examples	E-commerce platforms and examples
Exchange platforms – HomeExchange.com	Electronic payment platforms – Alipay, Paypal, M-Pesa, Visa, Mastercard	Incumbent companies' platforms – Caterpillar, Ikea, Zara
Donation platforms – freecycle, Nolotiro.org	Crowdfunding platforms – Caterse, Kickstarter	Third-party goods e-commerce platforms – Amazon, Alibaba, eBay, MercadoLibre, Etsy

Free services platforms – Couchsurfing	Social media – Facebook, Twitter	Third-party e-commerce platforms – • *Transportation* – 99, Uber, DiDi • *Delivery* – Deliveroo, Rappi • *Tourism* – Airbnb, Booking.com • *Financial services (lending)* – Zopa, Prosper • *Entertainment* – iTunes, Netflix • *Media* – Bloomberg, Reuters • *Advertising* – Facebook, Google • *Search* – Yahoo, Google search • *Information/reviews* – Yelp, Tripadvisor • *Learning* – edX, Lynda.com • *Health* – Doctor.com, MDLive, Doctolib • *Digital labour (gig work)* – Airbnb, TaskRabbit • *Digital labour (cloud work)* – Upwork, Amazon MTurk • *Apps Markets* – AppStore, GooglePlay • *Cloud Services* – AWS, Microsoft Azure, Tencent
Other sharing economy platforms – Goteo, Wikipedia		

Source: UNCTAD Digital Economy Report, https://unctad.org/en/publicationslibrary/der2019_en.pdf (accessed 7 April 2020).

Types of e-transaction for businesses

When we look at business-related transactions on the Web, we can distinguish three types:

- Commercial transactions external to the firm: e-commerce (selling), e-procurement (buying).
- External relational transactions other than buying and selling: e-partnering (coordinating, information-sharing, R&D with partners).
- Internal relations: e-management (planning and control, database sharing, recruiting, training, administration), information collection, knowledge management.

The contribution of the internet to globalization

The internet is, by design, a global network. It can be seen as an additional driver to globalization, but not a revolutionary one. As discussed in Chapter 1, globalization has been enhanced and fostered by political, technological, sociological and competitive factors. The additional contribution that the internet brings to globalization trends is the enhanced capability to decouple physical activities from the information exchange needed to support them. Evans and Wurster have argued that the internet breaks the traditional *reach versus richness* trade-off (see Insert 10.1) and, as a consequence, fosters the ability of companies to organize transactions and transfer data beyond national boundaries in real time.[17] The internet is a facilitator to globalization.

An UNCTAD report estimated that the global value of e-commerce sales (including both B2B and B2C) amounted to around US$ 26 trillion in 2018,[18] representing 30 % GDP with a growth of eight % over 2017. The value of global B2B e-commerce was estimated at US$ 21 trillion, representing 83% of all e-commerce.

Standardized products, such as commodities, are those that benefit most from internet transactions because most commodities were traditionally traded electronically. Traders in commodities were already used to anonymous, real-time transactions and the internet adds a convenient unified network for these.

Progressively semi-customized products, such as metal-engineered parts, can also find their way into the e-marketplace because once there is an agreement on technical specifications, reverse auctions can be organized for their procurement, as mentioned earlier.

Insert 10.1 The 'reach versus richness' trade-off

Evans and Wurster argue that, traditionally, economic activities are constrained by the difficulty of simultaneously achieving intense exchange of information (richness) with a large number of people (reach). Economic entities therefore have to choose between **volume** (reach) and **quality** of relationships (richness). See Figure 10.13. If a company wants to increase its volume and reach a larger number of people, it has to reduce the amount of information it exchanges with the customer and therefore standardize its product and customer interactions. Hypermarkets that can handle large numbers of customers provide no (or little) assistance to customers, for example. On the other hand, when a company wants to customize a product or service, it needs to exchange rich information with customers, but there is a limit to the number of customers it can handle. A specialized boutique giving expert advice to customers cannot handle as many customers as a supermarket. This reach/richness trade-off has induced companies to choose between two fundamental strategic positions: high-volume, low-cost **standardized products/services** or low-volume **differentiation** (see Figure 11.8).

The internet, because of its standard platform and connectivity, and because of its ability to carry very rich information in the form of text and video as well as voice and data, permits a certain degree of customization for a vast number of people, therefore increasing reach without sacrificing richness. It is possible, for instance, to work at a distance with suppliers or customers and still exchange customized information.

See Evans and Wurster (2000).

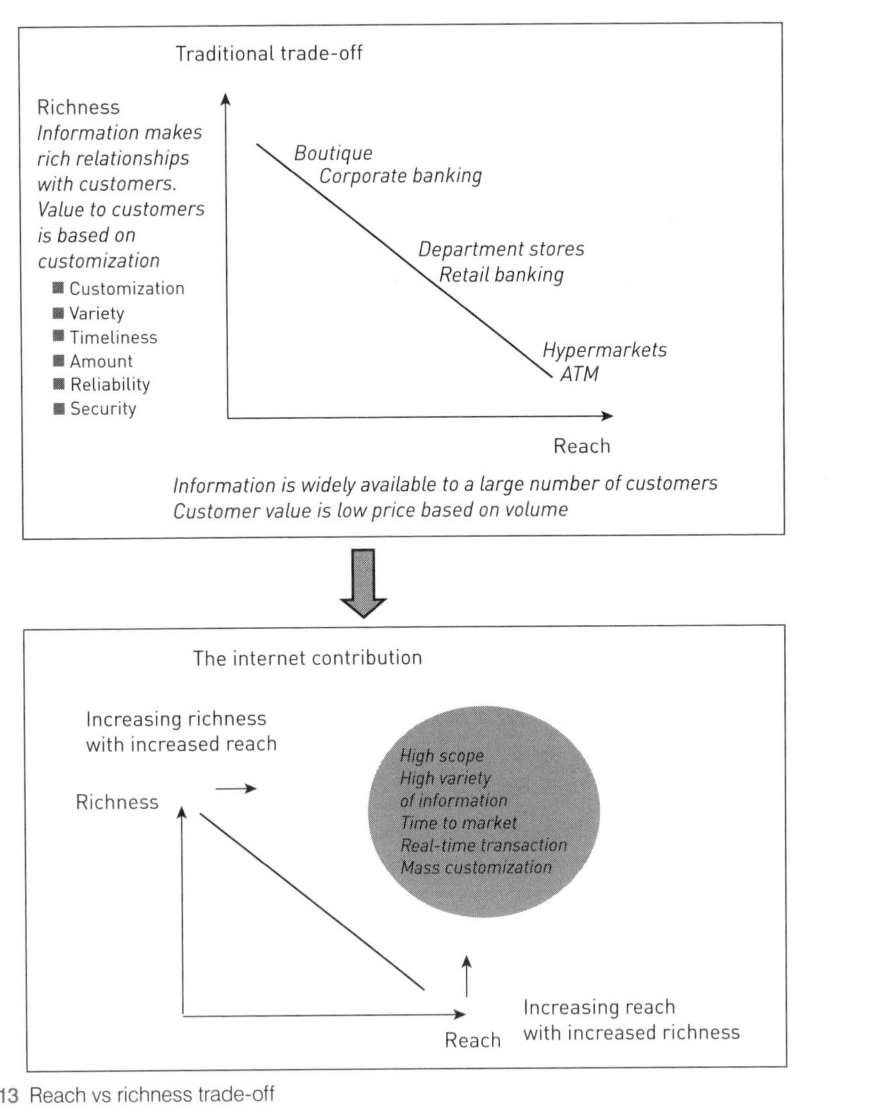

Figure 10.13 Reach vs richness trade-off

George Yip, amongst others, has made predictions for the impact of the internet upon global trade – such as increased globalization of markets and wider choice for individual consumers, global cost reductions, fiercer global competition and fewer governmental barriers to free trade.[19] See Table 10.5 for a summary of some of these predictions.

However, in spite of their global enhancement capabilities, internet transactions across borders are subject to potential limitations owing to regulatory and sociotechnical and cultural factors:

- Cross-border regulatory restrictions, such as customs duties and VAT taxes, still apply to the physical transfer of goods bought on the internet.

Table 10.5 Effects of the internet on globalization

For corporations	**Global markets** • Makes marketing communication and advertising more global (reinforcing global brands and branding) • Facilitates the management of global customers and global procurement • Facilitates access for small and medium-sized companies to global markets through e-commerce • Facilitates the development of global products **Global competitiveness** • Reduces costs of transactions and communications with customers, suppliers, partners, and employees across the world • Reduces costs of monitoring and organizing global logistics • Reduces costs of raw materials and other supplies (thanks to global e-sourcing) **Global innovation** • Global access to databases • Facilitates coordination of global research projects and global teamwork
For consumers	• Makes global brands more visible • Makes global purchasing feasible • Provides access to global information • Provides access to comparative assessments of competitive products from different countries • Provides easy and economical purchasing of global travel (e-tickets, e-lodging)

Sources: Authors' own table, drawn from text of McKinsey (2016); Yip (2000); Borcuch et al. (2012).

- Local legislation, such as the insistence of certain governments to restrict access to certain websites. A well-publicized example was provided by the experience of Yahoo! with French anti-racist legislation (see the example below).
- Sociotechnical and cultural factors, such as the propensity of customers to accept online payment, and attitudes towards electronic trade versus direct face-to-face relationships which may hamper or foster the development of e-business.

EXAMPLE 10.5 Yahoo! and anti-racist legislation in France

In November 2000, a French court ruled that Yahoo! should block French users from viewing and buying Nazi memorabilia on its American auction site, in accordance with French anti-racist regulations. The implication of the judgment was that Yahoo!'s parent company in the United States, and not just the French subsidiary, should make sure that access to auctions of Nazi objects should be banned to French citizens. Yahoo! counterattacked by asking the US court to declare that this decision could not be enforced in the United States because it violates the First Amendment of the American constitution and that US citizens were not obliged to follow French rules outside France. A US district court followed this argument, and decided that Yahoo! was not bound by the French judgment. Two French human rights groups appealed the decision. This series of events generated a polemic about the right of governments to regulate a 'global' medium such as the internet. Some analysts saw the French decision as a dangerous one for the future of the Web, others argued that the internet had to follow local rules.

Jack Goldsmith, a Professor of Law at the University of Chicago, wrote a commentary on the case in the *Financial Times*. Goldsmith refuted the concept of internet communication being inherently any less bound by geographical jurisdictions than any other medium, all of which 'facilitate transactions by someone in 'real space' in one nation with someone in 'real space' in another nation'. Goldsmith went on to assert that France had every right to clamp down on action on French territory that violated its laws or threatened its citizens.

Sources: Various press reports; Goldsmith (2000).

As companies such as Google, Amazon or Meta (formerly known as Facebook) have discovered, globalizing their businesses is not so different from the experience of traditional 'bricks and mortar' companies. It still requires the development of local alliances, acquisitions and an adaptation of the product offering to local conditions (see Insert 10.2).

Insert 10.2 How do internet companies globalize?

Internet companies, known as 'dotcoms', follow a classic pattern of international expansion in order to get global reach. They invest in countries and set up subsidiaries, acquire local players or enter into strategic alliances. Most of the overseas investment for dotcom firms is in the creation of sales offices. Some may set up software development centres in India. Amazon is present in 14 countries, Google in over 50, Meta in 37.

The internet and global firms

Overall, the internet was seen during the heady days of the 'new economy' in 1999 and 2000 as a new business paradigm, allowing firms to completely revolutionize the way they designed and implemented strategies.[20] This view was fuelled by the hyperinflation of stock valuations, when any dotcom newcomer could challenge the market value of well-established centenarian 'bricks and mortar' players. The subsequent bursting of the market bubble showed that traditional business strategy models are still valid, even in virtual space.[21]

For global or globalizing firms, the internet provides a tool to manage internal and external linkages, to run business processes more efficiently and to enhance their cross-border *management capabilities*, including:

- Real-time communication over all locations in various media: video, text and data
- Ability to field customer interactions, requests and feedback and to consolidate customer data
- Ability to serve as a platform for a global knowledge management system
- Ability to reach new suppliers through electronic global procurement
- Ability to identify and communicate with customers in low-density locations.

These capabilities are embodied in the recent technological development around the concepts of Web 2.0, internet of things (IoT) and Industry 4.0.

Web 2.0

The term Web 2.0, introduced in 1999, describes the evolution of the internet toward full interactivity among Web users who can share files in audio, text or video format, talk to each other, share programmes and store data remotely (cloud computing). According to a McKinsey research report:

> Web 2.0 technologies can be a powerful lure for an organization; their interactivity promises to bring more employees into daily contact at lower cost. When used effectively, they also may encourage participation in projects and idea sharing, thus deepening a company's pool of knowledge. They may bring greater scope and scale to organizations as well, strengthening bonds with customers and improving communications with suppliers and outside partners.[22]

Among the major benefits that the McKinsey survey highlighted are faster access to information, a reduction in communication costs and an increasing effectiveness of marketing. All of these benefits obviously appeal to global management, for which communication and knowledge management across borders make up an important feature of competitive capability.

Industry 4.0, the smart factory and the internet of things

Recently, the possibility of autonomous robots and machines communicating with each other through an internet connection (part of the 'internet of things' concept of networked devices communicating with their users and with each other) has given rise to the concept of the 'smart factory', a key part of the wider trend of increasing data exchange and automation in manufacturing that is known as Industry 4.0.

Outlined in the book *The Fourth Industrial Revolution* by Professor Klaus Schwab, Industry 4.0 encompasses 'new technologies that combine the physical, digital and biological worlds, impacting all disciplines, economies and industries [see Table 10.14 below]. These technologies have great potential to continue to connect billions more people to the web and drastically improve the efficiency of business and organizations.'

Through the combination and convergence of advanced technologies – including industrial internet of things (IoT), automation, artificial intelligence, the cloud and big data and analytics – Industry 4.0 is revamping business practices, transforming market dynamics across industries and generating collaborative approaches to innovation and the global supply chain.

The potential for achieving efficiency, productivity and sustainability gains becomes exponential as these technologies connect and communicate with one another together with machines becoming smarter as they continue to access and process more data.

The smart factory represents a combination of decentralized production sites operating in real time through online connections, with the possibility of local adaptation.

There are not as yet many concrete examples of such a smart factory in practice, but many global players are experimenting with the concept.

Table 10.6 The evolution of Industry 4.0

Date	Phase	Details
1800	INDUSTRY 1.0	Start of the industrial revolution with the invention of mechanical production with steam
1900	INDUSTRY 2.0	Mass production powered by electricity and combustion engines – assembly lines
1970	INDUSTRY 3.0	Electronics, IT for advanced automation of production processes – computers, IT and internet mark the beginning of the information age
2015	INDUSTRY 4.0	Data analytics as a core capability – internet of things, cloud, mobile devices, artificial intelligence, advanced algorithms, 3D printing, smart factory

Source: Table drawn by authors based on PwC (2016).

Siemens has a production centre in Amberg (Germany) that resembles this model of a smart factory. Set up in 1989, the factory is transforming from analogue manufacturing to analytical-fuelled digital production. The factory produces 1,200 different products from circuit boards to an entire production plant. The production line configurations need to be changed 350 times per day. In the past, this was done manually but now this laborious task has been replaced by a digital version created by a computer model of the products, production line and manufacturing process known as 'digital twins'. By making a replica of everything built, it helps streamline and speed up setting new configurations. This digital preview also helps identify possible bottlenecks and unforeseen requirements. The digitalization of the factory floor resulted in a 1,400 per cent increase in productivity.

Digital technologies and disruption to job and skills

The introduction of increasingly sophisticated digital technologies is transforming the nature of work and imposing a re-evaluation of corporate structures, workplace business practices and leadership paradigms. As AI technologies, robotics and cognitive tools develop, almost all jobs are reinvented. See Chapter 14 for a fuller discussion.

Industry 4.0 technologies and global supply chains

Advanced technologies are profoundly impacting traditional supply chains as they move from a linear model to an open, flexible and digitally interconnected ecosystem aimed at responding to fast changes in demand, increasing service levels and opening up integrated and collaborative approaches to suppliers' operations.

This digital supply network – whose components are being developed today – will enable companies at a global scale to be more resilient, efficient and closer to customers. This digital supply chain will enable companies to anticipate, adjust and respond to changes in the supply chain in real time as these changes happen.

The degree of adoption of supply chain 4.0 is likely to vary from firm to firm and from country to country but could be a factor influencing location and the distribution of firms (e.g. integrating multiple stages of production at a single location or using technologies such as 3D printing for a shorter, more localized value chain where manufacturing takes place closer to the end-user) (see Figure 10.15).

Comparison of the traditional supply chain model and the integrated supply chain ecosystem

Figure 10.14 Traditional supply chain model

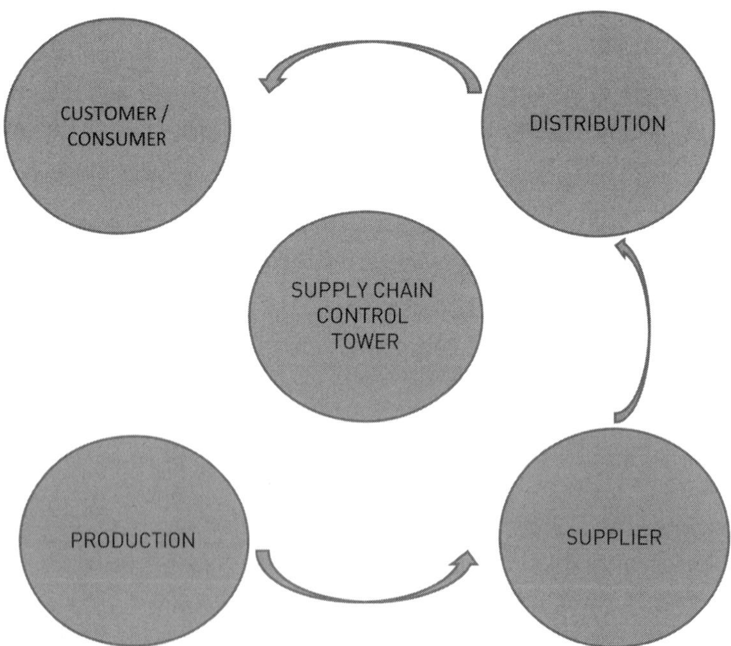

Figure 10.15 Integrated supply chain ecosystem

Table 10.7 Comparison of supply chains

Evolution	Traditional linear supply chain	Integrated supply chain ecosystem
Transparency	Limited view of supply chain	Complete view of supply chain
Communication	Information delayed as it moves through each organization	Information available to each supply chain member simultaneously
Collaboration	Limited visibility to the entire chain – hindering collaboration	Natural development of collaboration depth to capture supply chain value
Flexibility	End customer demand distorted as information flows along the material path	End customer demand changes are rapidly assessed
Responsiveness	Different planning cycles resulting in delays and unsynchronized responses across multiple tiers	Real-time response on planning and execution level (across all tiers to demand changes)

Source: Authors' own adapted from PwC (2016).

Internal implications

In order to harness the full potential of the internet, businesses need to develop several types of *web-enabling capabilities:*

- Partnering capabilities:
  - the ability to form partnerships and to activate them in real time
  - the ability to share information with partners so that the transaction can be executed automatically
  - the ability to make deals instantaneously
- A 'no secrets' management system: in order to make decisions quickly, the various internal processes of the company have to share information (in fact, automatically) horizontally
- Decision making: an ability to make important decisions, such as pricing, at increased speed, on occasion in real time, implying a very strong decentralization of authority
- Feedback: collecting, consolidating, interpreting and disseminating feedback from customers, so as to adapt and respond to local conditions
- IT: to develop an IT platform and telecoms network that can work in a seamless way.

In order to participate in the Web economy, firms are not only cataloguing their products on the Web and enabling 'one-click' sales, as currently happens on most of the B2C internet sites, but have had to completely rethink their managerial systems, structures and cultures. Table 10.8 summarizes these internal implications.

Table 10.8 Organizational requirements for e-business

Internal requirements	Consequences
Transparency	• Integrity and consistency of information • Clarity of data and procedures
Sharing culture	• Horizontal as well as vertical exchange of information • External partners have access to databases • No 'silos' of jealously guarded hoarded information
Process integration	• All management processes are compatible with each other to facilitate information flow
Pooled coordination	• Sequential coordination too time-consuming; therefore needs: – Ability to have different departments working together instantaneously instead of sequentially – Ability to bundle different parameters in real time
Real-time commitment	• Ability to make decisions quickly • No time for hierarchical checking
Horizontal processes	• Hierarchical communications and decision processes are inefficient

These organizational attributes may sometimes conflict with local cultures. The challenge for the global firm is to overcome these cultural differences among their employees, suppliers, customers and partners in order to make Web transactions effective.

MINI-CASE 10.1

The globalization of the sharing economy: Airbnb, Uber and BlaBlaCar

The development of the internet has considerably expanded the already well-established practice of making individually owned private assets or services available to other individuals. For instance, bed and breakfast accommodation or carpooling were commonplace concepts years before the appearance of Web-based platforms such as Airbnb, Uber or Blablacar. What is new with these concepts of the 'sharing economy' are their massive amplitude and their global spread. Short descriptions of three 'collaborative consumption' platforms and their global development follow.

Airbnb

Founded in California in 2007 under the name of 'Airbed and Breakfast' by three young, freshly graduated entrepreneurs, this Web-based platform puts private home owners in contact with individuals looking for temporary accommodation. The concept is simple: the owners of an apartment, a house or a room subscribes to the platform (later renamed 'Airbnb') which publicizes it on its Web page. Potential customers can contact the owner directly to arrange details of a rental. The website gets a commission from the transaction. Launched and refined in the USA, Airbnb rapidly expanded its service in 2011 to European tourism hotspots such as France and Spain, thanks to the acquisition of a small German platform. By 2019 the service was offering 7 million places to stay in more than 100,000 cities in 220 countries to 750 million guests.[23] In the process the company has developed tools such as translation software and online tourist guides. The company has, however, confronted local legal, administrative and taxation disputes provoked by what has been labelled 'unfair competition' by the traditional hospitality industry, and as a tax-evading device by local authorities.

Uber

Uber Technology Inc. was founded in 2009 in San Francisco and benefited initially from venture capital funding. The business model was based on direct contact (via a mobile phone application) between a customer looking for a ride and an Uber driver using either their own car or a company car but acting as an independent driver. Compared with traditional taxis, the service is personalized, more prompt and cheaper. The main feature is that the driver is not an employee of the company but acts on their own. Originally the market was limited to luxury cabs but rapidly expanded to all vehicles, competing directly with normal taxis. The first international expansion introduced Uber in Paris in 2011, London in 2012, Taiwan, Johannesburg and Bangalore in 2013, and China and Brazil in 2014. By 2020, Uber operated in 93 countries and 900 cities. The business model has attracted a lot of resistance from professional taxi drivers who claim that Uber competition is unfair because Uber drivers did not have to pay the normal extra taxes that taxis have to bear. However, Uber's success has yet to be confirmed. Several local governments are imposing restrictions on Uber's business model. According to a *Fortune* article, Uber recently revealed that it is losing more than $1 billion per year in China, and that 'Beyond its well-documented troubles in China, it is also struggling in Europe. The young tech company has committed a classic globalization mistake: it naively assumed that its business model and market approach, which ultimately solidified its market-leading position in the U.S., could translate just as seamlessly to other countries.'[24]

BlaBlaCar

In 2004 a group of young French MBA graduates created a website to bring together people looking for long-distance rides and people travelling in their own cars. The 'passenger' would contribute to expenses. The site was named 'covoiturage' ('carpooling' in French) and later became BlaBlaCar in 2012 when the young company started a significant expansion programme through Europe. In 2014 it raised $100 million from a Californian investment fund in order to finance its international expansion. In 2015 it acquired Carpooling.com, its German main competitor. By 2016 BlaBlaCar had expanded to Turkey, Mexico, India and Brazil and was present in 22 countries with more than 90 million members.[23] In its global expansion the company is looking for countries of more than 50 million inhabitants, good road networks and potential journey times between cities of one to four hours. In its expansion plans BlaBlaCar has to take into account local conditions, and cultures in which the concept of travelling with an unknown person in their car is not necessarily commonplace.

Questions:

1. Using these three examples, what is your assessment of the role of the internet in globalization?
2. Are the global expansion experiences of these three platforms similar to any other global expansion you know of?

MINI-CASE 10.2

Ericsson global value chain

Created in Stockholm in 1876 where Lars Magnus Ericsson designed telephones, Ericsson in 2021 is a global company that supplies communication infrastructure, services and software to the telecom industry and other sectors. With a global turnover of 233 billion SEK ($27.3 billion) and approximately 100,000 employees, it serves customers in more than 180 countries.

Ericsson operates in four major segments:

- Networks (71 per cent of sales): radio access networks solutions such as 5G, combining hardware products, such as antennae, and network deployment
- Digital services (16 per cent of sales): software-based solutions for business and operational support, communication services, core networks and cloud infrastructure
- Managed services (10 per cent of sales): networks and IT managed services, network design and optimization, and application development and maintenance to telecom operators
- Emerging business and others (3 per cent of sales): supports enterprises by providing reliable and secure cellular solutions that are easy to use, adopt and scale for global and local needs.

Geographically, Ericsson operates in 180 countries organized in five regional segments as represented below:

- North America: 32 per cent of sales
- Europe and Latin America: 24 per cent of sales
- North Asia: 14 per cent of sales
- South East Asia, Oceania and India: 13 per cent of sales
- Middle East and Africa: 10 per cent of sales

The total production of products and services relies on eight manufacturing sites worldwide, four service delivery centres and 15 R&D centres (see below).

Figure 10.16 Ericsson global sites and centres

In addition, Ericsson deals with around 30,000 suppliers worldwide, and their products and services often account for a large part of the deliveries to customers. The suppliers have been divided into around 300 categories. Each category has a leader, who is responsible for optimizing the category, so that the right suppliers are chosen based on their numbers, quality, geographical spread, price and risk. The target is to minimize the number to get the most out of the supplier base based on economical, value creation and risk perspectives. The idea is to concentrate on the thirty or so biggest categories, which together represent around 90 per cent of the total spend. Once their numbers have been reduced, the remaining suppliers are segmented depending on their importance and potential to Ericsson. A supplier relationship manager then makes sure that maximum value is extracted from the suppliers, and that they can contribute to Ericsson's business through their innovation and ability to complement the Ericsson portfolio. A range of tools and processes are developed for this purpose. The company has created a particular function, Sourcing Business Partner (SBP). According to the company,

> The SBP supports and works closely to the sales organization, adding value to the process by contributing their knowledge of the supplier base, the market and different business models. This could include identifying that a customer can improve the supply chain by using other suppliers in preparation for an offer to take over a service, or identifying suppliers that can contribute to a new solution.

Eriksson global value chain and the Covid-19 crisis

By the spring of 2021 the company announced that:

> All main Ericsson production sites were in operation. Ericsson continues to follow the situation of the coronavirus and recommendations from the local authorities and WHO, as the company assesses its supply chain. The supply chain has worked with limited interruption and was expected to continue to work to further improve resilience by, for example, increasing inventories of critical components. However, the longer the lockdown in many countries continues, the more disruptions we will likely see.
>
> Ericsson has a global supply chain set up, which ensures the company works close to customers through its European, Asian and American operations. Our main production facilities are in Estonia, Poland, China, India, Brazil, Mexico and the US.

Questions:

1 To what extent does the SBP function linking the suppliers' bases with the customer base make Ericsson better equipped to solve a customer's problem?

2 What constraints and costs are generated with this SBP organization?

Sources: Company website annual report 2020, https://www.ericsson.com/en/investors and https://www.ericsson.com/en/news/2020/3/coronavirus-disease_faq (both accessed 1 February 2022).

Summary and key points

1 Global operations:

  a Defined as an integrated network of facilities located across the world, performing the functions of procurement, production, distribution and servicing of products for customers

  b Four major decision dimensions:

  - Location
  - Production
  - Sourcing
  - Logistics

2 Offshoring and outsourcing

  a Offshoring: production in an international locality. Two types of offshoring:

  - Local for local: production for the local market
  - Local for global: production for the global network

b Outsourcing: buying products or services internationally. Two types of outsourcing:

- Local for local: sourcing for the local market
- Local for global: sourcing for the global network

3 Choice of location

a *Criteria for location* include:

- Costs
- Proximity
- Environment
- Learning

b *Ultimate choice* depends on:

- Kind of facilities
- Role of facilities in the network

4 Global production networks

a Set of integrated production centres deployed across the world

b Two kinds of global production networks:

- Global manufacturing networks
- Global service networks

c Global manufacturing networks:

- *Classifications*:
  - 'Network architecture model' based on the role of plants as information and knowledge creators. Four main types of plant:
    - Isolated – concentrate on production of products for specific geographical markets; do not communicate much with others; installed in import-substitution countries that require local production for their domestic markets
    - Blueprint – receive (but not create) a lot of innovation; produce goods according to blueprint received from elsewhere; located in low-cost countries or EPZs
    - Host plant network player – well-established factories serving large markets that have developed a high degree of competence in state-of-the-art manufacturing technology; not at the forefront of innovation
    - Innovator plant network player – play central role in product and process adaptation and innovation; source of inspiration for other factories
  - 'Strategic roles model' classified according to strategic role based on two main variables:
    - Primary strategic reason for setting up plant in a particular country, including accessing:

        - Low-cost production
        - Skills and know-how
        - Markets
    - Competencies of plant – tasks a given site is capable of doing:
        - Assume responsibility for production
        - Maintain technical processes
        - Purchase locally
        - Make process improvements
        - Develop suppliers
        - Develop processes
        - Make product improvement recommendations
        - Develop products
        - Supply global markets and become a global hub for product and process knowledge

- Types of global plants in a network:
    - *Offshore factory*: Produces low-cost items to be re-exported either for sales or to be reworked and integrated with other components
    - *Source factory*: Produces low-cost items but factory has larger responsibilities for procurement, production, planning, process modifications, redesign and logistics
    - *Server factory*: Produces products or components for local or regional markets, relatively autonomous in the network for production, planning and modification, but dependent on technology and critical components' input
    - *Contributor factory*: Produces for local or regional market but with wider range of responsibilities in local sourcing, product redesign and process modification
    - *Outpost factory*: Close to competition and key suppliers to learn about technological development
    - *Lead factory*: Factory design and producing products for the entire global network, responsible for the whole value chain of a product category
- Evolutionary path of a global plant:
    - An outpost factory evolves to become a lead factory either directly or indirectly through becoming first a source factory or contributor factory
    - An offshore factory evolves to a source factory and possibly becomes a lead factory in the long term
    - A server factory evolves to a contributor factory and possibly becomes a lead factory in the long term involving change of plant competencies

5 Global services network

a In the *back offices*, goods or support to services can be performed separately from their consumption; goods or services can be stocked

b Global services can be *classified* as:

- Offshore centres: Perform isolated act of production
- Source centres: Produce with certain degree of autonomy for supporting local markets – catering facility, distribution centres
- Contributor centres: May have regional role
- Outpost centres: Market intelligence
- Lead centre: Design centre

c *Front office* operations:

- In immediate contact with customers and need to be close to the market
- Physical front office and remote front office
- Require special attention to language, customs and social code adaptation

6 Global sourcing

a A *coordinated approach* to the selection of suppliers located across the world and the procurement of goods and services to be fulfilled in the global supply chain

b Various forms depending upon the degree of *centralization* and degree of *vertical integration* of the procurement function:

- *Outsourced global procurement model*: The firm delegates the procurement to an international buying or purchasing agent responsible for the whole procurement function
- *Internal central purchasing model*: A central department with its own offices located in the major sourcing countries centralizes the purchase; the purchasing division acts like an independent purchasing agent
- *Distributed procurement model*: Each production centre in charge of a product or component takes care of its own procurement based on centrally defined product specifications; applicable when there is local content requirement or when a subsidiary has complete responsibility for a product

c Electronic sourcing

- *EDI*: proprietary software which links corporations to their suppliers and permits exchange of information, automatic ordering and tracking of orders
- *E-procurement*: procurement on the internet:
  - Types of e-procurement sites:
    - *Horizontal marketplace* (*aggregators*) specializes in one category of product/service for all types of industries

    - *Vertical marketplace* specializes in one type of industry offering a 'one-stop shop' for a large variety of products/services
    - *Exchanges* organize spot markets between a large number of suppliers and a large number of buyers for certain types of commodity
  - Transactions can be one-to-one or made through reverse auctions
  - Provides reach and rich capabilities, opportunity to reach a larger number of suppliers than more traditional methods
  - Does not eliminate the need for the physical movement of goods

7 Global logistics

a *Allocation* function:

- Which products, what quantity, when and where
- Five major parameters:
  - Demand for the product
  - Degree of specialization
  - Capacity of production
  - Level of acceptable inventories
  - Estimated transportation time

b *Distribution* function:

- Selection of channels to be used in the chain
- Three major types of centre:
  - *Factory warehouse*: organizes grouping and supply of distribution centres and handling of large orders
  - *Distribution centres*: responsible for proximity storage/supply to dealers
  - *Advanced inventory*: dedicated to original equipment manufacturing that can be located in a factory

c *Transportation* function:

- Handles physical flow
- Three modes of transport:
  - Own fleet
  - Rented trucking services
  - Messenger services
- Two delivery modes:
  - Proximity zone (two deliveries a day)
  - Shipment zone (one delivery a day)

8 International infrastructure projects

a Various players – project managers, civil contractors, service providers, local suppliers, customers, government, financing institutions, operator and international institutions

b Phases:

- Pre-feasibility
- Feasibility
- Basic engineering
- Detailed engineering/tendering
- Expediting/site construction
- Training
- Start-up
- Operation

c Configuration of project management:

- Direct project management:
  - Customer fulfils role of project manager
  - If engineering firm supervises and manages the work, engineering project team is financially responsible for the amount of its fees
- Turnkey project:
  - Customer contracts whole project to specialized engineering firm or to consortium of equipment suppliers
  - Project manager:
    - Is responsible for completion at fixed price and delivery time
    - Hands over project to customer after the start-up phase
- BOT (Build, Operate and Transfer):
  - Has 'hostage risk', i.e. once infrastructure is set up, supplier has no bargaining power
  - Project manager:
    - Is in charge of construction and operation
    - Is responsible for output
    - Is paid on basis of a predetermined price per unit of output
- BOT variants include:
  - *BOO* (Build, Operate and Own): project manager keeps ownership
  - *ROT* (Refurbish, Operate and Transfer): similar to BOT but refurbishing old installations

9 The internet is a global network connecting millions of computers across the world

a The digital revolution

- Affects the way companies do business by cutting cost and getting closer to customers
- Digital platforms transform the ways consumers exchange information, buy products and services and pay for their purchases

b Internet players:

- Traditional companies 'old economy' or 'bricks and mortar'
- 'Pure plays' or 'dotcom companies'

c E-commerce companies

d Intermediaries

e Portals and browsers

- Traditional companies providing physical products/services

f Transactions:

- *Commercial transactions* external to the firms: e-commerce (selling), e-procurement (buying)
- *External relational transactions* other than buying and selling: e-partnering (coordinating, information-sharing, R&D with partners etc.)
- *Internal relations*: e-management (planning and control, database sharing, recruiting, training, administration etc.)

g The internet constitutes an additional driver to globalization thanks to its reach and richness capabilities:

- *Reach* is the ability to access a large number of people in real time owing to a standard platform and connectivity
- *Richness* is the ability to carry a high level of information in the form of text, video and voice

h Standardized and semi-customized products benefit most from internet transactions

i The internet:

- Increases globalization of markets
- Increases global costs reduction
- Fosters global competition
- Weakens governments' barriers to open trade

j Limitations to the globalization of the internet:

- Cross-border regulatory restrictions
- Local legislation
- Sociotechnical/cultural factors

k Provides a management tool that enhances global cross-border management capabilities:
- Partnering capabilities
- A 'no secret' management system
- Ability to make important decisions in 'real time'
- Ability to collect and consolidate feedback from customers
- Ability to develop an IT platform and telecoms network that can work in a seamless way
- Ability to rethink completely managerial systems, structures and cultures

l Web 2.0 allows the development of
- Industry 4.0 and smart factories give the possibility of autonomous robots and machines communicating with each other
- Traditional linear supply chains are replaced by integrated supply chains

m Cultural differences can restrain internet capabilities: the challenge for the global firm is to overcome those cultural differences among their employees, suppliers, customers and partners to make web transactions effective.

Learning assignments

1 Compare Singapore and Malaysia as a possible location for: 1) a PC assembly plant; 2) a semiconductor wafer factory; 3) a regional maintenance centre; 4) a customer training centre for international customers; 5) a chemical processing plant.

2 According to Ferdows (1997), what are the differences between a 'contributor' factory and an 'outpost' factory?

3 What are the new roles that De Meyer and Vereecke (1995) assign to 'foreign' factories?

4 What differentiates global manufacturing of goods from global production of services?

5 What are the three major functions of global logistics?

6 From the viewpoint of the client of an infrastructure project, compare the relative advantages and disadvantages of turnkey projects, direct project management and BOT.

7 What is the 'hostage' problem in BOT contracts?

8 Based on your personal experience, give concrete examples of the reach and richness capabilities of the internet.

9 Why do you think business-to-consumer (B2C) transactions are less likely to develop on the internet, both domestically and globally?

10 Do you know of any other cases similar to Airbnb's and Uber's problems with local government? What are the pros and cons of government regulation of internet platforms?

11 What do you think are the benefits and constraints of global e-learning platforms (education programmes offered through the internet)?

12 eBay is a virtual auctioneer. How do you think it can globalize its activities?

13 What new capabilities does 3D printing bring to global firms?

14 What is a smart factory?

15 Can you give examples of 'internet of things' in 1) medicine, 2) retailing, 3) a private home?

Key words

- Back office
- BOT (Build, Operate and Transfer)
- Distribution function
- Electronic data interchange (EDI)
- Electronic marketplaces
- Front office
- Internet of things
- Location
- Logistics
- Network architecture
- Plant competencies
- Procurement
- Smart factory
- Strategic role
- Turnkey project
- Web 2.0

Web resources

Global manufacturing index published by Deloitte Consulting: **https://www2.deloitte.com/content/dam/Deloitte/global/Documents/Manufacturing/gx-mfg-competitiveness-index-rank-by-country.pdf**

IT data information: **http://www.gartner.com/technology/home.jsp**

Social Media Landscape: **https://fredcavazza.net/2017/04/19/social-media-landscape-2017/**

Companion website

Visit the companion website at bloomsbury.pub/global-strategic-management-5e for a multitude of weblinks and resources, self-test questions for revision and appendices.

Notes

1 Milberg and Winkler (2009) and OECD (2007).
2 OECD (2010).
3 Kearney (2015).
4 Teboul (1991).
5 St George and Knoop (1998).
6 Rangan (1998).
7 Wells and Gleason (1995).
8 Wells et al. (1996).
9 McKinsey (2016).
10 Monteiro and Carrick (2019).
11 https://www.statista.com/topics/871/online-shop- ping/ (accessed 1 February 2022).
12 https://www.statista.com/statistics/330695/number-of-smartphone-users-worldwide/ (accessed 1 February 2022).
13 UNCTAD (2019).
14 https://www.statista.com/statistics/330695/number-of-smartphone-users-worldwide/ accessed 10 February 2021).
15 https://www.statista.com/statistics/264810/number-of-monthly-active-facebook-users-world-wide/ (accessed 1 February 2022).
16 https://wearesocial.com/uk/blog/2022/01/digital-2022-another-year-of-bumper-growth-2/.
17 Evans and Wurster (2000).

18 https://unctad.org/system/files/official-document/dtlstict2020d13_en_0.pdf (accessed 12 may 2022).
19 Yip (2000).
20 Mc Kinsey (2009).
21 Coleman et al.(2001), Porter (2001), Subramanian and Adner (2001).
22 Bughin et al. (2009).
23 https://www.stratosjets.com/blog/airbnb-statistics/ (accessed 12 May 2022).
24 Salomon, (2016).

References and further reading

Awate, S., Mudambi, R., Scalera, V. G. and Schotter, A. (2018) 'On the geography of emerging industry technological networks: the breadth and depth of patented innovations', *Journal of Economic Geography*, 18 (2): 391–419.

Bartmess, A. and Cerny, K. (1993) 'Seeding plants for a global harvest', *McKinsey Quarterly*, 2: 107–32.

Borcuch, A., Pilat-Borcuch, M. and Swierczynska-Kaczor, U. (2012) 'The influence of the internet on globalization process', *Journal of Economics and Business Research*, XVIII (1): 118–29.

Bughin, J., Chui, M. and Miller, A. (2009) 'How companies are benefitting from Web 2.0: McKinsey Global Survey results', *McKinsey Quarterly*, September.

Coltman, T., Devinney, T., Latukefu, A. and Midgley, D. (2001) 'Revolution, evolution, or hype?', *California Management Review*, 44 (1) 57–86.

De Meyer, A. and Vereecke, A. (1994) 'Strategies for international manufacturing', INSEAD Working Paper, 94/25.

Dornier, P. P. (1997) 'Michelin', ESSEC Case Study.

Ernst, R., Kawelis, P., Dornier, P. P. and Fender, M. (1998) *Global Operations and Logistics*: *Text and Cases* (New York, NY: John Wiley).

Ernst & Young (1992) 'Region of the new Europe: a comparative assessment of key factors in choosing location', *Report*.

Evans, P. and Wurster, T. (2000) *Blown to Bits* (Boston, MA: Harvard Business School Press).

Ferdows, K. (1997) 'Making the most of foreign factories', *Harvard Business Review*, 75 (2): 73–88.

Gereffi, G. (2020) 'What does the COVID-19 pandemic teach us about global value chains? The case of medical supplies', *Journal of International Business Policy*, 3 (3): 287–301.

Haigh, R. (1990) 'Selecting a US plant location: the management decision process in foreign companies', *Columbia Journal of World Business*, 25 (3): 22–31.

Kearney (2015) *US Reshoring Over Before it Began?*. https://www.atkearney.com/documents/10192/7070019/US+Reshoring.pdf/14777afa-0c14-460e-937b-11233be340b6 (accessed 21 June 2017).

Kiss, A. and Danis, W. (2008) 'Country institutional context, social networks, and new venture internationalization speed', *European Management Journal*, 26 (6): 388–99.

Kotabe, M. (1998) 'Efficiency vs effectiveness orientation of global sourcing strategy: a comparison of US and Japanese multinational companies', *The Academy of Management Executive*, November, 107–19.

Lindner, A., Cave, B., Deloumeaux, L. and Magdeleine, J. (2001) *Trade in Goods and Services: Statistical Trends and Measurement Challenges*, Statistics Brief, October, No. 1. www.oecd.org/std/statistics-brief (accessed 21 June 2017).

McKinsey (2009) 'How companies are benefiting from Web 2.0: global survey results', *McKinsey Quarterly*, September, 1–9.

McKinsey & Company (2016) *Digital Globalization: The New Era of Global Flows*, McKinsey Global Institute, March.

McWilliam, S. E., Kim, J. K., Mudambi, R. and Nielsen, B. B. (2019) 'Global value chain governance: intersections with international business', *Journal of World Business*, 55 (4): 101067.

Milberg, W. and Winkler, D. (2009) *Globalization, Offshoring and Economic Insecurity in Industrialized Countries*, DESA working paper, no. 87 (New York, NY: United Nations).

Miniwatts Marketing Group (n.d.) 'Internet world stats – usage and population statistics'. https://www.internetworldstats.com/usage/use007.htm (accessed 21 June 2017).

Monteiro, L. F. and Carrick, A. M. (2019) 'Digital transformation in Latin America: leapfrogging and social impact', INSEAD Case Study. https://publishing.insead.edu/case/digital-transformation-latin-america-leapfrogging-and-social-impact (accessed 1 February 2022).

OECD (Organisation for Economic Co-operation and Development) (2007) *Offshoring and Employment: Trends and Impacts* (Paris: OECD).

OECD (Organisation for Economic Co-operation and Development) (2010) *Measuring Globalisation: Economic Globalisation Indicators* (Paris: OECD).

Pananond, P., Gereffi, G. and Pedersen, T. (2020) 'An integrative typology of global strategy and global value chains: the management and organization of cross-border activities', *Global Strategy Journal*, 10 (3): 421–43.

Pélissié Du Rausas, M., Manyika, J., Hazan, E., Bughin, J., Chui, M. and Said, R. (2011) 'Internet matters: the Net's sweeping impact on growth, jobs, and prosperity', McKinsey Global Institute, McKinsey & Company. http://www.mckinsey.com/Insights/MGI (accessed 21 June 2017).

Porter, M. (2001) 'Strategy and the internet', *Harvard Business Review*, 79 (3): 63–78.

PwC (2016) Strategy and Analysis, 'Industry 4.0: building the Digital Enterprise 2016', Global Industry 4.0 Survey. https://www.pwc.ch/en/publications/2017/how-digitization-makes-the-supply-chain-more-efficient-pwc-2016.pdf (accessed 1 February 2022).

Rangan, K. (1998) 'FreeMarketsOnline', Harvard Business School Case Study 9598109.

Salomon, R. (2016) 'The real reason Uber is losing in China', 7 March. https://fortune.com/2016/03/07/uber-china-2/ (accessed 1 February 2022).

Sasi, V. and Arenius, P. (2008) 'International new ventures and social networks: advantage or liability?', *European Management Journal*, 26 (6): 400–11.

Schwab, K. (2017) 'The fourth Industrial Revolution', The World Economic Forum.

Skype (2005) 'eBay to acquire Skype', Skype Press Release, 12 September. http://about.skype.com/2005/09/ebay_to_acquire_skype.html (accessed 21 June 2017).

St George, A. and Knoop, C. (1998) 'Li & Fung: beyond filling in the mosaic, 1995–1998', Harvard Business School Case Study 9398092.

Subramanian, R. and Adner, R. (2001) 'Profits and the internet: seven misconceptions', *MIT Sloan Management Review*, Summer: 44–53.

Teboul, J. (1991) *Managing Quality Dynamics* (Englewood Cliffs, NJ: Prentice Hall).

UNCTAD (2016) 'In search of cross-border e-commerce trade data', UCTZD technical note for ITC Development no. 6, April.

UNCTAD Digital Economy Report (2019). https://unctad.org/en/PublicationsLibrary/der2019_en.pdf (accessed 1 February 2022).

Wells, L. T. and Gleason, E. S. (1995) 'Is foreign infrastructure investment still risky?', *Harvard Business Review*, 73 (5): 44–55.

Wells, L. T., Bhasin, A., Desai, M. and Srinivasan, S. (1996) 'Enron Development Corporation: the Dabhol Power Project in Maharashtra, India' (A), (B) and (C), Harvard Business School Case Studies 9-797-085 and 9-595-101.

WTO (World Trade Organization) (2015) *International Trade Statistics 2015*. https://www.wto.org/english/res_e/statis_e/its2015_e/its15_toc_e.htm (accessed 6 July 2017).

Yip, G. (2000) 'Global strategy in the internet era', *London Business School Review*, 11 (4): 1–14.

Chapter 11

Global innovation

At the end of the chapter you will be able to:

- Understand the logic and the limitations of the international product life cycle
- Appreciate the different designs of global R&D networks
- Recognize the different management issues in the global management of R&D
- Discuss the issues of the international transfer of technology
- Understand knowledge management
- Explain the recent development towards 'metanational' management of global knowledge creation
- Examine the latest developments on global open innovation
- Recognize the issues in the international protection of intellectual property

Introduction

The ability to create and quickly diffuse new products and processes is one of the main benefits of global management, as noted in Chapters 1 and 14. This chapter will look at the evolution of the management of innovation within multinational and global companies. It starts with a presentation and criticism of the classic model known as the *international product life cycle*, then examines the classic trade-off between centralized and distributed R&D using the case of Nestlé as an example. The issues involved in the international transfer of technology will then be discussed and the chapter will end by presenting a recent model of knowledge management and transfer of best practices within global firms, introducing the concept of global open innovation and examining the problems of intellectual property rights.

The international product life cycle model

In the 1960s, Raymond Vernon proposed the theory of the *international product life cycle*[1] to explain how product innovation and production could migrate from the country of origin of the innovative firm to other country subsidiaries (Figure 11.1).

The international product life cycle theory was built on observations of the TV set industry in the 1950s and 1960s. As shown in Figure 11.1, the theory identifies three stages in the international development of products and processes. In stage one, *new products and processes* are designed in the laboratories of firms located in the innovative country. In the 1950s TV set industry, the innovative country was the United States. RCA, Zenith, General Electric and Motorola were the innovators and, at this stage, the products were designed in the United States for the US market. Some production was exported, mainly to Europe. In stage two (1960s), some production was moved to industrialized countries such as Europe and Japan, either in the form of *local subsidiaries* of the innovative firms or through *technology transfer* to local firms (Matsushita, Sony, Thomson etc.). Some adaptations to fit local needs were made to the products. Finally, in stage three, *emerging developing countries* (South Korea, China) took the lead in the production of TV sets, because of cost advantages and market potential.

Stage One INNOVATION	**Stage Two FOREIGN PRODUCTION**	**Stage Three TRANSFER**
Innovative firms create new products and processes in their country of origin: an advanced industrialized country	Second-tier country subsidiaries receive products/processes from innovators and produce for local markets	Developing country subsidiaries receive products/processes from innovators and produce for local markets and global markets at low cost

Figure 11.1 The international product life cycle
Source: Authors' original figure based on text of Vernon (1966).

Criticism of the international product life cycle

In spite of its simplicity and appeal, the theory failed to explain the globalization of innovation that took place after the 1960s. Despite the fact that R&D resources are predominantly concentrated in developed, industrialized countries, there is no longer a major difference between the United States, Japan and Europe (see Table 11.1).

Today, a large variety of products are developed globally for world markets and launched at almost the same time in the key regions of America, Europe and Asia Pacific. The migration of R&D and production

Table 11.1 R&D capabilities, 2000 and 2018

	Research and development expenditure (% of GDP)		Researchers in R&D (per million people)		High-technology exports (US$ bn)		Patent applications, residents	
	2000	2018	2000	2018	2000	2018	2000	2018
EU	1.75	2.18	2,122.5	3,994.2	392.8	6,947.6	96,284	89,574
USA	2.63	2.84	3,496.4	4,412.0	197.5	1,563.7	164,795	285,095
Japan	2.91	3.26	5,078.0	5,331.2	128.9	1,110.2	384,201	253,630
India	0.76	0.65	109.7	252.7	2.1	202.7	2,206	16,289
China	0.89	2.19	538.6	1,307.1	41.7	7,318.9	25,346	1,393,815

Source: World Bank Development Indicators (2018) http://data.worldbank.org/data-catalog/world-development-indicators (accessed 1 February 2022) and UNESCO.

Table 11.2 Top ten R&D spenders as % of GDP

Position	Country	% of GDP
1	Korea	4.3
2	Japan	3.4
3	Finland	3.2
4	Switzerland	3.2
5	Austria	3.1
6	Sweden	3.1
7	Denmark	2.9
8	Germany	2.9
9	USA	2.7
10	Slovenia	2.4

Source: http://uis.unesco.org/apps/visualisations/research-and-development-spending/ (accessed 1 February 2021).

centres does not necessarily follow the sequential evolution predicted by the theory. Many research centres are set up where scientific and marketing resources are available, and global companies use global R&D networks to develop world products, as Example 11.1 illustrates.

Global R&D networks

Most large global innovators use distributed R&D labs involving the collaboration of multiple sites scattered around the world. In 2020 R&D expenditure amounted to $1.7 trillion with ten countries representing 80 per cent of the spend.[2] According to UNESCO Korea and Japan had the the highest R&D intensity, at 4.3 per cent and 3.4 per cent of GDP, respectively.[3]

Table 11.3 Total R&D spend US$PPP (purchasing power parity)

Position	Country	US$ bn
1	USA	476
2	China	372
3	Japan	170
4	Germany	110
5	Korea	73
6	France	61
7	India	52
8	UK	44
9	Brazil	42
10	Russia	40

Source: http://uis.unesco.org/apps/visualisations/research-and-development-spending/ (accessed 1 February 2021).

EXAMPLE 11.1 Nestlé – a global network

Nestlé is the leading nutrition, health and wellness company in the world. Its portfolio of around 2,000 brands encompasses a large array of products including leading brands such as Nescafé, Perrier, Maggi, Gerber and Nespresso. A Swiss multinational, Nestlé was one of the first to expand its operations worldwide. With its R&D expenditure in 2019 of CHF1.7 billion it operates the world's largest science and innovation network in the food and beverage industry. More than 3,900 employees working at 23 locations worldwide in R&D in four Fundamental Research Centres plus 31 Product Technology Centres and other R&D Centres, and 280 product application groups which adapt product ideas to local markets. See Figure 11.2 below.

The four fundamental research centres are: the Nestlé Institute of Health Sciences, which deals with biomedical research and science-based nutrition; the Nestlé Research Centre, which provides scientific knowledge and a research base for product renovation and innovation; the Clinical Development Unit, which provides medical expertise and manages worldwide clinical trials for the company; and the R&D Centre in Tours, France, which provides scientific expertise in plant science. The central research entity is supported by the plant science research hub in Tours, France, the Singapore Research Hub, which focuses on maternal and infant nutrition, and Nestlé Purina, which carries out petcare research in St Louis, Missouri, United States.

The Product Technology Centres provide a critical mass of technology expertise and product knowledge, for one or more of Nestlé's business categories. R&D centres have both a global role and a more local role by meeting regional needs or providing know-how in specific areas of technical expertise, such as system technology, and health sciences. To complement its internal capabilities, Nestlé works closely with a number of academic institutions and public organizations. The company launched the Nestlé R&D Accelerator at Nestlé Research in Lausanne, Switzerland to unite Nestlé scientists, students and start-ups to accelerate the development of innovative products and systems. Participants have full access to Nestlé's R&D expertise and infrastructure, with teams moving from idea to working prototype and shop test within six months. The company will extend this initiative to other R&D sites and categories, with its Lausanne site focused on cross-category and beyond-the-core innovation.

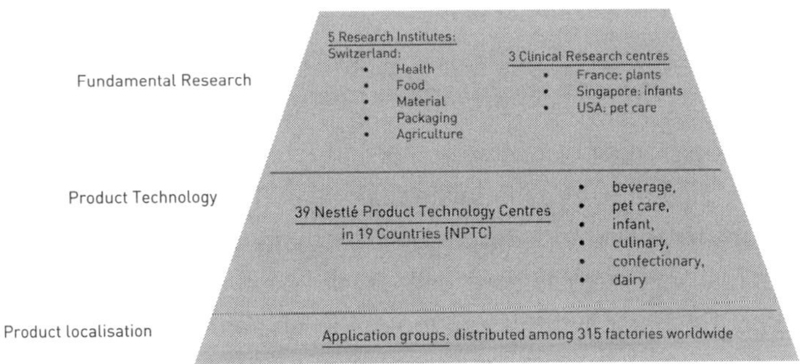

Figure 11.2 Nestlé's global R&D architecture
Source: Authors' original figure based on data from www.nestle.com.

Globalization of R&D: benefits and constraints

As illustrated in the Nestlé example, a global R&D network involves a decentralized, distributed approach to the management of innovation.

Benefits

There are four main potential benefits of decentralized as opposed to centrally managed R&D:[4]

- *Proximity to market* – the ability of a global firm to adapt or to create products that fit local customers' specificities.
- *Access to geographical clusters of knowledge creation and development* – universities, suppliers, researchers, start-up firms, venture capitalists. Michael Porter (1998) has illustrated the concept of technological centres as clusters of excellence such as Insulin in Denmark. Doz and Wilson argue that the more complex the type of knowledge needed, the more beneficial it is to have a geographically distributed network because of the richness of competencies that can be captured.[5]
- *Learning* – the ability of a global firm to leverage local knowledge across subsidiaries and to cross-fertilize this knowledge within a global network. De Meyer (1992) pinpointed the importance of 'learning' in international R&D: learning about different markets, different problem-solving methods, different sources of technological progress, different cultures and different competitors. Also, rapid diffusion of that learning throughout the organization is definitely enhanced by creating an international network of laboratories.
- *Access to low-cost and good-quality scientists and engineers* – some empirical evidence for this benefit is apparent when we look at the development of Bangalore as a centre for computer software or the science parks of Singapore, or Taiwan (Hinshu), which were developed originally on that basis. However, except for routine activities, this benefit is not sufficient to justify a decentralized R&D network.

Constraints

There are also two major constraints in implementing a globally distributed R&D network: the loss of critical mass and of face-to-face communication:

- *Critical mass constraints* exist when one activity needs to mobilize a minimum amount of resources in order to be performed efficiently and effectively. Research activities belong to this category – scientists and technologists are not lonely inventors; they need to benefit from the complementarities of colleagues in their field as well as in related domains. They also need assistance from technical staff, and they use more and more expensive laboratory instruments. Below a certain threshold of such resources, research projects have difficulty in taking off, hence the need for centralization and concentration of R&D activities. Having too many laboratories dilutes resources and hampers research performance. The solution to the problem is to be found in the creation of **centres of excellence**, specializing in one type of technological development, where scientific resources for that particular type of research are concentrated. Paradoxically, centres of excellence may solve the critical-mass problem, but do not particularly favour the internationalization of research activities concentrated in one location.

- *Communication constraints* result from the overwhelming evidence that innovative activities require face-to-face informal communication.[6] **Innovation** is based on a combination of well-defined methodological procedures as well as ill-defined, tacit, intuitive intellectual processes, personal encounters and conversations among researchers. Geographical distance, despite all information and communication technologies such as video-conferencing, is less conducive to inductive, intuitive and more complex and abstract discoveries. These communication constraints militate in favour of *co-located research*, where research projects are self-contained within a single geographical location in order to minimize communication between units and maximize it within units.

In total, the benefits of a distributed network of innovative centres outweigh the costs as more and more global companies decentralize their R&D networks. However, some research seems to indicate that there is a kind of inverse U-shaped relationship between the dispersion of R&D sites and the quality of innovation,[7] such that the quality of innovation tends to decline when R&D activities are too widely distributed.

Design of global R&D networks

Research centres in a global network belong to four main types:[8]

- *Research laboratories* in charge of long projects dealing with new technologies or scientific discoveries that are not necessarily related to a particular product. These laboratories are global by nature, and are most often, but not always, located near the corporate centre.
- *Development laboratories* in charge of projects whose objective is to lead to a product or process innovation.
- *Supporting/adaptive units* that provide product or process adaptation according to local contexts.
- *Scanning units* whose mandate is to monitor technological development and contribute to the knowledge platform of the company.

The way these units are set up and organized depends upon the global evolution of the firm over time, which usually follows the pattern shown in Figure 11.3.

When the company is past the stage of central R&D activities, local laboratories are set up in order to adapt local products or processes. In the next stage, centres of excellence that can specialize in basic research or certain products or process applications are established in innovative resource-rich countries. A **networked organization** is established to organize the exchange of ideas, technologies, people and information. As described in Example 11.1, Nestlé has reached this stage.

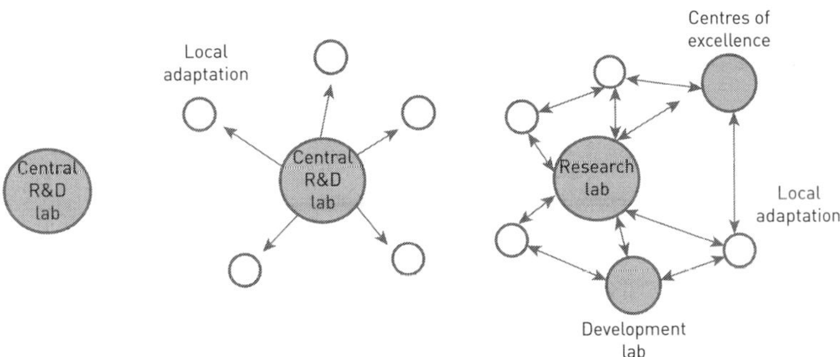

Figure 11.3 Evolution over time of global R&D activities

Management of global R&D networks

The management of global R&D or innovative networks requires adaptation in structure, systems and people/culture.

Structure

The structural aspects of R&D management relate to size, specialization, project organization and performance evaluation:

- *Size*: Research demands *communication* and *flexibility*. Large organizations are unsuitable to provide a proper innovative environment. In their research, Pearce and Singh (1992) found that 50 per cent of international laboratories employed fewer than 50 people and 80 per cent fewer than 200 people. In the case of Nestlé, the size of laboratories was between 20 and 200 employees. When a research site employs a larger number of scientists and technicians, it is usually divided into smaller, self-contained specialized units.
- *Specialization*: Specialization can be *discipline-centred* or *product-/process-centred*. The first case applies more to preliminary research, while the second fits more with development work where multi-disciplinary teams work on the many facets of product design, utilization, marketability and production.
- *Project organization*: The most common arrangement for R&D is the project management structure, in which a *project leader* is responsible for the planning, budgeting, control and completion of a particular development. Projects can be managed purely locally and then transferred to other units in the global network (projects are *co-located*), or can be organized by interdependent tasks distributed across units (*multiple-location projects*). As previously mentioned, co-located projects are likely to be more effective because of the communication constraints examined earlier, but co-location does not take advantage of the richness of a global network.
- *Performance evaluation*: Performance evaluation mechanisms may take various forms, depending upon the kind of performance that the company wishes to enhance. Table 11.4 gives some indication of the various methods according to the performance-enhancement objective.

Table 11.4 Performance evaluation criteria

Performance	Measurement
Scientific innovation	Number of patents
	Number of publications in research journals
Commercialization	Time to market
Profitability	Research unit as profit centre
Cost	Budgeting targets
Collaboration	Organization of conferences and internal seminars
	Internal presentation of papers
	Number of publications listed on the intranet

- Project management design within a global network can be categorized into:
- *Self-contained co-located independent projects*, in which one research unit in the network is responsible for the complete design and development of a product/process. In this case, the communication flow between engineers, technicians, marketers and manufacturers is entirely limited to the research unit located on one site in the network. On completion of the project, the product or process is transferred to other units. In the case of manufacturing an engine, a particular unit would be responsible for the whole design of a certain type of engine.
- *Integrated distributed projects*, in which several research centres each take responsibility for one different interrelated element in the design and creation of the product/process. For example, one centre will take care of the combustion chamber of an engine, while another will design the regulation. In such a case, inter-unit communication is maximized because researchers will have to exchange a lot of information to make the different parts fit together.
- *Parallel distributed projects*, in which a project is still divided between several units but in such a way that inter-unit communication is limited to only a few parameters. In the case of the engine, one unit would be responsible for the combustion chamber including the regulation, while another would take charge of the compressor system. There would still be some interdependencies to manage, but fewer than in the previous case.

The Global Innovation Index

One of the central drivers for economic growth and development is widely considered to be innovation. In 2007, the Global Innovation Index (GII) was created to provide insightful data on innovation that

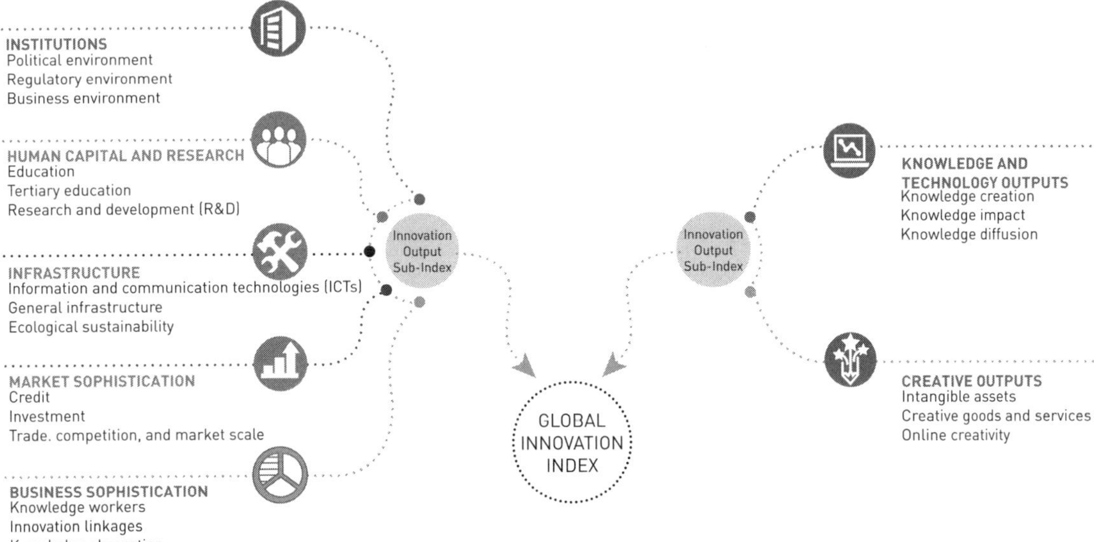

Figure 11.4 Global Innovation Index (GII) Framework
Source: Dutta, Lanvin and Wunsch-Vincent (2020).

could help economies evaluate their innovation performance and make informed innovation policies. The GII has had an impact on policymakers who refer to innovation and innovation rankings as part of their economic policy strategies. It also allows economies to assess their innovation performance and invest in resources to analyse their GII results in cross-ministerial task forces. GII can be used to design suitable innovation and intellectual property (IP) policies encouraging economies to prioritize and collect innovation metrics.

The GII is an evolving project that builds on previous editions while incorporating data – inspired by the latest research on the measurement of innovation. In 2020 the model included 131 countries/economies, representing 93.5 per cent of the world's population and 97.4 per cent of the world's GDP in purchasing power parity current international dollars. Table 11.5 below shows the top 20 countries in the GII 2021 ranking.

Table 11.5 Global Innovation Index top 20 countries

The Global Innovation Index top 20 countries 2021 report	
1	Switzerland
2	Singapore
3	The United States
4	Denmark
5	Sweden
6	The Netherlands
7	Finland
8	Luxembourg
9	Norway
10	Iceland
11	Australia
12	United Kingdom
13	Canada
14	Germany
15	New Zealand
16	Ireland
17	Belgium
18	Austria
19	France
20	Japan

Source: INSEAD Knowledge, October 2021.

Systems

The effective management of a global R&D network calls for the implementation of systems and processes for *planning and control* and *knowledge documentation and dissemination*:

- *Planning and control systems* consist of the orderly definition of research projects and their distribution across units, the allocation of resources to the projects and the control of resources utilization alongside the monitoring of project achievements. Project definition and attribution is generally done by a global central unit like that described for Nestlé in Example 11.1, on the basis of the overall project management philosophy described earlier. Project proposals are initiated either by the research units within the framework of their mandate or decided centrally and then delegated by the central coordination unit. Global product managers can initiate projects based on the assessment of market needs. An important consideration in the budgeting of research projects is to give research centres some 'free budgets', consisting of unallocated resources that can be used at the discretion of the unit head for contingencies or for the exploration of new unplanned investigations.

The degree of *standardization* of the planning system is a function of the nature of the research project. More fundamentally, advanced research programmes are given a 'budgeting envelope' without asking for too detailed a justification, while more applied, business-specific projects may require cash flow forecasts similar to any strategic investment.

Planning processes are not only useful for resource allocation but also as a *communication* mechanism. Planning can be linked with scientific conferences, during which various laboratories present their projects before the actual planning and budgeting exercise begins.[9]

Controls are exercised through *internal reporting,* measuring progress against technical and commercial milestones.

- *Knowledge diffusion and documentation.* Knowledge management is not limited to R&D, and the next section of the chapter considers this in more detail. For global R&D, knowledge diffusion and documentation are based on six main mechanisms or a combination of them:
  - People rotation
  - Conferencing
  - Databases
  - Publications
  - Personal networking
  - Electronic knowledge management platforms.

Research has shown that global companies tend to use a portfolio of mechanisms, usually coordinated by a central staff office.

People and culture

There are four people-related practices that are particularly conducive to global R&D:[10]

- *Temporary assignments* as a way for researchers to be familiar with the work of other laboratories and sometimes to be assigned to a marketing team. Training programmes, regular travel and conferences allow interpersonal exchanges and the inculcation of socialization and an 'open' culture of sharing.
- *Creation of 'gatekeeper' roles* in each laboratory, where the task is to translate the work from other laboratories into the language of the gatekeeper's own laboratory.
- *Creation of a small central staff* whose role is to ensure a proper diffusion of information and research results.
- *Promoting openness and sharing* as important corporate values.

International transfer of technology

Every component of globalization implies some process of technology transfer. During the 1960s and 1970s, international technology transfer was considered a critical issue because of the emergence of newly independent countries that aspired to industrialize and demanded an appropriate and complete transfer of technologies from multinational corporations. With the increased liberalization of economies, this topic has lost its geopolitical connotations but remains a managerial issue when dealing with the developing or emerging world.

Table 11.6 Classification of technology

	Physical	Informational
Product technology	• Blueprints • Formulation • Pictures, design • Models • Samples • Laboratory equipment • Databases	• Product development methodologies • Research heuristics • Creative methods • Testing methods • Data-mining research protocols
Process technology	• Plant layouts • Equipment • Process charts • Process handbooks	• Process control • Quality assurance • Maintenance processes • Logistics and supply chain
Management technology	• Handbooks • Flow charts • Manuals • IT equipment • Accounting documents • Planning templates	• Marketing management • Financial management • Strategic planning • Human Resource Management (HRM) • Project management

Table 11.6 gives a classification of the various forms of technology that can be transferred. Technology transfer takes place under five main *organizational and contractual* forms:

- Licensing agreements
- Projects (turnkey projects, BOT, etc.)
- Technical agreements with joint venture companies or local subsidiaries
- Joint projects
- Sales of equipment.

The typical issues in technology transfer are *appropriateness and completeness.* Technology transfer is *appropriate* if it fits with the local context. The classic trade-off is between modern, state-of-the-art technology that requires a solid infrastructure of human capital as well as support industries and a more modest, less advanced technology that can be more easily assimilated locally. Global companies have often been blamed for transferring old and obsolete technology in order to protect their competitive advantage, but on the other hand many cases of expensive, advanced technology – the 'white elephants' – have also been criticized as resource-wasting. At the time when Volkswagen set up the first Western factory of modern cars (the Santana) in China in the early 1980s, it would have been difficult to transfer the new models being manufactured and sold in Europe. The state of the roads, the network of available suppliers, the volume involved and the skill level could not have permitted the assimilation of such complex, advanced manufacturing systems. But, over time, the progressive improvement of local conditions made the transfer of modern technology feasible. SAIC, Volkswagen's Chinese partner, later entered a joint venture with General Motors to produce a more advanced model than the Santana with more sophisticated production technology.

A technology transfer is *complete* when the recipient of technology is able to perform by itself the product of the transfer. This raises the issue of the transfer of *informational technology.* The knowledge embodied in those elements is often non-explicit and calls for a 'coaching approach' to the transfer, instead of just shipping equipment or organizing a standard lecture.[11] Developing countries often regret that global companies restrict their transfer to physical content and limit information transfer to a strict minimum in order to maintain their future bargaining power. Although this interpretation is often too extreme, it is frequently true that engineers in global firms are not fully prepared to cope with the considerations of education and patience that a proper transfer implies.

Global knowledge management

Knowledge is the ability to understand and give meaning to facts and information. In the corporate world, knowledge applies not only to techniques and physical sciences, but to all aspects of corporate behaviour. **Knowledge management** consists of the ability for a firm to create, combine and share knowledge among its members. Global R&D management is only one sub-set of knowledge-based strategies. Beyond the strict management of R&D, the strengths of global companies are their capability to create, combine and share knowledge across borders. According to the Japanese social scientists Nonaka and Takeuchi (1995), knowledge can be created and shared at the individual, group and organizational level. They distinguish between **explicit knowledge** (i.e. knowledge that can be codified and explained verbally, in writing or with symbolic language) and **tacit knowledge** (that cannot be codified and that can be transferred only by imitation or observation, by 'teaching'). They distinguish four types of knowledge conversion:

- *Socialization* – the process of sharing tacit knowledge through social interaction, apprenticeship and observation.
- *Externalization* – the process of articulating tacit knowledge into explicit concepts through metaphors, pictures and theoretical formulations.
- *Combination* – the process of combining different elements of explicit knowledge into written, codified formats.
- *Internalization* – the process of transforming explicit knowledge into tacit knowledge; when knowledge is internalized it becomes part of the way of doing things and its explicitness may be lost.

According to Nonaka and Takeuchi, these four processes form a *knowledge spiral* of organizational knowledge creation from individuals to groups and then to whole organizations.

For global companies, knowledge management creates both opportunities and constraints (Table 11.7).

Table 11.7 Opportunities and constraints for knowledge management in global companies

Opportunities	Constraints
Diversity of contexts	Languages
Variety of experiences	Differences of cultures and mind-sets
Economies of scope in knowledge creation	'Not invented here' reactions Unwillingness and lack of motivation to share knowledge
Economies of speed by not 'reinventing the wheel'	Incentive systems reinforcing local performance and not rewarding 'global' citizenship 'Siloed', nationalistic perspectives Lack of trust between units

Transfer of best practices

Global companies build management processes in order to overcome the constraints and take advantage of the opportunities of knowledge management. One such process is the 'transfer of best practices', which has been documented by Szulanski (1996). Transfer of best practices comprises the *systematization of exchange of internal practices* developed in one unit and considered as 'superior' to other units. 'Practices' are the use of knowledge applied to all kinds of managerial activities – the running of a customer service centre, the management of a product launch, the training of salespeople or the control of accounts receivable. Szulanski found that three major factors can hamper transferring practices, what he calls *internal stickiness*:

- *Causal ambiguity* between the various elements of the practices that make it difficult to model precisely cause-and-effect relationships. Causal ambiguity exists when tacit knowledge is at the core of the functioning of the practice.
- *Lack of absorptive capacity* by the recipient unit which is not capable of interpreting the knowledge transfer and applying it. Here again, tacitness may constitute a barrier to knowledge transfer when the recipient unit has not got the internal resources to 'crack' the implicit, non-verbal elements of the practices.
- *Arduous relationships* that exist when tacit knowledge requires multiple interactions between individuals, particularly when geographical and cultural distance are present.

Szulanski's work challenges the classic views about knowledge transfer, as indicated in Table 11.8, and focuses attention on the predominant sources of stickiness, which are closely related to the amount of tacitness involved in knowledge.

The metanational corporation

Doz et al. (2001a, 2001b) have developed the concept of the 'metanational corporation' that puts knowledge transfer at the centre of a mode of managing global companies, beyond the classical

Table 11.8 Tools and approaches used for knowledge management in the metanational corporation

• Business units and team leaders trained and experienced in *D&D (disperse and diverse) practices*
• *Socialization* before teamwork implying 'non-productive' social interfaces
• *Transitional encounters* (conferences, seminars, workshops, etc.) with loose agenda to allow tacit knowledge to be shared
• Teams made aware of contexts through visits, education
• Strong, accessible, open, user-friendly knowledge management platforms (electronic libraries, case studies, chat rooms etc.)
• Deadlines for project completion
• Yellow pages staff directory (that lists who is responsible for what)

The risk of isolated subsidiaries

In a paper published in the journal *Organization Science* in 2008 entitled, 'Knowledge flows within multinational corporations: explaining subsidiary isolation and its performance implications', Monteiro et al. examine if, how and when MNC subsidiaries shared sales and marketing knowledge with each other. The authors discovered a phenomenon of isolated subsidiaries that top management and their teams might be unaware existed. Executives may believe that knowledge-sharing is rampant throughout the organization whereas the reality could be that some subsidiaries are working independently, unable to take advantage of the intellectual resources in other parts of the company.

The researchers surveyed 171 subsidiaries of which 22 per cent heard about new product ideas or practices from headquarters less than once a year, and 42 per cent sent new product ideas and practices to their headquarters or to other subsidiaries less than once a year. More than 10 per cent did neither.

The authors concluded that creating personal networks among subsidiary managers could improve contact and collaboration to ensure that no part of the organization is isolated from the knowledge-sharing process. A network could include, for example, an expatriate manager who is assigned to an underperforming foreign subsidiary to help tap into resources in other parts of the company. Language barriers also needed to be considered: these could prevent a subsidiary's manager from engaging with colleagues locally and at headquarters. Transparency is critical, for both the 'in' and 'out' crowd. Sharing information regularly about performance could address the reasons why subsidiaries' perceptions tend to vary when it comes to knowing which of their peers are successful and which processes are valuable. Lastly, the MNCs should recognize that the market for information can be flawed – sometimes knowledge is shared but MNCs do not realize that some employees share a lot of information while others none at all.

Source: https://knowledge.wharton.upenn.edu/article/popularity-contests-why-a-company-embraces-one-innovative-idea-but-shuns-another/ (accessed 1 February 2022).

organizational models described later in Chapter 16. The metanational corporation is capable of forgetting the concept of knowledge transfer and substituting the capability of knowledge 'melding' (a neologism comprising *melting* and *welding*). Melding knowledge implies that the tacit elements of knowledge are effectively *assimilated* and *put into practice*.

The metanational model is built on the interaction of two factors: the *location* factor (the place where knowledge is created, shared and *melded)* and the *context* factor (the intellectual foundations underlying knowledge creation such as language, mental mapping, codes, implicit rules and so on). The basic argument is that useful knowledge is frequently tacit and that tacitness is embedded in a particular context. Tacit knowledge creation, sharing and melding requires *co-location*: the ability for the people involved to benefit from frequent interactions, random encounters ('corridor' or 'coffee shop' interactions). This is precisely the reason why co-location is so important in the case of R&D projects. In global companies, locations between units can be distant and contexts very diverse (multiplicity of language, education, social codes and so on). The key problem for a global company is to take advantage of the *diversity* and at the same time resolve the *co-location* imperative. The various forms of knowledge creation, sharing and melding are represented in Figure 11.5:

- In the C&C (co-location and co-setting) model, knowledge is entirely co-located, with people sharing the same intellectual context transferred to other business units. This is the classic use of *centres of excellence*, in which one particular business unit is the creator of knowledge that becomes the 'best practice' to be transferred. This eliminates the problem of tacitness at the level of knowledge creation but not at the level of transfer. The issue of stickiness is still present.
- In the D&C (dispersion and co-setting) model, knowledge is created at different locations under the leadership of 'expatriates' who share the same intellectual and contextual background. They understand each other across cultures and they are able at the same time to adapt knowledge to local conditions and to share it, since the stickiness is reduced thanks to the common cultural background. This was the classic practice of multinational firms relying on a talented and mobile expatriate group. The problem with this approach is the difficulty of taking advantage of the contextual diversity of country units and may lead either to an inflexible application of 'central' recipes or a complete acculturation of the expatriate managers – the 'going native' syndrome.
- The C&D (co-location and diverse settings) model tries to take advantage of a *physical co-location* of managers coming from various parts of the world and working on a common project. This is the idea behind 'impatriation' practices. This can lead to 'Tower of Babel' consequences because of a lack of a common contextual background among participants and the lack of explicit management of the cultural differences.
- Finally the D&D (dispersion and diverse settings) model, the model of the 'metanational' corporation, is the one in which the creation, sharing and melding of knowledge in a dispersed and diverse world is explicitly managed. Table 11.6 lists the major organizational tools used for managing a D&D environment.

Global open innovation

As described above, a multinational company should be constantly trying to translate its multi-location presence into a source of competitive advantage. Achieving global competitiveness increasingly

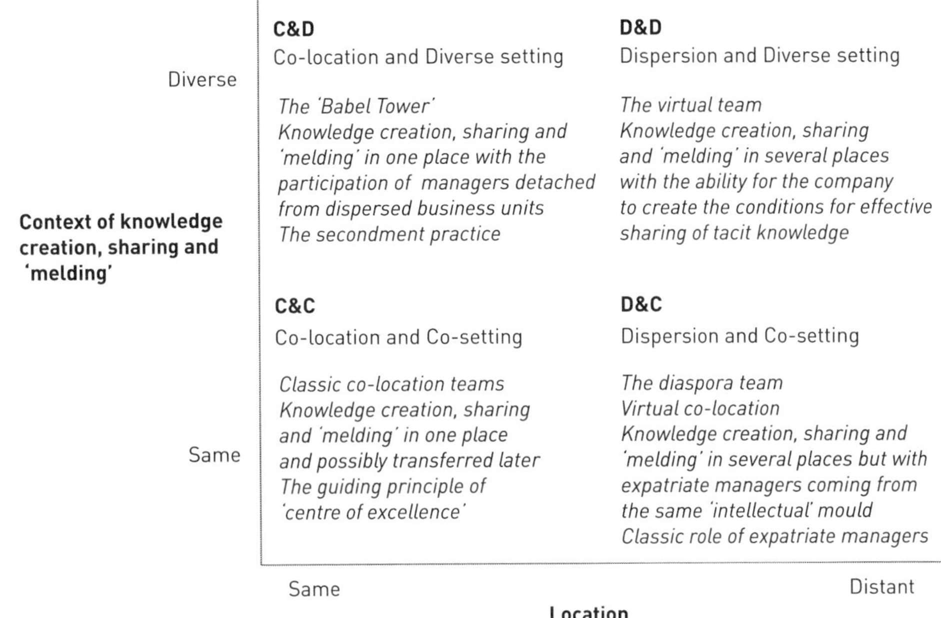

Figure 11.5 Knowledge creation, sharing and 'melding' in global firms
Source: José dos Santos, MS® Powerpoint presentation for MBA class, Singapore, 9 November 2001. Reprinted with permission from author.

requires integrating knowledge worldwide from its own subsidiaries and from sources beyond the firm's boundaries. Many MNCs can benefit from connecting with start-ups around the world that can offer novel solutions to existing issues or have knowledge which, combined with the MNC's existing intelligence, can lead to innovations. Start-ups can also help MNCs to identify developments that challenge existing beliefs or dominant logic. Access to different skill sets can also be a benefit to partnering with start-ups – with a fresh approach and more agile ways of working.

The concept of 'open innovation' with reference to the trend for embracing external cooperation has been increasingly applied at a global level: 'global open innovation'. As innovations largely come from outside rather than within an existing organization, the fundamental idea is that in a globalized world of widely distributed knowledge and fast-paced technology developments, firms can no longer rely purely on their own resources and research. It may be more cost-efficient for them to look externally to buy/license processes or inventions (i.e. patents) from other companies.

One example of this can be found in the INSEAD case study 'BT Group: Managing Open Innovation',[12] which describes how British Telecom set up an innovation hub in Palo Alto in 2000, with a mandate to identify new technologies and integrate them into BT's customer-facing units. International calls were its major source of revenue until the late 1990s, but the telecoms industry was transformed by the dot.com bubble, the arrival of WiFi and IP TV, competition from cable/media companies and the convergence of IT and communications. New revenues streams were required as landlines and other services were depleted. Innovation in companies like BT had traditionally emerged from in-house R&D, but in the early 2000s BT opened up to external sources, tapping into knowledge centres worldwide such as universities, high-tech start-ups, customers, other corporates and R&D labs.

Another example is the pharmaceutical industry when Merck tackled the issue of patent expiry on blockbuster drugs (known as 'patent cliffs'), after which cheap generic substitutes entered the market. Facing huge losses, Merck looked beyond the company to innovate and find cheaper ways to replace its blockbusters. By the end of 2011, Merck executives knew that to continue to grow the company's revenue stream, its in-house R&D efforts – the internal pipeline of drugs in development – would not be sufficient[13] (see Example 11.2 below).

In FMCG Procter & Gamble (P&G) used this approach when a scientist showed them the lollipop he had invented that spun when a button was pressed. The MNC adapted the technology to a toothbrush.[14]

However, the pull to an entrepreneurial ecosystem does not always yield the fruit expected at head office. Setting up a full innovation hub that absorbs new ideas and creates prototypes far from headquarters can be expensive, therefore some MNCs implement 'innovation outposts'. These are often small offices not designed to create innovations, but to 'pick' up the latest cutting-edge trends and report to headquarters, thus acting as a connection between the entrepreneurial cluster and the established firm. Outposts can help MNCs transform but require support from head office and the relevant business units to adopt and develop the new ideas.

Innovation outposts require people who can broker between the disruptive new ideas and the established methods at head office – effective brokers. In a *California Management Review* article, published in 2021, Benoit Decreton, Jean-Marc Frangos, Lisa Friedman and Felipe Monteiro describe three types of ineffective brokers: the loners, who lacked connectivity at both ends; the connected castaways who were completely tuned into the Valley but lacked connectivity to headquarters; and the VIP sightseers who were connected to headquarters but lacked connectivity to Silicon Valley or the local entrepreneurial ecosystem. Effective brokers cannot be created overnight – the connections needed require enormous investment, time and commitment.

For these outposts to be successful firms should have a clear purpose that is adapatable depending on how the outpost evolves. Effective brokers should engage with support teams closer to headquarters to direct the development of prototypes or build the business case for collaborations, like launching pads. Relevant processes need to be established to push external ideas from the ecosystem to head office whilst pulling problems from business units to search for external solutions. Commitment is also required at all levels in the organization. Finally an MNC needs to instil a culture of collaboration and humility – question whether it is really ready to engage in *open innovation*, which is a two-way street.

Also to be considered when collaborating on a new project is that secrecy can damage a good partnership. One example of how external knowledge can advance innovation is Procter and Gamble's Connect + Develop open innovation programme. Since its launch in 2001, the programme has formed more than 2,000 partnerships responsible for dozens of innovative products and new processes to increase the firm's productivity. Openness begins from within the company – P&G principles of open innovation in their business model enrich the company's knowledge pool and helps to find new ideas. In a book provocatively titled 'Gorillas can Dance', Prashantam (2022) documented different lessons from large corporations on partnering with start-ups to become more innovative.

MINI-CASE 11.1

FC Barcelona, Barça Innovation Hub (BIH)

Throughout its 120-year history, Barça has been a symbol of pride for Spain, Catalonia and the Catalan people. Its on-field success and star players have captured over 340 million fans worldwide who follow the club on social media. A behemoth of the sports world, Barça was valued at €3.72 billion on revenues of €840.8 million, making it the most valuable football club in 2019. It regularly featured among the world's top ten most valuable sports brands. It had over 1,450 official supporters clubs globally, 50 training academies in 49 countries, commercial offices in the USA and China with 39 sponsors and 19 official partners from around the world.

However, huge investments in football clubs from the USA, Arabian Gulf, Russia and beyond had precipitated a new era of competition. New media technologies, sponsorship networks, and an increasingly global fan base were changing football and sport more broadly. Innovations in player tracking, coaching technology, injury prevention and sports science gave early adopters an advantage.

Barça responded with the Barça Innovation Hub (BIH), a first-of-its-kind sports laboratory seeking to define the future of sport through global open innovation, launched in 2017. It was the brainchild of the Barça President and his Chief Strategy and Innovation Officer, Javier Sobrino, with three interlinked goals:

- To push the boundaries of cutting-edge sports industry knowledge
- Increase the visibility and impact of the Barça brand
- Develop new revenue streams.

With more than 2,000 athletes from five professional sports training at the club every day, 120 teams playing every weekend, the largest stadium in Europe and 3.5 million visitors per year, the BIH was gatekeeper of a data goldmine centred on athletic performance, fan engagement and smart facilities. Leveraging the club's position at the centre of a global ecosystem, the BIH worked with partners worldwide on R&D, innovation and knowledge sharing, giving life to Barça's motto, 'More than a club'. It partnered with universities, research centres, sports entities, sponsors, brands, investors, start-ups, athletes and fans. Barça Universitas, Barça's digital learning platform, organized conferences and academic programmes, and brought together 3,000 students from 65 countries in 2018.

It was assessed on several key performance indicators (KPIs), including the number of projects that the club implemented, consumers' associations between Barça and innovation, and the extent to which the BIH generated new financial resources. To achieve these goals, the BIH used Barça's position within a vibrant ecosystem of sports-focused businesses to identify and capitalise on new opportunities.

Open innovation was grounded in a belief that organizations should engage with external partners to develop innovations that they could neither develop internally nor acquire through a merger or acquisition. Throughout the club, all activities focused on improving the team or building its financial firepower to compete on player transfers and wages.

To meet the BIH's global ambitions, Barça identified seven locations for consideration: US, China, Tel Aviv, Sweden, Norway, Finland and Latin America.

Questions:

1 Did the club have access to the innovation that would yield the disruptive technologies and processes that would define the future?

2 Where, amidst the world's innovation clusters, should the BIH focus its resources and attention?

3 Where should the BIH look for inspiration to help Barça navigate the future?

4 How should it integrate and prioritise foreign ideas within an organization rooted in tradition, where trophies were the only real measure of success for its supporters?

5 How could global open innovation sustain its current on-field excellence and lay the foundation for future success?

This Mini-case is based on an INSEAD case study, Monteiro, Davies and Carrick, 2020.

Table 11.9 Intellectual property rights and their infringement

IPR	Infringement	Type of Business
Patents *Exclusive right granted for the protection of an invention*	Re-engineer the invention by reconstituting its components (reverse engineering)	Technology products, pharmaceuticals, chemicals, spares parts
Trademarks *Distinctive signs that distinguishes products or service of a company*	Usage of similar or confusing similar sign Imitation (with minor change)	All branded products
Copyrights *Original intellectual creation*	Plagiarism Reproduction without quotation	Books, articles, music, movies, software, video, art works
Industrial designs *Aesthetic or outward appearance of a product: shape, pattern, ornaments*	Imitation	Fashion, all industrial and household products, jewellery, packaging
Trade secrets *Confidential business information*	Leakage by employees Espionage Unauthorized diffusion: press, internet	Financial, legal, commercial, managerial documents used as internal strategic, managerial and organizational communication
Geographical indications *Signs on goods that have a specific geographical origin*	Copy Reproduction with similar shape, colour, graphism	Wines, foods, agricultural products, jewellery, watches, pottery, tableware
Integrated circuits *Layout and design of integrated circuits*	Copy Leakage by employees	Electronic industry, machinery, car industry, aeronautic

Source: 'Secrets of Intellectual Property', International Trade Centre, World Intellectual Property Organization (2003) https://www.wipo.int/edocs/pubdocs/en/intproperty/itc_p163/wipo_pub_itc_p163.pdf

Global knowledge and the protection of intellectual property rights

The protection of **intellectual property rights** (IPR) is a source of concern and sometimes an impediment to practising true global knowledge management. Global firms are often confronted with imitations, reverse engineering and trademark copies. Table 11.9 gives a list of the various forms of intellectual property and their infringement.

Protection against infringement of IPR can involve the measures summarized in Table 11.10.

Table 11.10 Protection of intellectual property rights

Parties involved	Protection methods
Employees	Restrict disclosure of IP to selected employees Require key employees to sign individual secrecy agreements Establish a strict catalogue of level of confidentiality Keep IP in secure location Educate employees on the rationale and the consequences of infringement Regularly interview employees Prepare handbook listing items to be protected, and what to do in case of leakage suspicion; give recommendations about best practices
Suppliers	Non-disclosure agreements Establish rules about what can and cannot be disclosed
Joint venture partners	Be specific in the joint venture contract Use 'black box' approach when technically feasible Screen partners' employees
Legal issues	Lobby governments Use diplomatic channels to support actions Engage in legal action as soon as possible, even if legal context is unfavourable

EXAMPLE 11.2 Global virtual lab at Merck Sharp and Dohme (MSD)

With revenues of $39.5 billion and 68,000 employees in 140 countries worldwide, MSD was the seventh largest global pharmaceutical company in 2016. Before 2000, R&D at Merck was predominantly done in house by laboratories scattered around the world. Early in 2000, the company decided to accelerate its partnership and licensing activities in order to boost the research pipeline. The concept of a 'virtual lab' was developed with the creation of a specialized World Wide Licensing group designed to support research done in-house by licensing-in complementary external technologies. This entailed the need to identify, contact and create relationships with small entrepreneurial firms.

In order to identify and get in touch with those firms, the World Wide Licensing group created a 'scouting organization' with seventeen scientific talent scouts covering the USA, Europe, Asia, Australia and South America. The task of these scouts was to identify and propose new opportunities for research partnerships.

The process used was made of five phases:

1. Needs identification: the 'franchise' for each therapeutic area (cardiovascular, oncology etc.) defines the domains in which technology partnerships would be useful. The franchise then publishes an 'area of interest booklet' to help guide the scouts' research.
2. The scouts look for new opportunities in those areas and identify potential firms to approach.
3. Evaluation and selection from amongst those opportunities and the initial contact and dialogue with the partnership candidates identified.

Table 11.11 Scout locations

USA	Asia
• North California • South California • South West • Midwest • New England **Europe** • UK, Ireland, Spain, Portugal • Germany, France • Italy, Switzerland • Denmark (Scandinavia)	• Korea • Japan • Hong Kong (China, Hong Kong, Taiwan) **Australasia** • Australia • New Zealand

4 The relationship is taken over by a group of franchise licensing integrators (FLIs) within each franchise. The FLIs evaluate the scientific and market potential of the selected opportunities and pass their evaluation to a Review and Licensing Committee (RLC) that gives the final green light for negotiations to proceed.

5 After approval, transactions managers take charge of negotiating the deal with partners.

This process was highly selective: it was estimated that, in 2011, of 7,000 opportunities generated by scouts only 20 per cent were transferred to FLIs; of those only 15 per cent were sent to the RLC who in turn approved just 6 per cent to go ahead. By 2010 this licensing process had achieved significant successes, to the extent that two-thirds of the company's sales for that year were attributed to in-licensing products.

Although this process brought the desired results some concerns were expressed internally. First, it was argued that it made the R&D process too dependent on external sources of knowledge and innovation. If this was not compensated by a strong internal research effort it would mean a loss of autonomous knowledge creation. Without strong internal R&D keeping up to date on new issues and trends, it would eventually become difficult to properly assess new external opportunities. Another issue was the reluctance of some in-house laboratories to accept external collaboration.

Source: Data used with permission from Klueter and Monteiro (2014).

Open innovation, however, is not just about getting contacts, firms must begin by creating the correct conditions within their organization. Firms need to partner with partnerships with the right mindset, with a willingness to share as well as absorb knowledge.

Reciprocity and trust are two key factors in achieving efficient and equitable outcomes in these partnerships. It is important to protect an organization's IP but if this is done in a clumsy manner it can lead to an ambiance of secrecy and tension. It is therefore preferable to rely on legal mechanisms such as patents and copyright to protect IP.

In the research paper 'Ready to be open? Explaining the firm level barriers to benefiting from openness to external knowledge', Monteiro et al. showed that using secrecy as a strategic tool can be a major barrier to open innovation. Their results show there is a trade-off between strategies aimed at accessing external knowledge through collaborations with outside parties and those using secretive behaviour such as a strategic knowledge protection mechanism: open innovation is a two-way street.[16]

MINI-CASE 11.2

Global giants' R&D networks – Siemens and BASF

R&D at Siemens

Siemens is a global electronics and electrical engineering corporation, operating in energy, healthcare, infrastructure and industrial solutions sectors. Founded in Germany in 1925, the company has 385,000 employees working at 1,640 locations around the globe, including 176 R&D facilities. Its revenue in 2019 was €86.849 billion. As of 30 September 2019, Siemens held approximately 68,300 granted patents, had 6,850 inventions and 3,750 patent applications pending. There were on average 45,100 employees that worked in R&D in 2019, in 44 countries including 14,100 in Germany. R&D expenditures climbed to €5.7 billion in fiscal year 2019, up from €5.6 billion in fiscal year 2018.

Its research and development activities were geared towards developing innovative, sustainable solutions for its customers – and the Siemens businesses.

Joint implementation of its operating units and Corporate Technology, the firm's central R&D department, ensures that research activities and business strategies are aligned. These units also benefit equally and in a speedy manner from new technological developments. Siemens focused on technologies including additive manufacturing, autonomous robotics, blockchain applications, connected (e-)mobility, connectivity and edge devices, cyber security, data analytics and artificial intelligence, distributed energy systems, energy storage, future of automation, materials, power electronics, simulation and digital twins, and software systems and processes.

Further technologies are currently being developed through its 'open innovation' concept. They work closely with scholars from leading universities and research institutions with the focus on its strategic research partners, and especially its eight Centres of Knowledge Interchange that they maintain at leading universities worldwide. Siemens' global venture capital unit, Next47, provides capital to help start-ups expand and scale and serves as the creator of next-generation businesses for Siemens by building, buying and partnering with innovative companies at any stage.

Technology

Technology (T) is the central in-house research unit at Siemens. T works alongside the business units to drive forward the basic technologies that are important for the company as a whole.

These core technologies are crucial to the long-term success of Siemens and its customers. Experts from the global research department of T and the various businesses work together here, consolidating the company's R&D activities.

The global network of experts comprises 2,400 employees, including 1,700 researchers and 350 patent experts. It acts as a strategic partner to support the executive units with R&D services, protect the company's intellectual property and coordinate the collaboration with top universities worldwide.

The main locations are in Germany, Austria, the US, China, Russia, and India.

R&D at BASF[17]

BASF SE is a German multinational chemical company founded in 1865. BASF is an acronym for Badische Anilin und Soda Fabrik (German for 'Baden Aniline and Soda Factory'). BASF Group is made up of subsidiaries and joint ventures in more than 80 countries and operates in 6 integrated production sites and 390 other production sites in Europe, Asia,

Australia, the Americas and Africa. Headquartered in Ludwigshafen, Germany, BASF has customers in over 190 countries and supplies products to a wide variety of industries.

At the end of 2019, the company employed more than 117,000 people, with over 54,000 in Germany. In 2019, BASF posted sales of €59.3 billion and income from operations before special items of €4.5 billion.

BASF's portfolio is made up of six segments: Chemicals, Materials, Industrial Solutions, Surface Technologies, Nutrition & Care and Agricultural Solutions.

The company is organized into 11 divisions that are grouped into 6 segments based on their business models. These divisions are responsible for operations and organized according to sectors or products. They manage the 54 global and regional business units developing strategies for the 76 strategic business units.

The regional and country units represent BASF locally, supporting the growth of the operation divisions in proximity to customers. The regional divisions are organized into four regions: Europe, North America, Asia Pacific, and South America, Africa, Middle East.

Eight global units form the corporate centre that is accountable for group-wide governance and supports BASF's Board of Executive Directors. Four global cross-functional service units offer services for individual sites or globally for business units of the BASF Group.

BASF has three global research divisions that are run from the group's key regions – Europe, Asia Pacific and North America: Process Research & Chemical Engineering (Ludwigshafen, Germany), Advanced Materials & Systems Research (Shanghai, China) and Bioscience Research (Research Triangle Park, North Carolina). Together with the development units in the operating divisions, they form the core of the global Know-How Verbund.

BASF developed a management approach called *Verbund* that integrates manufacturing and research. Production plants at large sites are closely interlinked and, in addition, the byproducts of one plant can be used as the starting materials of another. BASF considers that *Verbund* is the foundation of its competitiveness in all regions.

The group operates six Verbund sites as well as 361 additional production sites in more than 90 countries that 'create chemistry – around the globe'.[18]

Questions:

1 How does the global management of R&D at Siemens and BASF compare?

2 What are the potential benefits of the *Verbund* concept?

Summary and key points

1 International product life cycle

- **a** How product innovations and production *migrated* from country of origin of innovative firms to other country subsidiaries through a three-stage sequential process: 1) innovative country; 2) second-tier country; 3) third-tier country, mainly developing world
- **b** This model cannot explain the globalization of innovation that occurred after the 1960s

2 Global R&D network

- **a** Global firms more and more use a distributed network of R&D centres involving the collaboration of multiple sites scattered around the world

b Main motivations to set up a centre in a particular country are:

- proximity to local markets
- availability of skilled personnel
- R&D-supporting environments such as leading universities and local institutes

c Global Innovation Index (GII) provides insightful data on innovation that could help economies evaluate their innovation performance and make informed innovation policies. Main benefits of decentralized managed R&D:

- Proximity to market
- Access to geographical clusters of knowledge creation and development
- Learning from local knowledge

d Access to low-cost and good-quality scientists and engineers

Main constraints of decentralized managed R&D:

- Critical mass
- Communications

e Four categories of research centre:

- Research laboratories
- Development laboratories
- Supportive/adaptive units
- Scanning units

f *Issues in the management* of global R&D:

- *Size* of units: too big hampers communication
- *Role* of units: *discipline-centred* or *product/process-centred*
- *Degree of integration*: autonomous projects or integrated
- *Systems:* resource allocation, control, performance evaluation
- *Knowledge diffusion* and documentation: people rotation, conferencing, personal networking, electronic knowledge management platforms, databases, publications
- *People and culture:* small central staff, rotation, 'gatekeepers' in each laboratory, openness

g Typical evolution:

- First stage is central R&D laboratory
- Second stage is the set-up of local laboratories
- Third stage is the establishment of centres of excellence

3 International technology transfer

a Types of technology:

- Product

- Process
- Management

b Forms of *technology transfer*:

- Physical
- Informational

c *Key issues:*

- Appropriateness
- Completeness
- The risk of isolated subsidiaries
- Global open innovation

4 Global knowledge management system

a *Knowledge:* ability to decipher and give a meaning to facts and information

b *Knowledge management*: ability to create, combine and share knowledge among its members

c Knowledge can be *tacit or explicit*

d *Opportunities* for knowledge management: diversity of contexts, variety of experiences

e *Constraints*: languages, differences of cultures and mindsets, 'not invented here' reaction, unwillingness and lack of motivation to share knowledge, nationalistic perspectives, incentive system not conducive to sharing

f *Transfer* of best practices made less effective by: casual ambiguity, lack of capacity for absorption, difficult relationships

g *Models of knowledge creation*, sharing and 'melding':

- C&C model (co-location and co-setting)
- D&C model (dispersion and co-setting)
- C&D model (co-location and diverse setting)
- D&D model (dispersion and diverse setting) – major organizational tools:
  - Training for all relevant personnel
  - Socialization programme (informal team building)
  - Transition meetings (more formal team building and knowledge transfer)
  - Context-awareness training
  - Access to useful knowledge resources, especially a comprehensive staff and responsibilities directory
  - Clear deadlines for project completion

5 Intellectual property rights (IPR)

Types: patents, trademarks, copyrights, industrial design, trade secrets, genetic codes

Learning assignments

1. Why is the international product life cycle model no longer appropriate to explain global innovation?
2. What are the constraints on implementing a distributed R&D network?
3. What are the appropriate HRM practices conducive to global R&D?
4. When is technology transfer complete?
5. Give two examples of 'explicit' knowledge and two examples of 'tacit' knowledge in a business context of your choice.
6. What are the major challenges that the 'metanational' model of knowledge creation, sharing and 'melding' tries to address?
7. How can global open innovation help companies be cost efficient whilst remaining innovative?
8. How can research performance be measured?
9. How can you protect intellectual property rights (IPR) in a global firm through reciprocity and trust to achieve efficient and equitable outcomes in partnerships?

Key words

- Best practices
- Centre of excellence
- Co-location
- Combination
- Explicit knowledge
- Externalization
- Global open innovation
- Innovation
- Innovation outposts
- Intellectual property
- Internal stickiness
- Isolated subsidiaries
- Knowledge management
- Metanational
- Networked organization
- Socialization
- Tacit knowledge
- Technology scouting
- Technology transfer

Web resources

National Sciences Foundation:
http://www.nsf.gov/statistics/seind06/c4/c4s6.htm

Companion website

Visit the companion website at bloomsbury.pub/global-strategic-management-5e for a multitude of weblinks and resources, self-test questions for revision and appendices.

Notes

1 Vernon (1966).
2 http://uis.unesco.org/apps/visualisations/research-and-development-spending/ (accessed 9 february 2021)
3 Ibid
4 These categories are based on De Meyer (1992) and Wortmann (1990).
5 Doz and Wilson (2006).
6 Allen (1977).
7 Lahiri (2010).
8 This taxonomy is inspired by Pearce and Singh (1992) and Chiesa (2000: 341–59).
9 De Meyer (1991).
10 De Meyer (1992).
11 Lasserre (1995).
12 Monteiro and Decreton (2018).
13 Klueter and Monteiro (2014).
14 https://knowledge.wharton.upenn.edu/article/toys-and-spinning-brushes-how-john-osher-found-his-way-to-profits/
15 Monteiro, Davies and Carrick (2020).
16 Monteiro, Mol and Birkinshaw (2016).
17 Global Research at Siemens, https://www.siemens.com/global/en/home/company/innovation.html (accessed 29 June 2017).
18 https://www.basf.com/global/en/investors/ calendar-and-publications/factbook/basf-group/verbund.html (accessed 9 February 2022).

References and further reading

Books and articles

Allen, T. J. (1977) *Managing the Flow of Technology* (Cambridge, MA: MIT Press).

Augier, M. and Teece, D. J. (2007) 'Dynamic capabilities and multinational enterprise: Penrosean insights and omissions', *Management International Review*, 47 (2): 175–92.

Bogers, Marcel, et al. (2017) 'The open innovation research landscape: established perspectives and emerging themes across different levels of analysis', *Industry and Innovation* 24 (1): 8–40.

Boutellier, R., Gassmann, O. and Von Zedtwitz, M. (2009) *Managing Global Innovation: Uncovering the Secrets of Future Competitiveness* (Berlin: Springer).

Chesbrough, H. (2003) *Open Innovation: The New Imperative for Creating and Profiting from Technology* (Boston, MA: Harvard Business School Press).

Chiesa, V. (2000) 'Global R&D project management and organization: a taxonomy', *Journal of Product Innovation Management*, 17 (5): 323–409.

Decreton, B., Monteiro, L. F., Frangos, J. M. and Friedman, L. (2021) 'Innovation outposts in entrepreneurial ecosystems: why so many of them fail to be effective brokers and how to make them more successful', *California Management Review*. https://journals.sagepub.com/doi/10.1177/0008125621996494 (accessed 1 February 2022).

De Meyer, A. (1991) 'Tech talk: how managers are stimulating global R&D communication', *Sloan Management Review*, 49: 49–58.

De Meyer, A. (1992) 'Management of international R&D operations', Chapter 8 in O. Granstrand, S. Spölander and L. Häkanson (eds), *Technology Management and International Business* (New York, NY: John Wiley).

De Meyer, A. (1993) 'Nestlé SA', INSEAD Case Study 07/91-093.

Doz, Y., Dos Santos, J. and Williamson, P. J. (2001a) *From Global to Metanational: How Companies Win in the Knowledge Economy* (Boston, MA: Harvard Business Press).

Doz, Y., Dos Santos, J. and Williamson, P. J. (2001b) *The Metanational Corporation* (Boston, MA: Harvard Business School Press).

Doz, Y. and Wilson, K. (2006) *Innovation: Is Global the Way Forward?* (INSEAD and Booz Allen Hamilton).

Doz, Y. and Wilson, K. (2012) '10 rules for managing global innovation', *Harvard Business Review*, 90 (10): 85–90.

Dutta, S., Lanvin, B. and Wunsch-Vincent, S. (2020) 'Global Innovation Index 2020 who will finance innovation?' Cornell University, INSEAD, and the World Intellectual Property Organization (WIPO). https://www.wipo.int/edocs/pubdocs/en/wipo_pub_gii_2020.pdf (accessed 1 February 2022).

Garg, P. and Zhao, M. (2018) 'Knowledge sourcing by multidivisional firms', *Strategic Management Journal*, 39 (13): 3325–54.

Gómez, J., Salazar, I. and Vargas, P. (2020) 'The role of extramural R&D and scientific knowledge in creating high novelty innovations: an examination of manufacturing and service firms in Spain', *Research Policy*, 49 (8): 104030.

Huston, L. and Sakkab, N. (2006) 'Inside Procter & Gamble's new model for innovation', *Harvard Business Review*, 84 (3): 58–66.

Jaruzelski, B., Schwartz, K. and Staack, V. (2015) 'The 2015 global innovation 1000: innovation's new world order', *Strategy + Business*, 81, Winter.

Kim, S. and Lee, H. (2010) 'Factors affecting employee knowledge acquisition and application capabilities', *Asia-Pacific Journal of Business Administration*, 2 (2): 133–52.

Klueter, T. and Monteiro, L. F. (2014) 'Building the virtual lab: global licensing and partnering at Merck', INSEAD Case Study. https://publishing.insead.edu/case/building-virtual-lab-global-licensing-and-partnering-merck (accessed 1 February 2022).

Klueter, T. and Monteiro, L. F. (2017) 'How does performance feedback affect boundary spanning in multinational corporations? Insights from technology scouts', *Journal of Management Studies*. doi: 10.1111/joms.12252.

Klueter, T., Monteiro, L. F. and Dunlap, D. (2017) 'Standard vs. partnership-embedded licensing: attention and The relationship between licensing and product innovations', *Research Policy*. https://doi.org/10.1016/j.respol.2017.07.013 (accessed 1 February 2022).

Kuemmerle, W. (1997) 'Building effective R&D capabilities abroad', *Harvard Business Review*, 75 (2): 61–70.

Kumar, N. and Puranam, P. (2012) *India Inside: The Emerging Innovation Challenge to the West* (Boston, MA: Harvard Business School Press).

Lahiri, N. (2010) 'Geographic distribution of R&D activity: how does it affect innovation quality?' *Academy of Management Journal*, 53 (5): 1194–209.

Lasserre, P. (1995) 'Training: key to technology transfer', *Long Range Planning*, 15 (4).

Leonard-Barton, D. and Thill, G. (1994) 'Hewlett-Packard: Singapore', Harvard Business School Case 9-694-035.

Li, J. and Xie, Z. (2011) 'Global R&D strategies in an emerging economy: the development and protection of technological competencies', *European Management Review*, 8 (3): 153–64.

Meyer, K. E., Li, C. and Schotter, A. P. J. (2020) 'Managing the MNE subsidiary: advancing a multilevel and dynamic research agenda', *Journal of International Business Studies*, 51: 538–76.

Monteiro, L. F. and Birkinshaw, J. (2017) 'The external knowledge sourcing process in multinational corporations', *Strategic Management Journal*. doi: 10.1002/smj.2487.

Monteiro, L. F. and Decreton, B. (2018) 'BT Group: managing open innovation', INSEAD Case Study 05/2018-6397 2018. https://publishing.insead.edu/case/bt-group (accessed 1 February 2022).

Monteiro, L. F., Arvidsson, N. and Birkinshaw, J. (2008) 'Knowledge flows within multinational corporations: explaining subsidiary isolation and its performance implications', *Organization Science*, 19 (1): 90–107.

Monteiro, L. F., Davies, J. and Carrick, A. M. (2020) 'Barça Innovation Hub (BIH) goes global: innovation on and off the pitch', INSEAD Case Study. https://publishing.insead.edu/case/barca-innovation-hub (accessed 1 February 2022).

Monteiro, L. F., Mol, M. and Birkinshaw, J. (2016) 'Ready to be open? Explaining the firm level barriers to benefiting from openness to external knowledge', *Long Range Planning*. doi: 10.1016/j.lrp.2015.12.008.

Nonaka, I. and Takeuchi, H. (1995) *The Knowledge Creating Country: How Japanese Companies Create the Dynamics of Innovation* (Oxford: Oxford University Press).

Pearce, R. D. and Singh, S. (1992) *Globalizing Research and Development* (Basingstoke: Palgrave Macmillan).

Podolny, J. and Hansen, M. (2020) "How Apple Is organized for innovation", *Harvard Business Review*, 98 (6): 86-95.

Porter, M. (1998) *The Competitive Advantage of Nations* (New York, NY: Free Press).

Prashantham, S. (2021) 'Partnering with startups globally: distinct strategies for different locations',*California Management Review*, 63 (4): 123–45.

Prashantam, S. (2022). Gorillas Can Dance. John Wiley & Sons, Inc., Hoboken, New Jersey

Schotter, A. P. J., Mudambi, R., Doz, Y. L. and Gaur, A. (2017) 'Boundary spanning in global organizations', *Journal of Management Studies*. https://doi.org/10.1111/joms.12256 (accessed 1 February 2022).

Szulanski, G. (1996) 'Exploring internal stickiness: impediments to the transfer of best practices within the firm', *Strategic Management Journal*, 17, Special Issue: 27–43.

Ter Wal, A. L. J., Criscuolo, P. and Salter, A. (2017) 'Making a marriage of materials: the role of gatekeepers and shepherds in the absorption of external knowledge and innovation performance', *Research Policy*, 46 (5): 1039–54.

Terwiesch, C. and Xu, Y. (2008) 'Innovation contests, open innovation, and multiagent problem solving', *Management Science*, 54 (9): 1529–43.

United Nations (1993) *Intellectual Property Rights and Direct Foreign Investment* (New York, NY: United Nations).

Van Tulder, R. et al. (2007) *Private Sector R&D: Global View, Locomotive Project* (Copenhagen: Erasmus University/Interlace-Invent).

Vernon, R. (1966) 'International investment and international trade in the product life cycle', *Quarterly Journal of Economics*, 29 (2): 190–207.

Von Zedtwitz, M., Gasman, O. and Boutellier, R. (2004) 'Organizing global R&D: challenges and dilemmas', *Journal of International Management*, 10: 21–49.

Wortmann, M. (1990) 'Multinationals and the internationalization of R&D: new developments in German companies', *Research Policy*, 19 (2): 175–83.

Journals

California Management Review: https://cmr.berkeley.edu/

Journal of International Business Studies: https://link.springer.com/journal/41267/volumes-and-issues

R&D Management, Wiley-Blackwell: https://onlinelibrary.wiley.com/journal/14679310?gclid=Cj0KCQiAip-PBhDVARIs-APP2xc1CKBNzMTaP27mT1jNaVVaU3N9iXrN0TF-lo69oSD7eAzan5pnuXIN4aAiqsEALw_wcB

Research Policy: https://www.journals.elsevier.com/research-policy

Strategic Management Journal: https://onlinelibrary.wiley.com/journal/10970266

Chapter 12

Global financial management

At the end of the chapter you will be able to:

- Understand the nature of the risks generated by currency fluctuations
- Explain the hedging techniques available to manage currency fluctuations
- Compute the cash flow of an international project and assess its economic return using either the adjusted present value (APV) method or the cost of capital adjustment (CCA) method
- Recognize the benefits of crosslisting
- Appreciate the benefits and pitfalls of raising debt internationally
- Describe the mechanics behind, and some key tips for, using the various instruments of trade finance for global companies

Introduction

The world of global finance has evolved dramatically since 1980. Alongside traditional financing instruments such as international promissory notes that have existed since the Middle Ages, a vast array of facilities has been opened to firms operating across borders, ranging from hedging techniques to cross-border listing and swaps. Firms operating globally face several challenges related to the management of their cash flows, the cost of their capital and their exposure to risks. The domain of international finance is vast, and cannot be fully analysed within this chapter. We shall address some key issues in global financial management, but the discussion will be limited to managerial issues and will avoid the technical examples that more specialized books often provide.[1]

Four central global financial management issues are discussed in this chapter (Figure 12.1):

- *Currency risk*: exposure and hedging: how to protect against currency fluctuation
- *Project finance*: how to evaluate international investments, and how to finance them
- *Capital structure*: how to take advantage of global financial markets to raise equity and deal with debt
- *Trade finance*: the traditional instruments of financing exports/imports of goods.

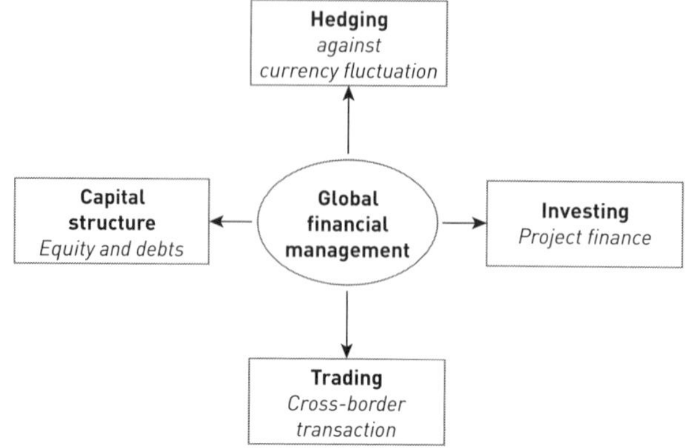

Figure 12.1 Key issues in global financial management

Currency risk

The most prevalent feature of international finance is that *currencies fluctuate in value against each other.* Figure 12.2 shows the fluctuation of four major global currencies (the US dollar, the yen, the pound sterling and the Chinese yuan) against the euro from 2000 to 2021.

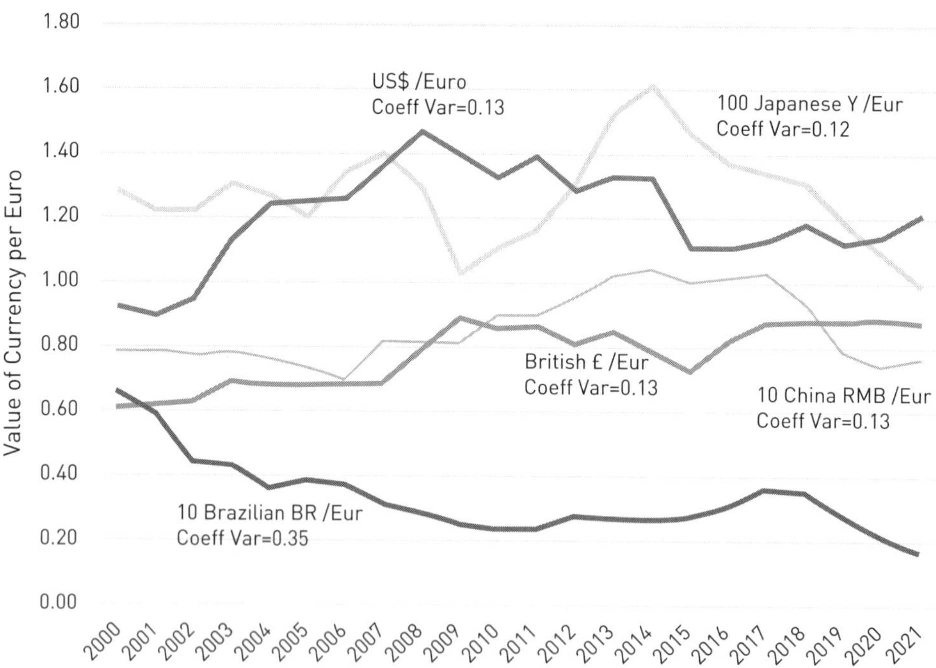

Figure 12.2 Variation of major currencies against the euro, 2000 to 2021, yearly average

Note: *Coefficient of variation = Standard deviation/mean.*

Source: Authors' own figure based on data from http://fxtop.com/fr/historique-taux-change.php (accessed 1 February 2022), reproduced from fxtop.com.

Companies operating globally are by definition exposed to different currency fluctuations. Their economic value can be affected in three ways:

- Their competitive advantage can deteriorate or be enhanced owing to the direct or indirect impact of a change in currency values. This is a **strategic exposure** that translates into a change in *future cash flow potential.*
- The short-term cash flow resulting from existing financial or commercial commitments can be affected positively or negatively. This is a **transaction exposure**.
- The reported valuation of assets and liabilities of global firms is also affected by currency variations; this in turn may affect market perception and ultimately the market value of firms. This is the **translation exposure**.

Strategic exposure

Currency fluctuations may have a direct or indirect effect on companies' competitive advantages by increasing their costs to an uncompetitive level or by giving competitors with weakened currencies a sudden competitive edge. This type of exposure is most significant in products or services that cater to price-sensitive customers, which is the case for most commodities. But even in differentiated products or services, such as aero engines or cars, a sharp increase in a country's currency value may lead to strategic disadvantage. In 2001 Nissan reduced the content of parts in its Micra model made in the UK to 55 per cent from 72 per cent due to the high value of the pound sterling. The group felt at a competitive disadvantage in maintaining a high level of local content in the country. Global firms are better positioned than domestic players to deal with strategic exposure because of their diversified market portfolio. They can also relocate production facilities, although that requires a lot of flexibility in resources transfer for effective implementation, and such willingness to shift location may affect their reputation as responsible citizens in the countries from which they exit. In practice, it is difficult to take drastic action of this type without being certain of the long-term *structural weakness* of a currency, which can be difficult to predict, as Figure 12.2 shows.

Hedging against this type of exposure is a matter of strategic product and geographic *positioning* and *global deployment of productive assets*:

- Hedging with strategic product positioning consists of developing products (or services) for price-insensitive market segments though *differentiation.*
- Hedging with geographical positioning consists of *balancing sales and production* within exchange zones; a pure global company whose revenues and productive assets are evenly distributed across the dollar zone, the euro zone and the yen zone would be sheltered, to a large degree, against the damaging competitive consequences of currency variations.
- Global deployment of productive assets would consist of *sourcing* either in-house or from external suppliers in low-cost countries such as China (which, despite its strong currency position, is still a low-cost manufacturing base for a large number of products).

Transaction exposure

Transaction exposure is the risk that currency fluctuation imposes on existing contractual engagements, one that may result in unexpected losses. Currency fluctuations reflect the differences in economic conditions between two countries: differences in inflation and interest rates particularly, as well as the confidence that investors will place in the stability of a country's economic and political conditions. This exposure occurs when a company borrows in a given currency to finance a productive asset that generates revenues in another currency. It also occurs when a company operating in a given country has signed a sales or supply contract that will be billed and paid in the future in a different currency. The positive or negative variation of the exchange rate will induce transaction gains or transaction losses. Obviously, transaction losses can damage company wealth while transaction gains give a speculative profit. Confronted with the probability of such gains or losses, the company can take two positions: a *speculative* attitude, betting on the probability that there will be a transaction gain; or a *hedging* perspective, making sure as soon as the contract is signed that the company will receive/pay a certain amount in its own currency whatever the exchange rate variation. There are several *hedging techniques* that can be used to guard against currency variation. The most frequently used ones are: forward contracts, future contracts, swap contracts and options. Other techniques such as *leading and lagging* or *netting* can also be used, but they are not considered as 'hedging' in the sense that there is still a certain degree of uncertainty.

Hedging techniques

- **Forward contracts** consist of buying at a fixed future date a fixed quantity of a given currency at a fixed exchange rate (the *forward rate*).

Forward rates reflect fundamentally the difference in interest rates between the two countries. For example, a European importer of Japanese goods will buy forward yen in order to be certain of paying the Japanese supplier at a known exchange rate. The same European company when exporting to the United States will sell the US dollars it will receive as payment at a pre-fixed exchange rate. An alternative method that produces exactly the same results is for the exporter to borrow euros, transform them into yen for the amount needed at the prevailing known rate of exchange on the day of the order. The yen are placed in a yen money market account and, at the date of the settlement, are used to pay the Japanese supplier; the interest gained is used to pay the interest due on the euro borrowing. The company will have to bear only the interest differential between the yen and the euros, which is exactly how the forward rate is calculated. In the case of the exporter to the United States, the company will borrow dollars and transform them into euros, put the euros in a money market account and, when it receives the money from the customer, use the dollars to pay back the loan; the interest gained on the euros pays the interest on the dollar loan. Forward contracts are the most common hedging techniques used by corporations. See Insert 12.1.

Insert 12.1 Hedging exposure to currency risk with forward contract

Piccadilly Wine and Spirits Ltd is a UK wine distributor that on 17 February 2022 ordered 3,000 bottles of Gigondas red wine from a vineyard in the Rhône valley (France) for €50,000 payable upon delivery, in three months. Hence the owner is exposed to exchange rate risk since he does not know what the pound sterling value will be in three months. He is subject to a transaction exposure for €50,000 since the GBP/EUR exchange rate varies. To protect himself, he can use one of several hedging techniques, of which the *forward contract hedge* is the most frequently used. In this case Piccadilly Wine's owner can fix *today* the rate at which he will buy €50,000 by guaranteeing the bank that he will be able to deliver the agreed fixed euro amount in three months. Banks publish each day's forward rates in multiple currencies. On 17 February 2022 the spot rate was £0.8353 per euro and so on that day the €50,000 are worth 50,000*0.8353 = £41,765. His bank gave him the three-month forward rate at 0.84 and in order to limit his risk he bought a forward contract by which he will, in three months, buy €50,000*0.84 = £42000, agreeing to take a £235 loss in comparison to the present spot rate (a loss of 0,5 %) . On 17 May 2022 (when payment came due) the £/€ exchange rate was 0.8446. If the company had not agreed the forward contract it would now have had to pay 50,000*0.8446 = £42,230, a loss of £465 (nearly 1.2 per cent of the order value).

An expanded case to explore and explain this topic in more detail can be found on the companion website to this book at bloomsbury.pub/global-strategic-management-5e

- **Futures contracts** are similar to forward contracts but they are standard financial instruments traded in *futures markets* such as London, Chicago or Singapore. They have a given size and a given expiry date.
- **Options** are contracts in which you buy the right to sell (*put option*) or buy (*call option*) a currency at a given exchange rate (the *strike price*) at the end of a maturity period. If at the end of the period the spot rate of the currency has varied unfavourably, you will not exercise your right. This option has a price (the *option premium*).
- **Currency swap** contracts are intermediated by a swap bank that matches long-term loans issued by two companies in their respective currency zones for use in the other company's currency zone. Company *X* borrows in currency *A* to be used in country *B* with loan repayment generated in currency *B*, while company *Y* borrows in currency *B* to be used in country *A* with loan repayment generated in currency *A*. The two companies can swap their loan. Assuming a perfect symmetry of the two loans, which the swap bank can arrange, there is a perfect hedging for companies *X* and *Y*. Swap contracts are good hedging techniques for long-term currency exposures.

Non-hedging techniques

Two other common forms of reducing transaction exposures are *leading and lagging* or *netting*:

- **Leading and lagging** is a technique by which you can collect receivables early (*leading*) if they are nominated in 'soft' currencies and delay collection (*lagging*) of receivables nominated in 'hard' currencies. Similarly, you would try to delay payment of payables nominated in 'soft' currencies and accelerate payment of payables nominated in 'hard' currencies.
- **Netting** is a technique used by treasurers of global firms that have centralized cash management for subsidiaries that trade with each other. Only the *net cash balance* resulting from the forecast inter-trade movement in their respective currencies is actually transformed and hedged into the currency that has a creditor position. If a German factory is planning to sell €1 million of components to a Singaporean company and the Singaporean factory is expected to sell 3 million Singapore dollars (S$) of finished products, the German factory will hedge S$650,000, which represents the net position at the rate of S$1.54 per euro at the time of the plan. This reduces the amount of currency exposed and the hedging costs. There are actually two different netting systems: *bilateral* netting (netting between pairs of subsidiaries) and *multilateral* netting (netting of all transactions and transfer of the net to a central centre).

Translation exposure

This type of exposure reflects the effects that changes in currency values have on the financial statements of global firms, and therefore on their *profits* and *book valuation*. There are several techniques to adjust income statements and balance sheets for currency fluctuations. The two main methods are the *monetary/non-monetary* method and the *current rate* method. In the monetary/non-monetary method, monetary items (e.g. cash, accounts payable and receivable, and long-term debt) are translated at the current rate while non-monetary items (e.g. inventory, fixed assets and long-term investments) are translated at historical rates. In the current rate method, assets and liabilities items are translated at the current exchange rate and income statement items are translated at the rate of the transaction or at an average rate over the period.

In practice, this type of exposure has relevance only to the extent that the economic source of value creation and valuation, the *cash flow*, is affected by the difference in reported translations. This may be the case concerning the tax consequences of currency fluctuation. Accounting standards require that translation exposure be reported, but market valuation is affected only to the extent to which reporting translation exposure reveals the strategic and transaction risks to which the firm is exposed.

Project finance

International project finance deals with the *valuation* and the *financing* of productive investments (different from financial portfolio investments) in different countries from that of the investor. In a global firm, there can be a multitude of configurations of international investments. A Swiss-based pharmaceutical firm may use a French subsidiary to implement a project in China jointly with a German subsidiary because it may relate to a product in which the French subsidiary has global responsibilities and for which the German engineering subsidiary has competencies in building plants. Project finance may concern greenfield wholly owned investments, acquisitions or joint ventures. The two key issues in project finance are: how to value these investments? How to finance them?

Project valuation

As in any economic valuation, the value of an investment for an investor is equal to the value of *future cash flows discounted by the weighted average cost of capital minus the discounted value of debts*. The only complexities that an international investment generates are the strategic and transaction currency exposures and any specific country risks. Table 12.1 gives an overview of the major types of risks involved in international projects and Table 12.2 lists some means of reducing those risks. Online Appendix 12.1 addresses the definitions of major risks involved in international projects.

Table 12.1 Classification of risk linked to infrastructure assets

<table>
<tr><th>Risk categories</th><th>Development phase</th><th>Construction phase</th><th>Operation phase</th><th>Termination phase</th></tr>
<tr><td rowspan="8">Political and regulatory</td><td>Environmental review</td><td>Cancellation of permits</td><td>Change in tariff regulation</td><td>Contract duration</td></tr>
<tr><td rowspan="2">Rise in pre-construction costs (longer permitting process)</td><td rowspan="2">Contract renegotiation</td><td rowspan="2"></td><td>Decommission</td></tr>
<tr><td>Asset transfer</td></tr>
<tr><td></td><td></td><td colspan="2">Currency convertibility</td></tr>
<tr><td colspan="4">Change in taxation</td></tr>
<tr><td colspan="4">Social acceptance</td></tr>
<tr><td colspan="4">Change in regulatory or legal environment</td></tr>
<tr><td colspan="4">Enforceability of contracts, collateral and security</td></tr>
<tr><td rowspan="7">Macroeconomic and business</td><td>Prefunding</td><td colspan="3">Default of counterparty</td></tr>
<tr><td colspan="2" rowspan="3">Financing availability</td><td colspan="2">Refinancing risk</td></tr>
<tr><td colspan="2">Liquidity</td></tr>
<tr><td colspan="2">Volatility of demand/market risk</td></tr>
<tr><td colspan="4">Inflation</td></tr>
<tr><td colspan="4">Real interest rates</td></tr>
<tr><td colspan="4">Exchange rate fluctuation</td></tr>
<tr><td rowspan="6">Technical</td><td colspan="4">Governance and management of the project</td></tr>
<tr><td colspan="4">Environmental</td></tr>
<tr><td>Project feasibility</td><td rowspan="2">Construction delays and cost overruns</td><td rowspan="2">Qualitative deficit of the physical structure/service</td><td rowspan="2">Termination value different from expected</td></tr>
<tr><td>Archaeological</td></tr>
<tr><td colspan="4">Technology and obsolescence</td></tr>
<tr><td colspan="4">Force majeure</td></tr>
</table>

As far as currency fluctuations are concerned, hedging techniques can possibly transform uncertainties into certainty in cash flow valuation, but what about country risks and currency risks when hedging is not available? There are two fundamental approaches for taking this type of risk into consideration: adjusting the cash flows or adjusting the cost of capital:

1 *Cash flow adjustment*, also known as **adjusted present value (APV)**, is a technique in which:
   - specific downside adverse risks are identified
   - their impact on the cash flow is calculated
   - the probability of their occurrence is determined
   - cash flows are adjusted using the probabilistic distribution
   - cash flows are translated into the investor's currency using purchasing power parity (PPP) differences as a proxy for currency fluctuations
   - cash flows are discounted using the investor's cost of capital.

Appendix 12.2 gives a simplified example of this method, which is usually considered the most appropriate technique by financial theorists.

Table 12.2 Financial risk mitigants and incentives for infrastructure finance

Type of measure	Instrument
Guarantees, realized directly by government or by its own controlled agency or development bank	Minimum payment, paid by contracting authority Guarantee in case of default Guarantee in case of refinancing Exchange rate guarantees
Insurance (private sector)	Wrap insurance, technology guarantees, warranties, commercial and political risk insurance
Hedging (private sector)	Derivatives contracts such as swaps, forwards, options etc.
Contract design, paid by contracting authority	Availability payment mechanisms Offtake contracts
Provision of capital, realized directly by government or by its own controlled agency or development bank	Subordinated (junior) debt Debt: at market condition at lower interest rate Equity: at market conditions at more advantageous conditions
Grants, generally delivered by contracting authority, even if some dedicated fund at national level may exist. Tax incentives can be delivered by national or local authorities	Lump sum capital grant Revenue grant: Periodic fixed amount (mitigating the demand risk) Revenue integration (it leaves the demand risk on the private player) Grant on debt interests Favourable taxation schemes for special purpose vehicle Favourable taxation schemes for equity investors

Source: Both tables reproduced from OECD (2015), *Infrastructure Financing Instruments and Incentives*, with permission.

2 *Cost of capital adjustments* are applied to the cost of capital by introducing a premium risk to the cost of equity. Professor Donald Lessard of MIT argues that adjusting the risk premium by introducing a 'country beta' to the cost of capital is more appropriate in the case of investments in emerging countries when risks are not diversifiable.[2]

Project financing

There are two sources of project financing:

- *Generic financing* provided by the corporation that uses its global equity and debt-financing capabilities
- *Specific equity* or *debt financing* provided by various financial institutions.

1 **Specific equity project financing** is usually provided for projects in emerging countries by development banks. Equity for projects in industrialized market economies is financed through normal market mechanisms, either public (stock exchange), private (venture capital) or directly by the corporation using its global financing capabilities. The major development banks that provide equity financing are listed in Appendix 12.3.

2 **Debt project financing** is provided by banking institutions, development banks, government aid, or suppliers' credits. When provided by banks or suppliers' credits, debt financing is backed by *credit risk insurance*. When projects are structured as joint ventures, financing can also come from local institutions and governments.

In some countries in which Islam is practised the rules of Islamic finance may also apply via specialized institutions[3] (see Insert 12.2).

Insert 12.2 Notes on Islamic finance

Islamic finance offers financial products that comply with *Sharia* principles. *Sharia* (the 'Way') is the set of laws derived from the *Quran*. Applied to finance, *Sharia* prohibits 1) the charging of interest on loans and 2) the financing of prohibited activities (*haram*) such as pornography, alcohol, pork-based food businesses or gambling. To satisfy the first requirement Islamic banking institutions offer a variety of products that are essentially structured as capital investments whose remuneration depends on the risky returns of the underlying activities. As far as the second requirement goes, questions of interpretation and enforcement depend on the opinion of the boards of directors of the institutions.

Global capital structure

The major financing issue for a global company is to decide where to generate equity and debt financing, and in what proportion. The overall objective is to minimize the cost of capital in order to enhance the *value creation capabilities* of the company. When the cost of capital of a company decreases, the value of the company increases. Finance theory tells us that the cost of capital, both equity and debt, is a function of macroeconomic factors as well as the systematic risk incurred by the company. Finance theory makes a distinction between *unsystematic* risks (that can be diversified) and *systematic* risks (that cannot be diversified). Unsystematic risks can be reduced by diversification: a global firm reduces its unsystematic risks by having a portfolio of investments across countries, but cannot avoid the inherent risks of investing in a particular country owing to the political and economic situation of that country (systematic risks). Since in a global economy different countries have different macroeconomic outlooks and different risk profiles, and different institutions to manage them, you can expect the cost of capital to be different from country to country, giving an opportunity to optimize your portfolio of financial sources in order to minimize cost. This creates the possibility of **crosslisting** and international bond issues.

In a purely global world in which free trade and free movement of capital, people and goods as well as market-based institutions prevailed, such international portfolio optimization would not exist: there would be one single capital market. The capital markets would be *integrated* and raising money in the United States, in Europe or Japan would cost the same. But since the world is not fully global, at least in the early twenty-first century, capital markets are still different in their structure, costs and risks, and are *fragmented.* Fragmentation can be observed in two ways. First, you can compare the cost of capital between countries. Academic researchers have found that the cost of capital has historically differed but has tended to converge, at least in the industrialized world (see Insert 12.3). Comparisons between indices of various stock markets show some high positive correlations among industrialized markets (see Table 12.3), except in Japan and France which show little significant correlation with the rest of the world. Emerging markets tend to correlate among themselves.

Insert 12.3 Academic research on international differences in the cost of capital

McCauley and Zimmer (1994) found that there were different costs of capital between Japan, Germany, USA and UK for the period between 1978 and 1992.

A study by René Stulz (1999) found that the effect of globalization on the decrease in cost of capital is significant but small. For globalization to reduce the cost of capital, the shareholder base has to become truly global.

Table 12.3 Correlation coefficients of monthly returns for selected stock markets, 1 January 2016 to 1 March 2021

	DOWJ USA	AORD Australia	Nikkei Japan	CAC 40 France	DAX Germany	BVSP Brazil	IPC Mexico	Hang Seng Hong Kong	SSEC Shanghai	KOSPI Korea	FTSE 100 UK	STI Singapore
DOWJ USA	1											
AORD Australia	0.73	1.00										
Nikkei Japan	0.60	0.47	1.00									
CAC 40 France	0.28	0.27	0.81	1.00								
DAX Germany	0.93	0.70	0.67	0.44	1.00							
BVSP Brazil	0.51	0.78	0.00	–0.13	0.54	1.00						
IPC Mexico	0.78	0.79	0.17	–0.12	0.76	0.89	1.00					
Hang Seng Hong Kong	0.76	0.86	0.39	0.22	0.82	0.88	0.88	1.00				
SSEC Shanghai	0.48	0.70	0.32	0.27	0.58	0.65	0.57	0.77	1.00			
KOSPI Korea	0.74	0.82	0.19	–0.07	0.73	0.92	0.97	0.91	0.61	1.00		
FTSE 100 UK	0.78	0.62	0.74	0.67	0.87	0.40	0.54	0.70	0.45	0.55	1.00	
STI Singapore	0.78	0.88	0.40	0.21	0.81	0.86	0.89	0.96	0.69	0.92	0.75	1

Note: *Correlation coefficients in bold are the ones above 0.60 showing a rather strong covariance.*

Source: Authors' own table and calculations, based on monthly returns data from Yahoo Finances, https://finance.yahoo.com/world-indices(accessed 1 February 2022).

Crosslisting

Crosslisting occurs when a firm lists its equity shares on one or more foreign stock exchanges besides its home country exchange. There are many reasons for a company to crosslist. Four proposed benefits are:

- The ability for a company to reach a *wider investor base*, which can potentially boost demand and hence liquidity for its shares. Increased demand for a company's stock may increase the share price, which can lower the cost of capital.
- The creation of a *secondary market* for the company's shares and recognition of the company in a new capital market, thus paving the way for the firm to source new equity or debt capital from local investors as demands dictate.
- As a secondary effect, *projecting the company's name and its products* in the foreign country where it is listed.
- By widening the investor base, there is potential for protection from a *hostile takeover* of the firm.

Crosslisting also raises some concerns. The company incurs costs in order to comply with the disclosure and listing requirements required by the foreign exchange and regulatory authorities. Secondly, the volatility of the stock in one stock market can affect the volatility of the same stock selling in another stock market. Crosslisting also provides an easy means for foreign investors to purchase a company's stock, which can potentially lead to a foreign investor challenging the domestic control of the company. Table 12.4 summarizes the country distribution of listed companies for various stock exchanges.

Table 12.4 Regional distribution of domestic and foreign listed companies for various stock exchanges, 2021

	TOTAL	Domestic companies	Foreign companies
AMERICAS	10,906	9,576 (88%)	1,330 (12%)
APAC	31,773	31,036 (98%)	737 (2%)
EMEA	14,930	13,021 (87%)	1,909 (13%)
WORLD	57,609	53,633 (93%)	3,976 (7%)
Major stock exchanges			
AMERICAS			
TORONTO TMX	3,559	3,501	58
NYSE	2,424	1,910	514
NASDAC	2,859	2,471	388
BOVESPA (Brazil)	359	345	14

ASIA PACIFIC			
Australian Securities Exchange	2,108	1,989	119
BSE India Limited	5,836	5,835	1
Hong Kong Exchanges and Clearing	1,866	1,770	96
Shenzhen Stock Exchange	1,746	1,746	0
EMEA			
BME Spanish Exchanges	3,651	3,623	28
London Stock Exchange	2,340	1,975	365
Euronext	1,068	944	124
Deutsche Börse AG	619	555	64

Source: Compiled by authors from World Federation of Exchanges members: https://focus.world-exchanges.org/issue/march-2021/market-statistics (accessed 1 February 2022).

Since 2015 the number of foreign listed companies in the world has increased from 2,704 to 3,976 in 2021 while the total number of listed companies went from 45,740 to 57,609. The increase in foreign listed companies came essentially from the Shenzhen and Shanghai Stock exchanges dominated by domestic listing.

International bond market

The international bond market is another way in which multinationals can source new debt capital. When markets are imperfect, international financing can lower the firm's cost of capital – for instance, Eurobond financing is usually cheaper than domestic bond financing.

The international bond market offers *foreign bonds*, *Eurobonds* and *global bonds*, which compete with domestic bonds for funding:

- A *foreign bond issue* is offered by a foreign borrower and the foreign bond issue is denominated in the local currency of the buyer of the bonds.
- A *Eurobond issue* is denominated in a currency foreign to the buyer – a German borrower issues a dollar-denominated bond to investors in the UK, for instance.
- A *global bond issue* is an offering by a single borrower to investors in North America, Europe and Asia.

Table 12.5 is a summary of various types of bond instrument.

Table 12.5 Types of international bond

Types of bond	Brief description	Payoff at maturity
Straight fixed rate	Fixed annual coupon payment as a percentage of the face value of the bond	Currency of issue
Floating rate note	Coupon payments which are indexed to some reference, such as three-month US dollar LIBOR*	Currency of issue
Convertible bond	Allows investors to exchange a bond for a predetermined number of equity shares of the issuer	Currency of issue or conversion to equity shares
Bond with equity warrants	Straight fixed-rate bond with an additional call option that allows the bondholder to purchase equity shares under specified conditions	Currency of issue
Zero coupon bond	Sold at a discount from face value No coupon payments over its life	Currency of issue
Dual currency bond	Straight fixed-rate bonds issued and coupon paid in one currency but principal repaid in another currency	Dual currency
Composite currency bond	Denominated in currency basket instead of single currency	Composite currency of issue

Note: * *LIBOR = London Inter-Bank Offered Rate.*

Benefits of raising debt globally

Global bond offerings widen the borrower's opportunities for financing at reduced cost, because with increased liquidity in global bonds, investors are willing to accept lower yields. With an increased pool of investors, global bonds also promote sources of financing.

Concerns with raising debt globally

A company may need to satisfy additional security regulations (e.g. information disclosure) required by overseas regulatory bodies.

International bond market credit ratings

Moody's Investors Service and Standard & Poor's (S&P) provide *credit ratings* on various types of international bond. Bond issues are classified into categories based upon the creditworthiness of the borrower. Potential bond ratings include investment grade, speculative grade or a grade which indicates a default risk.

Ratings providers assess the company's default probability based on current information and details of debt obligation. The ratings reflect only creditworthiness (not exchange rate uncertainty) and they are the result of an analysis of three factors:

- Likelihood of default and compliance with timely payment of interest and principal repayment
- Nature and provision of debt obligation
- Protection afforded by, and relative position of, obligation in the event of bankruptcy, reorganization or other arrangement under the laws of bankruptcy and other laws affecting creditors' rights.

There are a disproportionate percentage of international bonds which have high credit ratings when compared to domestic bonds. This can be explained by the fact that the Eurobond market is accessible only to firms that have good credit ratings and reputations.

Development finance

After the Second World War, following the Bretton-Wood conference, the World Bank was created to participate in the reconstruction of Europe. It was later expanded to the development across the globe by providing financing to public investments. This was the first International Financing Institution (IFI). Over the years multiple IFIs were created as well as Development Finances Institutions (DFIs) specializing in providing financing to the private sector in the developing world. For instance the World Bank created the International Finance Corporation for that purpose.

One may distinguish two kinds of DFIs: multilateral and bilateral (Tables 12.6 and 12.8).

Multilateral DFIs are private sector arms of international financial institutions (IFIs) that have been established by more than one country, and hence are subject to international law. Their shareholders are generally national governments but could also occasionally include other international or private institutions. These institutions finance projects in support of the private sector mainly through equity investments, long-term loans and guarantees. They usually have a greater financing capacity than bilateral development banks and also act as a forum for close co-operation among governments (see Table 12.6).

Table 12.6 List of the main multinational DFIs

AFDB (African Development Bank) ADB (Asian Development Bank) EBRD (European Bank for Reconstruction and Development) EIB (European Investment Bank)	IDB (Inter-American Development Bank) IFC (International Finance Corporation), a subsidiary of the World Bank ISDB (Islamic Development Bank) NDB (New Development Bank), ex-BRICS's Development Bank

Bilateral DFIs are set up in one country to implement foreign development and cooperation policy. They are either independent institutions, such as the Netherlands Development Finance Company (FMO), or part of larger bilateral development banks, such as the German Investment and Development Company (DEG), which is part of the German development bank KfW. They are both among the largest DFIs worldwide (see Table 12.7).

Table 12.7 The main bilateral DFIs

OeEB (Austria)	AFD/Proparco (France)	COFIDES (Spain)
BIO (Belgium)	KfW/DEG (Germany)	Swedfund (Sweden)
BMI-SBI (Belgium)	CDP/SIMEST (Italy)	SIFEM (Switzerland)
FinDev Canada (Canada)	FMO (Netherlands)	CDC Group (United Kingdom)
IFU (Denmark)	Norfund (Norway)	OPIC (United States)
Finnfund (Finland)	SOFID (Portugal)	

Source: OECD: https://www.oecd.org/development/development-finance-institutions-private-sector-development.htm (accessed 1 February 2022).

The BRICS's Development Bank (NDB) established in 2012 was renamed New Development Bank in 2014. It aims to provide financing to infrastructure and sustainable development projects in the BRICS countries. The Bank's membership is open to members of the United Nations and its original members were Brazil, Russia, India, China and South Africa. NDB admitted its first new member countries in 2021 with Bangladesh in September followed by United Arab Emirates in October.

Sovereign funds

Sovereign Wealth Funds (SWFs) 'are public investment vehicles that manage part of states' wealth due to the accumulation of exchange reserves by central banks linked with growing trade surplus and the constant rise of oil prices. These public funds invest internationally like other private investors in equity, bonds and real estate.[4]

According to a 2020 PricewaterhouseCoopers report, total assets from sovereign funds grew from $5,500 billion in 2007 to $15,000 billion in 2020.[5]

Table 12.8 provides a list of the ten largest sovereign wealth funds by total assets.

> SWFs do not borrow money or sell stock to the public, they incur neither a cost of debt nor a cost of equity, which potentially allows SWFs to demand a lower rate of return on their investments compared to a private or publicly listed fund.[6]

Table 12.8 Top ten largest sovereign wealth fund rankings by total assets

Rank	Fund	Total assets (US$ bn)
1	Norway Government Pension Fund Global	$1,323
2	China Investment Corporation	$1,045
3	Hong Kong Monetary Authority Investment	$580
4	Abu Dhabi Investment Authority	$579
5	Kuwait Investment Authority	$533
6	GIC Private Limited (Singapore)	$453
7	Temasek Holdings (Singapore)	$417
8	Public Investment Fund (Saudi Arabia)	$399
9	National Council for Social Security Fund (China)	$372
10	Investment Corporation of Dubai	$301

Source: Institute Fund Summit 2021 Earth Day Event, https://www.swfinstitute.org/fund-rankings (accessed 3 November 2021).

Targeted financing

Some financing initiatives have been developed to facilitate investments and developments with some specific objectives.

Green financing

Green financing is financing of investments that provide environmental benefits. The areas covered by this type of financing are targeted to:

- Energy efficiency, renewable energies
- Environmental protection
- Green products, materials, building
- Sustainable agriculture, forestry
- Transport (urban rail/metro, electric, hybrid)
- Waste management (recycling, waste management)
- Water efficiency, wastewater treatment
- Conservation, biosystem adaptation
- Carbon capture and storage.

According to an OECD report institutional investors held 1.04 trillions in infrastructure assets out of which 314 billion are attributed to green infrastructure. The green technology and sustainability market is predicted to grow from $11.2 billion in 2020 to $36.6 billion by 2025, at a compound annual growth rate (CAGR) of 26.6 per cent.[7]

Inclusive financing

Inclusive financing's objective is to provide individuals and businesses that have difficulties in opening banking services 'to have access to useful and affordable financial products and services that meet their needs – transactions, payments, savings, credit and insurance – delivered in a responsible and sustainable way'.[8] Inclusive finance is essentially geared to the domestic population, including small businesses.

Venture capital

Venture capital is a type of financing where private investors, investment banks, financial institutions and corporations target start-up companies and small businesses with long-term potential. An estimate from OECD valued the invested venture capital amounted to Start-up and other early stages at around $60 billion.[9] An example of corporate venture capital is provided by Intel.

Cryptocurrencies

Cryptocurrencies are a form of digital money, that is, transacted by individuals on a peer-to-peer basis through a coded mechanism ('crypted') using a denomination (e.g. Bitcoin) different from official currencies (dollars, pounds, euros, yen etc.). According to the creator of Bitcoin this type of currency 'allows online payments to be sent directly from one party to another without going through a financial institution'.[10] The value of those currencies is not guaranteed by central banks or by any organization. The guarantee of the currency is based on complex systems of internet-based mathematical procedures such as distributed ledgers and blockchains. Each transaction is registered on a file that only the individuals participating to the transaction can access. Since there is no official institution granting its value the cryptomoney price when translated into official currency is the result of market transactions made by the players in the market, hence its high volatility. Contrary to corporate shares quoted on stock exchanges whose value is based on economic anticipation, the value of cryptocurrencies is based only on the amount of money that cryptocurrencies holders want to sell and the amount of money that buyers want to put to purchase it.

Cryptocurrencies can be used for commercial transactions or for speculative investment. The number of cryptocurrencies available is limited, hence its volatility, as illustrated below:

25 January 2021 = $32,900
22 February 2021 = $48,233
29 March 2021 = $58,300
26 April 2021 = $55,682
24 May 2021 = $37,287

Figure 12.3 shows Bitcoin's price evolution from January 2021 to May 2021.

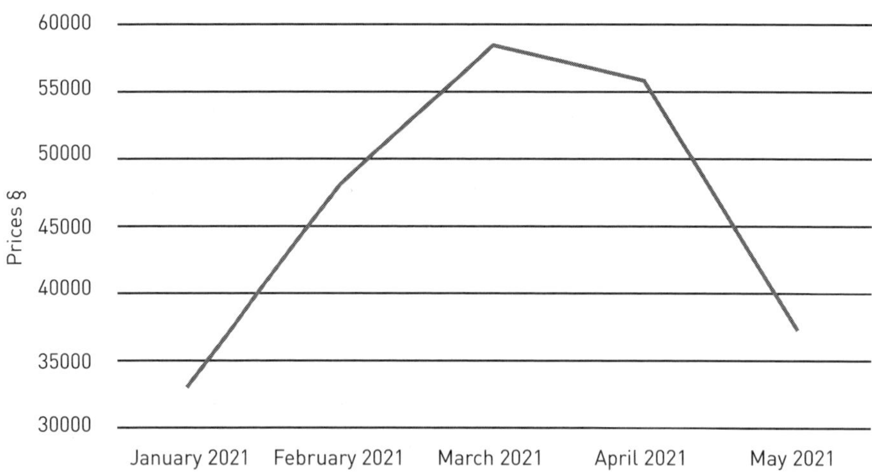

Figure 12.3 Bitcoin price (January–May 2021)

The two main cryptocurrencies are Bitcoin and Ethereum.

A technical note explaining cryptocurrencies in more detail is available in Appendix 12.3.

A fictional example is given in Insert 12.4.

Insert 12.4 The tale of a Bitcoin transaction

Fredrich Herman is the CEO of a medium-sized company specializing in machines for the butchery industry at a price of €50,000. One of his customers based in Turkey wants to use Bitcoin as the currency of transaction.

Friedrich went to the web and opened a Bitcoin wallet through one of the platforms available (e.g. Enterprise Wallet Solution, Exodus, Trust wallet etc.). Once he is properly registered and has paid a fee to the platform he is given a wallet with a code known only to himself. When the contract is signed on 17 February 2021, the €50,000 will be valued at 1.18 Btc at the rate of the Bitcoin on the day of signature (on 17 February 2021, 1 Btc = €42,300).[11] When the machine is delivered on 18 April 2021 (1 Btc = €46,800) his Bitcoin account will be credited at the price of the contract of 1.18 Btc in a secure transaction that nobody knows because it is encrypted with a code that only the buyers and himself know. This transaction is registered in a ledger to which nobody can access, and the ledger is the proof that the payment has been done. In this case, Fredrich is happy since if he can sell his 1.18 Btc on the Bitcoin market on the day of the receipt and he will receive 1.18 × 46,800 = €55,200 (minus fees) for a profit of €5,200.

However, Friedrich has seen the evolution of the Bitcoin and is interested in investing his Bitcoin until he needs cash by the end of May. On 30 May he sells his 1,18 Btc and receives €28,900 (on 30 May 2021, 1 Btc = €28,900). Alas he is now with a deficit of €21,100. Obviously Friedrich could have had the possibility to hedge on Bitcoin using various methods: short-selling, hedging with CDF or hedging with future.

Question:

What advantage is there to using Bitcoin instead of bank transfer?

Source: https://www.ig.com/en/trading-strategies/how-to-hedge-bitcoin-risk-190726#hedgingbitcoinwithcfdsandspreadbets (accessed 1 February 2022).

Trade finance

In addition to the classic financial facilities that exporters and importers can obtain in their respective countries from their banks, financing for international trade can take three forms:

- *Documentary credit* that benefits exporters of goods.
- *Credit facilities* offered to importers and exporters by export credit agencies that also mitigate the risks of exporters.
- *Countertrade* deals that ease the cash outflow of exporters.

Documentary credit

For exporters of goods, the most traditional method of trade finance is the documentary credit represented in Figure 12.4. The principle is that an importer of goods mandates his bank to issue a letter of credit that guarantees the exporter that they will be paid on receipt of shipping documents, establishing proof that the goods have actually been delivered to the transport company. The exporter can ask the importer's bank, through its own bank, to accept a *time draft* for the amount of the contract by issuing a *Bank Acceptance* (B/A). The exporter can discount this acceptance. Figure 12.4 gives a step-by-step simplified view of this process. There is a large variety of terms regulating the transactions and delineating the respective responsibilities of the exporters and the importers. Those terms, known as *Incoterms,* are defined by the International Chambers of Commerce (ICC) based in Paris.

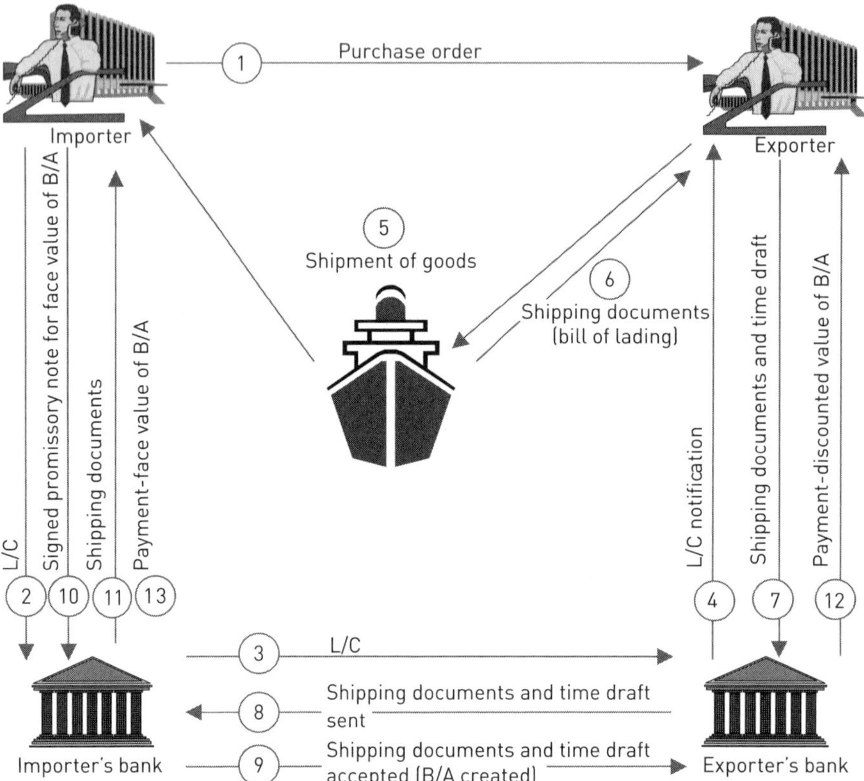

Figure 12.4 Documentary credit in international trade
Note: *B/A = Bank acceptance; L/C = Letter of credit application.*

Export credit agencies

Exporters, and sometimes importers, of goods can benefit from credits granted through export credit agencies such as the Eximbank (Export–Import Bank) backed by the Federal Credit Insurance Association (FCIA) in the United States, the ECGD (Export Credits Guarantee Department) in the UK or the Compagnie Française d'Assurance pour le Commerce Extérieur (COFACE) in France.

These agencies either provide credits directly or facilitate the granting of credits from banks or from the exporter's bank to importers by covering political risks and commercial risks up to a certain percentage of the contract.

In addition, these institutions may grant facilities to exporters to obtain *prefinancing* of their exports in contracts of long duration.

Appendix 12.5 has a list of export credit agencies in different OECD member countries.

Countertrade

Countertrade is another way of financing international transactions. It eases the pain for importers who have to find cash in hard currencies to pay for their imports. The principle of countertrade is that the buyer pays the total or part of the contract in products or services. Countertrade can take three main forms:[12]

- *Barter* trade, the most direct form of countertrade. The exporter is paid in products coming from the importer's country.
- *Buyback* contracts, in which the supplier of equipment agrees to buy part of the output of the exporter's facilities. In this case, there is cash outlay on both sides but the importer recoups its investment from the cash generated by the sales of products. A variant of buyback is known as a *counterpurchase* contract, in which the products sold to the exporter come from a third party.
- *Bilateral clearing agreements*, which exist at government level, are when two governments agree to trade, and the debit and credit of the trade are registered in an account whose balance is cleared at the end of an agreed period. In some cases, the balance can be 'sold' to a third party that can use it for purchasing goods in the debtor's country. This last arrangement is known as *switch trade*.

Countertrade agreements mostly involve developing countries that are short of hard currency. They were common practice in the era of state-controlled economies in communist countries until the early 1990s, but have decreased in importance with the liberalization of markets.

Global financial management and taxation

As indicated in Chapter 4, some global companies can use their multi-country presence to adjust their financial policies – to play with the differences in taxes between countries in order to minimize their tax exposure. Contractor (2016) describes seven methods of tax avoidance (see Chapter 4). In 2016 the European Commission imposed a penalty of €14 billion on Apple Corporation, arguing that the company benefited from Ireland's low tax rate of 1 per cent on profits achieved in the rest of Europe instead of paying at the already low official 12.5 per cent rate. The EU Commission's argument is that Apple effectively benefited from a government subsidy such as is forbidden in the EU. In April 2021 at the G7 Summit in Cornwall the participants agreed that a minimum global tax rate of at least 15 per cent would be applicable to multinational companies (MNCs). It was also decided that countries could tax the largest MNCs for profits generated in countries where they operate. This particular provision targets the companies operating through the internet such as Apple Music, Amazon and Google who had been benefiting from tax optimization though the transfer of profit in low taxation counties like Ireland or Holland.

MINI-CASE 12.1

Cleanwater in Vietnam

Cleanwater Inc. is an Australian public company involved in water treatment projects.

In early 2020 it was involved in negotiations with the provincial government of Da Nang in Vietnam.

Following the negotiation a proposed contract was submitted, as summarized below:

- Cleanwater will build a water treatment plant of 300,000 cubic metres/day capacity and serving 1 million people, via a joint venture company created with the Da Nang Water Supply Company (to put in a 10 per cent stake), and a private local conglomerate, the Jade Group (30 per cent stake), with Cleanwater holding 60 per cent of the capital. The joint venture operates as a concession of the project under a BOT contract.
- The capital cost is estimated at \$55 million of imported equipment and services plus 115 billion Vietnamese dong (VND) of local costs (rate of exchange is 23,000 VND to the dollar).
- The financing of the project is:
  - Shareholders: \$30 million
  - New Development Bank (ex-BRIC Development Bank): 10-year loan of \$10 million, with interest of 6 per cent, repayable in six instalments after the fourth year.
  - Export credit from EFIC, the Australian export credit agency: Spain: 8-year loan of \$15 million, with interest at 3 per cent, refundable after the second year
  - Asian Development Bank: local currency 10-year loan of 184 billion VND, with interest at 8 per cent, repayable straight after 10 years.
- The contributions of shareholders to the joint venture are the following:
  - Cleanwater: \$18 million cash
  - Da Nang Water Supply Company: \$3 million cash
  - The Jade group, a local conglomerate: \$8 million.
- The cost of operations and maintenance without depreciation and financing is estimated at 27,800 VND/m^3 plus 200 billion VND.

It has been agreed that the joint venture will charge for water at 34,500 VND/m.^{3}

Questions:

1 What are the risks in this project for Cleanwater?

2 What do you think of the financing of the project?

3 Cleanwater shareholders request a 15 per cent return on risky environments. Will they approve this project?

Summary and key points

1 There are four key issues in global financial management:

   a *Currency risk*: exposure and hedging against currency fluctuations

   b *Project finance*: how to evaluate international investments and how to finance them

   c *Capital markets*: how to take advantage of global financial market to raise equity and handle debts

   d *Trade finance*: financing exports/imports of goods and services

2 Currency fluctuations and hedging

Currency fluctuations can affect the economic value of companies that operate globally in three ways:

- *Strategic exposure*:
  - Change in competitive advantage of a company in terms of future cash flow owing to increased/decreased costs arising from changes in currency values
  - Hedging techniques include:
    - *strategic product positioning* through differentiation
    - *geographical positioning*: balancing operations within exchange
    - *sourcing in low-cost countries and strong currencies*
- *Transaction exposure*:
  - Positive or negative changes in short-term cash flows. Hedging techniques include:
    - *Forward contracts*: buying at a fixed future date a fixed quantity of a given currency at a fixed exchange rate
    - *Future contracts*: in recognized futures markets
    - *Options contracts:* acquire an option to sell (*put* option) or to buy (*call* option) a currency at a given rate
    - *Currency swaps*: the two companies, having borrowed in different currencies, can swap their loans
    - *Leading and lagging*: collect receivables early (leading) or delay (lagging) according to the strength of the nominated currencies
- *Netting*:
  - Centralized cash management among subsidiaries offsetting cash positions
  - *Bilateral netting,* netting between pairs of subsidiaries; *multilateral netting,* netting of all transactions and transfer of the net to a central account
- *Translation exposure*:
  - Currency movement affects valuation of assets/liabilities of global companies
  - Two main methods of adjusting financial statements:
    - *Monetary/non-monetary* method
    - *Current* method

3 Project finance

a International project finance deals with the valuation and financing of productive investments in countries outside the investor's country of origin

b Project valuation and financing are affected by three types of *risk*:

- Political and regulatory risks
- Macroeconomic and business risks
- Technical risks

c *Project valuation*: two approaches are available to take into account country risks and currency risks that are not diversifiable:

- *Cash flow adjustments* (APV-adjusted present value) cash flows are adjusted according to probability of risks
- *Cost of capital adjustments* (CCA) introduces a premium risk to the cost of equity

d *Specific project financing*:

- *Equity project financing*:
  - For *developing countries*, equity project finance is usually provided by development banks
  - For *industrialized market economies*, equity project finance is usually provided by development banks
- *Debt project financing* – provided by banking institutions, development banks, government aid or supplier credits

4 Global capital structure

a *Integrated capital markets*: cost of equity and debts is equivalent across stock exchanges

b *Fragmented capital markets*: cost of equity is equivalent across stock exchanges. Allows companies to benefit from *crosslisting* and *international bond issues*

- *Crosslisting*
  - Advantages:
    - Wider investor base
    - Creating a secondary market for the company's shares
    - Projecting the company's name and products
    - Some protection from hostile takeover with a widened investor base
  - Disadvantages:
    - Costs of compliance
    - Volatility in one stock market can affect volatility in another market
    - Foreign investors can challenge the domestic control of the company
- International bond issues
  - Benefits:
    - Means of financing at lower cost
    - Promotes diversified investor base
    - Financing of overseas subsidiaries
  - Disadvantages:
    - Additional security regulations

5 Trade finance

- **a** *Documentary credit*: an importer of goods mandates their bank to issue a letter of credit that guarantees that the exporter will be paid on receipt of shipping documents. Credit facilities offered by *export credit agencies* to importers and exporters
- **b** *Countertrade deals*: the buyer pays the total or part of the contract in products or services
- **c** *Barter trade*: exporter is paid in products coming from the importer's country
- **d** *Buybacks*: supplier of equipment agrees to buy part of the output of the exporter
- **e** *Bilateral clearing agreements*: governmental level when two governments agree to trade and the debit and credit of the trade is registered in an account whose balance is cleared at the end of the agreed period

Learning assignments

1. What are the three types of risk that a global company is exposed to as a consequence of currency fluctuations?
2. On 14 January 2002 it was announced that the US carrier JetBlue would buy ten Airbus 320 aircraft for $500 million. The planes were to be delivered over four years (two in 2002, two in 2003, three each in 2004 and 2005). Airbus incurs 70 per cent of its cost in euros. What can Airbus Industries do to cover its currency fluctuation risks?
3. In the UK referendum on EU membership in June 2016, why were most major British financial institutions against Brexit?
4. What are the benefits and problems for a Japanese firm being listed on the New York Stock Exchange?
5. Why is the adjusted present value (APV) method preferred to the cost of capital adjustment (CCA) method in valuing international projects?
6. How can a company deal with strategic exposure?
7. What is a letter of credit?
8. Why are the correlation coefficients between stock market returns so high (Table 12.3)?
9. What type of global financial management tools would a global firm have used to counteract the adverse impacts of the 1997 Asian financial crisis?
10. The central finance function is one of the central corporate functions of a conglomerate. Do you foresee a trend towards the formation of a global swapping bank account? What are the pros and cons of implementing such a financial tool?
11. Can companies take advantage of favourable exchange or tax rates to make purchases in different currencies/countries?
12. Name six commodity products which have forward and futures trades. Can you think of a commodity product not related to natural resources which has forward and futures trades?
13. When a global company originates from a country that may not have a sound financial system (e.g. Argentina), should its overseas offices/subsidiaries hedge their local currencies against the currency of the head office or hedge it against a foreign currency (e.g. USD), which is less prone to be affected by significant devaluations?

14 Why do you think the Japanese stock market, as shown in Table 12.3, has not correlated to other markets?

Key words

- Adjusted present value country risk (APV)
- Cost of capital adjustment (CCA)
- Country stock market beta
- Crosslisting
- Cryptocurrencies
- Currency swaps
- Documentary credit
- Export credit agencies
- Forward contracts
- Futures contracts
- Hedging
- Leading and lagging
- Netting
- Options
- Project valuation
- Strategic exposure
- Transaction exposure
- Translation exposure

Web resources

Euromoney:
http://www.euromoney.com
Global Capital:
http://www.globalcapital.com/
International Monetary Fund (IMF):
https://www.imf.org/en/Home
UNCTAD publications:
https://unctad.org/publications

Notes

1 See Eun and Resnick (2001); Eiteman et al. (2015); Hawawini and Viallet (2015); Madura (2015).
2 Lessard (1996).
3 Anwar and Millar (2008).
4 Amar (2016).
5 PricewaterhouseCoopers (2020).
6 Surendranath, Perry and Hemphill (2010).
7 OECD (2020).
8 https://www.worldbank.org/en/topic/financialinclusion/overview (accessed 1February 2022).
9 https://stats.oecd.org/Index.aspx?DataSetCode=VC_INVEST (accessed 1 February 2022).
10 Nakamoto (2008).
11 https://bitflyer.com/fr-eu/bitcoin-chart (accessed 1 February 2022.
12 See Hennart (1989: 243–70).

References and further reading

Amar, J. (2016) '*Sovereign Wealth Funds: major actors in the Global Economy*', Aix-Marseille University. Unpublished dissertation.

Ammer, J. and Mei, J. (1996) 'Strategic returns to international diversification', *European Financial Management*, 1 (1).

Anwar, H. and Millar, R. (2008) *Islamic Finance: A Guide for International Business and Investment* (London: GMB Publishing).

Bailey, W., Chung, P. Y. and Kang, J. (1999) 'Foreign ownership restrictions and equity price premiums: what drives the demand for cross-border investments?', *Journal of Financial and Quantitative Analysis*, 34 (4): 489–511.

Bank for International Settlements (2015) 'Digital currencies', Committee on Payment and Market Infrastructure. https://www.bis.org/cpmi/publ/d137.pdf (accessed 1 February 2022).

Botta, A., Tunon, A., Reema, J. and Mar, A. (2021) 'Reconceiving the global trade finance ecosystem', *McKinseyReport*. https://www.mckinsey.com/industries/financial-services/our-insights/reconceiving-the-global-trade-finance-ecosystem (accessed 1 February 2022).

Contractor, F. (2016) 'Tax avoidance by multinational companies: methods, policies, and ethics', *Rutgers Business Review*, 1 (1): 27–43.

Eiteman, D., Stonehill, A. and Moffett, M. (2015) *Multinational Business Finance, Global Edition*, 14th edn (New York, NY: Pearson Higher Education).

Eun, C. S. and Resnick, B. G. (2001) *International Finance Management*, 2nd edn (New York, NY: McGraw-Hill).

European Central Bank (2012) 'Virtual currency schemes'. https://www.ecb.europa.eu/pub/pdf/other/virtualcurrencyschemes201210en.pdf (accessed 1 February 2022).

European Parliament (2018) 'Cryptocurrencies and blockchain: legal context and implication for financial crime, money laundering and tax evasion'. https://www.europarl.europa.eu/cmsdata/150761/TAX3%20Study%20on%20cryptocurrencies%20and%20blockchain.pdf (accessed 1 February 2022).

Foss, N. J., Mudambi, R. and Murtinu, S. (2019) 'Taxing the multinational enterprise: on the forced redesign of global value chains and other inefficiencies', *Journal of International Business Studies*, 50 (9): 1644–55.

Giddy, I. (1994) *Global Financial Markets* (Lexington, MA: D.C. Heath).

Hawawini, G. and Viallet, C. (1999, 2011, 2015, 2019) *Finance for Executives*: *Managing for Value Creation* (Cincinnati, OH: South Western Publishing).

Hennart, J. F. (1989) 'Some empirical dimensions of counter trade', *Journal of International Business Studies*, 21 (2): 243–70.

Hicks, C. and Reeth, R. (2021) '7 of the best cryptocurrencies to invest in now', 10 May. https://money.usnews.com/investing/cryptocurrency/slideshows/whats-the-best-cryptocurrency-to-buy?slide=2 (accessed 1 February 2022).

International Finance Corporation (2001) *Project Finance in Developing Countries*: *Lessons from Experience*, 7.

Lessard, D. (1996) 'Incorporating country risks in the valuation of offshore projects', *Journal of Applied Corporate Finance*, 9 (3): 52–63.

Madura, J. (2015) *International Financial Management*, 12th edn (Boston, MA: Cengage Learning).

McCauley, R. and Zimmer, S. (1994) 'Exchange rates and international differences in the cost of capital', in Y. Amihud and R. Levich (eds), *Exchange Rates and Corporate Performance*, 119–219 (Burr Ridge, NY: Irwin).

Nakamoto, S. (2008) 'Bitcoin: a peer-to-peer electronic cash system'. https://bitcoin.org/bitcoin.pdf (accessed 8 February 2022).

Natarajan, H., Krause, S. and Gradstein, H. (2017) 'World Bank Group, Distributed Ledger Technology (DLT) and blockchain', *FinTech note, no. 1*. Washington, D.C. https://openknowledge.worldbank.org/handle/10986/29053 (accessed 8 February 2022).

OECD (Organisation for Economic Co-operation and Development) (n.d.) *Development Finance Institutions and Private Sector Development*. https://www.oecd.org/development/development-finance-institutions-private-sector-development.htm (accessed 1 February 2022).

OECD (Organisation for Economic Co-operation and Development) (2014) *Private Financing and Government Support to Promote Long-Term Investments in Infrastructure* (Paris: OECD).

OECD (Organisation for Economic Co-operation and Development) (2015) *Infrastructure Financing Instruments and Incentives* (Paris: OECD). https://www.oecd.org/finance/private-pensions/Infrastructure-Financing-Instruments-and-Incentives.pdf (accessed 1 February 2022).

OECD (Organisation for Economic Co-operation and Development) (2020) *Green Infrastructure in the Decade for Delivery: Assessing Institutional Investment*. https://www.oecd.org/environment/green-infrastructure-in-the-decade-for-delivery-f51f9256-en.htm (accessed 1 February 2022).

OECD (Organisation for Economic Co-operation and Development) (2020) *OECD/G20 Inclusive Framework on BEPS: Progress Report July 2019–July 2020*. https://www.oecd.org/tax/beps/oecd-g20-inclusive-framework-on-beps-progress-report-july-2019-july-2020.htm (accessed 1 February 2022).

PricewaterhouseCoopers (2020) *Sovereign Investors 2020: A Growing Force*. https://www.pwc.com/gx/en/sovereign-wealth-investment-funds/publications/assets/sovereign-investors-2020.pdf (accessed 1 February 2022).

Son, H. (2019) 'JP Morgan is rolling out the first US bank-backed cryptocurrency to transform payments business', *CNBC*, 14 February. https://www.cnbc.com/2019/02/13/jp-morgan-is-rolling-out-the-first-us-bank-backed-cryptocurrency-to-transform-payments--.html (accessed 1 February 2022).

Stulz, R. M. (1999) 'Globalization of equity markets and the cost of capital', NYSE Working Paper, 99-02, February.

Surendranath R. J., Perry, M. J. and Hemphil, T. A. (2010) 'The role of sovereign wealth funds in global financial intermediation', *Thunderbird International Business Review*, 52 (6), Nov/Dec.

Taskinsoy, J. (2019) 'The transition from barter trade to impediments of the dollar system: one nation, one currency, one monopoly', *SSRN Electronic Journal*, 6 March. https://www.researchgate.net/publication/331559802_The_Transition_from_Barter_Trade_to_Impediments_of_the_Dollar_System_One_Nation_One_Currency_One_Monopoly (accessed 1 February 2022).

Yescombe, E. R. (2014) *Principles of Project Finance*, 2nd edn (Cambridge, MA: Academic Press).

Journals

International Finance: https://onlinelibrary.wiley.com/journal/14682362

International Journal of Finance & Economics: https://onlinelibrary.wiley.com/journal/10991158

Journal of International Finance Studies: https://jifs-journal.org/JIFS-JOURNAL/Default.aspx

Journal of International Financial Markets, Institutions & Money: https://www.journals.elsevier.com/journal-of-international-financial-markets-institutions-and-money

Journal of International Money and Finance: https://www.journals.elsevier.com/journal-of-international-money-and-finance

McKinsey Quarterly: https://www.mckinsey.com/quarterly/overview

Chapter 13

Global human resource management

At the end of the chapter you will be able to:

- Appreciate the trade-offs in establishing a policy of reliance on expatriate global managers versus local ones
- Understand the causes of success and failure of an expatriate policy
- Contribute to the definition of an expatriate policy
- Contribute to plans for developing local management
- Participate in the design of global training programmes
- Understand the new trends on working from anywhere (WFA)

Introduction

The success of global strategies relies on the *quality of the people* who are in charge of their implementation. This chapter addresses four kinds of managerial issues that a global strategy imposes on human resources:

- First, there is a need to adopt a worldwide policy of *international movement of personnel,* differentiating within the pool of managers between those who will follow a 'global' career from those who will follow a 'local' career. This is the *assignment* issue.
- Second, there is a need to *manage the career* of the global managers. This is the *expatriate* management issue.
- Third, there is a need to *recruit and motivate local personnel.* This is the *localization* issue.
- Finally, there is the need to *develop skills* fitted to the requirements of global management. This is the *global skill development* issue.

These issues constitute the structure of this chapter (see Figure 13.1).

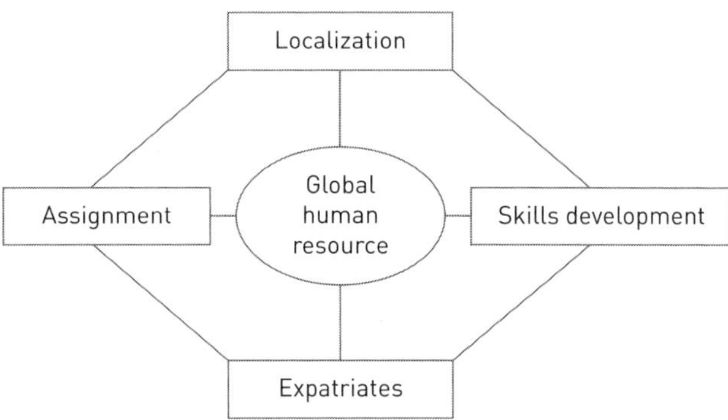

Figure 13.1 Global human resource issues

EXAMPLE 13.1 Appointing a divisional manager in France

Helvetica Chemical is a Swiss-based multinational company engaged in pharmaceuticals, agrochemicals, dyestuffs and industrial chemicals. It operates in more than sixty countries and is organized as a matrix of product and country divisions. The corporate headquarters in Basel is staffed with global central function services establishing and supervising policies in research, IT, legal, personnel and finance. In each country there is a group company managing director responsible for the total activities of local divisional units, and for the overall financial results of the country. Each divisional general manager has dual reporting: to the group company managing director (country head) and to the global division director in Basel responsible for the worldwide performance of the product line.

In France, the group company managing director, Lucien Boyer, was about to retire and the corporate headquarters designated Pierre Jourdan, general manager of the French Pharmaceutical Division, to replace him. Jourdan's promotion opened his own position at the Pharmaceutical Division in France, and the issue was whom to appoint as his replacement. Two potential candidates were identified.

- *Philippe Dupont*, a French national with a doctoral degree in pharmacy from Toulouse University, had been recruited two years previously from a competitor as marketing manager. He had spent his entire career in France and had in-depth experience of the French pharmaceutical industry. Since his recruitment to Helvetica, he had obtained excellent results. Dupont was Jourdan and Boyer's preferred choice.
- *Michel Garnier*, a Canadian from Quebec, who had extensive international experience as a marketing manager in Canada, Brazil and the United States. He had spent two years in Basel at the corporate office in the Strategic Planning Department, and was currently managing the Pharmaceutical Division of Helvetica Chemical in Morocco, where he too had obtained excellent results. Garnier was the preferred choice of the Basel Global Pharmaceutical Division.

Whom to appoint?

Answering this question provoked emotional reactions and very heated debates. For some, it was obvious that Dupont was the best choice, given his knowledge of the French market, his experience and the support of the French management structure. For others, Garnier should be appointed because he would bring a global perspective that could enrich the French subsidiary and position Helvetica Chemical as a true global player capable of transcending national barriers. After the first instinctive reactions, it became obvious that the appointment decision was more than a pure personnel management issue; it was really a *global strategic issue.* In practice, both choices were valid, but each would convey a fundamentally different message to employees, competitors and customers. Whichever candidate was picked, that decision would 'drive' the strategy of the company in a particular dimension.

Dupont was the perfect choice for a strategic orientation based on *local responsiveness.* His French education and experience with the market made him a perfect choice for the French subsidiary. No doubt, he would perform well, and Jourdan would be happy to supervise a colleague with whom he shared the same culture.

Garnier brought a global perspective and his appointment would be an opening into the walled city of a national subsidiary. His international experience would give him the capability to transcend national cultures and to introduce a truly global corporate mindset. From an operational point of view, he would bring different methods and approaches to the French subsidiary.

The final choice depended upon the strategic orientation that Helvetica Chemical wanted to give to its global operation. If, from a competitive viewpoint, there was little advantage to be gained in adopting cross-border integration, and the prime objective was to let local subsidiaries focus on their own market, the choice of Dupont would be the most effective. If, on the contrary, it became strategically important to adopt a worldwide coordinated strategy, then it was time to implement a global human resource management (HRM) approach that fitted with this objective and Garnier would be the recruit of choice.

This example illustrates the four kinds of issue presented in Figure 13.1: assignment of personnel, expatriate management, localization and skills development.

Source: Adapted with permission from the INSEAD case study 'Ciba-Geigy – management development', no. 11/1999-1153 authored by Yves Doz. Copyright © 1999 INSEAD. Revised Version Copyright © 1983 INSEAD.

Assignment of personnel: the global human resource wheel

In terms of personnel, a global company can be represented as a wheel, as in Figure 13.2.

At the centre is the corporate headquarters, where the board of directors and the key executives are located alongside the corporate staff. In many companies, the global business divisions are also located near the corporate headquarters, although this is not always the case.

The outer wheel is made up of the countries in which the company operates. Countries are staffed with three categories of personnel:

- **Local managers and staff** (host-country national, HCN), recruited at subsidiary level (the unshaded part of Figure 13.2). Their career is essentially within the local companies.
- **Global managers** (the shaded area in Figure 13.2). Their career is made up of successive appointments in different countries. Managers in this category are considered 'expatriates', although this terminology is progressively disappearing, to be replaced by the denomination of 'international' or 'global' managers.
- **Temporary assignees** (the arrow in Figure 13.2). These are referred as 'detached' personnel.

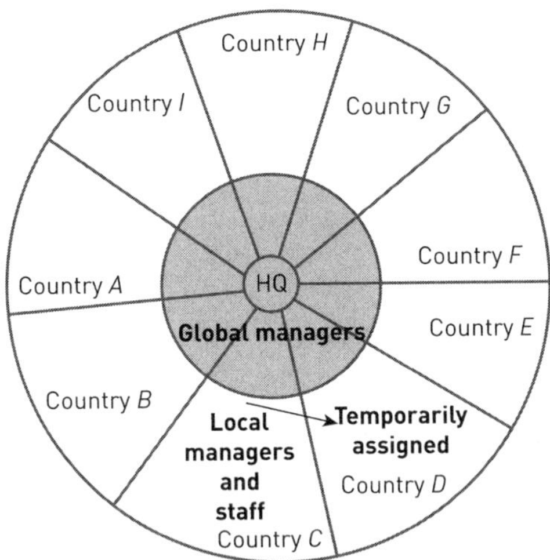

Figure 13.2 The global human resource wheel

The profile of the human resource wheel is not the same in a company that has adopted a global strategic position as in a company that operates in a multi-domestic mode (see Chapter 1). Figure 13.3 shows the difference between the two models. In a multi-domestic organization, global managers are relatively few and mostly from a dominant nationality (that is, the native one of the company). They move from place to place, generally in the most senior positions. Local personnel progress within their own subsidiary, although they may be seconded occasionally to other subsidiaries for technical support or learning purposes. A global organization will see a larger number of multi-cultural, global managers moving around. Those global managers will integrate local personnel aspiring to a global career, and temporary assignments of local personnel to other subsidiaries and to headquarters will be more frequent. Cross-cultural teams generate frequent travel.

Expatriate management

Expatriate personnel are employees living and working in a non-native country. They are often grouped into two categories: parent-country nationals (PCN), whose national origin is the same as that of the corporate headquarters, and third-country nationals (TCN) whose country of origin is different from both the corporate headquarters' and of the host country. An increasing number of TCN over PCN indicates that firms are moving from a traditional international management mode toward a global one (Table 13.1). American and European multinational firms employ a relatively larger number of TCN than Japanese or Korean corporations.

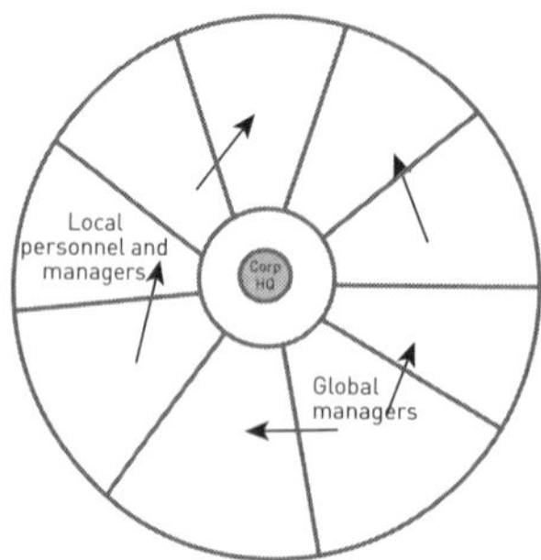

Multi domestic design

Only a few global managers move from subsidiary to subsidiary.
Local personnel have careers in their own countries.
Small corporate HQ.
Some temporary detachments.
Example: Colgate-Palmolive

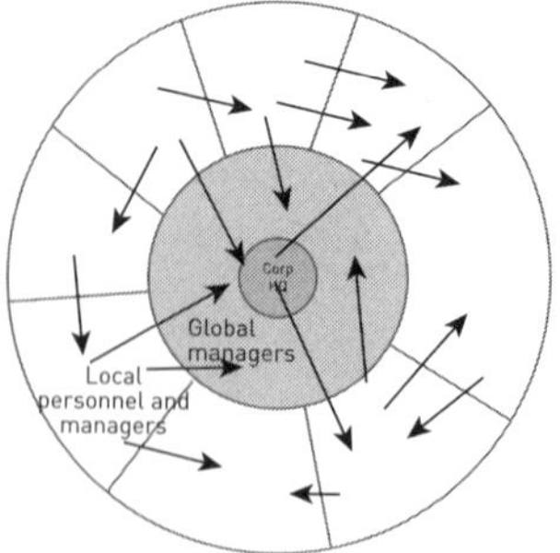

Global design

Many more global managers.
Local personnel have many detachment opportunities and can join the global manager group.
Large corporate HQ.
Example: Shell

Figure 13.3 Human resource wheels

Table 13.1 The changing nature of international staffing

Traditional international staffing The 'expatriate' model	Global staffing The 'global/international personnel' model
• Recruitment essentially from the headquarters home country (PCN) • 'Expatriate' compensation package • Local recruits stay local • Strong 'corporate style' spreads to the subsidiaries • 'Foreign office' type of career: expatriate personnel move from country to country • Performance appraisal based on local performance	• Recruitment from all over the world (TCN + PCN) • More and more local contracts instead of expatriate packages • Possibilities for locals to become global managers • A lot of job rotation • A lot of international management development programmes • Performance appraisals include local plus 'global' or 'regional' achievements

Success and failure of expatriation

Numerous studies have shown that expatriate personnel are confronted with a set of challenges, summarized in Figure 13.4. Rosalie Tung (1987, 1998), Dickmann et al. (2018) and McNulty and Brewster (2020) found that the main causes of failure among US expatriate managers were:

- Inability of the manager to adapt
- Inability of the manager's partner to adapt
- Family-related problems

- Manager's personality or emotional immaturity
- Manager's inability to cope with responsibility
- Manager's lack of technical competence
- Manager's lack of motivation.

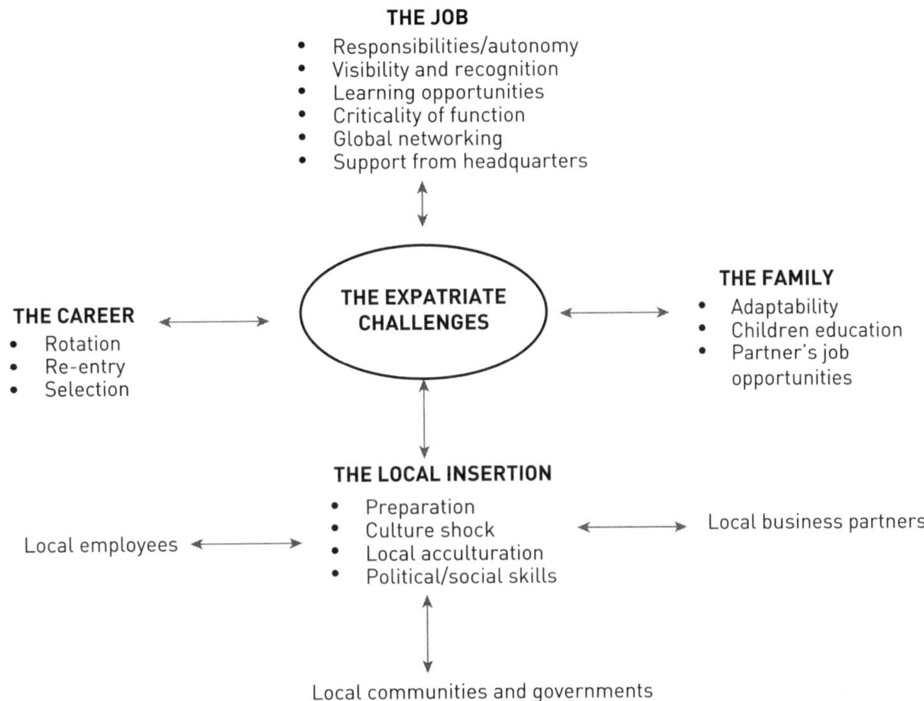

Figure 13.4 The expatriate challenges

Other studies have shown that recognition, understanding and support of cross-border assignments by central colleagues are crucial for the success of expatriation.[1] The research done on the topic all shows that extreme expatriate failure, as measured by the *recall rate* (i.e. the proportion of assigned personnel who fail to complete their predetermined contract) is relatively low (around 5 per cent). However, there are situations in which the assignments are less than satisfactory for both the firm and the individual manager.

Acculturation

Acculturation is the process by which group members from one culture adapt to the culture of a different group.[2] Acculturation can result in four different attitudes – the 'four Fs' described in Figure 13.5:

- The **flight** attitude is adopted by people who want to preserve their own cultural identity and, when confronted with a new environment, prefer to isolate themselves.

- The **fight** attitude bears some similarity to the previous one except that, instead of retreating and isolating themselves, the individual criticizes the host environment; militant expatriates claim the superiority of their own culture.
- The **fit** attitude describes people who are capable of immersing themselves in the local culture and, at the same time, preserving their own culture. They look for contacts with locals, get interested in host-country customs, arts and culture. They have a balanced perspective between global and local competitive requirements: they are 'cosmopolitan'.
- The **follow** attitude indicates excessive willingness to embrace local culture and assimilate oneself in the host environment. Assimilated expatriates progressively lose contact with the global headquarters and perspective, and have difficulty balancing global and local requirements.

Both the flyers and the fighters avoid socializing with the local community and prefer to live in areas solely occupied by expatriates. For the global corporation, these types of personnel lack the flexibility to adapt to local conditions: they may be good at defending the global aspect of business strategies but are poor at local responsiveness.

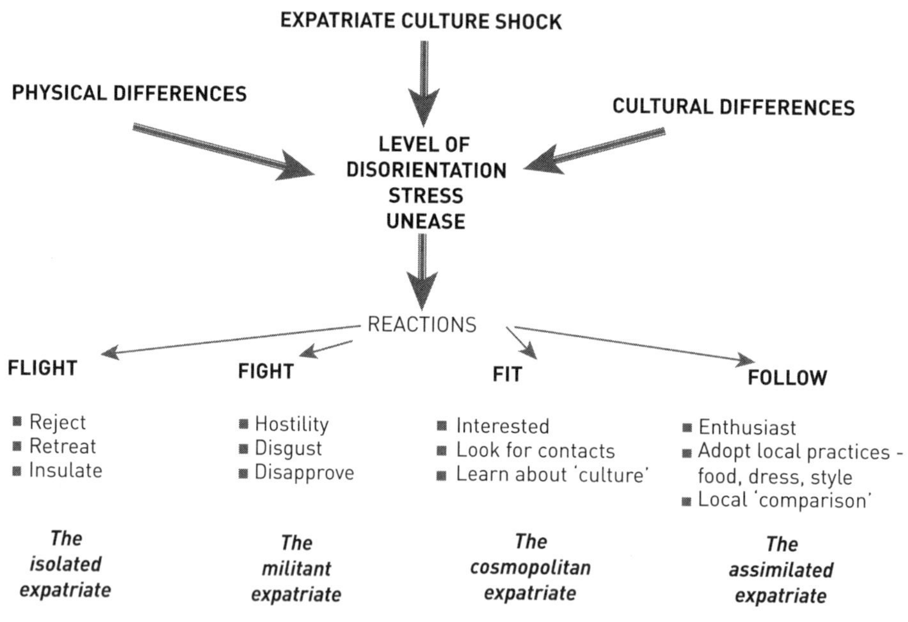

Figure 13.5 Expatriates' acculturation: the 'four Fs'

The expatriate and the company

For the company, the cost of expatriate personnel kicks in at around two to three times the equivalent position in the 'home' country (see Insert 13.1 and Figure 13.7 for cost elements). It is therefore necessary for global firms to put in place a coherent set of policies and practices that optimizes the benefits of expatriation for both the company and the individuals. Such a policy has six major components:

- Strategic vision
- Selection and preparation
- Compensation
- Tenure
- Support
- Career follow-up.

Strategic vision

A **strategic vision** places expatriate assignments within the framework of the company's global strategy. Assignment policies vary according to the global positioning and management style of the company (Dickmann et al. (2018); McNulty and Brewster (2020)). Edstrom and Galbraith (1977) identified three modes of transfer policies:

- **Filling position** – the classic policy of expatriation for key managers and technical support transfer.
- **Develop manager** – a policy designed to utilize international postings as an instrument for developing management talents and skills.
- **Develop organization** – a policy that embraces the 'transnational' management philosophy by which people move around in order to develop products and lead marketing campaigns with a view to developing the global strategic capabilities of the company.

A company of the 'multi-domestic' type from Figure 13.3 will focus more on the 'filling position' policy, while companies of the 'global' type will use the three policies conjointly. James Stewart Black and Hal Gregersen (1999) researched the management of expatriates at about 750 US, European and Japanese companies in the 1990s and one of their key conclusions was that: 'When making international assignments, companies should focus on knowledge creation and global leadership development.' In conclusion: global companies consider the worldwide movement of personnel as a tool to enhance their competitiveness through *knowledge transfer* and leverage of *cross-cultural richness.*

Selection and preparation

The **selection of expatriates** is a function of individual skills as well as the technical and competitive requirements of the company. Black and Gregersen conclude that: 'Successful companies assign overseas posts to people whose technical skills are matched or exceeded by their cross-cultural abilities.'[3]

Expatriates are required to exhibit what is referred to as *contextual intelligence* skills[4] that are primarily *sociocultural.* Figure 13.6 shows the ranking of skills that managers in Asia Pacific consider conducive to success.

Another study conducted by Günter Stahl on German managers (2001) revealed that seven factors were critical to success in international work assignments:

- **Tolerance of ambiguity:** the ability to function effectively in a foreign environment where expatriates experience ambiguity, complexity and uncertainty.
- **Behavioural flexibility:** the capacity to vary your behaviour according to the immediate requirements of the situation and the demands of the foreign culture.
- **Goal orientation:** the ability and desire to achieve your task goals despite barriers, opposition and discouragement.
- **Sociability and interest in other people:** a willingness to establish and maintain meaningful social relationships, combined with a genuine interest in people.
- **Empathy:** the capacity to accurately sense other people's thoughts, feelings and motives, and to respond to them appropriately.
- **Ability to be non-judgemental:** the willingness to critically re-examine your own values and beliefs, and to avoid judging other people by your own norms.
- **Meta-communication skills:** the capacity to clarify culturally different perceptions and to 'guide' the intercultural communication process.

The preparation of assignments involves several steps. First, and most importantly, international assignments must be part of a *career plan,* and the objectives of the assignment have to be clearly defined. If the assignment is only intended to 'fill a post', it is probably a one-off event and the expatriate

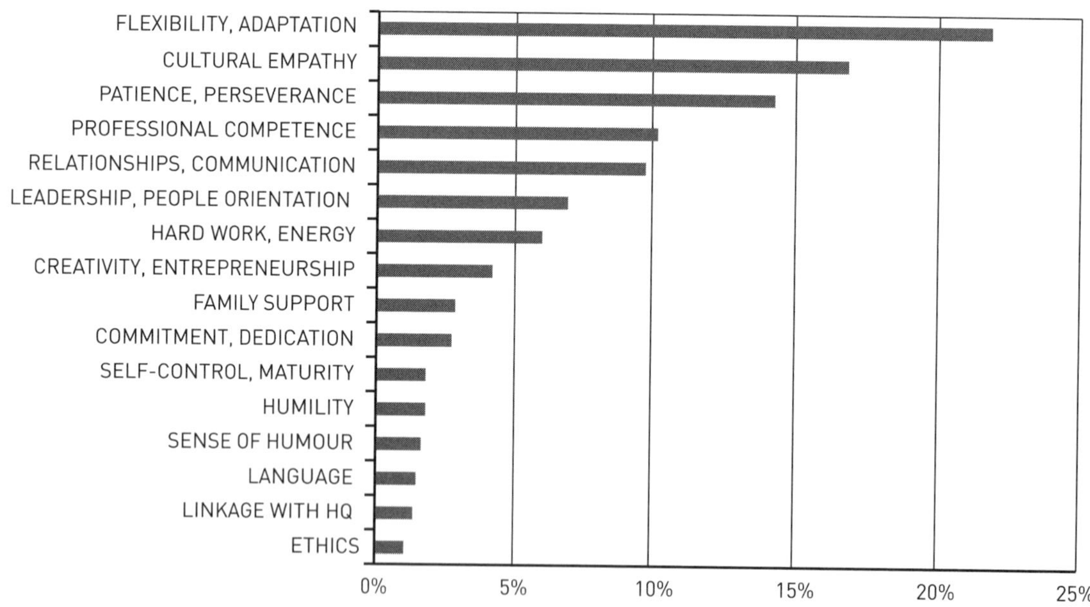

Figure 13.6 The primary ingredients of individual managerial behaviour required for success in expatriate assignments in Asia

Note: *The percentage is obtained by ranking how often these traits were selected in response to the question: 'What do you consider to be the three most important factors for success?'*

Source: Authors', from an unpublished internal report (Lasserre et al. 1997).

will be much more concerned about their future after the expatriation (a classic 're-entry problem') than about understanding the intricacies of the foreign environment. They, and their family, need to be informed about and prepared for the specific differences in living conditions and culture, but the primary concern remains the 're-entry'. If the assignment is a step in an 'international' career, the person should have a 'mapping' of their future career development path. Specific research about the foreign environment is necessary but, over the years and cumulative assignments, this aspect becomes relatively less important since the international manager 'learns to learn' when in place.

The second, perhaps rather obvious, step is *cultural and logistical preparation* for the employee and the family. Numerous organizations provide cultural training,[5] and most companies subscribe to them. They usually provide a pre-assignment trip for the expatriate and their family in order to have first-hand experience of living conditions. Some companies use short-term assignments or 'missions' of several weeks to immerse the future expatriate into the real working conditions.

Assessment centres are the third and probably the least-used step in assignment preparation. This consists of measuring the future expatriate's skills alongside certain predetermined dimensions that are considered important for the job and the country, and according to the results, tailoring a certain number of specific programmes designed to repair any deficiencies. DaimlerChrysler Aerospace ran such a programme named QUICK.[6]

Compensation

Classic expatriate contracts involve a series of clauses that, in addition to the normal remuneration attached to the job, are designed to compensate for the difference in living conditions and prices, the obligation for the person/family to change accommodation, pension systems, health insurance, schooling and cost of living, as well as any additional economic impacts on the family. Generally, a 'hardship' allowance is also granted in the case of countries that have a significant deficit in security, infrastructure or social/political context. Insert 13.1 shows two types of typical expatriate package. Figure 13.7 compares the cost of living in various cities of the world. An expatriate in Tokyo whose salary is based on New York living standards could expect to have the living standard component of their salary adjusted by 9 per cent if the rent is paid by the company. In most cases, housing and children's education are paid for by the company. Alternatively, if the same person were based in Johannesburg where the cost of living is 52 per cent that of New York, she/he would probably not receive compensation for cost of living (salary would not be reduced) but probably would receive a hardship allowance.

Tenure

The length of expatriate assignments in a given country is a function of four key factors:

- The time needed to *learn the local rules of business* and to *build relationships* with the various parties (customers, employees, government officials, partners etc.) with whom the person needs to interact.
- The importance of personal relationships in the job and the required *continuity* of the task (the task of building a new business requires more time than, for instance, setting up a factory).
- The *contextual hardship* of the country (difficult living conditions).
- The company's policy with regard to *career development*.

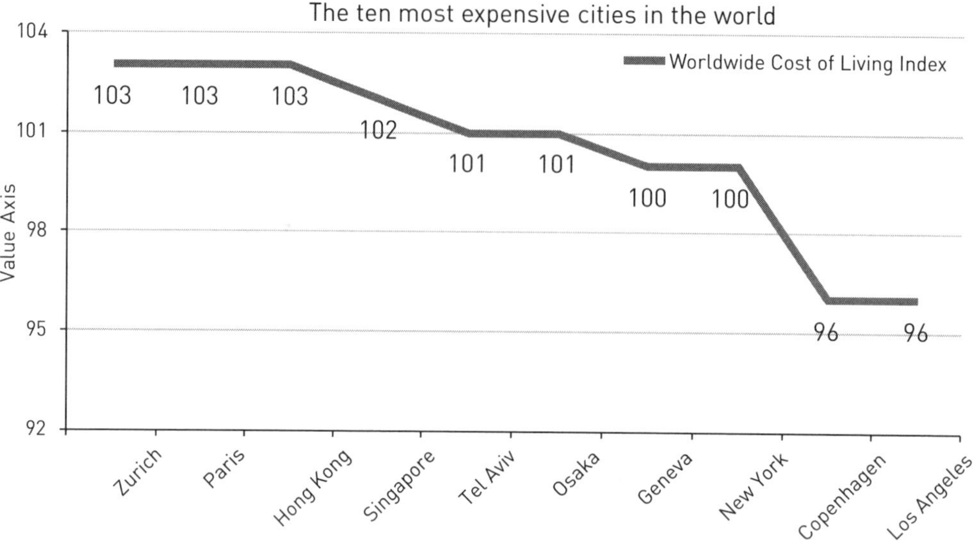

Figure 13.7 Selected indices of cost of living excluding rent

Note: *base = 100 for New York in 2020 taking into account the impact of Covid-19 pandemic.*

Source: Economist Intelligence Unit (2020).

Insert 13.1 Typical expatriate packages

There are two major types of package:

Home-based package: Employees receive compensation that is equivalent to what they would have received in their home country. In this case the adjustments are mentioned clearly in addition to the base salary. The legal contractual relationship stays in the home country.

Local-based package: Employees receive compensation in line with the compensation of equivalent jobs in the host country with some adjustment. In that case the adjustments are incorporated into the base salary (for instance, the salary would be increased to take into account the cost of living difference without being mentioned separately). The legal contractual relationship is in the host country; the legal contract with the home organization is suspended during the assignment tenure.

The packages may take into consideration the following adjustments:

Accommodation: Allowance to rent a house or apartment in the host country considering the local real estate market.

Car: In addition to a company car the expatriate family can be bought a car by the company or a fixed allowance can be added to the compensation.

Education: Allowance to cover tuition fees in international schools or local schools accepting foreign students. That allowance also may apply to universities.

Compensation for home residential expenses: Compensation for rental fees in the home country when the expatriate keeps their rental agreement.

Cost of living adjustment: Additional compensation to cover for the differences in cost of goods and services in the host country. Generally applied in one direction: if the cost of living is higher in the host country the allowance is granted but if the cost of living is lower there is no negative allowance. The issue for cost of living allowance is the evaluation of the host country's costs: whether it is considered that the expatriate lives like a local person (buys goods at local markets, for instance) or lives as in his/her home country (shops in expensive supermarkets).

Cultural and language training: Payment of tuition fees for language training and cultural training.

Hardship allowance: Allowance given to compensate for living in countries considered to be dangerous or subject to hard living situations such as climatic conditions or remote locations.

Health protection: The company covers health insurance and repatriation expenses in case of serious health problems, accidents or urgent or sophisticated treatment.

Installation: Company sources cover costs of moving and settling in, and of decorating the local accommodation.

Local employees: Payment of salary for servants, gardener, driver, nurses, if justified.

Pre-assignment visit: One or two trips organized and paid by the company for the family to visit the future host country.

Retirement: Pension plans are kept at a similar level to those in the home country. For instance, benefit-based retirement plans may be replaced by the equivalent capital-based allowance or vice versa.

Spouse assistance: A job may be provided locally for the spouse or the company may help the spouse to find a local job.

Taxes: Several solutions may apply: a) the company pays the local taxes in full; b) the company pays the local taxes but calculates what should be the normal tax rate in the home country and adjusts for the difference.

Trips for vacation: The company pays for the family trip to the home country for vacations at a predetermined frequency for a given airline class. In case of harsh environments, vacation trips may be provided at more frequent intervals.

Sources: *U.S. Expatriate Handbook: Guide to Living & Working Abroad* (West Virginia University, 2007); *Making Choices: The Expatriate Package*. RH Expat (2010); Expatica Communications B.V. (2010), http://www.expatica.com; plus authors' own research.

Given that in most cases acculturation – the process of getting acquainted with the other culture – takes three–twelve months, and that a managerial job requires at least two years to show meaningful results, a 'normal' expatriate assignment should last at least three years for non-technical jobs. The classic trade-off for determining optimal tenure is shown in Figure 13.8. The *local impact* of the expatriate, in terms of business results, is represented by curve *A*: it is a logistic function with a negative contribution during the learning period (acculturation). It progresses rapidly and then peaks when the person is in full control of the job.

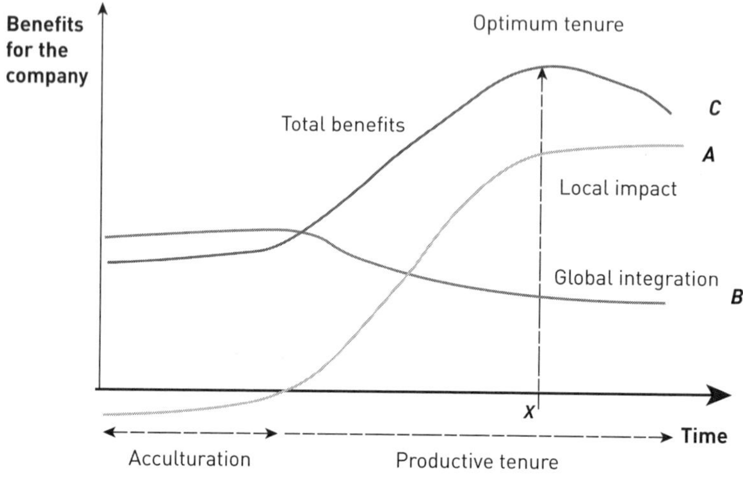

Figure 13.8 Expatriate tenure

Curve *B* in Figure 13.8 represents the *benefits of integration* for the expatriate – that is, being in tune with the overall culture of the company, its core values and competencies that are shared across the world. Over time, if the expatriate becomes rooted in the local specificities, the risk is high that they will lose the *global spirit* and become *localized.* The combination of the *A* and *B* curves is given by curve *C*, showing an optimum benefit for the company at time *X* that would theoretically be when the assignment finishes. As indicated earlier, several factors affect the shape of the curves: if the acculturation is difficult and the relationships with customers are important, curve *A* moves to the right, making the optimum assignment period much longer.

Support

The overwhelming empirical evidence coming from studies on expatriation shows that success is very closely correlated with the support and understanding coming from the parent company from which the person is detached. Support can take numerous forms, but it is the *psychological contact* – the feeling that you are not 'forgotten' or 'marginalized' – that matters the most. Some companies have put in place a process of **'mentoring'** by which a manager at 'headquarters' is in charge of regular communication with an expatriate about personal/career issues. Companies' internal communications should devote a large part of their editorial content to events in world subsidiaries. Visits of key executives should not only include 'business' meetings but also informal dialogues with the detached personnel. In broad terms, expatriate personnel should have the feeling that their assignment is important for the company. Figure 13.9 shows various practices that provide support to expatriation.

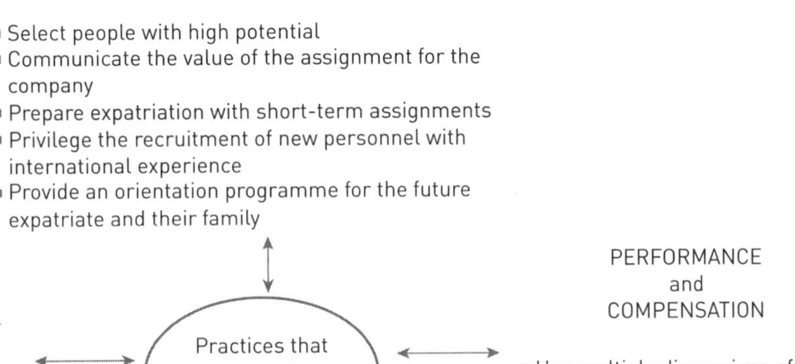

Figure 13.9 Human resources practices supporting expatriation
Source: Authors' own, derived from text in Evans et al. (2011).

Career follow-up

Traditionally, the career follow-up issue has been known as the *repatriation* problem. At the end of the assignment, the expatriate is concerned about finding a job at the parent company corresponding to their skills and performances. The repatriation problem assumes that the person is going to return to the 'home country'. This is the case for temporarily assigned personnel but is less probable in the global management context described in Figure 13.3 as the 'global design', where international managers move from position to position within the worldwide corporate network.

Both 'returning home' and 'going elsewhere', however, require from the company a *proactive international career management process.* In research conducted by Black and Gregersen (1999), it was found that 25 per cent of professionals returning from overseas assignments subsequently left the company because of a lack of job opportunities. The accumulated experience lost by such attrition is considerable. Companies such as Monsanto begin to prepare the employee for their return or next assignment at least six months before the end of the current placement: it involves the expatriate, human resources management and the line manager to whom the person reports. The returning employee indicates their preferences, the line managers and HR department monitor potential job openings during the coming year as well as assessing the returner's skills and knowledge. They propose several alternatives, generally including additional training in preparation for the next job.

Alternative forms of expatriation

Despite the fact that long-term assignments are still used extensively by global firms,[7] other forms of international assignments are increasingly common. These are:[8]

- *Short-term assignments*: more than a business trip and less than a year. This is used for specific problem-solving or control issues, to cover a person who is hospitalized or for management development purposes.
- *Commuter assignment*: the person commutes every week to another country. This can be quite frequent when time zone differences and transport duration are not significantly high.
- *Virtual teams*: a manager is in charge of a dispersed team. They do not commute often but uses internet and video conferencing. Although this practice was still relatively limited before the Covid-19 pandemic, it has been intensely used (and sometimes exclusively during lockdown periods) in global corporations.

According to KPMG (2020), 'there is a trend for long-term or standard expatriation (e.g. one–five years) to decrease while an increase of short term (e.g. less than twelve months), commuter (fly-in, fly-out and cross border) and permanent transfers' has been observed.[9]

The Covid-19 pandemic that struck in 2020 led to more people working from home as country lockdowns became a common occurrence to curb the virus spread. Global mobility decreased as borders were closed and entire countries were isolated for weeks and months. Business travel was avoided and video conferencing became the norm for many home workers.

Virtual assignments vs relocation

With more people working from home and developments in video conferencing technologies, employees are no longer required to relocate whilst working on international projects. Although frequent business trips may create issues similar to those when an assignee is relocated for the duration of the project, for example, tracking immigration laws, tax, social security and labour law regulations. For example, in 2020 Google asked 30 per cent of its 7,000 Ireland-based staff who had left the country to work remotely to return to Ireland due to tax and legal issues.[10]

Virtual assignments may differ to business travel in terms of cost allocation or how it is charged within the organization. An assignee's costs are often charged to the central project team and can have taxability implications for the employee and for the employer in payroll. Compliance can be triggered in the country where the employee usually lives and works despite not being the work location. It can lead to confusion for the employer with regards to tax, payroll tax and timings, while the employee may find calculating their net pay complex. The employee may need to apply for tax reimbursement and require support.

Although virtual assignments may appear easier and cheaper than relocation, they might well be more complex and incur other costs to those of relocating.

Destination challenges

Many issues should be considered, by both the employer and employee, before relocating. In 2020, the USA was considered the most challenging destination, followed by China and India. Brexit resulted in the UK, becoming a more difficult destination for relocation, especially for workers from the EU.

According to the *Santa Fe Repurpose Challenging Change Report 2020/21 on relocation*, the most challenging factors for employees are culture (38 per cent) and language (34 per cent). Support or preparation for the employees by the organization is key but often lacking. Now, more than ever, due to the Covid-19 pandemic, tracking employees is crucial. Immigration complications are also important in destination desirability (30 per cent). Global mobility professionals have always dealt with the complex issues of immigration but with the current changes in border rules, due to Covid-19, it is even more challenging.

All the different facets of relocation need to be considered to optimize cost. Tax costs represent on average 43 per cent of total expenditure (gross up taxes due on net compensation and employer social security costs) with the average gross up tax rate at 63 per cent. Tax planning is therefore key in reducing costs; knowing what is and is not taxable. Employer social security charges range from 36.8 per cent in Brazil to 0 per cent in UAE. Different agreements between countries affect costs massively depending on where social security costs are payable.

The future of global mobility

The 1980s and 1990s are considered by global mobility professionals as the 'golden years' with more predictable patterns of mobility. By the 2000s, global commerce became more complicated and so did the deployment of international talent, be it through business trips, short-term secondments, commuter or long-term arrangements.

The fourth industrial revolution led to organizational restructuring and transforming the way people interact. Online sales and home delivery increased further in 2020 when the Covid-19 pandemic hit the world. Retail giants looked to transform their businesses with a portfolio that balanced virtual sales with traditional, physical trading activities. Technology also affected the global mobility industry with services and solutions requiring a tailor-made approach, according to the organization's purpose, preferences and people. For example, in language/cultural prepping for employees, shipment of household goods or pre-move visits. Experts believe that although technology appears to be an alternative to relocation, there will be a mix of virtual and physical support for international assignments – technology cannot replace it totally.[11]

Support mechanisms have developed from those in the 1980s and 1990s when relocation companies often worked in silos. These businesses have sophisticated global, regional and local mobility supply chain partners who can deliver bespoke or integrated relocation and assignment management solutions. This means HR and global mobility teams can streamline communications and collaboration with human and digital processes and methods.

The Covid-19 pandemic without doubt has had a significant impact on global mobility, yet other risks including cyber-attacks, climate change, war, terrorism and the economic climate also affect the way people work. Given these factors, global mobility practitioners need to invest time in analysis and mitigation.

Source: Santa Fe Repurpose Challenging Change Report 2020/21 on relocation.

Table 13.2 Eight global trends for global mobility 2021 according to KPMG

Technology	Fully integrated technology solution that covers the whole spectrum of mobility
Talent not transactions	Focus on providing a great employee experience – outsourcing high-volume complex transactions such as tax, payroll, compensation, etc.
Work anywhere	Remote workforces created almost overnight
Legacy mobility types are shifting quickly	Traditional international assignee ('expat') replaced by short-term and commuting assignments and permanent transfers
Flexible solutions	Solutions need to be agile and accommodate different employee levels, needs and types
Managed moves are back on the upswing	Companies looking to be the most competitive in finding talent are willing to pay for managed moves
Immigration hurdles	Immigration has become a roadblock to mobility and many companies are reassessing their compliance risk tolerance as a result
Data and analytics	Seeking less data and more insight that is critical in 'telling the mobility story'

Source: https://home.kpmg/xx/en/home/insights/2016/04/global-assignment-policies-and-practices-survey.html?cid=van_gappsurvey-sx_xx-acx_tax-gappsurvey (accessed 1 February 2022).

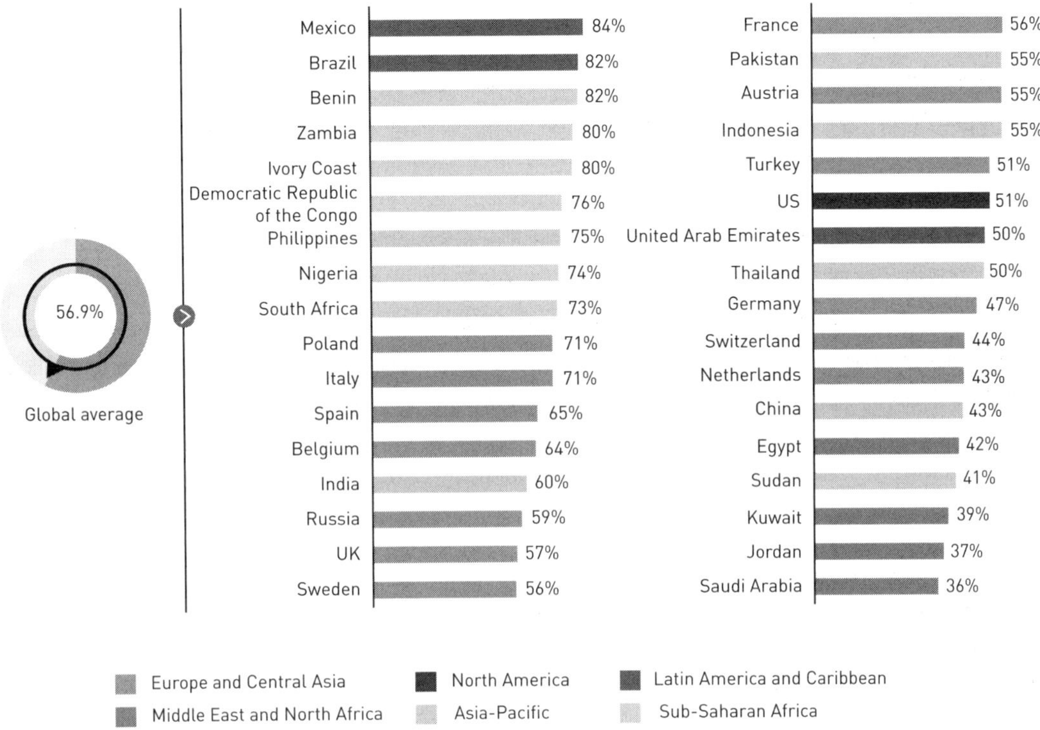

Figure 13.10 Percentage of respondents who would work remotely for an employer with no physical presence in their country

Note: *Countries displayed are the top thirty by either GDP or working population, or the top and bottom five outliers in percentage of respondents who would work for an international remote employer.*

Source: BCG, Decoding Global Talent, Onsite and Virtual, March 2021, https://www.bcg.com/publications/2021/virtual-mobility-in-the-global-workforce (accessed 26 January 2022).

Localization

Although expatriate personnel serve as vital links of communication and knowledge transfer in the network of worldwide business units, the long-term competitiveness of global firms relies more and more on the contribution and loyalty of *locally recruited personnel* (*host-country nationals*). Some studies suggest that the proportion of senior expatriates in global companies in the BRIC countries and in the Middle East declined by as much as 56 per cent to 12 per cent from the 1990s to the 2000s.[12]

- Local personnel play different important roles such as *cultural interpreters*, *communication facilitators*, *information resource brokers*, *talent developers* and *change partners*.[13] Localization of managers and staff helps global companies to 'break the language barrier' (literally and culturally) and develop the intricate network of personal and business contacts needed to build and consolidate a presence in the various countries. In China, for instance, the building of relationships (*guanxi*) is still recognized as a major requirement for conducting a business venture.[14] While expatriate managers may be able to build good contacts at senior levels, local managers can gain access to critical relationships, particularly among the medium- and low-level echelons of government and company hierarchies.

- Modern business development also demands a large quantity of talent that the pool of international managers alone cannot satisfy. A fast-moving consumer goods (FMCG) company found that, in order to maintain leadership in China, it had to recruit 2,500 local salespeople over a period of five years.[15]
- Localization is part of an overall global HR strategy, the aim of which is to attract talent everywhere in the world that the company operates, making the motto 'think globally, act locally' a reality.
- In some cases, localization is perceived by the authorities of emerging nations as a demonstration of the foreign enterprise's commitment to the country. Although in some cases government officials prefer to deal with high-ranking senior expatriates because of their greater decision-making power, they appreciate that below the very top jobs, foreign enterprises will increasingly be managed by local nationals. Localization is therefore an important way of developing beneficial goodwill.
- Localization reduces expatriate costs.

The main managerial issues in localization are in recruitment, retention and career management and performance evaluation, reward practices and cultural differences.

Talent also plays a part in deciding on location and has become a competitive factor. The Global Talent Competitiveness Index described below studies talent in different economies.

The Global Talent Competitiveness Index (GTCI)

The Global Talent Competitiveness Index (GTCI) was first published in 2013 as an action tool for continuous improvement in connecting talent to economic development. As talent has become increasingly important for wealth, the GTCI created an instrument for stimulating discourse between governments, academia, businesses and their associations, and citizens.

The GTCI model continues to evolve, covering national and organizational parameters. It generates insights that inspire action. The Index for 2020, published by INSEAD, in partnership with Adecco Group and Google, included 70 variables covering 132 national economies, across all groups of income and levels of development. It was a composite index, that relied on a simple but robust Input–Output model, composed of six pillars (see Figure 13.11). The seventh edition addressed the theme of 'Global Talent in the Age of Artificial Intelligence' exploring how the development of artificial intelligence (AI) is changing the nature of work and forcing a re-evaluation of workplace practices, corporate structures and innovation ecosystems. It showed that the gap between talent champions (almost all of them high-income countries) and the rest of the world is widening. It also concluded that turning AI into a force for good requires a proactive, cooperative approach. Introducing AI to organizations, communities or societies as a whole requires acceptability as a condition for sustainability. AI could be an opportunity for emerging countries to leapfrog. Reskilling the workforce is required as AI emerges in the workplace.

In 2018, the report 'Talent and 'Technology' examined how automation would influence the future of work. This was followed in 2019 by the report 'Entrepreneurial talent and global competitiveness' which attempted to identify the ways in which large and small firms, nations and cities could foster entrepreneurial talent in the era of digital transformation. In 2020, the report 'Global talent in the age of Artificial Intelligence' followed the path initially explored by the GTCI 2017 theme of Talent and Technology. The 2021 report 'Talent competitiveness in times of Covid' describes the ways in which the pandemic has changed the local and global talent scene.[16]

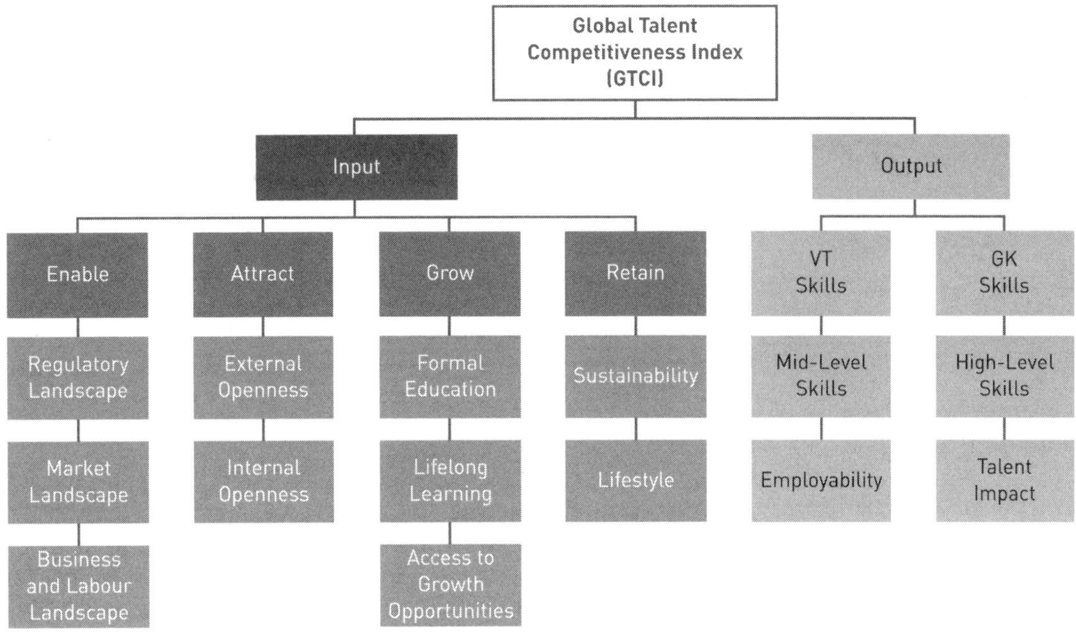

Figure 13.11 The Global Talent Competitiveness Index (GTCI) model
Source: GTCI (2021).

Table 13.3 Top twenty countries

COUNTRY	GTCI RANKING
Switzerland	1
Singapore	2
United States	3
Denmark	4
Sweden	5
Netherlands	6
Finland	7

Luxembourg	8
Norway	9
Iceland	10
Australia	11
United Kingdom	12
Canada	13
Germany	14
New Zealand	15
Ireland	16
Belgium	17
Austria	18
France	19
Japan	20

Source: GTCI (2021).

Recruitment, retention and career management

In some countries foreign firms are perceived favourably by the job market, but not in all. Japan and South Korea have traditionally been places where graduates from leading universities and institutions have shown a marked preference for domestic firms. As a consequence, the talent pool for foreign firms has been shallow and they have suffered a competitive disadvantage in recruitment. In fast-growing emerging countries such as China, the demand for skilled personnel far outpaced the supply, creating an unhealthy bidding process, and a high turnover rate. The global companies' ability to increase local recruitment depends on three main factors:

- The *image of the company*: firms with well-known branded products are better placed than unknown ones. The latter have to promote themselves by making presentations at universities, giving scholarships, contributing to good causes and engaging in public relations, such as the sponsoring of sporting events or academic contests at schools and universities.
- The *career prospects and training opportunities*. Firms that have a reputation of offering good development opportunities will be in a better position to recruit.
- A good understanding of *local qualifications and the education system*. Not all countries have the same technical and higher-education systems. A simplistic projection of the US undergraduate/graduate system onto the local model may overlook the best graduates in Germany, France or Japan. In Germany and Japan, enterprises compensate for the highly theoretical academic orientation of the school system by organizing on-the-job training. In France, the best graduate schools are not part of the university system at all.

Financial incentives have to be in line with normal practices – it is illusory to think that overpaying on salaries will ultimately produce a higher retention rate. The loyalty of local personnel to a global firm will be based more on career prospects and a subjective assessment of 'fair treatment' than on pure financial compensation. *Fair treatment* is the perception that local employees receive equal treatment to expatriates of a comparable level, and that their career prospects are not limited by a *glass ceiling.* 'Fair treatment' thus implies:

- The ability for local personnel to be able to join the group of 'global managers' if they have the competence and the desire
- Equal opportunities for development (training and career)
- Compensation based on the principle of 'equal job, equal pay' (expatriates' compensation for relocation excluded)
- Comparable involvement of local personnel and expatriates in information-sharing, meetings and decision-making sessions. Local personnel should not get the feeling that they are being excluded from important matters.

Performance evaluation, reward practices and cultural differences

The main difficulty in implementing global HRM practices is the need to align performance evaluation and reward processes with cultural differences. A global firm would prefer a standardized approach that fosters the diffusion of a common corporate culture and values as well as facilitating cross-border transfer of personnel. Recent studies suggest that more companies are adopting a globally standardized approach[17] but at the same time trying to adapt it to local conditions through a process of 'hybridization'.[18] Because of cultural differences, standard processes may not have the desired unifying impact and their implementation can be ineffective. In Asia, for instance, the most pronounced cultural divergences are found in four domains:

- *Giving and receiving feedback.* Most Western performance evaluation processes are based on the assumption that objective, open feedback between supervisors and employees is desirable. East Asian cultures have difficulty in accepting these assumptions. These are 'high context' cultures,[19] meaning that it is difficult to untangle the extent to which performance is due to the individual or to their situation. In addition, feedback only goes one way: employees do not challenge their boss. Therefore, any 'unjust' judgement is not openly discussed, allowing the supervisor to think that the judgement has been 'accepted'; this may generate frustration and resentment, and even covert dissident behaviour from the employee.
- *Individual versus group performance.* As mentioned in previous chapters, most non-Western cultures place a higher importance on group belonging and assimilation than on individualism. Too great a focus on individual performance may encourage perceptions of favouritism, and ultimately induce group resistance or sabotage of management policies.
- *System-led versus personalized evaluation processes.* In the Asia Pacific region, loyalty is often to a person or a group (clan) rather than to an organization. Neutral, mechanical systems based on numerical ranking and statistical distributions are not well understood. People prefer to be appreciated and evaluated by their supervisors through a holistic rather than an analytic approach.

- *Social impact of rewards or sanctions (importance of saving face).* Rewards and sanctions not only affect individuals in their private life but also affect their standing in their community, hence the importance of saving face: receiving blame in front of colleagues is considered unacceptable.

The dilemma is obvious: how can a company manage globally and still take into account the many cultural specificities of the countries in which it operates? There is no single answer to this, but the examples of leading global firms such as Hewlett-Packard, IBM, Unilever, ABB and Shell indicate that the progressive reinforcement of a strong corporate culture through education and career management gradually fosters a worldwide acceptance of common practices.

An example of localization within an overall framework is given in Example 13.2.

EXAMPLE 13.2 ABB's localization programme in China in the late 1990s

Asea Brown Boveri (ABB) had 15 joint ventures and 8 representative offices in China in early 1997, and employed a total of 80 expatriate managers. The company reckoned that by 2000 it would have 25 joint ventures, and its number of expatriate managers would then have ballooned to 250. If, on average, an expatriate manager cost an additional $200,000–300,000 per year on top of their normal salary, 250 expatriate managers would increase the compensation bill by more than $50 million per year.

The company set up a 'localization of management committee' with the intention of staffing its middle-management positions locally within three years and its top management positions within five years. To show the company's commitment to the goal, its vice-president of human resources for China sat on the committee as chairman. The committee, among other things, had the key task of identifying high-potential candidates among its China operations, and ensuring that these candidates received the necessary training and demonstrated good communication with the operating units. More importantly, the company explicitly required its expatriate managers to set targets of localization in their operations. Although ABB understood that expatriate managers were under pressure to meet short-term business goals, top management thought that the development of local managers was a long-term strategic concern and should be given priority. The expatriate managers were thus assessed not just on their business performance, but also on their ability to develop local managers. ABB believed that management must continuously scout for, identify and keep track of internal talent. High-potential staff at ABB were identified through a performance appraisal system. Then they were prepared for higher positions or greater responsibility by providing them with the necessary training and promoting them to more challenging positions as early as possible. Upper-level managers were also instructed to support and coach newly promoted managers. The company reported potential local managers to its corporate headquarters in Zurich.

Although most companies embraced the goal of localization of managers and tried to implement it, ABB went one step further by systematically collecting and reporting data to monitor local performance. Its HR department in the Beijing holding company had to provide management with a monthly report which detailed the development of HR in the company, such as the training and promotion of local staff, and also positions available in the company. It also had to complete a monthly international expatriate assignment form, explaining to its regional headquarters why certain positions were filled by expatriates rather than by local Chinese. This reporting system provided feedback on how well the company was implementing its goal, and also served as a reminder of the pace and urgency of the localization programme.

ABB achieved some tangible success with this programme. At its China holding company in early 1997, there were three local Chinese divisional managers (compared with none a year earlier), five local Chinese departmental managers and twenty local Chinese segmental managers.

At its joint ventures, the company in 1997 had nearly 100 local Chinese divisional managers, departmental managers and section managers. By 2000, it had only 70 expatriate managers instead of the projected 250.

Source: Lasserre and Ching (1997). Adapted with permission from Linda Lim at the University of Michigan.

Complying with regulations

Labour markets are regulated. The aspects of employment that are subject to the most regulations are:

- The contractual terms and elements of employment
  - Fixed versus undefined terms. The use of fixed contracts can be limited or prohibited for permanent functions
  - The maximum working days per week and the number of hours per day that are allowed
  - The conditions and restrictions of night work
  - The minimum wage
  - The premium for overtime
  - The minimum age of employment
  - Gender and race discrimination in employment
  - Holidays and paid leave
  - Retirement schemes
  - Healthcare contribution
- The firing process
  - Termination conditions
  - Legal recourse
  - Severance pay
- Employees' rights institutions
  - Trade union rights
  - Representation of personnel
  - Employment tribunals.

The International Labour Organization (ILO), the World Bank, the United Nations, the World Economic Forum and the World Federation of Trade Unions, amongst other bodies, give some useful information concerning variations in labour regulations. Figure 13.12 illustrates the countries located at both extremes of employment regulation (the most and least tightly regulated). Insert 13.2 is an illustration of the difficulties in global human resource management.

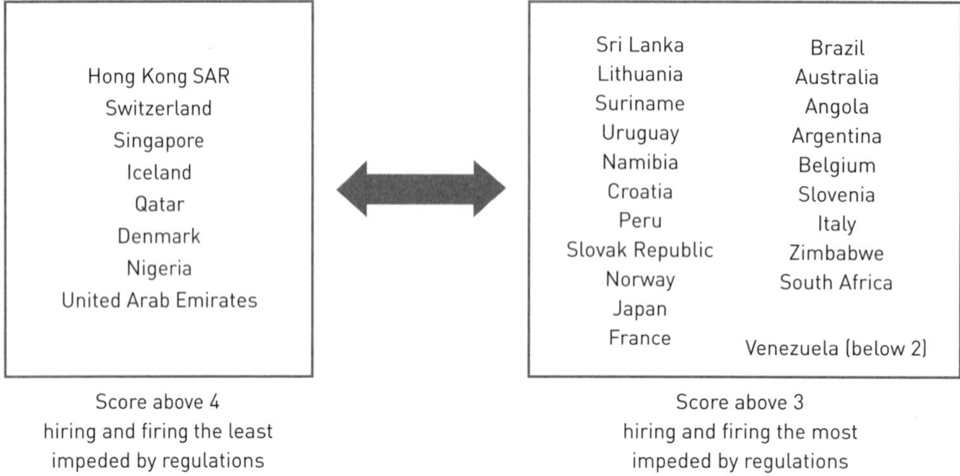

Figure 13.12 Hiring and firing practices

Note: *Scores in reply to survey question: 'Hiring and firing of workers is … 1 = impeded by regulations, 7 = flexibly determined by employers.'*

Source: Authors' own figure, based on data from the Global Competitiveness Index Historical Dataset © 2005–2014 World Economic Forum.

Insert 13.2 The Polish plumber

The idea of the cheap 'Polish plumber' has long been a much-discussed and divisive figure in the EU debate – and he became especially important in 2005 when the French public were called upon to vote in a referendum on a newly drafted European constitutional treaty. Opponents of the treaty argued that if it were to be adopted, workers from Eastern Europe could come and work in France for less than the minimum wage that French law demanded for French nationals and would not pay the social security charges that are applied to French workers. The result would be a severe loss of employment for French people. A similar argument – the threat to British jobs posed by cheap labour from other EU states – was one of those most often used in the UK in 2016 by 'Leave' supporters in the referendum on European Union membership (the so-called *Brexit* decision). In both cases the same reaction happened; the French voted 'No' to the treaty and the British said 'Yes' to Brexit. The 'Polish plumber' is now a mythical figure who represents anti-globalization sentiment as well as an illustration of the difficulties that a global company may encounter in the global management of its workforce.

Skills development

Global managers' required skills are based on a combination of the *organizational roles* they have to fulfil and some key *individual characteristics*.

Roles

Bartlett and Ghoshal (1992) have identified three main roles for the global manager:[20]

- Business managers operate in global business units and 'further global scale efficiency and competitiveness'. Their task 'requires not only the perspectives to recognize opportunities and risks across national and functional boundaries but also the skills to coordinate activities and link capabilities across those barriers'. This demands a combination of *strategic thinking*, *organizational design*, *resource allocation* and *coordination.*
- Country managers operate in local subsidiaries. Their role is to meet local customer needs, to defend their market position and to satisfy local government requirements. This needs a combination of *entrepreneurship*, *competitive and market intelligence collection* and *local resource acquisition.*
- Function managers sit at *corporate or regional headquarters.* Their primary role is to be *organizers* and *coordinate worldwide learning.* They make sure that technologies and best practices are transferred across businesses and countries. 'Using informational networks, they create channels of communicating specialized information and repositories for specialized knowledge.'

During their career, global managers will normally experience all three roles in different locations and businesses. In case of conflict, it helps to create an attitude of mutual understanding and conflict resolution if you remember that, during your own career path, you are likely to be in the position of the other party at some time.

Individual skills

The desirable individual skills for managers most frequently cited in research can be split into eight facets:[21]

- *Professional*: strong mastery of business knowledge in the relevant field (marketing, technology, finance, operations)
- *Cultural*: ability to respect and deal with cultural difference and avoid stereotyping
- *Negotiating*: ability to balance conflicting objectives with internal and external parties
- *Relational*: ability to relate easily with other people and show empathy
- *Leadership*: ability to set objectives, organize and motivate subordinates
- *Intellectual*: ability to balance global objectives with local realities
- *Courage* and *determination*
- *Flexibility* in moving from one role to another.

Figure 13.13 shows another set of global leadership capabilities that are identified in much research on the subject.[22]

Insert 13.3 shows how Percy Barnevik, the former CEO of ABB, described the characteristics he expected from global managers in his company.

Figure 13.13 Global leadership capabilities
Source: Author's own, based on text in Jokinen (2005).

Insert 13.3 Ideal characteristics of global managers

- Tough-skinned
- Fast on their feet
- Good technical and commercial backgrounds
- Ability to lead
- Open-minded: show respect for other ways of doing things
- Patience
- Stamina
- Humility
- Respect for other cultures
- Work experience in two or three countries
- Incisive
- Ability to sort out the debris of cultural excuses
- Generous
- People developers

Source: Taken from Kets de Vries (1994). Copyright © 1994 INSEAD. Reused with permission.

Developing skills through job rotation and training

Global skills development, known also as 'global leaders' development', mixes career management with formal training, facilitating skills acquisition as well as coaching in the various global roles that managers are likely to play during their careers. Figure 13.14 shows how a global oil company has orchestrated the development of its international managers.

In management seminars at various levels, global firms make sure that a mix of country managers, global managers and function managers of various nationalities participate, favouring the expansion of a 'networking culture'.

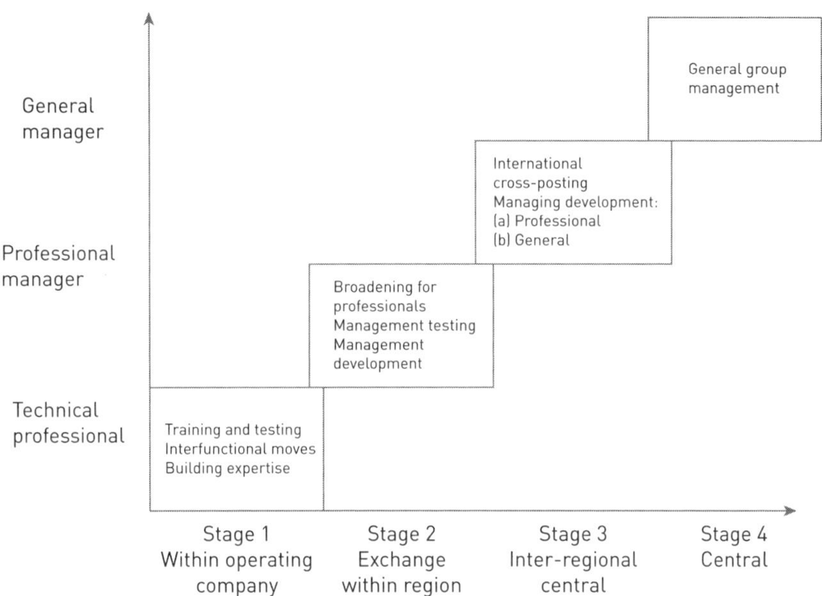

Figure 13.14 Global management development in a global oil company

An increasing trend is remote and flexible working. The following sections looks at these phenomena, in particular the impact of the Covid-19 pandemic on working practices and how organizations see the future workplace.

Working from anywhere (WFA)

Advances in technology and digital connectivity have affected the way in which people work. Prior to 2020, the workplace had become a more flexible environment with teleworking increasingly commonplace. The Covid-19 pandemic that began in 2020 forced employees worldwide to abandon traditional places of employment and work remotely. Global teams learnt to collaborate online successfully – a trend that was coined Work From Anywhere (WFA) and which affected multinational corporations across the globe.[23]

WFA has pros and cons for both the employees and global organizations. Real estate costs can be reduced or removed entirely. Multinationals can use talent from around the globe without dealing with challenges of relocation such as immigration regulations or work permits. Employees can also reap the benefits of WFA with geographical flexibility – living and working wherever they desire. Other advantages include savings made on travel, with commuting no longer required, and potentially a better work/life balance. The downside, however, for both employees and employer is potentially less efficient communication between colleagues, from problem-solving and socializing, to performance evaluation.

One of the leading multinationals in audio streaming and media services, Spotify, is one organization that is convinced that WFA is the way forward for its workers. Triggered by the pandemic, its leaders decided that Spotify should transition to a 'flexible/distribute first' company and introduced a WFA programme in February 2021. The company has a set of beliefs that state work is something you do, not something you come to the office for:

> How effective you are does not relate to the number of hours spent in an office – therefore employees should be given the choice of where they work. Being more flexible will give people a better work/life balance and help find new talent and maintain staff. Functioning as a distributed organization produces better and more efficient methods of working through intentional use of communication and collaboration practices and tools.[24]

Launched in the summer of 2021, Spotify offers employees more flexibility with a programme called 'My Work Mode'. This allows employees to work full time remotely, from the office or a combination of both. Geographical location is also considered, supporting workers with co-working space membership if they are not situated near a Spotify office. With this new programme, the company is building on its package for potential employees, which includes its flexible public holiday benefit[25] that was launched in 2017 and the Employee Incentive Mix of 2019.[26] According to Spotify's HR blog, a flexible working culture is built on trust, communication, collaboration and connection, together with acknowledging that staff are all individuals, with different needs. The company considered labour law, tax and insurance readiness for its workforce to be 'working from anywhere'.[27]

The acceleration of working flexibly and remotely has become more and more a part of a company's means of attracting talent. A report published in February 2021 found that 98 per cent of the 3,500 global remote workers surveyed preferred to work remotely in some capacity be it part time or full time.[28] Another survey in 2020 found that allowing remote work reduces employee turnover by an average of 25 per cent.[29] The increased adoption of flexible and remote working has shown that work does not necessarily need to be undertaken during office hours or in a 'physical' workplace. Other companies adopting the model include Twitter, Goldman Sachs, GitLab (the world's largest all-remote company, with 1,300 employees), Zapier (a workflow automation company with more than 300 employees, none of them colocated, around the United States and in 23 other countries) and MobSquad (a Canadian start-up that employs WFA workers).[30]

However, as vaccinations were rolled out in most countries, offering protection for employees from Covid-19, organizations started to reconsider their approach to office working. Microsoft 2021 Work Trend Index indicates that 66 per cent of surveyed leaders are considering redesigning office space for hybrid work, 73 per cent of employees want flexible remote work options to stay and 67 per cent of employees want more in-person work or collaboration post pandemic.[31] Reopening offices is still an attractive proposition for some employers. Even though the remote-work model has gained significant traction throughout the pandemic, many businesses are still not sure about embracing the practice permanently. J.P. Morgan's CEO in October 2020 questioned how people would learn the culture and build the character of a company if they were working remotely. He continued that much work takes place in meetings when people share ideas.

Netflix Co-CEO Reed Hastings also remarked in 2020 that 'Not being able to get together in person, particularly internationally, is a pure negative.'[32]

Other trends in the transformation of working practices have emerged which organizations should consider when attracting talent. There is a decreased desire for working in cities because of Covid-19 and the fear of future pandemics; together with the rise in the cost of urban living[33] plus increased incentives from organizations to attract remote workers, this could mean that these employees choose to live in isolation in more remote and even multiple locations – being 'extremely remote workers'.[34] Digital nomads in the past have been largely freelancers or contract workers in specific sectors such as web design or marketing. However, this mode of work could be the future for full-time employees. Offering employees the opportunity to work remotely (or extremely) is becoming less of an option for organizations but necessary if they want to attract the best talent.

While pandemics and high costs push professionals away from cities, some governments are establishing new initiatives to attract and *pull* global talent into cities. Finland is one such example that is offering foreign talent the opportunity to try out living in Helsinki for ninety days in a bid to lure more professionals. In 2020, 5,330 people from around the world applied for the free 90 Day Finn relocation package offered by Helsinki Business Hub. The international trade and investment promotion agency will provide the fifteen winners with airport pick-up, orientation, cultural training, Finnish experiences, remote-work facilities, introductions to local business networks and all the documentation needed for a three-month stay together with any housing, school or childcare requirements. The initiative helped put Helsinki on the map for global workers and fill a talent gap fuelling its growing tech sector. If it works, relocation packages like this could become a valuable new tool in the competitive race to win over foreign professionals. The unique opportunity that Finland is proposing could also be a proof of concept that helps the Finnish to design more effective relocation plans and attract talented employees who will stay longer.[35]

MINI-CASE 13.1

Global managers – Pedro Aguilar

Pedro Aguilar, twenty-nine, and John Anderson, thirty, graduated in 2017 from Caltech (California Institute of Technology), both obtaining a Master of Science in Electrical Engineering. Pedro, a native of Argentina, joined Central Electrica SA, the local subsidiary of Centerlec, a Texan-based multinational specializing in construction, operation and maintenance of electrical power plants. Since his recruitment Pedro had climbed the ladder of management positions and was appointed chief engineer in the Transformer Division in Cordoba in October 2020 with a monthly salary of 240,000 Argentine peso (ARS) ($2,620) plus a possible bonus of around 20 per cent at the end of the year. He was very happy with his promotion.

In December 2021 he met John at the company's headquarters. John told him that he had just been appointed chief engineer in Buenos Aires with basically similar responsibilities to Pedro's. They celebrated their encounter in a local pub and during their conversation, Pedro found out that John's salary was a tax-free $90,000 per year ($7,500 per month) plus a potential bonus plus a contribution to his accommodation of around 100,000 ARS ($1,092) per month.

Questions:

1. If you were Pedro, what would you think? What would you do?
2. What are the arguments that Pedro will hear if he complains to the HR director?
3. Can this type of situation be resolved? (You may find it helpful to refer back to Chapter 3 to find solutions for this situation.)

MINI-CASE 13.2

Global managers – Joseph Laval

In May Joseph Laval was appointed managing director of the French–Thai joint venture mobile telephony company Siammobile. The personnel in the joint venture were people who had transferred from the local partner (a traditional telephony firm) plus recruits from the local workforce. Joseph reported to the French parent company Gallicom, at regional headquarters in Singapore.

Gallicom implemented a global human resource management system. One part of the system evaluated the performance of personnel on a 1 to 5 scale (1 = Low performer, 5 = Outstanding performer). On that basis, bonuses were attributed and for low performers some painful lay-off decisions had to be made. A few months later, Joseph had to review the performances of the various departments.

One case that came to Joseph's attention was Sarawong, a senior client relationship manager who was one of the personnel transferred from the local partner to the joint venture three years previously. Sarawong was very devoted to the company, while his colleagues appreciated his kindness. In his early fifties, he was a senior person in the company. Over the years he had always had good evaluations; in Siammobile his rating was always 4 (High performer). This was satisfactory for him since his character was not to be an aggressive money-making manager. In practice his performances were not really so good. Joseph was surprised to see that his predecessor granted a 4 to Sarawong. He decided to give him a 3 (Average performer) even though he thought that a 2 would be more appropriate.

Sarawong was devastated when he received his evaluation. How could he keep face in the office with his colleagues? What did he do wrong?

He asked for a meeting with Joseph who rationally explained to him that the results of his departments were not on a par with others and that the company evaluation guidelines were very clear.

Joseph, as a senior member of staff, talked to Michel Journaux, the previous managing director of Siammobile with whom he had a good relationship, and who was now the head of Gallicom's Singapore regional office.

Questions:

1 What do you think of the situation?

2 What would you do if you were Journaux?

Source: Adapted with permission from de Bettignies (1996).

Summary and key points

1 There are four main issues in global HRM:

  a *Personnel management* and ratio of global to local managers: as seen in the *global human resource wheel*

  b *Expatriate management*: career management of global managers

  c *Localization*: need to recruit and motivate local personnel

  d *Global skills development*: need to develop skills appropriate for global management

2 There are two types of manager in global firms:

  a *Global managers*: career evolves by successive cross-border appointments

  b *Local managers*: career evolves within a country subsidiary

3 Global human resource wheel:

	Multi-domestic design	Global design
Number of global managers	Small	Large
Proportion of local personnel	High	Low
Proportion of temporary detachments	Relatively less	Relatively more
Can local personnel join the global manager group?	No	Yes

4 Expatriate management

  a There are two types of *national*:

    - Third-country nationals (TCN)
    - Parent-country nationals (PCN)

  b Expatriate *challenges* – four main aspects:

    - *Job*
      – Inability of manager to adapt
      – Inability of manager's partner/family to adapt

- *Local integration*
  - Preparation
  - Culture shock
  - Political/social skills
  - Local acculturation
- *Family*
  - Adaptation
  - Education
- *Career*
  - Selection
  - Rotation
  - Re-entry

c Expatriate *failure*:

- Measured by *recall rate* (proportion of assigned personnel who fail to complete their predetermined contract)
- Main causes:
  - Inability of manager to adapt
  - Inability of manager's partner/family to adapt
  - Family-related problems
  - Manager's personality or emotional immaturity
  - Manager's inability to cope with responsibility
  - Manager's lack of technical competence
  - Manager's lack of motivation

d Reasons for expatriate *success*:

- Recognition of cross-border assignments by corporate headquarters
- Corporate support/understanding given to expatriate personnel

e Four expatriate *attitudes* ('four Fs'):

- *Flight*: expatriates preserve own cultural identities, isolate themselves and avoid socializing with local community
- *Fight*: expatriates criticize host countries, claim superiority of their own cultures and avoid socializing with locals
- *Follow*: expatriates willing to embrace local culture and assimilate, gradually lose connection with global headquarters
- *Fit*: cosmopolitans who can immerse themselves into the local culture and simultaneously preserve their own cultures

f Expatriate *policy*:

- *Strategic – transfer policies* can:
  - Fill position
  - Develop manager
  - Develop organization
- Selection and preparation:
  - *Choice* of expatriates: identifying people with tolerance for ambiguity; behavioural flexibility; goal orientation; sociability and interest in other people; empathy; ability to be non-judgemental; meta-communication skills
  - *Preparation* of expatriates: clearly communicated career plan to avoid re-entry problems; cultural and logistical preparation for the employee/family (e.g. pre-assignment trips); assessment centres to provide tailored training after comparing current with required skills
- *Compensation*: additional compensation for the difference in living conditions, prices and burden on family (e.g. hardship allowance)
- *Tenure*:
  - *Duration*: company policy or function of time needed to learn business rules and build effective business relationships, depending on 'contextual hardship' of the country
  - Optimal tenure length is determined by the combined effect of the expatriates' local impact on business results (which *increases* over time) and the benefits of global integration (which *decreases* over time)
- *Support*: mentoring, communication and assurance that the staff are not 'forgotten'
- *Career follow-up*: proactive international career management process to ensure staff have a desirable job after the overseas posting and to avoid 'repatriation problems'

5 *Alternative forms of expatriation*

- Short-term assignment
- Commuter assignment
- Virtual team
- Global mobility is reduced due to digital revolution (remote work) and Covid-19 pandemic

6 Localization

a Importance of localization:

- Can build/maintain personal and business contacts without the potential problems caused by language barriers
- Local staff better qualified for business development which requires local sensitivity/knowledge
- Reduces expensive expatriate costs
- Allows a company to reap the benefits of implementing a 'think globally, act locally' policy

- Shows commitment to the country, which can be of concern to local government and/or people

b The Global Talent Competitiveness Index (GTCI)

- Talent plays a part in deciding on location and has become a competitive factor
- The Global Talent Competitiveness Index compares countries across the world on their talent competitiveness

c *Concerns*:

- *Recruitment*: International firms have more difficulty recruiting local talent when there is a scarcity of local talent
- *Retention*: loyalty of local staff may be hard to secure and companies can encourage loyalty through good career prospects and 'fair treatment' instead of financial compensation
- *Career management*: local staff need career management and equal opportunity to become 'global managers' with an absence of a 'glass ceiling' for local staff
- *Performance evaluation/cultural difference*: dilemma of implementing a standardized approach while taking cultural differences into account
- *Reward practices*: awareness of importance of rewards on private lives and social standing

7 Global skill development

Three main roles of global managers:

- *Business* managers operate in global business units:
  - Possess ability to coordinate activities and link capabilities
  - Role is to increase global-scale efficiency/competitiveness
- *Country* managers who operate in local subsidiaries:
  - Possess skills of entrepreneurship, capacity to build local resources and collect competitive intelligence
  - Role is to meet local customer needs, defend market position and satisfy local government requirements
- *Function* managers who operate at corporate or regional headquarters:
  - Have informational networks
  - Role is to organize/coordinate worldwide learning and transfer technologies and best practices
  - Global skills
- For individual:
  - Professional
  - Cultural
  - Negotiating
  - Relational

  - Leadership
  - Intellectual
  - Courage and determination
  - Flexibility
- Skill development:
  - Job rotation
  - Ongoing training

8 Working from anywhere

- Following the Covid-19 pandemic, global teams collaborate online
- Multinationals use talents from all around the world
- Offering employees remote working is attracting global talents

Learning assignments

1. What are the relative advantages and disadvantages of having a high proportion of global managers to local ones?
2. What are the main difficulties that confront expatriate managers when they are assigned to an emerging country?
3. What are the main problems of short expatriate assignments?
4. One of the main problems that confronts global firms in countries such as China is the turnover of local managers. How can this be prevented?
5. What are the benefits of mentoring an expatriate?
6. More and more Western countries' expatriation packages are disappearing and being replaced by local contracts. Why? What are the advantages and disadvantages?
7. What are the benefits and problems of applying a standardized performance evaluation system across the world?
8. Why is global mobility reducing in the 2020s?
9. Is digital remote working (working from anywhere) consolidating the globalization of enterprise? What is your answer If you are pro-globalization, and if you are anti-globalization?
10. What will be the key content of a management programme designed to train managers to become 'country managers'?

Key words

- Acculturation
- Career plan
- Compensation
- EU workers directive

- Expatriates
- Global leaders development
- Global managers
- Global talent competitiveness
- Local managers
- Mentoring
- Missions
- Relocation
- Remote teams
- Remote working
- Retention
- Roles
- Skills
- Tenure
- Virtual assignments
- Work From Anywhere (WFA)

Web resources

International Personnel Management Association for Human Resources:
http://www.ipma-hr.org/
Community website created for and by expatriates:
http://www.expatriates.com/

International online network for people who live and work abroad:
http://www.internations.org/

Companion website

Visit the companion website at bloomsbury.pub/global-strategic-management-5e for a multitude of weblinks and resources, self-test questions for revision and appendices.

Notes

1 Lasserre, Porter, Redding and Steward (1997).
2 This definition is from F. Rieger and D. Wong-Rieger, 'The application of acculturation theory to structuring and strategy formulation in international firms', a research paper quoted in Tung (1998: 125–44).
3 Black and Gregersen (1999: 4).
4 Khanna (2014).
5 Rottenberg (1999).
6 Stahl (2001): 206–7).
7 Brookfield Global Relocation Services (2011).
8 Collins et al. (2011): 221–5).
9 KPMG (2020).
10 https://www.irishtimes.com/business/technology/google-tells-workers-to-return-to-country-where-they-are-employed-1.4367674 (accessed 1 February 2022).
11 Santa Fe Repurpose Challenging Change Report 2020/21 on relocation, https://www.santaferelo.com/en/mobility-insights/global-mobility-survey/global-mobility-survey-2020-21-repurpose-challenging-change/ (accessed 29 January 2022).
12 Vance et al. (2009).
13 Holstein (2008).
14 Davies et al. (1995).
15 Hsiec (1999a).
16 Lanvin and Monteiro (2019, 2020, 2021).
17 Stahl et al. (2012); Yamagushi (2014).
18 Yahiaoui (2015).
19 Hofstede (1980).

20 Bartlett and Ghoshal (1992: 124–323), the skills quoted are from this article.
21 Jokinen (2005); Ghemawat (2012).
22 Adler and Bartholomew (1992: 52–65); Mendenhall (2001: 1–17).
23 Choudhury (2020).
24 https://hrblog.spotify.com/2021/02/12/introducing-working-from-anywhere/.
25 All employees can make a day-off trade: work on a day that is a public holiday in the country where they are employed, and then take out another workday as a holiday instead when it fits their values, beliefs, and celebration calendar better.
26 instead of creating policies and heavy administration. The company expects people to own their own growth plan - each individual to choose their own incentive mix.
27 https://hrblog.spotify.com/2021/02/12/introducing-working-from-anywhere/
28 https://lp.buffer.com/state-of-remote-work-2020
29 https://resources.owllabs.com/state-of-remote-work
30 https://hbr.org/2020/11/our-work-from-anywhere-future
31 https://www.microsoft.com/en-us/worklab/work-trend-index
32 https://www.forbes.com/sites/jackkelly/2020/09/08/netflix-ceo-reed-hastings-is-not-a-fan-of-working-from-home-and-wants-his-employees-back-at-the-office-12-hours-after-a-vaccine-is-approved/ (accessed 10 may 2022).
33 https://www.carbonbrief.org/solar-is-now-cheapest-electricity-in-history-confirms-iea
34 https://www.computerworld.com/article/3604736/remote-work-20-when-wfh-really-means-work-from-anywhere.html
35 https://www.bbc.com/worklife/article/20210121-finlands-radical-plan-to-lure-global-talent

References and further reading

Books and articles

Adler, N. and Bartholomew, S. (1992) 'Managing globally competent people', *The Academy of Management Executive*, 6.

Bartlett, C. and Ghoshal, S. (1992) 'What is a global manager?', *Harvard Business Review*, 70 (5): 124–32.

Black, J. S. and Gregersen, H. (1999) 'The right way to manage expatriates', *Harvard Business Review*, 77 (2): 52–63.

Brookfield Global Relocation Services (2011) 'Global relocation trends', Report.

Budhwar, P., Schuler, R. and Sparrow, P. (2009) *International Human Resource Management* (London: Sage).

Chalkiti, K. and Sigala, M. (2010) 'Staff turnover in the Greek tourism industry: a comparison between insular and peninsular regions', *International Journal of Contemporary Hospitality Management*, 22 (3): 335–59.

Choudhury, P. (2020) 'Our work-from-anywhere future', *Harvard Business Review*, 98 (6): 58–67.

Choudhury, P. (2020) 'Managing people. Our work-from-anywhere future. Best practices for all-remote organizations', *Harvard Business Review*, November–December.

Choudhury, P., Foroughi, C. and Larson, B. (2021) 'Work-from-anywhere: the productivity effects of geographic flexibility', *Strategic Management Journal*, 42 (4): 655–83.

Collins, D. G., Scullion, H. and Morley, M. (2011) 'Changing pattern of global staffing: challenges to the conventional expatriate assignment and emerging alternatives', in G. K. Stahl, M. E. Mendenhall and G. R. Oddou (eds), *Reading and Cases in International Human Resource Management and Organizational Behavior* (Abingdon: Routledge).

Davies, H., Leung, T. K. P., Luk, S. T. K. and Wong, Y. H. (1995) 'The benefit of guanxi: the value of relationships in developing the Chinese market', *Industrial Marketing Management*, 24: 207–14.

de Bettignies, H.-C. (1996) 'Evaluation', INSEAD Euro Asia Center, Case Study no. 03/1997–4677.

Dickmann, M., Suurtari, V. and Wurst, O. (2018) *The Management of Global Careers, Exploring the Rise of Global Careers* (London: Palgrave Macmillan).

Dowling, P. J., Festing, M., Engle, A. D. and Gröschl, S. (2009) *International Human Resource Management: A Canadian Perspective* (Scarborough, ON: Nelson Books).

Doz, Y. L. (1999) 'Ciba-Geigy management development', INSEAD Case Study no. 11/1999-1153.

Economist Intelligence Unit (2020), Worldwide Cost of Living 2020. https://www.eiu.com/n/campaigns/worldwide-cost-of-living-2020/ (accessed 8 February 2022).

Edstrom, A. and Galbraith, J. (1977) 'Transfer of managers as a coordination and control strategy in multinational organizations', *Administrative Science Quarterly*, June.

Elgan, M. (2021) 'Remote work 2.0 — when WFH really means "work from anywhere"'. https://www.computerworld.com/article/3604736/remote-work-20-when-wfh-really-means-work-from-anywhere.html (accessed 1 February 2022).

Evans, P., Pucik, V. and Barsoux, J.-L. (2011) *The Global Challenge: Frameworks for International Human Resources Management* (New York, NY: McGraw-Hill).

Ghemawat, P. (2012) 'Developing global leaders', *McKinsey Quarterly*, 3: 100–9.

GTCI (2021), The Global Talent Competitiveness Index 2021. https://www.insead.edu/sites/default/files/assets/dept/fr/gtci/GTCI-2021-Report.pdf (accessed 25 January 2022).

Hadley, C. N. and Mortensen, M. (2021) 'Are your team members lonely?', *MIT Sloan Management Review*, 62 (2): 36–40.

Harzing, A.-W. and Van Ruysseveldt, J. (2004) *International Human Resource Management* (London: Sage).

Hofstede, G. (1980) *Culture's Consequences: International Differences in Work-Related Values* (Beverly Hills, CA: Sage).

Holstein, W. (2008) 'The decline of the expat executive', *Strategy + Business*, July.

Hsieh, T., Lavoie, J. and Samek, R. A. P. (1999a) 'Think global, hire local', *McKinsey Quarterly*, 4: 93–101.

Hsieh, T., Lavoie, J. and Samek, R. A. P. (1999b) 'Are you taking your expatriate talent seriously?', *McKinsey Quarterly*, 3: 71–83.

Jokinen, T. (2005) 'Global leadership competencies: are view and discussion', *Journal of European Industrial Training*, 29 (3): 199–216.

Kets de Vries, M. (1994) 'Percy Barnevik and ABB', INSEAD Case Study 05/1994-4308.

Khanna, T. (2014) 'Contextual intelligence', *Harvard Business Review*, 92 (9): 58–68.

KPMG International (2020) Global Assignment Policies and Practices survey. https://home.kpmg/xx/en/home/insights/2021/10/global-assignment-policies-and-practices-survey-report.html (accessed 1 February 2022).

Lanvin, B. and Monteiro, L. F. (eds) (2019) 'The global talent competitiveness index 2019: entrepreneurial talent and global competitiveness' (Fontainebleau: INSEAD). https://www.insead.edu/faculty-research/research/gtci (accessed 13 April 2022).

Lanvin, B. and Monteiro, L. F. (eds) (2020) 'The global talent competitiveness index 2020: global talent in the age of artificial intelligence', (Fontainebleau: INSEAD). https://www.insead.edu/faculty-research/research/gtci (accessed 13 April 2022).

Lanvin, B. and Monteiro, L. F. (eds) (2021) *The Global Talent Competitiveness Index 2021: Talent Competitiveness in Times of COVID* (Fontainebleau: INSEAD). https://www.insead.edu/faculty-research/research/gtci (accessed 13 April 2022).

Lasserre, P. and Ching, P. S. (1997) 'Human resource management in China and the localization challenge', *Journal of Asian Business*, 13 (4): 85–99.

Lasserre, P., Porter, L., Redding, G. and Steward, P. (1997) *Managing International Assignments in Asia: Individual and Organizational Challenge*, The

International Consortium for Executive Education [internal report].

McNulty, Y. and Brewster, C. (2020) 'The expatriate cycle', *Global Business & Organizational Excellence*, May/June, 39 (4): 60–75.

Mendenhall, M. E. (2001) 'New perspectives on expatriate adjustment and its relationship to global leadership development', in M. Mendenhall, T. Mailman and G. Stahl (eds), *Developing Global Leaders* (Westport, CT: Quorum Books).

Parsons, A. J. (1996) 'Nestlé: the visions of local managers', *McKinsey Quarterly*, 2: 5–29.

Quelch, J. A. and Bloom, H. (1996) 'The return of the country manager', *McKinsey Quarterly*, 2: 31–43.

Reiche, B. S. and Minbaeva, D. (2019) 'HRM in multinational companies', in A. Wilkinson, N. Bacon, S. Snell and D. Lepak (eds), *The SAGE Handbook of Human Resource Management*, 2 edn, 541–56 (Los Angeles, CA: SAGE Publications).

Reiche, B. S., Lee, Y. and Allen, D. G. (2019) 'Actors, structure, and processes: a review and conceptualization of global work integrating IB and HRM research', *Journal of Management*. https://doi.org/10.1177/0149206318808885 (accessed 1 February 2022).

Rieger, F. and Wong-Rieger, D. (1998) 'The application of acculturation theory to structuring and strategy formulation in international firms', in R. Tung, 'American expatriates: from neophytes to cosmopolitans', *Journal of World Business*, 33 (2): 125–44.

Rosenweig, P. M. (1994) 'Colgate-Palmolive: managing international careers', Harvard Business School Case Study 9-394-184.

Rottenberg, S. (1999) 'Prepare for the overseas trip', *Harvard Management Update* (Boston, MA: Harvard Business School Publishing, U9904C).

Stahl, G. (2001) 'Using assessment centers as tools for global leadership development: an exploratory study', in M. Mendenhall, T. Kuhlman and G. Stahl (eds), *Developing Global Leaders*, 198–201 (Westport, CT: Quorum Books).

Stahl, G. K., Bjorkman, I., Farndale, E., Morris, S. S., Paauwe, J., Stiles, P., Trevor, J. and Wright, P. (2012) 'Six principles of effective global talent management', *MIT Sloan Management Review*, 53 (2): 30.

Tayeb, Z. (2021) 'The great divide: business leaders are split on long-term remote working. This is what Spotify, Twitter, Goldman Sachs, and others have announced'. https://www.businessinsider.com/what-spotify-twitter-goldman-sachs-said-about-long-term-remote-working-2021-3?r=US&IR=T (accessed 1 February 2022).

Tsedal, N. (2021) *Remote Work Revolution: Succeeding from Anywhere* (Boston, MA: Harvard Business School Press).

Tung, R. (1987) 'Expatriate assignments: enhancing success and minimizing failure', *The Academy of Management Executive*, 1: 117–25.

Tung, R. (1998) 'American expatriates: from neophytes to cosmopolitans', *Journal of World Business*, 33 (2): 125–44.

Vance, C. M., Vaiman, V. and Andersen, T. (2009) 'The vital liaison role of host country nationals in MNC knowledge management', *Human Resource Management*, 48 (4): 649–59.

Yahiaoui, D. (2015) 'Hybridization: striking a balance between adoption and adaptation of human resource management practices in French multinational corporations and their Tunisian subsidiaries', *International Journal of Human Resource Management*, 26 (13): 1665–93.

Yamagushi, T. (2014) 'Standardizing HR practices around the world', *Harvard Business Review*, September: 80–1.

Journal

International Journal of Human Resource Management: https://www.tandfonline.com/journals/rijh20

Chapter 14

Designing a global organization

At the end of the chapter you will be able to:

- Identify the benefits and issues for each organizational type
- Participate in a meaningful way in designing an appropriate organization in the context of a particular global firm
- Understand the characteristics of the transnational model and be able to introduce its features in a particular firm

Introduction

In Chapter 5 various models of organizational design were introduced. It has been argued that those designs were contingent upon the nature of the global industry context as well as the strategic positioning and business system selected by corporations. In practice, whatever the type of design chosen, companies engaged in global business have to cope with a dual requirement:

- They need to efficiently introduce and leverage their competitive advantages across borders; consequently their organizational design demands a certain degree of *coordination and centralization.*
- They need to adapt to local conditions; consequently their organizational design demands a certain degree of *decentralization* and local autonomy.

This chapter discusses the various organizational designs used by corporations in their international, multinational and global operations. Based on prior research, several organizational models can be identified:

- *Global*: a worldwide functional or global product structure
- *Confederation geographical*: a multi-countries structure
- *Multidimensional*: a matrix or transnational structure
- *Entrepreneurial alternative models*: customer-centred structures, complex dual structural models, the transnational model, the e-enabled model, holocracy.

These are described and illustrated in turn, showing their advantages and disadvantages. It can be argued that there is no single best structure and that the adoption of a particular structure is contingent upon the competitive imperative. A variety of structures can be derived from these models by mixing their features, but the chapter ends by advocating that global firms should develop a culture and management process of the 'transnational' model and by discussing the roles of regional headquarters (RHQs).

The merry-go-round organizational challenge

In a *Harvard Business Review* article published in 1983, Professor Christopher Bartlett observed that international companies were constantly reorganizing their operations and that their search to find the ideal international structure had shown poor results; this he called the *reorganization merry-go-round*. A similar observation was made more recently by a group of analysts from McKinsey who mentioned that the difficulty of finding an organizational model lies in the need to 'capture scale across borders while differentiating products and services to suit the needs of local customers all without letting complexity get in the way of speed and agility'.[1]

This phenomenon is illustrated in Example 14.1, detailing two companies in the same industry: Unilever and Procter & Gamble. These two firms have modified their global organizational structure over the years towards an increasing global business focus laying less emphasis on geographical decentralization.

EXAMPLE 14.1 Evolution of two global organizations

Unilever

Originally a British soap company created in the 1890s as *Lever,* the company became *Unilever* in 1929 after association with a Dutch margarine producer. Over the years the company developed a global presence through acquisitions and internal development. Originally the organization was based on strategically independent units on a country-by-country basis. During the 1980s four product divisions were established to coordinate regional operations: Foods, Personal Care, Home Care and Speciality Chemicals. The country autonomy of subsidiaries was still maintained. The 1990s saw a surge in international acquisitions that created organizational obstacles, confusion and excessive bureaucracy, leading to a much-needed corporate restructuring. Fourteen business presidents were appointed and operations were regrouped by business and products rather than geography. A matrix-type structure combining local initiative with some centralization was introduced. However, by the early 2000s, Unilever's market share had declined and its market shrank by 60 per cent from £51 billion (US$76 billion) to £20 billion (US$30 billion). Unilever was then split into two separate global business units: Foods and Home and Personal Care. It reorganized its 300 operating companies into 10 Regional Groups and gave more autonomy to subsidiaries. The company realized that it had too many brands and decided to reduce them from 1,600 to 400, 13 of which were global brands, that each generated more than £1 billion (US$1.8 billion). In 2005, the company launched a process of reorganization known as

One World aimed at aligning the entire company to a single strategy. Non-core products were divested. In 2011, the two global divisions were extended to four: Food, Personal Care, Refreshment and Household Care – these were later reduced to three: Beauty and Personal, Food and Refreshment, and Home Care. This goal was to foster growth in emerging markets. In 2020, Unilever operated 300 factories around the world, linked to a centralized controlled logistic network and seven main R&D centres, based in the UK (2), Netherlands, North America, China, Italy and India. Its turnover amounted to £52 billion (US$71 billion -58 per cent in emerging markets) and employed 149,000 people across the world. Its 400 brands are sold in 190 countries through a network of 25 million retailers.

Procter & Gamble

Founded in 1837 in Cincinnati (USA), as a candle and soap maker, Procter & Gamble created its first factory in Canada in 1915, but most of its international expansion started after the Second World War. It created an international product division in 1948 to manage its foreign business. By the mid-1950s, the operations were organized by product divisions in charge of managing brands on a worldwide basis, serving country subsidiaries. A reorganization in 1987 created 39 category business units in the USA, each managing product development, manufacturing, sales and finance. The international operations were run on a regional/country basis with autonomous country general managers (GMs) who adapted products to local conditions and were responsible for profits. Attempts were made to promote cross-border cooperation within product categories. Product category vice-presidents were given profit and loss responsibility.

In the late 1980s, P&G moved to a global matrix structure based on Products and Functions. Implemented first in Europe, this structure was extended to the world with the creation of four regions: North America, Europe, Middle East/Africa and Asia. Manufacturing, purchasing, engineering and distribution were integrated worldwide, but by the mid-1990s it became clear that this type of matrix organization created some conflicts and unnecessary expense. In 2005, P&G announced a restructuring plan reducing management layers and creating four interdependent global organizations: Global Business Units, Selling and Markets Operations, Functions, and Global Business Services for internal processes such as IT, HR and budgeting.

The ten Global Business Units (GBUs) were: Baby Care, Feminine Care, Family Care, Grooming, Oral Care, Personal Health Care, Hair Care, Skin and Personal Care, Fabric Care and Home Care. Within each category, Research & Development, Product Supply and Brand Organization develop, manufacture and market the brands and products provided to consumers.

The Selling and Markets Operations (SMOs) are responsible for developing and executing local sales and distribution. They are divided into six regions that reach consumers in more than 180 countries: Asia Pacific, Europe, Greater China, IMEA (India, the Middle East and Africa), Latin America and North America.

Functions provide expertise in the areas of Finance, Human Resources, Sales, Communications, Legal and IT.

Global Business Services (GBS) provides shared services such as payroll, purchases, real-time data analytics, benefits and facilities management.

In 2019, the ten product categories were contracted into six Sector Business Units (SBUs). The SBUs are responsible for global brand strategy, innovation and supply chain. They have direct profit responsibility for markets representing the majority of the company's sales and earnings (referred to as Focus Markets) and are responsible for innovation plans, supply plans and operating frameworks to drive growth and value creation in the six geographical markets mentioned earlier (referred to as Enterprise Markets). As of June 2020, P&G employed 99,000 people and generated sales of $70 billion, 35 per cent of which came from emerging countries.

Sources: P&G and Unilever websites annual reports 2020; Piskorsi and Spadini (2007).

Moreover, in an earlier survey another McKinsey team had observed that global firms that had adopted a global structure, instead of a local one, scored lower on several dimensions of organizational health than firms that had adopted a locally focused form of organization. They concluded that this *globalization penalty*[2] meant that locally based organizations were able to 'align around a strategy or change programme, to execute, and to renew the company faster' than globally structured firms.

In order to cope with the inherently conflicting demands of global integration and local responsiveness, multidimensional forms of organizational design have been proposed, ranging from the matrix to the networked models.

In this chapter you will encounter various models of global organizational design with discussions of when they are most appropriate. Each organizational design reflects the way companies meet this dual demand of integration/localization through the implementation of three interlocking elements:

- *Organizational structure*: how roles, responsibilities and power are assigned.
- *Organizational processes*: how decisions are made, resources allocated, policies enacted and rewards, sanctions and control exercised. Organizational processes include information, decision making, planning/control and performance evaluation processes.
- *Organizational culture*: the shared values and the dominant logic[3] of doing business; the 'dos and don'ts' and what behaviour is rewarded or sanctioned.

The various designs presented are usually seen at different stages of globalization. These are:

- The international division model
- The global functional model
- The geographical models: single business or multi-business
- The product division model
- The matrix model: single business or multi-business
- The transnational model.

In their seminal work, John Stopford and Louis Wells described this evolution,[4] as represented in Figure 14.1.

The international division model

The international division model can be described as the first organizational structure adopted by firms at an early stage of internationalization.[5] In this model, there is a clear distinction between the home-country business units managed by divisional executives in charge of product development, manufacturing, home marketing and exports, and the international subsidiaries which, under the leadership of an international division executive, oversee their countries' strategic development. The overseas subsidiaries possess a high degree of autonomy, but are dependent upon the home-country divisions for products and technical support. While international sales represent a small proportion of total sales and transactions between home divisions, and country subsidiaries are limited, this model

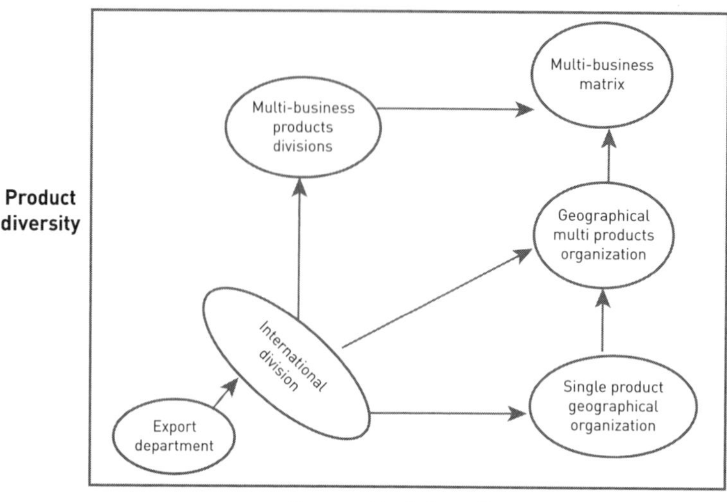

Figure 14.1 The evolution of global organizational models
Source: Authors' own figure, derived from text in Stopford and Wells (1972).

fulfills the requirements of global efficiency and local responsiveness. When international sales increase to represent a significant proportion of total turnover, the company begins to feel the need to integrate all activities in a global structure, either geographical, divisional or matrix.

The global functional model

The global functional design is based upon the worldwide centralization of decision making, coordination and control at the level of the key functional activities such as R&D, operations and marketing. All strategic decisions and operational policies are made at origin-country headquarters level. Country subsidiaries are local legal entities; the heads of country subsidiaries have responsibilities with regard to the laws of the countries in which they operate, but all key business decisions relating to products, production, operations and marketing come from headquarters. Managers within the subsidiaries take their instructions from the corporate vice-president or director in charge of their function. The only autonomous decisions are those related to the practical implementation of policies, such as sales management, or those with a strong local legal content, such as tax reporting or personnel management.

This organizational model best fits companies or business units within multi-business corporations operating in single business environments with strong demand for global integration and coordination.

The global functional organizational design is represented in Figure 14.2 and its characteristics are described in Table 14.1. An example of global functional design is provided below.

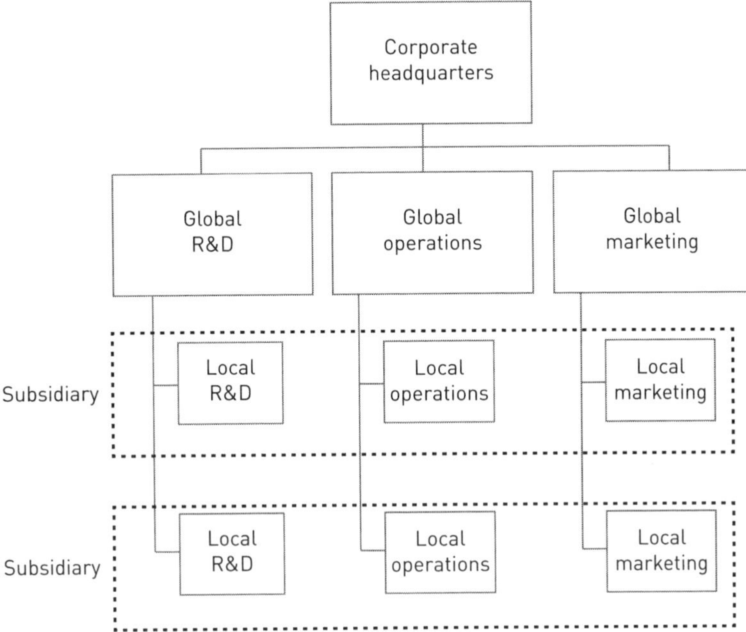

Figure 14.2 The global functional organizational design

Table 14.1 Characteristics of global functional organizational design

Organizational	Innovation	Efficiency of operations	Marketing impact dimension
Structure • Central functional executive exercises global power and responsibilities	• Central R&D function • In various research centres, research policies are centrally led • Subsidiaries' R&D managers report to central R&D • Sales function quite autonomous	• Central operational function such as vice-president manufacturing • Subsidiaries' operational managers report to central vice-president operations	• Central marketing function • Subsidiaries' marketing managers report to central marketing vice-president • Country managers are in charge of local interface with government and legal matters
Processes	• R&D strategy and budgets decided centrally • Control and reporting centrally organized • Worldwide R&D policies • Global standardized product development	• Global supply chain management • Global factories and operational centres • Central policies	• Key marketing policies set globally • Global advertising • Global pricing • Global sales policies • Some local adaptation of sales practices depending upon authorization by centre • Countries are nominally profit centres but without much power to influence profit

Organizational	Innovation	Efficiency of operations	Marketing impact dimension
Culture	• Careers are managed globally • High level of transfer of personnel • Expatriates are key transferrers of technology • Strong product/ technology identity	• Careers are managed globally • High level of transfer of personnel • Expatriates are key transferrers of best practice • Strong technology identity	• Marketing careers are managed globally • High level of transfer of personnel • Expatriates are key transferrers of best practice • Strong brand identity

EXAMPLE 14.2 Global functional organizational design at Apple

After the death of Apple's co-founder Steve Jobs, Tim Cook assumed the role of CEO of the company – but the essence of the organization did not change. The global organization is based on a pyramidal functional design. On the top level of the pyramid are the main function and product areas (Software, Industrial Design, Operations, Software Engineering, Product Marketing, Global Communication, Internet Services, Mac Hardware Engineering, Legal and Finance), each headed by a senior executive who oversees all global operations in that field.

Some other functions are headed by product-based vice-presidents, such as iPad and iPhone.

At the bottom of the pyramid are the international subsidiaries that have local responsibility for marketing and selling products, and sourcing components and devices.

Advantages of the global functional organizational model

The key advantages of this model are the efficiencies obtained through the consistency of decisions and policies. This leads to the optimal use, concentration and specialization of resources, which in turn produces economies of scale, avoids duplication of effort and enables rapid knowledge transfer from headquarters to the subsidiaries. These benefits are most felt when products are standardized and economies of scale and rapid transfer of central know-how are key determinants of competitive advantage – examples are commodities businesses such as oil or basic chemicals, and industries in which manufacturing or operational systems demand size optimization and complex supply chain logistics.

Disadvantages of the global functional organizational model

The drawbacks of this model are more visible when either the competitive context is fragmented into several segments, calling for distinct capabilities, or when the local markets and business environments vary significantly. In such cases a standardized, undifferentiated approach leads to inflexibility, local dysfunction and market rejection. Internally, it fosters excess bureaucracy and discourages initiative.

The geographical models

Geographical organizational design, unlike the global functional design, is based on the worldwide devolution of decision making, coordination and control to the subsidiaries. In such a model, central functions or product management roles can sometimes play an advisory, stimulating or coordinating role without much executive power. The relationships between the subsidiaries and the central functional directors or product managers are sometimes referred to as 'dotted-line' relationships, to signify that there are no firm, formal hierarchical links. Function managers within business units report to the national manager, who in turn reports either directly to the chief executive or to a senior manager in charge of international operations. In many cases, intermediary executive powers are given to regional executives located at regional headquarters in key world regions. National managers develop strategies and choose or adapt products to best fit with their local environment. Policies are decided and enacted locally. In many cases, national or regional managers sit on the corporate executive committee. The global strengths of this organizational model come from the flexibility that local managers have to adapt to their local characteristics. Its success relies, however, on the local degree of basic technological capabilities and knowledge (about product ranges in particular) that the corporation can call upon or install into the regional and country subsidiaries.

The geographical design may apply to single business companies or in multi-business companies. In both cases countries are generally grouped regionally.

Those two geographical organizational designs are represented in Figure 14.3 and their characteristics are described in Table 14.2.

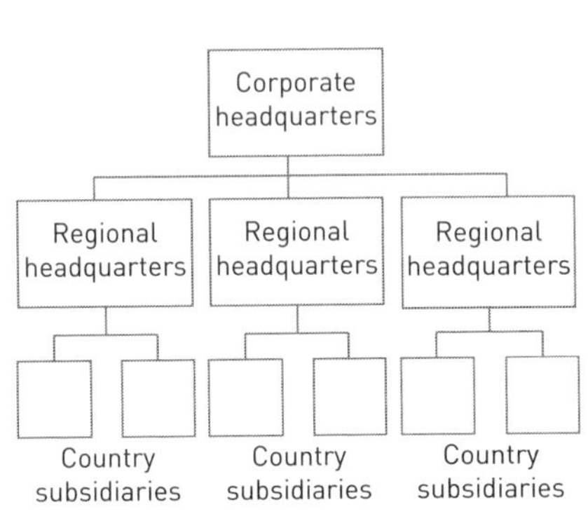

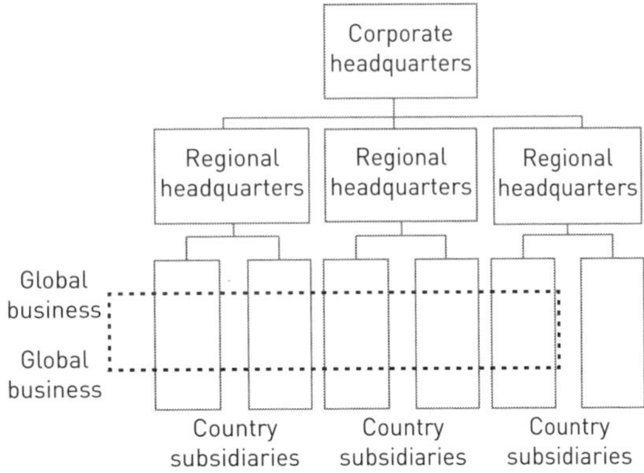

Figure 14.3 Geographical organizational models

Table 14.2 Characteristics of geographical organizational models

Organizational dimension	Innovation	Efficiency of operations	Marketing impact
Structure • National or regional subsidiaries have strategic and operational responsibilities • Global products or functions have a 'support' role	• R&D centres are distributed • Central R&D centre focuses on fundamental research • Central R&D centre and product managers propose products innovation but have no power to impose • Local companies have power to adapt products locally or have the discretion to choose from the corporate product portfolio the products they want to commercialize in their territory	• Self-contained operations at the level of countries/ regions • Scale efficiency obtained with country volume • Adaptation of products to local conditions • Optimization of product lines at country level	• Full localization of marketing mix • Optimization of marketing activities at country level • Local brands and promotion • Local pricing • Local distribution and maintenance
Processes	• Country-specific • Very little attempt to share and transfer best practices • Reliance on subsidiaries' self-interest • Regular information about corporate programmes through conferences and forums, but subsidiaries are free to decide what kind of innovation they adopt	• Country-specific • Arm's-length transactions among subsidiaries and between central factories and subsidiaries • Transfer pricing issues • Very often information systems are not compatible	• Country-specific • Marketing policies: subsidiaries' management has a high degree of discretion in implementation • Countries are profit and investment centres
Culture	• Pride in locally adapted products • Careers essentially local • Local identity	• Entrepreneurship • Agility • Autonomy	• Local image

In the single business geographical model, country managers are responsible for their profits and coordinate with central functions such as R&D, manufacturing and marketing in order to adapt to their local business realities.

In the multi-business geographical design, country subsidiaries are given full strategic and operational responsibilities for all product lines in their territory. In this design, the central global functions and product divisions have a 'support' or *dotted-line* role. National or regional units are profit centres and act autonomously.

EXAMPLE 14.3 Geographical organizations – Zee Entertainment and ISS

Zee Entertainment Enterprise

Founded in 1994 as a satellite TV and direct home transmission in India, Zee Entertainment Enterprise, part of the Essel conglomerate, is the largest producer and aggregator of Hindi programming in the world with around 1 billion viewers across the Middle East, Asia Pacific, North America, Africa and Europe.

Its internationalization process started by targeting the South Asian diaspora who wanted to remain connected to their original language programming. It launched its first subsidiary in the UK in 1995 followed by the USA, Africa and Southeast Asia. It offered its international audience Indian-produced movies and series chosen to suit local tastes. It then expanded its product portfolio to sport channels. It moved later on to produce local content for its various audiences. It offers a range of 46 domestic and 35 international channels. Its organizational structure is based on country management autonomy. Grouped into five regions (USA, Europe, Africa, Southeast Asia and Middle East/North Africa), country managers are in charge of their own research, programming and marketing, reporting back to regional managers.

Zee Entertainment's turnover in 2020 was $1,118 million and it employed 2,200 people. Its international operations represents 13 per cent of revenues.

International Service System A/S (ISS)

Founded in Copenhagen, Denmark, in 1901, ISS (International Service System) is a global facility services management company, offering facility management plus cleaning, support, property, catering and security services. In 2020 ISS had a turnover of $11 billion and 450,000 employees in 77 countries across Europe, Asia, North America, Latin America and Pacific. Its customers are from both public- and private-sector organizations ranging from industrial sites to administrative offices, offshore platforms, hospitals and retirement homes.

Poul Andreassen, who was the key architect of this organizational design, thought that the 'most profitable way to provide services is through small standalone companies led by a local manager who is encouraged to think of the business as his or her own'. He intentionally erected a barrier around the operational units which he called 'the Wall of China' to keep out top management. This original decentralized model was still in place in 2020. As stated on its website in its 2020 Annual report 'ISS is a country-centric organisation and rightly so. The vast majority of our business is originated locally. All business is executed locally, and all of our people are hired locally'.[6] Each country operates on local initiative and control, developing the local business according to market demand instead of following a 'one size fits all' approach. ISS has implemented a lean corporate structure, deliberately keeping overheads low and focusing solely on essentials. The role of the corporate centre is to provide financial and marketing expertise to the various countries.

Advantages of geographical organizational models

The main advantages of these designs are their *flexibility* and *adaptability* to local conditions. They encourage the optimization of the product and investment portfolio at country level, fitting with local tastes and regulatory conditions. Products tailored to consumer demands, advertising campaigns reflecting local culture and investment practices fitting with national policies enable companies to make more appealing value propositions. The ability to adapt and change competitive parameters without lengthy negotiations with the corporate centre gives geographically structured companies a better chance to capture emerging opportunities, or react rapidly to changing local conditions. Those advantages are more significant when customers' tastes and needs differ significantly across countries for economic, cultural, social or political reasons, and when scale economies can be attached easily within national boundaries. Traditionally, foods, cosmetics, personal services and government-regulated industries are those in which geographical design has worked well.

Disadvantages of geographical organizational models

Disadvantages arise when local autonomy creates too much duplication, erodes economies of scale or slows down the transfer of innovation. When customers become global and the market requires a 'global' pricing or service, geographically structured companies may lose their competitiveness if they do not introduce some element of global coordination. Sub-optimal resource allocation and delays in new product introduction are the main pitfalls of this model. In industries in which the pressures for globalization are high, this model leads to inefficiency and loss of competitive advantage. As seen earlier when discussing the 'reorganization merry-go-round' and 'the globalization penalty', since the 1990s those models have been abandoned, then reintroduced and given more predominance in the context of a matrix or transnational structure.

The multi-business global product division models

When a company has diversified into several business activities to become a multi-business corporation, it has the choice of three different organizational models to manage its global operations. Either it organizes itself along the *product dimension* or along the *geographical dimension* or with a *matrix*. The first organizational model is known as the multi-business global product division organization, which is represented in Figure 14.4 and its characteristics are described in Table 14.3. The example of Bombardier illustrates a multi-business global product division organization.

In this model, the company is divided into *business divisions*, each in charge of a product or service line. Each division chief executive is responsible for the global performance of the division's business and, as such, formulates its global strategy and puts in place the organizational design which best fits its competitive context. In some cases divisions act independently from each other and subsidiaries of one division in one country frequently do not interact at all with subsidiaries of another division. Within the division, the organizational design can be one of the three kinds described earlier: global functional, geographical or matrix.

If the competitive contexts of the division differ, one division can be organized geographically, for instance, and another use the global functional model. National subsidiary managers report to division heads. In this model, the divisional global headquarters of one business can be located in one country while the headquarters of another division are based in another country and the corporate headquarters in another one. The corporate headquarters' role is limited to overall strategic planning, financial control and executive career management.

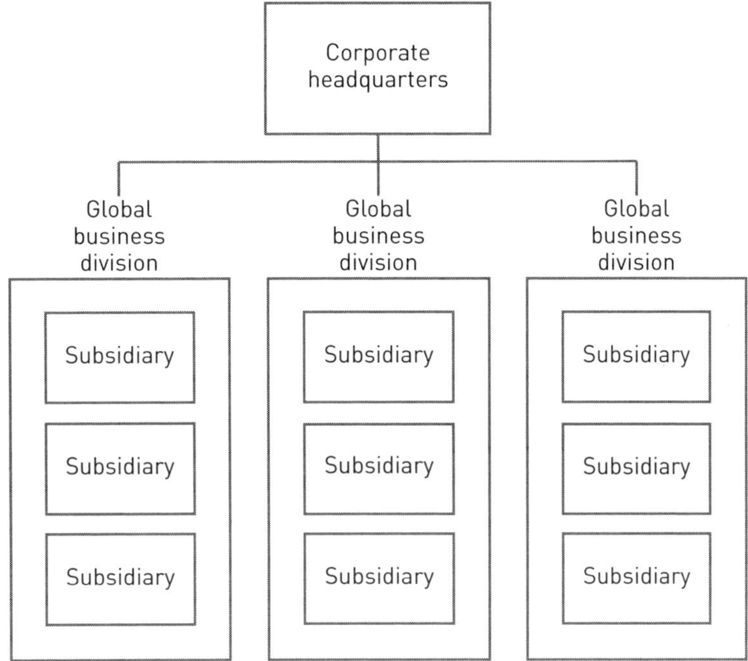

Figure 14.4 The multi-business global product division organizational model

Table 14.3 Characteristics of the multi-business global product division organizational model

Organizational	Innovation	Efficiency of operations	Marketing impact dimension
Structure • Global strategic and operational power and responsibilities given to separate product divisions	• R&D initiated by product divisions • Encourages global standardization	• Encourages coordination of activities within divisions • Strong efficiency and scale economies within divisions • Poor coordination among divisions	• Each division develops its own marketing approach • Marketing adapted to industry contexts
Processes	• Within divisions	• Within divisions	• Within divisions
Culture	• Careers and identity within divisions	• Careers and identity within divisions	• Careers and identity within divisions

EXAMPLE 14.4 Philips

The Dutch Philips group transformed itself from a diversified conglomerate involved in consumer electronics, domestic appliances and personal care into a multi-business global corporation involved in health-related products. In 2020, with a total revenues of €19.5 billion, the global segments were Diagnosis Imaging (41 per cent), Ultrasound (20 per cent), Image Guided therapy (37 per cent) and Enterprise & Diagnostic Informatics (8 per cent). It operates three market groups – North America, Greater China and International Markets (consisting of seven regions) – which are active in more than 100 countries worldwide. It employs 81,500 people.

Each global business segment's executive director is responsible for the management of its business worldwide. The country's head's objectives are to understand local market/customer needs and to develop and manage the relationship with existing and new customers. They have a country P&L responsibility.

Advantages of the multi-business global product division model

This model gives the global company the flexibility to adapt its structure to the competitive context of each business. By giving division executives the strategic responsibility for their business, this design provides the organizational mechanisms for global efficiency and coordination. This model tends to be favoured by the vast majority of multi-business corporations.

Disadvantages of the multi-business global product division model

The disadvantages of this model appear most clearly in regions or countries where big contracts require an integrated approach. In China or other emerging countries, customers do not understand why different propositions for different parts of a project come from different divisions of the same multinational and call for a single offer. The second obvious disadvantage of this model comes from the predominance given to *global efficiency* as opposed to *local responsiveness*.

The matrix models

The matrix model is an organizational design in which two (or sometimes three) managerial responsibilities are given equal power-decision and profit-and-loss responsibilities. In the global business environment, matrices can take several forms:

- *Function/geography matrix*: both functions and geography are given equal power and responsibilities. In such a case the R&D global vice-president would be responsible for the global R&D budget and would have some authority over the careers of scientists and designers, but national managers would have some authority over the allocation of resources, local laboratories and the careers of scientists or designers. A similar dual responsibility would apply for operations and marketing. This design is very often used by professional firms such as engineering companies, advertising or consultancy firms.
- *Products/geography matrix* in multi-business corporations. This design emphasizes dual responsibilities shared between the product divisions and the regions and countries.

- *Customer groups/geography matrix* in which responsibilities are shared between the customer-facing groups and the geographical units.
- *Tri-dimensional matrix* in which the power is distributed into three managerial areas: products (or customer groups), geography and functions.

The product/geography, customer/geography or tri-dimensional matrices are used in multi-business corporations.

The end result of these designs is shared executive power which puts middle managers in a situation of having 'dual' or sometimes 'triple bosses'.

The objective of such designs is to solve the requirements of efficiency, leverage and responsiveness through a dual structure. It aims to develop a culture of 'thinking globally, acting locally' by institutionalizing the tensions arising from the two competitive imperatives.

The single matrix organizational design is represented in Figure 14.5 and its characteristics are described in Table 14.4. Some examples of these structures follow.

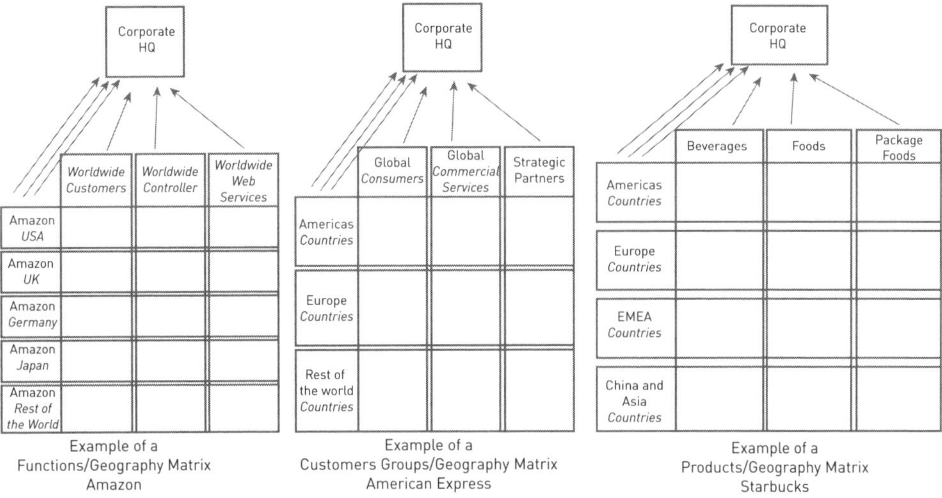

Figure 14.5 Matrix organizational simplified models

Table 14.4 Characteristics of matrix organizational models

Organizational dimension	Innovation	Efficiency of operations	Marketing impact
		Function/geography matrix	
Structure • Both functions and countries are given equal power and responsibilities	• Central R&D responsible for product innovation • Local subsidiaries responsible for product adaptation	• Central operations responsible for global operations and optimization • Local subsidiaries responsible for local results	• Central marketing responsible for global marketing strategies • Local subsidiaries responsible for local marketing strategies

Organizational dimension	Innovation	Efficiency of operations	Marketing impact
Processes	• Global research strategic plan and budget drawn up by global vice-president • Local budgets at subsidiaries level • Conferences for transfer of best practice	• Strategic investment in global factories or operational centres by global vice-president • Global best practice • Local operational responsibilities	• Global marketing plan • Local marketing plans • Reconciliation through strategic planning meetings
Culture	• 'Think global, act local' • Dual identity • Negotiation	• Local operating procedures • 'Think global, act local' • Dual identity • Negotiation	• 'Think global, act local' • Dual identity • Negotiation
Products: geography or consumer/geography multi-business matrices			
Structure • Strategic and operational responsibilities shared by product and geographical units	• Global product divisions lead global product development • National management adapt products and services locally	• Global factories and operational units • Local factories • Integration of supply chain	• Global marketing guidance/support • Local integration of product portfolio
Processes • Dual systems • Free flow of information • Multidimensional databases	• Dual strategic plans • Shared information systems • Transfer of 'best practices'	• Dual strategic plans • Shared information systems • Transfer of 'best practices'	• Dual strategic plans • Shared information systems • Transfer of 'best practices'
Culture • 'Think global, act local'	• Sharing and negotiating culture	• Negotiating	• Optimization

EXAMPLE 14.5 Matrix organizations – Olam and BASF

Olam International: a three-dimensional matrix

Olam International was established in Nigeria in 1989 for exporting cashew nuts from Nigeria into India. In 2016 Olam was a global integrated agri-business company cultivating or sourcing 47 products (staple foods, cocoa, coffee, spices, nuts, dairy produce, cotton, and industrial raw materials), from plantation and processing through to distribution. Production, sourcing and distribution centres are located in 70 countries worldwide to serve 21,000 customers.

Olam employs 80,000 full-time, seasonal and contractual personnel worldwide. In 2021, its sales totaled $Sing 47000Lillion (US$ 34000 million) with 47 per cent in Asia, the Middle East and Australia, 16.5 per cent in Europe, 19.5 per cent in Africa and 16.8 per cent in the Americas.

Its organization that was reorganized in 2020 is a three-dimensional matrix made of 3 Operating Groups, Country management and Functional teams as in Figure 14.6.

The three Operating Groups' directors are directly responsible for the profit and loss of a business or a section of business in more than one country. They are part of the team of global business heads overseeing global strategy, resource allocation and logistics coordination, as well as managing synergies and efficiencies for their respective businesses and the organization as a whole.

The country managers' role is to be in tune with and responsive to the local market and to manage sourcing, processing, logistics and distribution activities in their respective countries while controlling supply chain risks. Country management is grouped into four regions: 1) Asia, Middle East, Australia, 2) Africa, 3) Europe, 4) Americas.

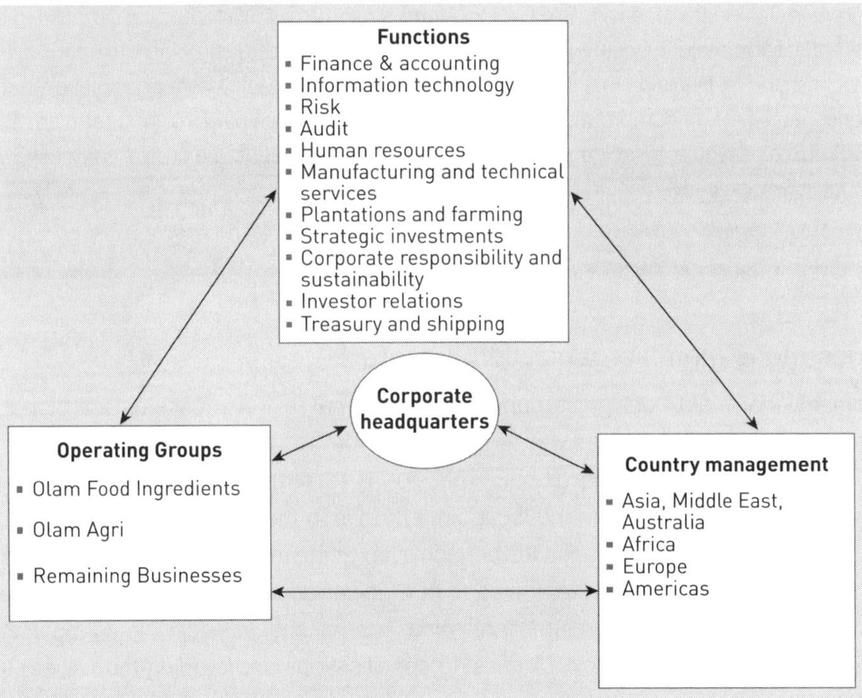

Figure 14.6 The Olam three-dimensional organization matrix

Functional teams include Finance and Accounting; Information Technology; Risk; Audit; Human Resources; Manufacturing and Technical Services; Plantations and Farming; Strategic Investments; Corporate Responsibility and Sustainability; Investor Relations; Treasury and Shipping. Although headed at a global level, functional team members are located in different tiers across various countries.

Source: Pant, Constantini and Pant (2011), and company documents. Reproduced with permission.

BASF

The BASF Group is one of the world's largest chemical corporations, with 358 sites scattered throughout 90 countries and customers in more than 170 countries. In 2021, the company's sales reached €79 billion (US$83billion) with pre-tax profits of €7.8 billion (US$8.2 billion). The group's activities are divided into five segments containing 13 global divisions. The segments are: Chemicals, Performance Products, Functional Solutions, Agricultural Solutions, and Oil and Gas. These products are organizationally balanced by four regional divisions: Europe, North America, Asia Pacific and South America/Africa/Middle East, with five research divisions and eight functional divisions including engineering and maintenance, global logistics, finance and human resources as well as seven corporate units providing management with strategic, financial and legal support. This provides BASF with a three-dimensional matrix. In the 1980s, most important business decisions were taken in the Ludwigshafen (Germany) headquarters; organizations with regional responsibilities remained sited in Germany, for the most part staffed by Germans. As part of a globalization drive since 2000, the BASF Group made a major effort to decentralize its international business, moving many of the company's operations and decision-making capabilities and key region-sensitive activities, such as marketing, as well as certain administrative functions, into three principal geographical areas: Europe, NAFTA (North America) and Asia. In accordance with BASF's long-term strategy, manufacturing capabilities in each region were targeted to receive major investments, with the eventual aim of increasing locally manufactured content to 70 per cent and above. Decision making was to be non-confrontational; where possible, executives sought to forge a consensus through compromise, with the overall aim of maintaining the long-term health and profits of the BASF Group as a whole. In fact, the ability to compromise represented a crucial career skill within BASF culture; without it, few executives could hope to advance!

Sources: Crawford and Schütte (2000); BASF Corporate information (2016). Reproduced with permission.

Advantages of the matrix organizational models

The multidimensional matrix design is supposed to internalize the pressures for global efficiency, leverage and local responsiveness, as well as achieving synergies among businesses. The mechanism is twofold: at the business level, the global dimension is represented by the executive in charge of the worldwide product division, while the local dimension is in the hands of the business units in the countries. The synergies among businesses are achieved at the region or country level by the regional or national manager. Take, for example, the case of a power-generation firm selling a large project to a public utility in Venezuela through international bids. The national salespeople will be in contact with the customer at the pre-bidding stage, discussing specifications and bidding modalities. To make an effective proposition, several divisions have to be involved: one for turbines, one for generators, one for transformation and one for regulation. A *bidding task force* will be gathered by the Venezuelan national manager in order to coordinate the bids of the various divisions. Assuming that the company wins the contract, the national manager will be credited with the sales and the profit on these sales, while each product division will be credited with the sales and the profits for their respective product offering. The project manager in Venezuela will effectively report to the national manager as well as to the different divisions, managing the tensions between the various 'bosses'. By forcing the project managers to make the necessary trade-off between the product divisions and national management, the matrix structure is intended to optimize the dual requirements of global efficiency and local responsiveness.

Disadvantages of the multi-business matrix organizational model

Matrix organizations are complex and may lead to power struggles that cancel out their expected benefits.[7] There are five main pitfalls of matrix structures:

- *Role ambiguity.* Middle managers operating in matrix structures are frequently placed in situations where their 'dual bosses' put pressure on them to achieve conflicting objectives. While, theoretically, the matrix organization is designed to force those managers to 'solve' these conflicts, in reality it does not. Managers will follow whatever instructions they consider come from the 'most powerful boss'. The matrix becomes an illusion.
- *Dilution of responsibilities.* In order to make a matrix work properly, numerous formal conflict resolution mechanisms must be in place, particularly committees, meetings and task forces. Decisions take a long time and, at the end of the day, it is very difficult to untangle who is responsible for what. In case of failure or mistake, it is always possible to find excuses for decisions made by an anonymous unaccountable committee.
- *Cost inefficiencies.* Coordination costs of matrix structures – such as travel, communication, time spent in meetings and delays in making decisions – tend to rise very rapidly without any compensation in competitive benefits.
- *Turf battles.* By design, matrix structures require product divisions and national managers to assert their power, leading to numerous territorial conflicts. The worst scenario is when customers themselves become involved in the conflict, receiving different value propositions, for instance, from different organizational units.
- *Costs of compromise.* The main danger of the dual tension resolution implied in the matrix design is that of compromise. In order to satisfy both of their 'two bosses', managers may adopt middle-of-the-road solutions, ultimately leading to mediocre decisions. To take an example of such an outcome, let us consider a lubricant company: the salespeople in Japan ask for eleven different sizes of cans to serve the motorist market. The global product division has decided that five sizes of can are sufficient to cover the market's needs and that it is more cost-effective to focus on those five types of can. Here is a typical conflict between global efficiency (five sizes) and local responsiveness (the Japanese market demands eleven sizes). A matrix structure may encourage the local lubricant manager to 'compromise' and propose seven sizes: a decision that will not satisfy the Japanese customer, but will still increase costs.

These pitfalls have encouraged many corporations to abandon this type of structural design and return to a simpler product or geographical organization structure. However, this does not overcome the fact that in a global company the tensions between efficiency, leverage and responsiveness are constant and inevitable, like 'breathing'. If the matrix structure that is supposed to achieve a symbiotic reconciliation between various competitive requirements does not fulfil this reconciliation, how can it be achieved?

Alternative structural models

Customer-centred structures

Since the 1990s, customer-centred structures have gained in popularity among companies who are especially conscious of their positioning and value proposition to customers. This strong customer focus has prompted some companies (e.g. Reuters and SingTel) to restructure their organization and form departments based on *customer groups* (defined by industrial sector for business customers, and by socioeconomic categories for private consumers). By having designated staff specializing in customer groups, customer needs can be better catered for, improving company responsiveness. Customer-centred structures are similar in concept to product divisional design described earlier.

With increased customer convenience and responsiveness, however, comes the trade-off of reduced technical competence among the staff of the service provider. Since each person is now serving a customer group, their knowledge is spread across the wide range of products which are being offered to that particular customer group. It could be argued that customers may not be expecting flawless technical advice (e.g. details of printer specifications) or may not be able to discern that ineffective 'expert' advice is due to a lack of knowledge or underlying uncertainty surrounding the advice (e.g. a bank's investment advice given to customers).

Complex dual structural models

As mentioned earlier, the logic behind dual models is to create within the global organization a mix of different designs. For instance, Citibank built an organization in which a global product division design (consumer banking and corporate banking), a geographical design (country subsidiaries) and a single matrix design for global account management co-exist. Another example is provided by 3M in Europe, which has adopted a global product division design in the form of European Business Centers (EBCs), which comprise pan-European product line organizations reporting to the US main product divisions in charge of R&D, manufacturing and technical services to customers. The geographical dimension is represented by regional subsidiaries, which are in charge of the operational results within the countries.[8] The ACER group had in the past similarly divided its global operations into two categories: strategic business units (SBUs) which essentially develop products and manufacture components in world-class factories, and regional business units (RBUs), which are locally based and in charge of assembling, marketing and sales (see Mini-case 14.2 at the end of the chapter). The dual complex designs offer the flexibility to take care of the many specifics of contexts and businesses without locking managers into the straitjacket of a unique organizational design. The obvious pitfalls of these designs are their complexity, which requires from managers a culture similar to that advocated by the 'transnational' model.

The transnational model

Contrary to the other models presented earlier, the transnational organizational design model does not focus on organizational structure but on *management processes and culture*.[9] The transnational design does not prescribe any particular organizational structure, but recognizes that a global organization is made up of four types of differentiated managerial roles:

- *Global business managers* act as strategists, architects of asset distribution and competencies leveraging, and coordinators of global activities
- *National managers* act as detectors of local opportunities and threats, builders of national resources and contributors to global competitive development
- *Functional managers* act as specialists, looking after new developments and making sure that best practices are shared and transferred across the organization
- *Corporate managers* act as overall organizational leaders and developers of talent.

These four roles can be distributed within a global product, a geographical or a matrix structure, the important thing being that managers develop a 'matrix in the mind'.

The seven key features of the transnational design are:

- Business units are part of a network, which follows the principle of *reciprocal dependencies*.
- *A non-dominant dimension* – all roles are important for competitive success and therefore no dimension, global, functional or geographical, predominates.
- A clearly defined and tightly controlled set of *operating systems*, and in particular of a transparent and multidimensional information system.
- Good *interpersonal relationships*.
- *Inter-unit decision forums* with active participation of global and functional managers in subsidiaries' boards.
- Strong *corporate values*.
- A culture of *sharing and willingness to collaborate*.

Since the transnational model does not rely on a formal organizational structure it is difficult to find companies that obviously and overtly assume the form of a pure transnational model. However, a variety of companies insert in their human resource and coordinating practices a lot of the features of this type of global design.[10]

As an example, the Acer group mentioned in 2011 that its organization was based upon 'the promotion of the spirit of teamwork to enhance company's overall competitiveness, and encourage closer communication between front-end and back-end management teams for better mutual understanding'.[11]

Since 1990, global corporations have come to understand that the search for an ideal structure is futile, and that what matters more is the way managers behave. Most of them have now invested in the development of attitudes, skills and behaviour in line with the 'transnational' model (see Figure 14.7).

An example of a transnational model of organization is provided by the globally integrated enterprise initiated by IBM and briefly described in Example 14.6.

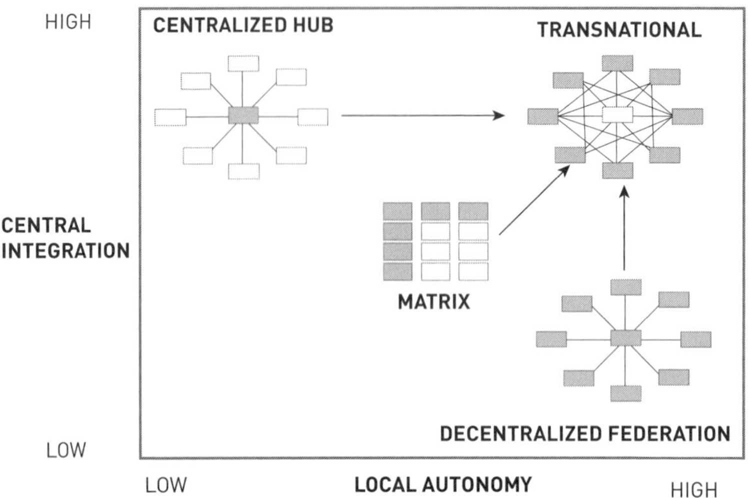

Figure 14.7 Convergence of global organizational designs

EXAMPLE 14.6 *Strategy and organizational structure: IBM from the 1990s to the 2020s*

International Business Machine (IBM), created in 1911 (under a different name) developed during the most part of the twentieth century as the leading multinational corporation in the computer industry. Since the 1960s the global structure was a product/services-geography products serving 150 countries.

In the early 1990s, confronted with strong competitive pressure, the newly appointed CEO, Louis Gerstner (1993–2002), introduced the strategic concept of 'going to market as one IBM' which was translated into a reorganization leading to the creation of a 'Worldwide Management Council' made up of geographical leaders as well as products/services divisions. One of the key decisions was to globalize the sales organization under the product/service groups. Sales people in countries were reporting to product divisions managers. The strategic focus was to transform IBM from a product company to a solution company implying the combination of several products and services.

In 2006, Sam Palmisano, the new CEO, continued the 'solution selling' strategy and accordingly reorganized the firm into two broad business segments:

Global Technology Services (GTS), concerned with the delivery of technology services (both hardware and software), including outsourcing the management of customers' information systems and equipment, integrated technology services and maintenance.

Global Business Services (GBS) dealt with professional services, delivering solutions to customers: consulting, systems integration and application management services.

Both segments are combined into what Palmisano called the 'globally integrated enterprise'.[12] The idea behind the globally integrated enterprise is to 'operate with one set of processes, shared services and broadly distributed decision making, carried out by a highly skilled global workforce managed by a common set of values'.[13]

Virginia Rometty succeeded Palmisano in 2012 and wanted to put IBM at the forefront of new technological development such as cloud services, artificial intelligence and cognitive computing. She undertook a massive business portolio by divesting some business (for instance PC business sold to Lenovo, retail stores to Toshiba) and acquiring others in healthcare, cloud computing, data analysis, security and weather. She reorganized the sales forces into unified, industry-based customer account and solutions teams.[14]

When Rometty's tenure was over and she was replaced by Arvind Krishna it appeared that performances between GTS and GBS had been unequal. The new CEO decided to split the company and on 8 October 2020 the spin-off of the Managed Infrastructure Services unit of the Global Technology segment became a new public company named Kyndryl:[15]

The two entities are due to operate according to their respective strategic focus:

- IBM, with $9 billion in revenues, concentrates on hybrid cloud and AI through five business segments: Cloud & Cognitive Software, Global Business Services, Global Technology Services, Systems and Global Financing. 175 counties are served with country-based operations that serve clients using the resources provided by the business segment specialists
- Kyndryl, with $19 billion in revenues and 90,000 employees, focuses on managing infrastructure and services to customers in 115 countries, with 4,600 big corporate clients supported by six global practices: Cloud; Applications, Data & AI; Security & Resiliency; Core Enterprise & zCloud; Network & Edge; Digital Workplace. According to Martin Schroeder, CEO of Kyndryl, 'Kyndryl is meeting customers where they are on their digital transformation journeys, with a lean and focused team that has the critical skills they depend on to succeed. Our country leaders and managing partners will be empowered to work closely with customers, make quick decisions and access the best global talent in the industry.'[16]

Digitally enabled organizations

Digital technologies have brought major structural change in the way of doing business, hence affecting the way global companies operate.

First, Industry 4.0 manufacturing technologies made it possible to locate smaller and more flexible facilities close to customers. Second, digital platforms, such as Airbnb or Uber, allow easy access to customers and local partners. Third, services such as online diagnostics and maintenance mean it is possible to provide customized solutions to customers.

These three digital developments give locally based customer facing teams more decision-making freedom. In a series of papers, the Boston Consulting Group (BCG) analysed the consequences of what it calls 'New Business Models for a New Global Landscape'.[17] According to this research, multinational companies will move from hierarchical vertical teams within businesses or regions, towards horizontal teams enabled by global collaboration platforms that allow members to communicate in real time. This leads to a dispersion of decisions to customer-facing teams without losing control of some products and services thanks to digitalization (see Figure 14.8). However 'digitization is enabling companies to centralize some functions and processes therefore allows for the simultaneous decentralization and centralization of processes, functions, and decision rights'.[18]

HOW AND WHERE DO I GROW GLOBALLY?	• Take a far more differentiated approach to prioritizing countries. • Directly target new global, borderless segments, such as digitally connected consumers and devices. • Shift to selling scalable, asset-light services at a lower cost per unit and value-added solutions. • Address risky markets with new business models and approaches.
WHAT IS MY GLOBAL PRODUCTION AND DELIVERY FOOTPRINT?	• Consider a multilocal manufacturing network. • Build hybrid global-local service delivery capabilities. • Leverage an ecosystem of platforms and local partners.
WHAT IS MY ORGANIZATION MODEL AND PHILOSOPHY?	• Become more customer centric; move beyond transactional relationships. • Become more country centric; increase local decision rights. • Centralize key functions driven by digital technologies and analytics.

Figure 14.8 New business models for a new global landscape
Source: Bhattacharya, Khanna, Schweizer and Bijapurkar (2017).

Digitalization also enables centralization of monitoring and control of some global processes such as distributed factories or global supply chains. An example of a digitally enabled organization is given in Example 14.7 and in Mini-case 14.1, at the end of the chapter.

EXAMPLE 14.7 Example of a digitally enabled structure: GitLab

GitLab was created in 2011 by Dmitriy Zaporozhets in Ukraine as an individual start-up to develop open source tools to automate software development cycles. Joined by Sid Sijbrandij as CEO, Gitlab was incorporated in 2014 in Holland with a team of nine people. In 2015, despite the company's working principle as an 'all remote company', almost the entire GitLab team flew to Silicon Valley. There were no headquarters (except for postal and legal purposes) – it was 'all remote' by design. Employees could work anywhere they chose, which applied to all levels in the hierarchy. Since they were spread across almost every time zone, there were no predetermined working hours – they could choose the time they preferred. Even hiring, onboarding and firing happened remotely. In 2014, Gitlab's team grew by another 100 people to more than 140 in total and in 2016 the number of people that contributed to GitLab grew to more than 1,000. More than 100,000 organizations and millions of users were using GitLab. By 2020, more than 3,000 people had contributed to GitLab. The GitLab Inc. team consists of 1,315 team members.

> We're the world's largest all-remote organization and we currently have team members in 66 countries and regions. With over 1,200 team members in more than 65 countries, GitLab is now the world's largest all-remote company. Every single team member is remote, with no central headquarters and no

company-owned offices anywhere in the world. GitLab has experienced 50x growth since 2016, reaching US$100M revenue in 2020 and the company was valued at $2.75 billion.

The organization is based on two settings:

1 Functions: The backbone of the organization: Engineering, Marketing, Sales, Customer support, Product, Finance, People, Legal
2 Working groups that are a temporary arrangement of people from different functions whose task is to achieve a particular business goal. A working group disbands when the goal is achieved (defined by exit criteria) so that GitLab does not accrue bureaucracy.

GitLab does not have an internationalization group. That responsibility is shared across many groups. GitLab documents the organizational processes in a handbook that describes how the company is run – it consists of over 10,000 pages of text.

Sources: https://about.gitlab.com/company/history/; https://about.gitlab.com/handbook/ (accessed 1 February 2022); Puranam and Minervini (2020).

Holocracy: an organization without structure

Defined as an organization where 'authority and decision making are distributed throughout a holarchy of self-organizing teams rather than a management hierarchy',[19] holocracy (sometimes referred as holacracy[20]) is based on three principles: 1) no job title or manager; 2) no hierarchy of managers; 3) every role is accountable. This concept was apparent in 2002 at Google when the company 'experimented with a completely flat organization, eliminating engineering managers in an effort to break down barriers to rapid idea development and to replicate the collegial environment they'd enjoyed in graduate school'.[21] The experimentation was abandoned because it created chaos: too many questions were raised with no priority (see https://www.compli.com/blog/what-google-learned-by-trying-to-eliminate-managers/).

In another case, in 2013 Tony Hsieh, CEO of Zappos, an online shoes and clothing company, introduced a new, complex self-management system inspired by holacracy.[22] This was progressively disbanded after Amazon's acquisition of the business. Most holocracy experiments were essentially carried out in the USA and were discontinued; there is no clear example of a global, multinational application of the concept.

Regional headquarters in global management

Many multinational corporations have established regional headquarters (RHQs) in order to support and control their global expansion. The motivation for setting up an RHQ is the recognition that there are significant regional differences which are too complex, too deep-rooted, and too large to be handled from a far-away corporate headquarters.[23] In essence the establishment of a regional headquarters is an intermediary organizational device between a purely global approach directed from the corporate headquarters and a fully decentralized structure based on national subsidiaries' autonomy. The classic locations for regional headquarters have been Brussels or Geneva for Europe, Hong Kong or Singapore for Asia and Miami for Central and South America. Africa and the Middle East have been traditionally integrated with Europe. However, some companies may choose different locations according to their business characteristics.

Regional headquarters have two main roles:

- *Entrepreneurship-enhancing roles*: such as scouting new opportunities, strategy development and implementation, strategic stimulation, intelligence gathering, new business development and, more generally, signalling the strategic commitment of the company to local governments and to the business divisions.
- *Integrating administrative roles* more directly with local operations: pooling resources for greater efficiency and effectiveness, benchmarking and spreading best practices, coordinating activities across borders and business divisions. The aim here is to achieve synergies and consistency.[24]

If we take those two dimensions separately we find four role profiles, as shown in Figure 14.9.

The first of these profiles, the *administrator*, is for RHQs limiting themselves to clerical activities such as taxation, legal services or finance. There are no or very few entrepreneurial functions, these being either directly governed from the corporate centre or left to the local subsidiaries.

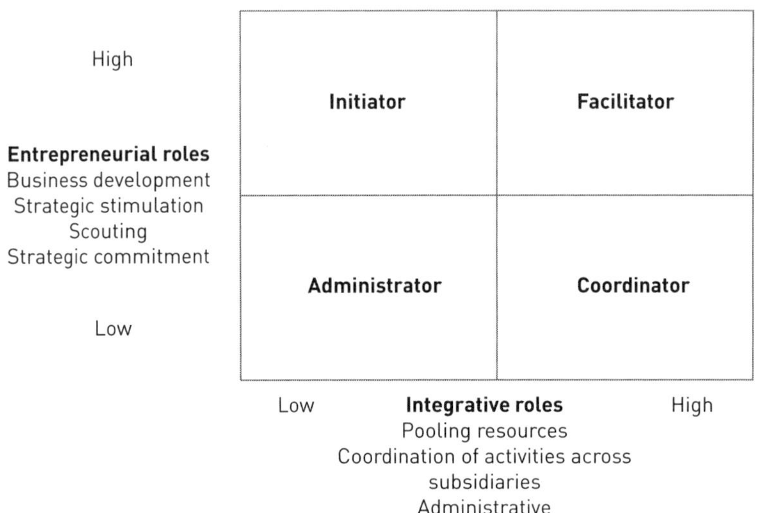

Figure 14.9 Profiles of regional headquarters in global firms
Source: Lasserre (1996).

The second profile, the *coordinator*, would describe an RHQ whose function is essentially to integrate and coordinate activities, to manage some central operations such as logistics, sourcing, training, and making sure that synergies across subsidiaries are taking place.

The third profile, the *initiator*, would consist of an RHQ in charge of only strategic development, information gathering and initiating deals.

Finally, the *facilitator* profile would describe an RHQ that fulfils both entrepreneurial and integrating roles.

Over time these roles may change. It would not be unusual for a company that wants to enter a region to start with a regional office that concentrates on entrepreneurial and strategic developments – an *initiator* profile. In time it may need to become a *facilitator* not only in order to stimulate strategic development but also to provide support and synergies to the operations.

When the businesses are well established in the region, the role of the RHQ may lessen to that of a *coordinator* or even an *administrator*.

Such a development is not always the case and in some companies the role of the RHQ increases instead of decreasing.[25]

Schütte[26] has identified three types of regional headquarter (Figure 14.10):

1 *The global RHQ is characterized by a strong alignment of its staff with corporate headquarters.* Global RHQs tend to be in charge of a limited number of global businesses and report to a senior manager who is responsible for these businesses on a worldwide basis. The RHQ can therefore be considered as an extension of the corporate HQ, staffed primarily by managers seconded from that HQ, who see themselves as enforcers and controllers. It will coordinate functional activities such as finance and human resource management, and can represent the corporate HQ in board meetings of the subsidiaries and during discussions with governments. It will, however, be less involved in synergy development between different businesses. It will also be relatively weak in representing regional concerns at headquarters. The advantage of the global RHQ lies in its simplicity: the organization is streamlined and focused. However, there are problems associated with the global RHQ. The main issue is that as an agent of corporate headquarters, the regional office downgrades the role of regional and national managers to implementers. This can lead to demotivation, the loss of local initiative and reduced feedback from the region.

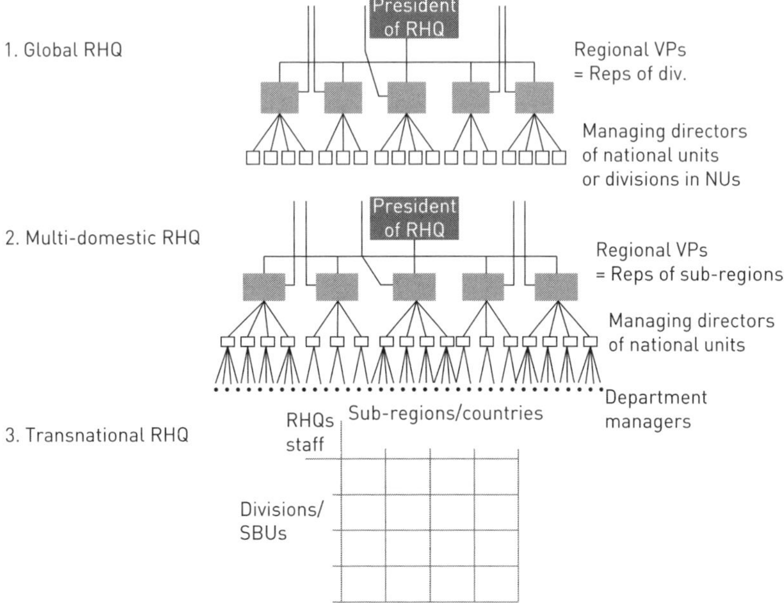

Figure 14.10 Organizational structure of regional headquarters
Source: Authors' own, derived from text of Evans et al. (2011).

2 *The multi-domestic RHQ operates in a geographical environment which is perceived to be different from other parts of the world.* The staff of the RHQ feel strongly committed to the region and obliged to fight for the region or defend it against pressures for globalization originating from HQ. The multi-domestic RHQ acts as a representative body of the operating units in the region and of their concerns. It therefore relies heavily on consensus between them and on their support. Its main purpose is to amplify the views of these local subsidiaries, which individually are too small to carry much weight at HQ. The advantage of this particular RHQ model lies in the devotion of the managers to the cause of the region. Ideally, the staff working in a multi-domestic RHQ will include managers from the region or at least expatriates with a long track record in the region. Strong advocacy of regional concerns may lead to a view of the world which is too one-sided and therefore not in the overall interest of the multinational corporation (MNC). The multi-domestic RHQ is a suitable model for an MNC needing to build a closer network in a region and win more recognition at HQ. It may be ideal for MNCs in which a region is not yet fully positioned on the mental map of the world or is still considered peripheral. The structure has the potential of creating a strong organizational unit in the corporation.

3 *The transnational RHQ is a structure in which there is recognition of the need for global integration but at the same time the characteristics of the region distinguish it from other regions and so an appropriate approach is required.* For practical reasons the transnational RHQ has to have an organizational structure which allows both the global and local forces to exert influence on decision making at the regional level. The matrix organization offers such a structure, with geographical concerns represented by sub-regions or countries and business concerns by product divisions or SBUs. The advantages of the transnational RHQ operating through a matrix organization are obvious. It serves as a regional forum where conflicting interests can be brought together for negotiation and solution. Over time, this experience leads to better understanding and a common spirit within the region. Synergies are possible between businesses and countries as well as across businesses and countries. When sufficient delegation takes place at HQ, the transnational RHQ emerges as a powerful organizational unit where decisions for the region are made without recourse to HQ. However, as mentioned earlier, the experience with matrix organizations in general is not wholly satisfactory. A second drawback of the transnational RHQ relates to the tendency to create a large, if not overblown, regional organization in order to accommodate all interested parties. In the extreme case an existing matrix at HQ level is simply replicated in the region, an arrangement which will not be well received in times of lean management and de-layering. Bearing in mind its advantages and disadvantages, the transnational RHQ emerges as a suitable model for large, experienced and diversified MNCs with mature regional managers. Through its flexible structure, it allows a multitude of perspectives, and maintains the balance between global and local needs without allowing one to dominate the other.

As indicated earlier, the organizational structure of RHQs may evolve over time according to the different roles assigned to them.

An alternative to regional headquarters: the gateway–hub structure

Proposed by C. K. Prahalad and Hrishi Battacharya[27] the gateway–hub model consists of a global company selecting ten gateway countries in the developed world and ten in the emerging world. These gateways have authority over most management decisions and serve as hubs for developing and coordinating activities in surrounding countries.

MINI-CASE 14.1

Siemens Vision 2020+

Telegraphenbauanstalt von Siemens & Halske was founded in 1847 by Werner von Siemens to produce telegraph pointers. In 2020, the Siemens Group generated revenue of €57.1 billion and employed 293,000 employees worldwide in 92 countries across Europe, Asia, the Americas, Africa, the Middle East and the Pacific.

In the early days the company defined itself as an international technologically innovative powerhouse. It expanded its business from telegraph to elevators, telecommunication, railways, medical devices, power generation, semiconductors.[28] Siemens was an early adopter of globalized business practices, opening offices in the second half of the nineteenth century in the major capitals of Europe, Russia and the Americas. Over the years Siemens has adapted its organizational structure in accordance with its global development. Starting from a centralized organizational structure overseeing countries subsidiaries, its major global structure was set up in 2008 around the three major global businesses called sectors (Industry, Energy and Healthcare), supervising 16 different business divisions serving various offerings (see Figure 14.11).

Countries were grouped in regional organizations. In 2014, the number of divisions was reduced from 16 to 10. However, the major organizational change

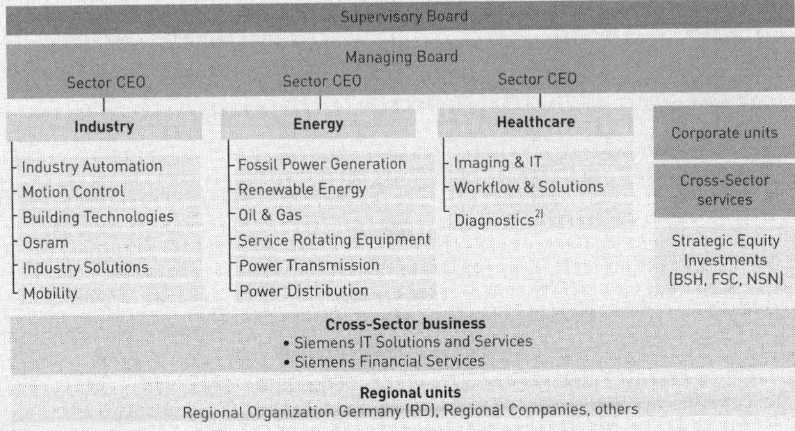

Figure 14.11 Siemens' new company structure on 1 January 2008

came with a major strategic redefinition named Vision 2020+ with the purpose 'to provide Siemens' individual companies with greater business freedom under the strong Siemens brand, in order to sharpen their attention in their respective market'.[29] In 2020, the company described its organization as a group of three major sectors: Smart Infrastructure (connected energy, building and industries), Digital Industries (Automation and Digitalization, Mobility (rail, electric infrastructure), plus Siemens Advanta (Consulting, business services, applications that offer comprehensive support to customers in their digital transformation)) and portfolio companies (six companies that are run independently). Siemens also created Next 45, an independent global venture to support new business developments. Each company has entrepreneurial freedom to sharpen its customer focus and orient its activities to the requirements of the industries in which it operates. The country subsidiaries act as one company in each country, with close collaboration between the businesses. They are empowered to serve customers, to create market opportunities and drive growth in the most efficient set-up.

This new business architecture relies on data mining and artificial intelligence through MindSphere® – an industrial information technology that provides solutions using advanced analytics and AI. According to BCG Consulting 'MindSphere, a data and analytics platform developed by Siemens, is being rolled out across all businesses, regions, and local offices to securely collect and analyze data from digitally connected equipment deployed around the world. Large, labor-intensive global plants are giving way to smaller, highly automated factories located closer to customers to provide greater flexibility and faster delivery.'[30]

SECTORS | **PORTFOLIO COMPANIES**

Digital Industries	Smart Infrastructure	Mobility	Siemens Healthineers	Portfolio Companies
Automation systems and software for industries Numerical and process control systems Integrated automation system production Management software	Energy systems and building technologies Intelligent gas and power grid control	Passenger and freight transportation Rail vehicles Rail automation systems Rail electrification systems Road traffic technology	Healthcare solutions and services Imaging, diagnostic and advanced therapies products and services Clinical consulting-services	Six companies providing products, software, solutions, systems and services for different industries: oil and gas, marine, mining, cement, water, fibre, wind, logistics and energy. Mechanical Drives Wind Energy Generation Siemens Logistics Siemens Energy Assets Large Drives Applications Valeo Siemens

- Siemens Advanta: Consulting for Digital Transformation
- Next45: Support New Business Developments

COUNTRIES

Europe, Commonwealth of Independent States (CIS), Africa, Middle East	Asia, Australia	Americas

SERVICE COMPANIES

Global Business Services	Real Estate Services	Financial Services

Corporate Development and Governance

Figure 14.12 Siemens' company structure in 2020

MINI-CASE 14.2

ACER's global organizational evolution

The ACER group, created in Taiwan in 1976, was by 2011 the second-biggest PC and notebook company in the world. With revenue of around $20 billion it employs 8,000 people worldwide. Since its creation, ACER has seen its global organization adapt to follow the management philosophy of its founder Stan Shih, as well as the industry's evolution.

The global organization has evolved in four stages:

- **Stage 1: Initial steps in globalization: 1976–1990**

  As early as 1979 ACER (known at the time as Multitech) started to export personal computers combining OEM contracts and sales under its own brand. To manage its operations American executives were recruited but were difficult to control. They acted quite autonomously and took many (often misguided) initiatives. A European office was opened in Germany to coordinate distributors and conduct market research. In emerging countries such as Thailand, Indonesia, Brazil, Chile, Argentina, South Africa, Mexico and India, ACER initiated a series of joint ventures. By 1990 it became obvious that the international operation needed to be reorganized.

- **Stage 2: Creating a multinational organization: 1990–2000**

  Stan Shih organized the global operation according to the client–server principle. The business units are divided into two broad categories: the SBUs, which essentially develop products and manufacture components in world-class factories, and the RBUs, which are locally based and are in charge of assembly, marketing and sales. Each unit is at the same time client and server, as shown in Figure 14.10.

  Stan Shih wanted local company managers to own a local shareholding of equity. 'At the heart of the client–server organization lies a closely linked team of mature and experienced managers committed to long-term success of their own piece of the ACER group. Mutual understanding and trust, communication and consensus are the cornerstone of ACER management.'[31]

- **Stage 3: The early 2000s**

  In December 2000, J. T. Wang was appointed as the president of ACER, responsible for turning around ACER PCs worldwide. At the time, the ACER group employed around 37,000 people in 232 enterprises

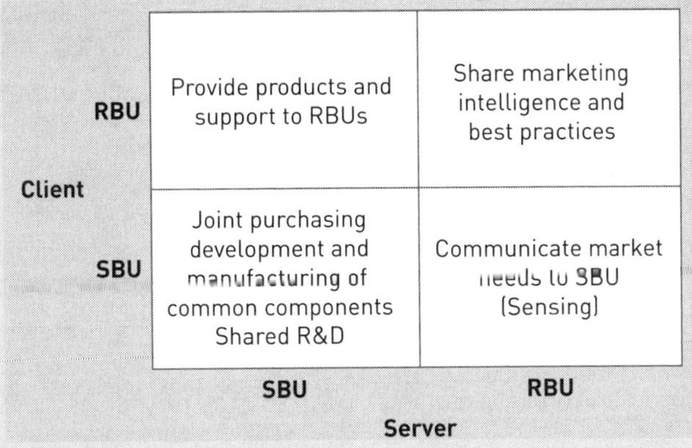

Figure 14.13 ACER's organizational model

in 41 countries supporting a network of distributors in 100 countries. In 2001 the bursting of the internet bubble precipitated a decline in PC sales. Wang initiated a profound restructuring. He introduced a more centrally integrated approach based on three global principles: One Global Company, One Global Brand and One Global Team.

- The principle of **One Global Company** led to the delisting of all locally listed international subsidiaries and the repurchase of all minority shares by ACER Inc. The group was reorganized: at first into three divisions, that ultimately were reduced to two, after the spin-off of one of them:
  - *ACER Brand Operation (ABO)* whose responsibility was to design, market and distribute products across the world.
  - The *Design, Manufacturing and Service Division (DSM)* in charge of R&D, manufacturing and service of all IT products. DSM was spun-off in 2001.
  - The third organizational leg was the *Holding and Investment Business* that was in charge of all financial matters, taking care of ACER's holdings in various businesses.
- The principle of **One Global Brand** stated that only the ACER brand could be used for IT products.
- The principle of **One Global Team** required that all managers abandon their parochial concerns.

- **Stage 4: Beyond 2010**

In 2007 ACER bought Gateway and Packard Bell and became the number two world provider of notebooks. It relies now on four global brands: ACER, Gateway, Packard Bell and E Machines. By 2011 the ACER organization was still based on the principle of One Global Team sharing strong corporate values, with operations divided into:

- Regional operations: Europe/Middle East/ Africa (EMEA), Pan America, Taiwan, China, Asia Pacific
- Global operations: PCs Global, Smart handheld Business, Channels, Marketing, E-Enabling Services
- Global functions: Finance, Human Resources, Legal, General Affairs.

Three key principles underpinned ACER's new management structure to ensure successful decision making:

- To promote the spirit of teamwork to enhance the company's overall competitiveness, and encourage closer communication between management teams
- To simplify operational systems and processes to boost effectiveness and speed
- To strengthen corporate governance and enhance company sustainability.

ACER in 2021

According to documentation provided by the company, the organizational structure and decision-making process were centred on five global businesses: IT Products, Digital Display, Smart Products, e-business and Value Lab, plus four regional offices: Asia Pacific and Europe, Middle East Africa, Americas and China.

Questions:

1. What were the major hurdles to ACER becoming a global company? How did it overcome them?
2. During its initial phase of global development, ACER relied on OEM, alliances and acquisitions, and had a decentralized management. Why? What are the pros and cons of such a strategy?
3. What do you think are the advantages and disadvantages of the client–server principle for global competitiveness?
4. What were the reasons behind ACER's strategic and organizational changes in 2001 and in 2020? Analyse the advantages and disadvantages of such changes.

Summary and key points

1 A global business organization should balance the following dual requirements:

  a To efficiently maintain *competitive advantages* across borders

  b To adapt to *local conditions*

2 Organizational designs

  a There are three main models of organizational design:
    - *Global hub:* a worldwide functional or global product structure
    - *Geographical:* a multi-countries structure
    - *Multidimensional:* a matrix or transnational structure

  b There are three key elements of organizational design:
    - *Organizational structure:* assignment of roles, responsibilities and power
    - *Organizational processes:* decision making, resource allocation, rewards and appraisal systems, planning and control
    - *Organizational culture:* shared values, reward system.

  c Types of *organizational design* (or model) (see the summary table of the common types of model in online Appendix 14.1)

  d The *transnational* model:
    - *Is different from* the other organizational designs because it focuses on management processes and culture instead of organizational structures
    - Possesses seven main features:
      - a network of business units
      - a non-dominant dimension
      - a clearly defined and tightly controlled set of information systems
      - good interpersonal relationships
      - inter-unit decision forums
      - strong corporate values
      - a willingness to share and collaborate

  f There are alternative models
    - Customer-centred structures
    - Complex dual structural models
    - Digitally enabled organizations
    - Holocracy

- **e** Most global companies have now realized that the search for an ideal structure is futile and have invested in the development of *attitudes*, *skills* and *behaviours* which are in line with the transnational model
- **f** Many multinational corporations have established regional headquarters (RHQs) in order to support and control their global expansion

  There are two major roles for regional headquarters: entrepreneurial and integrating, leading to four types of RHQ:
  - Initiator: high on entrepreneurial role/low on integrating
  - Coordinator: high on integrating role/low on entrepreneurial
  - Facilitator: high on both dimensions
  - Administrator: low on both dimensions

  - An RHQ's organization reflects the corporate design: global, multi-local or transnational
  - As an alternative to regional headquarters, a company can designate gateway countries serving as hubs in key parts of the world

Learning assignments

1. What are the benefits of having a geographical organization?
2. What are the typical difficulties in implementing a matrix organization?
3. What are the characteristics of the transnational model?
4. To what extent does the transnational model differ from the other organizational model?
5. Is holocracy a managerial illusion?
6. What does digital technology bring to global organizational design?
7. Does digital technology favour geographical decentralization or functional centralization?
8. What is the role of a 'coordinator' regional headquarters?

Key words

- Digitally enabled organization
- 'Dotted-line' relationship
- Global hub
- Holocracy
- International divisions
- Matrix
- Organizational culture
- Organizational processes
- Organizational structure
- Regional headquarters
- Transnational

Web resources

Booz Allen Consulting (see section on Ideas and Insights: strategy and organization):
http://www.boozallen.com/insights

BCG Consulting:
https://www.bcg.com/featured-insights/thought-leadership-ideas.aspx

Euromonitor Interntional (provides industry data):
http://www.euromonitor.com/

Companion website

Visit the companion website at bloomsbury.pub/global-strategic-management-5e for a multitude of weblinks and resources, self-test questions for revision and appendices.

Notes

1 Wouter et al. (2014).
2 Dewhurst, Harris and Heywood (2011).
3 Prahalad (1986).
4 Stopford and Wells (1972).
5 Ibid.
6 Ackenhausen (1993b).
7 Peters (1979); Bazigos and Harter (2016).
8 Ackenhausen (1993b). White Paper (2007).
9 Bartlett and Ghoshal (1989, 1990, 1992).
10 Bazigos and Harter (2016), Revisiting the Matrix, McKinsey Quarterly.
11 Acer appoints Jim Wong as Corporate President', April 2011, https://www.acer.com/ac/fr/FR/press/2013/72670 (accessed 28 January 2022).
12 IBM White Paper (2007).
13 Deviney et al. (2012).
14 Kanter and Cohen (2017).
15 IBM Newsroom (2021).
16 IBM Annual Report (202O).
17 Bhattacharya, Reeves, Lang and Augustinra (2018).
18 Bhattacharya, Khanna, Schweizer and Bijapurkar (2017)
19 Rud (2009).Robertson (2015).
20 Brian (2015à).
21 Garvin (2013: 75).
22 O'Rourke (2017).
23 Lasserre and Schütte (2006: Ch. 9).
24 Lasserre (1996).
25 Guey-Huey et al. (2010).
26 Schütte (1998).
27 Prahalad and Battacharya (2008).
28 von Karczewski (2018).
29 https://www.siemens.com/vision2020plus/en.html (accessed 1 February 2022).

References and further reading

Ackenhusen, M. (1993a) 'BS-International Service System A/S', INSEAD Case Study 11/ 93/4220.

Ackenhusen, M. (1993b) 'The 3M Company: integrating Europe', INSEAD Case Study 06/ 94/4317.

Aghina, W., De Smet, A. and Heywood S. (2014) 'The past and future of global organizations', *McKinsey Quarterly*, September: 1–10.

Bartlett, C. A. (1983) 'MNCs: get off the reorganization merry-go-round', *Harvard Business Review*, 61 (2): 138–46.

Bartlett, C. A. and Ghoshal, S. (1989) *Managing Across Borders: The Transnational Solution* (Boston, MA: Harvard Business School Press).

Bartlett, C. A. and Ghoshal, S. (1990) 'Matrix management: not a structure, a frame of mind', *Harvard Business Review*, 68 (4): 138–45.

Bartlett, C. A. and Ghoshal, S. (1992) 'What is a global manager?', *Harvard Business Review*, 70 (5): 124–32.

Bazigos, M. and Harter, J. (2016) 'Revisiting the matrix organization', *McKinsey Quarterly*, January: 1–87.

Bhattacharya, A., Khanna, D., Schweizer, C. and Bijapurkar, A. (2017) 'Going beyond the rhetoric: the new globalization', April. https://www.bcg.com/en-gb/publications/2017/new-globalization-going-beyond-rhetoric

Bhattacharya, A., Reeves, M., Lang, N. and Augustinra, J. R. (2017) 'New business models for a new global landscape', Boston Consulting Group Henderson Institute. https://www.bcg.com/publications/2017/globalization-new-business-models-global-landscape (accessed 1 February 2022).

Bhattacharya, A., Reeves, M., Lang, N. and Augustinra, J. R. (2018) 'Building the new global enterprise', Boston Consulting Group Henderson Institute. https://www.bcg.com/publications/2018/building-new-global-enterprise (accessed 1 February 2022).

Birkinshaw, J., et al. (2006) 'Why do some multinational corporations relocate their headquarters overseas?', *Strategic Management Journal*, 27 (7): 681–700.

Centre for Asian Business Cases (2001) 'Acer: the reorganization', Hong Kong.

Clyde-Smith, D. and Williamson, P. (1997) 'The ACER group: building an Asian multinational', INSEAD Euro Asia Centre Case Study 01/ 98-4712.

Crawford, R. and Schütte, H. (2000) 'BASF: working the matrix in Asia', INSEAD Euro Asia Centre Case Study 04/2999-4845.

Davis, S. M. (1979) *Managing and Organizing Multinational Corporations* (Oxford: Pergamon Press).

Decreton, B., Dellestrand, H., Kappen, P., et al. (2017) 'Beyond simple configurations: the dual involvement of divisional and corporate headquarters in subsidiary innovation activities in multibusiness firms', *Management International Review,* 57 (6): 855–78.

Del Carpio, L., Doz, Y. and Guadalupe, M. (2017) 'Embracing digital: ING's journey to a new way of working', INSEAD Case Study. 11/2018-6316.

DeViney. N. et al. (2012) 'Becoming a globally integrated enterprise: lessons on enabling organizational and cultural change', *IBM Journal of Research and Development*, 56 (6), Nov–Dec.

Dewhurst, M., Harris, J. and Heywood, S. (2011) 'Understanding your globalization penalty', *McKinsey Quarterly*, July: 1–17.

Doz, Y. (2016) 'Managing multinational operations from organizational structure to mental structures and from operations to innovation', *European Journal of International Management*, 10 (1): 10–24.

Doz, Y. (2017) 'The strategic decisions that caused Nokia's failure', INSEAD Knowledge. https://knowledge.insead.edu/strategy/the-strategic-decisions-that-caused-nokias-failure-7766 (accessed 6 June 2022).

Doz, Y. (2021), 'the fundamentals of transforming matrix to agile', INSEAD Knowledge. https://knowledge.insead.edu/strategy/the-fundamentals-of-transforming-from-matrix-to-agile-16181 (accessed 28 January 2022).

Flamant, A.-C., Fugjimura, S. and Willes, P. (2000) 'Renault and Nissan: a marriage of reason', INSEAD Case Study 10/2001-4928.

Franko, L. (1976) *The European Multinationals* (New York, NY: Harper & Row).

Garvin, D. (2013) 'How Google sold its engineers on management', *Harvard Business Review*, December: 75.

Ghazzawi, I. A. (2013/14) 'Café Britt: a Costa Rica pride', *Business Case Journal*, Fall/Winter, 21 (1).

Ghoshal, S. (1993) 'BS-International Service System A/S', INSEAD Case Study 11/ 93/4220.

Guey-Huey, L., Yu, C.-M. and Seetoo, D.-H. (2010) 'Toward a theory of regional organization', *Management International Review*, 50: 5–33.

IBM Annual Report (202O). https://www.ibm.com/investor/att/pdf/IBM_Annual_Report_2020.pdf (accessed 1 February 2022).

IBM Newsroom (2021) 'Kyndryl unveils new operating model and global structure'. https://newsroom.ibm.com/2021-07-01-Kyndryl-Unveils-New-Operating-Model-And-Global-Structure (accessed 1 February 2022).

IBM White Paper (2007) 'Developing global leadership: how IBM engages the workforce of a globally integrated enterprise', IBM Global Business Services.

Kanter, R. M. and Cohen J. (2017), 'IBM transforming: 2012–2016: Ginni Rometty steers Watson', Harvard Business School Case 9 317040.

Kennedy, R. E., Montgomery, C. A., Cladderton, L. and Hogan, H. (1998) 'Tyco International (A)', Harvard Business School Case 9-798-061.

Kets de Vries, M. (1994) 'Percy Barnevick and ABB', INSEAD Case Study 05/94/4308.

Kumar, N. and Puranam, P. (2011) 'Have you restructured for global success?', *Harvard Business Review*, October: 1–7.

Kunisch, S., Menz, M. and Collis, D. (2020) 'Corporate headquarters in the twenty-first century: an organization design perspective', *Journal of Organizational Design*, 9 (22). https://doi.org/10.1186/s41469-020-00086-9 (accessed 1 February 2022).

Lasserre, P. (1996) 'Regional headquarters: the spearhead for Asia Pacific markets', *Long Range Planning* (29): 30–7.

Lasserre, P. and Schütte, H. (2006) *Strategies for Asia Pacific* (Basingstoke: Palgrave Macmillan).

Levinthal, D. A. and Workiewicz, M. (2018) 'When two bosses are better than one: nearly decomposable systems and organizational adaptation', *Organization Science*, 29 (2): 207–24.

Malnight, T. W. and Yoshino, M. Y. (1995) 'Citibank: global customer management', Harvard Business School Case Study 9-395-142.

Nafei, W. (2016), 'Organizational agility: the key to organizational success', *International Journal of Business and Management*, 11 (5): 296. https://www.researchgate.net/publication/301535032_Organizational_Agility_The_Key_to_Organizational_Success (accessed 1 February 2022).

Nell, P. C. and Ambos, B. (2013) 'Parenting advantage in the MNC: an embeddedness perspective on the value added by headquarters', *Strategic Management Journal*, 34 (4): 1086–103.

O'Rourke, J., Golden, B. and Pandey, A. (2017) 'Zappos com: an experiment in holacracy', Case 17-13, Eugene D. Fanning Center for Business Communication, University of Notre Dame, Indiana. https://www.researchgate.net/publication/330125812_Zappos_An_Experiment_in_Holacracy (accessed 1 February 2022).

Pant, I., Constantini, J. and Pant, N. (2011) 'Olam International', INSEAD Case Study 09/2011-5786, and company documents.

Peters, T. (1979) 'Beyond the matrix organization', *McKinsey Quarterly*, 3.

Piskorsi, N. J. and Spadini, A. (2007) 'Procter & Gamble (A)', Harvard Business School Case 9-707-519, October.

Prahalad, C. K. (1986) 'The dominant logic', *Strategic Management Journal*, 7 (6): 485–501.

Prahalad, C. K. and Bhattacharyya, H. (2008) 'Twenty hubs and no HQ', *Strategy + Business*, 50: 24–9.

Pucik, V., Tichy, N. M. and Barnett, C. K. (1992) *Globalizing Management: Creating and Leading the Cooperative Organization* (New York, NY: John Wiley).

Puranam, P. and Minervini, M. (2020) 'GitLab: can "all remote" scale?', INSEAD Case Study 12/2020-6579 2020. https://publishing.insead.edu/case/gitlab (accessed 1 February 2022).

Puranam, P., Alexy, O. and Retzig, M. (2014) 'What's "new" about new forms of organizing?', *Academy of Management Review*, 39 (2): 162–80. http://dx.doi.org/10.5465/amr.2011.0436 (accessed 1 February 2022).

Robertson, B. J. (2015) *Holacracy: The New Management System for a Rapidly Changing World* (New York, NY: Henry Holt and Company).

Rud, O. P. (2009) *Business Intelligence Success Factors: Tools for Aligning Your Business in the Global Economy* (New Jersey, NY: John Wiley & Sons).

Salo, O. (2017) *How to Create an Agile Organization*, McKinsey & Company. https://www.mckinsey.com/business-functions/organization/our-insights/how-to-create-an-agile-organization (accessed 1 February 2022).

Schmitt, J., Decreton, B. and Nell, P. C. (2019) 'How corporate headquarters add value in the digital age', *Journal of Organization Design*, 8 (1): 1–10.

Schütte, H. (1998) 'Between headquarters and subsidiaries: the RHQ solution', in J. Birkinshaw and N. Hood (eds), *Multinational Corporate Evolution and Subsidiaries Development* (Basingstoke: Macmillan).

Shih, S., Wang, J. T. and Yeung, A. (2005) 'Building global competitiveness in a turbulent environment: Acer's journey of transformation', in W. H. Mobley and E. Weldon (eds), *Advances in Global Leadership*, 201–17 (Bingley: Emerald Group Publishing).

Stopford, J. and Wells, L. (1972) *Managing the Multinational Enterprise: Organization of the Firm and Ownership of the Subsidiaries* (New York, NY: Basic Books).

Taylor, W. (1991) 'The logic of global business: an interview with Percy Barnevik', *Harvard Business Review*, 69 (2): 90–104.

Von Karczewski, J. (2018) *1847–2017 Shaping the Future, Qualities that Set Siemens Apart – after 170 Years*. Siemens Historical Institute

Wouter, A., De Smet, A. and Heywood, S. (2014) 'The past and future of global organizations', *McKinsey Quarterly*, September: 1–10.

Yeung, A., Pu, B. and Qu, J. (2010) 'Acer: competitive advantage through global integration', *CEIBS Business Review*, August.

Part IV

Conclusions

Chapter 15 Current and future trends in globalization | This chapter is devoted to describing some of the most salient trends that are likely to affect firms' global strategic management. Many of the developments described are still ongoing, conjectural or incomplete. When one looks at the future one has to identify the ideological, social, demographic, political and scientific developments that affect the world of economics and business. Some of those are already visible today; some others are hidden or are present only in the form of 'weak signals' or 'black swans'. Finally the chapter will end by presenting some of the critiques of globalization and discussing the possible reversibility of the globalization process.

Chapter 16 Global strategic management in action: Haier – the building of a global champion, 1984–2020 | This concluding chapter comprises a long case study, tying together learning points from all the preceding chapters in an up-to-date, practical example of a global champion that has emerged over the last few decades.

Chapter 15

Current and future trends in globalization

At the end of the chapter you will be able to:

- Appreciate the major trends in the global economy
- Contribute to the building of future scenarios
- Identify some features of new models of global management

Introduction

As is often said, 'the future isn't what it used to be'. There are plenty of examples of predictions made by experts that turned out to be wrong. In 1989, Francis Fukuyama asserted that the world had entered a period that he called 'the end of history' in which, after the end of the Cold War, the world was increasingly dominated by liberal democratic societies.[1] This assertion was at best contentious, although Fukuyama stood by it in a 2014 *Wall Street Journal* article. The same can be said about globalization, the smooth progress of which had seemed inevitable and unstoppable. Geopolitical disorders following the September 11 attacks in the United States in 2001 and the increased momentum of nationalistic and authoritarian political regimes, as well as the financial crises of 1997 in Asia, the dotcom bubble burst of 2001, the subprime crisis in 2008, the Eurozone's over-indebtedness of 2011, the British decision in 2016 to quit the European Union (Brexit), the Covid-19 pandemic and the eruption of a major war in Ukraine in 2022 have shown that the road toward globalization is obstructed by many hurdles. Every year anti-globalization protesters gather at G8, International Monetary Fund (IMF) or World Economic Forum (WEF) meetings worldwide, in order to demonstrate against certain aspects of globalization. Joseph Stiglitz, a 2001 Nobel Prizewinner, criticized the global economic policies of the IMF, World Trade Organization (WTO) and the World Bank in his book *Globalization and its Discontents*.[2] At the same time, international conferences and meetings are organized by UNESCO, UN, G20, WEF and other international agencies or private initiatives to coordinate and promote multilateral programmes to cope with global issues.

Throughout the previous chapters, it has been assumed that globalization is ineluctable, and that most corporations are building strategies based on that assumption. The past thirty years have evolved in that direction. If we look at the future, however, the ongoing pursuit of globalization seems a likely scenario, but not the only one.

This chapter is devoted to describing some of the most salient trends that are likely to affect firms' global strategic management. Many of the issues described are conjectural and incomplete. When we look at the future we have to identify the ideological, social, demographic, political and scientific developments that affect the world of economics and business. Some of those are already visible today; some others are hidden or are present only in the form of 'weak signals'[3] or 'black swans'.[4]

Nevertheless, several organizations have projected future scenarios. All come up with three possible images: a globalized world, a fragmented world and an intermediate world in which globalization is partially achieved.

Figure 15.1 shows how this chapter is organized. First, some of the most significant global challenges will be briefly described. Then we will summarize the best-known scenarios. Finally, we will look at the emerging theories of *global management.*

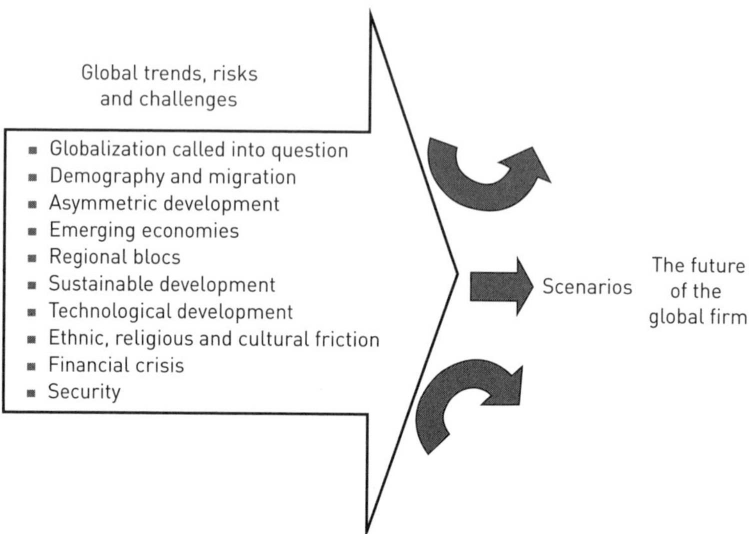

Figure 15.1 Global challenges and the global corporation

Global challenges[5]

Globalization called into question

The arguments in favour of and against globalization were introduced in Chapter 1 (Table 1.2). This dialectic tension between the zealots and the dissidents dominates the background of any future scenarios.

The *zealots'* point of view is best represented by a quotation from a report published by the US National Intelligence Council (NIC) entitled *Global Trends 2015: A Dialogue about the Future with Nongovernment Experts*.[6] Although published in 2000, the vision of the future is still the one these zealots foresee:

- 'The networked global company will be driven by rapid and largely unrestricted flows of information, ideas, cultural values, capital, goods and services, and people: that is, globalization. This globalized economy will be a net contributor to increased political stability in the world … , although its reach and benefits will not be universal. In contrast to the Industrial Revolution, the process of globalization is more compressed. Its evolution will be rocky, marked by chronic financial volatility and a widening economic divide between and within nations.'

- 'The global economy, overall, will return to the high levels of growth reached in the 1960s and early 1970s. Economic growth will be driven by political pressures for higher living standards, improved economic policies, rising foreign trade and investment, the diffusion of information technologies, and an increasingly dynamic private sector. Potential brakes on the global economy – such as sustained financial crisis or prolonged disruption of energy supplies – could undo this optimistic projection.'
- 'Regions, countries, and groups feeling left behind will face deepening economic stagnation, political, ethnic, ideological, and religious extremism, along with the violence that often accompanies it. They will force the United States and other developed countries to remain focused on 'old-world' challenges while concentrating on the implications of 'new-world' technologies at the same time.'

The *dissenting* voices are heard more and more in the countries that have benefited the most from globalization – the OECD countries – and their point of view can be best summarized by Rodrik:[7]

- 'First, reduced trade barriers and investment accentuate the asymmetry between the groups that can cross international borders (either directly or indirectly, say via outsourcing) and those that cannot.' These semi-skilled and unskilled workers can be replaced by other cheaper workers abroad. This undermines the social fabric in the developed world.
- 'Second, globalization engenders conflicts within and between nations over domestic norms and the social institutions that embody them' (such as pension funds, social security, values and culture).
- 'Third, globalization has made it increasingly difficulty for governments to provide social insurance.' The welfare state is under attack.
- 'The question therefore is how the tension between globalization and the pressures for socialization of risks can be eased. If the tension is not managed intelligently and creatively, the danger is that the domestic consensus in favour of open markets will ultimately erode to the point where a generalized resurgence of protectionism becomes a serious possibility.'

As might be expected, more extreme views are expressed by radical activist groups. Below is an extract from a talk given by Walden Bello, a representative of Corpwatch, during demonstrations in Melbourne against the World Economic Forum:

> What is *deglobalization*?
>
> I am not talking about withdrawing from the international economy. I am speaking about reorienting our economies from production for export to production for the local market;
>
> - about drawing most of our financial resources for development from within rather than becoming dependent on foreign investment and foreign financial markets;
> - about carrying out the long-postponed measures of income redistribution and land redistribution to create a vibrant internal market that would be the anchor of the economy;
> - about de-emphasizing growth and maximizing equity in order to radically reduce environmental disequilibrium;
> - about not leaving strategic economic decisions to the market but making them subject to democratic choice;

- about subjecting the private sector and the state to constant monitoring by civil society;
- about creating a new production and exchange complex that includes community cooperatives, private enterprises, and state enterprises, and excludes TNC [transnational corporations];
- about enshrining the principle of subsidiarity in economic life by encouraging production of goods to take place at the community and national level if it can be done so at reasonable cost in order to preserve community.

We are speaking, in short, about re-embedding the economy in society, rather than having society driven by the economy.[8]

This anti-globalization view has been gaining support in the early twenty-first century in places and among populations that had traditionally pushed for and benefited from globalization.

Geopolitics and globalization

As mentioned in Chapter 1, the interdependence between international politics and international trade, investment and movement of people was considered a factor conducive to globalization. Even so, Fukuyama's assertion about the 'end of history'[9] was an advocacy for a global democratic capitalism. Since then, history has taken its 'revenge':[10] nationalistic leaders, territorial and commercial wars, global religious assertion, 'soft cultural' interventions, economic sanctions and ideological boycotts during the past twenty years have impacted global trade and investment. Michael Witt[11] defends the perspective that the future of globalization will depend on the world's political configuration between 'liberalism' or 'realism'. Liberalism relies on states who manage possible conflicts of interest through negotiations via, and contracts with, transnational governance organizations such as the United Nations or World Trade Organization. Realism, on the contrary, relies on 'balance of power'. This approach leads to a struggle between dominant nations to reach some hegemonical position. The Cold War is a typical example of realism in international politics. Fukuyama's 'end of history' was based on the belief of a renaissance of 'liberalism'. The attitudes of leaders in China, Russia, USA, Turkey and even Britain seems to indicate that the time for 'realism' has come. In fact, most analysts believe that Russia's invasion of Ukraine in early 2022 will have long lasting effects on the global order. It implies that global firms will have to build and organize their operations on a country by country basis in a 'multi-domestic' mode. In the short-term the effects are visible in terms of trade, investments leading to various forms of 'reshoring' of major elements of value chains. Still debated are long term effects although it seems that there is a consensus that one may expect a more cautious approach to global investments, what the British newspaper *The Economist* calls 'slowbalisation' (*The Economist* June 19th 2022, p.17).

Demography and migration

Demography

In 2021 the world population was 7.87 billion; it is forecast to reach 9.7 billion by the year 2050 and is expected to reach 10.8 billion by 2100. As seen in Table 15.1, the increase in world population comes from the developing world of Asia, Africa and Latin America. Europe as a whole will experience a decline in population. The age pyramid in the industrialized countries of North America, Europe and Japan will shift towards ageing people. Japan's population shrunk in 2005 for the first time and is expected to continue falling. Even China will experience an ageing population because of its previous one-child policy combined with an increase in life expectancy. China will match the present European level of aged population in 2025 (20 per cent), and by 2050 both Europe and China will have more than 30 per cent of people over the age of sixty. This will create enormous pressures on healthcare, social services and pension management.

Table 15.1 World population, 2015 to 2100

	Population (millions)				Percentage of population aged 60 or over in 2050*
	2020	**2030**	**2050**	**2100**	
World	7,795	8,548	9,735	10,875	21.4
Africa	1,341	1,688	2,489	4,280	8.7
Asia	4,641	4,974	5,290	4,720	24.4
Europe	748	741	710	630	35
Latin America and the Caribbean	654	706	762	680	24.9
North America	369	391	425	491	28.5
Oceania	43	48	57	75	23.1
China	1,447	1,473	1,411	1,074	34.6
India	1,380	1,504	1,639	1,447	19.5

Note: * *WPP2019 – Percentage of total population by broad age group – both sexes.*
Source: United Nations Department of Economic and Social Affairs, Population Division (2019), World Population Prospects 2019, Total Population, Both Sexes – Medium Variant, https://population.un.org/wpp/Download/Standard/Population/ (accessed 1 February 2022).

By 2050, half of the world's population growth is expected to be concentrated in nine countries: India, Nigeria, Pakistan, Democratic Republic of the Congo, Ethiopia, United Republic of Tanzania, USA, Indonesia and Uganda.[12]

Populations tend to concentrate more and more in urban areas. In 2021, more than half (56.8 per cent) of the world population lives in urban areas and the proportion is forecasted to be 68 per cent by 2050, leading to the development of **megacities** of more than 10 million people: Beijing, Shanghai, Kolkata, Mumbai, Karachi, Dhaka, Jakarta, Cairo, Lagos, Mexico, São Paulo, Buenos Aires, Tokyo, New York and Los Angeles.[13]

Migration

Cross-border migrations, a perennial historical phenomenon, have taken new dimensions over the past years. This is mainly due to two phenomena: 1) economic and demographic imbalance, that is, people from South Saharan Africa moving to Europe; and 2) geopolitical disruptions in the Middle East (principally, since 2011, the ongoing Syrian civil war). One may anticipate a third driver of migration becoming increasingly significant – global warming and the incursion of ocean waters on coastal areas.

According to the UN population division 'The number of international migrants globally reached an estimated 272 million in 2019, an increase of 51 million since 2010'[14]

Public opinion is divided on the economic and social benefits of migration. Table 15.2 shows the main arguments.

Table 15.2 Pros and cons of migration

	Pros	Cons
Host countries	• Filling job vacancies • Sustaining economy • Servicing ageing population • Adding to innovation and cultural diversity • Re-equilibrate age pyramid for ageing societies	• Pressure on wages • Exploitation of migrants • Pressure on public services • Friction with local population • Transfer of diseases • Unfair distribution of national wealth • Population imbalance • Malpractices • Financial burden • Social friction
Home countries	• Remittances • Reduced unemployment • Innovation at return	• Loss of talent (brain drain)

Asymmetric development

The United Nations stated in 2020 that 'Since the 1990s total global inequality (inequality across all individuals in the world) declined for the first time since the 1820s. But while income inequality between countries declines, income inequality within countries has risen'.[15] The inequality between countries that increased from 1990 to 2000 has slightly decreased since 2005, mainly due to the emergent 'middle classes' of China and India (Figure 15.2). According to the World Bank, the number of people living below the poverty level of $1.90 a day had decreased from 1.9 billion in 1981 (40 per cent) to 1.1 billion (16.8 per cent) in 2010 and 689 million in 2020 (9.2 per cent). Globally, the trend is unequal but still towards an overall reduction (Table 15.3). The decline has been much more significant in East Asia than in the rest of the world. The income inequality within countries is continuing to increase. Data reveal that income inequality rose during 1980–2019. In Germany, the UK and France the average disposable income of the richest 10 per cent increased from around 29 per cent to 35 per cent in 2019. In the USA the increase went from 35 per cent to 45 per cent. In China it went from 28 per cent to 41 per cent, in Brazil from 54 per cent to 59 per cent and in India from 31 per cent to 57 per cent.[16]

This unequal development can generate conflicts, social unrest and may ultimately disrupt global trade and investments.[17] The war in Ukraine and its inflationary impact on food and energy prices is likely to accentuate these concerns.

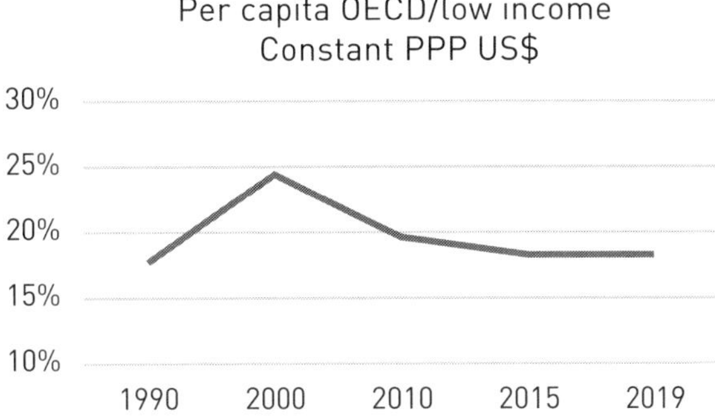

Figure 15.2 The global income gap, ratio of GDP per capita in OECD countries to low-income countries, 1990–2019
Source: Authors' own, based on data from World Bank Indicators, http://data.worldbank.org/indicator/SI.POV.DDAY?end=2012&locations=Z7&start=1990 (accessed 1 February 2022).

Table 15.3 Global and regional inequalities

Percentage of population with income below US$1.90 a day (2011 PPP)				
	1990	1999	2015	2019
East Asia and Pacific	60.9	37.9	2.1	0.98
Europe and Central Asia	2.5	7.8	1.5	1.03
Latin America and the Caribbean	15.2	13.9	3.7	3.75
Middle East and North Africa	6.49	3.53	5.24	7.03*
Sub-Saharan Africa	55.1	58.7	42.0	40.39*
Low and Middle Income[18]	44.8	35.1	12.1	10.74**
World	36.2	29	9.6	9.27**

Note: * *2018;* ** *2017.*
Source: http://iresearch.worldbank.org/PovcalNet/povDuplicateWB.aspx (accessed 1 February 2022).

Emerging economies

In Chapter 2, the characteristics of emerging countries were described, as well as their new role in the world. Economic projections indicate that the GDP, measured in PPP, of the seven largest emerging market economies (China, India, Brazil, Russia, Indonesia, Mexico and Turkey) will be around twice that of the group of advanced economies (USA, Japan, Germany, UK, France, Italy, Canada, Spain, Australia and South Korea) by 2050. When calculated in market rates the difference will be 50 per cent higher.[19] The impact of this will be felt in all kinds of industries and services. In industries reliant on low-skilled labour, de-localization to low-wage countries such as Asia (Bangladesh, Vietnam) or Africa will continue to force painful restructuring. Medium-level technology products will also be challenged by the ever more technologically advanced competitors emerging from China, Russia and India, forcing established companies to invest more in innovation. Another challenge raised by emerging economies is their future impact on resources. China's per capita consumption of resources is still far below the world average but its economic expansionism and population make the overall consumption very big in absolute terms. Already China is the largest consumer of steel and the second largest consumer of oil. Due its invasion of Ukraine in 2022 and the consequent and heavy economic sanctions imposed by the US, UK, EU, among others, Russia's role in the global economy was expected to decreased significantly.

Regional blocs

An alternative to globalization is regionalization. The argument put forward by Professor Alan Rugman to announce the 'end of globalization'[20] projects that instead of a free flow of goods, services, people and capital across the world, regional 'fortresses' may emerge as the dominant form of economic structure. Table 15.4 lists the various forms of such regional agreements. The most sophisticated regional organization that goes beyond a pure free-trade agreement is the European Union. Created after the Second World War by six European countries with the aim of reinforcing political and economic cooperation in order to prevent new continental wars, the Union progressively included more members, to reach twenty-eight as of 2016. The creation of the euro as a single currency that was adopted by 2016 by nineteen European countries reinforced the integration of some countries. However, the decision made by Britain to quit the Union illustrates the complexity of regional integration. Regional blocs facilitate the movement of goods, money and people between member states, and therefore are beneficial to global company strategies.

Table 15.4 Regional trade agreements

Region	Regional agreement	Countries involved	Content
Europe	EU (European Union) (previously EEC and EC)	Austria, Belgium, Bulgaria, Croatia, Cyprus, Czech Republic, Denmark, Estonia, Finland, France, Germany, Greece, Hungary, Ireland, Italy, Latvia, Lithuania, Luxembourg, Malta, Netherlands, Poland, Portugal, Romania, Slovakia, Slovenia, Spain, Sweden	• Created in 1957 as European Economic Community (EEC) by the Treaty of Rome by 6 countries • Enlarged in 1974, 1981, 1995, 2004, 2007, 2013 to 27 member states • Single Market (SEM) since 1992: free movement of people, goods, capital • Single currency, the euro, since 2002 for 19 countries (2016) • Beyond economic integration, the EU has political integration ambitions that are thrown into question by certain member states, in particular by the UK 'Brexit' decision of 2016. From 2011 the EU faced a financial crisis and several members needed bailouts

Latin America	MERCOSUR (Mercado Común del Sur)	Argentina, Brazil, Paraguay, Uruguay and Venezuela (suspended) plus associated members Bolivia, Chile, Colombia, Ecuador, Peru, Suriname	• Created by the Treaty of Asunción in 1991 • Aimed at establishing a common market
North America	NAFTA (North American Free Trade Agreement)	Canada, Mexico, United States	• Created in 1992 • Aimed at establishing a common market
Southeast Asia	ASEAN (Association of Southeast Asian Nations)	Brunei, Cambodia, Indonesia, Laos, Malaysia, Myanmar, Philippines, Singapore, Thailand, Vietnam	• Created in 1967 • Initial objective was to promote regional stability • Progressively transformed into economic cooperation • Implements an ASEAN Free Trade Area (AFTA)
Asia Pacific	APEC (Asia-Pacific Economic Cooperation)	21 countries from Asia, North and South America, Australia and New Zealand	• Created in 1989 • Begun as an informal dialogue group promoting open trade and practical economic cooperation • Goal is to advance Asia Pacific economic dynamism and sense of community
North Africa	MAU (Maghreb Arab Union)	Algeria, Libya, Mauritania, Morocco, Tunisia	• Created in 1989 • Aims at establishing a common market
Southern Africa	SADC (Southern African Development Community)	Angola, Botswana, Democratic Republic of Congo, Lesotho, Madagascar, Malawi, Mauritius, Mozambique, Namibia, Seychelles, South Africa, Swaziland, Tanzania, Zambia, Zimbabwe	• Created 1979 and expanded in 1992 to harmonize economic development among the countries of Southern Africa
Asia-Pacific region	RCEP (Regional Comprehensive Economic Partnership)	Australia, Brunei, Cambodia, China, Indonesia, Japan, Laos, Malaysia, Myanmar, New Zealand, the Philippines, Singapore, South Korea, Thailand, Vietnam	• Free trade agreement between 15 member countries that account for about 30 per cent of the world's population (2.2 billion people) and 30 per cent of global GDP ($26.2 trillion) as of 2020, making it the biggest trade bloc in history. Signed on 15 November 2020

Table 15.4 *(Continued)*

Africa	AfCFTA (African Continental Free Trade Agreement).	Angola, People's Republic of Burkina Faso, Botswana, Republic of Cameroon, Central African Republic, Republic of Chad, Democratic Republic of Congo, Republic of Côte d'Ivoire, Republic of Djibouti, Arab Republic of Egypt, Equitorial Guinea, Kingdom of Eswatini, Republic of Ethiopia, Gabonese Republic, Republic of Gambia, Republic of Ghana, Republic of Guinea, Republic of Kenya, Kingdom of Lesotho, Madagascar, Republic of Malawi, Islamic Republic of Mauritania, Republic of Mauritius, Republic of Namibia, Federal Republic of Niger, Republic of Rwanda, São Tomé and Principe, Republic of Senegal, Seychelles, Republic of Sierra Leone, Republic of South Africa, United Republic of Tanzania, Togolese Republic, Republic of Tunisia, Republic of Uganda, Republic of Zambia, Republic of Zimbabwe	• Free trade area founded in 2018, with trade commencing as of 1 January 2021. It was created by the African Continental Free Trade Agreement. As of 5 February 2021, 36 countries have ratified the AfCFTA agreement. The free trade area is the largest in the world in terms of the number of participating countries since the formation of the World Trade Organization

Sustainable development

In Chapter 4, sustainable development issues were presented: global warming and climate change, natural resource depletion and waste disposal in particular were discussed. This chapter will concentrate on future trends in these areas.

Global warming and energy

It is now well established that climate change is linked to greenhouse gas (GHG) emissions. According to the United States Environmental Protection Agency: 'Continued emissions of greenhouse gases will lead to further climate changes. Future changes are expected to include a warmer atmosphere, a warmer and more acidic ocean, higher sea levels, and larger changes in precipitation patterns'[21] (Figure 15.3).

The emission of GHGs is linked to the type of future energy consumption and production (Figure 15.4). By 2030, oil will remain the dominant source although oil reserves are likely to pass through what is known as 'Hubbert's peak'; the point at which the production of oil begins to decline as resources are increasingly depleted. Controversies remain about the exact time that Hubbert's peak may be reached.

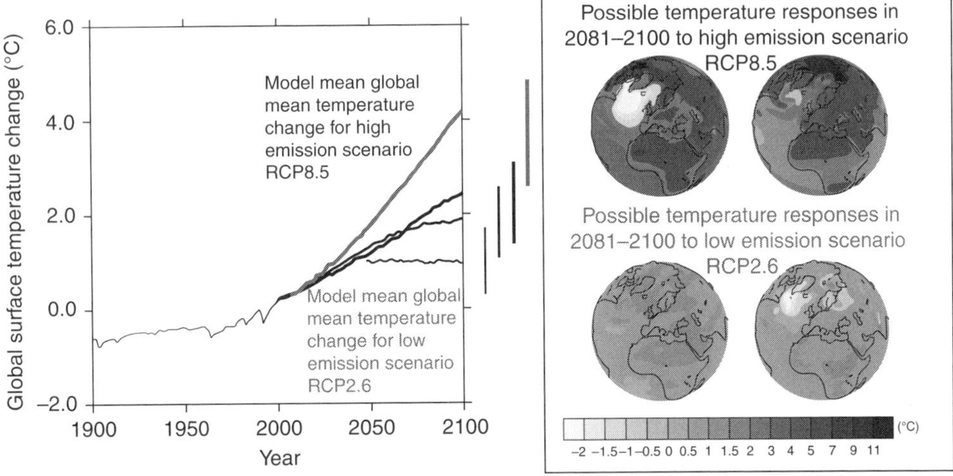

Figure 15.3 Projected changes in temperature according to different projected levels of greenhouse gas emissions

Note: *The lines show projected average changes across a range of climate models from high- to low-emission scenarios while the vertical bars on the right show likely final ranges in temperature by the end of the twenty-first century for each of these models.*

Source: Modified from FAQ 12.1, Figure 1 (Chapter 12) from Collins et al. (2013).

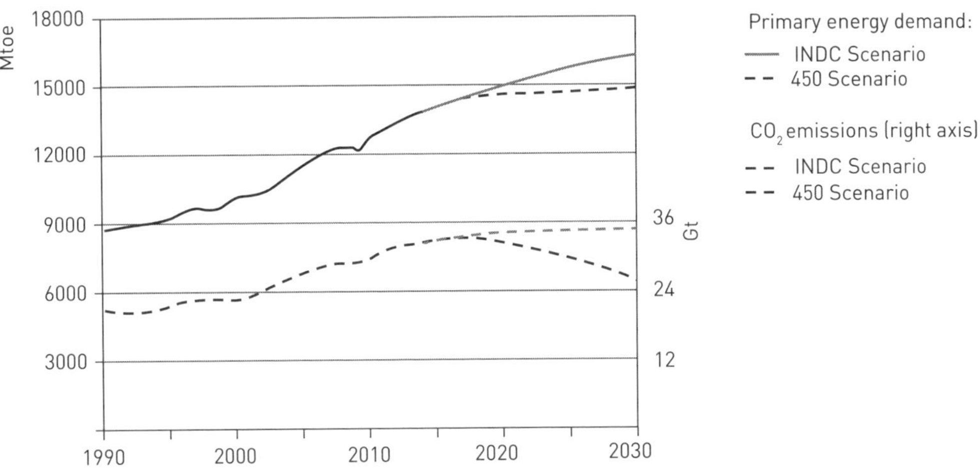

Figure 15.4 Energy demand and gas emission projections according to two scenarios

Notes: *Mtoe = million tonnes of oil equivalent; Gt = gigatonnes; INDC = Intended nationally determined contributions by countries prior to the 2015 Paris Conference on Climate; 450 = Energy evolution consistent with the goal of limiting the global increase in temperature to 2°C by limiting the concentration of GHGs in the atmosphere to around 450 parts per million of CO_2.*

Source: Reproduced with permission from International Energy Agency (2015) *Energy and Climate Change*, p. 37, https://www.iea.org/reports/energy-and-climate-change (accessed 1 February 2022).

Low-carbon-emission sources of energy such as hydroelectricity, nuclear and renewables such as solar energy, geothermal and marine are expected to represent 25 per cent of total energy demand by 2030. Energy consumption is dependent upon the adoption of energy-saving lifestyles, thermally insulated construction, greener types of vehicles and farming techniques.[22] Some analysts believed the energy crisis created by the war in Ukraine could accelerate the energy transition to more sustainable sources, notably in the EU.

Natural resources

Biodiversity

Biodiversity, defined as the diversity of living animal and vegetal organisms, is expected to decline by 10 per cent from 2010 to 2050[23] if no major changes in public policies and behaviour are implemented. Most of the losses will come from land-use management, climate change, infrastructure development, pollution and urbanization. Affected areas will be:

- The number of living terrestrial species
- Forests
- Marine fish stocks
- Water.

Under a 'business as usual' scenario, 4.7 billion people are expected to live in water shortage areas, that is, areas where water demand is higher than water supply. The affected regions are likely to be in North and South Africa as well as South and Central Asia.

Extractive resources

Again, given current usage rates, 'extractive resources (minerals, fossil fuels, metals and biomass) in 2030 will amount to 100 billion tons as compared to 72 million in 2015'.[24]

For oil and gas the peak of extraction, as mentioned earlier, is likely to have been reached by this date. For other commodities (such as rare earth elements), the peak is expected to be reached earlier.

Technological developments

We can expect to see major technological developments in the following four major areas: biotechnology, materials and nanotechnology, information technology, and renewable energy. The Covid-19 pandemic that hit the globe in 2020 has accelerated a number of these trends.

Biotechnology

Based on a better knowledge of cellular genetic codes (genomics) and the ability to manipulate genes, biotechnology is likely to develop a variety of innovations:

- *Genetic profiling* based on DNA comparisons can lead to applications in diagnostics and security. DNA analysis is already used for solving criminal cases but its possibilities extend well beyond that.
- *Cloning*, even limited to crops and animals without mentioning ethically problematic human cloning, finds its application in agriculture and animal breeding.
- *Genetically modified organisms* are likely to be used further, extending to medical and pharmaceutical applications.
- *Biomedical engineering* will allow the production of organic or artificial tissues or organs which can be used for therapeutic purposes.

Materials and nanotechnology

New materials based on the integration of composite substances with or without electronic sensors will give rise to a new generation of applications. Some materials will be made at nano scale (1/1,000,000 mm). Examples of applications are:

- Smart textiles and clothes that can react to weather conditions
- Buildings or vehicles that can adjust to weather conditions
- Faster and smarter semiconductors
- Integrated Microsystems: Systems-on-Chips (SoC) embedding electronic and mechanical or optical components (MEMS, Micro-Electro-Mechanical Systems)
- Self-assembling materials.

Information technology and big data

The combination of new materials and the increase in computing power as well as miniaturization and the extension of wireless communication will enable the development of:

- Pervasive information technology with computers everywhere, including homes, cars, public transport, workplace, streets etc.
- Embedded information technology will extend its traditional areas (computers, mobile phones and other 'obvious' electronic devices) to become part of all objects used for daily living: domestic appliances, lamps, blinds, clothes etc.
- Context-awareness IT, which is able to use information from the environment (location, neighbouring persons or objects, resources etc.) to inform the user
- Networking: most of the progress in this area will be the development of a pervasive wireless network
- Large-scale computing and big data storage linked with algorithms to produce the capacity to solve complex problems
- Web-based education and the development of Massive Open Online Courses (MOOCs) will considerably enhance the distribution of knowledge and change the format of traditional schools and universities.

Robotics and artificial intelligence

- In industry, robots have taken over an increasing number of tasks, improving productivity and displacing low-skilled labour. According to the Global Talent Competitiveness Index 2020, the top ten countries in terms of robot density in 2019 were Germany, Korea Republic, Singapore (joint first) followed by Japan, Sweden, Denmark, USA, Italy, Belgium and the Netherlands. Industrial robots can potentially go beyond industrial uses to revolutionize surgical treatments or drug delivery. Nanobots are likely one day to be used inside the human body for improved targeting of treatment. In hospitals handling Covid-19, robots have been used to disinfect air and surfaces, to answer patients' questions, to bring them medicine or food and to monitor their progress.[25]

- Artificial intelligence linked with large-scale computing is likely to replace a large variety of clerical and intellectual work.
- 3D manufacturing allows the production of customized parts.

Quantum computing

- Quantum mechanics is the basis of quantum computing. It refers to the scientific laws that affect the smallest dimensions of nature – molecules, atoms and subatomic particles. As a result, new physical phenomena arise (superposition, entanglement) which can be used for computing.
- Quantum computers use quantum bits, or qubits, that can be zero, one or a mixture of zero and one (superposition) that enables extremely quick processing – calculations that are not possible using conventional computers are a reality.
- Quantum algorithms: quantum computers can explore problems that are exponential in nature and are best suited to solving problems using three types of algorithms: 1) optimization Algorithms, 2) sampling algorithms and 3) machine learning algorithms.
- There are multiple possibilities for the use of quantum computers and some are already being applied in computer science, cyber security, financial services and logistics.

Renewable energy

Beside hydroelectricity, most of the expected progress in this area will come from:

- The development or improved harnessing of renewable energy sources:
  - Solar energy
  - Biomass or bioenergy
  - Ocean energy
  - Wind energy
  - Geothermal energy
  - Hydrogen[26]
- The utilization of energy-saving measures:
  - Hybrid or electric vehicles
  - Energy efficient insulated housing
  - Reduction of energy loss in production systems
  - Energy-saving illumination and appliances.

Global risks

Online Appendix 15.1 gives a summary of the main global risks, and Figure 15.5 presents an estimate of the probability of those risks occurring and their economic, as well as their human life, impact on the international community over ten years from 2021, identified by a team from the World Economic Forum.[27]

Ethnic, religious and cultural friction

An increased search for *communal identity* – religious, ethnic or linguistic – is expected to develop alongside, or in reaction to, globalization. Manifestations of such movements have been experienced in the Balkans, Chechnya, Mexico, Indonesia, China, Corsica and Spain. Communities that were living peacefully alongside each other are increasingly asserting their differences, at times with extreme violence as was experienced in Rwanda in the mid-1990s, and with Shiite–Sunni tensions in Iraq, the Lebanon and elsewhere in the Middle East since the 2000s.

Huntington has argued forcefully that future conflicts will be primarily rooted in cultural differences, and will thus occur between different 'civilizations'.[28] The terrorist attacks of 11 September 2001 in the United States gives some credence to this thesis. In 2014, a radical Iraqi group took over the city of Mosul and declared a caliphate named the 'Islamic State of Iraq and the Levant' based on Sharia law. The territory controlled by this group extended to Syria. A series of terrorist attacks in the Middle East, Europe, Africa and North America initiated by this organization were committed. Some citizens from various countries attracted by the religious rhetoric of this 'state' joined the ranks of 'jihadists'. As a result, in 2017 the Middle East was the centre of violent ethnic tensions based on religious grounds, which affected the political and social scenes of many countries. The so-called 'Islamic State' was defeated by an international coalition and lost its territorial footprint but in 2021 radical ideological terrorist forces are still active in various part of Africa (Mali, Burkina Faso, Mozambique).

Table 15.5 Selected global risks 2021

Low probability of occurrence/ high impact	High probability of occurrence/ high impact	High probability of occurrence/ low impact
• Weapons of mass destruction • IT infrastructure failure	• Infectious diseases • Climate protection failure • Biodiversity losses • Natural resources crisis • Extreme weather • Human environmental damages • Debts crisis • Livelihood crisis	• Digital power concentration • Digital inequality • Interstate relations fractures

Source: Adapted from WEF, *Global Risks Report* (2021).

Financial crisis

In 1997, four major Southeast and Northeast Asian countries (Thailand, Indonesia, Korea and to a lesser extent Malaysia) entered a massive depression due to highly leveraged financing and improper banking regulations. At approximately the same time, Argentina entered a period of turmoil due to its inability to service high government debts, and eventually defaulted in 2001. The situation in both Asia and Latin America stabilized, but in 2001 in the USA the highly inflated internet bubble burst, causing world stock exchanges to depreciate. By the end of 2007, a more pernicious crisis broke: the subprime crisis that destroyed Lehmann Brothers and threatened the financial community worldwide. Governments around the world injected money into their economies in order to avoid the nightmare of the Great Depression that followed the Wall Street Crash of 1929. By doing so, government debts increased up to a point where creditors realized that the Argentine scenario could happen in Greece and affect the whole of Western Europe. As pointed out in an IMF publication: 'The economic and financial turmoil engulfing the world marks the first crisis of the current era of globalization … The drivers of the recent globalization wave (open markets, the global supply chain, globally integrated companies, and private ownership) are being undermined, and the spirit of protectionism has reemerged.'[29]

In 2010, in what became known as 'the Eurozone crisis', massive budgetary deficits and high public indebtedness in Greece, Spain, Ireland and Portugal created tensions within Europe and forced the governments of these countries to implement budget deficit reductions that affected consumers and generated social unrest.

The Covid-19 pandemic in 2020–2022 created another set of global financial uncertainties. According to the IMF: 'Extraordinary policy measures have eased financial conditions and supported the economy, helping to contain financial stability risks. But actions taken during the pandemic may have unintended consequences such as stretched valuations and rising financial vulnerabilities.'[30]

Governments have injected masses of cash in order to support their economies. The following are the possible outcomes of these injections:

- Inflation
- Emerging market bankruptcies due to high interest
- Rising interest rates and corporate bankruptcies in vulnerable sectors
- Possible bank defaults.

Security

Since 11 September 2001, and particularly since the creation of the Islamic State, worldwide terrorist attacks have meant that security issues are affecting global transport and the movement of people. Although conflict with Islamic State has now deescalated, underground jihadist terrorist networks still exist in Africa and violence continues. The Uppsala Conflict Data Program (UCDP) notes that violence also continues in Afghanistan (accouting for 40 per cent of all fatalities from organized violence worldwide), and recorded fifty-four state-based conflicts in 2019, including seven wars. This report estimated that around 76,480 people were killed in organized violence in 2019, with the total number of deaths from armed conflicts being 2,523,676.[31] The first few months of war in Ukraine in 2022 already caused thousands of casualties.

The globalization of criminal activities

Illicit activities are increasingly crossing borders, ranging across:

- Human trafficking for sexual exploitation
- Smuggling of migrants
- Drugs commerce: primarily cocaine and heroin
- Trafficking of firearms
- Trafficking of natural resources
- Trafficking of human organs
- Maritime piracy
- Product counterfeiting, particularly pharmaceuticals
- Cybercrime
- Global terrorism
- Money laundering.

One may possibly add tax evasion to this list. Transnational organized crime takes advantage of globalization to increase its power. According to the Executive Director of the United Nations Office on Drugs and Crime: 'Organized crime has diversified, gone global and reached macro-economic proportions.' The estimated amount of money laundered globally in one year is 2–5 per cent of the global GDP, or in the range of $800 billion to $2 trillion.[32] Money-laundering activities cover a wide range of criminal activities such as drug trafficking, tax evasion, illegal political financing, corruption and all sort of crimes.

Future scenarios

The technique of **scenario building** is used to picture potential images of the future.[33] Scenarios are built upon contrasted configurations of key socioeconomic and political drivers. The configurations are based on expert opinion. Two to four possible futures are pictured – most scenarios contain two or three extreme representations and a middle one, although there is some argument for developing at least four scenarios in order to avoid the middle of the road choice.[34] Appendix 15.2 gives a simplified methodology for elaborating scenarios.

The main attractiveness of scenario building is that it expands the range of possible futures beyond pure extrapolation. It obliges decision makers to uncover the underlying drivers of change. Scenario building is not without pitfalls, however; the main criticism is that no scenarios can predict 'black swans', or unexpected events such as the terrorist attacks of 11 September 2001.

Appendix 15.3 summarizes some alternative scenarios that have been set out in the following publications: *Global Trends 2030*,[35] published by the US National Security Agency; the *State of the Future* reports from the Millennium Project,[36] initiated by the United Nations University; the *Global Scenarios to 2025 and the Global Energy Scenarios to 2050*, prepared by Shell Corporation;[37]

Global Scenarios Service prepared by Oxford Economics;[38] and *The World in 2025* prepared by the European Commission.[39]

Other sources of scenarios are given in the References at the end of this chapter.[40]

EXAMPLE 15.1 The Millennium Project

The Millennium Project, jointly founded in 1996 by the United Nations University, the Smithsonian Institution, Futures Group International and the American Council for the United Nations University, is an independent non-profit global participatory futures research think tank of futurists, scholars, business planners and policy makers who work for international organizations, governments, corporations, NGOs and universities. Its mission is to focus and collate the most cutting-edge thinking about the future and to make that thinking publicly available through a variety of media. Since 1996, about 2,500 futurists, scholars, decision makers and business planners from more than fifty countries have contributed their views to The Millennium Project's research.

Every year The Millennium Project publishes its latest report, *State of the Future*. Readers can view the most recent at http://www.millennium-project.org/publications-2-3/#sof19.

Table 15.6 Simplified list of the 15 Global Challenges identified by The Millennium Project

- Sustainable development and climate change
- Clean water access
- Population growth and resources equilibrium
- Democracy development in non-democratic societies
- Enhanced decision making in an accelerated changing environment
- Information and communications technologies for everybody
- Gap reduction between rich and poor
- Reducing threats from diseases
- Education as an instrument to address global challenges
- Reduction of ethnic conflicts, terrorism and weapons of mass destruction
- Improvement of women's status
- Stopping organized crime
- Accelerating of scientific and technological breakthroughs
- Meeting safe and efficient energy demand
- Including ethics in global decisions

Sources: Authors' based on http://www.millennium-project.org/projects/challenges/ (accessed 1 February 2022).

The same report identified the perceived progress identified as of 2021. Table 15.7 is an adapted version of those perceptions.

Table 15.7 The Millennium Project Global Challenges

Global challenges	Positive developments as of 2021	Negative developments as of 2021
• Sustainable development and climate change		
• Clean water access	• Improved water resources	
• Population growth and resources equilibrium	• Population growth slowing	
• Democracy development in non-democratic societies		
• Enhanced decision making in an accelerated changing environment		
• Information and communications technologies for everybody	• Increased internet users	
• Gap reduction between rich and poor		
• Reducing threats from diseases	• Increased number of physicians per capita • Improved health expenditures • Decreased child mortality • Increased life expectancy	
• Education as an instrument to address global challenges	• Improved literacy	
• Reduction of ethnic conflicts, terrorism and weapons of mass destruction		• Increased armed conflicts
• Improvement of women's status		
• Stopping organized crime		
• Accelerating of scientific and technological breakthroughs		
• Meeting safe and efficient energy demand	• Increased renewable energy • Improved energy efficiency	
• Including ethics in global decisions		• Increased level of corruption

Source: Authors' adapted from http://www.millennium-project.org/projects/challenges/ (accessed 1 February 2022).

In 2020, The Millennium Project was asked by the American Red Cross to create Covid-19 scenarios until January 2022:

- Scenario 1: America Endures (baseline, mix of good and bad developments)
- Scenario 2: Depression, Hubris and Discord (plausible worse case)
- Scenario 3: Things go Right! (plausible best case)

Further details are available at http://www.millennium-project.org/covid-19/

EXAMPLE 15.2 The 'Future Possibilities Report'

The UAE Government and the United Nations published the 'Future Possibilities Report 2020' which analyses six transformational trends for future economic growth and societal wellbeing. The six transformational trends are:

1 Exabyte Economy

Exabyte Economy focuses on the development of big data possibilities with computing power and storage becoming affordable and more efficient, and the roll out of 5G technology. The resulting flow of data will lead to improvement of artificial intelligence-based systems capacities to optimize processes and services that can disrupt business models across a range of sectors. This trend leads to an estimated total economic value of up to $8 trillion by 2025.

2 Circular Economy

Circular Economy focuses on an increasing public awareness in reducing the impact on the environment. It will continue to open up new possibilities for optimizing resource usage and reducing waste. This is estimated to bring new market possibilities totaling up to $4.5 trillion.

3 Wellbeing Economy

Wellbeing Economy presents opportunities emerging from an increased interest in physical and mental wellbeing as a result of adopting new approaches to wellbeing at individual, organizational and community levels. The combined value of wellbeing possibilities could reach $7 trillion within a few years.

4 Experience Economy

The fourth trend examines societies' interest in providing personalized experience services that are tailored to the needs of customers within *Experience Economy: From Ownership to Usership*. New trends could build an experience-driven economy worth up to $6.5 trillion by 2025, due to customers' desire to 'experience' rather than to consume.

5 Net Zero Economy

Net Zero Economy explores the general increase in energy demand and global efforts to reduce carbon emissions. This requires promoting the innovation of technologies and developing adaptable investment models and new markets. According to the report, it is expected that growing demand for renewable energy could yield over $2.3 trillion of possibilities by 2025.

6 Bio Growth Economy

Bio Growth Economy: New Agriculture and Biomaterials promotes new possibilities for various sectors worldwide relating to agriculture and emerging biological materials that could be worth over $1 trillion by 2025.

Source: *Future Possibilites Report 2020*, https://www.un.org/sites/un2.un.org/files/20200720_un75_uae_futurepossibilitiesreport.pdf (accessed 1 February 2022).

The future of global corporations

Academic and consulting research on the future roles, capabilities and organization of global firms is all based on the fundamental assumption that globalization is progressing and that global firms are the main vectors of that 'progress'. The main focus of organizational and strategic thinkers should be to imagine and craft the organization of the future in more innovative or 'revolutionary' ways[41] in order to lead, and adapt to, the changes brought by global competition. We can identify two major models or 'blueprints' for the future global firm: the **individualized corporation** model and the **metanational** model.

The individualized corporation

'The individualized corporation' is a term suggested by Ghoshal and Bartlett.[42] Based on the example of some leading global firms such as Canon, ABB or 3M, the authors argue that the future organizational form is best described by a *portfolio of three key processes*, embodied into a *new organizational model* in which *new management competencies and roles* are redefined:

1 The *new organizational model* is based on a network of relationships as opposed to the traditional hierarchical structure (Figure 15.5).

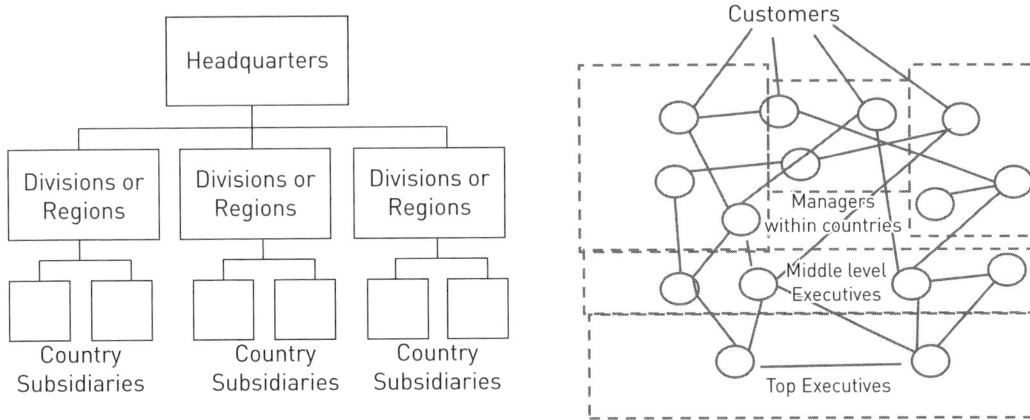

Figure 15.5 A new organizational model
Source: Authors' based on Ghoshal and Bartlett (1997).

2 The *key processes* are:

- The renewal process: developing a culture of moving away from incremental improvement to a culture of overall performance that combines both long-term and short-term achievements.
- The integration process: moving away from isolated dispersed competencies into a culture of linking these distributed competencies to build broad capabilities supported by cooperation and trust among units. The integration process is based on networking across units.

- The entrepreneurial process: moving away from an organizational model based on holding managers responsible, authoritarian and top-down control. This approach focuses on upward initiative coming from the commitment of front-line entrepreneurship supported by middle-level and top management.

3 The *new management roles* are described in Table 15.8.

Table 15.8 Management of new roles for the individualized corporaton

Managers and leaders	Roles	Competencies
Front-line entrepreneurs	Creation of opportunities Managing resources Engaging customers Performance achievers	Technical Curiosity Environment scanner Communicator People motivator
Senior Managers	Support of entrepreneurs Resources facilitators	Ability to delegate Ability to build teams Ability to negotiate resources
Top Executives	Organizational designer Inspirational strategist Organizational challenger	Ability to assess, select, inspire people Ability to connect with key stakeholders Ability to understand global trends and opportunities

Source: Authors' own adaptation of Ghoshal and Bartlett (1994).

The metanational corporation

The *metanational* corporation was mentioned in Chapter 11. This form of global organization, as proposed by Doz, dos Santos and Williamson,[43] is based on the assumption that in a globalized world competitive advantage is obtained at three levels:

- The ability to *identify* and access new competencies and innovative technologies and lead market knowledge.
- The speed and the effectiveness with which companies can connect scattered pieces of knowledge and use them to create *innovative products and services.*
- The ability to optimize the efficiency of global sales, distribution, marketing and supply chains to *leverage those products, services and process innovations* across global markets rapidly and cost effectively.

The traditional global firms were 'projectors', meaning that the source of their competitive advantage was to be found in their home countries, and their globalization was to *project those advantages* internationally. The metanational corporation is a 'prospector', meaning that the source of their competitive advantage is to be able to prospect, tap and leverage knowledge *scattered across the world* in a speedy and efficient manner. Although Doz and his colleagues did not identify any fully fledged companies that corresponded to the characteristics of their model, they found that companies such as

Nokia, the Finnish leader in mobile phones, or ST Microelectronics, a European microprocessor firm, were examples of metanationals in the making. The metanational firm has a dispersed internal and external network of design, production and customer relationship centres, each of which contributes to knowledge creation and leverage. The concept of a 'centre' or 'home headquarters' disappears in this type of organization – it is a *pure global firm within a global world.*

Both models are based on the form of a networked organization that implies the coordinated combined effort of 'unbundled' business units,[44] some of them being 'internal' to a corporation (subsidiaries), some external (partners, suppliers, distributors), and some in between (joint ventures, strategic alliances). The concept of the networked organization is not new but it gained momentum during the 1980s and 1990s because of the restructuring of firms, the forming of global strategic alliances and the development of IT.

MINI-CASE 15.1

Threat of a pandemic

The pandemic threat

Following the Covid-19 pandemic outbreak, which did not affect his territory, the Minister of Health of Pulau Vicente, a fictional South Pacific island, was concerned about future possible pandemic of flu carried by wild animals reaching his island.

He asked a group of health and economic experts to form a team in order to evaluate the potential economic and social consequences of a pandemic affecting the island under various contrasting scenarios.

The team gathered first in order to establish a plan of action. They determined that their study would be divided into four phases:

1. List the elements to be assessed in order to build a scenario:
   - **a** The impacted issues: what the minister wants to assess in terms of economic and social consequences, and a definition of a measurable variable of those issues (dependent variables).
   - **b** The most important driving forces either external or internal, direct or indirect that can possibly influence the selected issues in the future (independent or intermediate variables).
2. For each driving force, select its possible state of affairs (variables): either the variable is a number (for example, growth rate) or the variable is expressed as a range (high to low, frequent to infrequent). In both cases, no more than three discrete values for each variable would be assigned (the two extremes plus a middle value). The team planned to use a kind of Delphi technique (asking a group of experts to hypothesize on a given situation interactively and qualitatively).
3. Build a model in which the relationship between variables is represented and calculate the potential outcome of how the variables could affect one another for all value combinations.
4. Analyse each of the projected outcomes and reduce it to a small number of plausible and contrasted stories under the form of 'scenar-ios'. This is considered the most creative part

of the exercise, where two or three alternative futures have to be extracted from the data and described within a narrative.

Having adopted this methodology the team financed a series of research studies in order to collect data. Below are the results of their data collection:

a According to the health authorities, the anticipated flu could affect the population with various intensities. Assuming that the virus could be transmitted to humans it was deemed probable that one-tenth of the population could develop the flu, up to a projected maximum of one-third.

b Some experts say that there is no vaccine available but others think that a vaccine could be developed with an efficacy of 30 per cent to 70 per cent.

c The infected population, if not vaccinated or with failed vaccination, could receive a classic treatment to develop self-defence mechanisms (antibodies) but unfortunately around 2–3 per cent would die.

d Statistical data are shown in Table 15.9.

Table 15.9 Data relating to Pulau Vicente

Population (million)	27
Working population	40%
GDP (US$ billion)	195
Total hours worked/year	2,500
Total hours worked/week	48
GDP per employee (US$)	18,000
GDP per worked hour (US$)	7.2
Cost of vaccination per person (US$)	100
Cost of classical treatment per person (US$)	400
Death rate for non-vaccinated population	2%

Question:

Using the methodology of scenario building described in Appendix 15.1 can you describe the possible scenarios that illustrate the impact of a pandemic outbreak?

Summary and key points

1 The significant challenges to globalization include:

a Globalization called into question:

- *Zealot* point of view:
  - Globalization will drive networked global companies
  - Globalized economy will increase political stability but reach and benefits will not be universal
  - Globalization process will evolve with financial volatility and a widening economic divide
  - Potential brakes on global economy include sustained financial crisis or prolonged disruption of energy supplies
  - Regions, countries and groups feel left behind and will face deepening economic stagnation, political, ethnic, ideological and religious extremism
  - Developed countries will be forced to focus on ‘old-world’ challenges while concentrating on the implications of ‘new-world’ technologies

- *Dissenting* point of view:
  - Reduced trade barriers and investment increases asymmetry between groups that can cross international borders and groups that cannot
  - Globalization stimulates conflicts within and between nations over domestic norms and social institutions embodying them
  - Globalization makes it increasingly difficult for governments to provide social insurance
  - How to ease tension between globalization and pressures for socialization to minimize the possibility of a generalized resurgence of protectionism
- *Radical* point of view:
  - Re-embedding the economy in society instead of having society driven by the economy
  - Obtain financial resources for development from within instead of foreign investment
  - Implement measures of income and land redistribution
  - De-emphasize growth and maximize equity
  - Make strategic economic decisions subject to democratic choice
  - Subject private sector and state to constant monitoring by civil society
  - Create a new production/exchange complex that includes community cooperatives, private enterprises and state enterprises but excludes TNCs
  - Encourage production of goods at community/sub-national level

b Demography and migrations:

- Increase in world population will come from developing world
- Age pyramid in industrialized countries will shift towards ageing people, increasing pressures on healthcare, social services and pension management
- Increase in cross-border migration and intense urbanization will create megacities of more than 10 million people

c Asymmetric development – the unequal development of people living below a certain poverty level will generate conflicts and ultimately disrupt global trade and investment

d Emerging economies

- The output of the seven largest emerging market economies will be around twice that of the group of advanced economies by 2050
- Will affect low-tech and high-tech production

e Regional blocs:

- As an alternative to globalization, regional blocs emerging as the dominant form of economic structure
- Examples include EU, MERCOSUR, NAFTA, ASEAN, APEC, MAU, SADC

- **f** Sustainable development issues will become mainstream issues in the developed world
  - Main future concerns are:
    - Global warming and energy
    - Depletion of natural resources: biodiversity, water supply, extractive resources
    - Technological developments: biotechnology, materials and nanotechnologies, information technology and big data, renewable energies, robotics and artificial intelligence, renewable energies
- **g** Ethnic, religious and cultural friction
  - Increased search for community identity (religious, ethnic, linguistic) which will come into conflict with globalization, as evidenced in the Middle East and Africa
- **h** Financial crisis: prospect of a new global financial crisis is not insignificant
- **i** Security: terrorism increasing
- **j** Global criminal activities – increasingly cross-border, e.g. drug trafficking, piracy, cybercrime

2 Global risks

Affect the environment, the economy, the geopolitical stability, the societal well-being and technological adversities

3 Scenarios

- **a** *Scenario building* is used to picture potential images of the future
- **b** Scenarios are built upon contrasted configurations of key socioeconomic and political drivers
- **c** There are many publications that set out possible future scenarios
- **d** *The Millennium Project* from the United Nations is built around 15 Global Challenges

4 Emerging theories of global management with two major company models:

- **a** *Individualized corporation* with a portfolio of three key processes by which new management competencies and roles are defined:
  - Key processes are the entrepreneurial process, the integration process and the renewal process
  - The new organizational model is based on a network relationship instead of the traditional hierarchical structure
  - The new management roles are the operating-entrepreneurial role of front-line managers, the management-developer of senior and middle-level managers and the top-level institutional builder of top leaders
- **b** *Metanational*
  - The networked organization implies the coordinated combined effort of 'unbundled' business units, some 'internal' to a corporation (e.g. subsidiaries), some 'external' to a corporation (e.g. partners, suppliers, distributors), and some in between (e.g. joint ventures, strategic alliances)

- Assumes competitive advantage obtained at three levels:
  - Ability to identify and access new competencies, innovative technologies and lead market knowledge
  - Speed and effectiveness with which companies can connect scattered pieces of knowledge and use them to create innovative products and services
  - Ability to optimize the efficiency of global sales, distribution, marketing and supply chains to leverage those products, services and processes innovations across global markets rapidly and cost-effectively

Learning assignments

1. Why is globalization increasingly being called into question?
2. Does globalization increase the income gap?
3. What are the consequences for the global economy of the global economic/political power of China?
4. How will the 'global warming issue' affect the global economy?
5. Assuming that you are a global company producing cosmetics, what are the variables you would take into consideration to build a ten-year scenario for China?

Key words

- Asymmetric development
- Cybercrime
- Deglobalization
- Global warming
- Individualized corporation
- Megacities
- Metanational
- Regionalization
- Scenarios

Web resources

Institute for the Future (IFTF):
https://www.iftf.org/en/our-work/featured-projects/
Intergovernmental Panel on Climate Change:
https://www.ipcc.ch
The Millennium Project:
http://www.millennium-project.org/publications-2/
World Economic Forum, Reports:
https://www.weforum.org/reports
National Intelligence Council:
https://www.dni.gov/index.php/global-trends-home

Companion website

Visit bloomsbury.pub/global-strategic-management-5e for a multitude of weblinks and resources, self-test questions for revision and appendices.

Notes

1 Fukuyama (1989, 1992).
2 Stiglitz (2002).
3 Ansoff (1975: 3): In an article published in 1975 Professor Igor Ansoff define weak signals in the context of strategic planning as 'early in the life of a threat, when the information is vague and its future course unclear'..
4 Taleb (2007). Nassim Taled described black swans as 'highly improbable events'.
5 The term 'global challenge' is used in the United Nations University's The Millennium Projects report, published every year since 1997. The most recent edition at the time of writing is J. Glenn, E. Florescu and The Millennium Project Team (2015) *2015–16: State of the Future* (Washington, DC: American Council for the United Nations University). Most of the challenges discussed in this chapter are also part of the 15 Global Challenges of The Millennium Project.
6 NIC (2000: 20).
7 Rodrik (1997).
8 Bello (2000).
9 Fukuyama (2014).
10 Tertrais (2015: 7–18).
11 Witt (2019).
12 United Nations (2019): https://population.un.org/wpp/Download/Standard/Population/.
13 NIC (2000).
14 United Nations (2019), https://www.un.org/development/desa/en/news/population/international-migrant-stock-2019.html (accessed 11 May 2022).
15 United Nations (2020) https://www. un.org/en/un75/inequality-bridging-divide.
16 World Inequality database, https://wid.world/world. https://wid.world/ Accessed on January 29, 2022.
17 Piketti (2014); Stiglitz (2012, 2015).
18 World Bank: http://iresearch.worldbank.org/PovcalNet/povDuplicateWB.aspx (Accessed 21 February 2022).
19 PwC (2015). https://www.pwc.com/gx/en/research-insights/economy/the-world-in-2050.html (accessed 21 February 2021).
20 Rugman (2000).
21 EPA (2016).
22 IPPC (2012: 20).
23 OECD (2012).
24 OECD (2015b: 9).
25 https://hospitalityinsights.ehl.edu/robots-during-covid-19#:~:text=In%20hospitals&-text=A%20safe%20alternative%20is%20to,Robots%20to%20disinfect%20patients'%20rooms (accessed 1 February 2022).
26 There has been an increase recently in hydrogen as a potential revolutionary alternative for fossil fuels. For further information see https://www.ft.com/content/7eac54ee-f1d1-4ebc-9573-b52f87d00240?shareType=nongift (accessed 1 February 2022).
27 World Economic Forum (2021).
28 Huntington (1997). His original article, 'The clash of civilizations?' (*Foreign Affairs*, Summer 1993: 22–49), sparked a fierce debate about a new 'civilization paradigm', replacing the former demarcation of the First, Second and Third Worlds. (See *Foreign Affairs*, September–October 1993: 2–26, and Huntington's response, *Foreign Affairs*, November–December 1993: 186–94).
29 Pisani-Ferry and Santos (2009).

30 IMF (2021), https://www.imf.org/en/Publications/GFSR/ Issues/2021/10/12/global-financial-stability-report-october-2021 (Accessed on January 29, 2022).
31 https://ucdp.uu.se (accessed 1 February 2022).
32 https://www2.deloitte.com/content/dam/ Deloitte/in/Documents/finance/Forensic/in-fo-rensic-AML-Survey-report-2020-noexp.pdf (accessed 1 February 2022).
33 Wack (1985).
34 Roxburg (2009), pp. 1–9.
35 NIC (2012).
36 Glenn, Florescu and The Millennium Project (2016).
37 Shell (2005, 2008).
38 Oxford Economics (2011).
39 European Commission (2009).
40 On scenarios one may consult: Enriquez et al. (2015); PwC (2015); Attali (2006).
41 Hamel (2000). The author is not centred on the issues of globalization, but the book implicitly assumes that corporations will become more and more globalized.
42 Ghoshal and Bartlett (1997).
43 Doz et al. (2002).
44 Hagel and Singer (1999).

References and further reading

Acemoglu, D. (2021) 'Remaking the Post-Covid World', IMF: Finance and Development. https://www.imf.org/external/pubs/ft/fandd/2021/03/pdf/COVID-inequality-and-automation-acemoglu.pdf (accessed 1 February 2022).

Ansoff, H. I. (1975) 'Managing strategic surprise by response to weak signals', *California Management Review*, XVIII (2).

Aslam, A. (2005) 'Planet faces nightmare forecasts as Chinese consumption grows and grows', *One World News*, 10 March.

Attali, J. (2006) *Une Brêve Histoire de l'Avenir* (Paris: Fayard).

Bello, W. (2000) 'The struggle for a deglobalized world', *Focus on the Global South*, September. http://www.corpwatch.org/article.php?id=322 (accessed 4 July 2017).

Beneviste, G. (1994) *The Twenty-First Century Organizàtion: Analyzing Current Trends – Imagining the Future* (San Francisco: Jossey-Bass). (Presents two scenarios of the organization in the twenty-first century.)

Brown, L. R. (2005) *Learning from China: Why the Western Economic Model Will Not Work for the World*, March, Earth Policy Institute. http://www.earth-policy.org/plan_b_updates/2005/update46 (accessed 4 July 2017).

Collins, M., Knutti, R., Arblaster, J., Dufresne, J.-L., Fichefet, T., Friedlingstein, P., Gao, X., Gutowski, W. J., Johns, T., Krinner, G., Shongwe, M., Tebaldi, C., Weaver, A. J. and Wehner, M. (2013) 'Long-term climate change: projections, commitments and irreversibility', in T. F. Stocker, D. Qin, G.-K. Plattner, M. Tignor, S. K. Allen, J. Boschung, A. Nauels, Y. Xia, V. Bex and P. M. Midgley (eds), *Climate Change 2013: The Physical Science Basis. Contribution of Working Group I to the Fifth Assessment Report of the Intergovernmental Panel on Climate Change*, 1029–136 (Cambridge and New York, NY: Cambridge University Press). doi: 10.1017/CBO9781107415324.024.

Daugherty, P. R. and Wilson, H. (2018) '*Human + Machine: reimagining work in the age of AI*', Harvard Business Review Press.

Deloitte (2020) *Planning scenarios for resilient leaders: The world remade by COVID-19*. https://www2.deloitte.com/hr/en/pages/about-deloitte/articles/covid-19-svijet-preobrazen-pandemijom-koronavirusa.html (accessed 1 February 2022).

Devlin, C., Bolt, O., Patel, D. and Harding, D. (2014) 'Impacts of migration on UK native employment: an analytical review of the evidence', Home Office/Department for Business Innovation and Skills, March, Occasional Paper 109. https://www.gov.uk/government/publications (accessed 4 July 2017).

Doremus, P. N., Keller, W. W., Pauly, L. W. and Reich, S. (1998) *The Myth of the Global Corporation* (Princeton, NJ: Princeton University Press).

Doz, Y. L., Dos Santos, J. and Williamson, P. (2002) *From Global to Metanational: How Companies Win in the Knowledge Economy* (Boston, MA: Harvard Business School Press).

Enrique, L., Smith, S. and Ablett, J. (2015) *Setting Tides: Global Economics Scenarios for 2015–2025*, McKinsey Company, Strategy, September. https://www.mckinsey.com/business-functions/strategy-and-corporate-finance/our-insights/shifting-tides-global-economic-scenarios-for-2015-25 (accessed 28 January 2022).

EPA (United States Environmental Protection Agency) (2016) *Future of Climate Change*. https://19january2017snapshot.epa.gov/climate-change-science/future-climate-change_.html (accessed 7 July 2017).

European Commission (2009) *The World in 2025* (Brussels: European Commission). https://ec.europa.eu/research/social-sciences/pdf/policy_reviews/the-world-in-2025-report_en.pdf (accessed 4 July 2017).

Friedman, T. L. (1999) *The Lexus and the Olive Tree: Understanding Globalization* (New York, NY: Farrar, Strauss & Giroux).

Fukuyama, F. (1989) 'The end of history', *The National Interest* (Summer).

Fukuyama, F. (1992) *The End of History and the Last Man* (New York, NY: Free Press).

Fukuyama, F. (2014) 'At the end of history still stands democracy', *Wall Street Journal*, 6 June.

Gaub, F. (2021) *Conflicts to Come, 15 Scenarios for 2030*, European Union Institute for Security Studies. https://op.europa.eu/en/publication-detail/-/publication/84515f4e-5ebc-11eb-b487-01aa75ed71a1/language-en/format-PDF/source-207681264 (accessed 1 February 2022).

Ghoshal, S. and Bartlett, C. A. (1997) *The Individualized Corporation: A Fundamental Approach to Management* (New York, NY: HarperCollins).

Glenn, J. C. and The Millennium Project Team (2019) *Work/Technology 2050 Scenarios and Action*. http://www.millennium-project.org/projects/workshops-on-future-of-worktechnology-2050-scenarios/ (accessed 10 April 2021).

Guillen, M. (2020) *2030: How Today's Biggest Trends Will Collide and Reshape the Future of Everything* (New York, NY: St Martin's Press).

Hagel III, J. and Singer, M. (1999) 'Unbundling the corporation', *Harvard Business Review*, 77 (2): 133–44.

Hamel, G. (2000) *Leading the Revolution* (Boston, MA: Harvard Business School Press).

Hammond, A. (1998) *Which World? Scenarios for the 21st Century* (Washington, DC: Island Press, Shearwater Books).

Harari, Y. (2018), *21 Lessons for the 21st Century* (London: Jonathan Cape/Penguin Random House).

Harvey, M., Novicevic, M. and Kiessling, T. (2001) 'Hypercompetition and the future of global management in the twenty first century', *Thunderbird International Business Review*, 43 (5): 599–616.

Heilbroner, R. (1993) *21st Century Capitalism* (New York, NY: W.W. Norton). (Presents five scenarios of capitalism in the twenty-first century.)

Huntington, S. P. (1997) *The Clash of Civilizations and the Remaking of the World Order* (London: Simon & Schuster).

IBM (n.d.) 'What is quantum computing?' https://www.ibm.com/quantum-computing/what-is-quantum-computing/ (accessed 8 May 2021).

IBRD (International Bank for Reconstruction and Development) (2007) *Global Economic Prospects, Managing the New Wave of Globalization* (Washington, DC: The World Bank).

IBRD (International Bank for Reconstruction and Development) (2021) *World Development Report 2021: Data for Better Lives* (Washington, DC: The World Bank). https://www.worldbank.org/en/publication/wdr202 (accessed 1 February 2022).

IFTF (Institute for the Future) (2020) *Future Forces Disrupting Sustainable Business*. https://www.iftf.org/fileadmin/user_upload/images/ourwork/Sustainability/IFTF_GEMI_FutureForces_Report_2020.pdf (accessed 20 April 2021).

International Energy Agency (2015) *Energy and Climate Change. World Energy Special Report* (Paris, France). https://www.iea.org/reports/energy-and-climate-change (accessed 1 February 2022).

IPCC (Intergovernmental Panel on Climate Change) (n.d.) *Global Warming of 1.5°C*. https://www.ipcc.ch/sr15/ (accessed 20 April 2021).

IPCC (Intergovernmental Panel on Climate Change) (2012) *Renewable Energy Sources and Climate Change Mitigation: Special Report of the Intergovernmental Panel on Climate Change Renewable Energy Sources and Climate Change*, Intergovernmental Panel on Climate Change. https://www.ipcc.ch/pdf/special-reports/srren/SRREN_FD_SPM_final.pdf (accessed 9 July 2017).

IPCC (Intergovernmental Panel on Climate Change) (2013) *Climate Change 2013, The Physical Science Basis: Frequently Asked Questions*. http://www.ipcc.ch/report/ar5/wg1/docs/WG1AR5_FAQbrochure_FINAL.pdf (accessed 5 July 2017).

Kai-Fu, L. (2019) *AI Superpowers: China, Silicon Valley and the New World Order* (Boston, MA, and New York, NY: Houghton Mifflin Harcourt).

King, S. D. (2017) *Grave New World: The End of Globalization, the Return of History* (New Haven, CT: Yale University Press).

Loungani, P. (2021) *The Guru of Globalization*, IMF Finance and Development. https://www.imf.org/external/pubs/ft/fandd/2021/03/profile-of-economist-assaf-razin-telaviv-university.htm (accessed 1 February 2022).

Luebkeman, C. (2019) *2050 Scenarios: Four Plausible Futures* (London: Arup). https://www.arup.com/perspectives/publications/research/section/2050-scenarios-four-plausible-futures (accessed 1 February 2022).

Melander, E. (2016) *Organized Violence in the World 2015: An Assessment by the Uppsala Conflict Data Program*, Uppsala University. http://www.pcr.uu.se/digitalAssets/61/c_61335-l_1-k_ucdp-paper-9.pdf (accessed 7 July 2017).

Mitroff, I. I. (1997) *Business Not as Usual: Rethinking Our Individual, Corporate, and Industrial Strategies for Global Competition* (San Francisco, CA: Jossey-Bass). (Presents four scenarios of US development into the twenty-first century.)

NIC (National Intelligence Council) (2000) *Global Trends 2015: A Dialogue about the Future with Nongovernment Experts,* December. https://www.cia.gov/library/readingroom/docs/DOC_0000516933.pdf (accessed 5 July 2017).

NIC (National Intelligence Council) (2008) *Global Trends 2025: A Transformed World*. https://www.files.ethz.ch/isn/94769/2008_11_Global_Trends_2025.pdf (accessed 5 July 2017).

NIC (National Intelligence Council) (2012) *Global Trends 2030: Alternative Worlds*. https://globaltrends2030.files.wordpress.com/2012/11/global-trends-2030-november2012.pdf (accessed 7 July 2017).

NIC (National Intelligence Council) (2021) *Global Trends 2040: A More Contested World*. https://www.dni.gov/files/ODNI/documents/assessments/GlobalTrends_2040.pdf (accessed 1 February 2022).

OECD (Organisation for Economic Co-operation and Development) (2001) *Policies to Enhance Sustainable Development* (Paris: OECD).

OECD (Organisation for Economic Co-operation and Development) (2012) *Environmental Outlook to 2050* (Paris: OECD).

OECD (Organisation for Economic Co-operation and Development) (2015a) *Income Inequality: The Gap between Rich and Poor*, OECD Insights, December.

OECD (Organisation for Economic Co-operation and Development) (2015b) *Material Resources, Productivity and the Environment*. http://www.oecd.org/env/waste/material-resources-productivity-and-the-environment-9789264190504-en.htm (accessed 9 July 2017).

OECD, IMF, World Bank, UN (2000) *A Better World for All* (Paris: OECD).

Oxford Economics (2011) *Global Scenarios Service* (Oxford Economics).

Piketti, T. (2014) *Capital in the Twenty-First Century* (Cambridge, MA: Belknap Press/Harvard University Press).

Piketti, T. (2020) *Capital and Ideology* (Cambridge, MA: Belknap Press/Harvard University Press).

Pisani-Ferry, J. and Santos, I. (2009) 'Reshaping the global economy', *Finance & Development, A Quarterly Publication of the IMF*, 46 (1), March.

PwC (2015) *The World in 2050, Will the Shift in Global Economic Power Continue?*. www.pwc.co.uk/economics (accessed 4 July 2017).

Raleigh, C., Jordan, L. and Salehyan, I. (2014) *Assessing the Impact of Climate Change on Migration and Conflict* (Washington, DC: The World Bank).

Rodrik, D. (1997) *Has Globalization Gone Too Far?* (Washington, DC: Peterson Institute for International Economics).

Roldan, C., Brauer, D. and Rohbeck, J. (eds) (2018) *Philosophy of globalization* (Boston, MA: Walter de Gruyter). https://library.oapen.org/bitstream/handle/20.500.12657/29566/1000366.pdf?sequence=1&isAllowed=y (accessed 1 February 2022).

Roxburg, C. (2009) 'The use and abuse of scenarios', *McKinsey Quarterly*, November.

Ruane, J., McAfee, A. and Oliver, W. (2022) 'Quantum computing for business leaders', *Harvard Business Review,* 100 (1): 112–21.

Rugman, A. (2000) *The End of Globalization: A New and Radical Analysis of Globalization and What it Means for Business* (London: Random House).

Saari, D. J. (1999) *Global Corporations and Sovereign Nations: Collision or Cooperation?* (Westport, CT: Quorum Books).

Schoemaker, P. (1995) 'Scenario planning: a tool for strategic thinking', *Sloan Management Review*, 36 (2), Winter.

Schopfer, T. and Sajadi, R. E. (2021) 'The clever use of robots during COVID-19', *EHL Insights*, Ecole Hotelière de Lausanne. https://hospitalityinsights.ehl.edu/robots-during-covid-19#:~:text=In%20hospitals&text=A%20safe%20alternative%20is%20to,Robots%20to%20disinfect%20patients'% (accessed 1 February 2022).

Sheffield, C., Marceto, A. and Kaplan, M. A. (eds) (1994) *The World of 2044 – Technological Development and the Future of Society* (St Paul, MN: Paragon House). (A global economy scenario to the year 2044.)

Shell (2005) *Global Scenarios to 2025* (London: Shell). http://www.shell.com (accessed 4 July 2017).

Shell (2008) *Global Energy Scenarios to 2050* (London: Shell). http://www.shell.com (accessed 4 July 2017).

Stiglitz, J. E. (2002) *Globalization and its Discontents* (New York, NY: W.W. Norton & Company, National Intelligence Council).

Stiglitz, J. E. (2012) *The Price of Inequality: How Today's Divided Society Endangers Our Future* (New York, NY: W.W. Norton & Company).

Stiglitz, J. E. (2015) *The Great Divide: Unequal Societies and What We Can Do About Them* (New York, NY: W.W. Norton & Company).

Taleb, N. N. (2007) *The Black Swan: The Impact of the Highly Improbable* (London: Allen Lane).

Tertrais, B. (2015) 'The revenge of history', *The Washington Quarterly*, 38 (4): 7–18.

Thomas, N., Sheppard, D. and Hume, N. (2021) 'The race to scale up green hydrogen', *Financial Times*, 8 March.

Tonby, O., et al. (2019) *Future of Asia*, McKinsey Global Institute Discussion Paper. https://www.mckinsey.com/kz/sitecore/content/mckinsey/home/featured-insights/future-of-asia (accessed 1 February 2022).

UNEP (1999) *Global Environment Outlook* (Cary, NC: Oxford University Press).

United Arab Emirates & United Nations (2020) *Future Possibilities Report 2020*. https://www.un.org/sites/un2.un.org/files/20200720_un75_uae_future-possibilitiesreport.pdf (accessed 1 February 2022).

United Nations Department of Economic and Social Affairs (2011) *The Global Social Crisis. Report on the World Social Situation* (New York, NY: United Nations). http://www.un.org/esa/socdev/rwss/docs/2011/overview.pdf (accessed 7 July 2017).

United Nations Department of Economic and Social Affairs (2015) *World Population Prospects, 2015 Revision: Key Findings and Advance Tables* (New York, NY: United Nations). https://esa.un.org/unpd/wpp/publications/files/key_findings_wpp_2015.pdf (accessed 5 July 2017).

United Nations Department of Economic and Social Affairs (2019) *World Population Prospects*, Population Division (New York, NY: United Nations). https://population.un.org/wpp/Download/Standard/Population/ (accessed 10 April 2021).

UNODC (United Nations Office on Drugs and Crime) (2010) *The Threat of Transnational Organized Crime* (New York, NY: UNODC).

UNODC (United Nations Office on Drugs and Crime) (2016) *Organized Crime*. https://www.unodc.org/unodc/en/organized-crime/index.html (accessed 7 July 2017).

Wack, P. (1985) 'Scenarios: shooting the rapids', *Harvard Business Review*, 63 (6): 139–49.

White, J. (ed.) (1992) *Global Climate Change: Linking Energy, Environment, Economy, and Equity* (New York, NY: Plenum Press). (Energy scenarios to the twenty-first century.)

Witt, M. A. (2019) 'De-globalization: Theories, predictions, and opportunities for international business research', *Journal of International Business Studies* 50: 1053–77.

Woetzel, J., et al. (2020) *Climate Risk and Response*, McKinsey Global Institute. https://www.mckinsey.com/business-functions/sustainability/our-insights/climate-risk-and-response-physical-hazards-and-socioeconomic-impacts (accessed 1 February 2022).

World Bank (2015a) *Ending Extreme Poverty and Sharing Prosperity: Progress and Policies* (Washington, DC: World Bank). https://openknowledge.worldbank.org/bitstream/handle/10986/23604/Ending0extreme0rogress0and0policies.pdf?sequence=1&isAllowed=y (accessed 29 January 2022).

World Bank (2015c) *World Bank Forecasts Global Poverty to Fall Below 10% for First Time; Major Hurdles Remain in Goal to End Poverty by 2030*. http://www.worldbank.org/en/news/press-release/2015/10/04/world-bank-forecasts-global-poverty-to-fall-below-10-for-first-time-major-hurdles-remain-in-goal-to-end-poverty-by-2030 (accessed 5 July 2017).

World Bank (2016) *Global Monitoring Report 2015/2016: Development Goals in an Era of Demographic Change* (Washington, DC: World Bank).

World Bank (n.d.) Regional aggregation using 2011 PPP and $1.9/day poverty line. http://iresearch.worldbank.org/PovcalNet/povDuplicateWB.aspx (accessed 1 February 2022).

World Bank (2015b) 'South Asia extreme poverty falls, but challenges remain', 15 October. https://www.worldbank.org/en/news/press-release/2015/10/15/south-asia-extreme-poverty-falls-but-challenges-remain (accessed 8 February 2022).

World Economic Forum (2006) *China and the World: Scenarios to 2025*. http://www3.weforum.org/docs/WEF_Scenario_ChinaWorld2025_Report_2010.pdf (accessed 5 July 2017).

World Economic Forum (2016) *The Gobal Risks Report 2016*. https://www.weforum.org/reports/the-global-risks-report-2016 (accessed 1 February 2022).

World Economic Forum (2021) *The Global Risks Report 2021*. https://www.weforum.org/reports/the-global-risks-report-202 (accessed 1 February 2022).

Zakaria, F. (2020) *Ten Lessons for a Post-Pandemic World* (London: W. W. Norton & Company).

Journals

European Journal of Future Research: https://eujournalfuturesresearch.springeropen.com

Futures: https://www.journals.elsevier.com/futures

Journal of Future Studies: https://jfsdigital.org

Chapter 16

Global strategic management in action: Haier – the building of a global champion, 1984–2020

This in-depth case study on the globalization of Haier illustrates most of the subjects that have been covered in this textbook. The company represents its pathway to globalization in a graph that is reproduced here as Table 16.1.

Table 16.1 Haier's six strategic stages

Strategy Phase 1 Building the brand	Strategy Phase 2 Diversification	Strategy Phase 3 Internationalization	Strategy Phase 4 Multi local global presence	Strategy Phase 5 Global integrated network	Strategy Phase 6 Global ecosytem
1984–1991	1991–1998	1998–2005	2005–2012	2012–2019	2019–
Quality products created by quality talent	Liquid assets driven by motivated people	An international brand built by international talent	A globalized brand developed by localized Haier people	From products to solutions through community of interest	Micro enterprises organized around users' needs

Source: Based on information from https://www.haier.com/global/about-haier/intro/?to=2&spm=net.32024_pc.header_141698_20200720.2. (Accessed 13 April 2022)

Introduction

In 1979 Chairman Deng Xiaoping, Leader of the People's Republic of China, introduced the new economic philosophy *Socialism with Chinese Characteristics* with his famous sentence 'It does not matter if a cat is white or black so long as it catches mice' now being reused to show an acceptance of some features of capitalist economic thought. This announcement opened the way to introducing a form of market economy into a highly regulated and bureaucratic system. Before 1979 Chinese enterprises were all state-owned, operating in a centrally planned economy. Enterprises were called 'working units'; clearly split into Technical Centres (for research), Factories (for production) and Distribution depots and stores. The 'cat' revolution allowed the progressive transformation of those entities into integrated firms, capable of taking charge of the whole value chain. Company ownership was distributed between state-owned (by central government or local authorities) and collective enterprises; an open door to privatization that was used by senior party members and bureaucrats who increasingly took over these ex-collective enterprises and floated them on stock exchanges. This was the context that saw the 1984 merger of two factories in the municipality of Qingdao – the Qingdao General Refrigerator Factory and the Qingdao Air Conditioning Factory. The new entity kept the name Qingdao General Refrigerator Company, but this was changed in 1992 to Qingdao Haier Refrigerator Company, and later shortened to *Haier.* The first manager of the newly formed company was an engineer from the Qingdao municipality, Mr Zhang Ruimin.

Phases 1 and 2: building the brand and diversification (1984–1998)

Zhang's first stated objective was to make Haier the best refrigerator manufacturer in China. His method of achieving this objective can be characterized by three means: a) good management practices, leading to quality products and high productivity; b) acquisition of modern technology; and c) taking the opportunity to consolidate a fragmented industry. In addition, he quickly moved to expand the product offering by entering the market for related household appliances.

Good management practices

Before 1979 and the movement towards more of a market economy, Chinese management practice was characterized by a limited concern with quality, poor productivity and a total lack of concern about the consumer experience (since the concept of the consumer was alien to the Marxist vocabulary). Qingdao General Refrigerator was typical of this environment. Zhang was quick to perceive the radical strategic shift that would be needed in this new market-driven atmosphere. Buyers who had previously queued to buy whatever was coming out of factories would progressively be attracted by products of good quality at a good price. Zhang realized that if Haier could provide such products it would benefit from the opportunity for growth in sales and profits. That would require a radical change in management practices.

Zhang dramatized the quality issue in 1985. Following a complaint from a customer about the quality of the refrigerator he had just bought, Zhang had seventy-six refrigerators brought out from the warehouse to the street in front of the factory, ordered the 800 factory workers outside to watch and had the seventy-six units sledgehammered to pieces in public.[1] Following up on that gesture, he reorganized the workplace and introduced a series of management practices based on Six Sigma[2] concepts and the goal of 'zero defects'. Quality control was introduced throughout the manufacturing process, instead of only being applied to the end products. He introduced the technique of OEC (Overall, Everyone, Everything and Everyday, Control and Clear) to induce workers to focus on rigour and quality. Under this philosophy, management would introduce and retain '**Overall Control** of and **Clarity** on **Every**thing that **Every** employee finishes on his or her job **Every** day'. To ensure this on the productivity front, he introduced a wage calculation card system based on the daily performance of a series of seven attributes ranging from quality to production planning, efficient use of materials, and discipline (the '*everything, everyone, and every day*' performance record).[3] Over the years Zhang continued to reorganize frequently as was necessary to keep improving quality, costs and innovation.

Technology acquisition

Poor manufacturing technology had characterized Chinese firms, so Zhang decided to turn to foreign technology to change Haier's manufacturing process. He bought a manufacturing line under licence from the German refrigerator firm Liebherr and a year later Haier was able to introduce its first modern refrigerator, the 'Four-star', which became a leading brand.

Industry consolidation

When Zhang took over in 1984 there were more than 110 local refrigerator manufacturers in China. This was due to the introduction of the market economy and the huge consumption eagerness of Chinese families that it unlocked. Many companies wanted to benefit from the boom in demand for refrigerators, but not all of them had the economies of scale and the management and technical capabilities to compete when the market matured and began to demand quality products at good prices. Haier and a few other companies that were able to raise their productivity and quality, and thus achieve better financial results, could acquire their weaker competitors. Haier acquired seventeen enterprises in China between 1988 and 1998.[4]

Product-related diversification

In 1988 the company expanded its product line by acquiring a microwave oven factory in Qingdao. Between 1988 and 1995 it entered the wider market of 'white goods' appliances: air conditioning, washing machines, vacuum cleaners and cooking stoves. For instance, in 1995 Haier acquired Red Star Electric Appliance Company, a leading white goods manufacturer run by the Qingdao municipality. In 1996 it moved into 'black goods' – products such as TVs, video recorders and DVD players. These moves allowed the company to offer customers the whole range of household products from the same supplier, and to reposition the brand name Haier as a broad provider of home appliances, instead of just being known for refrigerators. These acquisitions also allowed Haier to achieve operational synergies in manufacturing, procurement and distribution.

The competitive battlefield of China in the 1990s

By the 1990s China's appliances market was clearly divided into two categories of player: domestic and foreigners.

Domestic players

As mentioned earlier, during the 1980s and the early 1990s the number of domestic players in household appliances increased massively. The majority of these firms had originally been initiated and run by local government. Their products were of poor quality but the newly unlocked demand was such that they could sell whatever they produced despite this. When private investors and foreign firms entered the industry, price competition increased and profit margins decreased. As we have seen, this provided a golden opportunity for the leading, more efficient companies such as Haier and Midea to make acquisitions amongst these struggling firms and consolidate the market. (See Table 16.2 for a short factual description of Midea Group.) By 2019 the market was nearly a duopoly, with Haier and Midea controlling over 50 per cent market share in the major appliances market (see Table 16.2 and Figure 16.1).

Table 16.2 Head-to-head comparison of Haier Smart Home and Midea groups

	Haier Smart Home	Midea
Place of origin	Qingdao (Shandong Province)	Beijiao (Guangdong Province)
Year of creation	1984	1968
Revenue in 2019 (billion yuan)	200.76**	278.22
Number of employees 2019	99,757	134,897
Number of factories worldwide*	25	21
Number of countries present*	160+	200
Chinese market share (2019)	30.6%	19.8%***

Note: * *We will discuss Haier's global investments and foreign market strategy in the following section, 'Phases 3 and 4: internationalization and global brand strategy (1998–2012)'; ** Haier Smart Home Annual Report 2019, p. 7 (http://smart-home.haier.com/en/yjbg/P020200604564589608928.pdf?appdesc=Haier%20Smart%20Home%20FY%202019%20Annual%20Report); *** Midea Annual report 2019 (https://www.midea-group.com/asset/Midea-Group/Financial%20report.zip/Midea-Group-2019-Annual-Report.pdf) (accessed 1 February 2022).*

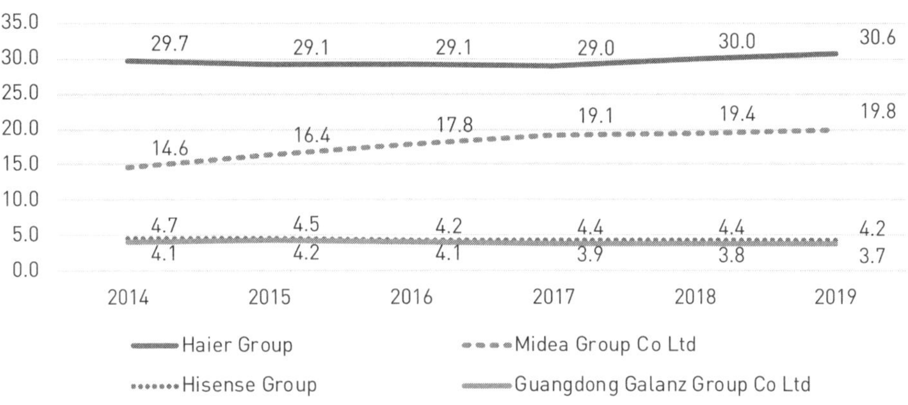

Figure 16.1 Evolution of market share in China in major appliances (2014–2019)

Source: Consumer Appliances: Euromonitor from trade sources/national statistics (date exported 10 January 2020). © Euromonitor International.

Foreign players

The sheer size and untapped potential of the Chinese market attracted several foreign companies from the USA, Europe, Japan and South Korea to enter, especially in the 1990s. Their strategy was to rely on their experience in their existing markets, their technological superiority and the reputation and reach of their globally known brands. They focused their efforts and expectations mainly on the high-end market. By the early 2000s the Chinese market was showing signs of the overcapacity that would lead to a price war.

Whirlpool (from the USA – see Chapter 5) entered the Chinese market in 1994 with four joint ventures: 1) with Snowflake in Beijing for refrigerators; 2) with Narcissus in Shanghai for washing machines; 3) with

MVC in Shendu for microwave ovens; and 4) with Reibo in Shenzen for air conditioners. Lack of product and management adaptation led to disappointing results, which saw the company close its refrigerator and air conditioner joint ventures as early as 1997.

Electrolux (from Sweden) entered the market in 1997 with the acquisition of Zhongyi Refrigerator and Hangzhou Wanbao Air-Conditioner. Electrolux did acknowledge regional conditions as far as localizing its management, but found itself struggling in the price war against local Chinese players, and despite several reorganizations was only able to achieve 0.5 per cent market share in 2016.

Bosch-Siemens (a powerful German conglomerate) entered in 1994 by establishing a joint venture with a domestic washing machine manufacturer in Wuxi. It had only managed to obtain a poor 3.2 per cent market share by 2016.

Japanese brands enjoyed a good reputation for quality and performance but again their market share remained modest. Panasonic, for instance, only achieved 1.4 per cent in 2016.

Figure 16.2 shows the strategic positioning of the various players in the Chinese appliance market in early 2010. Chinese players are competing on price and their local knowledge while international competitors are competing on differentiation based on technology and marketing.

Phases 3 and 4: internationalization and global brand strategy (1998–2012)

In the 1990s, having achieved domestic success and diversified its product offering, Haier Group was able to start on the third stage of its strategic development (see Table 16.1) – internationalization.

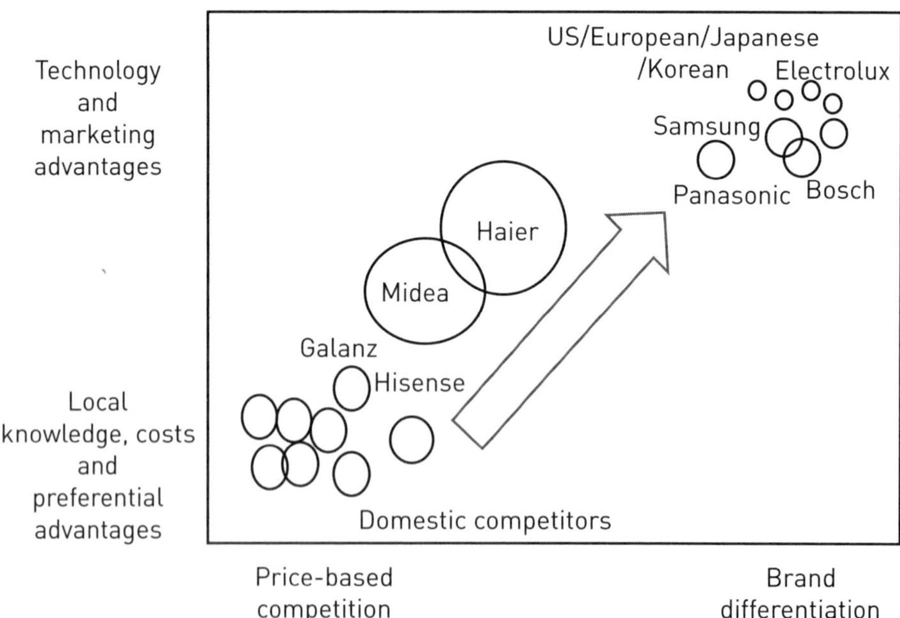

Figure 16.2 The competitive battlefield in China, 1990s to 2010

Note: *Circle size indicates market share.*

Table 16.3 Haier vs. global competitors, 2018–2021

	2018	2019	2020	2021
Haier	1	1	1	1
Whirlpool	2	2	2	2
Midea	3	3	3	3
BSH Hausgärate	4	4	4	5
Electrolux	5	5	6	6
LG	7	7	7	7
Zhuhai Gree	8	8	8	8
Panasonic	9	9	9	9
Hisense	10	10	10	10

Source: Haier website.
Note: Sales projections based on seventy-eight countries.

Internationalization

Haier's internationalization strategy followed a three-step approach of:

> Going out, going in and going up. First, gain ground in the traditional major household appliance markets like Europe, USA and Japan by making [inroads] into the niche markets, then with the advantageous positions obtained in these major markets, rapidly expand the market presence in the developing countries. Next, take to the main channels of local markets with localized products that meet mainstream local user needs, and ultimately become the market leader of high-end and innovative products.[5]

'Going out': export

In the early 1990s Haier exported its products by contracting original equipment manufacturing (OEM) arrangements with large distributors or local producers, as well as some agents in Europe and the USA, to manufacture goods for rebranding and resale. In Southeast Asian countries that imposed a legal requirement on local content manufacturing, the company entered into local OEM joint venture agreements. Very soon – by 1992 – the company decided to adopt the common international brand name 'Haier' for all its products, and progressively move its export drive away from the OEM model.

'Going in': breaking into overseas markets

One way Haier discovered to establish its brand and to gain brand recognition against giant US and European competitors was to gain a foothold by focusing initially on niche products that were not well served in the existing market. The positioning philosophy was to offer quality products at an affordable price in markets that were neglected by leading manufacturers.

Haier gained some success with small refrigerators for hotels and students' bedrooms, home wine-chiller cabinets and, later on, small freezers for small kitchens (established players in the USA especially were focused on making big family-sized refrigerators or chest freezers). Zhang later explained how Haier had identified this unsatisfied market demand, based on a market survey it had done on university and college campuses in order to understand the problems of students living in small rooms. In the fields of these small refrigerators and wine cabinets, Haier quickly took a leading market share in the USA.

'Going up': foreign investment and becoming a dominant international player

The first major greenfield direct investment by Haier was in 1999 with the establishment of a $30 million, wholly owned refrigerator factory – *Haier America Refrigerators Co.* – in Camden, North Carolina, USA. This became the home of the Haier America Industrial Complex, and was subsequently expanded over the years. The bold choice to go straight into a sophisticated, crowded market like the USA was justified by Chairman Zhang Ruimin, who explained that Haier's strategy was deliberately very different from that of other Chinese enterprises which tended to first go after the easier markets of Southeast Asia – 'our strategy is the other way around: we go to easier markets after we first penetrate difficult markets such as the United States and Europe'.[6]

In Europe Haier had already established local offices in most major market countries and was marketing its China-made products through a network of local distributors. In 1993 a joint venture with Merloni, an Italian appliances manufacturer, was established to manufacture front-loading washing machines designed for the Chinese market. In 1997, Haier made an investment in Croatia (at that time, still part of Yugoslavia) in the form of a small joint venture to manufacture air-conditioning units for the European market.

Table 16.4 lists the international acquisitions, joint ventures and greenfield investments made by Haier since 2000.

Table 16.4 Haier's key international industrial investments

Year	Country	Mode of investment/partner	Product lines
2000	Bangladesh	Joint venture (JV) with Hayes	Refrigerators, air-conditioning units
2000	Iran	OEM JV	Refrigerators, air-conditioning units, washing machines
2000	Vietnam	JV	Refrigerators
2001	Italy	Acquisition of Meghetti	Refrigerators
2002	Japan	JV with Sanyo – this became a full acquisition in 2011	Refrigerators, washing machines
2006	Pakistan	JV with Ruba Group	Industrial zone
2007	India	Greenfield investment at Pune	Refrigerators
2012	New Zealand	Acquisition of Fisher and Paykel	Multiple appliances
2013	Italy	JV with Fagor	Multiple appliances
2013	Poland	JV with Fagor	Refrigerator factory
2016	Russia	Greenfield, $50 million investment	To build refrigerators (capacity: 500,000 units p.a.)
2016	USA	Acquisition of General Electric Appliances Business	Multiple appliances
2019	Italy	Acquisition of Candy	Home appliances

Global marketing: global brand, localized brand name

The fourth stage in Haier's plan (Table 16.1) was to address global brand strategy. According to Zhang Ruimin, 'All success relies on one thing in overseas markets, creating a localized brand name. We have to make Americans feel that Haier is a localized US brand instead of an imported Chinese brand.'[7] By the mid-2000s, in addition to local manufacturing, local distribution and marketing, Haier had started to implement a local design strategy to make products that fitted more closely to local market characteristics. For instance, it introduced a flat refrigerator for the Indian market and a three-door refrigerator for the European market. Design centres were set up in France, Germany and Italy while marketing headquarters were established in the major European countries. This approach to localization demonstrated on a larger scale the intelligent market research and local market sensitivity that had worked so successfully for Haier's initial entry into the USA by filling the vacant compact refrigerators niche.

With its localized products, Haier approached the main distribution channels in each market to expand its market presence, operating under and promoting the Haier brand regardless of the product type. In 2016 the company claimed that it was present in the top ten chains in the USA and Europe. Its presence by then covered more than 160 countries.

However, in August 2016 following the acquisition of GE Appliances, the global branding approach was dramatically changed with the introduction of the 'Haier Kitchen Appliances Matrix'. This consists of five major brands: Haier Cooking, GE Appliances, Fisher & Paykel, Casarte and Leader.

During the two phases of global development, Haier came into contact with, and quickly had to adapt to, a wide variety of customer preferences. Zhang thus recognized the need to change the culture of Haier from a manufacturing orientation to a customer orientation. He wanted to create a service-oriented company designed to achieve 'zero distance to the customer'.[8] This move was referred to as *market chain management* or, according to Zhang, *Rendanheyi* (connecting user value to the value that employees shared). The philosophy was to make sure that everyone in the company would be in contact with a customer all along the value chain. So, for instance, a design department working on a freezer would be the customer of a technical laboratory working on the necessary cryogenic technology, while the freezer product manufacturing unit would be the customer of the design department and so on until the final customer (the purchaser of the unit). Each department would become a strategic business unit (SBU) having autonomy in making operating decisions and measuring performance. Those units were called ZZJYTs (*Zi Zhu Jing Ying Ti*: literally translated as 'independent operation units'). There were three kinds of ZZJYT unit: a) those in direct contact with customers, which were in charge of understanding the market, designing the products and manufacturing and distributing them; b) support functions such as logistics, running the facilities, quality assurance and control, and human resources management; c) strategic and corporate management functions.[9] By 2012 there were around 2,000 ZZJYTs, containing 60,000 employees, spread across the five continents.

Phase 5: global integrated network (2012–2019) – consolidating global leadership

Over the first five phases of strategic development (Table 16.1), Zhang Ruimin, the chairman of Haier, showed his willingness to radically change management systems, and even the whole culture of the company, to fit with changing competitive requirements.

In 2012, Zhang introduced a further change in management culture and processes with the view 'to transform the company from an enterprise that manufactures household appliances to become a networked enterprise that fits into the internet age'.[10] A central component of this new business model, *Rendanheyi 2.0*, is its reliance on a community of interests (COI) grouping of the ZZJYTs, users and partners into a network as a platform for development and market responsiveness. Users are linked to the COI via internet forums in which they discuss product features and usage, and propose innovation and changes. *Rendanheyi 1.0* had encouraged a similar openness and sharing of ideas amongst Haier staff. Under 2.0, partnerships are sought with universities, technology companies or even with competitors, while the ZZJYTs are in charge of integrating those agreed changes into the design, development, production and distribution of the products themselves.

An example of this type of collaboration is Haier's development of a water purification product. The specialized purification technology, which was outside Haier's existing expertise, comes from collaboration with Strauss, an Israeli technology company, as well as via the sharing of patents with Dow Chemical of the USA. Haier also collected and distributed information online about water-quality problems in various places in China. This combination of detailed information and access to the cutting-edge technology and expertise of its partners allows Haier to offer customers the best possible water purification product, designed and modified for the specific water impurity issues in their area.[11] See Figure 16.3 for a schematic representation of this model in operation.

In 2017 the company stated: 'Haier has managed to turn a traditional closed hierarchical system into a networked node organization, integrating first-class resources from around the world in an open way; and in manufacturing, Haier has explored replacing traditional physical plants with inter-connected factories and making the transformation from mass manufacturing to mass customization.'[12]

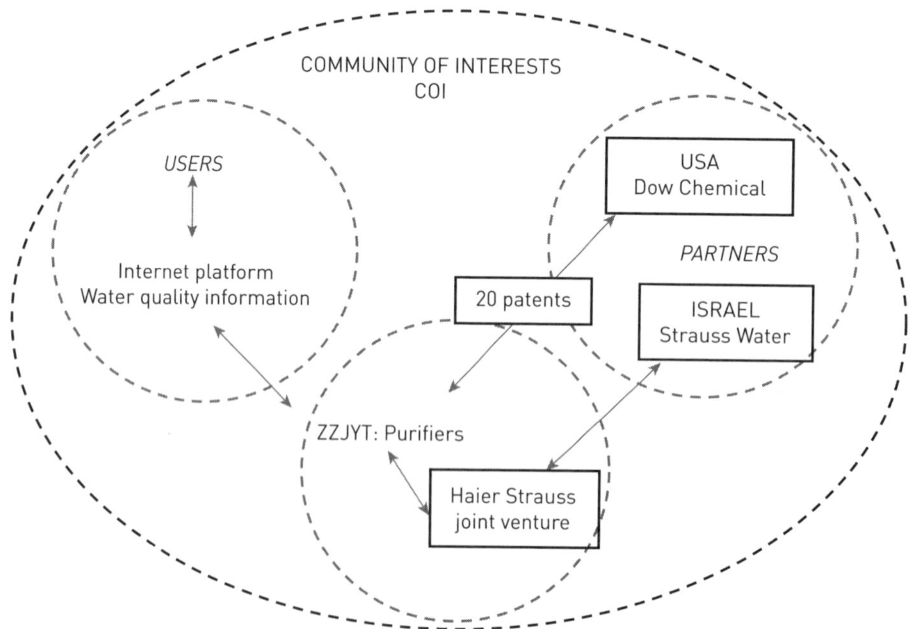

Figure 16.3 Schematic representation of *Rendanheyi 2.0* as applied to water purifiers

By adopting *Rendanheyi 2.0*, Haier nurtured entrepreneurial talent and achieved great financial performance. For example, Haier's incubation, investment and acceleration platform, HCH Ventures, was a platform that helped entrepreneurs start and run their business. By the end of 2017, 2,483 entrepreneurship projects were on its HCH Ventures with 256 of these moving on to incubators, and 4,325 entrepreneurship and innovation incubation resources were available on the platform. Haier established 24 incubators in 9 countries around the world. By 2019, Haier had more than 200 micro enterprises, 3,800 service and support micro enterprises and 1.22 million micro-stores that were creating an open platform to attract human resources and investment from society.[13]

Transformation was disruptive by nature but Haier's employees in Asia and North America embraced Zhang's business model. In January 2019, Haier acquired the Italian appliance manufacturer, Candy, where *Rendanheyi* was introduced next.

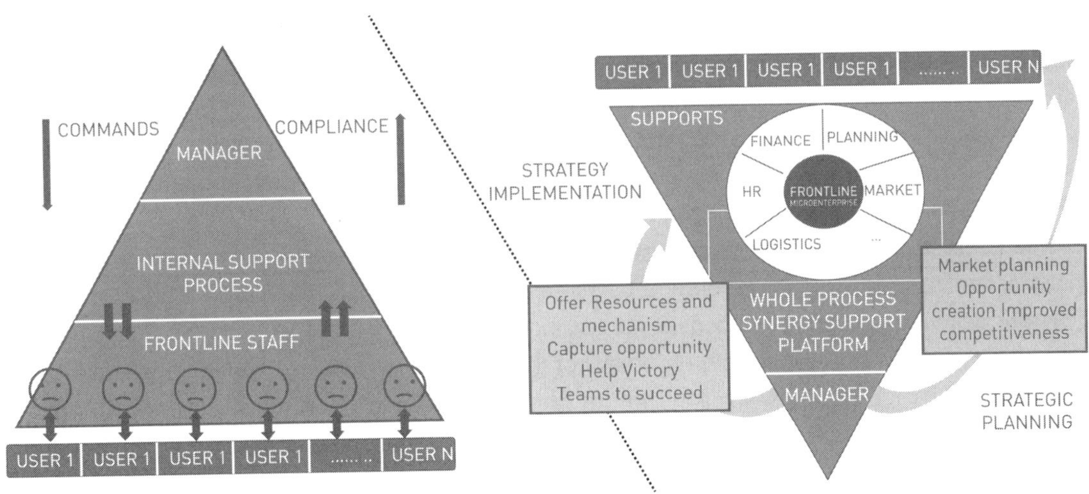

Figure 16.4 Haier's inverted pyramid organizational structure
Source: Haier presentation at INSEAD 2018.

Phase 6: ecosystem strategy (2019–)

According to a case by Koo, Lee and Minnaar (2022):

> The consumer landscape Haier faced had become increasingly complex and competitive ... Companies that would become dominant in this landscape were not those that built products and services for a single customer use, but those that created ecosystems around their products and services to deliver integrated experiences.
>
> Around 2015, top managers at Haier became increasingly aware of the potential of an ecosystem strategy in the home appliances business.

On 8 August 2016, at the tenth Davos Brand Day held at the Davos Convention Center in Dalian, Liang Haishan, Vice Chairman of the board of directors and Rotating President of Haier Group, delivered a keynote speech entitled 'Haier Builds Ecosystem Brand in the Internet Era with the Rendanheyi Model'.

According to Zhang Ruimin, Chairman of the board of directors and CEO of Haier Group, Haier is not only a product brand and enterprise brand, but is gradually developing into a leading ecosystem brand under the model of community economy.

On 10 May 2018, China Brand Day, Zhang proposed the concept 'ecosystem brand' for the first time. This was considered an iteration and innovation to the brand connotation that followed the product brand and platform brand. It was the world's first definite plan to build an ecosystem brand in the Internet of Things (IoT) age.[14]

A year later in June 2019, Haier announced it would change its name from Qingdao Haier Co Ltd to Haier Smart Home Co. Ltd, indicating Haier's smart home-centric strategy was leading the company's development. This was followed in December 2019, with Zhang's announcement on the beginning of the sixth strategic development stage – Ecosystem Brand stage.

After a few years of development, in October 2020 Haier unveiled the 'Three-Winged Bird' – an instance of what Haier referred to as a 'scenario brand'. Unlike a traditional brand, which encompasses a series of products that fall under the same umbrella but are promoted and sold separately, Haier's conception of a scenario brand consisted of an interconnected set of products that were promoted as a package.

For example, with Haier's Three-Winged Bird scenario brand, a user could announce in their living room that they wanted to take a nap. This announcement would then activate three appliances and devices – the electric curtain, the air conditioner and the humidifier.

The Ecosystem Brand system consists of breaking the organization into approximately 4,000 micro enterprises (ME) organized around users' needs for a scenario referred as 'Ecosystem Micro Communities' (EMC). Each EMC consists of two parts: the Experience EMC and the Solution EMC. The Experience EMC is responsible for obtaining the user needs. These are then transferred to the Solution EMC which provides solutions to the issues. These micro enterprises are linked through contractual agreements that define the amount of profit to be shared. The IT platform Haier developed (EMC Workbench) ensures the accountability of the teams in the MEs, taking on the traditional role of a manager. The platform automates the bidding process for jobs and contracts. It also tracks employee performance relative to goals and subsequent bonuses that are calculated and dispersed through blockchain technology.[15]

> EMCs were temporary structures that connected various MEs as well as external partners. What made EMCs unique was their ability to quickly and flexibly bring different stakeholders together with different expertise to collaborate on a new product or service.
>
> For example, the Internet of Food (IoF) Ecosystem brings together different EMCs: smart cooking, storage, ingredients, cleaning, dishes, mother and infant food.
>
> Anybody could propose an EMC by submitting a long-term vision, an estimate of resources required and potential profit to an internal committee called the Great Shared Platform. This was comprised of members of different functional areas, such as HR, legal, finance and others. Upon approval, the EMC was formally registered in Haier's internal digital platform. Once registered, EMCs could start to attract the right resources to help them achieve their vision.[16]

By the beginning of 2020, Haier had successfully incubated four listed companies (Haier Smart Home, Haier Electronics, Haier Biomedical, INKON Life), five unicorn companies (a privately held start-up company valued at over $1 billion) and 23 gazelle companies (a high-growth company that has been increasing its revenues by at least 20 per cent annually for four years or more, starting from a revenue base of at least $1 million). It owns a number of ecosystem brands including Haier, Casarte, Leader, GE Appliances (US), Fisher & Paykel (New Zealand), AQUA (Japan), Candy (Italy), COSMOPlat, RRS Logistics, Yingkang Life, Haier Biomedical, Haina Cloud, HCH and Haier Brothers.

By early 2022, initial returns on the most recent evolution of the Rendanheyi model – and the EMC structure – were positive and indicated that it was supportive of Haier's strategy.

Learning assignments

Phases 1 and 2

1. Explain how the two leading players in the Chinese appliances market were able to obtain such a dominant (nearly 50 per cent) market share by 2016.
2. Why were foreign firms not able to gain a significant market share in China?
3. Can you comment on the mini-fridge example? What does it demonstrate about Haier's approach and philosophy?

Phases 3 and 4

1. What were the benefits and risks for Haier in the decision to concentrate first on entering advanced markets such as the USA or Europe while most Chinese firms tended to enter emerging markets first?
2. What were the risks for Haier in undertaking costly international acquisitions and joint ventures?

Phase 5

Give your critical views on the ZZJYT's organization and community of interests model. How different are these from the decentralized organization and strategic alliances approaches?

Phase 6

Do you think that Haier's organization around micro enterprises (MEs) and Ecosystems Micro Communities (EMCs) will allow Haier to succeed in a competitive environment increasingly based on ecosystems and platforms? Why or why not?

Notes

1 See http://www.bbc.com/news/business-24622247 (accessed 6 July 2017).
2 Six Sigma is a set of quality management techniques which aims to ensure that 99.999 per cent ofarts manufactured will be free from defects.
3 Fisher, Lago and Liu (2013: 51).
4 Crawford, Zend and Schütte (2000).
5 Haier website: http://www.haier.net/en/about_haier/haier_global/OverseasMarket/(consulted 29 March 2017).
6 Wu (2000).
7 Ibid.
8 Campbell, Meyer, Xin and Stack (2015).
9 Fisher, Lago and Liu (2013: Ch. 4).

10 CEO profile, company website: http://www.haier.net/en/about_haier/Leadership/introduction/ (consulted 4 April 2017).

11 http://www.haier.net/en/about_haier/news/201505/t20150508_268224.shtml (accessed 13 April 2017).

12 Ibid.

13 https://smart-home.haier.com/en/gsgk/?spm=inverstor.31557_pc.irheader_20200506_1.1 (accessed 1 February 2022).

14 The Internet of things (IoT) describes the network of physical objects — a.k.a. 'things' — that are embedded with sensors, software and other technologies for the purpose of connecting and exchanging data with other devices and systems over the internet.

15 Bernstein, Lee and Minnaar (2022).

16 Koo, Lee and Minnaar (2022).

References and further reading

Bernstein, E., Lee, M. and Minnaar, J. (2022), 'How companies are using tech to give employees more autonomy', Boston Harvard Business Review. https://hbr.org/2022/01/how-companies-are-using-tech-to-give-employees-more-autonomy (accessed 1 February 2022).

Campbell, D., Meyer, M., Xin Lee, S. and Stack, K. (2015) 'Haier: zero distance to customer (A)', Harvard Business School Case, no. 9-115-006, June.

Crawford, R., Zend, M. and Schütte, H. (2000) 'China's Haier Group: growth through acquisitions', INSEAD Case 03/2001-4898.

Fisher, B., Lago, U. and Liu, F. (2013) *Reinventing Giants How Chinese Competitor Haier has Changed the Way Big Companies Transform* (San Francisco, CA: Jossey Bass).

Hamel, G. and Zanini, M. (2020) 'Humanocracy: creating organizations as amazing as the people inside them', *Boston Harvard Business Review*.

Koo, W. W., Lee, M. Y. and Minnaar, J. (2022), Haier: organizing to build a smart ecosystem brand, INSEAD case, 03/2022-6724

Wu, Y. (2003) 'China's refrigerator magnate', *McKinsey Quarterly*, 3: 106–16.

Zohar, D. (2022) *What Makes a Quantum Organization? In Zero Distance* (Singapore: Palgrave Macmillan).

Glossary[1]

[1]This glossary is the sole responsibility of the authors

Absorption mode of integration.
According to Jemison and Haspeslagh, absorption acquisitions take place between companies operating in similar industries and business contexts. The objective here is to achieve as rapidly as possible the necessary synergies through consolidation and rationalization of activities.

Acculturation
Is the process by which group members from one culture adapt to the culture of a different group.

Adjusted Present Value Country risk (APV)
A technique of discounted cash flow in which specific downside adverse risks are identified, their impact on the cash flow is calculated, a probability of their occurrence is determined, the cash flows are adjusted using the probabilistic distribution, the cash flows are translated into the investor's currency using the Purchasing Power Parity differences as a proxy for currencies fluctuation and cash flows are discounted using the investor's cost of capital.

Advertising agency
Is an external supplier of design and sourcing of advertising and promotion instruments for a company or a particular brand.

Alliance
An alliance is the sharing of capabilities between two or more firms with the view of enhancing their competitive advantages and/or creating new business without losing their respective strategic autonomy. Alliances can take several legal forms from simple long term contracts to equity joint ventures.

Arbitrage
Economic arbitrage exists when it is possible to buy a product in one market and simultaneously sell it in another market at a higher price. Dealers in foreign exchange often use arbitrage on foreign currencies that are not exactly quoted at the same rate of exchange on different markets. With electronic transactions it is possible to buy and sell simultaneously. Commodities traders use also arbitrage. By extension the concept is often used even if there is no simultaneity: for instance difference in taxation between countries in a free trade area may take advantage of arbitrage opportunities.

Asymmetric Development
In international economics, economic development is considered as asymmetric when countries develop at considerably different rates. For instance the gap in revenues between African and Western countries has increased over time, showing a strong asymmetry.

Back office

Refers to those activities of a firm that are not in contact with customers such as warehousing, IT, accounting or the kitchen in a restaurant.

Bargaining range

In a negotiation the difference between the buyer's and the seller's reservations prices. If the seller's reservation price is higher than the buyer's reservation price there is no feasible negotiation.

Best Practices

Any practice, knowledge, know-how or experience that has been proven to be valuable or effective within one organization that may have applicability to other organizations (this definition is thanks to Chevron Corporation). For instance if one subsidiary of a multinational company has developed a successful way to launch a product, this may be considered as a best practice that can possibly be transferred to other subsidiaries. Professor Sulanzki pinpointed that there are a lot of difficulties in transferring best practices between units of the same company. He called it 'stickiness'.

Biodiversity

The diversity of living animal and vegetal organisms.

Blue Ocean strategy

A term coined by Professors Chan Kim and Renée Mauborgne to define innovative strategies based on redefining the components of a business system and creating a new market space.

Bottom of the Pyramid

According to Prahalad the 'Bottom of the Pyramid' in emerging countries is constituted by the largest proportion of the population, located at the lower end of income, who are willing to consume goods that are of good quality but a lower price level, adapted formulation and packaging.

BOT

B.O.T (Build Operate and Transfer) is an infrastructure construction or maintenance contract by which the project manager is not only in charge of the construction but also of the management of operations. At the end of a given period the infrastructure is handed over to the customer. The project manager is responsible for the output and is paid on the basis of a predetermined price per unit of output ($ per kilowatt/hour, $ per toll fee, $ per cubic meter of water, etc.). For instance, a Western electricity company that builds or takes over a power generation plant in China or a water treatment company manging the water distribution network in Jakarta. There are many derivative to BOT:

- BOO (Build Operate and Own): the project manager keeps ownership.
- BOOT (Build Own Operate and Transfer): the project manager has full ownership of the infrastructure during the period of operation.
- ROT (Refurbish, Operate and Transfer): similar to BOT but with old installations to refurbish.

Bribe

A form of direct corruption, generally a cash payment or a bank transfer to an overseas account.

Bricks and mortars

As opposed to internet based operations, brick and mortar operations are those that require tangible fixed assets to operate: factories, branches, stores etc.

BRICS

Refers to Brazil, Russia, India, China and South Africa but has increasingly become a term to name emerging countries.

Browsers

A software application used to locate and display web pages. The most popular browsers are Google Chrome and Microsoft Edge. All of these are graphical browsers, which means that they can display graphics as well as text. (Definition from GreatNexus Webmaster Resources.)

Business etiquette

The set of body gestures, clothing codes, ways of expressing oneself, social behaviors and attitudes that are considered as proper in a given business circle. For instance, business etiquette in Japan requires a ceremonial exchange of business cards.

Business strategy

There are many definition of business strategy. In this book we offer the following definition:

A company business strategy is a set of fundamental choices, which define its long-term objectives, its value proposition to the market, how it intends to build and sustain a competitive business system and how it organizes itself.

Californisation

This word has been used by Kenichi Ohmae, in his book *Triad Power* to describe the world convergence of consumers' tastes, particularly among young people.

Carbon trading schemes

Market mechanisms through which carbon credits are exchanged. The most utilized market mechanisms are the *cap-and-trade* schemes, under which a regulatory body sets a limit (the cap) on the amount of CO2 that companies are allowed to emit. Companies that emit more than their cap have to purchase credits from a company that has kept below the cap.

Capabilities fit

In an alliance or an acquisition, capabilities fit assessment consists of determining whether the respective contributions of the partners in an alliance or the combination of assets, resources and competences in a merger or acquisition are supplementing or complementing each others'. When performing a capabilities fit analysis one should first determine the required resources, assets and competencies needed for competitiveness of the alliance or the merged entity. Then one draws for each partner the specific contribution in each element of the value chain. Then in the last phase one determines the potential gap to be filled by joint investment and one evaluates whether the mutual contributions plus the additional investments make the future alliance effective.

Career plan

The planned evolution of a person in an organization in terms of potential future functions, job rotation and training.

Centre of excellence

An organizational unit (plant, laboratory, product development centre, etc.) that has developed a particular high quality in expertise that can possibly be transferred to other units.

Clusters

Professor Michael Porter in his book *Competitive Advantage of Nations* uses the term 'clusters' to describe regions of the world in which some industries have developed a high level of competitiveness thanks to a supporting demand, supply and competitive context.

Coalition alliance

Coalitions are alliances in which competitors, distributors and suppliers in an industry put together their capabilities to develop markets or to establish a common standard.

Code of conduct
What a particular organization regards as good practice in its operations with regard to its social and environmental responsibilities.

Co-location
Where people or organizational units are physically located at the same site.

Combination
The process of combining different elements of explicit knowledge into written, codified formats.

Comparative advantage
The Theory of Comparative Advantage is commonly referred to as the 'Ricardian model'. The original description of the idea can be found in an *Essay on the External Corn Trade* by Robert Torrens (1815). David Ricardo formalized the idea using a compelling yet simple numerical example in his 1817 book, *On the Principles of Political Economy and Taxation*. According to the principle of comparative advantage, the gains from trade follow from allowing an economy to specialize. If a country is relatively better at making wine than wool, it makes sense for it to put more resources into wine, and to export some of the wine to pay for imports of wool. This is even true if that country is the world's best wool producer, since the country will have more of both wool and wine than it would have without trade. A country does not have to be the best at anything to gain from trade. The gains follow from specializing in those activities which, at world prices, the country is relatively better at, even though it may not have an absolute advantage in them. Because it is relative advantage that matters, it is meaningless to say a country has a comparative advantage in nothing. The term is one of the most misunderstood ideas in economics, and is often wrongly assumed to mean an absolute advantage compared with other countries. (These definitions come from the International Study Centre at http://internationalecon.com/v1.0/ch40/40c000.html for the first part and the World Trade Organisation web site for the second part.)

Compensation
Remuneration and benefits given to a person for specific work. Refers to remuneration of employees.

Competencies
Refer to the collective know-how of an organization. This know-how can be technological or managerial. Competencies can be a source of competitive advantage if the know-how is difficult to buy, replicate or imitate by competitors. Some competencies are called 'core competencies' when they are specific to a firm.

Constellations
A form of alliance with multiple partners. Doz & Hamel identified three types of constellations: networks, portofolios and webs. Alliance networks are those in which multiple partners contribute to one goal, increase reach, adopt a common standard or promote a new technology. Alliance portfolios are those in which a company enters into a partnership with multiple companies. Alliance webs are those in which multiple partners contribute and benefit interdependently.

Convergence
A theory according to which societies become more and more similar. This concept is used in international marketing to describe the fact that consumers tend to progressively behave the same way across the world.

Corporate culture
The set of values and beliefs that are shared by employees in a corporation.

Corporate Strategy

In a multi-business corporation, the corporate strategy consists in defining its long term objectives, selecting its business portfolio, allocating resources across businesses and design its organizational structure, processes and systems.

Corruption

The definition of corruption given by Transparency International is: 'the abuse of public office for private gain'. Corruption involves a corruptor (the person who delivers the private gain) and a corrupted (the person who receives it). As compensation the corruptor expects some favor or gain from the corrupted.

Co-specializations

Co-specialization alliances are alliances in which partners combine complementing capabilities.

Cost of Capital

The cost of capital is the cost at which future cash flows are discounted in order to obtain the net present value (NPV) of an investment. Generally the cost of capital is calculated as the weighted average of cost of debts (interest on loans) and cost of equity (the minimum return that shareholders are expecting from their own investment).

Cost of capital adjustment (CCA)

A technique of discounted cash flow in which the adverse risks are taken into consideration by adding a specific risk factor to the cost of capital used for the calculation.

Cost Leadership

According to Professor Michael Porter, Cost Leadership is a strategy by which firms gain and sustain competitive advantage thanks to a lower cost position than their competitors. Generally cost leadership is linked to size: the higher the size, the higher the economies of scale and hence the lower the costs.

Country Diamond

Term used by Professor Michael Porter in his book *The Competitive Advantage of Nations* to describe the four context dimensions that characterize the competitiveness of a country (or a cluster - see above). The four dimensions are: 1) a Context that encourages vigorous competition and investment, 2) the presence of related and supporting industries, 3) demanding customers and 4) the quality of resources (human capital, natural resources, infrastructure etc.).

Country life cycle

The theory according to which countries follow a development path from emerging to maturity.

Country risk analysis

Set of techniques used to assess how risky a country is. The four dimensions of country risks are: political, economical, competitive and operational.

Country stock market beta

A measure of risk developed by Professor Don Lessard comparing the volatility of a country's stock market with another one.

Cross-listing

Refers to the listing of a corporation to several world stock markets.

Cryptocurrencies
A form of digital money that is transacted by individuals on a peer-to-peer basis through a coded mechanism ('encrypted') using a denomination (e.g. Bitcoin) different from official currencies (dollars, pounds, euros, yen etc.).

Cultural fit
In an alliance or an acquisition, cultural fit assessment consists of determining whether the companies involved exhibit similar or dissimilar values and ways of doing business.

Cultural heritage
The values and norms that are the results of past historical experience.

Currency swaps
A technique of currency risk hedging. It consists of contracts intermediated by a swap bank that is matching long terms loans issued by two companies in their respective currency zones for use in the other company's currency zone. Company X borrows in Currency A to be used in country B with loan repayment generated in currency B, while company Y borrows in currency B to be used in country A with loan repayment generated in currency A.

Customer value curve
The set of factors that customers explicitly or implicitly consider valuable for them in a product or service. Also called 'customer utility curve'. A customer value curve can be used by firms to compare their product or service offering with that of their competitors. Customer value curves are one of the main tools used by the strategic approach designed by Professsors Kim and Mauborgne called 'Value Innovation'.

Cybercrimes
Attempts to exploit property (or sometimes human integrity) through the internet. The most frequent cybercrimes are the diffusion of electronic viruses and illegal access to databases to steal money or information.

Death valley
A frequent phenomenon encountered in joint ventures and alliances at the early stages of implementation when partners discover unexpected behavior or surprises. Death Valley can generate deep conflicts.

Deglobalization
A neologism used by ATTAC, an anti globalization NGO, to recommend that countries (particularly developing countries) re-orientate their production to serve local markets and not global ones.

Differentiation
How firms position themselves differently to their competitors. According to Professor Michael Porter, differentiation is a strategy by which firms gain and sustain competitive advantage thanks to superior product functionalities, superior service and superior quality that create 'barriers to imitation'.

Distribution function
The part of a logistical process that organizes the channels for the physical distribution of parts and products.

Documentary credit
A well established technique of trade financing. The principle is that an importer of goods mandates his bank to issue a letter of credit that guarantees the exporter that he will be paid on receipt of shipping documents establishing the proof that goods have actually been delivered to the transport company.

Dotcom companies
Companies operating essentially though the internet.

Dotted lines relationship
A term used to describe a non-hierarchical relationship between individuals or organizational units that need to establish some kind of mutual reporting.

Due diligence
The investigation that a potential acquirer carries out in order to value a targeted asset. Originally due diligence was essentially financial. More recently it is also applied to non financial elements such as managerial capabilities and culture.

E-Commerce
A generic term to describe commercial transactions through the internet.

Eco-friendly capital investments
Factories and facilities designed and built with a low environmental impact perspective.

Electronic Data Interchange (EDI)
The sharing of data between a supplier and a customer used to place orders and settle transactions electronically.

Electronic Marketplaces
Internet based procurement web sites.

Emerging countries
Countries that exhibit: a) high economic growth, b) an increasing development of a middle class, c) a high degree of infrastructure investments and d) an opening of their market to international trade and investment.

Emerging countries champions
Companies based in emerging countries and that can pretend to be globally competitive.

Entry modes
The kind of operation that a foreign investor is setting in order to operate in a country. Entry mode describes the legal form of the operation as well as the size of the investment that the foreigner is willing to make. The main types of entry modes are: wholly-owned investment, acquisition, joint venture or licencing.

Environmental crisis
An ecological disaster.

Ethics
The codes of conduct that guide non-corrupted behavior.

Externalization
The process of articulating tacit knowledge into explicit concepts through metaphors, pictures and theoretical formulations.

Expatriates
People employed in one country with a contract originated in another country. Frequently designates managerial personnel sent by corporate headquarters to work in a foreign subsidiary.

Explicit knowledge
Knowledge that can be documented precisely and therefore that can be communicated and transferred.

Export credit agencies
Government agencies that act like insurers and cover the risks associated with international trade and investments. As a result the exporter and the foreign investor can benefit from export credits.

Extractive agenda

When partners are primarily motivated to enter into a strategic alliance in order to learn something from their partner or to obtain resources that they would otherwise have difficulty obtaining by themselves.

Fair trade marketing

A form of international trade promoting rules and practices that provide better terms of trade for small and medium-sized producers from the developing world.

Fair process

A management practice that consists of a) Engagement: Involvement of relevant people, seeking inputs and allowing them to challenge ideas, b) Explanation: everybody who is involved or affected should understand why a particular decision was taken, and c) Expectation: clearly defining someone's role and responsibilities. According to Professors Kim and Mauborgne, fair process is needed in order to get people involved in difficult or innovative decisions.

First mover advantages

The competitive advantages that a company gains by being the first or among the first to enter a new market. First mover advantages can be due to the preemption of existing resources, the creation of a standard or the ability to rapidly create entry barriers for newcomers.

Fit analysis

The study of the possible compatibility between partners in an alliance or between buyers and sellers in an acquisition. There are four types of fit: strategic, capabilities, cultural and organizational.

Forward contracts

Contracts by which the contracting parties commit to buy or sell goods or currency at a given price at a predetermined date. Foreign exchange forward contracts are a classical way to hedge against exchange rate fluctuation.

Franchise

A contract by which the owner of a brand (the franchiser) grants an individual or a company (the franchisee) the right to operate under its brand. Franchise contracts are generally granted under the condition that the franchisee respects a certain number of quality practices defined by the franchiser.

Front office

Designates activities that are in direct contact with customers.

Future contracts

Contracts by which the contracting parties agree carrying out a transaction at an anticipated date at predetermined conditions. Forward contracts are one category of future contract but future contracts can also cover agreements that are not necessarily based on a financial transaction.

Global accounts

Global accounts are customers that are operating globally and for whom the suppliers negotiate and manage the delivery of goods or services in an integrated way across borders.

Global business strategy

A business strategy that defines the ways and locations in which a company decides to compete across borders.

Global Capability Index

An index to measure to what extent a company has globalized its assets and personnel: how assets or personnel are distributed across the world.

Global chess

The ability for a multinational company to cross-subsidise one country by another in order to compete more effectively in that country. For instance selling at a loss in country A to oblige a competitor in country B to lower its profits in country A.

Global hub

A highly centralized organisation such as worldwide functional or global product structure.

Global industries

Industries in which, in order to survive, competitors need to operate in the key world markets in an integrated and co-ordinated way.

Global leaders development

Is the way careers of leaders are enhanced through practices that mix formal training, facilitating skills acquisition as well as coaching in the various global roles that managers are likely to play during their careers.

Global Managers

Managers whose career is made up of successive appointments in different countries.

The Global/Multi-local mapping

Analytical and graphical tool developed to position industries and industry segments according to the relative importance of global and local forces.

Global positioning

Global positioning consists of the definition of the various value propositions for the products or services of the company, corresponding to the type of segments and countries in which the company wants to compete.

Global Revenue Index

An index measuring the distribution of sales of a company across the major regions of the world relative to the distribution of markets across the same regions.

Global solution selling

The sales of a valuable solution to a client located in a particular country that implies the mobilization of resources and competencies of several subsidiaries across the world on the part of the seller.

Global warming

Increasing warming of the planet due to greenhouse effects resulting from emission of CO2.

Globalization

The progressive change in competitive structures from multinational (country by country) to global (worldwide).

Grand Tour

The fact finding trip of corporate executives in countries where the company is considering foreign investment in view of assessing the countries' attractiveness.

Hedging

A technique of reducing risk by settling risky transactions at predetermined fixed terms. Often used to manage risks resulting from currency variation.

Hierarchy of needs

A theory developed by Maslow according to which humans start by satisfying their primary needs and progressively move up to more intellectual and artistic needs when the primary needs are satisfied.

Holocracy

Defined as an organization where authority and decision making are distributed throughout self-organizing teams rather than a management hierarchy. Holocracy is based on three principles: 1) no job title or manager; 2) no hierachy of managers; 3) every role is accountable.

Hub

In the context of global business a hub is a location that serves and supports several other locations in a region. Typically in a hub services and logistical activities would be concentrated: for example Singapore or Hong Kong for Asia; Geneva, London or Brussels for Europe.

Inclusive financing

Financing systems that serve individuals and businesses that have difficulties in opening banking services.

Individualism

Individualism is a cultural characteristic of a society in which individual interests are emphasized over collective ones.

Individualized corporation

A new organizational model proposed by Ghoshal and Bartlett in which new management competencies and roles are redefined in a portfolio of three key processes: the renewal process, the integration process and the entrepreneurial process.

Industrial ecosystem

A group of interacting firms that depend on each other's activities.

Industry 4.0

Manufacturing systems based on data exchange and automation. Industry 4.0 technologies may use connected mobile devices, advanced algorithms and 3D printing, for example.

Industry analysis

The systematic analysis and forecast of demand, competitive forces and risk in an industry.

Industry culture

The norms and ways of thinking that are common to people operating in a given industry.

Innovation

The process of inventing and developing new concepts, products or services.

Institutional void

Institutional void occurs in a country when information problems, misguided regulations and inefficient judicial systems fail in the proper functioning of economic activities (i.e, market failures).

Integration process

The process by which various firms and activities are made to work together. Following a merger, acquisition or an alliance, the post merger integration process organizes the way two firms are working together from partial to full integration of their activities.

Intellectual property

The legal ownership of a patent, a design, a brand, an artistic or a literary production.

Internal stickiness

The difficulty for different units of an organization to exchange ideas and practices.

Interface management
Defines the mechanisms by which two or several partners organize their relationships and communication in an alliance.

International division
An organizational design for managing international operations by centralizing the control of geographical subsidiaries in one division reporting to top management.

International product life cycle
The theory according to which new products are launched sequentially over time internationally from developed countries to less developed ones.

Internet of things
Describes networked devices communicating with their users and with each other (smart factory, for instance).

Joint venture
The legal form by which two or more companies organize their collaboration. Joint ventures can be conducted under the form of equity contribution or under a contractual arrangement.

Joint venture decay
The phenomenon that typically occurs in a joint venture after several years when partners have obtained what they wanted from their collaboration and no longer see the value of the joint venture.

Joint venture for market entry
A joint venture that allies a foreign investor and one or several local partners with a view to creating or developing a business in the country.

Knowledge management
A managerial process by which companies capture and internally distribute strategic, commercial and technical information.

Leading and lagging
A technique of international cash management consisting of delaying or accelerating the payment of expenses and the receipt of income according to the strengths and weaknesses of the currencies involved.

Learning alliances
Alliances whose main purpose is for the companies involved to generate new knowledge or to gain knowledge from each other.

Licensing
A contract by which the owner of a product, a service or a process (the licensor) authorises another party (the licensee) to manufacture the product, deliver the service or use the process for its own benefit.

Location
The choice of place to set up an economic activity (offices, plant, distribution centres, research activities etc.)

Local Manager
A manager recruited and operating within a country.

Logistics
The physical handling, transportation and storage of goods.

Macroeconomic indicators

Measures that indicate the economic characteristics of a country, for instance production, growth, income, trade and investments.

Market segmentation

The division of consumers into categories according to different criteria and who exhibit different demand characteristics.

Marketing Positioning

The choice made by a company of the market segments in which it wants to compete and the definition of the various elements of its approach to those segments (its 'value propositions').

Matrix

An organizational design by which the line of command is shared by two or more decision makers. In global firms the typical matrix is either function and geography or business and geography.

Megacities

A urban area in which 10 million or more people live.

Mentoring

In global firms, the human resource management process by which expatriate personnel are coached by a 'mentor' at the corporate level.

Metanational

A global firm that leverages innovation across countries.

Middle Class

In economic terms, the population that can afford to purchase goods and services beyond what is needed for subsistence, but who do not belong to the country's wealthy elite.

Middle Class Effect

The effect by which the size of the middle class increases more rapidly than the average of the economy.

Missions

Short-term international assignments.

Modularization

The technology of producing goods and services by subcomponents that can be assembled according to various configurations.

Multinational companies

Companies that operate in different countries.

Nanotechnology

Technologies using materials with a nano scale (1/1,000,000 mm).

National and ethnic culture

Norms and values that are characteristic of a nation or an ethnic or religious group.

Netting

An international cash management system by which only the net cash movements are transferred across borders. Netting minimizes foreign exchange risk exposure.

Network architecture

Defines the role of plants as information and knowledge creators in addition to the traditional roles of foreign factories as supply bases.

Network Externalities

The economic benefits accrued to a product or service derived from the number of existing users of this product or from related products. Examples of network externalities are products based on technical standards such as mobile phones, video discs, IT systems or services such as auctions.

Networked organization

How an organisation manages its activities through a strong exchange of information and co-ordination of actions between internal and external units through partnerships and alliances.

Offsourcing

The purchasing of goods and services outside the country in which a company is located. Generally offsourcing takes place in low-cost countries.

Offshoring

The production of goods and services outside the country in which a company is located. Generally offshoring takes place in low-cost countries. It is also known as 'de-localization'.

Options

The ability to make an investment with the possibility to pull out with minimum costs.

In the financial sector an option is materialized by a tradeable instrument that allows the investor to exercise its full investment if the conditions are favorable or not to exercise if the conditions are not favorable.

In the non financial world options are called 'real options' and consist of making a minimum investment with the option of pulling out if the conditions are not favorable.

Organizational culture

The set of values, beliefs and behavioral norms that are pre-dominant in an organization.

Organizational fit

The ability for two organizations in an alliance, a merger or an acquisition to synchronise their structures, sytems and processes.

Organizational processes

The way decisions are made and actions are controlled in an organization: processes can be bureaucratic, mechanistic, participative, top-down, bottom-up etc.

Organizational structure

The way the chain of command, the roles and functions are defined in an organization. An organization can have a centralized or decentralized structure, flat or hierarchical structure, structure by functions, by products, by country or matrix structures.

Piggybacking

The practice for large multinational firms to help their smaller sub-contractors or suppliers to set operations close to their own foreign investments.

Plant competencies
Are the sets of know-how and technical capabilities of a plant.

Pre-acquisition process
The process by which the decision to acquire is made, the acquisition target selected and the valuation and negotiation conducted.

Political power
Political power is the ability of one person or group of people to influence government.

Post-acquisition process
The process by which an acquisition is integrated after the deal has been signed. Also referred to as the 'Post Merger Integration'.

Power distance
A dominant social value in a group or a society by which group members accept authority. In a high power distance society one is obedient and respectful of leaders while in a low power distance one can openly challenge the views of the leader.

Preservation mode of integration
A mode of post-merger integration that consists of keeping the acquired company autonomous from the acquiring company.

Procurement
The purchase of good and services.

Professional culture
The dominant values, beliefs and norms that members of a profession share. Examples are medical culture, engineering culture, accounting culture and academic culture.

Project valuation
The techniques used to calculate the return or the price of an projected investment. Discounted cash flow is the most used valuation technique.

Quantum computing
Computers using quantum bits, or qubits, that can be zero, one or a mixture of zero and one (superposition) that enables extremely quick processing – calculations that are not possible using conventional.

Real option
See **Options** above.

Regionalization
The concentration of the international expansion of a company in a particular region of the world.

Regional headquarters
Are offices based in regions in order to support and control activities of local subsidiaries of global firms.

Representative offices
A limited form of implantation in a foreign country. In a representative office people make contacts, collect information and negotiate contracts but do not sign nor implement the contracts.

Reservation price
In a negotiation the economic limit above which a buyer will not buy, or below which the seller will not sell.

Retention
Is the way global firms encourage the loyalty of local staff through good career prospects and 'fair treatment' instead of financial compensation.

Reverse auction
A process by which potential buyers of goods or services invite potential sellers to bid online in a given time frame.

Roles
Definition of the position, the task and the responsibilities that a person has within an organization.

Sharing agenda
When partners in a strategic alliance are primarily motivated to maximize efficiency in sharing certain elements of the value chain through economies of scale and scope.

Scenarios
The descriptions of possible anticipated future states of affairs.

Segmentation
The division of a market or a business into sub-components that share similar features. Examples are the division of consumers by income levels.

Silent languages
The non-verbal expression of opinions, emotions and decisions. Silent languages are an important mode of expression in certain societies and for people external to that society it becomes critical to understanding the meaning of physical gestures and facial movements that express opinions, emotions, decisions.

Skills
The know-how that an individual possesses in the accomplishment of their tasks.

Social Network
For sociologists a social network is a group of individuals that are connected to each other. Recently, websites like Facebook, Twitter or Linkedin are platforms that connect people via the internet.

Socialisation
The process by which newcomers in a group or an organization is initiated to the norms, values and practices of the group.

Socially responsible investing (SRI)
Investment in companies that are respectful of the environment and human rights.

Sprinkler model
The simultaneous launch of a new product in all markets.

Stand Alone value
The value of an acquisition calculated without the potential synergies that the acquisition may bring. If the acquired company is listed on a stock market, the stand alone value is the market value. Alternatively the stand alone value has to be calculated by the classical valuation techniques: discounted cash flow, net assets, comparables, etc.

Strategic exposure
The way competitive advantage of a firm can deteriorate or be enhanced owing to the direct or indirect impact of a change in currency value.

Strategic fit
In an alliance or an acquisition, strategic fit is where the parties engaged have compatible objectives and are committed to the success of the association.

Sub–optimization
The negative or lower economic performance resulting from one or more decisions to ignore the overall effect on a sytem. An example of sub-optimization would be to adopt a global price while ignoring the adverse effect it could have in different markets that have different demand curves.

Sustainable development
Development that meets the needs of the present without compromising the ability of future generations to meet their own needs.

Symbiotic mode of integration
A mode of post-merger integration that consists of first keeping the acquired company autonomous from the acquiring company and progressively integrating the functions for which real synergies exist.

Synergies value
The calculation of the additional value brought in as a result of a merger, an acquisition or an alliance by the integration of the entities concerned.

Tacit knowledge
Knowledge that cannot be codified.

Technology transfer
The process by which knowledge is transferred from one individual, group or organization to another individual, group or organization. Technology can be transferred through documents when the knowledge is codified or though apprenticeship and collaboration when the knowledge is tacit.

Tenure
The length of time in a given position.

Time Incompressibility
When a capability, in order to be replicated, needs as much time as originally spent to create it. Time incompressibility makes imitation difficult and gives the creator of the capability a first mover advantage.

Transaction exposure
Transaction exposure is the risk that currency fluctuations impose on existing contractual engagements and that may result in unexpected losses.

Translation exposure
Translation exposure reflects the effects that changes in currency values have on the financial statements of global firms, and therefore on their profits and book valuation.

Transnational
Two meanings: 1) the meaning given by the United Nations to designate multinational corporations; 2) an international organizational design model described by Bartlett and Ghoshal that does not focus on organizational structure but on management processes and culture.

Triple Bottom Line
Measures the financial, social and environmental performance of a company in three dimensions: profit, people and the planet.

Turn Key Project
A project in which the customer contracts out the whole project to a specialised engineering firm or to a consortium of equipment suppliers. The project manager takes care of completion at a fixed price and delivery time and hands over the project to the customer after the start-up phase. The project manager is financially responsible for the whole amount of the contract.

Uncertainty avoidance
Uncertainty avoidance occurs when risk taking, change, ambiguity and deviance are all negatively viewed when making decisions.

Valuation
Defines the financial method used to evaluate the value of an economic entity, either a particular asset or a complete company.

Value chain
The set of activities needed for the creation, production and commercialization of a product or service.

Value curve
The set of product or service attributes that customers value such as performances, quality, responsiveness, price, convenience etc.

Value proposition
The set of products or services attributes such as performances, quality, responsiveness, price, convenience etc. that companies propose to customers.

Values
Set of beliefs and codes of conduct that a person or an organization adheres to.

Venturing agenda
When partners in a strategic alliance are primarily motivated by a desire to engage in collaboration to create a business.

Venture capital
A type of financing where private investors, investment banks, financial institutions and corporations target start-up companies and small businesses with long-term potential.

Washington Consensus
A series of prescriptions established in 1989 at the Institute of International Economics Conference in Washington, DC that reflect liberal policy recommendations for emerging countries.

Waterfall model
The sequential launch of a new product market after market.

Wholly-owned operations
An organization that is controlled entirely by another organization.

Window of opportunity
The timespan at the beginning of a market when the market is not saturated and it is possible to enter without creating overcapacity.

Index of subjects

A

absorption mode of integration 301, 346
acculturation xxv, 438, 487–488, 494, 514, 517, 518, 521
adjusted present value country risk (apv) 478
advertising agency 131, 362, 378
alliance xxiii–xxiv, xxix, xxxiv, 31, 63, 186, 199–200, 219, 278, 284–285, 292, 307–330, 333, 338–342, 344–346, 348–350
arbitrage xxxvii, 23–25, 33, 198, 323, 364, 366, 376, 378
arbitrage benefits xxxvii, 24, 33
asymmetric development xix, 562, 566, 585, 587

B

back office 14, 191, 383, 387–388, 421
best practices 14, 24, 292, 302, 326, 341, 351, 359, 424, 436, 443, 448–449, 452, 507, 516, 519, 530, 541, 546, 551
blockchain 445, 479–480, 604
born digital xiii, 209, 220–221
born global xiii, xxviii, xxxiv, xli, 10, 17, 57, 173, 175, 208–211, 220–221, 224, 271
BOT (build, operate and transfer) 418, 421
bottom of the pyramid 52–53, 67, 528
bribe 127–128, 130, 141, 159, 162–163
brics 40–42, 46, 67, 70, 467–468
business etiquette 96, 107–108
business strategy xiii, 173, 175–177, 179, 217, 221, 224, 238, 270, 380, 405

C

cage distance framework xxiii, 243, 252–254
californization 11, 354, 378
capabilities fit xiv, 285, 290, 293–294, 310, 314, 317, 335, 344, 346
career plan 490, 515, 517
centre of excellence 449
child labour 16, 112, 115, 124, 135–136, 146, 161, 163, 168, 171
clusters xxvii–xxviii, 73, 79, 81, 105, 181, 188, 217, 225, 233–234, 239, 248, 252–253, 331, 428, 442, 447
co–location 430, 438–439, 448–449
combination 5, 21, 53, 90, 190, 231, 237, 248, 259, 263, 272, 278, 284, 357, 370, 386, 397, 406, 429, 433, 435, 449, 494, 506–507, 510, 542, 573, 602
comparative advantage xxxvi–xxxvii, 6, 16, 33, 50
compensation 85, 116, 268, 282, 486, 489, 491–493, 495, 497–498, 503–504, 515–517, 539
constellations xxiv, 326–328, 346
convergence xv, xxvi, xxxvii, 6, 8, 11–12, 15, 32, 110, 351, 353–354, 374, 378, 406, 439, 542
corporate culture 73, 108, 155, 196, 201, 295, 337, 503–504
corporate social responsibility (csr) 141, 144, 163
corporate strategy 177, 203, 217, 221, 223
corruption xxi–xxii, xxviii, 1, 16, 47–49, 66, 102, 112–113, 115, 126–134, 138, 141–143, 147–148, 151–154, 158–160, 162–163, 164, 168–171, 244, 250, 252, 349, 577, 579
cost leadership 176, 189, 193–194, 202, 218, 221
cost of capital adjustment (cca) 453, 477–478
country ‘diamond’ 239, 253
country life cycle xxviii, 234, 253
country risk analysis xiv, xxiii, 173, 226, 244, 252–253
country stock market beta 478
covid–19 xxxvi, xl, 3, 11, 15, 22–23, 31–33, 36–39, 107, 127, 149–153, 162–165, 167–168, 215–217, 287–288, 341, 363, 374, 413, 422, 492, 496–498, 509–510, 515, 517, 572–573, 576, 579, 583, 588–589, 592
covid–19 green recovery 163
crosslisting xvii, 453, 462, 464, 476, 478
cryptocurrencies xvii, 469–470, 479
cultural distance xiii, 242, 251–252, 254, 262, 436
cultural fit 278, 285, 290, 293–295, 310, 314, 335, 345–346
cultural heritage 77, 88, 108
currency swaps 475, 478
customer value curve 232, 354, 378
cybercrime 577, 586–587

D

death valley xxiv, 279, 323–324, 335–336, 346
deglobalization xxxvi, xl, 3, 17, 20–22, 33, 563, 587
differentiation 53, 73, 76, 176, 178, 190, 194, 202, 218, 221, 238, 292, 295, 356, 402, 455, 475, 598

digitally enabled organization 544, 554
digital space xiv, 271
distribution function 417, 421
documentary credit xvii, xxv, 471–472, 477–478
due diligence 266, 290, 296, 343, 346

E

economic cultures xii, 73, 83, 108
ecosystem xx, xxiv–xxv, 61, 71, 114, 125, 145, 331–333, 345–347, 350, 361, 407–409, 440–441, 479, 544, 603–605
electronic data interchange (edi) 382, 390, 421
electronic marketplaces 390, 421
emerging countries champions 67
emerging country 40–41, 52, 67, 266, 517
entry modes xiv, xxiii, xxix, 263–264, 270–271, 280–281
environmental crisis 163
ethics xii, 113, 130, 133–135, 141, 143, 148–149, 152, 159, 163, 166–167, 169, 171, 479, 490, 578–579
EU workers directive 517
expatriates xxv, 109, 192, 265, 438, 483–484, 488–490, 499–500, 503–504, 514–515, 518–519, 521, 528, 548
explicit knowledge 435, 449
export credit agencies xvii, 471–473, 477–478
externalization 435, 449
extractive agenda 316, 334, 345–346

F

fair process 306, 346, 349
first mover xiv, xxix, 197, 221, 260–262, 277, 280, 282
foreign direct investment xxiii, 10, 38, 47, 65, 225, 247, 310
forward contracts 456–457, 475, 478
franchise 263–264, 266, 279–280, 443–444
front office 387–388, 416, 421

G

global/multi-local mapping xi, xxii, xxxvi–xxxvii, 3, 25, 26, 33, 202
global account xv, xxiv, 10, 12, 198, 351, 353, 365–368, 376, 378–380, 540
global business strategy 177, 221
global capability index 185, 218, 221
global companies xii, xxii, xxviii, xxx, xxxvii, 1, 10, 14, 25, 33, 72, 87, 112, 130, 135, 143, 158, 160–162, 175, 184, 196, 198, 201, 220, 326, 351, 361–362, 390, 424, 426, 429, 433–436, 438, 453, 473, 475, 489, 499, 502, 543, 554, 584
global corporate strategy 177, 203, 221
global hub 385, 415, 553–554
global industries xxxvii, 4, 10, 26, 33, 225
global integration 10, 14, 20, 202, 494, 515, 525–526, 548, 558
globalization ix–xii, xvi, xix, xxi–xxii, xxvii, xxix, xxxii–xxxiv, xxxvi–xxxvii, xl–xliv, 1, 3–17, 19–25, 27–29, 31–33, 35–40, 52, 57, 62, 71, 73, 75, 77, 79, 83, 85, 87, 89, 91–93, 95, 97, 99, 101, 103, 105, 107, 109, 112–113, 118–119, 121, 123, 125–127, 129, 131, 133, 135, 137, 139, 141, 143, 145, 147, 149, 151, 153, 155, 157, 159, 161, 163, 165, 167, 169, 171, 173, 175–176, 180–181, 183–184, 186–187, 192–193, 199, 203, 205, 215, 219, 223, 287, 308, 338, 349–351, 353, 380–382, 401–404, 410–411, 419, 422, 425, 428, 434, 446, 462, 480, 506, 517, 525, 532, 538, 548, 551, 556, 559, 561–565, 567–569, 571, 573, 575–577, 579, 581–587, 589–594
global leaders development 518
global managers xxxiii, 112, 482, 484–486, 503, 506–509, 511–513, 516, 518, 527
global open innovation vii, 169, 424, 439, 441–442, 448–449
global positioning xxviii, 175–176, 180, 187, 190, 200, 203, 217–218, 221, 489
global revenue index 176, 184–187, 218, 221
global solution selling xv, xxiv, xxix, 351, 353, 367–369, 376, 378
global talent competitiveness vii, 500–501, 516, 518, 520, 573
global warming 113, 114, 118–119, 142, 158–159, 565, 570, 586–587, 591
grand tour 247–248, 252–253
green recovery 149–151, 163

H

hedging xvii, 344, 351, 453–458, 460, 471, 474–475, 478
hierarchy of needs xxiv, 354–355, 378
holocracy 522, 545, 553–554
hub xxxiii, 61, 156, 181, 188, 202, 220, 234, 253, 260, 276, 385, 415, 427, 439–441, 451, 511, 542, 549, 553–554
human rights 1, 112–113, 115, 124, 135–139, 142–143, 146–148, 158, 161–163, 166, 170, 404

I

incentives xxx, 86, 173, 207, 229, 238, 241–242, 252–255, 296, 384, 460, 480, 495, 502, 511
individualism 75–77, 85, 104, 108, 503
individualized corporation 581, 586–587, 590
industry analysis xxviii, 238, 252–253
industry culture 73, 108
innovation vii, ix, xvi, xxix, xxxiii, xxxv, xliv, 24, 31, 36, 68, 115, 151, 154–156, 169, 180, 201, 213–214, 216, 218, 225, 229, 261, 269, 280, 292, 308, 312, 327, 351, 385, 387, 398, 404, 406, 412, 414, 424–425, 427–433, 435,

437, 438–452, 500, 524, 527–528, 530, 532–533, 535–536, 556, 566–567, 580, 589, 595, 602–604
innovation outposts 440, 449–450
institutional voids xxvii, 49, 51, 66–67
integration process xxix, 299–300, 302, 304, 343, 346, 581, 586
intellectual property xxx, 55, 351, 424, 432, 442–443, 445, 448–449, 451–452
interface management 303, 346
internal stickiness 436, 449, 452
international divisions 554
international product life cycle xvi, xxv, xxxvii, 24, 33, 424–425, 446, 449
internet of things 406–407, 420–421, 604–605
isolated subsidiaries 437, 448–449

J

joint venture xv, xxiv, xxix, 14, 56, 84, 88–89, 116, 123, 131, 133, 210, 258–259, 261–267, 269–272, 275, 277–280, 285, 309–310, 312–314, 317–320, 322, 325, 333–337, 342–344, 346, 349, 367, 434–435, 443, 474, 512, 598–600, 602
joint venture decay xv, 279, 336, 346
joint venture for market entry 285, 313, 333, 346

K

knowledge management xvi, xxx, 351, 401, 405–406, 424, 433, 435–437, 442, 447–449, 521
knowledge sourcing 451
knowledge transfer 436, 438, 448, 489, 499, 528

L

leading and lagging 456, 458, 475, 478
leapfrog 500
learning alliances 309, 311, 317–318, 324, 329, 345–346
licensing 56, 89, 142, 173, 192, 200, 219, 238, 258, 263, 266, 268, 270–272, 275, 280–282, 308, 329, 337, 358, 434, 443–444, 451
local adaptation 189, 356, 370, 374, 406, 527
localization xi, xviii, xxi, xxxv–xxxvi, xl, 1, 3, 11, 13–16, 25, 29, 32, 53–55, 66, 192, 201, 351, 382, 388, 427, 482–484, 499–500, 504, 513, 515, 520, 525, 530, 567, 601
local managers 130, 484, 486, 500, 504, 513, 517–518, 529
location xxix, 4, 7, 14, 23, 190–191, 195–196, 199, 218, 229, 234, 238, 252, 260, 262, 276, 282, 351, 381–384, 408, 413–414, 420–422, 428–430, 437–439, 443, 448–449, 455, 495, 497, 500, 510, 516, 573
logistics xvi, xxiv–xxv, xlv, 11, 21, 30, 55, 191–194, 199, 234, 237, 272, 292, 294, 304, 330, 338, 355, 371, 377, 381–384, 389, 391–395, 404, 413, 415, 417, 420–422, 434, 528, 537–538, 546, 550, 574, 601, 603, 605

M

macroeconomic indicators 229, 253
marketing positioning xv, 370, 377–378
market opportunities xiii, 52, 173, 205–206, 208, 226, 228–229, 251, 253, 272, 550
market segmentation 232, 253
matrix xviii, xxvi, xxx, xxxv, 3, 26, 57, 155, 201–203, 220, 351, 358, 483, 522–526, 532, 534–542, 548, 553–554, 556–557, 601
megacities 565, 585, 587
mentoring 495, 515, 517–518
metanational xxx, xliv, 424, 437–438, 449, 450, 581–583, 586–587, 590
middle class xxi, 40, 42–43, 52–53, 65–69, 100, 231–234, 251, 254–255
middle-class effect xxiii, 42, 231–232, 253
missions 491, 518
modularization 356, 378
multinational companies xxvii, xxxvii, 5, 10, 18, 23, 33, 57–58, 77, 92, 135, 139–140, 153, 193, 205, 364, 366, 422, 473, 521, 543

N

national/ethnic culture 108
netting 456, 458, 475, 478
network architecture 386, 414, 421
networked organization 429, 449, 583, 586

O

OEM 55, 57, 66–67, 179–180, 236, 551–552, 599–600
offshoring xxii, xxiv, 55, 67, 381–383, 387, 398, 413, 422–423
offsourcing xxii, 55, 67
options 61, 90–91, 106, 131, 270, 282, 291, 309, 315–316, 350, 456–457, 460, 475, 478, 510
organizational culture 102, 110, 351, 525, 553–554
organizational fit 278, 285, 293, 295, 310, 314, 335, 345–346
organizational processes 525, 545, 553–554
organizational structure xxvi, 10, 155, 198, 202, 295, 305, 329, 339, 523, 525, 531, 540–542, 547–549, 552–554, 556, 603

P

pace of entry xiv, 257–258, 262, 277, 280
pestel 228
piggybacking 197, 205–206, 208, 221, 223, 225, 390
plant competencies 415, 421

platform 92, 145, 155, 167, 176, 188, 221, 282, 316–318, 324, 327–329, 341, 372, 398–399, 402, 405, 409–411, 419–420, 429, 441, 471, 550, 602–604
political partner 333–334, 346
post-acquisition process 290–291, 346
post-merger integration 284, 290, 350
power distance 75–76, 80–81, 104–105, 108
pre-acquisition process 290–291, 346
preservation mode of integration 301, 346
procurement xxxiv, xl, 22, 55, 98, 133–135, 153–154, 169–170, 191, 196, 236, 263, 269, 280, 294, 302, 310, 320, 338–339, 351, 366–367, 376, 382–383, 388–392, 395, 399, 401–402, 404–405, 413, 415–416, 419, 421, 596
professional culture 73, 108
project valuation xvii, 459, 475–476, 478

R

real option 258, 270, 280
regional headquarters xviii, xxvi, 87, 105, 179, 203, 211, 260, 262–263, 370, 504, 507, 512, 516, 523, 529, 545–547, 549, 554, 557
regionalization 36, 568, 587
relocation xviii, 496–498, 503, 510–511, 518–519
remote teams 518
remote working xl, 510, 517–518, 521
representative offices 192, 200, 206, 261, 269, 277, 280, 504
retention 299, 500, 502, 516, 518
roles xxx, 77, 303, 305, 322, 381, 383, 385–386, 414, 420, 433, 499, 506–507, 509, 516, 518, 523, 525, 529, 541, 546–548, 553–554, 581–582, 586

S

scenarios xxvi, 561–562, 571, 577–579, 583–584, 586–587, 589–593
segmentation xv, xxiv, 19, 53, 190, 232–234, 253, 353–355, 358, 378, 385
sharing agenda 316, 346
silent language 72–74, 104, 107–109
skills xviii, xxiii–xxiv, xli, 84, 86, 95, 133, 149, 151, 191, 205, 224, 236, 249, 261, 265–266, 278, 311, 320–322, 326, 336–337, 371, 385, 407, 415, 482–484, 487, 489–491, 495–496, 501, 506–509, 513–516, 518–519, 541, 543, 554, 589
smart factory 406–407, 420–421
socialization 21, 433, 435, 437, 448–449, 563, 585
socially responsible investment (sri) 163
sprinkler model 361, 375, 378
stand-alone value 298, 346
strategic exposure xvii, 455, 475, 478
strategic fit xiv, xxiii–xxiv, 278, 285, 290, 293, 310, 314–316, 334, 337, 344–346
strategic role 414, 421
sub-optimization 364, 376, 378
sustainability xl, 113, 117, 118, 125, 134, 144–145, 149, 154–157, 168–170, 172, 176, 195–197, 338, 406, 431, 469, 500–501, 537, 552, 590, 593
sustainable development goals (sdgs) 149, 154, 163
symbiotic mode of integration 301, 346
synergies value 298, 346

T

tacit knowledge 435–439, 449
technology scouting 449
tenure xxv, 85, 489, 491–492, 494, 515, 518, 543
transaction exposure xvii, 455–457, 475, 478
translation exposure xvii, 455, 458, 475, 478
transnational xxxvi, xliv, 5–6, 34, 36, 69, 123, 169, 172, 176, 184, 201, 223, 254, 256, 351, 489, 522–523, 525, 532, 540–542, 547–548, 553–554, 555, 564, 577, 593
transparency international (ti) 127, 132, 163
triple bottom line 144, 162–163
turnkey project 367, 395, 418, 421

U

Ukraine war xxxix, 15, 17, 21, 22, 38, 41
uncertainty avoidance 75–76, 80–81, 104–105, 108

V

valuation xvii, xxiii, 173, 255, 290–291, 296–298, 309–310, 319, 322, 343, 346, 349, 455, 458–460, 475–476, 478–479
value chain xxii, xxxiii, xxxvii, 13, 18–19, 26, 29, 32, 37, 52, 55, 154–155, 175, 181, 191–194, 199, 205, 217–219, 221–222, 294, 316–317, 408, 412–413, 415, 422, 594, 601
value curve xxii, 16, 189, 194, 218, 221, 232, 354, 370, 377–378
value proposition xxii, xxiv, 142, 175–178, 181, 188–190, 193, 217–218, 221–222, 292, 332, 540
venturing agenda 316, 334, 346
virtual assignments xviii, 496–497, 518

W

WACC (Weighted adjusted cost of capital) 276, 297–298
waterfall model 361, 375, 378
web 2.0 399, 406, 420–422
wholly owned operations 258, 263, 280
window of opportunity 261–262, 265, 277–278, 280, 282
work from anywhere (WFA) 509, 518

Index of names

A

Aaker, D 379
Abida, Rib 254
Ablett, Jonathan 590
Ackenhusen, Mary 555
Adil, Asif 281, 347
Adler, Nancy 108–109, 519
Aguilar, Frank xxxiii, 228, 254, 511
Aharens, Nathaniel 347
Akadar, Adhwin, 347
Albert, Michel 73, 83, 87, 108–109
Albuquerque, Tulio 154, 169
Alexander, Marcus 224, 306
Allen, Thomas 450, 521, 555, 589, 592
Almodóvar, Paloma 225
Altman, Steven xxxvii, 34
Ambos, Bjorn 254, 557
Ammer, John 479
Andersen, Torben 521
Anderson, Erin 281
Anderson, Kim 223
Anderson, Terry 166
Ansoff, Igor 176, 223, 588–589
Anwar Habiba 479
Arvidsson, Niklas xliv, 451
Ariño, Africa 281
Ashkenas, Ron 347
Arnold, David 281
Asin, Amy 350
Asmussen, Christian 224
Attali, Jacques 589
Augier, Mie 450
Austin, J vii, 35, 254
Awaysheh, Amrou 164, 166

B

Baden, Fuller, C 329
Bader, T 223
Bailey William 479
Baker, M xxxvii, 34
Baker, Wayne 110
Banalieva, Elitsa 223
Banerjee, Neela 166
Barkema, Harry 281–282
Barnett, Carole 557
Barnevick, Percy 557
Barney, J 7, 34
Barsoux, Jean-Louis 72, 87, 110, 520
Barth, K 164, 167, 379
Bartlett, Christopher xliii–xliv, 34, 202, 223, 507, 519, 523, 555–556, 581–582, 589–590
Bartmess, A 422
Barton, D 43, 68
Bastian, Caroline xxxvii, 34
Battilana, Julie 164, 166
Bazigos, M 555–556
Benavente, Jose Miguel 169
Beneviste, Guy 589
Berck, Jonathan xliii
Berger, Peter 73, 83, 87, 108–109
Berger, S 109
Berggren, C xliv
Berry, Heather 254
Besanko, David 178, 223
Besouri, Christopher 68
Bettis, Richard 245, 254–255
Beugelsdijk, Sjoerd 254
Bhattacharyya, Asit 164, 169, 557
Biver, Jean-Claude 240–241
Birkinshaw, Arnold 399
Birkinshaw, Julian 379, 450–452, 556, 558
Bjorkman, Ingmar 521
Bleeke, Joel 347–348
Bloch, Nicolas 69
Bloom, Helen 521
Bode, Christiane 164, 167
Boele, Richard 171
Bolt, Olivia 589
Borcuch, Artur 404, 422
Boutellier, Roman 450, 452
Brake, Terence 275
Brammer, Stephen 167
Branicki, Layla 167
Brett, Jeanne 93, 108–109
Brewer, Thomas 254, 288

Brodbeck, Felix 109
Brown, Lester 99, 504, 589
Brusoni, S xliv
Buckley, Peter 7, 35, 222, 224
Budhwar, Pawan 519
Bughin, J 422–423
Burbano, Vanessa 164, 167
Burns, Jennifer 167

C

Cadbury, A 141, 165, 167
Cadot, Olivier 167
Campbell, Andrew 34–35, 223–224, 606
Cannice, Mark xliii
Capron, Laurence 168, 347–348
Carr, Chris 223
Carrick, Anne Marie 68, 224, 241, 255, 393, 398, 400, 421, 423, 451
Casanova, Lourdes 57, 68
Casson, Mark 7, 34
Castells, Manuel 6, 35
Cave, Bill 422
Cavusgil, Tamer 69, 281
Cennamo, Carmel 349
Cerny, Keith 422
Chaddick, Brad 254–255
Chattopadhyay, Atava xxxix, 53, 68
Chen, Guoli 68, 274, 281
Chen, Yougan xxxix, xliv
Chenh, Simon 254
Cheng, Yang xliii
Chesbrough, Henry 450
Chetty, Sylvie 109
Chiesa, Vittoria 450
Chhokar, Jagdeep 109
Chi, Tailan 224
Chu, Chi, Ning, 109
Chui, M 422–423
Chung, Peter 479
Choudhury, Prithwiraj 355, 38
Cirjevskis, Andrej 348
Cladderton, Lisa 557
Ciarlante, Deana
Clyde, Smith, Deborah 556
Collis, David 557
Coltman, Tim 422
Connell, Julia 281–282
Connely, Catherine 139, 281–282, 473
Contractor, Farok 89, 152, 404
Coviello, Nicole 358–359, 380
Cowking, Philippa 109
Coyle, Donald 109
Cramer, Jacqueline 167
Crane, Andrew 136, 167, 538, 606
Crawford, Robert 167
Cuervo-Cazurra, Alvaro 254
Cunha, Olao 254
Cunningham, Mark 348
Cushman, John 167
Cuypers, Ilya 109

D

Danis, Wade 422
Daher, Nick 109
Dathe, Tracy 109
Daugherty, Paul 589
Dastmalchian, Ali 109
Davidson, William 223, 347–348
Davis, Stanley 556
Dawar, Niraj 53, 68
de Bettignies, Henri, Claude xxxix, 513
de la Torre, Jose 347
de Meyer, Arnoud 350, 385–386, 420, 422, 428, 450–451
De Smet, Aaron 555, 558
Decarli, Massimiliano 282
Decreton, Benoit 440, 450–451, 556, 558
Delmas, Magali 164, 167
Deloumeaux, Lydia 422
Demarzo, Peter xliii
DeMonaco, Lawrence 347
Deng Xiao Ping 45
Dent, Stephen 347–348
DePamphilis, Donald 348
Devinney, Timothy xliii–xliv, 422
Devlin Clarian 589
Dewhurst, Martin 555–556
Dhanaraj, C 223
Donalson, Thomas 166, 167
Doherty, Robert 348
Dore, Ronald 73, 83, 87, 108–109
Doremus, Paul 223, 590
Dorfman, Peter 109
Dowling, Peter 520
Doz, Yves xxxix, xliii–xliv, 35–36, 202, 222–223, 225, 308, 313, 315, 325–326, 329–330, 347–349, 428, 436, 450–452, 484, 520, 556, 582, 589–590
Dragonetti, Nicolas 379–380
Dranove, D 223
Dunchin, Faye 167
Dunfee, Thomas 164, 168
Dunning, John xxxvii, xliv, 7, 35, 181, 222–223
Dyer, Jeffrey 348

E

Eccles, Robert 347–348
Edstrom, Anders 489, 52
Eiteman, D 478, 479
Edward, Ron 223
Eizaguirre, Almudena 168
Eldar, Ofer 164, 167
Elkington, John 144
Engels, Friedrich 6, 35
Engle, Allen 520
Enrique, Luiz 590
Erdmenger, Christoph 170
Ernst, David 281, 347, 348
Erns, Ricardo 422
Eun, Cheol xliv, 479
Evans, Paul xliv, 402, 422, 495, 520, 547
Evenett, Simon xxxvii, 35

F

Fadiman, Jeffrey 164, 168
Falcao, Horacio 108–109
Fang, Tony 96, 109
Farndale, Elaine 521
Farooq, Sami xliv
Farrell, Diana 68, 254
Faulkner D 223
Felter, Claire 166, 168
Fender, Michel 422
Ferdows, Kasra 385–386, 420, 422
Festing, Marion 520
Fisher, Roger xxii, 90, 108–109, 600–601, 605–606
Flamant, Anne-Claire 556
Florescu, Elizabeth 588–589
Francis, S 223, 347, 561
Frangos, Jean Marc 440, 45
Franko, Larry 556
Frankopan, Peter 35
Fraser, Jane 34–35, 68
Freeling, Anthony 361, 379–380
Freeman, S 172, 223
Friedheim, Cyrus 348
Friedman, Lisa 440, 450
Friedman, Thomas 590
Frieman, Milton 141
Fukuyama, Francis 561, 564, 588, 590

G

Gahuri, Pervez 109
Galbraith, Jay 489, 52
Ganson, Brian 168
García-Canal, Esteban 68
García-Feijoo, Maria 168
Gasman, Olivier 452
Gates, Bill and Melinda 330
Gatignon, Hubert 168, 281
Gawer, Annabelle 349–350
Gee, Francesca 347, 349
Geertz, Clifford 72, 109
Geringer, M xliii, 347–348
Gersh, Ulrich 68
Ghadar, Fariboz 348
Ghauri, Perez 165, 168, 281
Ghemawat, Pankaj xliv, 7, 34–35, 223–224, 243, 254, 348, 519–520
Ghoshal, Sumantra xliii–xliv, 34, 202, 223, 348, 507, 519, 555–556, 581–582, 589–590
Ghosn, Carlos 348
Giddy, Ian 479
Glen, Jack 282
Glenn, Jerome 588–590
Gompers, Paul 281–282
Gongming, Qian 35
Goodwin Jason 35
Goold, M 224
Gravelle, Jane 165, 168
Greenwald, Gleen 166, 168
Gregersen, Hal 489, 496, 519
Greve, Henrich 321, 347, 349
Gröschl, Stefan 520
Guey, Huey Li 555, 556
Guillén, Mauro 69, 254
Guisinger, Stephen 254
Gupta, Anil 68, 109
Gwartney, James 68

H

Habeck, Max 299, 347
Hadjikhani, Amjad 165, 168
Haigh, Ronald 385, 422
Halevy, Tammy 348
Hall, Edward xxxvii, 68, 73–74, 108–110, 380, 423
Hamel, Gary 224, 308, 313, 315, 325–326, 347–349, 589–590, 606
Hampden Turner, Charles 77, 109, 111
Hammond, Allen 590
Hanges, Paul 109
Hankinson, Graham 358–359, 380
Harbison, John 350
Harding, D 589
Harrigan, Kathryn 347, 349
Harris, Bryan 166, 168

Harris, Jonathan 555–556
Harris, Lloyd 168
Harter, Jim 555–556
Harvey, M 590
Harzing, Anne 520
Haspeslagh, Philippe 299, 301, 347–349
Hawawini, Gabriel xxxix, xliii, 347, 479
Hayton, J xliv
Hazan, Eric 423
He, Honwei 168
Hebert, Louis 347–348
Heblich, Stephan 168
Hedlund, Gunnar xliv
Heenan, D 202, 222, 224
Heike, Fabig 171
Heilbroner, Robert 590
Helmold, Marc 109
Henisz, Witold 168–169
Hennart, Jean Francois 224, 478–479
Hennebel, Ludovic 137, 168
Herbig, Paul 96, 109
Heron, Randall 166
Hess, David 164, 168
Hesterly, William 348
Heywood, Suzanne 555–556, 558
Hill, Charles xliii
Hitt, Michael xliv
Hofstede, Gert xxvii, 73–76, 108–109, 518, 520
Hogan, Harold 557
Holliday, Charles 168
Holstein, Williams
Hopkins, Raymond 36, 282
Hoskisson, Robert xliv
Hoque, Nazamul 282
House, Robert 109
Howell Lieweyn 254–255
Ho-Won Jeong 109
Hsieh, Tsun, yan 109, 520, 545
Huang, Yascheng 68–69
Humes, Samuel 35
Hummel, Florian 109
Huntington, Samuel 71, 73, 79, 108–109, 575, 588–590
Husted, Bryan 164, 168
Huston, Larry 451
Hwang, Peter 281–282
Hyde, Dana 347, 349

I

Ifzal, Ali 68–69
Inglehart, Ronald 110
Inkpen, Andrew xliii–xliv, 349
Ireland Duane xliv
Isono, James 348

J

Jackson, Terence 110
Jacobides, Michael 347, 349
Jasperen, Frederick 282
Jaruzelski, Barry 282
Javidan, Mansour 109
Jeffrey, William 222, 224
Jemison, William 299, 301, 347, 349
Jenkins, Rhys 165, 168
Jensen, Karina xliv
Jin, Ami 68
Joachimsthaler, Erich 379
Johansen, John xliv
Johanson, Jan 34–35, 37, 223–224, 258, 281–282
Jokinen Tiina 508, 519–520
Jones, Geoffrey 34–35
Jones, Jeannette 225
Jordan, Lisa 499, 592

K

Kaetzler, Backy 349
Kaha, Harun 282
Kandemir, Destan 69
Kang, Jun, Koo 479
Karch, Nancy 379
Kaplan, Norton 592
Karmokolias, Yannis 282
Katsoulakos, P 165, 169
Kaufmann, Daniel 164, 169
Kawelis, Pavos 422
Keller, William 223, 590
Kelly, Nataly 224, 255, 379–380
Kennedy, Robert 557
Kess, Pekka 350
Kessler, Benjamin 224
Kets de Vries, Manfred 520, 557
Khanna, Tarun 49–51, 68–69, 518, 520, 544, 555–556
Kharas, Homi 43, 67, 69
Khou, Julia 349
Kiessling, Timothy 590
Kim, Chan 194, 195, 222, 224, 282
Kim, Deckman 69
Kim, Jung Kwan 422
Kim, Soonhee 451
Kinnumen, Tuomo 350
Kiss, Andrea 422
Kitching, John 289, 347, 349
Klincewicz, Krzysztof 349

Klueter, Thomas 451
Knight, Gary 223–224
Kogut, Bruce 281–282, 347, 349
Kolk, Ans 169, 171
Koller, Thimothy 255, 348
Kordestani, Kameron 349
Koontz, Harold xliii
Kostova, Tatiana 170, 254
Kotabe, Masaaki 422
Kotler, Philip xliv
Kremenyuk, Victor 110
Krishna, L. N 347, 349, 543
Kröger, Fritz 349
Kuemmerle, Walter 451
Kulatilaka, Nalin 281–282
Kumar, Amit 164, 169
Kumar, Nirmalya 451, 557
Kundu, Summit 224

L

Lahiri, Nandini 451
Lanes, Kersten 348
Lang, Austin 35, 555–556
Lange, Glenn, Marie 167, 235, 255
Langlet, François 35
Lanvin, Bruno 431, 451, 520
Lasserre, Philippe iii–v, vii, 69, 255, 334, 349, 450–451, 490, 505, 518, 520, 546, 555, 557
Latukefu, Alopi 422
Laurent, André 73, 75–77, 107–108, 110
Lavoie, Johanne 520
Lawrence, Paul R 36, 73, 109–110
Lawson, Robert 68
Lazzarini, Sergio 69
Leal, Donald 166, 172
Lee, Hyangsoo xxxix, 451, 521, 603, 606
Lee, Matthew 164, 166
Lehmacher, Wolkgang xliv
Lehni Markus 126, 164, 169
Leite, Carlos 164, 169
Lenin, Vladimir 35
Lessard, Donald 347, 349, 461, 478–479
Leviagängas, Pekka 350
Levi-Strauss, Claude 72, 11
Levitt, Theodore 353–354, 380
Lewis, Richard 83, 11
Lhabitant, F Serge 70
Li, Chenguang 169, 349
Li, Jiantao 451
Li, Lee 34–35
Lieberman, Marvin 281–282
Liesch, Peter 224
Lindner, A 387, 422
Linhares, Joao 166, 168
Linnenluecke, Martina 167
Liu, Ben 282, 606
Lloyd Reason, Lester 223
Long, Gideon 168
Lorenzoni, Gianni 329
Lorsh, William 73
Lowell, Bryan 34–35
Luermann, Timothy 281–282
Luk, S.T.K 519
Luo, Yadong 281–282
Luostarinen, Reijo 225
Luyrens, J xxxvi, 27, 37
Lynn, Isabella 321, 347, 350

M

Ma, Jieqiong 282
Madura Jeff 480
Malnight, Thomas 367, 379, 380, 557
Magdeleine, Jocelyn 422
Mankin, Eric 325
Magni Max 67, 70
Mamun, Abdulah 282
Manyika J 423
Marano, Valentina 170
Marceto, Alonso 592
Martin, Drew 96, 109, 347–348, 358, 372–373, 543
Marx, Karl 6, 35
Matten, Dirk 167
Mauborgne, Renée 194–195, 222, 224, 347, 349
Mauro, Paolo 169
McDougall, Patricia 224
McKee, M 27, 37
McLaughlin, Kathleen 379
McLuhan Marshall 6, 34–35
Mead, Margaret 110
Medina, Danielle 109
Mei, Jianping 479
Melander, Erik 591
Mellahi, Kamel 224
Mendenhall, Mark 110, 519, 521
Meng, B 37
Mesquita, Louis 69
Meyer, Erin 73, 75, 78–79, 95, 107–108
Meyer, Klaus 224, 451
Meyer, Marshall 606
Micklethwait, John 35
Middleton, Stuart 224
Midgley, D 422, 589

Miguel, J xxxviii
Mikko, Kosone 222–223
Milberg, William 421–422
Millar, Roderick 479
Minkov, Michael 76, 109
Minor, S xliii
Miroux, Anne 57, 68
Mirza, Hafiz 36
Mischke, Jan et al 36
Mitchell, D 299
Mitchell, Will 347–349
Mitroff, Ian 591
Mol, Michael 451
Moffett, M 479
Monaghan, Sinhead 169, 223, 224
Monteiro, Felipe iii–v, vii, 68–69, 154, 156, 169, 224, 241, 255, 398, 421, 423, 437, 440, 444, 450–451, 520
Montgomery, Cynthia 557
Montgomery, David 282–283, 557
Moore James 349
Morley, Micael 519
Moro, Sergio 151–153, 168, 170
Mowla, Mohamad Masrulul 282
Mudambi, Ram 282, 422, 452, 479
Musacchio, Aldo 69

N

Narasimhan, Laxman 68
Narayandas, Das 380
Narayanswamy, Subbu 69
Narula, Rashneesh 224
Neeley, Tsedal 108, 11
Newenham-Kahindi, Alosius 170
Nichols, Martha 135, 165, 169
Niron, Hashai 222, 224
Noda, Tono 379–380
Novela, Selly 36
Novicevic, Miroland 590
Nugent, C 166, 169

O

O'Loughlin, Emily 349
Odziemkowska, Kate 169
Ohmae, Kenichi 11, 34, 36, 225, 354, 379–380
Olshavsky, Richard 36
Onofre, Renato 166, 17
Oppenheim, Jeremy 35
Ormiston, C 69
Oviatt, Benjamen 224
Oxley, Joanne 349

P

Palepu, Krishna 69
Parker, Philip xxxix, 158, 380
Parsons, A 111, 521
Patel, Dhiren 589
Patton, Bruce xxii, 90, 109
Pauly, Louis 223, 590
Pearce, Robert 430, 450, 452
Paauwe,Jaap, 521
Pélissié du Rausas, Matthieu 423
Peng, Mike xliv, 36, 282
Perkins, Helen 282
Perlmutter, Howard 224
Pernia, Ernesto 69
Perry, Tod 166, 48
Philips, Dom xxxv, 24, 166, 170, 186, 190, 211, 534
Pieper, Jan 109
Piketty, Thomas 34, 36
Pilat,Borcuch, Mardalena 422
Pimentel, Marta 224
Pinilla, Vincente 223
Pinson, Christian 379–380
Piscitello, Lucia xliv
Piskorsi, Nikolaj 524, 557
Pitta, Fabio 172
Plas, Geraldine 164, 170
Pope, Jeremy 165, 17
Porter, Michael xxviii, 36, 177, 189–191, 193, 222, 225, 238–239, 252, 254–255, 422–423, 428, 452
Prado-Wagner, Carmen 36
Prahalad, C. K xliv, 36, 52–53, 68–69, 202, 222, 224–225, 245, 254–255, 325, 349, 549, 555, 557
Prashantam, Shameen 452
Probert, Joselyn 350
Prud'homme, C 111
Pucik, Vladimir xliv, 520, 557
Puranam, Phanish xxxix, 451, 545, 557
Purshe, William 350

Q

Qian, Zhengming 423
Qualls, William 36
Quelch, John 358, 379–380, 521

R

Raiffa, Howard 108, 11
Raleigh, Clionadh 592
Ramaswamy, Kannan xliii–xliv
Rangan, Subramanian 36, 170, 321, 347, 350, 421, 423
Rastogi, Vaishall 69

Redding, Gordon 73, 83, 108, 110–111, 254–255, 520
Reed Hall, Mildred 109
Reich, Robert 223, 325, 590
Reinert, Uwe 69
Reinhart, Forest L 146, 165, 170
Rennie, Michael 223, 225
Resnick, Bruce xliv, 479
Retchman, René 171
Reuer, Jeffrey 169, 349
Ricardo, David xxxvi, 6, 16, 34, 36
Ricks David 71, 108, 110
Rieger, F 521
Riesenbeck, Hajo 361, 379–380
Rigman, Tom 282
Ritzer's George 6
Robertson, Roland 6, 36, 555
Robinson, William 6, 36
Rodrik, Dani 21, 34, 36, 563, 588, 592
Rogers, Jerry 254–255
Ronen, Simcha 73, 79, 110
Root, Franklin 282, 397
Rosenweig, Philip 521
Ross, Jerry 349
Rottenberg, Stephanie 518, 521
Rouse Ted 69
Rowley, Tim 349
Roxburg, C 589, 592
Rudnicki, Jeff 350
Rugman, Alan 36, 225, 592
Russ, Meir 225

S

Saari, D 592
Sachs, Jeffrey 8, 34, 36, 40–41, 70, 510, 521
Said, Rémi 34, 37, 152, 289, 423, 506, 521, 561
Sakkab Nabil, 451
Salacuse, Jeswald 92–93, 108, 110
Salehyan, Idean 592
Salle, Robert 35
Samek, Robert 520
Sane, P 170
Santos, Jose xxxix, xliv, 152, 439, 450, 582, 589–590, 592
Sarala, M 350
Shenkar, S 73, 79, 110
Schaefer, Scott 223
Schein, Edgard 72, 11
Schipani, Andres 166, 168, 170
Schmidheiny, Stephan 168
Schneider, Suzan xxxiii, 72, 87, 110, 273–274, 282, 366
Schroder, Bill 223
Schütte, Hellmut 380, 451
Schwartz, Gordon xxxix, 65, 131, 170, 255, 354–355, 379–380, 538, 555–558, 606
Schwartz, Kevin 451
Scullion, Hugh 519
Sheffield, C 168, 259, 592
Shenkar, Oded 73, 79, 110
Shih, Stan 551, 558
Shipilov, Andrew xxxix, 349–350
Sigala, Marianna 519
Sinatra, Alessandro 350
Singer, Mark 589–590
Singh, Jasjit xxxix, 54, 164, 167, 274, 282
Singh, Harbir 167, 348, 350
Singh, Satwinder 430, 450, 452
Sinha, Jant 69
Sklair, Leslie 6, 36
Smith, Craig 165, 170
Smith, Kenneth 350
Smith, Shi 379–380
Smit, Sven 590
Soubbotina, Talyana 68–69, 170
Spadini, Alessandro 524, 557
Spar, Deborah 143, 167, 349
Spekeman, Robert 321, 347, 350
Staack, Volker 451
Stahl, Gunther 87–88, 110, 489, 518–519, 521
Stalk, Georges 222, 225
Starace, Francesco 154–156
Steen, Mattheew 224
Stefanini, Marco xxxii, 60–62, 68
Steinhubl, A 348
Stevens, Charles 170
Steward, Pamela 520
Stiglitz, Joseph 592
Stiles, Philip 521
Stonehill, Arthur 479
Stopford, John 202, 222, 225, 525–526, 555, 558
Stoyan, Tanev 223, 225
Stumpf, Siegfried 110
Sun, Tzu 176
Sunshine, Russell 94, 108, 110
Szulanski, Gabriel 436

T

Tahilyani, Naveen 69
Taleb, Nassim 588, 592
Tallman, Steven xliii–xliv
Tamboto, Eddy 69
Tan, Ja 69, 97
Tanev Stoyan 34, 36
Tang, Jin'han 282
Tanzi, Vito 170, 17

Tao, Z 350
Tashman, Peter 170
Taylor, William 223, 558
Teece, David 450
Tell, Fredrich xliv
Terwiesch, Christian 452
Thill, George 451
Tichy, Noel 557
Tippmann, Esther
Toulan, Omar xliii–xliv, 165, 349
Träm, M
Trevor, Jonathan 521
Tribewalla, Vikas 379–380
Trompenaars, Alfons xxvii, 73–74, 76–77, 83, 87, 108–109, 111
Träm, Michael 349
Tung, Rosalie 486, 518, 521

U

Uddin, Mohammad Rahim 282
Ury, William 109
Usunier, Jean Claude 109

V

Vahlne, Jan, Erik 35, 37, 224
Vaiman, Vlad 521
Vaish, Paresh 281, 347
Valla, Jean Paul 35
Van de Ven, A xliv
Van Ruysseveldt, Joris 520
Van Tulder, Rob xliv, 169, 171, 452
Vance, C 521
Vanhonacker, Wilfried 281–282
Varma, Suvir 69
Vereecke, Andreé 385–386, 420
Vermeulen, Freek 281–282
Vernon, Raymond 424–425, 450, 452
Vestring, Till 69
Viallet, Claude xliii, 349, 479
Viscio, Albert 299–300, 350
Vitaro, Richard 350
Von Krogh, George 347, 350
von Zedtwitz, Maximilian 450, 452

W

Wack, Pierre 593
Walker, Thomas 109
Wallerstein, Immanuel 6, 37
Wang, Anne 65
Wang, Chen Tang 551–552, 558
Wang, Chuanfu 64–65
Wang, Haiyan 68
Wang, Peter 381–282
Wang, Zhi 37
Watson, George 272
Watts, Philip 168
Weaven, Scott 272, 282
Weber, Max 83, 108, 111
Weerawardena, Jay 224
Wei Shang, Jin 169, 171
Weihrich, Heinz xliii
Weiman, Jens 169
Welch, Lawrence 223, 225
Wells, Louis 202, 222, 225, 397, 421, 423, 525–526, 555, 558
Welters, C 169
Weerawardena, Jay 224
Wheeler, David 116, 171
White, J 593
Whitley, Richard 73, 83, 87, 108, 111
Wild, John xliv
Wild, Kenneth xliv
Willes, Pierre 556
Williamson, John 68, 70, 281–282
Williamson, Peter xliv, 47, 332, 347, 350, 380, 450, 556, 590
Wilson Dominic 70
Wilson, Jared 166
Wilson, James 589
Wilson, Keeley 428, 450, 451
Wilson, Thomas 348
Winer, Russ xliii
Witt, Michael xxxix, 37, 83, 108, 110–111, 254–255, 588, 593
Wong Rieger, D 518, 521, 555
Woo, H. S 111
Wooldridge, A 35
Wouter, Ahina 558
Wouters, Olivier xxxvi, 27, 37
Wright, Patrick 521
Wurster, Thomas 402, 422

X

Xavier, Carlos 166, 172
Xie, Zhenzen 451
Xin Li 34, 37, 606
Xu, Yi 224, 452

Y

Yahiaoui, Dorra 521
Yamagushi, Takeo 518, 521
Yandle, Bruce 172
Yang, Jie 282
Yeung, Arthur 558

Yip, George xliv, 23, 34, 37, 379–380, 403–404, 422–423
Yoshino, Michael 321, 347, 350, 557
Youval, Alsmon 68, 70

Z

Zaheer, S 223, 225
Zahra, S 282
Zainulbhai, A 43, 69
Zeutchel, U 108, 11
Zhang, Ruimin xxxviii, 595–6, 600–604
Zhao, H 282
Zhengming, Q 35
Zhou, N 254
Zhuang, X 274, 281
Zoubir, Y 70
Zulkarnain, Z 350

Index of organizations and companies

A

AAFLA 143
Accenture 61, 149, 368, 400
Acer xxvi, xxxiii, 56, 190, 540–541, 551–552, 555–556, 558
Asian Development Bank (ADB) 467
Adidas 147
Advent 8, 11, 20, 287, 289, 325, 399
Air France 302
Airbus xxii, xxv, 132, 182, 185–186, 309, 327–328, 331, 366, 394, 477
Airtel 289, 291
Alcatel 289, 306–307, 400
Alcatel-Lucent 289, 306–307
Alfa 289
Alicorp 59
Allergan 29, 289, 291
Allianz 361
Alstom 368
Alza 291, 318, 348
Amazon xxiv, xxxiv, 14, 31, 33, 124, 184, 331, 357, 361–362, 392–394, 398–401, 405, 473, 535, 545
Amnesty International 135, 137–139, 148, 166
ANZAM (Australian and New Zealand Academy of Management) 223
Asia Pacific Economic Cooperation (APEC) 569, 585
Apple xxiv, xxxiv-xxxv, 6, 10, 33, 147, 179, 184, 197, 240, 306–307, 331, 353, 357–359, 361–362, 392–393, 452, 473, 528
Asahi 359
Asea Brown Boveri (ABB) 504
Association Of South East Asian Nations (ASEAN) xli, 14, 569, 585
Aspen Institute 149
AT&T 200, 366
AtKearney 422
Aventis 287, 303

B

Bangladesh 41, 147, 235–236, 468, 567, 600
Basf xxxiii, xxxv, 445–446, 450, 536, 538, 556
Bayer xxxvi, 17, 27, 29, 288, 291
Bayer Monsanto 288
Benetton 268, 363–364, 380
Bharti Airtel 289
Bhopal 143
Bank for International Settlements (BIS) xxxvi, 4, 34, 479
BlaBlacar xxxiii, 410–411
Blackstone 289
Boeing 182, 366, 393
Bombardier 133, 532
Booz Allen 450, 555
Boston Consulting Group xxxvii, 34, 58, 68, 543, 555–556
BRF 59
Bridgestone 184
British East India Company 7
Brookfield 110, 519
British Telecom (BT) 200, 366, 439–440, 451
Business Impact 146
BYD xxxii, 59, 64–65

C

Canon 182, 581
Cap Gemini 366, 368
Cargill xxxiv, 259
Carrefour xxxvii, 33, 55, 145, 188, 190, 199, 389
Caux Roundtable
CDC Capital Partners 467
Centre for Asian Business Cases 556
Charoen Pokphand xxxii, 62
Chrysler 293, 341
Ciba Geigy 348
Cinven 289
Cisco 306–307, 320, 398, 400
Citibank 12, 198, 366, 380, 540, 557
Cochlear xxxiv, 209, 211
Compagnie Française d'Assurance pour le Commerce Extérieur (COFACE) 472
Coca-Cola (Coke) 357
Colgate 486, 521
Columbia 8, 36–37, 167, 255, 290–291, 349, 422, 566

Cornhill 361
Corning 327, 329
Corpwatch 142, 163, 563, 589
Cosan xxxii, 123
Council of Europe 134

D

Dabhol xxxiv, 397, 423
Daewoo 52, 342
Daimler 65, 293, 340
Daimlerchrysler 491
Dangote Cement 59
Danone 145, 184, 370
Dell 60, 118
Deloitte 68
Deutsche Telecom 399
Disneyland 25, 35

E

Earth Policy Institute 589
Ebay 399–400, 420, 423
European Bank for Reconstruction and Development (EBRD) 467
ECGD (Export Credit Guarantee Department) 472
European Economic Community, (EEC) 9, 18, 568
Economic Intelligence Unit (EIU) 520
Electrolux 186, 190, 348, 357–358, 598–599
Embraer 39, 101
Enel xxxii, 154–156, 166, 169
Enron xxxiv, 368, 397, 423
Ericsson xxv, xxxiii, 182, 306, 366, 380, 412–413
Ernst & Young 222, 385, 422
Essilor xxiii, xxxii, 213–215
EssilorLuxottica 215, 288
Etisalat xxxii, 59, 156–157
EU Emissions Trading Scheme (EU ETS) 121
Euromedia 131
Euromoney 478
Euromonitor 68, 253, 374, 378, 555, 597
European Foundation for Management Education (EFMD)
European Union (EU) xli, 9, 150
Eximbank (Export-Import Bank) 472

F

Facebook (Meta) 11, 33, 210, 272, 353, 357, 373–374, 398–401, 405, 421
Food and Agriculture Organization (FAO) 168
FCIA 472
FEMSA 59
Fiat 293, 341
Fiat-Chrysler 293
Fitch 31, 35, 246–247, 251, 253–254
Forrester 400
Foster 144, 207, 329, 332, 359, 404, 501, 524
Framatome 268
France Telecom 203
Francolor 350
Fraser 34–35, 68
FreemarketsOnline 423
Fuji Xerox 318

G

Garments 12
Gartner 400, 421
GATT (General Agreement on Tariffs and Trade) 9,13–14
Global Vaccine Alliance (GAVI) xxiv, 330
GE-Snecma 309, 322
Gemplus xxxiv, 209–210
General Electric (GE) 7, 289, 349, 387, 425
General Motors (GM) 309, 341–343, 435
Global Compact xxviii, 146–147, 171
GLOBE (Global Leadership and Organizational Behavior Effectiveness) 79,80–82,108–109
Global Sullivan Principles 146
Globe xxvii, 4, 11, 28, 79–82, 105, 108–109, 118, 132, 150, 183, 190, 197, 353, 356, 445–446, 467, 509–510, 572
Golden Agri Resources 59, 536
Goodyear 184, 198
Google 117, 145, 147, 240, 357, 361–362, 373, 398–401, 405, 473, 497, 500, 518, 545, 556
Greenpeace 142–143
Gucci 52, 364

H

Haier x, xix, xxvi, xxx-xxxi, xliii, 39, 289, 559, 594–606
Harvard Business School vii, xlii, xliv, 35–36, 49, 95, 146, 170, 189, 197, 223–225, 254, 282, 348–349, 380, 422–423, 450–451, 521, 556–557, 590, 606
Heineken 357
Helvetica Chemical 483–484
Hewlett Packard (HP)
Holcim-Lafarge 288, 291
HSBC xxviii, xxxii, 10, 145, 147, 182, 211–213, 360
Huawei 15, 184, 274, 306–307, 362, 400
Human Rights Watch 135
Hyundai 12, 23l
IBM xxxv, 11, 36, 60–61, 75, 118, 305, 326, 357, 364, 366, 368, 398, 400, 504, 541–543, 555–557, 590
International Bank for Reconstruction and Development (IBRD) 591
International Chamber of Commerce (ICC) 472

International Finance Corporation (IFC) 34, 467
IKEA xxxiv, 117, 258–259, 400
International Labor Organisation (ILO) 135–136, 138, 148, 165, 168, 505
IMD (International Institute for Management Development) 37
IndoMedia 131
Infosys 39
INSEAD vii, xxxvii, xxxix, xlii, 34, 54, 61, 68–69, 108, 110–111, 149, 154, 156, 158, 166, 167, 169–170, 224, 241, 255, 281–282, 343, 348–350, 361, 373, 379–380, 422–423, 432, 439, 450–451, 484, 500, 508, 513, 520, 555–557, 603, 606
Institute For The Future (IFTF) 587
Intel 11, 190, 240, 357, 359, 362, 469
International Finance Corporation 224, 467
International Herald Tribune 166
Intergovernmental Panel on Climate Change (IPCC) 587, 591
International Service Systems A/S (ISS) xxxv, 531, 555
Isuzu 342

J

Jardine Matheson 269
JP Morgan 349, 48

K

Kennedy Round 9
Kenya Flower Council 147
Kyoto Treaty 48

L

Lenovo 39, 305, 543
Li & Fung xxxiv, 388–389, 423
Light Up The World (LUTW) xxxii, 157
Lockheed 143
Lucent 289, 306–307, 400
Lukoil 59
LUTW xxxii, 157–158
LVMH 52, 68, 240

M

3M 147, 540, 555, 581
Maastricht 17
Marks & Spencer 147
MAU 569, 585
McDonald 190, 197, 268, 356, 358–359, 370, 389
McKinsey xxxvii, 17, 23, 34–36, 43, 68–70, 108, 163, 222, 225, 254–256, 281, 290, 347–350, 368, 378–380, 397, 404, 406, 421–423, 479, 481, 520–521, 523, 525, 556–558, 590, 592–593, 606
Mercado Libre 59
Mercedes-Benz 52
Mercosur 569, 585
Michelin xxii, 184–186, 198–199, 422
Microsoft xxxviii, 24, 117, 222, 272, 307, 357, 364, 368, 401, 510
Midland Bank 302
Millennium project xxxv, 577–578, 586–590
Miniwatts Marketing Group 423
Mitsubishi 56, 62, 182, 341
Monsanto 288, 291, 496
Moody's 466
MOSOP 116
Motorola 64, 307, 326, 425
Merck Sharp and Dohme (MSD) xxxv, 443

N

National Intelligence Council (NIC) 562
NEC 306
Nestlé xxii, xxiv-xxv, xxxv, 5, 7, 10, 17, 147, 182, 184–186, 327, 357–358, 424, 427–430, 433, 450, 521
Nike 11, 143, 167, 360, 363, 389
Nissan xxiv, xxxiv, 182, 305, 311, 313, 315, 318, 322–323, 325, 338–340, 455, 556
Nokia 10, 64, 182, 274, 289, 306–307, 400, 556, 583
Nortel 306, 4
North American Free Trade Agreement (NAFTA) xli
Nummi 309, 318, 342

O

OCP group 59
Organization for Economic Cooperation and Development (OECD) xxvi, xl, 8, 11–12, 21, 30–31, 34, 36, 39–41, 43–44, 47, 49–50, 66–69, 119, 126, 128, 131, 134, 140, 148, 150–151, 164–166, 169–170, 204–205, 207, 222–223, 225, 229, 233, 248–249, 253, 382, 421–423, 460, 467, 469, 473, 478, 480, 563, 567, 588, 591
Olam International 536
Oracle 60, 366, 390, 400
Orange 366, 399–400
OtiS xxi, xxxiii, xxxvii, 17–20, 24, 33, 35
Oxford xliii–xliv, 31, 35, 109–111, 167–168, 170–171, 223–224, 255, 452, 556, 578, 589, 591–592

P

Panasonic 12, 598–599
Paris agreement on Climate Change
Petronas 39
Peugeot 182, 293, 341
Pew Center on Global Climate Change
Philips xxxv, 24, 166, 170, 186, 190, 211, 534

Pirelli 184
Pixtech 329
Prince of Wales Business Leader Forum (PWBLF) 146
PricewaterhouseCooper 346–347, 350, 407, 409, 423, 480, 588–589, 592
Procter & Gamble xxxv, 5, 182, 190, 363, 440, 523–524

Q

Qualcomm 288
Quinta do Vallado xxxii, 215–217, 224

R

Ranbaxy 39, 282
Raytheon 182
RCA 425
Renault xxiv, xxxiv, 182, 305, 311, 313, 315, 318–319, 322–323, 325, 338–341, 556
Renault Nissan 338–339
Reuters 147, 289, 400–401, 540
Robina 59

S

Saatchi 363, 366
Sabanci 59
SADC 569, 585
Shangai Automobile Industrial Corporation (SAIC) 342, 435
Samsung xxii, xxxiv, 6, 52, 175, 179–180, 182, 274, 306–307, 358, 362–363, 598
SAP 60, 368, 390–391, 399–400
SASOL 59
Sasol 59
Saurer 54
Schneider Electric xxxiii, 273, 282, 366
Shell (Royal Dutch Shell) xxxii, xxxiv, 116, 123–124, 143, 146, 165, 170–171, 182, 389, 486, 504, 577, 589, 592
Siemens xxvi, xxxiii, 7, 182, 326, 329, 366, 407, 445–446, 450, 549–550, 555, 558, 598
Smithkline and Beecham 303–305
Snecma 309, 322, 349
Sony 11–12, 24, 56, 182–183, 190, 290–291, 349, 357–358, 425
South African Brewery 288, 360
Standard & Poor's 466
Star 169, 200, 308, 327, 441, 596
Starbucks 147, 535
Stefanini xxxii, 60–62, 68
Sunna Design xxxiv, 210
Suparicom 59
Suzuki 342
Swatch 190, 363–364, 370
Swift 327
Swire 269

T

TAG Heuer xxxii, 239–241
Tata 61
Tesco xxxvii, 33, 199, 374
Teva 29–30, 289, 291
Teva-Allergan 289
The Economist, 166
Thomson Reuters 289
Time Warner 400
Tokyo Round 9
Total 137, 143, 168
Toyo Ink 350
Toyota 56, 64, 182, 309, 318, 342
Transparency International 127–129, 132–133, 163, 164, 170–171
Transsion Holdings 274
Treaty 9, 17–18, 120, 148, 506, 568–569
Tyco 557

U

Uber xxxiii, 10, 398, 401, 410–411, 420–421, 423, 543
UBS 393
United Nations Conference on Environment and Development (UNEP) xxxvi–xxxvii, 4, 34, 37, 39–40, 44, 58, 67–69, 184–185, 236, 242, 247, 253–256, 281, 401, 422–423, 478
UN Environment Program (UNEP) 123, 163–164, 166, 171, 592
UNESCO 122, 171, 240, 425–426, 450, 561
UNICEF 135, 163, 165, 171, 330
Unilever xxxv, 5, 10, 17, 24, 54, 145, 182, 190, 357–358, 363, 370, 373, 378–379, 504, 523–524
Union Carbide 143
United Nations (UN) xli, 113, 164
Universal 59, 72, 116, 136, 138, 147, 368, 562, 584
Unocal 137, 168
United Nations Office on Drugs and Crime (UNODC) 593
Uruguay Round 9
US Fireman's Fund 361V
Visa 327, 329, 400
Vodafone 366
Volkman 54

Volkswagen 184, 342, 435
Volvo 319, 358–359

W

Walmart xxii, xxxvii, 33, 55, 184–186, 197, 199
Washington Consensus 46, 7
Westinghouse 268, 358
Whirlpool xxii, xxxiv, 186–187, 262–263, 597, 599
Wipro 59
World Bank xxxvi, xli, 4, 9, 35, 39, 41–42, 44–46, 48, 50–51, 66, 69, 70, 102–103, 111, 129, 134, 142, 149, 163–165, 170, 171, 229–232, 245, 251, 253–256, 330, 378, 398, 425, 467, 480, 505, 561, 566–567, 588, 591, 593
World Business Council for Sustainable Development 113, 171
World Economic Forum (WEF) 147, 153, 236–238, 254–255, 423, 505–506, 561, 563, 574, 587–588, 593
World Resources Institute 119, 163, 167, 171, 254
WPP Group, Young & Rubicam 362, 565, 592–593
World Trade Organisation, (WTO) xxxvii, xli, 6, 9–10, 12, 14, 17, 34, 37, 281, 423, 561
WWF (World Wide Fund for Nature) 122, 164, 172

Z

Zain 289, 291